SECRETS OF THE FLESH

SECRETS OF THE FLESH

A LIFE OF COLETTE

JUDITH THURMAN

BLOOMSBURY

First published 1999 by Bloomsbury Publishing Plc, 38 Soho Square,
London W1V 5DF

First published in the USA in 1999 by Alfred A. Knopf Inc., a
subsidiary of Random House Inc., 201 East 50th Street, New York,
NY10022

A CIP catalogue record is available from the British Library

ISBN 0 7475 4309 7

10 9 8 7 6 5 4 3

Printed in Great Britain by Clays Ltd, St Ives plc

For Charlotte (Arkie) Meisner

When my body thinks . . . all my flesh has a soul.

—COLETTE,
Retreat from Love

Contents

INTRODUCTION

Biographers generally believe that it is easy to be a "monster." It is even harder than being a saint.

—COLETTE,
Lettres à ses pairs

IN MARCH OF 1900, a forty-one-year-old Parisian man of letters published a novel that purported to be the journal of a sixteen-year-old provincial schoolgirl named Claudine. Henry Gauthier-Villars was best known as an amusingly opinionated music critic who had championed Wagner and insulted Satie. His paunch and top hat had endeared him to the cartoonists of the penny press; and his duels, his puns, and his seductions of women managed to generate almost as much copy as he wrote himself.

Gauthier-Villars used his own name for scholarly non-fiction and one of many pseudonyms when a work was light. He and his alter egos—Willy, Jim Smiley, Boris Zichine, Henry Maugis, and the Usherette—had a bibliography which already included a collection of sonnets, another of essays on photography, several comic almanacs, a monograph on Mark Twain, and a number of salacious popular novels. It was not a very well kept secret that most of these works had been improved by other hands, if not entirely ghostwritten. In an ironic bow to this reputation, Willy claimed that the new manuscript had arrived in the mail tied with a pink ribbon—the literary equivalent of a baby girl delivered by the stork.

Claudine at School was not the first authorial travesty of its kind, and certainly not the last, although Claudine herself was something new. She was the century's first teenage girl: rebellious, tough talking, secretive, erotically reckless and disturbed, by turns beguiled and disgusted at her discovery of what it means to become a woman. In his preface to the book, Willy calls her "a child of nature," a "Tahitian before the advent of the missionaries," and he pays homage to her "innocent perversity" even while regretting "this word 'perversity,' which subverts the idea that I wish to give of . . . Claudine's special case—for the very reason that I insist one cannot find any conscious vice in this young girl, who is, one might say, less immoral than she is 'amoral.' "[1]

The novel languished for a few months until Willy rallied his influential friends, who duly produced reviews hailing *Claudine at School* as a masterpiece. By autumn, it had sold some forty thousand copies, becoming— including its four sequels—one of the greatest French best-sellers of all time. There were five *Claudines* in all, two successful plays, and a range of product spin-offs in the modern sense, including Claudine cigarettes, perfume, chocolates, cosmetics, and clothing. The "author," notorious to begin with, became something of a brand name himself. "I think that only God and maybe Alfred Dreyfus are as famous as [Willy]," said Sacha Guitry.[2]

The man who signed *Claudine at School* is now best remembered as the "deplorable" first husband of the woman who wrote it. Madame Henry Gauthier-Villars, née Sidonie-Gabrielle Colette, was then an athletic beauty of twenty-seven who could pass easily for seventeen. She concealed her feelings and her talent, but she flaunted her rustic accent and a plait of auburn hair as long as she was tall. Her family in Burgundy still called her "Gabri," but in Paris she went by the waifish moniker of Colette Willy. She had rejected her own first name long before she married, insisting that her school friends— rowdy village girls like herself and like Claudine—call one another by their patronyms, *comme des garçons*. When she married for the second time, Colette Willy became Colette de Jouvenel, and finally, triumphantly, syncretically, just Colette.

COLETTE BEGAN WRITING in her early twenties, living turbulently and working tirelessly, her powers waxing as she aged. In the course of half a century, she produced nearly eighty volumes of fiction, memoirs, journalism, and drama of the highest quality. Her published correspondence fills seven volumes, and at least three important collections of letters remain unedited. Her critics and biographers have been more prolific than she was.

Digesting this colossal banquet was not the greatest of my challenges as her biographer. Colette's friend Jean Cocteau liked to say: *"Je suis un mensonge qui dit toujours la vérité":* I am a lie that always speaks the truth.

To which Colette's American anthologist, Robert Phelps, would add: she is a truth who always speaks a lie. A French critic would note more expansively: "Colette's art is that of the lie. But the great game she plays with us is, precisely, to stuff her best lies with great flashes of truth. To read her with pleasure thus consists of disentangling, with a deft pair of tweezers, the true from the false."[3] The autobiographical candor of Colette's best writing is an illusion, just as her celebrated physical immodesty is misleading. She has, as Dominique Aury puts it, "a fierce modesty of sentiment."[4] She actively disdains all forms of empathy and resists being known.

MY TITLE, *Secrets of the Flesh*, comes from a fan letter which André Gide sent Colette after reading *Chéri*. "What a wonderful subject you have taken up! And with what intelligence, mastery, and understanding of the least admitted secrets of the flesh!"[5] It's darker in the French—*des secrets les moins avoués de la chair*—and I recognize it as the kind of compliment that is more significant for the envy and unease with which Gide makes it.

Secrets of the Flesh sounds rather louche, and that, of course, is intentional—my own ironic bow to Colette's reputation. Her novels were locked away from young Frenchwomen of good families and put on the Vatican's Index of proscribed texts. Simone de Beauvoir had to read Colette for the first time on the sidewalk outside a Paris bookstore. The critics called Colette soulless and perverse, reproaching her for an art "based solely on the senses." Even Colette's lover the marquise de Morny—a lesbian transvestite and former drug addict—would complain of her to Willy: "Colette is an impulsive child without any moral feeling." The child, who was thirty-three at the time, was amused rather than defensive. "I was quite surprised," she told Willy, "to see the words *moral feeling* in Missy's handwriting."[6]

Some of the condescension that the world reserves for the acting profession—a bias against its perceived narcissism—has also rubbed off on Colette, who, as a young woman, acted and mimed on the music-hall stage, sometimes half-nude, sometimes in drag. She played a gypsy, a gigolo, and a cat; a faun in a torn chamois loincloth; and an Egyptian mummy who comes back from the dead in a jeweled bra. Every time in later life that her name was proposed for some official honor, a chorus of elders protested.

This fallen young Colette, in the prime of her beauty, was as attractive to potential saviors as she was to libertines of both sexes. The monkish poet Francis Jammes offered to play Jesus to her unrepentant Magdalene. The priestly François Mauriac would later give her unsolicited absolution for her sins of the flesh, claiming that "this pagan and carnal creature leads us irresistibly to God."[7] How? By offering, in characters like Léa and Chéri, such a desolate example of hedonism unredeemed by any higher spiritual aspirations. I'm not sure that many readers have fled in disgust from Colette to God, and it could be that a fair number have turned with relief from Him to her. But Mauriac isn't wrong about Colette's existential pessimism: "Senses, intractable masters, as ignorant as the princes of old who learned only what was indispensable: to dissimulate, to hate, to command . . ."[8]

LIKE HER MOTHER, Sido, who claimed that she had been born three hundred years too early for the world to understand her, Colette was an anachronism in her own generation. "O bourgeoisie of 1880," she exclaims almost sixty years later, "idle and cloistered young girls . . . sweet-tempered cattle ruled by men, incurable feminine solitude, ignoble resignation, the young adolescent generation of 1937 looks upon you with incredulity."[9]

What we look upon with incredulity in 1999 is Colette's invention of the modern teenager in 1895, when she began to write *Claudine at School*. She was not a sweet-tempered cow; she thought she wanted to be ruled by a man, but she hated her dependence and marginality; resignation was alien to her, and so, if we are to believe her friend Natalie Barney, was solitude.

Describing her isolation in the Paris of the fin de siècle among the brilliant men and women she met through her husband, Colette would say, "I was maladroit at making myself noticed."[10] The expression in French—*me faire valoir*—literally means "getting myself valued." Writing was the way she began to assert her value, first in the eyes of her husband, then publicly, and more slowly, to herself. She then laid down her pen only when she could literally no longer hold it. Husbands and lovers came and went; maternity was an ephemeral occupation for her at best; she was "a tough and honest little businesswoman,"[11] as she puts it, who never had the luxury to consider talent its own reward, and never ceased to haggle over her contracts—a realism that was (and still is) dismissed as "peasant shrewdness" in a country that lavishes every possible honor upon its great writers except for cash.

It is not hard to see why Colette always felt more of an affinity with the courtesans, actresses, and artistes she had frequented in her youth than she did with the bluestockings, the militants for women's rights, or the gentlewomen of letters living on their allowances. She respected those ambitious entrepreneurs of her own sex whose notion of a bottom line would never be Virginia Woolf's five hundred a year and a room of one's own, but fifty thousand a year and a villa of one's own, with a great chef, a big garden, and a pretty boy.

The most successful actresses and courtesans also came closest to fulfilling a radical Amazonian ambition: to live uncoupled yet sexually fulfilled. Most of them were bisexual, kept younger lovers, and were single mothers. Like Léa and Charlotte in *Chéri,* they managed, very competently, their hard-earned fortunes. Their careers, as de Beauvoir remarks, enhanced their erotic prestige rather than taxing it, and that was one of their great charms for Colette, who so often struggles to impersonate a "real" woman while feeling, as she puts it, like a "mental hermaphrodite."[12]

The feminists had less to attract her. By 1900, the women's-rights movement in France had a solid history, a daily newspaper, and a distinguished following. But the combination of utopianism and puritanism which marked so much feminist theory—and the denunciation of women who "collaborated" sexually with their oppressors—deterred many women otherwise eager for liberation from joining the cause. Colette's antipathy to feminism was, in her youth, outspoken. In 1910, an interviewer asked if she were a feminist, and she looked at him, incredulous. "Me, a feminist? You're kidding. The suffragettes disgust me. And if any Frenchwomen take it into their heads to imitate them, I hope they'll be made to understand that such behavior isn't tolerated in France. You know what the suffragettes deserve? The whip and the harem."[13]

The demimonde, and in particular the homosexual demimonde, was Colette's real theater of resistance. "When all is said and done," writes the historian Alain Corbin, "the pederasts of the nineteenth century were the first to develop the model of a strictly hedonistic sexuality"[14]—an eroticism liberated from monogamy or procreation. Cavafy would call them "the valiant of voluptuousness," and it's a useful and lovely epithet for Colette. For her, as for Epicurus, hedonism was something much more purposeful and, one could say, more ethical than a greed for sensation. It was the expression of an active faith—a credo without a god, a devil, or an afterlife, but with the power of all true faith to inspire ecstasy, and reverence for creation, and to console.

COLETTE CAME OF AGE as a woman and a writer during the Dreyfus Affair, which dominates the history of the French fin de siècle. The anti-Semitism, homophobia, and misogyny of the period prove to have much in common. The Jew, the "New Woman," and the homosexual were at once fascinating and repulsive figures who obsessed the popular imagination. In each case, the danger that they posed to the established order was the same: miscegenation. They threatened to corrupt the old fixed categories of national identity in one case, gender in the other two, at a moment when all kinds of boundaries, external and internal, were being transgressed. It was around 1900 that the Cartesian religion of objectivity came under attack by the greatest minds of the age, and this extraordinarily anarchic and fertile moment generated the anxieties about meaning, and about the integrity of the self, that we still live with. The Impressionists had challenged objective perception; now Freud was taking on objective consciousness, Proust the truth of memory, and Einstein the absolutes of matter and energy, time and space.

What is so subversive about Colette's first novels is their suggestion that gender, too, is subjective. She perceived instinctively that the child of either sex has desires classified too strictly as masculine or feminine: urges to penetrate, devour, and possess; to be cherished, dominated, and contained. The character of Claudine offers one of the first critiques of a society that demanded too much conformity; that assigned the privilege of doing and being done to exclusively to one sex or the other. The damaged girls, child-women, feminized men, lost boys, inverts, and sexual impersonators Colette describes have been forced to deny or renounce the forbidden aspects of themselves—their impure true feelings—and they've experienced a split that seems impossible to heal.

COLETTE'S GREAT TREATISE on gender is called *The Pure and the Impure*.[15] It tracks the course of the forbidden desires which go underground to resurface as perversions, and the search of a fragmented self for another, symmetrically fragmented, to complete it. "I'd like your opinion of what I'm writing about unisexuals," she tells a friend, halfway through the composition. ". . . One could treat the chapter as follows: Unisexuals/One and only chapter/ There are no unisexuals."[16] Gender is impure.

Pure and impure are, for Colette, what Kierkegaard's Either/Or was for my first subject, Isak Dinesen: battle lines, personal and cultural. A dialectic is a useful construct for a biographer, but it exists to be transcended. A coherent personality aspires, like a work of art, to contain its conflicts without resolving them dogmatically. The writer's solution is to find a narrative structure for them, and the process often begins, as Proust's does, with the mistaken notion or memory of two divergent paths in life, which wisdom and time rejoin.

The ideal of purity for Colette is an Edenic state of harmony enjoyed by wild animals, flora, birds of prey, certain sociopaths, and by ordinary humans only as fetuses. To be pure means to be unhindered by any conscious bonds of need or dependence, or by any conflict between male and female drives. As Colette believes that there is no authentic androgyny in the fallen world, there can be no wholeness, and for a woman no autonomy—a male privilege—without an unacceptable erotic sacrifice. "How to liberate my true hope?" she asks. "Everything is against me. The first obstacle to my escape is this woman's body barring my way, a voluptuous body with closed eyes, voluntarily blind, stretched full out, ready to perish. . . . I'm she, this woman, this brute beast so stubborn in her pleasure."[17]

Colette's "true hope" was revolutionary. She may or may not have read Nietzsche, but she absorbed his exhortation, which was the byword of her generation: "Become thyself." But how, around 1900, could you possibly become an individual—yourself—and a *woman?* That question is at the heart of everything she writes.

In middle age—at menopause, to be exact—Colette would embody her notion of purity, which is to say of wholeness, in the powerful, pagan earth mother to whom she gives her own mother's name. This Sido (who should not be confused with the real Madame Sidonie Colette) is complete, fierce, belligerent, gay, utterly sovereign in her chosen, female domain, and contemptuous of love's frivolity and servitude. Sido's effortless chastity, as Colette describes it, has nothing of the nun's or the virgin's renunciation. Sido is a person and a woman both.

HAPPY CHILDHOODS ARE as scarce in biography as they are in fiction. Colette laid claim to one, noting dryly that it had been a bad preparation for human contacts. Before she met Willy, she says, her life had been "nothing but roses." In *My Apprenticeships,* she represents her marriage as the stroke of an executioner that severed her from the idyll of her girlhood. "I had a great deal of trouble accepting that there was such a difference between the existence of a daughter and of a wife, between country life and life in Paris, between the presence—at least the illusion—of happiness and its absence, between love and the laborious, exhausting game of the senses."[18]

Colette's accounts of her early happiness are important but questionable documents for a biographer. They conflict with the evidence provided by other sources, including her fiction, and they often contradict or undermine themselves internally, as does the sentence I have quoted. In an essay by Dominique Aury, who has also written one of the most troubling and truthful books about a woman's secrets of the flesh—*Story of O*—I found a passage which suggests a way to understand the paradoxes of Colette's writing about her formative years. Aury is discussing Longus and his version of Daphnis and Chloe—an important story for Colette:

Two handsome adolescents in love, forever adolescent, forever in love—is there any more universal royalty, whether they live in tales, ballads, or fables, frescoes or tapestries, or even on wallpaper? That the height of artifice should lead to simplicity . . . is much less a proof of true simplicity or convention than of a strange and obscure trust of man in man and of man in the earth, of a faith without dogma, time or place which the worst denials of barbarism or civilization have never been able to root out entirely from his heart. Nothing, nothing at all, not even experience, will prevent the hope that the secret of happiness is there.[19]

The secret of happiness: there it is in all its innocence. Aury has dared to say it, just as she dares, from behind the mask of Pauline Réage, to avow that in the pursuit of that secret, a certain kind of woman—Aury, like Colette, is mostly if not exclusively interested in a certain kind of woman, the masked, tenacious one—will stop at nothing: no taboo, sacrifice, or convention; no threshold of decency. Yet people who know where the secret of happiness is to be found do not, as a rule, become writers. Aury formulates the commonplace about a writer's experience in its most extreme form where she writes of Marcel Proust: "[His] was that most stupendous of bargains, a life for a life."[20]

"To receive happiness from someone—," Colette muses in *The Pure and the Impure*, "I'm obliged to use this word that I don't understand—is it not to choose the sauce in which we want to be eaten?"[21] Yet she never satisfies her hunger for it, or for the theme of adolescent love—the fable of Daphnis and Chloe—who are sometimes two teenagers, but more often an aging woman and a young man, a middle-aged roué and a girl, a mother and child, a butcher boy and an old queen, a spoiled husband and his cat. This is not, is never, parody. Whatever their real ages, Colette's lovers are engaged in that futile adolescent quest for happiness—for reunion—which, in the classical version of their love affair, pits them against a rapacious world, but in Colette's modern retellings, against the rapacity and reticence they encounter in each other.

COLETTE ACCEPTED Willy's definition of her as "a child of nature," in quotation marks. So, on the whole, did the French literary establishment, without the marks. *"Colette, notre plus grand écrivain naturel,"* Montherlant calls her—our greatest natural writer. But beware when the French admire something as natural. It touches on their deepest fear: looking ridiculous. Colette's vitality was in a way too truculent; her speech, as she says herself, too "brutal and familiar"; and her fiction, too popular for the taste of the mandarins. She never dropped her Burgundian accent. She got fat and didn't worry about it. She wrote an advice column for a women's magazine. She was one of the first writers to describe the pathology of an anorexic and the poignance of a faked orgasm. In her sixties, Colette opened a beauty salon, sold her signature products in provincial department stores, and did makeovers in a lab coat. (Natalie Barney noted that her clients came out looking twice as old as they went in.) But that is an image to retain: of female science operating with feigned benevolence on female nature—Colette the fixer.

The "child of nature" took great pains to give herself an unwriterly past. "Vocation, sacred signs, childhood poetry, predestination? I can't find any such things in my memory. . . . In my youth I never, *never* wanted to write. No . . . I didn't get A's for the style of my homework between the ages of twelve and fifteen! For I felt, each day better . . . that I was, precisely, born *not* to write."[22]

These vehement protestations, coming from one of France's greatest prose stylists, are most important for the claim that they stake to what Willy calls "Claudine's special case." Colette wants us to believe that, however voracious a reader she might have been, she was never bookish. Bookish children, it is true, read with a hunger which she reserves for her carnal pleasures. General ideas, she liked to say, were like dangling earrings: they didn't suit her. "I'm not worthy of politics," she told an interviewer after the Second World War, when he observed that "we have yet to meet a character in any of your novels who worries about anything other than himself."[23] "A 'child of nature' such as I am," she asserts elsewhere, ". . . cherishes the arbitrary, prefers passion to goodness, and combat to discussion."[24]

The ability to generalize from one's own experience is the basis for a conscience. But conscience for Colette is what living *dans le vrai* was for Flaubert—a dangerous distraction, and a choice between conflicting devotions: to self and destiny, or to other lives and their burdens.

"THERE'S ONLY ONE PERSON in this world you can count on, and that's yourself,"[25] Sido told Colette at the time of her divorce from Willy, and she took this stark advice to heart. Her egoism, which she calls "my monstrous innocence," and which is—like the shell of the tortoise—armor, plumage, camouflage, and refuge all in one, does not make her easy to approach. Yet it's tremendously compelling, as is all heresy, the more so, perhaps, to modern women torn between their own conflicting devotions.

The subject of love was, as Colette puts it, "the bread of my life and pen."[26] But the experience of love aroused her profoundest mistrust, and perhaps that is why the men in her works tend to be weak, or very young, or contemptible except for pleasure. A man really worth loving would be an invitation to perdition, and she doesn't want to put temptation in her own path, even in the form of a character. Mother love was a more dangerous and regressive temptation for Colette than romantic love. Children, herself included, were those "happy, unconscious little vampire[s] who drain the maternal heart."[27] And here I should begin her story.

PART I

CHAPTER I

Balzac has invented everything.
—COLETTE,
The Evening Star

1

IN THE MIDDLE of the last century, the village of Saint-Sauveur-en-Puisaye was a rustic backwater despite its proximity to Paris, three hours by train to the nearest station followed by a rough cart ride. The Puisaye was called "the poor Burgundy" to distinguish it from the rich Burgundy of the great vineyards. The landscape was dotted with ponds which bred malaria and smelled of caltrops and marsh mint. Coppice grew thickly in the ravines, where the wild strawberries and lilies of the valley were guarded by pitiless brambles. Game abounded in the woods. There were ancient stands of pine, which Colette loved for their scent. The spongy paths she followed when she gathered wild mushrooms or hunted for butterflies with her brothers were carpeted with violet heather. It was a secretive, inbred region of casual morals, hard winters, poaching, and poor farms. Wet-nursing was, as late as the fin de siècle, a lucrative sideline for the farmers' wives.

Saint-Sauveur had once been a fiefdom of the counts of Auxerre. It is built on a hill, with houses, writes Colette, which "come tumbling down the slope into the valley." There are two noble edifices at its peak: a château of medieval provenance, reconstructed during the reigns of Louis XV and XVI,[1] and a "Saracen" tower dating from the twelfth century. The streets are steep and narrow. They were unpaved in Colette's youth and would flood after a violent rainstorm. Walls of ferruginous sandstone enclose the gardens of the houses,

3

two stories high, for the most part, with ochre and gray façades and rust-colored grillwork. The autumnal colors of the earth and the architecture give the village an air of decline, even in summer. "It's not very pretty," admitted Colette, who claimed to "adore" her birthplace at the same time that she called it "mean, close-fisted, and confined."[2] Once she left it, she never returned, except on business, or to refresh her memory for a piece of prose.

BUT SAINT-SAUVEUR HAD a chronicler long before Colette. His name was Crançon, and he was a local magistrate during the last decade of the Second Empire. One imagines him as a haughty little man in a frock coat and pince-nez, bored and embittered but vain of his probity. One of his duties was to pass along to his superior, the imperial prosecutor in Auxerre, such village scandal as he deemed worthy of interest. His reportage, comic in the Balzacian style, makes delightful reading. It focuses, naturally, on the village notables, and one in particular: a troublesome bachelor named Jules Robineau-Duclos.

Colette describes Jules Robineau—Sido's first husband—as a striking figure on a fine horse; dark and haggard; courteous but aloof; a Don Juan among the serving maids. He was known to his fellow villagers, says she, as the Savage. But the real nickname of this appealing Burgundian Heathcliff was the Ape. There are no surviving portraits of him, but Crançon calls him "monstrous to look at."[3] He suffered from a curious deformity—fourteen extra teeth growing in a double row—and as a boy of sixteen, he had submitted to the torture of having them extracted in one sitting. The year was 1829. There was no anesthesia except alcohol.

Jules Robineau and his younger sister, Louise, were the heirs to a handsome fortune[4] in farmland, forests, vineyards, and village real estate. In 1836, their mother died in a lunatic asylum, and they lost their father later that year. By the terms of his will, the sixteen-year-old girl became the ward of a cousin, M. Givry—a provision that suggests her brother, at twenty-two, was already markedly unstable. Givry promptly married Louise to his own son. If the groom had any qualms about the taint of madness in his wife's blood, they were assuaged by her dowry.

The tormented brother lived a lonely, dissolute, and chaotic life. He "declined to wed," writes Crançon, "taking a concubine, who was not in the least impoverished under his roof." This doesn't seem quite fair: surely no local girl of his own rank would have had him. His peasant mistress, Marie Miton, ruled his household, suffered his violence, and in 1843 bore him a son, for all of which she was promised ten thousand francs in his will. At the time of his marriage to Sido, Robineau found Marie a husband, fourteen years her junior, and Colette knew this "old Cèbe" as a widowed neighbor with whom her mother traded rose cuttings.

The decades passed slowly, as they do in the provinces. "The passion for drink," Crançon continues, "increasingly consumed M. Robineau until it had stupefied him completely. He ceased going to bed. From morning to night he sat numbly at a table before a bottle of eau-de-vie, which was no sooner emptied than it was refilled." The "romantic pallor" Colette attributes to the "Savage" was a symptom of these sleepless alcoholic binges. He barricaded his house against imaginary African mercenaries, took potshots at his servants, and threatened to hack one of his maids into small pieces as bait for crayfish.

The Givrys were impatient for Robineau to die, he was doing everything to oblige them, and by the late 1850s, "his death seemed to be imminent. It was a matter of waiting perhaps a month or two. . . . But M. Givry, his brother-in-law, didn't have that much patience." He sued, in his wife's name, to have Robineau declared insane.

There were two competency hearings, which must have been enthralling to a village which, as Colette puts it, "vegetates all the year round in peace and inanition and has to content itself with meager scandals."[5] The servants testified to their master's violence. But Robineau was not without his well-wishers, including, of course, his "concubine," who stood to lose her inheritance if the judge ruled in favor of the Givrys. There was also, more important, a dissident faction of the Robineau family, who "seized with delight upon an opportunity to thwart Monsieur Givry, whom they disliked."

These prominent relations "joined forces to shake M. Robineau out of his lethargy so that he could make a decent impression in court. . . . Watched over and deprived of drink, [he] recovered a bit physically and morally." The judge concluded that the Givrys were petitioning in bad faith, and ruled in the defendant's favor, noting, however, that he did seem "precociously senile."

The story might have ended here. But Robineau's defenders "knew perfectly well that, left to himself, he would succumb to his old drunken ways, and that M. Givry would get his hands on the inheritance. . . . They resolved then . . . to marry off M. Robineau. It is true that he was already old [forty-two], that he was ugly, that he stammered and was more or less an imbecile, but he was rich, which compensates for a great deal."

Now, it happened "by chance" that a respectable young lady who had spent her childhood in the neighboring village (Mézilles), "whose family lived in Belgium and who, I believe, had not always paid her expenses" (dixit Crançon), had returned to visit her peasant wet nurse, Mme Guille.[6] According to Colette, Sido was out walking and Robineau was inspecting his estates, astride his strawberry roan, when they crossed paths. "The passing vision of this man . . . with his youthful black beard and romantic pallor was not unpleasant to the young woman."[7] But according to Crançon, it was one of the anti-Givry conspirators who engaged Sido in a conversation, which led to an "inspection," which was followed by a proposal, which entailed all of that lengthy haggling central to every middle-class betrothal of the period. Robineau, in the meantime, went on another shooting spree and would have murdered his servants had his aim not been so unsteady. The police commissioner deprived him of his firearms. This embarrassment did not retard his wedding plans.

"After her brothers had discussed, for eight days, the terms of her marriage contract," Crançon concludes, Adèle-Eugénie-Sidonie Landoy and Jules Robineau-Duclos were wed at the town hall of Schaerbeek, a suburb of Brussels, on January 17, 1857. It was the week that Gustave Flaubert went on trial, charged with obscenity, because he had failed to condemn adultery in his *Madame Bovary*.

2

SIDO WAS BORN in Paris on August 12, 1835. She never knew her mother, née Sophie Chatenay, who died of puerperal fever two months later. Her father made inquiries in the Puisaye and found Mme Guille. "If I was keeping [her] awake," Sido told Colette, "she could have seen [Halley's] comet." This is Sido's only extant reference to the woman who raised her, although it was presumably to her nurse that she owed her encyclopedic knowledge of provincial housekeeping and gardening, and perhaps, too, some of the ferocity of her character. Her hardiness, physical and moral, was certainly not that of a bourgeoise. But as an *orpheline de mère,* like so many of Colette's heroines, Sido could never understand those well-off Parisians who left their babies with a country wet nurse, sometimes for years. "Children are their parents' joy for all of their lives," she told Colette, even though her own childhood suggested otherwise. "As for me, I brought nothing but grief to my father, because my birth had cost my mother her life, and I reminded him too vividly of this event."[8] It would later be said in the region that as a little girl, "Mme Colette never knew she had a family. . . . The village believed her people had abandoned her."[9]

Sido's father, Henry Landoy, was the first of the unfaithful and profligate men in her own life and in her daughter's. He was "ugly but well-built!" Sido told Colette, with "pale, contemptuous eyes and a long nose above the thick Negro lips that had inspired his nickname,"[10] the Gorilla. At the end of her life, in a passing phrase, Colette describes her mother's antecedents as "cocoa harvesters" from the colonies, "colored by island blood," with frizzy hair and purple fingernails.[11] She was a little more expansive in an early letter to Francis Jammes, where she calls Henry Landoy "a quadroon": "My ancestors also came from a warm island, long ago, like yours, except that mine had to be darker. . . . At home we've kept nothing, neither documents nor souvenirs, only a daguerreotype of mama's father, a kind of gingerbread-colored gorilla who sold cocoa. There! I have a stain of black in my blood. Does that disgust you?"[12]

The Landoys' parish records suggest no plausible explanation for the "stain of black" in their blood. But in a 1997 French biography of Colette, Claude Francis and Fernande Gontier assert that the records are faulty, and perhaps fraudulent. According to their new research, the family came originally from Champagne, where they were literate but humble farmers and converts to Protestantism. During the seventeenth century, the persecution of heretics was particularly intense in their native province, and like many of their coreligionists, some Landois—as they originally spelled their name—sought refuge in Martinique, prospered in the spice trade, and acquired slaves. Their children were of mixed descent, Creole and African, and a number of these sons of color were sent back to France to apprentice in the Guilde des Épiciers—the Grocers' Guild—which controlled the lucrative colonial traffic in tobacco, chocolate, rum, sugar, pepper, and other exotic products.

In the late eighteenth century, non-white colonial immigrants were subject to strict surveillance and, if they were not of French birth, deportation. Many provided themselves with false identity papers or borrowed the parish records of relatives who had stayed in France. This seems to have been the case with Colette's direct forebear, Pierre Landois, a Martiniquais who, by the time of the Revolution, had established himself as an *épicier* in Le Havre. His two sons were also in the grocery business: Pierre in Paris, and Robert—Colette's great-grandfather—in Charleville, a city in the Ardennes that was a hub for the import-export trade with the Antilles. Here Robert married Marie Mathis, the daughter of a bargeman. Their son Henry—the "Gorilla"—was born in 1783, and the family was "rich enough" to give him a "solid education."[13]

Henry served in an elite lancer regiment of Napoleon's army, and while he was stationed in Versailles, he courted a pretty girl with golden hair—Colette's grandmother—whose father managed the local clock factory. "No doubt," writes Colette, "before having betrayed her twenty times, her husband, a shade *'colored,'* had been seduced by the pallor of that Parisienne."[14]

Their marriage was hasty because Sophie was pregnant. She eventually gave birth to seven children, of whom four survived. Sido's brothers, Eugène and Paul, were her seniors by nineteen and twelve years, respectively. Her sister, Irma, was her elder only by fourteen months. But Irma barely figures in Sido's letters or Colette's biographies. She made her living as a milliner in Le Havre, where she was born, and in 1907 died destitute in a Brussels hospice.

Francis and Gontier speculate that her fate was a well-kept family secret, and that for a decade before her late marriage to a much older man, she had lived by her charms.

After his wars, Henry Landois worked in his father's grocery, prospering sufficiently to become a wholesaler, which meant a gentleman.[15] But he lived beyond his means, and at the time of his wife's death, he had amassed such pressing debts that he was forced to flee the country to escape his creditors. He then took up residence in Belgium, married a rich widow of whom nothing more is heard, and after several more upheavals and reversals of fortune, resettled his family in Lyon, with a pet monkey named Jean, in a large, richly furnished house, where he manufactured chocolate.

It was here, according to Colette, that an eight-year-old Sido—recalled from the Puisaye—tortured an infant of unknown provenance who had arrived one morning with *her* wet nurse. "Bring her up," Landois—or, as he now signed himself, Landoy—told Sido; "she's your sister." Her maternal instincts weren't compelling enough to resist the jealousy of the last born for the new arrival, and with that "cruelty of childhood" which both Sido and Colette secretly admired and which neither entirely outgrew, she proceeded to "taper" the child's insufficiently elegant little fingers by squeezing and pinching them. "My father's daughter started out in life with ten little round abscesses," Colette claims Sido told her. ". . . Now you realize what a wicked mommy you've got. Such a lovely newborn. How she screamed!"[16]

THE CHRONOLOGY OF Sido's adolescence is murky. She apparently spent 1848, the year of the liberal revolution, living in Mézilles with Mme Guille. It has often been said that her brothers used her residence there to facilitate their own covert political activities. The Puisaye was a refuge for partisans of democracy and illegal secret societies, and they were both passionate freethinkers and republicans.

The brothers had taken Belgian citizenship, and sometime between 1849 and 1854, when their father died, Eugène brought Sido to Brussels. He was, by now, a successful publisher and a distinguished liberal journalist who, after the coup d'état of 1851, opened his house to writers, artists, and intellectuals fleeing the repressive climate in Second Empire France. Sido told Colette that she spent the happiest years of her life in this emancipated, literary milieu, whose loss she never ceased to mourn, and that Eugène had "initiated" her "to the art of loving and understanding the rare and the beautiful."[17]

Francis and Gontier go further, advancing the theory that Sido's "philosophy"—and, through osmosis, Colette's—were definitively colored by the "audacious" ideas of the atheists, bohemians, and sexual revolutionaries she met at her brother's, and in particular, those of Victor Considerant, Eugène's great friend and the "standard-bearer" for the utopian communalist Fourier. "According to Fourier," they write, "the repression of the passions is at the origin of all the evils, crimes, and pathology of civilized societies. . . . Fourier predicted that it would take three centuries to transform our civilization into Harmony. Sido saw herself as a pioneer of this new social and erotic order. 'I have always been a bit mad,' she told Colette in 1909, 'though not as much as you think. But here's how it is: I came into this world three hundred years too early, and I'm not understood here, not even by my children.' "[18]

"WHEN A YOUNG GIRL is without fortune or profession," writes Colette of her mother's first marriage, "and is, moreover, entirely dependent on her brothers, what can she do but hold her tongue, accept what is offered, and thank God for it?"[19] But holding her tongue was never Sido's style. Her "liberty of speech," her independence of spirit, and, not least, her lifelong fondness for her brothers all suggest that she hadn't listened "scared and silent" as the men decided her fate. Robineau was so notorious that she and her family couldn't have been ignorant of his character, but he was also so decrepit that perhaps they took a practical view of their devil's bargain: her virginity and a few years, at most, of unhappiness in exchange for a lifetime of security.

"We're all so dumb at twenty," Sido told Colette, speaking of women. As an old widow, she held marriage in contempt: it was "a forfeit," which can also mean, in French, a workman's contract or a heinous crime. And of husbands, in general, she would rage: "God, but they are stupid!" To the daughter whom she regarded as a second and better self she would insist that she, Sido, had been "meant for a life of liberty!" . . . "I wasn't able to shake off the yoke as you have. . . ." "I never wanted to have children."[20] Nor was Colette, childless until forty, ever encouraged by her mother to procreate. Perhaps, however, the Gorilla's daughter saw something alluringly familiar and challenging in the Ape: that "deep-rooted misogyny which women," according to Colette, "find so attractive."[21] There are many versions of the romance between Beauty and the Beast, though in most of them, a virgin's bellicose ambitions to conquer and domesticate a predator are piously disguised.

3

JULES ROBINEAU OWNED a good-sized house in Saint-Sauveur, at 6, rue de l'Hospice. In 1925, a small rose-marble plaque was affixed to the façade. It reads, simply: COLETTE WAS BORN HERE, and she was grateful, she said, for the discreet omission of a date. The opening lines of *My Mother's House* have made this "solemn, rather forbidding" dwelling a literary monument. Generations of French schoolchildren are, from their *dictées,* on intimate terms with the blackened, crooked steps, the carriage entrance bolted "like an ancient dungeon," the desolate sound of a doorbell "like that of an orphanage." It was a house, writes Colette, "that smiled only on its garden side."[22] These are images worth remembering.

Robineau used regularly to beat his concubine, Marie Miton, and two months into his marriage, drunk as usual and "mocking the pain he was causing me," he tried to beat Sido, too. "There was a charming scene of carnage," she told Colette, and she was always indignant at those women who were not ready to leave, expel, or murder the unfaithful and violent wretches they had married. "Aiming for his head," she continued, "I began to throw everything on the mantel, including an oil lamp with sharp edges. It hit him smack in the face, and he took the scar to his grave. I was very pleased with myself. That straightened him out, you know, once and for all. You would never have believed such a thing of your old mommy, *n'est-ce pas,* little one?"[23]

In her fairy tale version of Sido's life, Colette never alluded to Robineau's brutality, or to her mother's unhesitating and remarkably brave readiness to defend herself. Instead she describes how the Savage—perceiving that his bride was "bored"—saddled his mare, rode off to Auxerre, and returned with a cashmere shawl and a mortar of rare marble. Sido left these treasures to Colette, who cut up the shawl for lingerie bags and used the mortar to make almond paste. They were only the relics—the symbolic trophies—of her mother's real legacy, or the best part of it: "The will to survive [that] is so alive in us women" and "the lust for victory [that] is so female!"[24]

Robineau was humbled, and Sido had enough good will to pity this emotionally destitute creature who had never, she said, "known how to give."[25] They shared a contempt for the prigs of the village, and at least one other deep affinity. Writing to Colette about a Biblical rain of frogs that fell one summer day on a road between two water holes, Sido notes that this strange phenomenon hadn't surprised her: "J. Robineau—who had a profound knowledge of all things connected with the fields, the woods, and the ponds—had already spoken to me about it."[26] The love of nature in a virile, unsociable male would only have endeared him to Colette.

If Sido was, as Crançon maintains, an "unloving" wife, she was also, if we believe both the evidence of her own letters and Colette, an "uncomplaining one." An orphan with no dowry, she had yet acquired a name and connections she remained proud of all her life. They brought her a fine estate and a trousseau of silver, china, cut glass, copper cooking pots, and sheets woven from the flax of her own farms. She enjoyed what local high life there was— balls and dinners with the rural gentry—and she kept house lavishly, employing five servants, and teaching the kitchen help to cook the robust Flemish dishes that reminded her of her brother's home. Her friendship with Victor Gandrille, the millionaire proprietor of the château, was a source of gossip. Crançon, who kept track of Madame Robineau's income and debts, calls her "a woman incapable of thrift or order." At the end of her life, still stuck in a provincial backwater and living on a meager pension, Sido would sigh to Colette: "I love luxury." "It's very tiresome not to be rich."[27]

If Robineau was still fornicating with the maids, he probably didn't dare to do so at home. Francis and Gontier suggest that he continued to depend on Marie Cèbe, who lived next door, to nurse him through his binges. In the early years of her marriage, Sido "tried to combat" her husband's alcoholism, but she abandoned the battle once her own affections were engaged elsewhere. At the time of his death, they had separate bedrooms. "I have always considered it neither fitting nor proper to sleep with one's husband," Sido told Colette.[28]

But it was apparently not against her principles to sleep with someone who was not her husband. We shall meet her second lover shortly. Her first, according to Crançon, was the village notary, Adrien Jarry, "who, it is said, has ever only half-denied it." On August 14, 1860, M. Jarry registered the birth of Mme Robineau's first child, a daughter, Héloïse-Émilie-Juliette, to whom Colette would give the deceptively romantic epithet "my sister with the long hair."[29]

At least there were no questions about Juliette's paternity, as there would be about her brother's. According to Sido, the girl had Robineau's character "completely." Colette describes her sister's "strange little head, attractive in its ugliness," with Mongol cheekbones and a broad, "sarcastic" mouth. Her forehead was low, her eyebrows were thick, her dark hair was "abnormal in length, vigor, and thickness,"[30] and it is not unlikely that the arms and legs of the Ape's daughter were hairy, too. This disconcerting infant, Sido told Colette, "was infatuated with the night . . . and as she grew up she remained faithful to the shadow."[31]

Sido felt an almost moral repugnance for ugliness. She would set enormous store by Colette's beauty and vitality, and she never ceased to remark how much they were alike. Juliette was a girl and later a woman alien to her mother in every respect, and an outsider, a freak—even an orphan—in her own family. She never shared her mother's passions for the house and garden, her father's love of nature, or her brothers' of music. Colette describes her as a ghost wandering through the house with her nose buried in a novel—an "intoxicated victim" of romantic fiction.[32] "I feel this child is unhappy, I feel she is suffering," says Sido anxiously, in Colette's memoir. But her maternal pride was also, it seems, deeply offended.

Chronic depression and perhaps even psychosis were part of Juliette's patrimony. But for a troubled child who feels rejected by or invisible to a parent, the unwillingness to thrive can also be a form of revenge. Colette describes how the teenage Juliette, having caught typhoid, refused to let her mother nurse her: "I don't know anyone around here,"[33] she cried in her delirium, addressing Catulle Mendès—Colette's future friend—who was one of the literary celebrities Juliette consorted with in her world of fantasy. Later on, she wrote vapid and uncultivated letters to a mother conscientious about her own prose style and exalted by the literary talent of her other daughter. She married a man whom Sido loathed, and whose demands for his wife's marriage portion would ruin the family. Juliette gave birth to her only child in a house across the street while Sido, banished, listened for the newborn's cry from her own garden.

Juliette was thirteen when Colette was born. The disparity of temperament was as alienating as the difference in age, and the two sisters were virtual strangers. But then no one, according to Sido, had ever really known Juliette. "I was the only one," she would claim in a letter to Willy a few days after Juliette, at forty-eight, had killed herself by taking strychnine in her second suicide attempt. Sido was mistaken, however, for one meets the shade of Juliette over and over in Colette's work, and particularly in her journalism. She portrays depressed, abused, violent, and betrayed women—victims of their families, of their men, and of their own weakness—with an eloquence that belies her own distaste and detachment. The sense of sisterhood is there, furtive and shameful but deeply felt, as it must have been at Saint-Sauveur.

There are many examples I could quote, but the finest and most familial is Colette's study of the infamous parricide Violette Nozières:

> I regarded this young girl's face, which seemed gentle, almost without interest until the day the photographs revealed its striking resemblance to the paternal effigy. Violette Nozière is, to the exclusion of all maternal echoes, her father's daughter: compare the architecture of the two heads . . . the plaintive but timid mouth, and in the eyes, the same reproach—the reproach of the weak, the discontent of those who have never struggled against themselves. . . .
>
> Am I pleading the cause of a criminal of whom I know nothing except her crime? No. I give less thought to her than I do to her adolescence, and . . . its hidden seething. . . .
>
> Subtle and wounded senses, suffocated souls, admit almost nothing. Beneath the still waters, no monster's scales appear to ruffle the reflection of a placid landscape. . . . Few parents have any genius, how many have a foreboding of catastrophe? They never intervene by pure divination. . . . One has seen captives whetting the instruments of their escape practically under their warders' eyes.

Before us in the courtroom sit two strangers, two enemies, mother and daughter. . . . The mother will curse her in vain. But at least the daughter will put an end to her confused, atrocious dream, which she ripened for so long before those two: her mother, the stranger, and her father, the cipher.[34]

CHAPTER 2

Without a doubt, she was Madame Bovary.
—CLAUDE PICHOIS, on Sido

1

$\mathcal{I}$N AUGUST OF 1860, a new tax collector arrived in Saint-Sauveur. This former captain in the Zouaves, Jules Colette, immediately became an object of curiosity to the village. His accent marked him as a southerner, and his diction as a gentleman. The coincidence of a red ribbon in his buttonhole—the Legion of Honor—and a wooden stump protruding from the slack left leg of his trousers signified that he was a war hero.

The men in the café would quickly have heard the outlines of the Captain's valorous career, recounted with *gaillardise*. He had served in Algeria, in Turkey, and with General Canrobert in the Crimea. He had led a victorious charge against the Russians at the Battle of Alma, and had been wounded at Sebastopol, but had survived the cholera epidemic which decimated his regiment and the infamous horrors of that winter. "The snow, the famine, the grass harvested from beneath the corpses of the horses and eaten raw—he spoke of these," wrote Colette, "as of so many special favors personally granted him by fate."[1]

In 1859, Napoleon III had ordered the Zouaves to Italy to help Victor Emmanuel expel the Austrians. It was there, on the battlefield at Melegnano, that a cannonball had splintered Captain Colette's thighbone. He was rescued by two of his men and taken to a field hospital in Milan, where a surgeon with a hacksaw had performed the amputation, just below the groin. The Milanese were passionately grateful to their liberators. "Ah, the women of Milan!" he sighed to his new friends. "What memories. It was the best year of my life!"[2]

Jules Colette was still convalescing there when the emperor visited his ward. "I would like to do something for you," he told the Zouave, who replied that a crutch, Sire, was all the recompense he required. That, a Croix de Guerre, and a sinecure as the tax collector of Saint-Sauveur were his rewards for what he liked to call *"mon égratignure"* (my scratch).[3]

Mme Robineau was nine months pregnant with Juliette when Captain Colette became her neighbor, lodging with a widow a few doors away. She was probably too anxious about her confinement and too swollen by the August heat to have paid him much attention. But he liked to sing at his open window—the Italian love songs he had learned in Milan—and she could have heard him from her own. The voice was a baritone, agile and mellow. She would learn that it could also give vent to terrible "sham southern rages"; "to growls and high-sounding oaths"; and, when the fury was sincere, to tones of honeyed menace.[4]

Perhaps by the beginning of September, when she was on her feet again, Sido discovered that this expressive organ belonged to a handsome man of thirty with Cossack cheekbones and feline eyes. Their gaze was ribald and challenging. The Captain made it a point to let the village know that the surgeon's hacksaw had spared his manhood. His great muscular strength was "controlled and dissimulated like that of a cat,"[5] and he was remarkably athletic on his crutches. Crançon would also report that Jules Colette had impregnated a local girl and sent her away so as "not to sabotage his plans"[6] to conquer the heart and fortune of Mme Robineau.

In the beginning, Sido had been amused when the Captain's landlady complained about his barracks language, his incessant smoking and coquetry, and his eccentric eating habits. Perhaps the Crimea had given him his taste for salads in preference to red meat. He didn't touch alcohol. This must have impressed the wife of Jules Robineau. The Captain, in turn, was charmed by the aplomb of the young northerner with the plush figure and the marvelous hair, whose feline features—so like his own—were more striking for their fire than their perfection. Sido's glance was penetrating. So was her irony. From her first sentence, she betrayed her otherness to the village. He would have heard her story in the café: the drunken old brute she had married for his fortune; the republican brothers in Belgium; the superior airs. They often met in the château society that would later spurn them. Perhaps he paid her a New Year's Day visit, and they played music or chess while Robineau went to fetch another bottle from his cellar, tossing out his favorite bit of philosophy: "If you drink you'll die, but if you don't drink you'll die anyway."[7]

"A droll man," writes Claude Pichois, "with the melancholy gaiety of amputees and southerners, attentive, gallant, fervent, and relatively cultivated, [Captain Colette] would not have found it difficult—in the desert that was Saint-Sauveur—to inspire Sido's tenderness."[8] Theirs was the complicity of two literate castaways stranded among philistines. However their affair began, one infers that it was precipitous. "There are people who fling themselves into the path of your existence, and plunge it into chaos," Sido told Colette. "Thus your father acted with me."[9]

2

THE COLETTE FAMILY CAME originally from the Moselle, but Jules Colette, like his father, was a navy brat born in Toulon, and on his mother's side he was a Provençal. When Sido was exasperated with her second husband's jealousy, she would call him "the Italian." She also blamed his passivity, which would prove so fatal to their fortunes, on his "Italian side." It was a weakness that her son Léo would inherit, and she was always grateful that the roulette wheel of genetics had vouchsafed Colette her own "need to act. You don't get that from your father," she boasted. "He was meant to be a pasha or a priest, which as far as I'm concerned amounts to the same thing."[10] Sido would have been astounded to hear Colette declare, as an old woman: "I was born 'under the sign' of passivity."[11]

The Captain's father had been a naval infantry commander, retiring with honors to a small estate at Le Mourillon, outside the city of his birth. It had a picturesque situation on a rocky promontory overlooking the sea. When Colette was a music-hall artiste, playing Toulon on one of her tours, she found a postcard of the spot and sent it to her mother.[12] Sido recalled a vacation there with her three older children, and it would have given Colette, in later life, a charming alternative to Brittany or Saint-Tropez. But a nasty dispute with his niece over their patrimony forced Jules Colette to sell the cliff house, along with "a pretty piece of country" that his mother had "been so happy to possess."[13]

The Captain's parents considered him their prodigal son, and his mother resented him publicly enough for Crançon to quote her complaint that Jules had "ruined" them. His children, in turn, called Mme Colette *mère* their "wicked" grandmother, to distinguish her from the "good" (dead) one. Sido, of course, knew her mother only from her brothers' stories, and from a single image—a miniature painted on a piece of ivory with a hairline crack. It passed to Colette, and was stolen from one of her many apartments in Paris, but she recovered it at a flea market some thirty years later. (Impressed by the coincidence, the vendor gave her a good price.) The portrait showed a pale, smiling young woman in an empire gown with a sausage curl at each ear. But all that Colette really knew about Sophie Landoy was that she had died "prematurely" and so terribly "deceived."[14]

Impartiality was never one of Sido's virtues. She detested in-laws in general, and this little bulldog of a mother-in-law in particular. Having members of her family marry strangers was a martyrdom she always found hard to endure. "My sons-in-law are all pigs and my daughter-in-law a fat beast," she told Colette.[15] The only one of her children's consorts for whom she seems to have had no reproach was Colette's lesbian lover, the marquise de Morny.

The Captain's mother had "green eyes shaded by low, gingery brows, and in her big, black taffeta skirts, she moved with a dense, corporeal majesty."[16] Her jealousy was legendary, and it disgusted Sido all the more because it was another worthless legacy to her husband from his Latin ancestors. Colette, on the other hand, understood it perfectly. In *The Pure and the Impure,* she relates how her wicked grandmother would follow her septuagenarian husband to a public toilet and stand guard outside the door until he emerged. "A man who wants to deceive you," she told Colette, "can escape through even smaller holes!"[17]

If one were inclined to credit Sido's views on the importance of ethnic heritage in the formation of character, one could illuminate much about Colette by citing Theodore Zeldin's masterful portrait of the Provençals:

> They saw themselves as heretics in Christendom . . . heirs of the Cathar creed . . . which still survived among them . . . Provençals, they claimed, did not see good and evil as contradictory; they had no hierarchy of values, no moral imperatives; they saw life as an art, to be played with coquetry and dilettantism. . . . They did not judge the ideal. Unlike the northerner who believed in absolute truth . . . lying was not disapproved of in the Mediterranean. Lying indeed was neither a game nor a psychosis, but a rite and a ceremonial. . . . Mediterraneans do not think about death. . . . They [did] not live to obtain rewards in the next world, but sought to enjoy the present, to please themselves, to create an image of themselves as agreeable, noble, beautiful. Love in the south was different from what it was in the north. Provençals did not condemn passion.[18]

In 1847, at eighteen, Jules Colette entered St. Cyr, the French military academy. Early the next year, he was stripped of his commission and demoted to private—officially for "indiscipline," although Francis and Gontier speculate that he had killed a fellow student in an illegal duel, and Pichois, that he had participated in left-wing political demonstrations. That February, France was convulsed by the liberal revolution that toppled the July Monarchy and established the brief-lived Second Republic. Years later, running for local office as a republican, the Captain would boast of "having stood on the steps of the Hôtel de Ville with Lamartine, Arago, and Ledru-Rollin," the heroes of the day.[19] The immediate result of their bloodless and enlightened uprising was the institution of universal male suffrage, and five million Frenchmen, including peasants and workers, voted in the first election. What great democrat did they choose as their president? Prince Louis-Napoleon.

In the meantime, the well-connected father of the troublesome private arranged to have him posted to a naval infantry regiment shipping out to French Guiana. After a year of rehabilitation in the tropics, Jules Colette was permitted to finish his training at the École Spéciale Militaire, and was recommissioned as a second lieutenant in the Zouaves. By 1851, the people's prince had become a reactionary emperor, and the fervent republican from Toulon, a foot soldier in his pointless wars. Rereading her father's letters to his commanding officer, Colette would discover that his greatest ambition had been to die gloriously in public. But it was the Captain's fate to botch everything he attempted, even dying. Marriage, a family, politics, literature, and the pastimes of a country gentleman could never console him for a bitterness no civilian can readily understand: the secret humiliation of survival.

3

JULIETTE WAS THREE and Sido had been married to Robineau for six years when she gave birth to her first son, Edmé-Jules-Achille. "If there were any doubts about her liaison [with Jarry]," wrote Crançon, "there is scarcely a one as to her relations with M. Colette, nor is there a soul in Saint-Sauveur who is not convinced that the second child of Mme Robineau is [his] handiwork."[20]

Sido never said anything on the subject, except for a cryptic remark to Colette: "You're not like me. I resist my passions,"[21] which doesn't mean that she could resist someone else's. Achille would be buried in the tomb of the Colettes, but in his lifetime, he always went by the name of Robineau-Duclos. He inherited his third of the disputed fortune, became a doctor, and eventually married very well. His wife, Jane de la Fare, was the daughter of a viscount whose ancient family owned land and castles in the province. It would have been considered a grave *"mésalliance"*[22] for the bride had her relations suspected that Achille was the bastard of a penniless former tax collector and the Madame Bovary of Saint-Sauveur.

Sido enjoyed the de la Fare connection and depended on Jane in her old age, but also ridiculed and despised her. She had always doted on Achille, whom she called "my beauty," who had the Captain's features and, as he grew up, a much more passionate sense of filial loyalty than his younger sister.

Colette, probably aware of his paternity, would claim Achille as "a whole brother by virtue of heart, choice, and resemblance." But he was also her first—and her greatest—romantic rival.

Achille had just turned two and Juliette was five when "their" father died in his sleep of a massive stroke, which wasn't discovered until the morning. Crançon blamed Sido for "confining" her husband to an isolated bedroom on the "pretext" that his loud snoring kept her awake. "I'm surprised," he continued, "that I've never heard anyone suggest that the unfaithful wife and her lover did not help speed [Robineau's] end. At least it is certain that they let him commit suicide in peace."23

After the funeral, the helpful M. Jarry made an inventory of Robineau's property and possessions. He left an estate of some three hundred thousand francs, to be shared equally by his widow and his two children.24 Managing her property was a burdensome practical responsibility for a woman "incapable of thrift or order," and Captain Colette was only too willing to intervene on Sido's behalf. She made no secret of their intimacy, telling one of her noble friends at Saint Fargeau that she planned to remarry as soon as the official mourning period was over. The village was outraged, as much, one suspects, by the Robineau fortune's going to the two outsiders as by their "immodesty and disrespect."25

Sido would later describe widowhood as "a black veil, and underneath a monkey's smile."26 Eleven months after her husband's funeral, on December 20, 1865, she married her lover at the town hall. The Captain's parents had come from Toulon for the quiet civil ceremony, and were perhaps meeting the bride for the first time.27 Ten more months passed—they were no doubt counted backwards on every hand in the village—before the birth of Sido's second son, Léopold Jean, called Léo by the family and lazzarone—lazybones—by his mother.

Except for their love of luxury and their propensity for debt and for attracting the animosity of a provincial village, the resemblance between Mme Bovary and Mme Robineau ended with Sido's second marriage. She was neither a sucker for romantic love nor a victim of romantic disillusionment, and she was vigilant as Colette would never be against their enslavements. "I don't understand how one can let oneself be 'victimized' [qu'on se laisse 'victimer']," she writes to Colette about a husband murdered by his wife's lover: "It's a state that I could never have endured."28 Her own husband's single-minded devotion to her was entirely "frivolous," in her estimation, just as the love in novels was "a great bore. . . . In life, my poor Minet-Chéri, folk have other fish to fry. Did none of these lovesick people you read of have children to rear or a garden to care for?"29

The garden was Sido's metaphor for motherhood, and she was always indignant when her human plants pulled up their roots and left her. She was a gardener and a mother of the French school: more concerned with form and control than with abundance. Ceres herself was the mother of an only child, and the mythical earth mother of Colette's oeuvre was never in favor of big families. She felt the distaste of a meticulous artisan for mass production, and it depressed her to see women with prolific broods of "slapdash" offspring. When Colette objected that there were four of them, Sido replied warmly: "I beg your pardon! I've had two husbands. So I am only two times the mother of two children."[30]

But rearing children and caring for a garden were never enough for this powerful character three hundred years too advanced for her time. After the birth of Léo, her first official Colette, Sido would wait seven years before she had another. Perhaps by then she had understood that none of her three offspring would help her to participate, at least vicariously, in the creation of "a new social and erotic order." One was a bizarre and moody pubescent daughter, and the other two were elusive male "savages" who tested her conviction—pure in theory, ambivalent in practice, and ahead of its time—that the proprietary mother is a disgrace, and the only maternal love worthy of the name is the one that lets go.[31]

CHAPTER 3

If a child could tell about his childhood while he is passing through it, his true childhood, his account would perhaps be nothing more than one of intimate dramas and disappointments. But he only writes having attained adulthood. However, he believes that he has preserved the memories of his childhood intact. I mistrust even my own.

—COLETTE,
Belles Saisons

1

THE SPIRIT OF the Second Empire was embodied in a line from Zola's working notes for *Nana*, which defines the novel's "philosophical subject as follows: a whole society hurling itself at the cunt."[1] Zola makes Nana's "cunt" the symbol of all that was degenerate in the body politic: new money, vulgar consumption, and foreign influences; an aristocracy prepared to abandon honor, religion, and prudence, indeed to commit suicide for its carnal pleasures; a proletariat debased by poverty, alcohol, and bad genes, and eager to pollute its oppressors; a parasitic Fourth Estate—the press—profiting from the debauchery of Parisian high life and goading its bacchants toward their ruin.

The Second Empire collapsed with the Franco-Prussian War of 1870–71, a desperate gamble with disastrous consequences for Napoleon III, who lost his throne, and for France, which was unprepared to fight an army superior in every respect—armaments, leadership, strategy, and morale. The defeat at Sedan was followed by a civil war; a five-billion-franc indemnity; the loss of

Alsace, part of Lorraine, and, in the minds of many Frenchmen, an inestimable portion of their manhood and honor. The reverberations of this humiliation would affect Colette in profound if insidious ways.

TWO YEARS LATER, at the age of thirty-seven, Mme Colette conceived her last child. By the end of her pregnancy she was "as big as a house." Her labor lasted "three days and two nights"[2] which suggests a distressed and perhaps very large baby. It ended on the twenty-eighth of January, 1873, toward ten o'clock in the evening, with the birth of a daughter: Sidonie-Gabrielle.

Sido would later tell Colette that children who have been carried high in the womb and refuse to descend become the best loved, because they have "lain so near their mother's heart and have been unwilling to leave her."[3] Colette was fourteen at the time, and she had been reading an illicit Zola novel—probably *Pot-bouille*—one of the rare books her parents had deemed unsuitable and locked away from her. It contained a graphic description of childbirth, and she had come to Sido to have the image of "the flesh split open, the excrement, the polluted blood . . . exorcised."[4] But her mother's reply did nothing to allay her sense of horror. All Sido would say was that she had never regretted her own suffering. Like Colette herself, who relished the occasional choice gory detail—the dagger in the eyeball—Sido had a streak of "divine cruelty,"[5] by which Colette means implacable realism. She refused to make a cult of her daughter's innocence.

Sido's midwives, Colette wrote, were so distracted that they let the fire die, and "since I had entered the world blue and silent, nobody thought it worth while to bother about me." The "half-choked" baby defied their indifference, "showing a determined will to live and even to live long."[6] The most interesting aspect of this dramatic if dubious account of cold and neglect is that it permits Colette to take sole credit for her own survival.

The near tragedy of the lying-in was ephemeral. Sido recovered, and the infant began to prosper. If her famously insatiable appetite wasn't born with her, it was probably tempted, if not actively bullied, into being. "The lover may resign himself to the monotony of lovemaking," Colette would write in an essay on children's nutrition, "but the fresh and noble child does not even accept the routine of an egg a day. One cannot succeed in seducing the child, in nourishing him, without diplomacy and ingenuity."[7] Feeding and seduction were always synonymous for her.

Her mother breast-fed her for a while, then delegated the job to a peasant wet nurse named Émilie Fleury, whom Colette would immortalize in the *Claudine*s as Mélie, the nanny of her motherless heroine. She adored this beautiful and good-natured body servant, and bossed her around, as toddlers do, although Mélie was also responsible for her "first great grief of heart and stomach: weaning."

> How can I explain that [the scene] should remain so intact and vivid? Nothing of it escapes me: the square kitchen, the russet copper pots, the linen cupboard facing the antique bread bin. . . . Two massive mahogany chairs exiled from the dining room, lyrically gothic, in the Restoration style. . . . The guilty one, the traitor, my wet nurse Mélie, sitting on one of those chairs, opened her blouse and freed her peerless breast, white and blue like its milk, pink like that strawberry they call "June beauty." I ran up to her, agile on my sixteen-month-old legs, and standing upright, I leaned on her knees, disdaining to sit because I gave suck, Mélie assured me, "like a grownup." . . . Horrors! The celestial breast had been besmirched with mustard!
>
> . . . It wasn't for my burned lips that I wept so long. I wept because, in the face of my tears spilling over her white neck, the neck of a beautiful blond that was younger than her sunburned face, Mélie my slave, source of my greatest bliss, Mélie two times a traitor, Mélie was laughing.[8]

The traitor was forgiven and became the family cook, although she never ceased to be Colette's "faithful she-dog, [my] blond and white slave."[9] Nor did Colette ever lose the association of bliss with a voluptuous, feminine pliancy, and with the pleasure of domination—a pleasure that became purer for her with age, and toward which she expresses an infant's sense of entitlement.

But Colette's maternal image for her first years of life was split into two personae, and Mélie-the-slave had a formidable counterpart in Sido-the-master. Colette's mother was, for all her "humor and spontaneity," a stickler for control, cleanliness, continence, and obedience. She disapproved of cuddling or caressing infants on the ground, said Colette, that human touch might "wilt" their "intact" beauty.[10] She chastised Gabrielle for her greed, her impudence, or even for her timidity in a "maternal, which is to say humiliating, manner."[11] Displays of temper were forbidden; she considered her children's tears "wanton"; they were taught to be "silent before all else." "To look happy," writes Colette of her family, "was the highest compliment we paid each other."[12]

Sido boasted of her ability to housebreak pets and children. Her kittens never soiled the floor, "and all four of you," she told Colette proudly, "were trained to be just as clean. No pooping in your beds."[13] She was as proprietary of her children's bodies as she was "oversolicitous" about their feelings. Her daughter's hair, for example, was *her* "masterpiece," and she complained when Colette—a woman of thirty—cut it without permission.

Colette remarked that her mother could "see through walls,"[14] and her own art of opacity probably evolved to foil Sido's mind-reading. She would be just as, if not more, physically possessive of her own daughter. When the five-year-old girl took a running fall on a flight of steps and scratched her face, Colette gave her a "pair of slaps" and this rebuke: "I'll teach you to ruin what I've made."[15]

Maternal love is earthly, therefore impure. There may have been cruelty, but there wasn't any malice to Sido's domineering. "Her one idea," Colette also says, "was to give."[16] Yet her great warmth and perceptiveness, combined with her fierce penchant for repression, confused and damaged, to different degrees, all four of her children. The boys became secretive vagabonds. Léo was an eternal waif, at times suicidally depressed. Achille had a streak of sadism; he once marinated, then roasted, the family puppy, and tried to serve it for Sunday dinner.[17] Juliette withdrew into her world of fantasy, then wreaked her vengeance by ruining the family, although her guilt was so extreme that she tried to kill herself shortly thereafter. Colette was awed by the force and superiority of Sido's character, and throughout her life, she found it difficult to regard intimacy with another human being as anything other than a choice between submission and domination.

Like everyone, Colette would replay her earliest experiences of dependency in her adult sexual life. There would be a slave—sometimes Colette, sometimes her lover—who did the child's bidding, indulged her greed, absorbed her fury, and who could be exploited. And there would be a master who wielded a seductive power to deprive, punish, and reward. Throughout her life, an ideal of omnipotence and a penchant for tyranny coexist with a conviction, equally isolating, that she is a helpless thrall.

2

"G A B R I," the much doted upon baby of the family, was an enchanting creature with blue eyes which turned gray-green as she aged, and which the French call *les yeux pers.* Her mother fussed over her golden hair, which darkened to auburn, shampooing it with rum and egg yolk, and brushing it for hours. It grew into a Rapunzel-like plait, famous in the village and later in Paris. Sido boasted that her daughter talked at eight months and "sang at a year," having, apparently, inherited her father's love of music and his propensity to be swept away by it, which, she would acknowledge, posed a danger to her prose.

Baby Gabrielle had a roster of pet names. She was Sido's Minet-Chéri (her darling kitten), her sunshine, her Beauty, her golden jewel, and occasionally, her *pauvre toutou blanc*—poor white pup. Her father, more romantic and less familiar, called her Bel-Gazou, which means, in Provençale, "lovely babble," and this was the nickname she bequeathed to her own daughter and namesake, Colette de Jouvenel.

Colette's first decade was an era of prosperity for her parents. The family had a *banc de notable*—a front pew—in church, which they attended despite the fact that Sido was an avowed atheist who liked to read Corneille under the cover of her missal. On New Year's morning, Mlle Gabri, with a sense of her own importance, distributed bread and pennies to the poor, who received them, she notes, "without humility and without gratitude."[18] Sido was generous to the indigent, and in particular to their children. She fed tramps at her kitchen door, and scandalized the village by hiring a series of unwed, pregnant maids (including Mélie), "contemptuous of a narrow provincial judgment on this morality" which, Colette boasted, was "too elevated for it."[19] Sido was, however, always rather caustic about Colette's infatuations with working-class village idols and their finery, and she lumped her daughter's brief enthusiasm for cathechism classes and feasts of the Virgin into the same category as a passion for servants' weddings.[20]

Like most members of their class, the Colettes sent their older children to boarding schools in the county seat, Auxerre. Juliette lived in an expensive pension for young ladies, where she learned to draw and to do *broderie anglaise*. Achille and Léo were interned in a spartan college whose rigors they endured "in dumb hatred" and from which they returned "dirty, emaciated."[21] Gabrielle, as a result, was for long periods that "queen of the universe," an only child.

In those halcyon days, the family still owned a private carriage—their blue victoria. They kept at least three full-time servants in addition to a part-time laundress, so Mme Colette could devote herself to the finer points of domesticity, horticulture, charity, and motherhood. She believed that a child should learn to read by three, and in addition to the alphabet and the scales, she taught her daughter to embroider. She supervised those elaborate seasonal house-cleanings which take place in the provinces, preferring live spiders to camphor for keeping the moths out of her woolens. She dried violets and chamomile for infusions, and made necklaces of the wild mushrooms which Colette gathered in the woods. She put up her own preserves and fruit liqueurs, and was particularly proud of her cassis. In the cool of the dairy house she pressed cheeses, and from her own fine butter she made the short-crust pastry for her *tartes au citrouille*.

But Sido's greatest joy and refuge was her garden. Her flowers were famous, and she had a weakness for showy red and purple blooms.[22] She grew hibiscus and double violets, and her roses had indecent names like *cuisse-de-nymphe-émue* (thigh of the aroused nymph). If she shared her cuttings with "old Cèbe" next door, she begrudged them for such banalities as Catholic

pageants and village funerals. "My roses," she protests, "have not been condemned to die at the same time as Monsieur Enfert!"[23] Often the cleverness is
actually Colette's, who could elaborate several pages of dialogue from a single line in one of her mother's letters. But Sido was perfectly capable of such
verbal elegance, and of such pagan indignation.

Even as a child, Colette was struck by the difference between her mother's
two faces. Her "anxious indoor face" was humbled by its cares and "weighed
down by a husband and children who clung to her." Her "radiant garden face"
gleamed with a "wild gaiety, a contempt for the whole world, a lighthearted
disdain which cheerfully spurned me along with everything else." Those
gleams, Colette believed, were "kindled by the urge to escape from everyone
and everything, to soar to some high place where only her own writ ran."[24]

Colette, too, would become a passionate gardener. If she never became a
professional housewife, it was, in part, Sido's doing. Her ambitions for her
daughter did not include drudgery. What Colette retained of her education in
homemaking, much of it received from Mélie, was a fund of knowledge about
food that she would retail in exquisite homilies to her women readers, and a
profound love of order which nothing in her life—not war, passion, divorce,
vagabondage, or literary eminence—could alter.

But the flash of defiance Colette saw in Sido's garden face became the light
she wrote by. It had shown her, very young, that a woman's domestic burdens
are incompatible with her creative freedom. And with Sido's encouragement,
she rejected those aspects of her mother's experience that Sido let her feel
were demeaning, confining, or sacrificial—including motherhood itself.

"It was not from her," wrote Colette as an old woman, "that I learned that
between mothers and children there exists an immutable and rigid love called
sacred, which cannot be broken except at the price of curses and scandal. On
the contrary, she detached me, she shook me free with an imperious hand, dis-
missing the fruit of such teachings as I had acquired from books and school."[25]

3

BY 1879, the six-year-old Colette was a rugged little urchin with two blond
braids like "reins" or "whips"; a "well-built little body" that gave her great
pleasure; and as often as not a dirty face, which Sido told her was beautiful, "although my mother and the pictures of me at that period do not
always agree."[26] She started school that October, wearing a black pinafore
that enveloped her "like a sack," and lace-up boots with hobnailed soles that
helped her to navigate the vertiginous streets, slippery first with leaves, then
with ice, then mud. That winter, she recalled, the snowdrifts were higher than
she was tall. The children carried metal footwarmers to class, which they filled

with hot coals and sometimes used for roasting potatoes, and whose smell and heat put them to sleep.

The girls occupied two "unbelievably dirty and ugly" rooms on the ground floor of the old schoolhouse. In *Claudine at School,* Colette describes her fellow pupils as the daughters of shopkeepers, farmers, policemen, and laborers, "the whole bunch rather unwashed."[27] Their first-grade teacher was "the old Miss Fanny [Desleau]," "an insubstantial phantom" who liked to declaim passages from the Bible while rapping a ruler against her desk. She was replaced the next year by Mme Viellard, the wife of a carpenter, who "wept at the indiscipline"[28] of her rambunctious pupils. They pocked the schoolyard with holes, where they buried marbles; vandalized a neighbor's garden; rang doorbells and then hid; climbed trees in their pinafores, flashing their legs. Colette was the ringleader of this mischief. But Mme Viellard treated her with the deference owed to a rich man's daughter, and let her pay a poor classmate a penny or two to take her turn at sweeping the room.

The French had (and still have) a six-day schoolweek, with Thursday afternoons off. On those afternoons, Colette and her friends would gather in Sido's garden, where, for five hours, they played rough and loudmouthed games, impersonating the more grotesque village characters and cheating at cards. "All the filth of a squalid village street has poured forth from six child-ish mouths," writes Colette. "Hideous tittle-tattle of rascally and low love life."[29]

When they tired of mimicry, they discussed their futures. "A sort of resigned wisdom, the peasant terror of adventure and distant travel, already keeps them all—the clockmaker's child, the grocer's little girl and the off-spring of the butcher and the laundress—chained to their parents' shops." Jeanne, "it's true," proclaims that she will be a tart, "but that sort of thing," Gabrielle reflects contemptuously, "is simply childish nonsense. Having no special wish when her turn came," she announces that she will be a sailor. "And that was simply because she sometimes dreamed of being a boy, and wearing trousers and a blue beret."[30]

"I never had friends of my own kind," Claudine laments, or boasts, in *Claudine at School.*[31] And the voice that narrates the novel is of a young girl precociously critical of and amused by the little world she stage-manages, plays along with, and knows herself not to belong to. However much Colette would rhapsodize about her sense of place, and define herself as a woman who belongs "to a native village I have left behind,"[32] her character was shaped by her conviction of being "a special case," and her feeling of superiority to that village and its inhabitants. She would always remember the note one of her teachers had attached to a composition: "Imaginative, but one senses a stub-born determination to set herself apart."[33]

Her brothers shared this *"parti pris de se singulariser,"* and Colette describes the pleasure they took in tormenting a school friend who had the impudence to become "passionately attached to them," and the misfortune to be "a commonplace child of commonplace parents, whom no dark mood ever touched."[34] The pride which Colette and her brothers took in their singularity—and their darkness—seems to have been actively nurtured by their mother, who "found it quite natural, and indeed obligatory, that the children she produced should be miracles."[35] Her own relations with the village dullards (all those insufferable people who, as she puts it, believe in Hell)[36] were superficially cordial at best, and as Crançon's reports suggest, she and the Captain were both considered upstarts, even pariahs. One neighbor, Sido would recall, "spewed venom" at them for thirty years, and another delighted in sending them anonymous letters. It is Juliette's abstraction from (or surrender of) the family idealization of the uncommon that sets her apart. And when Colette describes her own "shame," on Juliette's wedding day, at seeing her sister's face assume "a swooning look of . . . submission," it is, in part, because Juliette is submitting to the village as embodied in a man.

French intellectual life is, in its way, also a provincial village—rivalrous, gossipy, and homogeneous. The place Colette will occupy in that village won't be unlike her mother's in Saint-Sauveur. She refuses to assimilate; she remains indifferent to her neighbors' proprieties, quarrels, and conventions; she situates herself outside their culture and asserts her uniqueness: "I was the only one of my kind, the only [writer] put on earth not to write." And even though she dresses up for church and occupies her *banc de notable,* she does so as an unbeliever in the religion of literature (of which politics is but a sect) and the gods of men in general.

SUMMER WAS a slow season for the children. The heat "quivered up" from the burning gravel of the road, and the garden was bathed in yellow light. Colette's brothers were home from school, and they had glamorously queer pursuits, from most of which they excluded her. They hid from their mother in the trees of the garden, where they "read to excess," or they escaped to the woods and meadows, where they hunted butterflies, sometimes deigning to take Colette with them. It was from their field guides that she first learned to name the flowers.

All three Colette children were gifted musicians, and among the Robineau heirlooms was an Aucher piano. Colette took lessons and would become an excellent pianist, although in later life she would only rarely, and then not willingly, exhibit her skill. Léo was the undisputed musical genius of the family. He had perfect pitch and could just as easily sight-read a Schubert sonata as he could reproduce the songs he heard at a village minstrel show.

But there was always something screwy about Léo. He liked to dismember clocks and watches, and he erected a cardboard cemetery at the foot of the garden, each headstone meticulously inscribed with an epitaph and genealogy for the imaginary corpse. Sido, who fretted all her life over Léo's morbid dreaminess, was horrified to discover this city of the dead among her roses, and she destroyed it "with an angry rake." His only protest was to Colette. "Don't you think it looks sad," he asked her, "a garden without graves?"[37]

Léo never grew up, and apparently never wanted to. He studied to be a pharmacist, but spent his life as a humble clerk in a working-class suburb of Paris because, says Colette, it was a job that left his mind free for puerile daydreams while his body sat at a table looking "deceptively like a man." The man was, as the boy had been, frugal, elfin, unkempt, depressive, and "attached to nothing but his native place."[38]

4

JULES COLETTE WAS as quixotic as his younger son. He spent most of his life in the country unable to identify the trees in his garden. He assured Sido he could economize on corks when bottling their wine, and the wine spoiled in six months. The husband of the chocolate maker's daughter also failed, Sido notes, at making chocolates, and at ridding the kitchen garden of its pests. He couldn't get the family dog to obey him, and he even had trouble controlling the unruly pages of the evening newspaper. "Everything you touch diminishes like Balzac's *peau de chagrin*," Sido told him, with her usual withering candor.[39]

The Captain's superiors had been critical of his "lack of zeal" as a tax collector,[40] and in 1880, he resigned the dull job he had neglected in order to run for the district council. His patriotism, his war wound, and his battle-field decorations were the only qualifications that he could present to his would-be constituents. Colette describes his campaign platform: He traveled the countryside preaching, in country schoolrooms, against alcoholism, and giving "instructive" lectures and magic-lantern shows on natural history, physics, chemistry, and geography, which bored his peasant audiences into a stupor. Afterwards, he invited the "mayor in clogs" and the members of the municipal council for drinks in the local tavern, abstaining himself, but allowing his "campaign manager"—the eight-year-old Colette—to "warm herself " with a thimbleful of wine, and to charm her countrymen with a rustic toast in that local accent the candidate didn't possess.

In the first round of voting, Colette's father lost both to the Bonapartist and to his republican rival, Dr. Merlou—of whom we have not heard the last. In the second round, Merlou was elected by 1,460 votes to the Captain's ten.[41] This resounding defeat should have discouraged him, but it didn't. While the village laughed behind his back, he prepared—with more magic-lantern shows and lectures on geography—to run for mayor. "[He] is more unpopular than ever," the Colettes' neighbor, Mme de Saint-Aubin, wrote to her son. The "absurdity [of his machinations] does not escape the workers. . . . At heart, M. Colette knows perfectly well that all this is a farce and a big joke—he says as much—but he absolutely wants to be something."[42]

JULES COLETTE WOULD SEEM to be the model for the marginal male figures in his daughter's novels who are good for nothing but love, and in the final analysis, perhaps not so good at that. Paternity was another of his failed careers, and the children, says Colette, considered their father more of a sibling rival than a parent. He never bothered about their studies or their whereabouts. He never kissed them. He had his own toys, which they coveted: pens, fine papers, and sealing wax that he sometimes shared, but more often locked away. The boys knew that if they wanted to finagle a small loan, they should ask, as they might an older brother, for cigarette money.

Colette reasons that the Captain took so "little interest" in them because of his exclusive passion for their mother. That passion suggested to her that older women could be more compelling than their younger rivals. It was a not entirely unwholesome notion she could bank and draw upon later, in both her life and her fiction. But if an overly seductive father does one kind of damage, a sexually indifferent one does another. His daughter will probably feel insecure or fraudulent in her femininity, and she may also seek from her mate the paternal containment that she never had as a child.

When Colette was little, the Captain had enjoyed roughhousing with her—throwing her up to the ceiling—and that excited her. In addition to their campaign trips around the province, which ended the night a furious Sido smelled alcohol on her breath, he took her to Brussels for a few days when she was six, and twice, briefly to Paris. But she says that she had no memories of these excursions beyond the bedbugs in one of their hotels. There was obviously no romance attached to being, as she calls herself, her father's "favorite." "We were," she writes, "on a fraternal footing."[43] He seemed, in other words, barely conscious that she was a little girl.

In some ways, that was lucky. Unlike most daughters of her generation, Colette never had a father whose honor was invested in her virtue. He was too oblivious to be possessive. His sense of propriety seems to have been nonexistent. Sido would remind him to watch his language around Gabrielle, and he would retort: " 'Oh, the child, it doesn't matter about her.' Well," Colette concludes, "that was frank enough."[44]

When Claudine escapes from the pension in Auxerre where her class is staying during exam week, the teacher threatens to report "this extravagant conduct" to her parent. "Papa?" Claudine shrugs. "He'll say, 'My God, yes, this child has a great love of liberty,' and he'll wait impatiently for the end of your story so that he can resubmerge himself [in his book on snails]."[45] His snails were much more interesting to Claudine's father than his only child. Never meddled with but also never courted or cherished by Jules Colette, the daughter who loved her liberty would be ripe to surrender it to a mature rake "turned on," as she puts it, "by *le vice paternel*."[46]

CHAPTER 4

I was still a child and none too pure-minded, being exercised, as one is at thirteen, by all those matters concerning which ignorance is a burden and discovery humiliating.

— COLETTE,
My Mother's House

i

BEFORE THEY BECOME boy-crazy (if they ever do), girls between eleven and thirteen cultivate those passionate and often stormy friendships among themselves that the French call *amitiés de pensionnaire*. They compare the little swells of flesh pushing out their nipples and the relative bushiness of their pubic hair. If they're not sophisticates, they give their first periods some cute and friendly code name. We used to say, "My cousin from Redhook has come for a visit." Colette's visitor was "cousin Pauline."[1]

The competition and solidarity among pubescent girlfriends take many forms, some of them violent, some erotic. All help to reassure the girls about the changes in their bodies which presage the loss of childhood and its illusions, and to cushion the coincidental discovery of what is involved, anatomically and culturally, in giving oneself to a man. No one understood or described the mixed emotions of this "most troubled age," as Colette calls it,[2] better than she did. She writes of, and perhaps suffered, "the neuroses of puberty, the habit of eating clay and charcoal, of drinking mouthwash, of reading dirty books, and sticking pins into the palm."[3] These mortifications of the flesh are extreme but common, especially among girls whose parents discourage any frank expressions of feeling. They seem to prick a taut-to-bursting container. Along with her bodily fluids, a teenager can thus release, in a relatively controlled manner, without necessarily knowing why, some of her anxiety about sex, menstruation, childbirth, and separation from her mother.[4]

In *Claudine in Paris,* the peasant wet nurse, Mélie, scoffs at the importance bourgeois families give to virginity and advises her nursling to " 'do as we do . . . try them out first; that way, the deal's honest and no one's fooled.' . . . Good advice," Claudine muses. But then she adds: "Honest girls . . . stay that way, despite all the Mélies in the world."[5]

Thanks to her own Mélie, and to her country life, Colette was familiar enough with the facts of reproduction, and she had certainly seen her cats mate and give birth. But she balked at imagining humans in the same acts. The sight of her pregnant sister filled her with "embarrassment and disgust."[6] The Zola novel left her feeling "credulous, terrified, threatened in my dawning femininity."[7] When she caught her father ardently kissing her mother's hand, she turned away in "confusion." She was overcome by "uncomprehending repulsion" at the sight of the hired man embracing the kitchen maid.[8] After one of those servants' weddings which she adored (her passion wasn't for the dancing or the romance, but for the food), her best friend, Julie, pointed out the lighted window of the room where the newlyweds were to spend the night. "I had not thought of that," writes Colette: "Between them will be enacted that obscure encounter of which my mother's outspoken simplicity and the lives of the beasts around me have taught me too much and too little. And afterwards? I am frightened of the room, of the bed. . . ." Her immediate impulse was "to go home to mother."[9]

If Colette knew about her mother's scandalous youth, she never admits it. She makes a point of describing her parents' "widely separated" beds and her mother's prudishness about displays of attraction, even of affection, between men and women. In her descriptions of Sido across the years the word "chaste" recurs like a leitmotif. Her vested interest in her mother's sexual purity—her "innate innocence"—has its universal aspects, which are too well known to need mention, and its particular ones, to which I shall return. But Colette resumes all of them simply where she writes that her glimpse of the two servants' lovemaking left her with a sense of "childish trust betrayed."

It is worth remembering that Colette knew Sido only as a middle-aged woman who had loosened her stays, who had taken, somewhat prematurely, to wearing an old lady's ruched bonnet, and who, unlike her daughter, accepted the loss of youth and muscle tone without a struggle. A budding girl whose mother considers love "frivolous" if not indecent and renounces vanity will look for a more tolerant mentor, a woman whose sexual confidence and glamour she can take as a model. Colette didn't have to search far, for around the corner, on rue de la Roche, lived Adrienne de Saint-Aubin.[10]

Adrienne, "dreamy" and "strange," was the sister of the notary, M. Jarry. She was three years younger than her friend Sido, and had four children of roughly the same ages as the Colettes', the littlest Saint-Aubin boy just two months older than Gabrielle. In a playful moment, the mothers had exchanged sucklings, and Adrienne liked to remind Colette of it: "You," she would call out in her husky voice, "the one I once fed with my own milk." This teasing, says Colette, made her blush violently, because she was terrified that Sido would read her mind and find there the "image that tormented me: . . . Of Adrienne's swarthy breast with its hard purple knob."[11]

Colette also candidly admits that she was "chiefly attracted" to Mme de Saint-Aubin "by all those things in her that least resembled my mother."[12] Adrienne was sultry, mischievous, nonchalant, and sardonic. She had "tawny eyes," "sunburned arms," and "frizzy hair" with a scent of musk—giving her a remarkable likeness to the mature Colette. Compared to her friend, poor Sido—smelling of "laundered cretonne"—must have seemed frumpish and tame.

Mme Colette's unfaithful daughter loved Adrienne's beguilingly untidy house, which she would visit surreptitiously, like a "cat." When she heard her mother calling her from beyond the yew trees, she would "rush home at once" and feign breathlessness, as if she had come from afar. But Sido wasn't fooled, and even though her friend was careful, Colette says, "never to entice or to detain me," her mother's "acute perception and jealousy on the one hand, and my excessive confusion on the other," led to a gradual cooling of the friendship. It took Colette a long time "to associate a disturbing memory, a certain warmth in the heart, and the enchanted transformation of a person and her dwelling, with the idea of a first seduction."[13]

2

WHILE COLETTE WAS slinking off to visit her idol, Juliette was betraying Sido with a mother surrogate of her own. Mme Pomié lived across the street, next door to Adrienne. Her husband was the village doctor and a local councilman, and they had no children. She and Sido were "enemies" (Mme Pomié was the previously mentioned spewer of venom), and perhaps one cause of their feud was Juliette, for Sido claimed that Mme Pomié had always coveted her own firstborn as a daughter.

In 1884, Dr. Pomié retired, selling his practice to a young physician named Charles Roché, who became engaged to Juliette the same year. The wedding took place on April 14, 1885. Achille and Léo volunteered to provide the music, escaping the more fatuous duty of being attendants. Colette "swaggered about in a pink dress, highly delighted" with everything but the "swooning look of submission" on her sister's face.

Sido, writes Colette, had not dared "to prevent this unfortunate marriage," although "she made no secret of what she thought about it." The reasons for her misgivings in 1885—beyond her dislike of in-laws and marriages in general—aren't immediately obvious. Roché, it's true, was a pompous ass, but he was a respectable professional with some well-born relations who owned a château, and Juliette was peculiar. To a more conventional mother—a Mme Pomié—he might have seemed like a godsend.

The marriage was initially less "unfortunate" for Mme Roché, who worshipped her husband, than for the Colettes. Juliette was an heiress, and all of Saint-Sauveur knew, probably down to the last sou, pine tree, and chicken, what her portion was or ought to have been.[14] But the inheritance was mostly in land, and Jules Colette had no knowledge of farming. Over the years, the peasants had persuaded him to make a long-range investment in expensive new equipment and improvements. In order to do so, he had borrowed money "at interest rates that should have alarmed him."[15] He also apparently used some of this money to finance his politicking and to speculate on the stock market. It is easy to understand why the Captain's daughter was such an admirer of Balzac.

When her mother and stepfather signed Juliette's marriage contract, they were obliged to give an accounting and to make a distribution of the Robineau estate. At first, the Captain managed to conceal his losses and manipulations. To raise the cash for Juliette's dowry, he borrowed a hundred and twenty thousand francs from the Crédit Foncier, using the Robineau farms as collateral. But almost immediately after the wedding, Roché, probably egged on by the Pomiés, became suspicious and asked for a review of the books. The Colettes refused. Their son-in-law then consulted several lawyers and threatened to sue the Captain for "improvident guardianship."[16] Tormented by her divided loyalties, Juliette swallowed a dose of poison, and her stepfather threatened to shoot her husband if he failed to save her. In the meantime, a family council was convened to negotiate a settlement. The estate was revalued, amends were paid, and Sido's portion, originally half, was reduced to a third.

Achille was so furious with his sister that he never spoke to or saw her again. He was convinced that had she only been patient "for a few years, everything could have been arranged."[17] But no one else had much sympathy for the arrogant, perhaps larcenous spendthrifts who had gambled away a fortune that wasn't theirs to begin with—not even Sido's brother's wife, Caroline Landoy,[18] who sided with Juliette. "Achille's conduct is the worst," she told her niece. "Waiting only would have given Colette time to spend the rest." Aunt Caro also spoke her mind to Sido, who resented her candor. "All this surpasses anything I could have imagined," wrote Caro, "and I have no esteem left for M. Colette, and . . . no desire ever to see him again."[19]

By now, Juliette had recovered, and was pregnant. At the urging of her husband and surrogate parents, she ceased speaking to her mother, and when they met on the street, she cringed like a "child expecting a blow." The village reveled heartlessly in this melodrama. "We were," writes Colette, "the only topic of conversation."[20]

Consumed by the loss of her daughter, the enmity of her neighbors, the criticism of her relatives, the folly of her husband, and the specter of bankruptcy, Sido began falling apart. She suffered "nervous fainting fits," heart palpitations, and bouts of nausea. "With so much to bear courageously every day in secret," wrote Colette—no doubt with considerable understatement—"my mother had less time for her garden and her last-born."[21]

3

THAT SUMMER, Colette took the exams for her primary school diploma. She got a nearly perfect mark on the dictation—a passage from Victor Hugo about his love of pigeons—and a perfect mark in mathematics. Her "piece of ordinary sewing" was acceptable, and she did very well on the oral. But the best writer in her class earned only a three out of ten on the essay question, largely because she didn't have a clue about the subject, "Germany's ancient claim to Burgundy."[22] In 1944, it would come back to haunt her.

At this point, there was no further education to be had in Saint-Sauveur, and to continue her studies, Colette's parents would have had to send her to Auxerre. It is understandable that, having lost one daughter, Sido would be extremely reluctant to part with the other. It is also likely that they simply couldn't afford the tuition.

The house on the rue de l'Hospice was part of Achille's inheritance, and the Colettes lived on there for the next five years, selling off Sido's farms one by one to cover their interest payments. The Rochés were ensconced across the street in the Pomiés' old place, which Sido could see from her upstairs windows. After the wedding, Colette had moved from a garret adjoining her parents' bedroom to Juliette's bigger room on the ground floor. She was overjoyed to have inherited a real young lady's boudoir with a dressing closet and a bed canopied in lace. But her happiness and privacy there were "threatened," she writes, because Sido—distraught and perhaps a little paranoid—was having recurring nightmares that her youngest daughter would also be "abducted" by some strange man. Her dreams, which excited Colette, were fueled by the lurid accounts of ravishments and elopements that were a staple of the provincial press, and by a sequence of events which, to the Captain's mind, seemed harmless enough: a tramp had attempted to force his way into the kitchen; a band of gypsies had offered "with flashing smiles" to buy Colette's hair; an old man in the village plied her with candy. But Sido was obsessed, recalling that a Belgian girlfriend[23] had, at sixteen, suffered just such a fate: abduction by a stranger in a post chaise.

One night, says Colette, a wind was rattling the doors and shutters of the old house and keeping Sido awake worrying about predators. She arose and carried her sleeping daughter back upstairs to the garret, where she could guard her. Whether this scene was real or imagined, it marks a crossroads in Colette's life: a parting of the ways. Sido's nightmare of loss and violation would become Colette's reverie of escape: of a demonic liberator ruthless and unscrupulous enough to pry her from the trap of her mother's arms, house, power, anxiety, and solicitude—and not least, from her own claustrophobic attachment to Sido.

CHAPTER 5

Only a dream could waft a little girl right out of her childhood and place her, neither surprised nor unwilling, in the very midst of a hypocritical and adventurous adolescence. Only a dream could thus turn a loving child into the ungrateful creature that she will become tomorrow, the crafty accomplice of the stranger, the forgetful one who will leave her mother's house without a backward glance. In such wise was I departing for the land where a postchaise, amid the jangling of bells, stops before a church to deposit a young man dressed in taffeta and a young woman whose ruffled skirts suggest the rifled petals of a rose. I did not cry out.

—COLETTE,
My Mother's House

1

SIDO MAY HAVE BEEN a modern, but the nineteenth-century novel is full of country gentlemen like Jules Colette, romantics in an age of materialism, defeated soldiers and idealists who ward off their melancholy by keeping busy with inventions, poetry, and amateur science. Colette's father had ideas on national defense. He wrote an ode to his good friend Paul Bert, the radical republican from Auxerre. He loved geography, and sometimes sent his hand-colored maps to the Geographic Society. He belonged to the International Society of Electricians and contributed his equations to the *New Annals of Mathematics*.

This review and others of interest to M. Colette were distributed by the firm of Gauthier-Villars, the leading scientific publisher in France. Jean-

Albert Gauthier-Villars, who had acquired the company in 1864,[1] was another typically nineteenth-century figure: the military engineer. Colette claimed him as a school friend of her father's, but while Jules Colette was at St. Cyr, Gauthier-Villars went to the École Polytechnique, the most elite of the cadet academies and a stepping-stone, for its old boys, to the highest positions in industry and the civil service.[2] He and the Captain had, however, served contemporaneously in the Crimea and Italy.

The two veterans had their wars in common, and their devotion to "order and progress." But they could not have been more different in their roles, real and symbolic, as fathers. Gauthier-Villars was the kind of feared and respected patriarch extolled by all the conservatives of an era in which "family values" was as much the battle cry of the right as it is today, for many of the same reasons,[3] and the French were polarized by their attitudes to the Church more than by any other issue.

Here a gulf—almost an abyss—opens between Colette's and Willy's milieux. Sido was an atheist from a family of freethinkers, held to be a sinner by her neighbors, and proud of it. An adulterer herself, she had not raised either of her daughters to consider virginity, marriage, motherhood, or even respectability as a woman's sacred duty. Mme Gauthier-Villars was morally exigent, socially ambitious, and, one gathers, extremely tiresome in her piety. Having married her younger son to a banker's daughter and her daughter to a Polytechnician, she had an heiress lined up for Willy when he announced his intention to make a misalliance with Gabrielle Colette.

The Gauthier-Villars belonged to, indeed embodied, *la bourgeoisie absolue*. They were rich and ultra-Catholic, voted with the right-wing nationalists, feared the pululating masses, supported the army hierarchy, deplored the influence of Jews and foreigners, and opposed the anticlerical reforms which were the legislative centerpiece of the Third Republic. The most important of these, at least for Colette's first novel, was the institution of secular, secondary public education for both sexes.

While it sounds enlightened, the new law wasn't designed to prepare women for paying jobs, except in teaching, or for political equality— Frenchwomen didn't get the vote until after World War II. The republicans were engaged in a struggle with the Catholic Church for the hearts and minds of the next generation of French mothers. "Republican companions for republican men" was one of Jules Ferry's slogans, and contemporary feminists understood very well that the new schools would just prolong their marginality by releasing a little steam from their frustrated ambitions.

Secular education for women, however, was a red flag to the Catholic right, which perceived, justly, that it opened a door, that it boded a revolution in morals, and particularly in the "morals"—the relationship to authority—of women who were educated outside convents. In the early 1880s, several new normal colleges had been founded, the most prestigious one at Sèvres, to train women teachers for the *laïques*—the public girls' schools—and their critics imagined them to be hotbeds of sexual misconduct that sent regiments of lascivious lesbians into the French countryside, spreading their vice among the innocents entrusted to their care.

This anxiety was highly contagious, and not confined to the Catholic right. Historians associate the rout by Germany with the period of corruption, loss of faith, and cultural turbulence that followed, and lasted well into the new century. The manhood of France had been dealt a blow, and Frenchmen, both impressed and humiliated by the machismo of the enemy, were said to be suffering in their collective pride. The press was filled with jeremiads about the declining birthrate, proposed changes in the divorce laws, and the stirrings of feminism. It was an age of misogyny—"a whole society," in Zola's words, "hurling itself at the cunt" with a fervor in which lust, rivalry, and aggression mixed with a fear of impotence. Male writers and politicians from the most reactionary to the most avant-garde were haunted by the specter of an "emasculating" and "virilized" New Woman, of whom there were many versions: Huysmans's ventriloquist; Valéry's "pure abstraction"; Wilde's Salomé; and countless less exalted dykes, nymphomaniacs, vampires, bluestockings, and *sévriennes*—"the best of them," in the words of Willy, "not worth much."

2

In October of 1887, one of those terrifying creatures, a professional schoolmistress, penetrated Saint-Sauveur. She took over from the underqualified Mme Viellard, in whose classroom Colette had been vegetating for two years, and briskly began teaching a course designed to prepare the village girls for a *brévet*, the equivalent of a high-school diploma. Olympe Terrain was twenty-four, and a graduate of the normal college at Auxerre. The child of peasants, she had taken the only virtuous route to advancement available to poor women, and she would encourage all of her best students—Colette among them—to pursue a teaching degree. But the life of a schoolmistress was in itself too harsh a lesson. Colette evokes it briefly and compassionately in *Claudine at School:* the grueling competition for places, the subsistence wages in the village, the unheated dormitory above the classrooms, the knowledge that failure meant going back to tend the pigs. Willy, in the same novel, exploits the contemporary fantasies about the Olympe Terrains of France and their *laïques*. It was a book that would have confirmed the worst fears of his mother, had her modesty and her confessor permitted her to read it.[4]

Like her fictional counterpart, Olympe Sergent, Mlle Terrain arrived in the village with her mother, an old peasant woman in a bonnet. The portrait Colette gives of her in the novel was in most of its particulars drawn from life.[5] The new *institutrice* was an excellent pedagogue with a "lively, exigent" manner.[6] Although well prepared for her job, which she would keep until her retirement thirty years later, she had landed it through the patronage of her protector and Captain Colette's old nemesis, Dr. Merlou—who is caricatured as the slimy Dr. Dutertre in the novel. This connection made her, initially at least, a target for Colette's resentment. "For the Colette family," Mlle Terrain told Jean Larnac, Colette's first biographer, "I was an intruder. I was told, at first, that Gabrielle wouldn't be coming back to school, then one fine day she appeared [in the yard] a bit before the bell rang, neglecting to take her place in line to go in. Not a word from me. During the first period, the girls—under Colette's influence—were playing with marbles and calling themselves by their last names. When she started reading her newspaper, I told her, more or less: 'My child, public school must be thoroughly disagreeable for you, as the rules must be followed by all the pupils, and I can't permit them to read newspapers.' That was all, and thereafter Colette showed herself as she was, which is to say an agreeable young girl, very intelligent, perfectly gifted in French, worthless or nearly so in the sciences, extremely musical, and mischievous and witty in a remarkable way."[7]

Olympe Terrain goes on to say that henceforth Colette had to take her turn at sweeping, and never again claimed special privileges as a "rich man's daughter." She describes Gabrielle, at thirteen, as notably crazy about cats and their love affairs. Thanks to the influence of her literate parents, she had "read everything." Colette would later observe that she had never liked fairy tales or children's books, and had begun reading *The Human Comedy* at the age of seven. "I was born in Balzac," she told an interviewer as an old lady. "He was my cradle, my forest, my travels." And she called herself "one of those people who, from childhood, devote themselves to a single author." But she also read Alphonse Daudet, Hugo, Mérimée, Labiche, Zola, Taine, Voltaire, Musset, the tales of H. C. Andersen—and Shakespeare (in translation).[8]

The young Colette was a precocious literary critic. She "laughed" at Balzac's sometimes careless prose (but her objections later "melted in the fire of my devotion"). She listened "sternly" to her father's recitations of his odes and eulogies—the Captain was something of a specialist in funeral oratory[9]—and objected to the excesses of his style: "I told you the same thing last week. . . . Too many adjectives!"[10] Her own prose, says Mlle Terrain, was already notable for its originality, and even then she revised it prodigiously, "without help." It was only because she had turned in such a "brilliant" essay that she passed the exam for her diploma in 1889, as her insolence at the oral had been spectacular.[11] "We loved her roguish repartee," the old teacher recalled fondly, even as she blamed Colette's foul mouth on a father famous for his profanity and a mother for her cynicism: "Mme Colette liked to say of Gabrielle, 'She'll marry an old man with lots of money.' "

Mlle Terrain's opinion of the Colette family (*"sens moral très attenué"*—a very attenuated moral sensibility) was, naturally, biased by the village gossip, her intimacy with Merlou, and her outraged sense of betrayal at her subsequent treatment by Colette in *Claudine at School*.[12] "If Colette was really like Claudine," said Olympe Terrain, "she knew how to hide her weaknesses, for she never showed herself to be a wicked creature." The *Claudine* books, she concludes, were the product of greed and opportunism, and of a "diabolical imagination"—probably Willy's.

3

THE MAN Colette would refer to with mock deference as M. Willy was already a celebrity by the time they met, although not yet as famous as her talent was to make him. He was fourteen years her senior, and the figure she cut in his world was, at first, that of a morose provincial schoolgirl with a five-foot-long braid and flashes of uncouth charm. He, according to his friend Rachilde, was "a man of the world, and of the best world; the very model of a brilliant Parisian rake."[13]

To their contemporaries, the age difference wasn't troubling or even significant. Teenage virgins routinely married dissolute older men, and Colette's models for the gamine and the playboy whose romance she would describe in *Gigi* were, one is somewhat startled to learn, eighteen and sixty, respectively. But it was central to their scenario as a couple, an exchange to which she brought the vitality and he the prestige. Tomboyish and supple, undecorous in speech and appetite, Colette would be taken for a minor, or at least a "false minor," into her late twenties, and Willy, as she noted, "went to a good deal of trouble to appear old"[14]—an aging satyr—even as a youngish man.

Their romance conformed to a fin de siècle taste for the kinky retelling of mythic love stories, Colette playing Beauty to Willy's Beast. "If many a young girl puts her hand into the velvet paw," she wrote of her initiation, "offers her mouth to the gluttonous spasm of an inflamed mouth, and stares serenely at the shadow on the wall of an enormous masculine stranger, it is because sensual curiosity whispers potent counsels to her."[15] But there was much more than sensual curiosity to Colette's first marriage. She loved Willy better and longer than she would ever publicly avow, and in understanding what he meant to her, we should not forget how often in her life and in her fiction she would restage their unequal contest—and reverse the roles.

Willy was vain of his image, famously so, and with a touch of perversity considering that in the mirror held up by the world he was even more obese and bald than in the flesh. In *My Apprenticeships,* Colette makes a mischievous inventory of the photographs, caricatures, sketches, effigies, academic portraits, drawings, postcards, statuettes, figurines, silhouettes, and even souvenir items, like an inkwell in the shape of his trademark top hat, that her husband had collected, and in many cases commissioned. He was not above commissioning his own literary portraits, too, in the form of reviews that were paid for in cash or kind; items of gossip and publicity for his books; and biographies that leavened their flattery with just enough low-minded ribbing to give it a credible edge.

His self-portraits belong to this genre. They tend to contrast Willy's high culture with his low appetites, and his sexual charisma with his unprepossessing and, as he aged, gross appearance. The year he met Colette, for example, he described himself as "a freckled blond, baby-faced, conceited, with the thick lips of a hedonist and eyes that are myopic though still lively. Has great success with women and lets it be known." Twelve years later he confessed: "I would have liked to be dark, tall, and slim, with a fatal allure in the style of 1830; instead of making me a prince of darkness, Nature cast me in a rather dumpy mold, piercing my pudgy face with eyes whose washed-out blue was reassuring—too much so—to timid creatures inclined at first to take fright before the illusory swagger of an off-to-the-wars mustache."[16]

The most definitive of these self-portraits was the figure of a Parisian rake named Henry Maugis who first appears in *Claudine in Paris,* and later, as Colette puts it, "promenades through the entire oeuvre, if I dare call it that, of M. Willy. This Maugis," she continues, "turned on by *'le vice paternel,'* lover of women, of exotic liquors and puns, musicographer, Hellenist, man of letters, duellist, sensitive soul, scoundrel, who banters while he hides a tear, puffs out his chest like a bullfinch, calls every little shopgirl 'babe,' prefers the state of partial undress to nudity and the anklet to the silk stocking—this Maugis doesn't belong to me."[17]

All of these descriptions and hundreds more one could cite conform to Willy's own penchant for mystifying his sex appeal. But the naked Willy, or nearly naked Willy, comes as a revelation, and must have been so to his many mistresses. In an album of photographs that belonged to Madeleine de Swarte, Willy's last companion, there is a snapshot of him on the beach at Cabourg dated August 1890, exactly a year after he met Colette. He is wearing a knitted bathing suit and a big straw hat. He has his arms crossed over his chest. He's paunchy, it is true, but he has a virile, confident body—a body all the more surprising because the head on its shoulders looks much older in comparison.

Thirty-five years later, Colette would be photographed on the beach at Saint-Tropez, in a similar pose, in a similar bathing suit. She was living, at the time, with a lover fifteen years her junior. She was quite tremendous. They had the same kind of allure.

4

HENRI GAUTHIER-VILLARS WAS BORN on August 10, 1859, at his grandmother's house in Villiers-sur-Orge, while his father was off organizing the telegraphic services for the Emperor's army in Italy.[18] While he was preparing for his First Communion, the Communards mounted their insurrection, and briefly took his father captive. At this point he still was, he says, "as religious as it is possible to be."[19] He thereafter became as irreligious as it is possible to be, the choirboy gone to the devil, in relation to both his mother's faith and his father's intellectual seriousness.

They sent Henri first to the famous Lycée Fontanes, where he misbehaved, and then to the equally renowned Jesuit Collège Stanislas. Here he received an excellent classical education, which he perverted with enormous gusto and brilliance for his puns. Comfortable in Greek, fluent in Latin and German, Willy applied himself, he said, only to subjects which "enticed" him. One of his passions, inherited from his mother, was for music. Another was for very young girls. There were a number of Parisian brothels that specialized in procuring them for elderly clients, and as a student Willy frequented one on the rue Montmartre. The gamines liked him, he claimed—his youth was so refreshing—and the madam didn't charge so long as he agreed to wear his schoolboy's kepi when he went upstairs to the bedrooms. "I have since understood that the [old voyeurs] must have been watching my boyish revels through a hole."[20]

In 1879, Willy entered the army to do his obligatory twelve months of service. It was the year that Zola finished *Nana;* that the Ferry administration tabled its education reform bill; and that Colette, then six, made her first trip to Paris with the Captain. The young Gauthier-Villars was an excellent shot and swordsman—skills that would prove valuable in the many duels of his career—but he pretended so successfully to be a cretin that he was excused from the more onerous maneuvers. A visiting general, an intimate of his father's, put a stop to the farce, and Willy finished his stint with no further disgrace and only one distinction, not yet significant: that of having served in the same artillery battery as a young lieutenant from Alsace named Alfred Dreyfus.

When he left the army a year later, Willy was ripe for the seductions of Paris. He enrolled in law school, but spent his evenings in the cafés and brasseries of the Left Bank, where his contemporaries met to debate literary theory and to pick up girls. It was as contentious a moment in French literature as in politics. There was general agreement that the culture was in decline, but a fractious diversity of opinion about what would regenerate it. Schools of poetry and esthetics, each with its own ephemeral review, were formed, merged, and dissolved like speculative stock companies in a boom. There were the Zutistes (Phooeyists), the Hydropaths, the Jemenfoutistes (Damn-it-alls), and the Hirsutes, among others. When Rodolphe Salis of the Café de l'Avenir took his bohemian clientele across the river and opened the literary cabaret Le Chat Noir, Willy was one of the inner circle, along with Verlaine, Henri de Régnier, and Jules Laforgue. It was here, writes Willy's biographer, François Caradec, "that Symbolism was born."[21]

In 1885, Willy received his law degree, which, notes Caradec, served mainly to embellish his calling card. His father gave him a job in the family publishing firm, housed in a building on the quai des Grands-Augustins. Willy's office on the ground floor, behind the bookshop and below the printing plant, became a famous stop on the intellectual party circuit. Catulle Mendès wrote a feature about it, and Mallarmé a poem. It was also frequented by Debussy, Rémy de Gourmont, Pierre Louÿs, and the anarchist Félix Fénéon, a great admirer of Willy's puns.

Eager to "assert himself as a savant in the eyes of a father who kept a tight rein on the purse strings, and with the staff . . . which didn't take him seriously,"[22] Henry, as he now signed himself, began to publish the kind of scholarly books which could be expensively printed by "Daddy's workers," all of them, it was said, ghostwritten by penniless provincial teachers like Olympe Terrain. In the meanwhile, "Gaston Villars" and "Henry Maugis" were contributing impious drama and music criticism to a review called *Lutèce,* in which, to quote Colette, "my future husband . . . fought strenuously against bad literature and bad music."[23] He was filled with contempt for the Realists, Decadents, Naturalists, and Parnassians, championing the "Anglo-Saxon humor" of Mark Twain and Laurence Sterne, and eventually labeling himself an *auteur gai.* "Cant" was a favorite pejorative in his circle, and in Willy's case, it was a synonym for "sincerity." Freud's remark that a joke is an epitaph on the death of a feeling was never more apt than in the case of the Belle Époque's most relentless and talented coiner of puns.

The pun was an anarchic form—a little bomb lodged in a serious text which exploded its pretensions. There was just enough of the vandal in Willy's work and persona to make them fashionable in an era when the political anarchists, as Roger Shattuck notes, had a "dynamic" effect on the artistic experiments and behavior of the avant-garde. Willy's erudite buffoonery, his well-bred taste for lowlife, his cynicism, and his career of scandal and provocation were much more significant to his contemporaries than they seem at this remove. For one of his sillier dirty novels, he would be prosecuted for pornography, whereupon his reputation enjoyed one of those festive trials that rally the literary heavyweights of an era.

Willy, however, was never one of the heavyweights. Great literature translates a local dialect into a language comprehensible outside the borders of an era, a class, or a culture, and in this regard Willy was the provincial and Colette the woman of the world. He might have been writing in Udik: without considerable effort, very little of it rewarded, he is unintelligible today.

In her *Portraits of Men*, Rachilde calls Willy, rather too kindly, "the almost great man."[24] He would claim, dubiously, that his "penchant for happiness" distinguished him from his contemporaries, and that he had never been "drunk enough [even more dubious] to consider the incoherence of dreams interesting."[25] Here he was perhaps thinking of his friend Alfred Jarry, who took nihilism to such hallucinatory extremes that it became mystical, so that one might say that to Jarry, nothing *was* sacred.

True anarchism required more austerity, commitment, and discontent with society than Willy could muster. His desire to be thought original was always paralyzed by his *"crainte du ridicule"*[26] (fear of being ridiculous). The almost great man spent his life in revolt against his absolutely bourgeois family, and he could still describe himself, well into middle age, as a *potache vieilli* (an aging schoolboy) obsessed with naughty schoolgirls. But if he was disappointing as a son, he remained a faithful member of his class, who once told a friend that "for men as [well-] born as we are, it is acceptable to commit a moral outrage, but not to suffer a lapse in good breeding."[27] The same writer who admires Claudine's "amorality" would defend Wagner's Christianity against Nietzsche's paganism. He accepted his parents' politics, becoming, like them, a militant anti-Dreyfusard and anti-Semite, and later, a right-wing nationalist. And in his own perverse way, he also accepted the politics of their marriage. The "paternal" authority that Willy would exercise, not only over Colette, but over a series of other nubile young protégées, whom he liked to call his "daughters" or his "nieces," was a parodic homage to the real thing.

5

THE 1880S ARE, as Claude Pichois points out, "the most mysterious period in Colette's life," and the documents are missing which would conclusively establish the chronology of her earliest relations with Willy. He would tell Rachilde that he had known his wife since she was ten. Colette says that she was twelve when she indulged in the "forbidden pleasure" of reading Willy's reviews in her father's copies of *Lutèce*. Elsewhere she notes that she had spent a week in Paris with her father in 1884, when she was eleven.

In handwritten notes for a biography that was never published, Willy's secretary and friend, Pierre Varenne, gives what we may presume is Willy's account of their meeting, and while the dates are faulty, the facts seem credible enough. "It was probably to forget his reversals," writes Varenne, "that [Jules Colette] threw himself into the most diverse, not to say baroque, studies. These brought him, one day, accompanied by his daughter, to the publishing house of Gauthier-Villars" in search of a certain work on higher mathematics and the almanac of the Bureau of Longitudes. They were received by Willy. The Captain, in his gregarious southern manner, happened to mention that he had lost his leg at Melegnano during the Italian campaign.

"Really!" said Willy. "Did you know my father . . ."

"Your father?"

"Yes, Gauthier-Villars . . ."

Willy, Varenne continues, summoned his father, who neither recognized nor remembered the Captain, and asked him "rudely and ironically" where they had met. It was not, they established, at Melegnano ("damn well possible you're right," allowed the Captain) but elsewhere in the Crimea and Italy. And while Gauthier-Villars continued to insist that he had never laid eyes on Captain Colette, he consented to make his acquaintance.

In spite of Sido's objections to her husband's expensive "craze" for science, Jules Colette, says Varenne, subsequently came to Paris "fairly often" to visit the bookshop and to recall his wars with Jean-Albert Gauthier-Villars, "an obliging listener and witness." The young Colette, with her "magnificent hair," sometimes accompanied her father, and Willy showed great consideration for both of them, "bombarding the father with puns and stuffing the daughter with candy."[28]

According to Colette, her decisive meeting with her future husband took place five years later, in the summer of 1889. It was the year Cocteau was born, and his schoolmate, Colette's third husband, Maurice Goudeket. Rachilde published *Monsieur Vénus*—a novel in which a rich and virile noblewoman named Raoule de Vénérande sexually enslaves her working-class lover. The Eiffel Tower was finished, and the world's fair opened in Paris. In Auxerre, Captain Colette's ode to Paul Bert was read aloud at the ceremony dedicating his statue. The Colettes had just liquidated one of their last remaining farms, and in July, Gabrielle passed the exams, oral and written, for her *brévet*.[29]

She and her father celebrated with a trip to the capital, perhaps to visit the fair. As an old woman, Colette would tell a friend that the Captain had caught a splendid fish in one of the ponds near Saint-Sauveur and had decided to present it to Gauthier-Villars.[30] If this was true, they must have rushed straight to the quai des Grands-Augustins from the train station with their offering packed in melting ice. But what, one has to wonder, were Willy and his father doing in the office at the height of the summer holiday, when all self-respecting Parisians were in the country?

Wherever they met again—and supposing, for the sake of the poetic contrast, that it was among the stacks of dry journals in the bookshop—it is easy to imagine the irresistible impression that a Colette of sixteen made on a Willy of thirty. Everything about her was designed to ravish him: the whiplash braids, the cat's eyes, the supple waist, the slangy patois, the incredible freshness (begging to be corrupted), and not least, the self-conscious singularity. With that instinct for the superior and the vital which made him such a discriminating critic, such a successful predator, and such a hopelessly blocked writer, he would have sized up her potential for giving pleasure.

AT WHAT POINT does the sexual timidity of the young girl give way to that bravura which Colette describes so intimately? Perhaps the first time she has an occasion to test her power.[31] The summer before Colette met Willy, according to her own vague chronology, her mother began to suspect that a family friend—"a man above reproach" in whose household Colette was spending her school vacation—"had designs on my little pointed face, my tresses that whipped about my ankles, my shapely body."[32] Wasting no time, Mme Colette put on her bonnet, boarded a train, and went off to retrieve her. When she arrived, she found her daughter playing in the garden with the man's daughters as he contemplated the scene in silence. "Such a spectacle of harmony couldn't deceive Sido. For one thing, she noticed that I was prettier than I was at home. Thus do girls change color in the warmth of masculine desire, whether they are fifteen or thirty."[33]

The man has never been identified, nor the anecdote confirmed, but in a late letter to her friends Francis and Éliane Carco, Colette mentions a suspect: Paul Bert, who had the added attraction of being "my father's intimate friend. He lived in Auxerre in a beautiful house with a garden, and I knew his four daughters. Raised by their mother in the English fashion, they had bare arms and legs no matter the season."[34]

Perhaps his were the garden, the daughters, and the transformative desire she alludes to. It would, in any case, make a lovely irony. Bert was one of the architects of the public school system, and he was known as "the father of the teaching colleges." He would thus, indirectly, also be a godfather of the *Claudine*s.

COLETTE CAME HOME from Paris madly in love with the jaded and paunchy but charismatic man of letters who was also her father's friend, and began writing to him in secret. "Only certain distinguished-looking gray-blue paper seemed worthy of my love letters," says she. But where "to hide myself to write them?" Not in her room, where her mother might barge in on her; not in the library, where the neighbors dropped in to consult the dictionary. "Better, for its romance, for the beating of a young heart, for the deception," a bench on the road between the train station and the town.[35]

Colette pretends that she didn't think much of her own letters. "Except for the great love she believed was in her heart, this girl of seventeen had nothing to say." She liked her lover's replies, "the other voice of the duet." And yet a duet requires two players, two voices fairly balanced. Willy told her that he "trembled" at the mere thought that she would read his lines. The lines themselves trembled. He wrote in the margins and on the flaps of his envelopes in a spidery, microscopic hand, "aggressive and agile . . . I envied the ease, the ardent and personal style, that was contained in handwriting so condensed that to decipher it I often needed a magnifying glass."[36] So she envied his style! Let Colette deny that she ever had any literary ambition: the envy betrays her. Envy is the desire to possess. It makes their romance more intelligible and more interesting, for it wasn't only as a lover that he seduced her, but as a writer.

Many years later, Colette would say that she had cast her love letters, and Willy's too, one presumes, into the fire. "Born of the flame, the greater part have already perished in the flame. . . . Oh, it wasn't a matter of a grand auto-da-fé. Just a modest burning of the stubble. . . ."[37] One burns the stubble of last year's crops to fertilize the field for its new growth, and it's a useful image. Colette, provident and pitiless, would scorch the earth of each old love, and of each old love story, before plowing on.

THAT BENCH between the station and the town was also a convenient place to meet someone descending from the train. " 'Why didn't you come?' writes the loving girl." And: "My very dear darling, I didn't sleep a wink the entire night, you were both too close and too far from me."[38] So they met in secret, too. She says nothing of those rendezvous, and neither do her biographers. But in *The Tender Shoot,* one of her last and greatest novellas, Colette's narrator defends his predilection for "green fruit" by reminding her of her own first passion: "Didn't you tell me that at sixteen, you yourself fell madly in love with a bald man of forty [sic] who looked twice that age?"[39]

The story takes place in the Franche-Comté, where Willy's family, and later Willy and Colette, had a country house. A middle-aged libertine is staying on the estate of some friends, and goes out walking. He meets a girl of fifteen who saves him from an angry goat. Her social position is ambiguous: she seems to be "half-peasant, half middle-class." He returns to the spot the next day and begins to woo her. She refuses his presents with an absolute "inflexibility." Their little chats must be kept secret from her vigilant, possessive mother.

Toward the end of his holiday, the roué and the girl arrange a rendezvous at twilight, and when she arrives, she throws herself impetuously into his arms. "I think an ordinary man, I mean an ordinary lover," says the narrator, "would have thought that, in Louisette, he'd met the most shameless of semi-peasant girls. But I was not an ordinary lover."

"Without going into a lot of details that would embarrass us both," the narrator describes to "Colette" how Louisette gives herself up to the pleasure of being kissed. "She treated sensual pleasure as a lawful right, but nothing gave me reason to think that she had had any previous experience." Soon they are meeting at night, after the girl's mother (who, like Sido, rises at five) is sure to be sleeping. Yet Louisette's filial loyalty is so ferocious that her lover becomes jealous of it, and he even comes to feel that she may be exploiting him for her pleasure "like a lecherous man who's found a willing girl."

At the end of the tale, the formidable mother finds them together. "Her resemblance to Louisette left me no doubt, no hope," says the narrator. She takes in the scene "with a wide, magnificent gaze Louisette perhaps would never have." He protests that he has "not behaved . . . in a way that could . . ." but she cuts him short. "Monsieur . . . may one know your age?" And "plunging her hand into her daughter's hair, she forced her face around toward me." Louise buttons her open blouse, buckles her belt, and "mutter[s]" to her mother, "Do you want me to go for him, Mother? Us two'll 'chaäse' him, shall we?"

6

COLETTE MAY HAVE known or guessed that Willy was a ladies' man, but in August of 1889, she probably had no idea that his affections were seriously committed elsewhere. He was, in fact, sharing an apartment on the rue de l'Odéon with "his first great love,"[40] a woman of twenty-five named Germaine Servat. They had been lovers for three years, and that summer Germaine was pregnant with Willy's child, although still legally married to a photographer and caricaturist named Émile Cohl. On September 19, she gave birth to a son, whom she named Jacques.

Mme Cohl was subsequently divorced, and Willy legitimized his child, although he continued to conceal his existence—and Germaine's—from his parents. His literary career was flourishing. Music empassioned contemporary audiences the way film would in a later era, and Willy had noticed "the astronomical sums that music publishers spent to launch their concert series and to stage their operas. I knew," he told a friend, "that the music columns of the great dailies were in the hands of boring writers . . . which distanced the reader. . . . My idea was to produce a column that was gay, mocking, droll, and fun to read."[41]

He had just left *Lutèce* to become the music critic of *Art et critique*, signing his weekly reviews "the Usherette of the Cirque d'Été." Caradec dates the birth of the Usherette to an evening that Willy spent with Emmanuel Chabrier at the première of Massenet's *Le Cid*. " 'Old boy,' " said Chabrier to Willy, " 'this is second-rate shit.' This definitive word gave me a taste for music criticism."[42]

The Usherette's début was also definitive for Willy's career. In 1892, "she" moved to the widely circulated *Écho de Paris*, making Willy one of the best paid, most influential and controversial journalists in Paris. His reviews were passionate, erudite, larded with puns, and quite often vicious. As one man couldn't possibly cover and report on as many concerts as his columns suggested he had attended, Willy hired help, and the list of his "collaborators" is nearly as long as the bibliography of his publications. Some of his helpers furnished "technical information," among them Debussy, Fauré, and Vincent d'Indy. Others were obscure or impecunious young writers and musicians— Léo Colette would be one—who drafted the reviews, which Willy then embellished. Sometimes he acknowledged them, sometimes he didn't, and if they felt exploited, very few protested. "When we old ghosts recall our past as dupes," Colette would write, "we're in the habit of saying: in the days when we worked in the *shop* . . ."[43] Henry Gauthier-Villars, in the meanwhile, was reviewing music under his own name and publishing studious books on photography, while Maugis, Jim Smiley, Boris Zichine et al. were churning out lascivious comic almanacs and articles.

While the pudgy erotomane was abroad every night exercising his "gift for ubiquity," as Caradec so nicely puts it, and racking up his conquests—among them, apparently, a child of nature in the Puisaye—the mother of his son was at home, living in the shadows of her transgressions. As a divorcée with a bastard, she would not have been received by any respectable Parisian hostess. On New Year's Eve of 1891, Germaine Servat died suddenly. Many years later, Colette would suggest that "the mother of [Willy's] son" had committed suicide.[44] "I weep shamelessly for her," he told a friend, "and I curse the obligation to furnish amusing copy which I write with a heart in tears."[45] Her parents refused to acknowledge the liaison or its fruit, and buried her under her married name. Willy's parents, or at least his mother, had still not been told. Alone with his grief and his two-year-old, and perhaps searching to assuage the one in the same place he lodged the other, he confided in a family which did not share the Servats' or the Gauthier-Villars' bourgeois prejudices. A week or two after the funeral, he asked the Colettes to find Jacques a wet nurse in their village.

CHAPTER 6

In a few hours, a man without scruples turns an ignorant girl into a
licentious prodigy . . . Disgust is never an obstacle. It comes later,
like honesty. . . . But she is frequently astonished: "And what else do
we do? Is that all? Don't we start over at least? . . . Let her not con-
template, for too long, the flattering shadow of Priapus surging on
the moon-washed or lamplit wall! This shadow will ultimately
unmask the shadow of a man, already marked by age; a watery
glance, troubled and unreadable; the tremulous gift of tears; the
marvelously veiled voice; that strange lightness of an obese body;
the hardness of an eiderdown stuffed with stones.

—Colette,
My Apprenticeships

1

ACHILLE ROBINEAU-DUCLOS HAD by now received his medical degree and bought a practice in the cathedral town of Châtillon-
sur-Loing (now Châtillon-Coligny) in the Loiret. Sido's income had
diminished with the loss of her remaining farms, and the Colettes were living
on the Captain's modest pension—three hundred francs a month. In the summer of 1890, they moved in with their older son, sharing his small house off
the main square. Colette etched Willy's name into the glass of a top-floor window, and it is still there.

Their removal was traumatic for her, although not quite as ignominious as
she describes it. The house on the rue de l'Hospice wasn't sold out from under
them, but rented. Nor was the furniture seized by creditors and dragged into

the street by their bailiffs. The family auctioned what they couldn't accommodate in their new and smaller quarters. It seems a little petty to quibble with Colette over these facts. Every examined life has its fall, or falls, and the departure from Saint-Sauveur serves that function for her. Describing Claudine's less humiliating move from Montigny to Paris, she would write: "The physical horror of seeing the furniture moved about and of packing up my little habits made me as shivery and bad-tempered as a cat in the rain. To watch the departure of my little mahogany desk stained with ink, my narrow walnut sleigh bed, and the old Norman dresser that I used for my underwear made me nearly hysterical. Papa, more affected than ever, paced in the middle of the disaster, and sang. . . . I never hated him as much as I did that day."[1]

Before they left, though, she was chosen to give the official speech at the dedication of Saint-Sauveur's new schoolhouse. Dr. Merlou, who had been elected mayor, presided over the ceremony. This valedictory, delivered in a dress of virginal white, was not her last word on the subject.

ACHILLE, says Colette, was remarkably "beautiful and seductive" as a young man. He would marry relatively late—at thirty-five—and as a bachelor, glamorous to his patients and picky about women, he had adventures. He had confided to a friend some five years earlier that he was recovering from a venereal disease, probably contracted in the brothels of Paris. Colette would describe how a beautiful peasant girl offered her virginity to him in his consulting room. "She displayed a body so majestic, so firm, so smoothly sheathed in its skin that my brother never saw another to compare with it." They made love in his office and in the fields. She had a child, a boy with his father's curly hair, of whom she was insanely proud. Sido saw this grandchild of hers once, and "went away. Otherwise I should have taken him."[2]

Sido would claim that she had "no rival in [Achille's] heart," but even Colette had to admit that her mother was made "ordinary," which is to say humbled and impure, by his affairs. "Oh, if only I could see her again thus diminished," she writes in *Break of Day,* "her cheeks flushed red with jealousy and rage!"[3] One of her own first and formative passions was jealousy of her mother's jealousy of Achille.

But Colette had by now outgrown "the most troubled years" and embarked upon "the age of great devotions, of vocations."[4] Achille took her with him on his rounds and taught her to help him. She weighed out medications and learned to suture wounds, tying the knots his fingers were too thick for. "I wanted to become a woman doctor," she states, an ambition all the more extraordinary as there were only seven in all of France.[5]

These rounds were Colette's finishing school, in which she discovered that nothing natural would ever be alien to her (except, perhaps, maternity), but not the "impetuous blood spurting from a vein" as she threaded a stitch, nor "the peaceful corruption of country morals that is born and satisfied in the depths of ripe grass . . . or between the warm flanks of sleeping cattle. If Paris and the Latin Quarter had not prepared [Achille] for so much knowledge, secrecy, and variety" in erotic matters, or for so much "impudence . . . at least in the girls,"[6] she was in the element of her future fiction.

2

COLETTE WAS RECOVERING from a bad case of the flu when Willy arrived in Châtillon, with Jacques, a week before her seventeenth birthday. By now her family knew about the romance, and considered her unofficially engaged: "It's a beautiful twenty-eight-month-old baby [sic]," wrote Sido to Juliette, "whose mother is dying [sic]. . . . It's this child who should get Gabri into the Gauthier-Villars family by the front door, because his grandfather is wild about the little one, and he has to consent to his son's marriage with a young girl with no dowry because of this little one, and if it were not for that, I think that a respectful reading of the riot act would be necessary."[7]

Colette would claim that Sido had always hated Willy, and had never wanted her to marry him. This letter suggests quite the contrary. Not only was she unfazed by the fact that Willy had a mistress, however moribund, and a son; that he had been courting (and if one reads between the lines, seducing) her daughter while living with his concubine in Paris; that he had entered her own house through, so to speak, the back door; she saw these as tactical strengths.

Varenne's unpublished notes only add to the confusion of overlapping dates, obscure motives, and lies: "Colette learned from her father, in whom Willy had confided, that he was a widower [sic] and the father of a three-year-old [sic], whose mother . . . had just passed away, a fact that only heightened [her romantic] feelings. . . . The trip that he made to Châtillon-Coligny with his little boy, to meet Sido and to ask for the hand of Gabrielle . . . was the charming prelude to the marriage that took place . . . [sixteen months] later."[8]

Willy was an attractive prospective in-law not only to the Captain, but in fact to all the Colettes. Sido was fiercely proud of belonging to a family of writers, and Willy had much in common with the Landoys, who found him congenial, too. Her elder brother Eugène had died in 1880, but her younger brother Paul was also a prominent journalist, editor, and theatrical impresario. Raphaël Landoy, Eugène's son, was a humorist, who entertained Willy in

Brussels and called him *"mon cher alter magot "*[9]—a pun on "alter ego," which translates as fellow worm. Willy had long since charmed Achille and Léo, who helped with his columns and shared his passion for music.

The engagement was announced, much to the horror of Willy's family. That April, Colette went up to Paris on her own. She stayed with a family friend, Mme Cholleton, the widow of a general with whom Jules Colette had attended St. Cyr and served in Algeria and the Crimea. "If the Colettes, ruined provincials, were unimpressive," writes Claude Pichois, "the widow of the general . . . as Gabri's chaperone, could inspire trust in the Gauthier-Villars family."[10]

One thus imagines a stern figure in black taffeta clutching her rosary. Not a bit. The Algerian-born widow Cholleton had met her husband in Algiers, where he was serving with the Zouaves and she was singing in the opera chorus. According to Colette, "Madame la Générale" was "a converted Jewess" who "instructed me in many a nicety practised by inmates of the harem, among them the regular use of kohl. In her widowhood, she still affected some peculiarly African forms of adornment, such as hair-curlers of leather, ropes of blue pearls or necklaces of gazelle-droppings, and other magical fetishes." She fed Colette "couscous and the plump sweetmeats of Oran" and scandalized her by flirting with the houseboy. "I was then at that uncompromising age when one denies to persons of advanced years the right to indulge in amorous love."[11]

As for her discretion as a chaperone, Mme Cholleton indulged Gabri with as many late nights at the theater as she wanted—in the company of her fiancé. Colette drew on these outings for a famous scene in *Claudine in Paris*. As she tells it, Claudine and her "uncle" Renaud have been to a play, and it is midnight by the time it ends. Claudine wants to walk along the boulevards. They pass a café, and she asks to go in—she's thirsty. Renaud demurs: it's a noisy bohemian hangout. "So much the better!" replies Claudine. She orders a glass of Asti, and then another, and the "musky and treacherous heat" of the wine goes to her head. "You drink like a suckling," Renaud tells her: "all the grace of the animal kingdom is within you."

In the cab, on the way home, she begs him to kiss her. When he resists the temptation, she accuses him, in a jealous rage, of wanting to get rid of her so he can go off to sleep with his other women. Moved and trembling, he drives her to her door, and the next day—certain of her "destiny"—she decides to offer herself: "Because of my noble father, the lunatic, I need a daddy, I need a friend, a lover. . . . Good lord, a lover! My liberty weighs on me, my independence exasperates me; what I have been looking for for months—for a long time—is, I have no doubt of it, a master."[12]

Willy would later claim that the fictional scene was a precise transcription of the actual events, with one small difference: Colette hadn't waited until the morning to exclaim: "I'll die if I can't be your mistress!"[13] And who knows? Perhaps he behaved as honorably as Renaud. But the adventure of her woman's life began, Colette would write, "with the help of . . . a guilty intoxication, an appalling and impure adolescent élan. They are numerous, those barely nubile girls who dream of being the spectacle, the plaything, the erotic masterpiece of an older man. It's an ugly desire which they expiate by fulfilling."[14]

JACQUES GAUTHIER-VILLARS REMAINED in Châtillon until July of 1892, living with a wet nurse next door to the Colettes and "taking up," as Sido told Juliette, "a great deal of my time."[15] Willy had by now persuaded his mother, who had never laid eyes on her grandson, to raise him. He came to fetch Jacques home to Paris and then left for Bayreuth, to cover the Wagner festival for *L'Écho de Paris*. He was suffering from an unidentified malady which "tormented" Sido, who was afraid that "all this won't turn out for the best."[16]

Colette has written very little about this period except to note that "the infatuation of a girl in love is neither as constant nor as blind as she tries to believe. But her pride keeps her brave and self-contained."[17] Willy paid her infrequent visits, bringing books or candy. Her parents, somewhat belatedly solicitous of her reputation, had forbidden him to offer her expensive presents, which no doubt suited his miserly inclinations. When he departed, she always walked him the half-mile to the station, to have some time alone. Her brothers teased her about his baldness, and their mother said, "Will you shut up? . . . Are you absolutely determined to hurt the poor girl?" To which Achille replied, "it's very good for her. . . . She'll get plenty of it when she's married. This is good training."[18]

Colette needed all the pride and self-containment she could muster, because her future in-laws continued to look upon the engagement as "deplorable," and it was stalked by scandal. Both the Colettes and Willy began to receive anonymous letters postmarked Saint-Sauveur. Those addressed to the family "ran down" Willy, as Sido told Juliette, and they felt obliged to pretend the marriage had been postponed. Those addressed to Willy may have impugned Colette's honor, for many years later, when he was happy enough to impugn it himself, he would describe a character named "Vivette Wailly" as "that smart, cunning little country wench, expiring from poverty and unmarriageable in her own province"[19] because she had run away with a (female) music teacher.

In November of 1892, Colette and the Captain made a trip to Paris, where she was finally introduced to Willy's parents, and he showed her their future apartment, completely furnished "down to the pots and pans."[20] Many years later, Colette would tell a friend that "without the Gauthier-Villars, [who were] profoundly honest, [Willy] would not have married me after our three-year [sic] engagement."[21] His own letters tell a contrary story. In April of 1893, he wrote to his friend Marcel Schwob from Châtillon to say that he was "dreaming of marriage and completely blown away by the acrobatic grace of my pretty little Colette. In a month I will have wed her. And there you have it. I won't have a sou. *All right!*"[22] And a few days later he announced his wedding plans to his brother, Albert:

Just a word . . . to inform you of an imminent event which, perhaps, you have heard spoken of at the house. . . . I'm marrying the daughter of the Captain (of Châtillon), happy to avow my gratitude to a family which has been so absolutely and touchingly kind to Jacques. She doesn't have a dowry, by the way, which does not thrill our Parents. From their point of view, they're right to balk. I, in all good conscience, could not act otherwise. Please announce this news to Valentine [Albert's wife], whose family, I think, will shriek in horror. But a marriage like yours is so rare, combining the most exquisite tenderness and, how shall I put it, the most serious comfort. . . . As for me, I'm not, far from it, making a marriage of money. And if I ask myself what right I have to pronounce the words "marriage of love," I might have to answer, maybe none. Love, the grandiose kind that stings and pierces you, is, I think, the bunk of fiction. And when one inters the fragments of that ideal thing at Bagneux [the cemetery where Germaine was buried], one doesn't replace them, old boy.

Albert Gauthier-Villars was quick to reply, and Willy to address his objections:

You say that this young girl will have a very difficult position. But where? You don't think I'm so feeble-minded as to impose her on my relations. Come on! My parents are convinced that it's a deplorable marriage. I'm less convinced. If they change their minds, so much the better, and she will, no doubt, do her best to modify their opinion. If they persist, and it is their absolute right to show her the cold shoulder, without her having in the least deserved it, I will never manipulate them to alter their attitude. . . . Finally, you say that I'm getting married without great joy. You're right, it's true, I can't help it, the whole world believes that I've shaken my ears like a wet dog after the blow [of Germaine's death] and that it's forgotten. That's a bit untrue.[23]

Even in 1893, a man was not obliged to marry a young lady simply because her family had helped him to find a baby nurse for his son. If Willy could not, "in all good conscience," do otherwise, he had to have felt a more pressing sense of duty. Perhaps, like the lover of Louisette, he had "not behaved . . . in a way that could . . . ," but he had probably done enough. Colette would tell her third husband, Maurice Goudeket, that Willy had raped her before their marriage.[24] This accusation is impossible to verify, much less to date. But Sido's talk of "reading the riot act" to the Gauthier-Villars implies a serious compromise. In her less infatuated moments, Colette seems to have taken a practical attitude toward her first marriage, not unlike her mother's: "What do you want!" she told a friend in her old age. "I didn't have a choice: either stay a spinster or become a schoolteacher."[25]

The banns were published the last week in April, and the ceremony was set for the second week of May. On the fourth, the gossip column of *Gil Blas* carried a nasty little inset: "The talk of Châtillon is the intense flirtation between one of our wittiest Parisian clubmen and an exquisite blond [sic] famous in the region for her marvelous hair. It seems that the word marriage has not yet been pronounced. Thus we strongly advise the lovely owner of two incredible golden braids to withhold her kisses—according to the advice of Mephistopheles—until there's 'a ring on her finger.' "[26]

Willy challenged the editor to a duel, and wounded him in the stomach. "The wounded one could have been Willy," Sido told Juliette, "and Gabri is almost as moved as if it had been."[27]

SIDONIE-GABRIELLE COLETTE AND Henry Gauthier-Villars were married on May 15, 1893. The groom's parents had given their consent but did not attend the wedding. They divested Willy of his job in the family company and reduced his financial interest in it to a hundred thousand francs' worth of non-voting stock. The bride's half sister and her husband had not been invited, even though they and Sido were on speaking terms again. Achille, Sido explained to Charles Roché, wouldn't have them, "and if it were not for him and his help, this marriage wouldn't have happened."[28] It is not clear what kind of help he supplied, but perhaps he paid for Colette's trousseau, which was, according to the marriage contract, worth five thousand francs, and provided her with a small trust, good for another three.[29]

"Did anyone ever see a quieter wedding?" asked Colette rhetorically. There were no photographers, perhaps because of all the adverse publicity. The civil ceremony took place at the town hall, and the religious service— "a simple benediction" rather than a Mass—later that afternoon. The bride wore a dress of white muslin with a corsage of red carnations, and in lieu of a veil or a diadem, a wide satin bandeau—"*à la Vigée-Lebrun*"—around her forehead.

In the interval between the two formalities, Willy and his witnesses, Pierre Veber and Adolphe Houdard, and Colette's witnesses, her cousin Jules Landoy and Achille, went off to write one of his columns, while the bride, "accustomed to taking a back seat," slipped off into the garden: "Could it be that there, with the tomato seedlings and the calico cat, I glimpsed for a moment the mistake I had made and reassured myself as to my courage?"

Returning from church, they sat down to a simple though copious wedding "breakfast" (at six o'clock), whose most memorable course was a sea pike in a *sauce mousseline*. The champagne made Colette sleepy, and she conked out at the table. Sido woke her in time to cut the cake, "deflating the nougat bastion, and ruining the molded pink and green ice cream with a silver spade."

It was an unseasonably hot evening. The dusk had fallen and the guests had dispersed by the time the newlyweds retired to their chamber. By morning, "a thousand leagues, abysses, discoveries, irremediable metamorphoses" stood between Colette and her childhood. But there is a coda to this chapter of her life: the morning after.

The bride came downstairs, she says, to find Sido in the kitchen, stirring the morning chocolate. She was still wearing her black faille party dress, and she had an expression of unutterable sadness. It is worth pausing to consider that figure of a Ceres in mourning, and the anxiety that envelops it. In the small house where her daughter was losing her virginity, at least officially, the mother had not undressed for bed; had spent the whole night awake, evidently tormented and unhappy. She was unable to bear the thought of Colette's "going off with a strange man," or her initiation into an adult sexual life, and Colette was nearly unable to bear her mother's sadness.[30]

When I came to this scene, I thought of Isak Dinesen's image for the ordeal of separation—the Bible story of Jacob wrestling with the Angel. "I will not let thee go," says Jacob to the Angel, "until thou blesseth me." Sido gave her daughter many inestimable gifts, but never the blessing of letting go.

PART II

CHAPTER 7

So many women want to be corrupted, and so few are chosen!
—COLETTE,
The Pure and the Impure

1

*J*T IS A SUNDAY in the autumn of 1893. The streets of Paris are empty, the cafés full, the horse chestnuts turning amber under a violent sky, and dusk is falling. Colette and Willy have lunched with his parents in Passy. The nanny brought little Jacques into the drawing room, and the young stepmother—his *"petite maman"*—put him on her lap. She was wearing a dress of *lie-de-vin*—the blackish red of claret dregs—with a fluted linen collar, and her string of bridal pearls. The auburn braid that nearly everyone remarked on ("that hair is to get attention") was coiled like a sleeping python on the armchair beside her. Did the child want to touch it? He must have. And perhaps they played horsie, she bouncing him hard on her knees as he cracked the whip.

They took their leave, and walked a little to shake off the Sabbath stupor of too much food and too much stilted pleasantness, which would have left Colette desperate for a tender gesture, while Willy, lighting a cigar, might have thought about the sacrifices he had made in marrying a girl with no money, and—as he hailed a cab and she gathered up her skirts to mount it— their compensations.

They traveled north as the lamps were being lit and church bells tolled the hour, through streets of what were then country houses with vast gardens. Their cab approached the Arc de Triomphe and descended the avenue Hoche, stopping at a mansion from the Second Empire, with a flashy marble façade. A naked Venus stood in the Pompeiian vestibule, and here they gave their coats to a footman in livery. Then they ascended to a vast reception room on the first floor, hung with Old Masters and short on chairs. By now, it was quite crowded.

André Billy has described the salon of Mme Arman de Caillavet as a "chapel," and her Sunday gatherings a "service" officiated at by the high priest, Anatole France, who was Mme Arman's lover. Élisabeth de Gramont, duchesse de Clermont-Tonnerre, compared the room to a "train station" and France to the stationmaster, although in the same chapter she also refers to it as a "stock exchange," whose raison d'être was, she says (her aristocratic distaste masquerading as democratic admiration), "utility, the exchange of services." The ambitious journalists, writers, and politicians whom the duchess met there gave her "a flash of insight into the ingredients of the [very different] milieu from which I came. That milieu solicited nothing because it had nothing to offer. . . . But it retained the prestige of the past, of elegance, sport, and the art of pleasure."[1]

Colette's milieu was as remote from Mme Arman's as was that of Mme de Gramont, although their two paths—from the village and the château— would merge, as they do in Proust's masterpiece, in the classless sanctuary of Lesbos.

WILLY'S MARRIAGE WAS a great curiosity to his vast circle of acquaintances gathered at Mme Arman's for Sunday tea. It was not a marriage of convenience, nor one, apparently, of obsessive love. Nor was it the sort of "ignominious union" Proust so admired, which detaches a defiant man of the world from the society in which he has taken such pains to cultivate his standing. It seemed to be a caprice, and Colette was aware, as she shook hands in the salon, that the august men and women she was meeting were looking for some clue to her secret value, which—as much out of pride as from her own ignorance about it—she refused to provide.

Willy's sense of "utility" was uncommonly sharp. He had few relations he did not exploit. And because Colette's talent and its earning power had not yet made her "this precious child," as he called her to Rachilde, he treated her with an offhandedness that reinforced her own sense of having little value in his world. Intent on his business, he would have introduced her to some kind friend—a man, no doubt; an erudite, melancholy connoisseur of beauty. After a few words, he would have gone off to work the room, leaving them to discuss the worldly subject on which Mme Willy could best hold her own: M. Willy.

2

ACCORDING TO COLETTE, the first year of her marriage to Willy was the unhappiest period of her life, except for the six weeks at the end of 1941, when her third husband was interned by the Nazis. But 1893 is also virtually undocumented—she left almost no letters. She wrote regularly to her mother, but Achille or his wife burned that correspondence after Sido's death. She must, at least, have written dozens of thank-you notes, for she was, like most of her contemporaries, a fairly scrupulous social bookkeeper. But she was a nobody—"to some people worthless and invisible, to others too conspicuous and vaguely dishonored"[2]—and the somebodies of Paris whose archives have been preserved didn't save them. So we have only her own highly selective memories.

Colette's self-portrait as a bride—written at sixty-two—isn't convincing, in part because it is rather too limp and lifeless to be true. More intriguing is the young girl's relation to the terribly crafty and self-possessed old woman telling her story. "With Willy dead," writes Claude Pichois, one of Colette's most astute critics, "she narrates . . . her married life, blackening it as it suits her and leaving a caricature of her husband that her talent has imposed on the general public. The truth is other."[3]

It is certainly dangerous to take the word or trust the memory of anyone about the character of a former spouse. Indignation matures slowly, and sometimes the fruit is ripe only when the tree is dead. In Colette's case, passion was often an anesthetic. When it wore off, it left her feeling furious at the pain and forgetful of the perverse pride with which she had once endured it. "It is not happiness that one asks of the man whom one loves," she would tell a young friend in a candid moment. "It's only the possibility of existing in his presence and of suffering from it."[4]

After their divorce, Willy took the occasional potshot at Colette in a novel. His caricatures were violent, though so badly aimed as to be relatively harmless. His memoirs contain a few unflattering though believable "rectifications" of their old feuds. But he balked at the idea of writing any definitive portrait of the woman he called "my widow," and whose talent he never ceased to extol. Colette wasn't so reticent. She published *My Apprenticeships* four years after his death. Voluptuous in its detail and its rancor, it is one of the most damning elegies ever pronounced over the dead body of a husband, or an oeuvre.

Yet even if we don't accept *My Apprenticeships* as the truth, we should accept it as Colette's truth. It opens with four puzzling little fin de siècle portraits to which she gives—the expression is important—"without love, a privileged place." They resemble nothing so much as the bronze idols, the deities of love and death, which Freud, at the same period, kept in his consulting room as talismans of human strangeness.

The first is a nameless young man whom she describes as an "ascetic," and who would now be called a co-dependent. He spends his life in the company of addicts, pretending to drink and to smoke opium as they do, hearing their confessions, holding their heads, and deriving from these "transient friendships" with the living dead a "mournful bliss." "It is easier to smoke and drink," notes Colette, "than to fake it, and abstinence, rare in all domains, reveals a gift for defiance and virtuosity."

The second figure is that of an eight-year-old girl who "already knew too much . . . about the different ways of giving oneself terrible pleasure." She hides in the garden, letting her mother search frantically for her, listening to the maternal voice grow hoarse and desperate, then appears at a run, feigning breathlessness, and full of false excuses for her absence. (The description recalls the portrait Colette gives of herself in *My Mother's House,* appearing at a run and "feigning breathlessness" as she returns from the house of Adrienne de Saint-Aubin.) Colette asks her what worse mischief she will perpetrate at twenty, and she replies, boastfully, "Oh, I'll think of something."

The third figure is a professional kept woman named Zaza whom Colette describes as a "fertile prairie, man's hayloft of abundance." Her lover's best friend warns him that she is a femme fatale who is destroying him. When the friend himself comes on to her, Zaza takes her revenge. "She drew him close, pushed him away, called him back, engraved on the wrist of the poor man, with the help of a broken glass, the four letters of her name; gave him assignations in a taxi . . . wore black lace blouses, and most scandalous of all, refused herself to him." The man dies, and with an "insouciance . . . that would have chilled a more sensitive listener," she tells Colette: "One shouldn't tempt the devil, even as a joke. That fool . . . tempted the devil."

The fourth, last, and finest of her talismans is the Spanish dancer Caroline Otéro, the most famous courtesan of the Belle Époque, and the mistress of five kings. Colette explains to those readers who may be surprised to find Otéro's name at the beginning of her memoirs that its purpose is "to give these pages their tone." One anecdote gives the tone best of all. Colette has been invited to a private supper at Otéro's mansion. The guests are a handful of aging women. The hostess, dressed in her peignoir and mules, consumes enormous quantities of stew, then picks up her castanets and dances, for her own pleasure, until two in the morning, working up a sweat, and with it a dark and musky smell that is "more refined than she is." Apropos of nothing ("she delivered her great truths to no purpose"), she tells Colette: "Kid, you don't seem very bright. Remember that there is always, in the life of a man, even a miser, a moment when he shows you an open hand." "The moment of passion?" asks Colette. "No, the one when you twist his wrist."[5]

Colette invites us to consider these four figures—a necrophiliac of sorts, a sadistic child, a murderous tease, and a mercenary sex goddess—as the caryatids who support her memoir and the era to which it refers, an era which, like the little girl, knew too much about giving oneself terrible pleasure. What do they share with one another and with their author? Mistrust, defiance, spiritual emptiness, and the virtuosity of their lies.

3

IN 1893, a journalist named Georges Lecomte, one of Willy's many serviceable friends, published an account of Gauthier-Villars's life which his subject probably helped him write:

> Up a little after dawn, he rustles through the gazettes that are still moist from the press, scans the reviews, plumbs the . . . depths of the most hermetic poems . . . reads articles on philosophy and science . . . manages a serious publishing house [sic], sends telegrams, writes twenty letters to friends, women, scientists, theater directors, ministers, showmen, professors at the Collège de France; jumps into a cab, from the cab to an exhibition, from there to a dress rehearsal, hears the play, then travels to the four corners of Paris to console anguished women, investigates, by letters, the vices of the provinces, observes those of Paris, turns up at musical teas, plays whist at the officers' club . . . writes half a dozen articles on the most various subjects . . . lunches, dines, finds the time to be devoted to his friends, to be hard on his enemies, to lash out at those who annoy him; finally, ever fresh, joyful, amusing, he settles into the theater, from which he emerges to visit a press that is about to roll . . . to write his account of the evening. Then come the beers, the free meals, and the kisses. . . .
>
> In the midst of this feverish chaos, he conserves enough energy to be ever witty and unfettered . . . to send flowers and theater tickets, to engage in duels when necessary, to help his friends when they're in trouble, to command an artillery unit a month a year and make an annual pilgrimage to Bayreuth and much more often, one to Venusberg.[6]

"Venusberg"[7] was Willy's garçonnière on the top floor of the building which housed the Gauthier-Villars bookshop and printing plant. Colette describes this "encampment" with exquisite distaste in *My Apprenticeships*. It was furnished with all the clichés of bachelor dissolution: the clubby color scheme—walls painted chocolate brown and bottle green—balls of dust and hair beneath a sagging bed, a set of "disgraceful" file cartons holding Willy's press clippings, and a collection of pornography. Here the young girl who had dreamed of a demonic liberator and had offered so gamely to become Willy's "erotic masterpiece" discovered, instead, that she was supposed to pose—in her socks and panties—for a dirty postcard.

UNLIKE CLAUDINE, Colette didn't have a honeymoon: Willy traveled only when he could get his expenses paid for by a publisher. He took his wife to the Jura for two weeks to mooch on his parents. His mother was horrified by the quantities of butter and jam that her new daughter-in-law consumed, and when they returned, Willy moved her (as she describes herself, she has the dead weight of a sofa) to the apartment he had rented for them on the rue Jacob.

Here they had three "somber" rooms on the third floor, between two courtyards. The square salon connected with the dining room. It was heated by a white enamel stove whose toxic fumes, Colette says, made her sleepy. The bedroom was furnished with an immense mirrored wardrobe which made her "sad," and one can imagine why. Off the bedroom was an alcove filled with junk where she installed a washbasin and its accouterments— plumbed bathrooms were still an unusual luxury. These lodgings were "agreeable enough," she allows, at least in comparison to the garçonnière, except for one sinister eccentricity that would probably now be considered, by a realtor with a clientele of design students (the faculty of the École des Beaux-Arts is down the street), marketably kitschy: The woodwork, mold- ings, doors, and the niche behind the stove had been decorated by the previous tenant with crude *pique-assiette* mosaics made from some two hundred thou- sand tiny "lozenges" of colored glass. "A good cleaning got the best of them," but not before Colette declared herself "appalled" at "the thought of living between walls that had witnessed such secret folly."[8]

THE NEWLYWEDS' DAY began with an early breakfast at a dairy bar frequented by delivery men across the river on the Right Bank. Then Willy went to work as Lecomte describes it, and Colette returned to her grotto, where she enjoyed, she says bitterly, the leisure of a prisoner and the rest of an invalid. She wrote those lost letters to her mother and helped Willy tackle his voluminous correspondence. Like every wife of the period, she kept a house- hold ledger, and no purchase—stamps, buttons, a clothes brush, a pound of cherries—was too trivial to be recorded. She had a maid and later a cook, so her assertions of having lived like a pauper and of filling up on sugar instead of meat should be read as the expression of a poetic, rather than a literal, deprivation of nourishment. She groomed herself meticulously, played with her cat, read by her oil lamps, and "dug myself in," she writes, "so as not to know Paris."[9]

Willy reclaimed her company in the early evening, when his real work began—the tireless self-promotion which had begun to make him a literary brand name. There was not a cultural event of any importance that the couple did not attend, and after a performance that the Usherette was reviewing, Colette waited in the corridors of *L'Écho de Paris* while he corrected his galleys ("he was very sensitive about typos"), coming to life when the playwrights Courteline or Catulle Mendès arrived and paid her some attention. Then she followed her husband, famished and tired, to the Napolitain, d'Harcourt, Weber's, or Pousset's, where he met his cronies, delivered the puns he had been polishing all day, and ogled the young actresses and models who were as busy as he was advancing their careers.

Colette told her mother that the first time she was obliged to wear a low-cut dress at a grand dinner she was "embarrassed" to parade her naked arms and shoulders "under the noses" of so many strangers, and Claude Pichois observes that this showed "an amiable modesty, or an affectation of modesty, which she would transcend." He also justly notes that she protests too much about her passivity and estrangement. "Of course, to be seen at Longchamp [the races], at the Palais de Glace [the fashionable skating rink], at the theater, at the concerts, at the clubs, to frequent the [salons] . . . may not constitute a profound pleasure. But proud, unsociable, or pretending to be so to pique the general curiosity, Colette had some real friends."[10]

She had them in time. A year or eighteen months into her marriage, she had found her sea legs in the swell of Parisian society and had discovered her "taste for survival and self-defense."[11] Until then, however, she was less self-conscious of her décolleté than she was galled by her insignificance as Willy's penniless, provincial child bride. And in the cafés, on the landings of the Opéra, in the crowded drawing rooms that smelled, by midnight, of rancid caviar and spilled drinks, Colette, like Claudine, "harvested . . . looks and glances" that were "not entirely full of good will toward me: 'It's awfully young' . . . 'Where's it from?' . . . 'It's from Montmartre' . . . 'It's Slav . . .' " And of her husband: "Is [he] already so old that he takes his pleasure with little girls?"[12]

Those who took the trouble to observe the young Mme Willy give contradictory impressions of her. Some, like the society painter Jacques-Émile Blanche, who gave a luncheon in honor of the newlyweds, met a cowed young girl whom his cousin Willy scolded for her table manners (she rolled her bread into pellets and launched them) and patronized like a child. Others found her vivacious and *sans gêne*—cheeky—and a skillful purveyor, when it suited her, of her rustic charm.

4

IN ASSESSING Colette's unhappiness, we should take a closer look at Willy's. "It's that man's story which should be written," she allows. "The trouble is that not a soul knew him intimately."[13] Yet Willy was capable of more candid self-awareness than Colette. "I have too much contempt in my heart," he told a friend, "for too many people and too many things not to suffer from it, all the while finding it amusing, which is only an illusory consolation. I feel, however, that my solitude is a force which no other force can counteract. It's for that reason that I shut myself up in the midst of three thousand intimate friends who envy me, malign me, and whose names I've forgotten."[14]

In marrying a vital girl who was, at the same time, inexperienced and completely beholden, Willy may have hoped to find a "force" to balance what was, in fact, his chronic depression. If he was unknowable, it was because so much of his energy went into dissembling the disarray of his soul.

Willy's malaise had a contemporary name, the *mal du siècle,* and his symptoms—enervation, loss of faith, a feeling of doom, a sense of isolation, discomfort with society, and the mistrust of relationships—affected nearly every artist and colored every important literary work of the period. For his friend Marcel Schwob, "the internal crisis" was mirrored by the "external crisis"—the rash of anarchist bombings and assassinations which had so profoundly unsettled Paris. The tension was palpable in the cafés and at every public gathering.

Indeed, the established order was under siege in the broadest sense. Legitimate authority, religious dogma, scientific truth—the very notion of objectivity—were being discredited by the greatest minds of the age. "Literature in this period," writes Theodore Zeldin, "was above all concerned with revealing the nature of man," and "originality . . . acquired a moral value."[15] But if the individual was redefined as paramount, without a god, he was also perceived as innately selfish and alone, and this was a shock whose horror we have accepted, though not, perhaps, ceased to feel.

Men and women of the fin de siècle sought to redress their solitude "in the midst of three thousand intimates" according to their means and temperaments. Some, like Alfred Jarry, took refuge in hallucination; others, like Willy, in debauchery. His friends Léon Daudet, Charles Maurras, and Maurice Barrès would propose reactionary political solutions to this loss of cohesion and identity. Movements and cults proliferated. So did violence, mysticism, drug use, and suicide. Alone in her grotto, Colette dreamed of dying and of being resurrected back in Saint-Sauveur (how aptly named is her imagined Eden), where butter is cheap and the sun is shining.

Those who weren't completely contaminated by their pessimism would subscribe, with Nietzsche and Ibsen, to the belief that there was still, in a corrupt, stifling, and godless bourgeois world, something worthwhile: "the will to give expression to one's personality."[16] Willy's career was a perversion of that ambition. His goal was to be as notorious as possible—for his utter moral worthlessness.

As for Colette, she was a Nietzschean without knowing it. From her village life, her unconventional mother, her appetite for work, her own vitality and egoism, she had developed an unusual degree of resistance to the notion that life was not worth living. It didn't suffice to preserve her "innocence," but it helped to fortify her detachment and resolve. "In the era of my high youth," she wrote at sixty, "it befell me to hope that I could become 'someone.' If I had had the courage to formulate my hope in its entirety, I would have said, 'someone else.' But I quickly renounced that. I have never been able to become someone else."[17]

THE MOST OBVIOUS SYMPTOM of Willy's sense of destitution was his obsession with money. He was profligate and miserly by turns. He ran up debts, perpetrated scams, borrowed large sums from rich women and small ones from poor friends; "parked his assets" under other names, and was eventually forced—like Colette's grandfather—to flee the country to avoid his creditors. "No one," she says, "was wise to his secret holdings. . . . His most often repeated word—I know whereof I speak—was: 'Quick, little one, there's not a cent in the house.' "[18]

In the beginning, she says that she found it natural—the child of bankrupt parents—to live with empty pockets, without a winter coat, and with the occasional windfall of allowance money that had to last for months. She may not have been aware of the extent to which Willy was, with these small indignities, punishing her for his sacrifice—noble, as he saw it—of taking a bride without a dowry. "My wedding?" he wrote to a friend in 1893. "But yes, you did drop me a line about it. And between old pals . . . it wasn't worth the trouble. . . . I have married a woman absolutely destitute of cash, and I am no longer anything at all in the paternal book business."[19]

Money was Willy's real fetish, and its worship eventually sapped his strength, degraded his character, and destroyed his marriage to Colette. "Money matters, money matters," she muses. ". . . Where have they led me, I who didn't bother about them? A year, eighteen months after our marriage, M. Willy says to me: 'You should jot down your memories of elementary school. Don't be afraid of spicy details, perhaps I can make something of them. Funds are low.' "[20]

5

EARLY IN THE WINTER of 1894, Colette received an anonymous letter indicating an address in Montmartre where she could surprise her husband with his mistress. She took a cab to the boulevard Bochard-de-Saron and knocked on the door of a ground-floor apartment. When she was admitted, she found herself in a room that was bare but neat, with a sunny window, a birdcage, and an open pot cupboard. Beyond it, in an alcove, she could see one corner of a big bed. But the bed was empty, for Willy and a young woman with ferocious eyes were sitting at a kitchen table "poring over a book—yet another one!—of accounts."

At the sight of Colette, the woman seized a pair of scissors that lay on the table. Willy wiped the sweat from a brow that was "vast, pink, and powerful" and said, with an air of only casual surprise, "You've come for me?" Colette replied, "Of course I have."[21] And then he hustled her out the door.

The woman was Charlotte Kinceler. Willy had known her well before his marriage. There is a photograph of a young Lotte in one of his albums, dated October 29, 1888, and inscribed: "I will love you always."[22] Lotte—a well-known character in Montmartre—had been taken up by the artists and writers of Le Chat Noir. She was one of those "wild girls" who haunt the romantic fiction of the era: tough, volatile, melancholy, "rather nasty on occasion but fundamentally good"[23]—a "daughter of the people," as the sons of the upper classes liked to call them. Her father was an alcoholic former Communard. Her sister was a prostitute, according to Colette, who muddled the story, which came from Willy's memoirs. One day he had taken a friend with a taste for slumming, the critic Jules Lemaître, to meet the famous Lotte Kinceler. Lemaître questioned her about a mutual acquaintance: "a bleached blond named Alberte . . . currently employed, if I'm not mistaken, in the gallant profession."

"The ga-what? The gallant profession?" Lotte snorted. "The only Alberte I know is a whore."[24]

This style of repartee gave Lotte some modest fame. She inspired a play by Brieux, *Les Hannetons,* in which she was played by Polaire, the actress who would immortalize Claudine. One of the Symbolists wanted to introduce her to the president of the Republic. Willy speaks of her "instinctive fineness, physical and moral." Colette admired her speech, which was that of a fortuneteller; her strength and suppleness, which were those of a python; and her caustic wit, which was that of a "hunchbacked child."[25]

They eventually became friends, and their rapprochement taught Colette, she says, many useful things: deception, humility, and the art of making peace with a rival. Some of their letters have survived. Most of them concern Lotte's affair with an unnamed general who had been keeping her, and with whom she was negotiating a parting settlement. Colette consoles Lotte for her ills, "physical and mental." She gives her beauty advice: "glycerine ruins the hands, use lanoline instead." And she adopts a tone of feminine complicity as the polygamist's senior wife: "Is he going to play the pasha, this Willy, in his virginal dressing gown! The pasha with nine cocks? No, but 'one's enough' [he says], provided it's a good one."[26]

Some of Willy's letters to Lotte have been saved, too (she defied his command to burn them), but they are not so lighthearted. "I'm bored to death," he tells her:

> [It's] a boredom that is dense and tenacious, that weighs me down and eats me up, and I . . . do everything to distract myself, without succeeding. . . . I add, my honest tiny one (for I've always said that your frank little soul was the most honest of all), I add that the other day, my troubles had made me drunk like a bad wine; I'm struggling with myself in a jungle of inextricable difficulties. That's why I'm bitter, and sad. . . . Destroy, as soon as possible, this letter, which is a confession, but a confession of which I'm proud. When we see one another again, may nothing in our respective manners let on that there is something confidential between us.[27]

Charlotte Kinceler saved her money and opened an herbalist's shop on the rue Pauquet. Here she sold teas, pomades, and potions to induce abortion. One afternoon, in a driving rain, she went into the back room to write a note: "When it shits buckets like this, it's amazing how everything disgusts me."[28] Then she washed the ink stains from her fingers and shot herself—in the head, says Willy; in the mouth, says Colette—with a small revolver.[29]

6

COLETTE WENT BACK to Châtillon alone shortly after the discovery of Willy's infidelity.[30] On her first day home, she drove out with her brother on his rounds, and in the evening, after Achille and her father had gone to bed, she sat up late with her mother telling tales of Paris. Sido loved music, and Colette no doubt described how Fauré and Debussy had improvised duets at the soirées of Mme de Saint-Marceaux. She adored the theater, and Colette would have regaled her with the first-night gossip, comparing the elegance of certain courtesans to the vulgarity of certain duchesses. She probably took her mother on a house tour of the salons: Judith Gautier's red-lacquered attic with its exotic pets, poets, and Wagnerians; the ancien régime grandeur chez Mme de Polignac; the parvenu splendor chez Mme Arman; the dense and smoky gatherings at the Mercure de France, presided over by Rachilde—so shocking in her fiction, so astute in her criticism, and so bourgeois in her marriage.

Colette was a gifted mimic. Perhaps she took off the novelists with "socialist pretensions" and the ones who "specialized in the plumbing of female souls"—types she would mock gleefully in the *Claudines*. Sido would have enjoyed an account of the art students' high jinks at their Bal des Quatz'Arts; of the Montmartre nightclubs; of the famous "inverts," local and foreign, of both sexes. Just as Colette played up her rustic charm in Paris, she flaunted her worldliness in the country, and her mother would tease her about it: "Look at you, proud . . . as a flea on his hind legs because you've married a Parisian."[31]

Some of this storytelling was, like Scheherazade's, a way of warding off a fatal moment: the moment of weakness, which was also the moment of greatest intimacy, when Sido rose from the armchair to tuck Colette in. She says that she gave her mother "the gift of a lie"—the lie of her happiness—and was proud of having done so. Yet even Colette admits that Sido probably wasn't deceived.[32] So this heroism was also, and perhaps primarily, self-protective. Many daughters of loving but intrusive mothers—mothers greedy for vicarious pleasure and ready, presumptuously, to take on their adult children's battles—have armed themselves with the same shield of pride.

CHAPTER 8

1

EARLY IN THE WINTER of 1894, the Willys attended the annual Polytechnic Ball, presided over, that year, by Jean-Albert Gauthier-Villars. Colette recalled having danced with her father-in-law, and wearing a pale green dress the color of her complexion. Shortly thereafter, she came down with a high fever, stomach pains, and swelling, and was put to bed. Her symptoms, she said, didn't respond to treatment, and Dr. Jullien told his patient that she wasn't cooperating with her cure. "There is always a moment, in the life of young people," she wrote, "when dying is just as normal and seductive to them as living, and I hesitated."[1]

The doctor wrote to Mme Colette, who came to Paris with a modest wardrobe of black dresses and cotton nightgowns, slept in the "dark dining room," addressed her son-in-law coolly as "Monsieur Willy," groomed Colette's hair, and cajoled her—in the course of the sixty days she remained in bed—back to life.

Willy wasn't thrilled to be living with his mother-in-law. Writing to Juliette's husband sometime toward the end of his wife's long convalescence, he reports: "Tomorrow they'll get her up, not for long, and she is so happy about it, the poor little thing! For that matter, now that she's doing better, she's becoming unrestrainable: she stirs, she kicks up her heels, eh! the little minx!" And he concludes: "My mother-in-law is still here. I don't know when she'll return to Châtillon. What prevents me from wishing too ardently for her departure is that she'll take my wife along with her."[2]

Colette has implied, and most of her biographers have accepted the implication, that her illness was, if not a nervous breakdown, a psychosomatic episode of some kind, triggered by her discovery of Willy's infidelity, and intensified by the stress of concealing her humiliation from Sido. This point needs to be reexamined. First, there is the high fever, which one medical specialist attributes to typhoid.[3] Then there is an unpublished letter from Colette to Lotte Kinceler, written in 1896, when Lotte was very ill. "Two years ago," writes Colette, "I had my whole insides so badly damaged, and I am so well cured, that I wish the same happy outcome for your ills."[4] Then there is the rigor of the treatment: sixty days of bed rest and mustard plasters to reduce the abdominal swelling. Finally, there is the secret she would confide to her third husband, Maurice Goudeket: Willy, she said, had given her a venereal disease.[5] Considering his promiscuity, this seems not only plausible, but likely.

A century after the illness, relying on a secondhand confession and some sketchy circumstantial evidence, we can only speculate as to what venereal disease, if any, Colette contracted. Francis and Gontier confidently assert that it was syphilis, but Colette had none of the enduring complications of syphilis in later life. The high fever, sickly complexion, inflammation of her lower "insides," and doctor's prescription of bed rest and mustard plasters suggest acute gonorrhea, which was nearly epidemic at the time. In *Claudine Takes Off*, Colette attributes a case of "chronic genital herpes" to Maugis, Willy's alter ego, and throughout her life, she mentions painful "pelvic inflammations" that recur at moments of stress. But recurrent pelvic inflammations— salpingitis—are also symptomatic of gonorrhea, especially in women. And the disease sometimes causes severe eye pain and photophobia. Colette notes that her eyes were "still" weak and sensitive to light in the letters she writes from the Breton island of Belle-Île that spring, and she would suffer an attack of what Willy would call "hysterical blindness" toward the end of the year.[6] But whatever the malady, it would help to explain Sido's silent fury.

2

BY THE TIME she fell ill, Colette already commanded the devotion of some real friends, and the three she singles out for her specific gratitude were perfect specimens of the age in which she served her apprenticeships.

Paul Masson, who wrote under the name of Lemice-Térieux *(le mystérieux)* and who appears in Colette's fiction as Masseau, came daily to the rue Jacob: he was working at the Bibliothèque Nationale, just across the river. He would sometimes cross paths on her landing with Marcel Schwob. These two men, both good friends of Willy's, "pretended to hate each other," Colette wrote, "and played a game of insulting each other politely under their breath. . . . Then they would declare a truce and talk at immense length, and I was stimulated and excited by the battle of wits between those two subtle, insincere minds."[7]

Schwob was partly crippled, so Colette's three flights cost him considerable pain. He sat at her bedside, "wasting his time on my behalf with magnificence," and she was too young, she says, to have been astonished. "I treated him as my possession. At twenty, one accepts exorbitant gifts royally."[8]

From his ancestors, Talmudic scholars, Schwob had inherited his hawkish profile and his passion for the esoteric. He was an anglophile like his friend Willy, a dandy like his friend Oscar Wilde, and a champion of the Symbolists. The brilliance of his talk was always greater than that of his prose. He earned his living as a literary critic and translator, and in addition to the works of Twain, Dickens, and Defoe, which he read aloud to Colette, he had translated *Hamlet*. His erudition was profound, and he loved slang.

Schwob was twenty-five when he met Colette. He and Willy were already acquainted through *L'Écho de Paris*. By the time the newlyweds were settled into the rue Jacob, Schwob was living around the corner on the rue de l'Université. He shared his gloomy apartment with a squirrel, a griffon, and a Japanese dog. His mistress had just died, the sort of mistress who was, like the exotic pets, de rigueur for a man such as Schwob: a tubercular young prostitute named Louise.

One of Colette's earliest published letters is a note to Schwob on his bereavement:

> Willy scolds me, and shoves me around, and cries; he would have done better to inform me [of Louise's death]. . . .
>
> If I have never spoken with you of your poor [friend] during her long illness, I have never forgotten to ask after her every time you left our house. But Willy didn't want to let me speak to you of her because, he said, I would only increase your pain. . . . And now he tells me very harsh things which I truly do not merit. You know me enough, my dear Schwob, to know that I would have found other words to say to you, returning from the cemetery, than a report on my bronchitis. . . . I ask your forgiveness for having been so base a little while ago.[9]

One day, on a whim, and defying his frailty, Schwob decided that he would make a pilgrimage to Kipling's grave in Samoa, accompanied by the Chinese manservant who doubled as his nurse. He didn't find what he had sought there. Depressive and doomed (he would die at thirty-seven), Schwob became, in the course of a long illness and many operations, a morphine addict. But despite his decadence and his nihilism—or perhaps because of them—he was also a connoisseur of vitality. He defined the true poets (thinking of his friend Verlaine) as those "who are neither theoreticians nor grammarians but who listen to themselves live, and sing what they hear."[10] This explains his attraction to Colette, and his precocious recognition of what was so fine about her.

COLETTE'S THIRD REGULAR VISITOR was a *femme du monde*, "kind to such a young and defenseless patient, confined so long to a sad bed . . . in a room where nothing spoke of choice, comfort, or love."[11] (Self-pity would seem to have been her only luxury.)

Mme Arman de Caillavet arrived at the third floor breathless—she was fat—with a basket of exquisite fruit or a box of chocolate wrapped in a shawl. One day she also brought Colette the galleys of Anatole France's latest novel, *Le Lys rouge*. The master, she said, would value their young friend's opinion, and Colette made some minor corrections. The subject was apt: the destructive passion of jealousy.

Mme Arman was one of Proust's models for Mme Verdurin.[12] She was fifty when Colette met her, an imposing woman with piercing blue eyes and a double chin who hennaed her hair and dressed flamboyantly. Born Léontine Lippmann to a family of bankers, she had converted from Judaism at the time of her marriage to the son of an arms dealer who owned a vineyard in Bordeaux. Caillavet was one of the family estates, and M. Arman had annexed the particle to his name, along with a certain amount of ridicule. He was a jovial man, a Gascon, somewhat clownish, a bon vivant and a yachtsman, who played the rather thankless role of a French Teddy Wharton to his wife's Edith.

Mme Arman, whom Colette describes as "Minerva's bird" (a reference to both her intelligence and her nose), was famous for her letters and for her uncredited contributions to the work of her lover. It was she who had ghostwritten the preface—which France had signed—to Proust's first work of fiction, *Les Plaisirs et les jours*. Her son, Gaston, was to become one of the most successful comic playwrights of the era.

Although their friendship ended bitterly, Léontine Arman de Caillavet was Colette's first mentor in Paris. She had endured her own share of condescension from society, had noted Colette's inelegance and distress, perceived the defiance and repressed fury behind her reserve, and sympathized. She seems to have offered the kind of maternal solicitude and approval for which Colette was starved, and with it a shrewdness of which Sido would have approved gratefully. A few years later Mme Arman would tell her daughter-in-law, Jeanne Pouquet: "You must take the world for what it is, despise it and exploit it."[13] She probably gave Colette the same advice.

3

ON JUNE 25, the French president, Sadi Carnot, was assassinated by an anarchist in Lyon. In one of her rare comments on world events, Colette mentions the news to Marcel Schwob. It made her feel sorry for the caricaturist Caran d'Ache, "who will have to mock up a new type of president." Then she goes on to a more cheerful subject: the little jewel that Mme Arman has sent her, a fly with ruby eyes.[14]

Colette had recovered from her illness, or "nearly," and her doctor had recommended a change of air. Feeling guilty, no doubt, Willy decided he could afford two months by the sea. They had left for Belle-Île, an island off the coast of Brittany, early that month, accompanied by Paul Masson, and found rooms close to the shore in a "wooden house that smelled like a ship."[15] It had a balcony of pink brick, and here, in the evenings, by the glow of the lighthouse and the moon, they could watch the sardine women dancing on the beach. One of them took notice of the somber, unattached Masson and called up to him: "Don't you need anyone?" "What for?" "To sleep with."[16]

Masson, "Lemice-Térieux," seems, at first, an odd companion for such a wholesome holiday. He was a frail man, "prematurely aged"; learned, dessicated, with perfect manners and an opium habit he had brought home to France, Colette believed, from his short career as a judge in India. In "The Kepi," she captures the flavor of his friendship with Willy. They shared an obsession with puns, and they liked to bait her innocence with their contempt for love and women. "I had not yet become inured to the mixture of affected cynicism and literary paradox," she writes, "by which, around 1900, intelligent, bitter, frustrated men maintained their self-esteem." She enjoyed Masson's "caustic wit," though, and his malice: "the way he attacked people on the least provocation."[17]

Masson had been an assiduous visitor to the rue Jacob during Colette's illness, and when Willy was out for the evening, they would dine tête-à-tête. She wore her favorite velvet dressing gown for him, which was supposed to look "vaguely" like something from Botticelli, and let down her hair. He fed her the latest gossip, and together they invented "fantasies" about a mistress he didn't, "thank God," have. These games were in line with Masson's specialty as a writer: the elaborate literary hoax. He had published "Bismarck's" adolescent diary, which was supposed to have caused a brief diplomatic crisis between France and Germany, and "General Boulanger's" *Thoughts and*

Reflections. When Colette met him, he was "attached to the catalogue [of early printed books] at the [Bibliothèque] Nationale, and because it seemed short on certain titles—royal letters, sixteenth-century German manuscripts—he had decided to insert them. "But the books don't exist?" Colette asked him. "Ah, he replied, I can't do everything."[18]

THE "EARTHBOUND" COLETTE was now seeing the ocean for the first time: "I'm swimming in waves of joy,"[19] she wrote to Schwob. On the west side of the island, the thunderous high Atlantic crashed against a rocky coast; the air was thick with mist, and the rain hard as hailstones. This romantic scenery would beguile Marcel Proust, who summered there briefly the next year, and Sarah Bernhardt, who would renovate the old fortress at the Pointe de Poulain.

On the east side, where the Willys and Masson were lodging, the climate and sea were practically Mediterranean. There was a port for sailboats; the terraced hills were planted with vines and fig trees; and the water, a transparent green close to the shore, was "blue velvet" at the horizon. "Trolling" the beach, Colette found creatures she had never seen: white sand crabs; exotic shellfish, little monsters "with leaves on top and naked, shining legs underneath . . . all my flesh creeps when I think of them."[20]

This idyll on Belle-Île left such a deep impression that Colette would reshuffle her memories of it several times, most notably in the last Claudine, *Retreat from Love,* and much later, in *My Apprenticeships.* Both versions attest to the happiness of a young woman who is restored to her element—nature— and who recovers that physical eloquence stifled in the salons of Paris. In her memoir, Willy is a marginal figure, absorbed in his secretive correspondence, pursuing women and money, and she spends her time with Masson. There is no third party in the novel, where Claudine and Renaud enjoy a kind of "splendid, self-indulgent" honeymoon. He combs the beach with her, jumps the waves, plays with the sand crabs. They go sailing, and he teaches her to work the ropes and trim the jib. She wears the sailor suit from Colette's own childhood daydreams, and Renaud impulsively makes love to his "ship's boy" on the beach, shocking two bathers who mistake them for a homosexual couple.

Colette's letters to Schwob from Belle-Île contain the raw material for both versions, but without the self-conscious poignancy or the explicit eroticism. Willy and Masson play Jules and Jim—paternally. She is their doted-on and recalcitrant only child. With nature as an ally and a backdrop, she reclaims her power. Her naiveté is a foil for Masson's cynicism; and her brutality, for his refinement. She drags him out to the cliffs on his "weak legs" and down to the beach in his dark suit. When he loses a journal containing a story by

Schwob, she claws him with her nails so that his wrist bleeds, and threatens to drown him. "I've teased him so unmercifully that we get angry with each other for real."[21]

Willy is busy, but not invisible or detached. It is he who takes Colette sailing and teaches her the ropes. They climb the rocks and find a beach with soft, warm sand between the boulders. Colette is wearing a beret and a pair of bloomers, like Claudine's. She takes off her shoes, and then her garters and stockings, and begins running in the surf. A big wave topples her, and Willy takes a tumble, too: "I blotted myself in the soft sand to dry off, and then I recommenced my struggle with the treacherous element, which rolled me, I tell you, like a common cigarette.... And then, you know, Willy got undressed and took a dip himself, and scandalized the seaweed. We got caught by the sea, too, and if you had seen me mount the cliffs, my Schwob, it was something rather fine! I got the skin scraped from my knee and a gashed hand. I'm full of pride."[22]

The Belle-Île Willy treats his wife as a wild but adorable child, and she, for once, has him (mostly) to herself. The Belle-Île Colette is privileged to satisfy two of her deepest yearnings: to be free as a tomboy, and cherished as a Daddy's girl.

4

WILLY AND COLETTE visited her family before returning to Paris toward the end of September. She describes her activities to Schwob: she kills a snake; she catches frogs and salamanders in the river; she picks plums and makes jam ("that is, I watch it made"); she drives her brother's carriage and kills the horseflies; she reads Schwob's translation of *Moll Flanders,* admiring the scene in which Moll "goes to bed chastely with that gentleman, and is pleased but disappointed, and says, 'I can't say I was as charmed as he thought I was, because I was a good bit more corrupt than he was.' " Sido, she tells him, "bustles around, puts on her pince-nez, spills water, and fights with Willy all day long. It makes me laugh with joy."[23]

On a photograph of his wife, in braids, from Châtillon, taken about this time, Willy would write: "not yet hiding her ears or her feelings."[24] He was wrong, or perhaps deluded, because the cheerful lack of introspection and the unflagging, almost willful display of high spirits conceal her dark moods and the resentments that she is saving up for *My Apprenticeships*. But for now, Colette passes up every opportunity, and they are numerous, to commiserate with the gloominess of her friend. "As for your stupid stories from the abyss and about the flagrant futility of living, I won't even respond to them, it's so dumb! ... Ah! So Mr. Schwob is in a funk? irritating and reprehensible habit, Mr. Schwob. I used to know a train conductor who died of it."[25]

CHAPTER 9

This first-night crowd was a spectacle of general infamy. They leaned on the edges of their boxes, displaying their diamonds—the spoils of their crooked fortunes and their prostitution. All the grand marshals of vice were there, half undressed in their parade clothes and . . . flanked by a mafia of scribblers and politicians, apprentice ministers or academicians of the future. . . . In the stalls and the stage boxes sat the starlets and the part-time hookers gussied up in their vaporous gowns . . . little women of frail and tormented grace, with feverish, tiny heads weighed down by thick hair, all of them exuding an air of insolent pageboys and of obsessive and perverse charm. . . . And to cap it off, the complete nullity of the men, their complexions like boiled carp . . . their slack grins, their exhausted languor, the ugliness of their crooked eyes. What an orgy.

—JEAN LORRAIN, on the fin de siècle *tout Paris*,
from *Jean Lorrain*, by Philippe Jullian

1

*T*HAT OCTOBER, Captain Alfred Dreyfus, Willy's former fellow grunt and the only Jewish officer on the French General Staff, was accused of offering to sell French military secrets to the Germans. He was court-martialed behind closed doors, convicted by a unanimous verdict, and sentenced to life imprisonment on Devil's Island.

The Dreyfus case wouldn't be reopened for two years, and in the interim it lay dormant. Anti-Semitism, writes Eugen Weber, was as French as the croissant, and it had always been a fact of life even for prominent Jews, whether they were lapsed, like Schwob; converted, like Mme Arman or Sarah Bernhardt; converted and anti-Semitic, like Catulle Mendès and Henry Bernstein; or half Catholic, like Proust.

Hannah Arendt's view of the Jews' "route to assimilation" helps to illuminate how, in fact, all outsiders—homosexuals, provincials, foreigners, and ambitious women—carved out their niches in the salons. During their period of emergence, the Second Empire, they "followed the precepts Goethe had proposed for the education of his *Wilhelm Meister.* . . . In this book the young burgher is educated by noblemen and actors, so that he may learn how to present and represent his individuality, and thereby advance from the modest status of a burgher's son into a nobleman. For . . . those who were actually outside of high aristocratic society, everything depended upon 'personality' and the ability to express it. To know how to play the role of what one actually was, seemed the most important thing."[1]

By the fin de siècle, the ante has been upped. The mere possession of an "interesting" personality is no longer the ticket of admission to a terminally sated and bored society which has developed, as Arendt puts it, "a morbid lust for the exotic, abnormal and different, as such."[2] It is the era of cranks and séances. Alchemists have their followings. So do Krafft-Ebing and Sacher-Masoch. It is chic to have a violent or perverse death. The emperor Nero and the eighteen-year-old barbarian king Amalric are the new role models for young gays. High-born rebels like Colette's future lover Missy shoot up their morphine (the spot just above the garter on one's right thigh is the place of choice) between courses at dinner. Jean Lorrain wears kohl and serves ether with his tea cakes. Huysmans describes a black Mass in the suburbs at which "old queens are the choirboys and nymphomaniacs the parishioners."[3]

The ranks of Gomorrah swell with the wives of bankers and politicians, as well as with the cabaret singers and laundresses of Montmartre. Like everyone else, Schwob provides himself with an exotic servant and an opium pipe. Like everyone else, Judith Gauthier embraces the Orient and takes a female lover. Wild animals, especially felines, become popular pets. Rachilde prefers two sewer rats named Kyrie and Eleison. They help preside over her "Tuesdays" at the Mercure de France, perched on her shoulder, and when she is sentenced to two years in prison for *Monsieur Vénus,* Verlaine consoles her with the comment: "Ah, my dear child, if you have invented a new vice, you are the benefactor of humanity!"[4]

ON EVERY STORM-TOSSED VESSEL filled with retching bodies, there is usually one passenger, freakishly sound, who strolls the pitching deck on steady feet while insolently eating a ham sandwich. Colette was that sort of freak at the fin de siècle. She drank for pleasure, not to get drunk. She smoked an occasional cigarette, but was never addicted to tobacco and pitied people who were. She described herself as "incapable of enjoying" drugs.[5] Toward the end of her life she would tell a friend that, apart from her three husbands, she had taken only three lovers.[6] She had her own standards of sexual propriety, and when Willy, who had a penchant for threesomes, brought home a "notorious model," who made herself comfortable in Colette's bedroom and proceeded to "confide her taste in pleasure to [us] and to the birds . . . the blood of 'the daughter of Mme Colette' rebelled."[7] It surely didn't always rebel, but even when she was earning her living by dancing half nude on the music-hall stage and flaunting her liaison with the notorious Missy, Colette behaved as if her way of life were the most natural in the world.

To be natural was not, however, to be normal—on the contrary. In her fashion, Colette was as rebellious toward convention and as ambitious to be "unboring" as the most flamboyant of her contemporaries. Rather than shake off the earth clinging to her provincial roots, she began to cultivate it. She had not spent a year in the salons to no purpose, and her illness had given her the advantage of private lessons (in playing herself) with two masters, Masson and Schwob, who prized her most for her truculent, poetic, animal vitality.

That winter, Colette described her prowess as a "cabin boy" (and probably as a snake killer and frog catcher) to Mme Arman's daughter-in-law, and one evening she made a grand entrance at Mme Arman's Wednesday dinner with her hair tucked under a pompom cap and her supple, still adolescent body outfitted in the sailor suit from her anecdotes. This costume did more than reveal, thrillingly, a pair of muscular legs. It introduced her persona—an impudent little androgyne with a resemblance to the marble cupids who had also found their niches in Mme Arman's dining room.

The men in evening clothes and women with bare shoulders who paused, forks in the air, to applaud and titter at the apparition knew perfectly well that public cross-dressing was forbidden to women by law, except on the stage. The law made some exceptions: a woman who wanted or needed to wear trousers for professional reasons could petition the prefect of police for a special permit, and among those who did, successfully, were Sarah Bernhardt, Mme Dieulafoy the archeologist, and Rachilde.

Rachilde's experiments with transvestism in life and fiction were by now legendary. Her father, Colonel Éyméry, had wanted to marry her, at fifteen, to one of his fellow officers. When she refused, she was sent to a convent and given the choice of marriage or the veil. She continued to resist and was brought home, where she threw herself into a pond on the family estate. Her father fished her out, and she lived under his roof for a few more years, secretly contributing articles, signed with a man's name, to a local paper. The

Colonel, ignorant of their author's identity, read them aloud with relish at the dinner table.

But the minute she reached her majority, Rachilde escaped to Paris, her equivalent of running away to sea. She arrived in the early 1880s to pursue a literary career and wore men's suits, according to her biographer, "to escape sexual advances, cover news stories more easily, and . . . save money on dresses, which were very expensive."[8] Rachilde was also one of the first women of the era to bob her hair, which she sold to a famous fetishist, who kept it in a sculpted coffer. She shot, rode, and fenced with great skill, "and she took her travesty . . . to the point of having printed on her visiting cards: Rachilde, man of letters."[9]

The precautions that were taken to repress such behavior (and the frustrations which inspired it) are a measure of the anxiety it aroused in an era when each new improvement in women's status—the right to an education, a profession, a divorce, a bank account, authority over their minor children—was experienced by the men of France as another blow below the belt. They needed, writes Edward Berenson, "to restore their collective masculinity, and they sought to do so by stemming the tide of women's emancipation. If the French woman could become a real woman once again . . . submissive, obedient, emotional, unthreatening sexually or otherwise," then "French men would necessarily regain the virility believed to characterize the Napoleonic age."[10]

It was impossible for Colette's male contemporaries—and Freud was not the least of them—to conceive that a young woman might yearn for the freedom symbolized by a pair of trousers, a sailor suit, or a short haircut without yearning to be a man. Women themselves—Colette included—were confused and troubled by such yearnings, and that, in part, would be the subtext of the *Claudine*s. Indeed, Colette's early work is a fascinating and baroque form of transvestism. She is a woman writing as a man, Willy, who poses as a boyish girl, Claudine, who marries a "feminized" man, the aging Renaud, who pushes her into the arms of a female lover, Rézi, with whom she takes the virile role.

2

A SUCCESSFUL SELF-IMPERSONATION IS both gratifying and desolating—a hollow triumph of the false self at the expense of the true one. This, according to Arendt, was the devil's bargain made by the Jews, homosexuals, and other upstarts who played up their abnormality for the entertainment of a society that welcomed exhibitionists even while it despised them. "Such were the conditions from which arose the complicated game of exposure and concealment, of half-confessions and lying distortions, of exaggerated humility and exaggerated arrogance."[11]

Those conditions also gave root to Colette's elusiveness, and to the game of peekaboo (to give it its common and primal name) that she plays with her readers. Her earliest experiences in the salons confirmed her isolation and her need to playact—to expose and conceal herself at the same time. They aligned her, forever, with those who labor behind the footlights and are separated by a breach of class, trust, and experience from the spectators in the hall.

In such a predicament, one searches for an ally and soulmate in the form of a fellow actor, someone able to see through one's performance, admire its bravura, and discount it. Early in 1885, Colette found such a person: Catulle Mendès introduced her to his mistress, Marguerite Moreno.

Moreno, half Argentine and half French, was two years Colette's senior and a rising star at the Comédie Française. She was a dark, willowy young woman with the features of a Clouet madonna, and when Colette met her, she had a baby son—blond and luminous like his father—who was shortly to die from a peril which had obsessed Sido: meningitis. "Everything about her," wrote Colette—her wit, her pallor, her marvelous suave voice—"humbled and enchanted the displaced provincial that I still was."[12]

Moreno forgot that luncheon in Mendès's light-filled apartment. "Marcel Schwob introduced us," she recalled. He—her future husband—had brought her to the rue Jacob, where they found Colette curled up with a book on her divan: "You turned to me that face which has only been made more beautiful by all you managed to steal from life. Life was depriving you of so much in those days! . . . After three sentences we were friends."[13]

Moreno became something very rare, if not unique, in Colette's life: a peer. Their correspondence has a candor missing from nearly all of her exchanges with other friends, whom she would address in a voice that was maternal, filial, or collegial, but not confiding. Her familiar speech and her un-Parisian physicality often misled casual acquaintances to think that they and Colette were on intimate terms when she was, on the contrary, a fiercely guarded woman who was discovering that she was good at fooling the world: "People who've only met me three times are taken in," she says of Claudine:

When they see me with windswept hair, my skirt brushing the ground, my solid stance and my steady gaze, they say to themselves: "There's a nice little woman for me! Buoyant, lively, and so easy to live with!" . . . You try, then! If I were a man and knew myself profoundly, I wouldn't like myself very much: unsociable, revving with enthusiasm, or hostile at first sight, a nose that claims to be infallible and makes no concessions, faddish, pseudobohemian, very "good-girlish," at heart jealous, sincere out of laziness, and untruthful out of modesty. . . . I say that today, and then tomorrow, I'll find myself charming.[14]

In an age when there were ten writers at every dinner party, and each one rushed home to confide the clever or outrageous behavior of his fellow guests to a journal, everyone was, to some degree, a performer, courting posterity by cutting a figure worth recording. Colette's fictional version of her encounter with the young Proust at Mme Arman's gives us a glimpse of the way she was beginning to project an exaggerated stage version of herself in public.

> One Wednesday [she writes], at the house of old Ma Barmann [Mme Arman], I was cruised, politely, by a young pretty-boy of letters.[15] (Beautiful eyes, that kid, a touch of conjunctivitis, but never mind . . .). He compared me . . . to Myrtocleia, to a young Hermes, to a Cupid by Proud'hon; he ransacked his memory and secret museums for me, quoting so many hermaphrodite masterpieces that . . . he almost spoiled my enjoyment of a divine cassoulet, the specialty of the house. . . .
>
> My little flatterer, excited by his own evocations, didn't let go of me. . . . Nestled in a Louis XV basket chair, I heard him, without really listening, parade his literary knowledge. . . . He contemplated me with his long-lashed, caressing eyes and murmured, for the two of us:
>
> "Ah, yours is the daydream of the child Narcissus; it's his soul, filled with sensuality and bitterness . . ."
>
> "Monsieur," I tell him firmly, "you're delirious. My soul is filled with nothing but red beans and bacon rinds."[16]

"If we are to trust Proust's judgment," writes Arendt, "[the outcasts and pariahs] were the only ones in fin de siècle society who were still capable of passion."[17] And the encounter Colette describes so frivolously was more significant than she knew. The "young pretty-boy of letters" who wasn't yet "Proust" had recognized the true face and impure true feelings of the young misfit who wasn't yet "Colette" and understood the narcissism forced upon her by her imposture.

PROUST FREQUENTED Mme Arman's in part because he was enamored of her son, Gaston, and of Gaston's wife, Jeanne—two of his several models for Saint Loup and Gilberte. Colette had also begun to cultivate a friendship with the young Caillavets. He was still an amateur playwright, darkly handsome and "not very gay. But he laughed with his eyes."[18] His wife, who starred in his drawing room comedies, was a stagestruck beauty exactly Colette's age whom Willy would nickname "the cabbage rose." They had a

year-old daughter, Simone. Colette told Jeanne that if she could be guar-
anteed such a fetching baby, she wouldn't hesitate to "ask Willy to make
her [one]."[19]

According to Jeanne's granddaughter and biographer, Michelle Maurois,
the two couples were together a great deal that winter and the next. Colette
"always addressed Jeanne as 'the resplendent one' or 'the magnificent,' " and
the tone of their banter "is proof of a gay and joking intimacy." It was proof
of an attraction: intimacy is another matter. The Willys applauded Gaston's
plays; the two husbands flirted with each other's wives, the wives flirted with
each other—or at least Colette did: she signed her letters to Jeanne "with
an amorous embrace." When the Caillavets went to London for a week that
September with another couple, Colette teased them: "Nocturnal London
brawlers, are you going to bring home another daughter from this little trip as
a foursome? It's very bad, I know about it, when one is part of a young foursome, you excite one another mutually."[20]

There's a good deal of poignancy to this assertion of complicity with the
Caillavets and their friends, because for all her youth, Colette wasn't part of a
young couple, and the emotion they excited in her was envy. It wasn't envy for
a baby or a conventional marriage so much as for a wholesome erotic life with
a husband whose appetite didn't need all kinds of heavy spice to pique it. She
envied Jeanne, just as she envied the little tarts at the d'Harcourt their "virile"
bohemian lovers with full heads of hair, and it was the same privation she
would feel one night some years later when Polaire summoned the Willys to
her apartment to intervene in a quarrel she had been having with Pierre
Louÿs. He had been beating her; she was hysterical and indignant. But the
quarrel ended, before their eyes, with the beast gathering his willing victim in
his arms and carrying her back to their disheveled bed. Colette was left, she
says, with the haunting image of "a spectacle unknown to me, love in its youth
and brutality, an offended lover, his naked torso, the play of his perfect muscles beneath his soft, feminine skin, the bulges and hollows of his proud and
indifferent body, the confident manner in which he had knelt, then lifted
Polaire from the floor."[21]

In the aftermath of the Kinceler affair, Colette might have resolved, like so
many other deceived wives of the era, to pay Willy back in kind by taking one
of his protégés as a lover. She says she didn't, although she joked with Schwob
about his escorting her to Mme Arman's: "Willy only asks that you descend
from the carriage a few yards before her door, so that people won't say that
we're 'flaunting our liaison' too much. Okay? . . . We'll have fun there."[22]

In *My Apprenticeships* she takes great pains to explain her fidelity, blaming
it on Willy's "extreme skill" in discouraging "male or female friends of my
own age"; his tyranny, which she found seductive; her own "native savagery,

common to Sido's children"; a village childhood "which inhibits the formation of intimate bonds"; her "tomboyish nature."[23] But these excuses are
intended to distract us from a truth which, by the time she wrote her memoirs,
Colette chose to forget: she was still and would be for years, in spite of her privations and Willy's cruelties, obsessively in love with the abductor "who possessed me . . . before I was a woman."[24]

3

THE THEATER of the salons can't be understood without reference to the
importance of theater in general at the fin de siècle. The early 1890s were
the heyday of the great art houses, directed by men like Antoine, Paul Fort,
and Lugné-Poe, which introduced French audiences to the avant-garde
plays of Ibsen and Strindberg, as well as to the work of "the more daring
of French authors, from Courteline and Brieux to Alfred Jarry."[25] It is worth
noting that Lugné-Poe would collaborate with Willy on the stage version of
the *Claudines*; that Oscar Wilde's *Salomé*—the great theatrical sensation of
1893—had been written in French with the help of Marcel Schwob and Pierre
Louÿs; that it was Schwob who gave Jarry's *Ubu Roi* its first reading, and that
Colette and Willy were in the audience at its tumultuous and now legendary
first night—he calling the riotous crowd to order so that the show could continue, and she "roaring" so loudly "with joy" that her laughter could be heard
above the unholy din.[26]

"If you really want to be known in literature, you have to be on the stage,"
wrote Edmond de Goncourt in 1892, "because the theater is all the literature a
lot of people know."[27] By theater he meant popular theater—the theater of
the boulevards. Half a million Parisians (out of three million) went to a play
once a week, and twice that number, writes Eugen Weber, went once a month:
"The stage . . . provided the primordial subject of conversation in society."[28]

No one would understand the commercial relationship between theater
and literature better than Willy, and if you look at his career more dispassion-
ately than Colette could, he appears less a failed writer with a "neurotic"
(her word) fear of the blank page than a remarkably successful impresario of
the entertainment business. He was part agent, part mogul, part hustler. He
developed and commissioned properties, dramatized his novels, novelized
his dramas, managed a large creative stable, and took credit for its collective
productions. He aimed his publicity as much at a consumer of entertainment
as at a reader and, having secured that consumer's brand loyalty, supplied him
with a product consistent in its ingredients, if not its quality.

Colette surmises that her husband wrote letters, which he did manically, to
avoid writing books. But in fact he used the mails the way a contemporary

producer uses the phones and the fax machine: to make his deals; to pitch his projects; and most important, to "buff" his contacts. He courted and manipulated his celebrity in a modern fashion. "The ironical Willy," wrote Henry de Madaillon, "was surely the first to understand the importance—solely financial—of the obstinate repetition of a name or a title . . . of the shameless reproduction and dissemination of the most scabrous photographs by every means available to the press. He knew, was the first, to guess and exploit the public taste for suggestive indiscretions on the life of 'stars,' for spicy ancedotes, for 'love' stories with an intimate smell. He only made use of all that as an ironic virtuoso who had all of human Folly at his disposition."[29]

COLETTE CAME of age among performers, amateur and professional, her husband prime among them. Almost every man or woman she commemorates in *My Apprenticeships* was associated with the theater in some way. Otéro was a music-hall star. Polaire started in the music hall, then went on to become the leading comedienne of the boulevards. Moreno was the greatest classical actress of her generation, and according to some critics, of the century. Courteline made his mark as a satirist, first with Antoine and his art theater, later with the Comédie-Française. Schwob was essential to both Wilde and Jarry, and *Ubu Roi* was dedicated to him. Catulle Mendès was one of the most influential drama critics of the period. Jean Lorrain wrote for the theater, and chronicled its vices and pretensions. Even poor, doomed Lotte Kinceler had her moment of glory on the stage, when Polaire played her in Brieux's *Les Hannetons*. Colette spent more of her early life in a stage box or an orchestra seat than she did in her study. She would later adapt a striking number of her novels for performance, and much of her fiction is structured theatrically or cinematically. She learned the art of self-dramatization from the masters. By the time she embarked on her own professional career in the theater—acting in it and writing for and about it—it was her lifeblood.

4

IN 1895, Willy's career took a new direction: fiction. The first of his more than fifty novels was called *Une Passade,* and like the rest of them, it was just dirty enough—and the dirt was just arty enough—to be objectionable to the kind of bores and prudes whose outrage was in itself a mark of distinction, and a boost to sales.

Une Passade was also, typically, a collaborative effort with another writer, in this case, Pierre Veber, one of the witnesses to Colette's marriage. Veber wrote the text and Willy "corrected" it, which is to say, he supplied certain elements of the plot and added his trademark puns. Three years later, he renounced his rights to the book; a second edition was signed by Veber (his name came first) and Willy; a third by Willy (first), then Veber.

By then, however, the two men had had a violent quarrel, which Colette reports in *My Apprenticeships*. Veber had called at the rue Jacob to collect royalties that he was due, and Willy had refused to pay. Veber then shouted from the bottom of the landing: "There are judges, sir, for people who kick their creditors into the hallway instead of paying their debts!" To which Willy replied, "My creditors, sir, are men I honor and respect. . . . But I refuse that title to a little scumbag who comes to badger me twice a week on the pretext that I owe him thirty-two francs, and in reality to pinch the ass of my maid!"[30]

The tone of the disputed property is not much higher than that of the dispute. *Une Passade* is a roman à clef in which Willy's alter ego, Henry Maugis, falls under the spell of a man-eating literary groupie named Monna Dupont de Nyeweldt. She is a nymphomaniac who doesn't wear a corset and whose taste for low life is nearly as insatiable as her appetite for sex. Among her victims is a decadent novelist modeled on Rémy de Gourmont and an anarchist modeled on Félix Fénéon. In the course of his five days as her sex slave, Maugis becomes impotent—as a writer. He manages to escape to his friend Jim Smiley, who gives him the courage to break with his dominatrix. It is hardly surprising that the real Monna (Mina Schrader de Nysolt) "wanted to strangle Veber and wrote Willy thirty-page letters" before, as Caradec tells us, she attempted to murder a politician, "which got her locked up."[31]

The extremely popular subject of the female vampire who preys on the male artist was one that Willy would tackle in the two novels that precede the *Claudines*: *Maîtresse d'esthètes* (1897) and *Un Vilain Monsieur!* (1898), both ghostwritten by Jean de Tinan. By then, Wilde's *Salomé* (banned in London) had been produced in Paris. Colette and Willy were almost certainly at the première.[32]

Willy's novels and Wilde's play treat, as Pichois puts it, "an old bugaboo shared by Vigny, Balzac, and Baudelaire, an old bugaboo which was no less current for Willy and for . . . the Decadents, whom he despised."[33] Huysmans describes the contemporary femme fatale as "the symbolic incarnation of undying Lust, the goddess of immortal Hysteria, the accursed Beauty exalted above all other beauties by the catalepsy that hardens her flesh and steels her muscles, the monstrous Beast, indifferent, irresponsible, insensible, poisoning, like the Helen of ancient myth, everything that approaches her, everything that sees her, everything that she touches."[34]

But the voracious, castrating woman in Willy's fiction is always too cartoonish to be frightening. Much more convincing is the sense of brotherhood among the men who share her body, and with it, the secret fear that their potency—and perhaps even their heterosexuality—is in peril. "Fin de siècle Clubland," writes Elaine Showalter (and the world of Willy's novels is nothing if not a literary men's club), "existed on the fragile borderline that separated male bonding from homosexuality and that distinguished manly misogyny from disgusting homoeroticism."[35]

IN MAY OF 1895, Marcel Proust had not yet begun to explore the clandestine common ground between Sodom and Clubland when he wrote what seems to have been a fan letter to Willy, probably in response to the collection of his reviews which had, with *Une Passade,* been published that year. Willy was too busy to reply. He delegated that duty to Colette: ". . . You are the only one (although I think Fénéon made the same observation) who has so clearly seen that for [Willy] the word is not a representation, but a living thing, and much less a mnemonic signifier than a pictorial translation. I'm rambling a little, but I know very well what I mean to say, and I feel that you will understand me marvelously well, because you know, your letter proves it, that my Willy is an original (even though he goes to pious lengths to hide it)."[36]

By now, however, Colette was writing something more substantial than touchingly pretentious thank-you notes for her husband. Earlier that year she had signed her name—Colette Gauthier-Villars—to six brief articles of music criticism that appeared in Maurice Barrès's short-lived review, *La Cocarde.* Pichois speculates that Willy had supplied the technical and historical references, as he probably had for her letter to Proust, but that she was responsible for both the prose and the opinions. Twenty years later, Barrès's friend and collaborator, Charles Maurras, would dedicate a book of essays to Colette "in memory of *La Cocarde,*" and he gives us a glimpse of the literary debutante "wearing a Basque beret over her ear, her braid flapping at her heels," and listening to him hold forth while "pretending to correct her husband's galleys (and her own!)."[37]

Colette had also by now given Willy the proof that her ear for prose was as natural as her ear for music and that, when she tried, she could be an extremely compelling and amusing raconteur. "I believe what Willy told me," writes Sylvain Bonmariage, "and which was subsequently confirmed by Alfred Vallette and Rachilde. The young Colette had an exceptionally lively imagination. At the time of her marriage she lacked both the vocation and the knowledge to create a publishable manuscript. On the other hand, she had a biting sense of humor, the gift of repartee, which was all verve and off-color wit. She was listened to, and she liked to be listened to. She had related to Willy, and apparently to others, among them Vallette, some of the episodes that Willy invited her to set down on paper."[38]

In 1907, Colette told a journalist that it was she, not Willy, who had suggested that she write a book. Her husband, she continued, had laughed "at my pretention," so she had set to work on her own "without saying anything."[39] This assertion was published at a moment when the couple were quarreling bitterly over their communal property, including the *Claudine*s, and Colette never repeats it, perhaps because it contradicts her vehement disavowal of any literary calling. Yet it would be strange if she *hadn't* thought of writing a book. It's the common dream of the writer's consort—the unpaid typist, sounding board, muse, and galleys slave. Dominique Aury wrote *Story of O* to dazzle Jean Paulhan, and Mary Shelley created *Frankenstein* on a dare. The same dare—erotic and literary—would have appealed to Colette, who was aroused, motivated, focused, indeed inspired, by rivalry all her life.

Her chronology for the composition of her first novel is as unreliable as her versions of its genesis. But the meticulous Colette scholar Paul D'Hollander makes a convincing case that it was during the winter of 1895–96 that she began to "jot down" her memories of the village school at Saint-Sauveur—and Claudine was conceived.

CHAPTER 10

l

OLETTE HADN'T SEEN her native village for six years, and in May
of 1896, Willy took her back to do some reconnaissance. Olympe Terrain wasn't there to receive them, but her teaching assistants gave the
couple lunch, and "they had some good laughs."[1] Willy wrote to thank the
headmistress for her hospitality in absentia, and she responded with an invitation to the graduation ceremonies, which were to be held in July.[2] Colette
accepted in a bantering note addressed to "Mmmzaîle," signing herself "your
ex-scourge."[3]

On their second visit, the homegirl and her famous Parisian husband
caused a stir both in the village and in the school. Mlle Terrain told Jean
Larnac that "Colette insisted I put her up, saying that she would be, among
us, a role model of all one shouldn't do."[4] They dined with the students,
and afterwards Colette and Willy played duets on the piano. She described
their sleeping arrangements in an unpublished letter to Marguerite Moreno.
Because the beds were so narrow, Willy slept alone, in one of the master's
bedrooms, while she bunked with the girls. "In the morning, eruption of
Willy in the dormitory. . . . Paternity!" He crowned a twelve-year-old with a
laurel wreath, telling her solemnly, "Work is freedom, work is the future"—a
joke that Colette would have good cause to remember.[5]

If Mlle Terrain saw anything improper in the behavior of Colette and
Willy, it did not deter her from inviting them back for the prize ceremonies in
1897. "In a few days I'm returning to Saint-Sauveur (for 48 hours)," wrote
Willy to one of his ghosts, "to stay in an adorable girls' boarding school.
I paw [them] while waiting for (sexual) parties, I kiss the assistant teachers,

too. . . . I find it madly amusing, and my exquisite, depraved, loving kid finds it even more amusing."6

At the last minute, however, they didn't go. Colette begged off with the excuse that her stepson had chicken pox. "Write to console me," she entreats Mmmzaîle.7 But Willy gave Olympe Terrain a franker explanation. They were not coming, he writes, because "people have been stupid enough to tell Colette that our comportment scandalized Saint-Sauveur. The kid has been aggrieved to hear it. As for me, I dare say that I don't give a good g-d, having, for a long time, become inured to the opinions of my contemporaries. But, I repeat, my Colette has a heavy heart. That's why your girl is silent."8

2

COLETTE AND WILLY SPENT the rest of that summer traveling. They went first to Champagnolle, in the Jura mountains, staying at a modest inn with peeling wallpaper, narrow iron beds, and a pair of curtains fit "for wrapping up fetuses."9 Colette reported to Schwob that her cat was no longer a virgin *("elle connaît la vie");* that she was getting Willy up and out to explore the country at four in the morning ("the cold pinches" but "the colors are very beautiful at that hour"); and that if he didn't write to her, she would, on her return, roll up a copy of the *Revue franco-américaine* and stuff it down his throat.10

From here they repaired to Willy's parents' house, an experience of which Colette observes: "Before my marriage I had never stayed 'with anybody,' as I used to say, and I was slow to break through the constraint which restrained me, not from liking those who welcomed me, but from surrendering to the simple pleasure of showing myself as I really was."11 The syntax is tortured in the French, too, perhaps because Colette really wanted to stuff rolled-up newspapers down the throats of her in-laws, or—as she threatened Schwob—to wrap them in flypaper: "a very amusing [invention]. You see them land and struggle until they're immobilized. They must suffer frightfully."12

Instead she played the demure young wife. When she could, she escaped from the drawing room to the fields. When she couldn't, she nodded off over her embroidery in an armchair. She listened to Mme Gauthier-Villars's parish lore and Lenten recipes, and to her sister-in-law's pieties on the subject of childrearing: "When my daughters are older, I'll teach them to starch men's shirts."13 She was an attentive and charming aunt, teaching Willy's nieces and nephews to make flutes and daisy chains, and to start fires with a piece of glass. "I never confessed to them how well-behaved and easy I found them . . . how astonished I was to perceive the profound difference between their childhood and my own. They had been broken to a superficial obedience, which I admired as much as I did their neat curls, their clean nails, their scent of English soap, the way that they raised their little pinkies eating a boiled egg. . . . They were sweet to me," she concludes, "and perhaps I was, without knowing it, missing a child who would have come from me."[14]

But this conclusion is as sentimental as it is dubious. She is much more convincing about her maternal instincts in *Retreat from Love:* "A child? Me?" exclaims Claudine. "What end do you pick it up by? If I delivered something, it would surely be a beast-baby, furry, with tiger stripes; with soft paws and claws already hardened; ears well-set and horizontal eyes, like its mother."[15]

COLETTE KEPT in touch with Mlle Terrain until her manuscript was done, and her letters, said the schoolmistress, "were very filial."[16] That September, the couple made what would become an annual pilgrimage to Bayreuth, where they were entertained by Wagner's widow and son. Willy, wrote Colette, was gorging on so much opera that it had "unhinged him. . . . Hide your eyes! Willy, the odious tyrant, the gentle master, the fat cat, wept like the offspring of a heifer from the Twilight of the Gods. As for me, I'm more solid; I made fun of him while rubbing my eyes but only because I had a dust mote in them. Exactly!"[17]

Finally, a series of scribbled notes inform Mlle Terrain that Colette and Willy are "back to the bustle of Paris"; that she is suffering from migraines; that she has been entertaining an old schoolmate, Marie Duban. "Last night I took her to the opera, and for the entire four acts of *Aïda* she cowered in my shadow. . . . What was I supposed to do? Fill the hall with her acquaintances?"[18]

With the exception of this glimpse of Colette playing the exasperated woman of the world to her provincial friend, there are very few documents to account for her activities that autumn and winter in Paris, probably because she was writing. She had found a stationer's with a supply of school note-books. They were small, nearly square penmanship exercise books with covers of black canvas. The cheap, lined paper had a watermark which "brought me back six years." She worked at one end of a cluttered desk with the light behind her, hunched at an angle, with twisted knees, and wrote, she claims, "with application and indifference."[19]

She may have written with detachment and without ambition; with the "passivity [one feels] in accomplishing a commission"; with that sense of free-dom and impunity conferred by anonymity. She may have written with a debutante's uncertainty about her powers and the anguished skepticism that nearly every writer feels toward the first draft of a first book. But indifference? "I have discovered an astonishing young girl," Colette told Olympe Terrain in October of 1896. "Do you know who she is? She's exactly me before my marriage."[20]

3

WILLY'S WORKSHOPS WERE expanding. One of his new recruits was a student named Edmond Maurice Sailland, who rebaptized himself Curnonsky, and who was to become more famous for his gastronomy than for his prose. In 1896, he abandoned the university to devote himself to literature full-time, and he would remember that some of the articles he wrote for Willy paid extremely well—"a hundred gold francs."[21]

"You were a nice boy of twenty-one with a sweet face," Colette would remind him when they were both eighty, "and I was a cold, unobliging little girl whose provincial origins could be read in her features, her silence, her long braids, and those dresses worthy of their village. But it's not nothing to have been twenty at the same time and it took me only a few days to call you *tu*, while you always addressed me, tenderly, as *Madame*."[22]

Curnonsky, in turn, brought his friend Paul-Jean Toulet into the fold. A dandy and a cynic who would make his own mark in literature as a "fantasist," he was Willy's landscape specialist. Toulet's drinking and whoring companion, the handsome and gifted Jean de Tinan, signed on for *Maîtresse d'esthètes* and *Un Vilain Monsieur!* He lived near the Luxembourg Gardens in an apartment furnished, ahead of its time, "in the most precious Art Deco style," where he received such friends as Jean Lorrain, Rachilde, Pierre Louÿs, Henri de Régnier, Jarry, and, of course, Colette.[23]

Michèle Sarde puts it nicely when she observes that "a novel by Willy was turned out like a Renault."[24] He would begin with what in Hollywood is now called a "concept." This was pitched in a letter of several pages to the appropriate "nigger" (*nègre*—"nigger"—is the French word for ghostwriter, still in use):

> "Old Cur, what do you think of this? The hereunto-attached sweet little notion has thrust itself upon me. Cast your connoisseur's eye on this larva, and in fifty pages either sketch its future or crush it stillborn under your proud heel. . . ." On its return, the Idea was purged of its new form and the traces of a stranger's handwriting; it reappeared as a typescript, changed envelopes—and addressees: "Petipol, help! Here's my latest hatchling. Can you, in a month's time, make a light volume of it, setting: little north coast beach, wet bathing suits, casino . . . leggy girl, etc." The mysterious Petipol having distilled the aforesaid "elements," the manuscript . . . was

launched . . . to a third therapist: . . . "You wanted to know about my next book? Here it is. Doesn't it make you want to bang your head against a wall? Only your adroit good graces, that lightness of touch, that felicity of expression . . . are capable of transfusing into this 'poor man's child' a rich and joyous blood which" etc. etc. "It goes without saying that I'll know how to repay . . ."[25]

Willy's methods were well-known, and while his slaves were sworn to discretion, they were, on the whole, philosophical about their anonymous labors. "Like everyone else," wrote Ernest Lajeunesse, "I made my literary debut by calling myself Willy." "If I had published a novel under my own name," wrote Curnonsky, "it would have sold three thousand copies. With Willy's signature, we sold two hundred and fifteen thousand copies of *Maugis en ménage*. And Willy was very fair: half of the royalties for him, half for the nigger."[26]

On this point, there has been quite a bit of disagreement, notably from Colette, whose legal and financial battles with her husband we shall consider later. But as D'Hollander concludes: "We may venture with confidence to believe that Willy's generosity was a function of his resources—which were eminently unstable."[27]

4

COLETTE WAS JUST, or perhaps not quite, twenty-four when she finished the manuscript of her first novel and submitted it to her husband. According to Curnonsky, it ran to some six hundred closely written pages. According to Colette, Willy gave the work a cursory reading and declared to her: "I was wrong. There's nothing here." He then stuffed the notebooks into a drawer.

Paul Masson committed suicide that October. He dosed himself with ether and then fell or jumped into the Ill River. He did not have time to publish a survey he had been conducting: "What are the phrases, interjections, or onomatopoeic sounds," he asked a range of correspondents from the literary world, "which most habitually escape your lips at the moment of ecstasy?"[28]

Marcel Schwob was convalescing after an operation. Colette wrote to him from Châtillon, called him "my dearest enemy," asked if he had cried out under the knife, or if they had put him under. She was reading his *Imaginary Lives*, and she told him in the tone of one professional to another that "the irritating perfection of some of them gives me a pain in my hair and a tingling in my ankles."[29]

But by the end of the year, she herself was in an extremely fragile state of mind and health. Willy tells Lotte Kinceler on December 2 that "Colette has been suffering an extremely violent hysterical fit: she is obliged to rest in a closed room, without light—and she's suffering a great deal. As soon as she can, I'll ask you to come. All my kisses, my Lolo, Kiki."[30]

This time, Lotte had nothing to do with Colette's crisis. For the better part of the year, Mme Arman had refused to receive her. The preceding February, Jeanne de Caillavet noted in her diary that "Mother has had a long, a too long visit from the little Willy [Colette]. The unhappy woman is holding on to us. It's too late. We've heard some vile things about them. They're false, they're treacherous. It's better never to see them again. . . . Mother wanted a frank explanation from Willy; that can only lead to disagreeable complications and new lies. We have to make a break gently and politely. How much Willy must hate me now! He'll have to take revenge by dragging me in the mud. Damn!"[31]

In another journal passage, Jeanne explains the break. Colette and Willy, she says, "tried to profit from what they thought was an opportune moment to instigate a quarrel between me and Mother, or at least to cause an unpleasant scene between us. . . . Mother claims that Willy was in love with me. It's a strange way of paying court."

Their exclusion from the avenue Hoche was "devastating" for the couple: professionally for Willy and personally for Colette, who lost her society godmother. She made a last, brave attempt to salvage the friendship, going alone to ask Mme Arman the reason "for her cooling off." The lady replied that she had proof Willy was the author of "a cruel story" about her which had appeared, anonymously, in two journals. Colette denied the allegations. Mme Arman then confronted her with the gossip about Willy and Jeanne. "It would be disagreeable," she concluded, "for her daughter-in-law to have to meet them" in her salon.[32]

A fortnight later, Jeanne notes that her husband has received "a fantastic letter from the said Willy." He tells Gaston de Caillavet that Colette "has been badly shaken" by his mother's "scene"; that she has been "very ill, 'in mortal danger,'" in the throes of an hysterical fit which has left her nearly blind; she can't move without a thick black blindfold." He closes by asking Gaston what he thinks of all this.[33]

Gaston didn't answer, but he did discuss the case with Marcel Proust. "As [Colette and Willy] had always been very kind to me," Proust told his friend Louis de Robert, "and I felt that they had been mistreated, I paid them my first and only call (which I in no way concealed from Mme Arman, who always bore me a mortal grudge on that account), and I offered them my services in finding an oculist. *I believe*, however, that Willy thought this gesture was not spontaneous, but in any case the fact that they had, at that moment, been dismissed, which did not diminish them at all in my esteem, was not, I believe, pleasant for them to recall."[34]

In time, Colette and Willy took their revenge on everyone who had played a role in their humiliation: on Mme Arman, on Anatole France, on Jeanne, even on Proust, who are caricatured in the *Claudines*, respectively, as "old Ma Barmann," the vulgar and bitchy Jewess with the hooked nose; Gréveuille, the windbag; Rose-Chou, the flighty society belle; and that unnamed, loquacious, "pretty-boy of letters" who presumes to analyze Claudine's soul.

Were Colette's eye problems "hysterical," as Willy suggests? Had the "pain" caused by Mme Arman's rejection really "almost caused her to lose her sight," as he told Proust?[35] Or were these symptoms of the gonorrhea he may have given her? It is impossible to say. She recovered, and as far as I know, her blindness never recurred. But one might also observe that there are certain blind spots in her work, in her heart, in her vision of others, and these may invariably be traced to a traumatic experience of rejection and jealousy. A few years later, Jacques-Émile Blanche was painting her portrait when she heard the wheels of a carriage outside his studio window, and caught a glimpse of Willy bidding a tender farewell to the lady who had delivered him. "She had real convulsions," he wrote, "hysterical crying fits, one had to lay her on a sofa and bathe her temples with cologne because she believed herself abandoned forever."[36] And thirty years later, she would write: "I have had occasion to descend to the very depths of jealousy . . . in my writings of bygone days I believe I compared it, as everyone does, to a sojourn in hell. . . . Jealousy is not at all low, but it catches us humbled and bowed down, at first sight. For it is the only suffering that we endure without ever becoming used to it."[37]

CHAPTER 11

1

IN JULY OF 1896, Colonel Picquart, the new head of intelligence for the army's General Staff, told his commanding officer that he had compelling evidence to show that Captain Dreyfus had been framed by a fellow officer, Major Esterhazy.[1] A year later, no action had been taken on his confidential report except that he had been transferred to a frontline post in Tunisia, where his first act was to write his will and his second to go public with what he knew about the conspiracy against Dreyfus. Picquart's bravery had two consequences: he was cashiered ignobly, and Clemenceau, in defiance of the fear or hostility of politicians from all parties, called for a new investigation of the whole case.

Esterhazy asked for a trial and was acquitted. Two days later, on January 13, 1898, Clemenceau's newspaper, *L'Aurore*, published a special edition of three hundred thousand copies which ran Émile Zola's open letter to the president of the Republic, famously entitled *"J'accuse."* Zola was immediately put on trial himself—for libeling the army—was convicted, barely escaped with his life from an angry mob of anti-Dreyfusards waiting outside the courtroom, and went into exile in London.

In the meantime, Esterhazy was enjoying his celebrity as a "victim of the Jews," and huge posters with his image decorated the boulevards. Like all the central figures in the Affair, he was, as Arendt observes, a creature out of Balzac: an aristocratic rake, gambler, daredevil, blackmailer, and thief. Shortly after Zola's trial, Esterhazy was charged with embezzling the bank account of a relative and fled—also to London—where he confessed to the

British press that he had, indeed, framed Dreyfus—on orders from his superiors in the intelligence division. One of the officers he accused, Major Henry, confessed to forgery, then committed suicide.

Early in 1898, there were almost no politicians[2]—even on the left—not that many Jews,[3] and very few intellectuals active in the camp of Dreyfus, Clemenceau, Picquart, and Zola. Anatole France was among the first, and when Dreyfus was stripped of his Legion of Honor, France renounced his own. Charles Péguy, who would later found the *Cahiers de la Quinzaine*, rallied to the cause a little later. So did the Natanson brothers, Alfred, Thadée, and Alexandre, who published the prestigious *Revue blanche*. Willy, writing as Henry Gauthier-Villars, was at the time their chief music critic, and Thadée's wife, Misia—a society hostess, pianist, and patron of music—was a friend of Colette's. This friendship would acquire an ironic symmetry. During the Occupation, Misia's third husband, José-María Sert, used his influence with the Nazis to help get Colette's third husband, Maurice Goudeket—a Jew—released from the detention camp at Compiègne.

The Affair now began to enforce a drastic triage of alliances, even within families. Sarah Bernhardt, an ardent Dreyfusard, stopped speaking to her son, a confirmed Anti. Proust's Prince and Princess de Guermantes discover that they have both secretly been buying Masses for Dreyfus, while their cousins the duke and duchess revile him. Marcel's Jewish mother supported the Captain, her Catholic husband opposed him, as did M. Arman de Caillavet, whose wife's salon nevertheless became a Dreyfusard stronghold. Gaston was a Dreyfusard like his mother, while Jeanne and her parents were anti-Semites. She kept her true feelings from her husband but, summering at Puteaux, she confides to her diary that "the Jews are looked upon askance here, and they scarcely dare to promenade their insolence or their vapidity in these pretty avenues."[4]

The feminists, led by Marguerite Durand of *La Fronde*, supported Dreyfus,[5] as did most of the literary avant-garde, including Gide, Mallarmé, Saint-Pol Roux, and Apollinaire—although Valéry gave twenty francs to the fund established for Major Henry's widow ("not without reflection"). Most of the Impressionists were Dreyfusards, although not Renoir and Cézanne. The Affair reconciled Monet and Zola, who had quarreled over a review, but Degas fired one of his models who was a Protestant, because "all Protestants," he claimed, "are for Dreyfus."[6] Bicycle enthusiasts were divided, and there were two rival cycling journals, one pro, one contra.

Colette's future friend the couturier Paul Poiret broke with his father, a draper and anti-Dreyfusard, and it is worth noting that most of the shopkeepers and artisans of Paris sided on this and most issues with the right. Among her other friends, Jean Lorrain and Pierre Louÿs, like most of the

Decadents, were Antis, and so—vehemently—were Gyp (the countess Martel de Janville), the author of several best-selling anti-Semitic novels, and Rachilde. Jules Lemaître, Lotte Kinceler's old admirer, helped to baptize the reactionary League of Patriots, which was quickly joined by Colette's former mentor at *La Cocarde*, Barrès. The Affair buried, for Barrès, the last vestiges of that romantic socialism for which *La Cocarde* was the vehicle. He adopted the battle cry of "France for the French," and converted to the violently anti-Semitic, anti-German, and anti-republican nationalism of his friends, the future leaders of L'Action Française Léon Daudet and Charles Maurras.

There wasn't a salon in Paris not riven by the Affair. "While the countess de Greffulhe was a republican," writes Michelle Maurois, "and from the outset had defended Dreyfus, Mme Aubernon took the other side. However, when she was asked, 'What are you doing with your Jews?' she replied: 'I'm keeping them,' and Mme Normand said, 'I'm dropping my little Jews and keeping the big ones.' "[7]

On the other side, the Natansons did not break off relations with every one of their anti-Dreyfusard friends and authors, but did draw the line at receiving any further contributions from Henry Gauthier-Villars. Willy's embrace of the anti-Dreyfus party and its rhetoric[8] was particularly enthusiastic. From the outset of the Affair, he had larded his articles and novels with contemptuous remarks about the Jews. One of these had provoked a duel with the poet Ferdinand Hérold, who invited one of Dreyfus's defense attorneys to be his second. When Édouard Drumont, a proto-fascist and future leader of the Antisemitic League, began collecting money for Mme Henry, Willy made a donation.

It was hardly a surprise, therefore, that when the *Revue blanche* asked the leading intellectuals of Paris to sign a petition supporting Dreyfus, Henry Gauthier-Villars declined to add his name. What was memorable was the joke that Pierre Veber made of it: "It's the first time Willy has refused to sign something he didn't write."[9]

IT WOULD BE interesting to know how the Colette family felt about the Affair. The Captain should, in principle, have been a Dreyfusard, at least after '98, as the crisis developed into a clash between the republicans and anticlericals on one side, the Catholic hierarchy and the conservatives on the other. Sido was casually anti-Semitic, although no more so than most of her neighbors. She considered politics only slightly more frivolous than love—but she came from a staunchly liberal family. Achille had just married a nobleman's daughter, and if he were a Dreyfusard, he would have been, among students and alumni of the Faculty of Medicine, an exception.

As for Colette, her anti-Semitism was never rabid, but it was, as her close friend Renée Hamon would observe, "native."[10] "I was hoping to find you [at a play]," she writes to Rachilde around 1900. "But instead of [your] short, impatient nose, all I could see were the appendages of the Natansons. I couldn't confuse you."[11] Otherwise she says nothing that reveals her sympathy for one side or the other. But the course of the Affair coincides almost exactly—1894–1906—with the years of her extended adolescence and servility to Willy as a woman and a writer. She was still, and for years to come would remain, his creature, and she probably demurred to the biases of his politics as she did to the kinks of his libido.

Many years later, Colette would confess her shame for the caricature she gives of Mme Arman in *Claudine in Paris*. But her shame was toward an individual who had been kind to her, and whom she had wronged, and she never acknowledged either having, or having betrayed, a civilized principle: of resistance to baseness. One can't overlook Colette's complacence, not simply toward politics, but toward the more fundamental forms of ethical maturity, because time wouldn't change it.

2

WILLY'S CAREER FLOURISHED in the last years of the century, and early in 1897, the couple moved from the rue Jacob to a more luxurious Right Bank apartment, on the sixth floor of 93, rue de Courcelles, where they were up the street from Proust, still living with his mother at number 45. It was one of those fashionable artist's studios which were, at the turn of the century, built on the top floors of the new bourgeois apartment buildings, mostly around Montparnasse. Even then, such lodgings were too expensive for most working artists, but attractive to expatriate Americans, gentlemen painters, and divorcées of a bohemian temperament.

In addition to gas, running water, and an elevator upholstered in red velvet, the Willys' new digs enjoyed a northern exposure, a large, skylit drawing room with a balcony, and several smaller rooms of more conventional proportions. The walls were painted "hospital green"; the parquet was strewn with goatskins; and Colette's cat, Kiki-la-Doucette, who was shortly to take his place in French literature, "roamed around depositing his wastes everywhere except in the designated receptacle."[12]

Colette's account of her hand in the décor varies according to the text one consults. In *Three . . . Six . . . Nine* (*Trois . . . six . . . neuf*) she claims that her taste wasn't confident enough for her to insist on the kind of furnishings she longed to install, and which would remind her "warmly . . . of my beloved province."[13] In "The Kepi" she allows that "I wanted to show my sophistication, to satisfy my newly born—and modest—cravings for luxury."[14] It was she who chose the goatskins, the color scheme, and the white divans, but Willy was responsible for the pseudo-Gothic dining room suite and the collection of Wagnerian bric-a-brac. "Let us leave these marvels of impersonality to their oblivion," writes Colette, "these café curtains, this lacquerware, that portrait of mine—in a Pre-Raphaelite gown, by a young painter of the moment—all of it, in short, so ultra-Parisian."[15]

With the manuscript of *Claudine at School* also consigned, momentarily, to oblivion, Colette returned, she writes, to her "divan, to the cat, to books, to new friends, to the life that I tried to make sweet, ignorant of the fact that it was unwholesome for me."[16] What was unwholesome was her subservience to "the extraordinary man I had married," who "deployed the gift, exercised the tactic, of occupying, without respite, the thoughts of a woman."[17] Their daily life, however, was rather athletic.

They rose early two or three mornings a week to ride in the Bois. They skated at the Palais de Glace. Every summer, they took a long vacation, dividing their time between Willy's parents' house and a spa-casino at Uriage-les-bains, where Jacques Gauthier-Villars would remember that Colette walked her angora cat on a leash in the vast and shady park. In July, they made their annual pilgrimage to Bayreuth. On Sundays in the spring, they and a party of bohemian friends took long bicycle trips to the countryside outside Paris, dining in one of those little *guinguettes*—the taverns with pleasure gardens along the Marne or the Seine immortalized by the Impressionists.

Colette would have liked, she says, to "imitate the somnolence of the scarlet-faced diners in their tennis vests and their shirtsleeves. But I was already suffering from the vertical midday light, the embankments bald of grass, the gravel mixed with cigar butts under the tables . . . and I took my distance to cultivate a homesickness for my village which was revived, sharply, beneath the poplars, and by the smell of the river."[18]

But the unhappiness that she evokes so potently in *My Apprenticeships* was not apparent to her friends from this period. Indeed, Colette and Willy seemed to be the ideal modern couple whom Jean de Tinan depicts as "Silly and Jeannette" in his novel of 1899, *Aimienne*. Silly is "a well-known humorist." He is "married. He calls his wife Jeannette . . . you think that it's because her name is Jeanne? Not at all, her name is Renée; Jeannette is her family name. In exchange she calls him Silly like the rest of the world. . . . No one has ever known Silly's given name. She also calls him 'sweet Master,' 'fat Cat,' 'la Doucette,' and 'Blue one.' . . . These appellations suit a particular set of circumstances. . . . Jeannette is graceful and pretty. It's a marriage of comrades. Uptight people find them a bit bohemian; others find them charming. I think that the former are jealous."[19]

IT WAS IN September, Colette remembered, or thought that she remembered—a "russet" September late in the century—that Willy, back in Paris from a visit to his parents, decided to clean up his desk. The desk was a "hideous" piece of furniture whose drawers "vomited a mess of balled-up papers." Among them, Willy found the notebooks Colette had filled with her novel, and which he thought he had thrown out. As she tells it, he began reading:

"Nice . . ."

He opened a second notebook, said not another word, a third, a fourth . . .

"Christ," he grumbled, "I'm an ass . . ."

He shuffled the notebooks together, threw on his top hat, and ran to a publisher. . . . And that is how I became a writer.[20]

Not quite, for the publisher he ran to thought the novel had no merit, and so did a second, and perhaps a third, until, finally, Ollendorff agreed to take a chance on *Claudine at School*. But before the deal was cut, Willy put his wife back to work "with urgent and precise suggestions":

"You couldn't . . . warm this up a bit? . . . For example, between Claudine and one of her girlfriends, an overly close friendship . . . (he used another, briefer expression to make himself understood). And then some rural slang, lots of rural slang. . . . Some girlish high jinx. . . . You see what I mean?"

I saw very well. I also saw, later, that M. Willy orchestrated something rather better than silence around the subject of my collaboration. He acquired the habit of summoning me to hear the praise that wasn't stinted on his behalf, laying his hand on my head softly, to say:

"But you know this child has been precious to me? So, so precious!"[21]

THE SUBJECT OF Colette's "collaboration" with Willy on the *Claudine*s has filled thousands more pages than are contained in the novels. This much one can say with certainty: Willy exploited his wife. He signed Colette's first novel, and three of the sequels. He owned their copyrights, and he eventually sold them, outright, for a paltry sum, for reasons we shall consider later. He received and kept the royalties, which were handsome, paying Colette a small allowance and buying her a country house, which she loved, but which he also reclaimed and sold.[22] After Willy's death, she would sue for, and win, the right to drop her husband's name from the title pages of the disputed fictions, though after *her* death Jacques Gauthier-Villars would sue for, and win, the right to have his father's name restored.

There is also no serious question about the true authorship of the *Claudine*s. Colette wrote them, and they are in every sense, including morally, her intellectual property. Willy edited them; helped to shape them, influenced their tone. To what degree? One can never answer satisfactorily because the manuscript of the first *Claudine* has vanished, having been either destroyed or acquired by a collector who won't admit to having it. The manuscripts of the sequels are conserved at the Bibliothèque Nationale, and they are inconclusive.

"Entirely in my hand," writes Colette; "a very fine script appears in them at long intervals, changes a word, adds a pun or a dry reprimand."[23] This is partially true, but then these manuscripts are clearly not first drafts. Colette also claims that Willy's contributions vulgarized her work, but a careful reading reveals that they sometimes refined it. And sparse as they are, Willy's margin notes suggest that their collaboration was a duet, even a lovers' discourse, and that some of Colette's most erotic moments with her husband took place between sheets of paper.

Paul D'Hollander has weighed the arguments made by both parties; listened to the witnesses; examined the documentary evidence; checked the chronology; compared the adjectives; counted the commas; and he concludes that "we can't accept Colette's version absolutely. In our opinion, Willy's . . . interventions were numerous and sometimes important."[24]

It sometimes takes a heroically minute scientific effort to establish a truth that appears rather obvious to common sense. Colette was a brilliantly gifted young amateur who had never written a book before, and was doing so anonymously, and on command. She was unsure of herself and eager to please. Her husband was a seasoned writer and editor who took her first manuscript in hand. It is apparent, even from the existing evidence, that he helped her develop the characters both on and off the page; that he fine-tuned her prose; that he supplied references and opinions; that he added words, sentences, even passages.

Willy calls himself "the father of the *Claudine*s," to which Colette retorts: "but they are my daughters, too."[25] One could say fairly that he engendered the work, but that she bore it, birthed it, nurtured it with her own substance, and when there was no longer any love between the progenitors, she wanted her daughters to have their mother's name.

More essential to Colette's dispute with Willy over the *Claudine*s are the questions of identity and self-possession which it both raises and obscures. In a richly anecdotal and quirky book published in 1961, the novelist and critic Armand Lanoux sets out to understand the culture of the fin de siècle in terms of what he is far from unique in seeing as its abiding obsession and defining conflict: "the battle between the sexes." He moves from class to class of French society, analyzing the beginnings of "women's revolt." If 1900 marks the "parting of the waters," as he puts it, then "with Colette, one is on our shore, just as with Maupassant one is still on the banks of the Second Empire."[26]

Colette's struggle with Willy, he continues, is against the notion of man and husband as "bourgeois proprietor."[27] Their case is the more dramatic because Willy was also the proprietor of Colette's creative productions. But if she refuses to be owned, Lanoux remarks, she also refuses to renounce her desire to be possessed, and her tolerance of this "insoluble" and "turbulent" contradiction strikes him as modern, courageous, lucid—and greedy.

IF COLETTE WAS an exemplary daughter of the fin de siècle, she was also the specific and unique child of Sidonie Colette, and her struggle with Willy magnifies the paradoxes of her childhood. She claims sole authorship of the novels, but in the same breath disavows their esthetic servility. She denies Willy's role in her evolution as a writer, but complains indignantly of his total domination. And this was her predicament with Sido, who had also insisted on improving her daughter's self-image and claimed co-title to her identity.

It's no coincidence that Claudine is motherless; that when we meet her she is a charming and lonely schoolyard bully, "mean and avid for emotions,"[28] who dreams of obedience to a lover who will beat her, and declares, "I don't like the people I dominate"; that she enters her marriage to a "husband-daddy" yearning naively for an infant's sense of oneness; that she embarks on a love affair with a beguiling but treacherous woman, and suffers a double betrayal; that by slow stages, and unwillingly, she is forced to accept her solitude. "Hélas! Claudine," she cries to herself, "must you always remain your own mistress?"[29]

For Sido's daughter and Willy's child-wife, there was no middle ground between her terror of abandonment and her fear of being consumed. Her only choices, and they were both fairly desperate—or, to use Colette's epithet for herself, monstrously innocent—were to obliterate the master or surrender to her/him.

The lack of a sympathetic imagination tends to reproduce itself in the next generation, and Colette was a tyrant to her own child. She broke free of her servility through writing, and she eventually outgrew her need for a master, but what she couldn't transcend was the scenario of domination and submission. There is only one kind of love missing from the exhaustive, wise, and often revolutionary exploration of the subject contained in her oeuvre, and that love is mutual.

CHAPTER 12

To become nothing but a woman! It's not much, and yet I threw myself toward this ordinary end.

—COLETTE,
Paysages et Portraits

1

DREYFUS HAD BEEN LIVING on Devil's Island for four years when he was pardoned, in October of 1899, by the newly elected president, Émile Loubet. Loubet succeeded Félix Faure, who died an exemplary fin de siècle death: after a large lunch, he had a heart attack in the arms of his mistress, Mme Steinheil—a true femme fatale, who, in her distress, forgot her corset at the Élysée.[1]

The pardon was opportune. International opinion was running so high against the miscarriage of French justice in the Dreyfus case that there was a movement to boycott the Paris Exposition of 1900. The same parliament which had unanimously rejected a retrial the year before now acted swiftly to censure the anti-Dreyfusard government. The Exposition opened in April, a few weeks after the publication of *Claudine at School*, "under the brightest of commercial skies."[2]

The visitors who came from around the world to tour the exhibits were greeted at the main gate by a young beauty wearing an evening dress and an ermine cape designed by Paquin. La Parisienne, as she came to be known, was a stucco goddess twenty feet tall, perched atop a golden ball with her eyes turned rapturously toward heaven and her corseted figure—wasp waist, rounded arms, and voluptuous bosom—offered up to the view of man. This kitsch Venus on a pedestal was the French woman as the French man of the period wished to perceive her.

There were, of course, exceptions. Maupassant, for all his misogyny, created a memorable modern heroine in Mme Forestier, who is infinitely more intelligent, capable, and cunning than the mediocre husbands whose careers are underwritten by her talents. The Symbolist Jules Laforgue—"revolted," Lanoux tells us, "by the insane mythification" of women—declared that "out of laziness and corruption we have created a being set apart, unknown, having no arm other than her sex . . . adoring or hating but not a candid friend, a being . . . [whose spirit of defiance] is that of an eternal little slave."[3]

"The widespread adulation of women," writes Michèle Sarde, "was also an implacable way of subjugating them."[4] More implacable was the Napoleonic Code, still in effect, which gave a husband complete control over his wife's assets and wages, and absolute discretion over her choice of profession or domicile—even if they were legally separated.

If they did work—and women accounted for 37 percent of the labor force—they were paid half of what a man earned for the same job. The average salary for a female worker was two and a half francs a day,[5] but a seamstress or laundress doing piecework could earn as little as a single franc; a street sweeper, one franc fifty; a chambermaid, forty francs a month; a nanny, between thirty-five and fifty a month. The invention of the telegraph provided a new category of jobs for women—operators—nearly all of whom remained unmarried, and who started at nine hundred francs a year. Shop work was better paid, a hundred and fifty francs a month, but for a working day of fifteen hours. A chorus girl at the Moulin Rouge took home two hundred francs a month, minus stiff fines for any absences, infractions of the rules, or damage to her costumes.[6]

The legal workday in the 1890s was eleven hours; the weekly day of rest did not become obligatory until 1905; there were no vacations or benefits, and of course there was no job security. That misery was one of the reasons that the sex industry flourished so luxuriantly. At the fin de siècle, there were approximately a hundred thousand Parisian prostitutes serving a population of slightly under three million. The great bordellos, like The Sphinx, were pornographic theaters offering lavish spectacles to a heterogeneous audience that sometimes included children. The morals of milliners, like Sido's sister, or of herbalists, like Charlotte Kinceler, were suspect because so many small *boutiques à surprise* were in fact fronts for freelance sex work. Child prostitution wasn't outlawed until 1909, and girls as young as eight or ten circulated in the café-concerts and the brasseries, ostensibly selling flowers, but in fact offering themselves to men and women equally. Lesbian prostitutes cruised the Champs-Élysées. Wretched creatures sold themselves for a few sous on the outer boulevards. Destitute provincials wrote desperately to Paris madams, begging for a situation.

Léo Taxil, the author of a contemporary study on prostitution, reproduces some of their letters—their résumés, in effect. These decorous, agonizingly misspelled documents detail "the unhappy circumstances which had led them into a life of sin." Some had aged parents; some had children whom they had to leave behind, as the law prohibited prostitutes working in registered brothels from living with offspring older than four or five. All the women had enormous debts to other madams which their new employer would, by custom, assume, and which could probably never be paid off. "I'm a big brunette with my own linen," writes one, "clothes for day and evening, and a debt of four hundred francs." "I send you a fotograf so that you can playce me," writes another. "I owe 450 francs plus expenses for linens and dresses I am sure to be sootable having always been."

"Exploited by the brothel keepers," Taxil continues, "who rented them clothes and jewels at usurious prices, [the women] are, by turns, angry, combative, irrational, generous, loyal to their companions. They consider themselves, with good reason, abandoned by the entire world, and expect commiseration only from their peers."[7] It was an expectation Colette would come to share when she divorced her husband, lost her standing in respectable society, and went on the stage.

The flesh trade also flourished because the displaced rural laborers who flocked to Paris couldn't afford to marry. It flourished because the fin de siècle was an era of gourmandise—of insatiable, even bulimic, consumption of carnal pleasures.[8] It flourished because the ideals of wifely virtue were incompatible with a decent sex life for either spouse. A young girl's virginity was the prime though unwritten clause of every marriage contract, and she was kept in total ignorance of what would be expected of her on her wedding night (much less at the term of her first pregnancy).

That ignorance supplied amusing copy for certain memoirists of the period, like André Billy, who recalls that after having given a young girl an imprudent kiss in a hansom cab, she wrote to ask him: "Now that you have possessed me entirely, what will become of us?" But some of the anecdotes were more sinister. Lanoux describes the attempted suicide of one young bride, brutally deflowered, and Dumas *(fils)* evokes her state of mind: "On the wedding day, the eloquent, well-bred, tender young man was suddenly transformed. Where the young girl had been dreaming of a radiant god, she saw, leaping upon the altar, a sort of fearsome, velvety beast, mumbling hoarse sounds, ravenous for her flesh, his blood altered. This isn't love, it's legalized and consecrated rape."[9]

The obsession with virginity and fidelity only increased as women became more conscious of their rights to pleasure. By the fin de siècle, innovations in contraception and abortion were making it possible to contemplate sex without procreation. Improved hygiene and the increasing popularity of sport—the advent of the bicycle and the bathing suit—were giving maidens like Proust's "young girls in bloom" a greater awareness of their bodies. And as men and women yearned for sexual compatibility but failed to find it within their arranged marriages, the temptations of adultery increased for both sexes and were chronicled relentlessly by the theater, the fiction, and the press of the period. Willy sums up the contradiction nicely: "I won't tell you again," he says to the heroine of his novel *Suzette veut me lâcher*, "that adultery is the foundation of society, because in making marriage tolerable, it assures the perpetuation of the family."[10]

Considering the era half a century later, Simone de Beauvoir would conclude that the loosening of moral standards taxed women more than it served to free them. It was still, in principle, a woman's duty to be virtuous and submissive, but never before had she felt such an obligation to be alluring. "It's this very complexity of woman that enchants [man]," writes de Beauvoir: "here he has a marvelous domestic servant who can dazzle him without great expense. Is she an angel or a demon? The uncertainty makes her into a sphinx. This was the symbol over the door of one of the most famous brothels of Paris."[11]

BY 1900, French feminism was into its second generation. In 1881, Hubertine Aucler, one of the most tireless campaigners for reform of the divorce laws, began to publish *La Citoyenne*, a suffragist journal whose slogan was We Dare Resist.[12] In 1897, the socialist trade union leader Marguerite Durand founded *La Fronde*, the first daily published entirely by women. The first woman lawyer was admitted to the bar in 1900. "Women doctors can no longer be counted," wrote a hyperbolic conservative in 1901. (There were fewer than a hundred.) "They're invading every speciality, even the most scabrous ones." The same year, René Viviani raised the question of women's suffrage in parliament, although he took it for granted that the vote would be granted only to widows, spinsters, and divorcées.

By 1904, however, even a decorous ladies' magazine like *La Vie heureuse*, filled with articles on taste, fashion, and society, was running features on female pioneers of accomplishment. In one issue alone there were tributes to a painter, Mlle Dufau; a mountain climber, Mme Vallot; and five doctors who ran a clinic for women and children and whose lives were "stories of tenacious will and supple intelligence."[13]

Literature, of course, was one of the few careers accessible to a woman without specific technical training, and the striking number of French women writers in the last quarter of the nineteenth century[14] was noted with alarm and derision by contemporary polemicists. In the face of this onslaught, the Goncourt brothers stipulated that no women would be admitted to their newly constituted Academy. Maurice Donnay ridiculed the emancipated woman in his successful play *L'Affranchie,* and it is worth noting that *affranchisseur* translates both as emancipator and castrator (of cattle). Barbey d'Aurevilly spoke for many of his contemporaries where he concluded, in his essay "The Bluestocking," that a woman writer is but "a man manqué."

The ambitious women of the fin de siècle were faced with a choice as drastic as it was contrived: between retaining the prestige of their femininity, which left them at the mercy of their men; and renouncing it for the sake of a man's autonomy and creative freedom, which set them adrift in an environment hostile both psychologically and economically to emancipated women. Convention presses against the character of an outsider like the weight of the ocean pressing against a diving bell. It takes an equal inner pressure, a kind of single-mindedness, to resist it. Perhaps that is one reason so many literary women were attracted to Lesbos, and chose never to have children: the temptations of marriage and motherhood were too regressive. And their predicament still hadn't been resolved by the time de Beauvoir described it in *The Second Sex:*

> For the young woman . . . there is a contradiction between her status as a real human being and her vocation as a female. And just here is to be found the reason why adolescence is for a woman so difficult and decisive a moment. Up to this time, she has been an autonomous individual: now she must renounce her sovereignty. Not only is she torn, like her brothers, though more painfully, between the past and the future, but in addition a conflict breaks out between her original claim to be a subject, active, free, and, on the other hand, her erotic urges and the social pressure to accept herself as passive object. Her spontaneous tendency is to regard herself as the essential: how can she make up her mind to become the inessential? But if I can accomplish my destiny only as the *Other,* how shall I give up my Ego? Such is the painful dilemma with which the woman-to-be must struggle. Oscillating between desire and disgust, between hope and fear, declining what she calls for, she lingers in suspense between the time of childish independence and that of womanly submission. It is this uncertainty that, as she emerges from the awkward age, gives her the sharp savor of a fruit still green.[15]

This is precisely Colette's terrain in the *Claudines.* In the first novel, the heroine revels in her freedom and the native violence of her character. She is still heretically devoted to what de Beauvoir calls the adolescent female's "cult of the self ": "One can't please the whole world and oneself, too. I prefer to please myself first." As she grows up and is initiated into womanhood, Claudine discovers that femininity, like all cults, demands certain stark renunciations in exchange for the privileges of inclusion. "To obey, to obey! It's a humiliation I have never submitted to—I was about to write, savored. Savored, yes."[16]

2

WHEN THE INSPECTOR of schools visits Claudine's classroom in Montigny, he assigns, as the subject for a composition, a pensée of Franklin's: "Laziness is like rust; it wears things out much more than use does." "Let's go to it," Claudine tells herself, and she produces a perfectly hypocritical little essay that illustrates the theme, while reflecting to herself: "So it's not nice to laze in an armchair? And what of the workers who labor all their lives and die young and exhausted? But hey, you can't say that. In the world of exams, things don't happen as they do in life."[17]

Claudine at School is a novel about hypocrisy told from the point of view of an innocent—which is to say a young girl who has not yet lost her candor. Paradoxes don't intimidate her, and that, perhaps, is the real source of the "amoralism" noted by so many contemporary critics. The title has a double sense, for Claudine is always contrasting the vapidity of her lessons with the schooling she gets from the world. "Lower your eyes, Claudine," Mlle Sergent commands her, as if this would prevent her from seeing.

What she sees is the harsh life that awaits a woman like Mlle Sergent—an intelligent, passionate, ugly woman with no independent means. What she sees is the self-abnegation that will be her own fate as a female. What she also sees is the craven sentimental vanity of women who have accepted the myth of their "purity." The comic spectacle of male lust arouses her contempt, disgust, shame—and her sense of superiority. But looking into her heart, she also sees how much she yearns to become its object. "Would you believe it," Claudine reflects when the slimy deputy Dutertre tries to paw her in the hall, "that since his 'immoral advances' ... I've been feeling what could be called a vague pride? Pretty humiliating for me, that observation. But I know why. 'Because he's known a lot of women in Paris and everywhere and I please him ... There you have it. ...' "[18]

AT THE BEGINNING of *Claudine at School,* the old school buildings are torn down and the girls witness, writes Colette, "the discovery of double walls, walls we thought were full and thick, and which are hollow as armoires, with a kind of black corridor between them, where there's nothing but dust and a frightful, repulsive old smell. I amuse myself by frightening Marie Belhomme, telling her that these mysterious hiding places were contrived in the olden days to immure women who had deceived their husbands."[19]

By the end of the novel, the new school has been erected, and the last scenes describe its dedication ceremony. They are full of Flaubertian echoes—references to the agricultural-fair scene at the heart of *Madame Bovary,* in which Rodolphe's cynical wooing of Emma and the pieties of bourgeois morality and rural life are juxtaposed in an exquisitely savage counterpoint. The same pieties are evoked here: toward the flag, the Republic, and the "maternal soil." And the girls who have spent two hundred pages comparing breasts, fighting in the dust, lusting for each other and for their teachers of both sexes, struggling for their places in a pecking order as vertical as that of any barnyard or corporation, listen to the speeches with lowered eyes, in dresses of First Communion white, and lift their off-key voices in *The Hymn to Nature.*

The demolition of the obsolete old school is a useful metaphor for the novel itself, and for its importance in the history of women's writing. Colette deconstructs a myth which had already begun to crumble when she sat down to write: the myth of the chaste vessel, selfless and will-less. Woman's true character, she insists, also has its double walls, and between them is a dark hiding place with a carnal stench where their forbidden desires are entombed.

Claudine at School was published by Ollendorff in late March of 1900. The reviews were somewhat slow to come, and it was largely due to three influential essays by friends of Willy's—Charles Maurras in the *Revue encyclopédique,* Rachilde in the *Mercure de France,* and Henri Ghéon in the *Revue blanche*—that the novel began to attract notice. Once it started to gather, however, the momentum was tremendous—and Willy did everything in his considerable power to capitalize upon it. Forty thousand copies were sold in two months and, according to Colette, some three hundred and fifty thousand in the course of a few years. In purely commercial terms, as Pichois notes, the success of the *Claudine* novels as a series "is one of the greatest, if not the greatest, in all of French literature."[20] In literary terms, the words of Rachilde were prescient:

> Yes, [Claudine] is a very slight personage of fifteen, her hair down her back, her fists on her haunches, and she is woman herself, howling from the height of puberty, with all her instincts, her desires, her willfulness, and . . .

her *crimes!* . . . Claudine . . . is a modern, she's a delinquent, she's a classic, and she has emerged from the eternal. No, women of letters, old or young ones, can't write things like that. . . . By Willy, the book is a masterpiece. By Claudine, the same book is the most extraordinary work that could possibly burst from the pen of a debutante, and it promises something a bit more than glory to its author: *martyrdom,* for there will never be enough stones or crowns of thorns to throw at her.[21]

CHAPTER 13

_i_

L ATE IN THE SUMMER of 1900, Willy and Colette, flush with their
success, set out from his parents' house for a drive in the country.
Their carriage climbed the steep dirt road that wound up from the city
of Besançon into the hills, turned into a drive, and stopped in front of a small
manor with a slate roof and an elegant, Directoire façade the color of a "yellowed cameo." "All this is yours," Willy told his wife, gesturing toward the
house, its lawns and garden, and the surrounding park. Two years later, he
bought the adjacent farm and vineyard. "Three years later," says Colette—
though, in fact, it was seven—"he reclaimed them from me."[1]

The manor on the hill was called Les Monts-Bouccons, and it had been
built as a hunting lodge in the eighteenth century. Its gardens are gone, but it is
still surrounded by a park of ten acres, meadows, fruit trees, a beautiful woods
with a stand of old and very tall sycamore trees. At the bottom of the woods
lies a grotto—a kind of natural amphitheater reputedly once used by Druids.
The house is perfect in its proportions, but diminutive. One crosses the salon
in three giant steps. There is a little study to one side, which still has its fin de
siècle linoleum floor, and a paneled dining room to the other, dark and almost
Gothic in feeling. Upstairs are five bedrooms. Colette's had the balcony one
can see in photographs of the house, and from it she enjoyed the view,
breathing in the scent of mown hay, damp earth, and roses. Her sense of loss
endowed Les Monts-Bouccons, as it endowed Saint-Sauveur, with a beauty, a
grandeur, a depth—at least of character—which neither quite possesses, or at
least not any longer. Their reality, which is small and a little shabby, suggests
Colette's powers of idealization, and the idealizing tendency of memory.

Except for her annual visits to Bayreuth and to her in-laws, Colette spent most of her summers and early autumns, between 1901 and 1905, at Les Monts-Bouccons. She worked and gardened, rode her horse, answered her mail, drove her little gig, gathered cherries. Friends occasionally came to see her. Captain Colette stayed with her in the autumn of 1901, and wrote an ode to the house, although this visit isn't reported in her published recollections. Willy, like a modern husband—a workaholic—came and went, "arriving dead tired, departing overwhelmed, cursing his excessive 'labors' and the obligation, at the height of summer, to remain 'nailed' to Paris." When he was gone, he left her feeling jealous and abandoned, still dreaming "that old and normal fantasy of living as a couple, in the country." Yet this abandonment was also a tonic: she felt herself slowly "become better, that is to say, capable of living on my own, and punctual, as if I had already known that discipline cures everything."[2]

Part of Colette's discipline was rising at six in summer, at seven in autumn, to work out in the portable gym she'd installed in a shady spot. Her equipment included a trapeze, parallel bars, poles, ladders, a platform, and "on all of this," she told Marguerite Moreno, "I perform the timid flying tricks of a lady who fears breaking something and being beaten by her husband." Then there were the tricks, less timid, she performed in her study: "I assure you that I work in a different manner with Willy-la-Doucette. For it is absolutely necessary to eat this winter. And this mania of dining today on what one will earn tomorrow is the most pernicious thing one could imagine. I'm sad to remain here," she concludes, "thinking that I have to leave. There's a divine odor of mushrooms everywhere. . . . It's the moment of the year when I amuse myself by thinking of things which cause me terrible pain, simply for the pleasure of coming to, again, as myself and seeing that it's not true."[3]

2

I N *My Apprenticeships,* Colette gives her readers the mistaken impression that she had been toiling in Willy's workshops for a long time before she was able to persuade him, with the cunning of the slave, that he would get more value for his investment by settling her somewhere in the country. Les Monts-Bouccons, however, was bought less than six months after the publication of *Claudine at School.* But whether the property was the gift of a grateful husband or the ploy of a shrewd master, it earned back its price many times over. Between 1901 and 1906, Colette wrote Willy at least a book a year. She thus became his most valuable and productive collaborator, the wellspring of their prosperity. The first *Claudine* was succeeded by four others and two wildly successful plays, which were followed by the adventures, in two volumes, of another and less compelling erotic ingenue named Minne, whose career was, "happily for the honor of the French novel," says Colette, cut short only by the author's divorce.[4] And the combined value of these "properties"—a word Willy would have approved—finally made a more splendid dowry than almost any Polytechnician's daughter could have brought him.

Invested soundly, that literary capital might have provided both its creator and its titleholder with the security that neither enjoyed. Willy would die nearly penniless, and while Colette always made more money than she admitted to, it wasn't until the end of her life, when she sold the theatrical and movie rights to *Gigi,* that she had a commercial success on a par with that of the *Claudine*s. So it is hard to fault her, as Willy's friends would, when she exaggerates her husband's avarice—even though she does. By the time she wrote *My Apprenticeships,* during the Depression, she'd come to reckon the extent to which her talent had financed his infidelity. "For what I've spent on free love," he joked, "I could have gotten laid regularly by a professional."

For each of those precious volumes, Willy rewarded Colette with "a number of pearls for her bridal necklace"[5] and an allowance of three hundred francs a month, suspended for the summer, which she considered princely and spent on expensive chocolate and fine woolen stockings for her mother. On the other hand, her allowance wasn't intended to cover her bills at Lewis, the famous milliner, where she bought her hats; or at Redfern, the couturier from whom she ordered her suits, riding habits, and evening dresses; or to pay for their carriage, their coachman, and their cook or the other expenses of their two households. And then there were installment payments of another kind. Willy, wrote Colette, doled out "my share of precise torments and confused pleasures."[6]

3

A PRECISE TORMENT lends itself to an objective description more readily than a confused pleasure. Colette tells us that Willy not only received his other women in their apartment, but expected her to entertain them socially and even sexually. Having "sized up" her potential earning powers, he furnished her with a comfortable study, but locked her into it four hours a day—returning at an appointed time to exact his ogre's toll in finished pages. (This story has been endlessly repeated, but was it true? It seems unlikely. There were servants in the house, and a telephone. Colette told Francis Jammes that Willy provided a "squirrel's cage" for her, but that its door was open. At the end of her life, she explained to an interviewer that she was only locked up in the country, and then at her own request, because she found it so hard to concentrate there.)[7]

Nevertheless, Willy was by turns indulgent and cruel, distant and seductive, admiring and dismissive. He kept her beholden not only for her meals, her clothes, and the roof over her head, but for her emotional sustenance, too. He discouraged any friendship that might rival or undermine his authority, and they lived, she admits, "despite appearances . . . in a unique state of isolation. Isolation that it took the two of us to support and to preserve."[8]

In *The Vagabond*—a novel that her own mother read as an autobiography—Colette goes further. "No one understood a thing about our separation," she writes of Renée Néré's divorce from the unfaithful painter Adolphe Taillandy. "But would they have understood, beforehand, my long, cowardly, and complete complacence? . . . Oh, what a savant master I had in him! How he measured out his indulgence and his exigence! . . . It came to pass that when I showed myself too restive, he beat me, but I don't think he really liked to. A man who gets carried away doesn't hit that well, and this one struck me, now and then, simply to reinforce his prestige."[9]

Locked up, forced to write, beaten, exploited, made to perform degrading sex acts, systematically humiliated—it's a scenario of bondage for which Colette offers a simple and heartfelt excuse: "My God!" Renée exclaims, "how young I was, how much I loved that man, and how I suffered."[10] But a more objective analysis of her marriage must give Colette's complicity in her suffering—her "confused pleasures"—more attention than she was able to.

There are, of course, women who innocently fall prey to brutal men. They are forced into marriages that render them helpless, enduring their tortures because they have no means to escape them. They hate their degradation and dream of revenge or rescue while putting on a stoic face, and sometimes, if the chance comes, they seize it—as Sido did—with a well-aimed lamp or gunshot.

But there are others—spunky girls, self-supporting women of accomplishment—who willingly and inexplicably obliterate themselves for the sake of a second-rate Svengali. The most famous fictional example of such a woman is Réage's O, who, of course, is not locked up for a mere four hours a day to write best-sellers. She is sequestered by her lover in a Sadean château, submitting her orifices to any use her anonymous masters wish to make of them, and they dole out the exigence without any of the indulgence. But they, too, impose "a skillfully managed progression" of "precise tortures," asking her at each level, "O, do you consent?" And they remind her that her "being whipped is less for our pleasure than for your enlightenment."[11] Like Willy-

Taillandy, but much more so, they remain dispassionate, calculating, and rational.

Because so many of Colette's readers and biographers have accepted her accounts of sexual martyrdom, it is worth considering Jessica Benjamin's objection to the conventional feminist reading of Réage's novel, which is "simply as the story of a victimized woman." O, she argues, isn't bullied into submission: she consents to it. What draws a masochist to a sadist is her vicarious experience of his control, virility, power, and detachment, and what draws him to her is his forbidden yearning to share in her "feminine" capacity for surrender. One lover does the holding on for the couple, one does the letting go.

The slave of love as Benjamin describes her has often been a young girl trapped, like Colette, in an "emotional hothouse" with a chaste, possessive mother who has "rejected sexuality . . . in favor of control and self-control." A daughter in such a bind can sometimes differentiate herself by "fighting maternal power with paternal power," and indeed the daddy's girls of this world seem to become the women most at ease with their desires. But that was not the fate of Captain Colette's daughter.

In a culture where autonomy is a male privilege, as is an unfettered sense of entitlement to pleasure, it is not so hard or so unusual to become an invisible woman who struggles with her voracity and aggression while posing as a baby-doll and feeling, as Colette puts it, like a "mental hermaphrodite."

Benjamin concludes that masked women like O and her sisters have sought release in the various forms of voluntary sexual bondage—with idealized love at one end of the continuum and masochism at the other—from their feelings of fraudulence and isolation; that it has provided them, however perversely, with paternal containment; and that in submitting to his will, a woman enslaved to her mother's image seeks recognition for her true self from a father, and identifies with his freedom.[12]

Claudine, whose only maternal image is that of a peasant nurse and body servant, will marry a man twenty-five years her senior—a *"papa-mari"*— because, she says, her own oblivious, distracted father has been "useless" to her. But her husband will prove to be a disappointing master. Why? He is too weak, frivolous, and above all too "feminized" to provide the vicarious experience of virile autonomy: "You have to help me, Renaud," Claudine will plead with him at the end of the third novel in the series. "Yes, I'm your child—nothing other than your child—a daughter who has been too spoiled and to whom you must sometimes refuse what she demands. . . . You have to teach me that some forms of greed are toxic. . . . It gives me pleasure to depend on you, and to fear you."[13]

As Colette's respect for her own unfaithful and disappointing master began to wane, her jealous resentment of his other women swelled to fill the void. Her jealousy, as she herself admits in a number of texts, was obsessive. It inspired fantasies of murder and suicide, although she reassured Willy she would never "turn the gas on." More often, she would try to master her fury by annexing her husband's mistress as a friend, an accomplice, even as a lover—"betraying" Willy with the agent of his own perfidy. These bouts of anxiety and despair alternated with ecstatic and generally brief moments of reunion, like the idyll on Belle-Île.[14] The astounding success of *Claudine at School* ushered in such a period: of indulgence and attentiveness on Willy's part, and of renewed vitality on Colette's.

The sequel she began writing at the end of 1900, *Claudine in Paris,* was composed fast, in less than a year—"in a state of joy," Willy remembered. Paul D'Hollander asks an apposite question: "Has it ever been sufficiently remarked that *Claudine in Paris* is the only novel about love that Colette ever wrote?" By which he means the only novel in which she treats romantic love uncritically; in which love holds out the hope of healing and restitution. Of all the *Claudine*s, asserts Willy, Colette liked *Claudine in Paris* best of all. At least, he adds, "she used to."[15]

AS THE NOVEL BEGINS, the heroine, her cat, her useless father, and her old nurse, Mélie, move to the capital so that he can pursue his research on the snails of Burgundy in scientific libraries. They look up his sister, Claudine's aunt, who sponsors her début in a society she observes with the same candor and detachment she once deployed to skewer her village. Too refined for Montigny, she's too crude for Paris, and her "ironic sagacity" as an outsider provides, says D'Hollander, the novel's only real literary interest.

But it also hasn't been sufficiently remarked that the psychological interest of the novel lies in Colette's elaboration of a story—frivolous on the surface but bleak at its core—in which absent, neglectful, or abusive parents produce love-starved, sexually perverse, and damaged children. There are three such children, all seventeen, in the novel. First there is Claudine, motherless and father-hungry, who discovers that what she has been yearning for is a father, a lover, and a tyrant rolled into one. Then there is her former classmate Luce, the daughter of a "brutal" stonecutter and his greedy peasant wife.

In *Claudine at School,* Luce's beauty and docility aroused Claudine's "voluptuous meanness," and she kept her slave in line with daily beatings that Luce both sought and received gratefully. When they meet by chance in a Paris park, Claudine is amazed at her old friend's transformation into a young lady of fashion. They go back to Luce's suspiciously sumptuous apartment, where Claudine proceeds to solicit her friend's story between threats, blows, and caresses. Luce had been thrown out of the school at Montigny by her older sister, the assistant teacher, Aimée. Her mother had no sympathy for her plight, offering only one option: to come home and tend the pigs. Destitute and abandoned, Luce fled to Paris and looked up her one relation, a rich old uncle. He offered to keep her in style if she would sleep with him—provided, that is, that she was still a virgin. Claudine, fascinated and disgusted, extracts the sordid details of this fin de siècle Cinderella story in which the prince is an old lecher, and it is worth noting that one of the uncle's favorite erotic pastimes is dressing Luce in her old school apron and sitting her at an ink-stained desk while he plays the professor—a parodic version of Willy's role with Colette.

Poverty plays a central part in the fall of Luce, as it did in the lives of so many provincial girls who sold themselves to the rich old lechers of Paris. Poverty also played a central part in Colette's version of her marriage to Willy, and it's very wishfully that she provides her heroine with a dowry from her dead mother—a hundred thousand francs prudently invested with the notary in Montigny. It is telling, too, that Claudine is shocked when Luce declares with smug vindictiveness that she would rather see her mother starve than send her any money. Unlike Claudine, and unlike Colette, Luce has lost, with her innocence, the hope of reunion—the restitution of parental love central to the novel. In denying her mother's need, she gives up on the fulfillment of her own as a child.

Renaud's son, Marcel, is the third and perhaps the most poignantly damaged child in the novel. Marcel is the grandson of Claudine's Aunt Coeur. His mother is dead. His parents separated when he was still a baby because, Colette suggests, the combination of his mother's sexual prudishness and her excessive maternal zeal alienated her husband. Renaud has long since abandoned him to the care of his grandmother, who has "raised him like a girl"— obsessively overprotecting and indulging him. Marcel has turned into a spoiled and flamboyantly queer "little marvel," a "ninny in trousers," "a girl manqué," and Colette implies that the boy is courting this father who loves seductive females by trying to play one.

Renaud may be a miserable father to his son, but he becomes an irresistible, indulgent "uncle" to Claudine, and a foil for Luce's uncle, the gross despoiler. Renaud falls in love with Claudine's wild youth and beauty, her "animal grace," and her ingenuous wit. She falls in love with his paternal tenderness.

The last part of the novel is devoted to Renaud's courtship of Claudine, or rather hers of him—for it is she who can't contain her impetuous desire to be "your daughter, your friend, your wife, everything!" In the carriage on their way home from the restaurant where she gets drunk on Asti, she leans her head on his shoulder "with the security of someone who has finally achieved the goal of a long march."

The day after this fateful evening, Marcel, passionately curious about its outcome, visits Claudine. "Tell me," he asks. "My father was his exquisite and witty self? He didn't treat you like a 'dirty child,' 'a little piece of trash,' like he does me?" Guessing the truth, he can't contain his bitterness, and congratulates Claudine on her "deftness" in snagging such an eligible bachelor. Wild with indignation, she attempts to scratch out his eyes. But there is a grain of truth to Marcel's accusation, which Colette only half allows. For while she considers herself (and is) innocent of any mercenary interest in Renaud's fortune, she does usurp, without pity and without sympathy, that part of Marcel's patrimony which consists of his father's love.

In the last scene, Claudine insists that she can't marry Renaud: she will become his mistress so that no one can accuse her of trying to steal Marcel's money. Renaud tells her she'll be his wife or nothing and convinces her without undue effort. When he asks Claudine's "sublimely unconscious" father for her hand, the malacologist accedes with a few affectionate and confused profanities, noting that Claudine is too flat-chested to be his type. Then the fiancés retire to her room, "me wrapped in his arms, which carried me away as if he were stealing me, both of us winged and dim-witted, like lovers in a tale."

Here is Sido's old fantasy of abduction, with the difference that the child wishes fervently to be stolen. Colette's mistrust of love had not yet conquered her hope that in submission her wounds and losses would be healed. Whether or not it was written in a "state of joy," *Claudine in Paris* is certainly the last time—until the very end of her life—that Colette would so happily unite a woman and a man.[16]

CHAPTER 14

1

JN AUGUST OF 1901, Colette and Willy spent their usual two
weeks at Bayreuth, with a stop at Carlsbad. They were not traveling
alone. A charming lady added her name to the postcards they sent to
their friends. Both husband and wife mention her in their letters. "The music
is good, the food is mediocre . . . and Georgie is vivacious," writes Colette.
"Georgie—what a bitch!" exclaims Willy with enthusiasm. He had fallen
"hard" for her. So had Colette. For a while now, Georgie had been sleeping
(sequentially) with both of them. The affair ended, with bitterness all around,
when the trio returned to Paris.[1]

Georgie Raoul-Duval, née Urquhart, was an American from a rich
Louisiana family, born in Paris in 1866, educated in Europe, and married to a
French mining engineer of distinguished lineage. Her dowry, reports Pichois,
was two hundred thousand francs; his income, a million.[2] The couple moved
in the highest society on both sides of the Atlantic, and Raoul-Duval had
helped to arrange the union of Boni de Castellane to Jay Gould's daughter,
Anna. According to Cocteau, he and Georgie's son had shared a tutor in the
years they were both students at the Lycée Condorcet (along with Maurice
Goudeket, Colette's future husband).[3] Impressed by Georgie's beauty,
charisma, caprice—and by her monstrous narcissism—Cocteau would use
her as his model for the mother in *Les Parents terribles*.

Colette had met Georgie the preceding spring, in the salon of Lucien and
Jeanne Muhlfeld. Lucien was a novelist and Willy's collaborator at *L'Écho de
Paris;* Jeanne was a famous literary hostess. By then, Willy, who had a garçon-
nière in Passy, near Georgie's apartment, may already have been her lover.

His memoirs tell one side of the story: "Colette has claimed, as is only too natural, and I haven't prevented her, the high ground in this murky tale. She has described her anxious hesitations, her refusals that were bit by bit disarmed. . . . Bull! bull! In reality, it was she—seduced from the moment they met at the Muhlfelds, who courted [Georgie], a passionate, brutal, and tenacious courtship whose impudence scandalized . . . all the literary couples."[4]

Colette took the high ground (a figure of speech) in the novel she began writing on her return from Germany. For three years now she had been channeling her life into her fiction almost as fast as she lived it, and *Claudine in Love* recounts Claudine's seduction by a beautiful, treacherous redhead named Rézi, who betrays her with Renaud. While there is no reason to believe that Willy had any more, or any less, a hand in writing it than he did the two earlier *Claudine*s, it is by far the steamiest, most reckless and controversial book in the series, and it came close to embroiling its collaborators, or at least Willy, in lawsuits for both libel and obscenity.

In a letter to Jeanne Muhlfeld written shortly before the novel was published, Colette complained that Willy "(that vengeful boy) is in the process of transforming—retouching—the Rézi of Claudine with such overly brutal strokes that she's Georgie. There she is. There she'll be . . . horribly recognizable. It mustn't be. It's a procedure unworthy of him and of nearly everyone."[5] But in a letter to Lucien Muhlfeld written just after their publisher, Ollendorff, had balked at the "immorality" of the text, she protests: "There isn't the shadow of a monstrosity, and not a single *word* that one could attack."[6] It's difficult to explain the turnabout, except to note that moral criticism always piqued Colette's defiance, and the couple had probably already spent the advance. ("I need money," she had told Jeanne bluntly earlier that winter. "We're near the end of our tether.")[7]

IN THE BEGINNING, Colette, like Claudine, wasn't aware that she and her husband were sharing a mistress. Willy, who calls Georgie "dangerously seductive," explains that she loved unnecessary risks, and would fix successive rendezvous with Colette and with him in the same room, an hour apart. He didn't mind, but he knew how jealous his wife was, and one afternoon, when the scent of Colette's perfume was still fresh on Georgie's skin, he warned her that such reckless indiscretion could get her shot. Georgie was incredulous, then indignant. Why should Colette shoot her, she asked, and not him?

But Willy understood that however smitten Colette might be, Georgie was dispensable to her while he was essential, a fact Colette confirms. She tells Jeanne: "I'm worried, above all, you understand, for him. I have reasons to concern myself a little less with . . . the friend of Claudine."[8] Mme Muhlfeld apparently couldn't deter Willy from his (or was it Colette's?) desire for "vengeance," and of course in exposing Georgie, he was exposing his wife, and she was, despite her protestations, helping him do it.

According to Willy, the novel was already typeset when someone alerted Mme Raoul-Duval that her lovers were about to reveal their threesome in lurid detail and so thinly veiled that no one in Paris could mistake her identity. She protested to Ollendorff, and Pierre Valdagne, the editor in chief, vainly appealed to Willy to modify his text. He refused, and Georgie then offered a "hefty sum" to buy up and pulp the entire first printing. Ollendorff accepted—neglecting, however, to inform Mme Raoul-Duval that Willy still held the copyright and could resell the book elsewhere. Rachilde's husband, Alfred Vallette, was willing to risk the scandal, and gave him a new contract. In May, the Mercure de France published *Claudine in Love* with a different title: *Claudine Married*. A few weeks later, Sido reported to Juliette that Willy's new book was enjoying "a wild success," and indeed, it sold— according to Colette—some seventy thousand copies by the summer.

Claudine Married is a compromising novel, not least for the reader, who feels like a voyeur. Its transposition of real (and extremely well known) personalities to the page with almost no disguise prefigures those modern documentaries in which a family opens its doors to a film crew and lives its most intimate moments in front of them. It calls the world to witness a wife lending her talent as she lent her body to her husband's exhibitionism, at the same time—and in his name—chastising him for corrupting her.

The novel begins with an account of Claudine's wedding night, which has widely been read as a description of Colette's—rightly or not one cannot say, but the sensual intensity and the psychological acuity of the prose both ring true. "Feel a bit like crying," Claudine admits in short, unfinished phrases that reproduce the voice of someone too anxious and excited to take deep breaths, "vague malaise, rib cage tight and painful. Ah! let my friend take me fast and free me from this stupid apprehensiveness, which is neither fear nor modesty."[9]

Alone in the bedroom with her husband, Claudine typically tries to master her reticence by taking the initiative. She undresses while Renaud watches from a distance. He keeps his clothes on, "without his body ever touching me, his mouth and hands don't let me go, from my agitated revolt through my crazed consenting, to the shameful sobs of pleasure that my pride would have preferred to withhold. Afterwards, only afterwards, does he throw off his clothes as I have done mine, and he laughs, pitiless, to vex a stupefied and humiliated Claudine."[10]

Claudine is grateful, later, for her husband's "self-abnegation," although she also admits that the moment of penetration, when it eventually happens, leaves her with "a bit of terror" in the face of "what is called 'conjugal duty.' " But it also leaves her with an inexpressible feeling of dissatisfaction. For all Renaud's skill, tact, and experience—for all the "authority" of his caresses—sex is a matter of technique for him. For Claudine, it's "a mysterious despair that I seek and fear." *"La fêlure est là, "* she says—the split is there.[11] To know Colette, or attempt to know her, one must ask what it is she despairs of. Her work of a lifetime suggests an answer: an ecstatic experience of reunion, in which the split between two bodies, sexes, and generations is repaired.

AS THE STORY PROGRESSES, Claudine begins to grow restive in her marriage: "Regarding the world through [Renaud's] eyes, the great things become smaller, the serious in life diminishes; the useless, the futile, and the negligible assume an enormous importance. But how to defend myself against the incurable and seductive frivolity that transports him, and me along with him?"[12]

When she defiantly refuses to play hostess for him, Renaud establishes his own reception day, and at one of his parties, he introduces Claudine to an unhappily married Viennese beauty named Rézi. Her English husband is a kind of zombie, a hollow man, probably impotent, who has left the better part of himself in India. As money means everything to Rézi, she can't leave him, and as she is terrified of his jealousy, she cuckolds him only with women.

Claudine and Rézi begin meeting every day, usually in Rézi's boudoir, and after several months of superficial intimacy but progressively hotter flirtation, they become lovers, Claudine playing the virile role. She admits the affair to her husband, who professes to be "charmed" by it, and when she protests that he has a curious double standard—abhorring his son's homosexuality but sanctioning his wife's adventures with another woman—he tells her that an affair between two women doesn't "count," to which she objects, in an aside to the reader (which must also be read as a warning to Willy) "for Renaud, adultery is a question of gender."[13]

The indulgent husband proceeds to rent a garçonnière for the two women so that they can pursue their pleasures without fear of intrusion. Renaud begins to meet Rézi there himself, and when Claudine finds out, she realizes that she has been doubly betrayed: by her mistress and her master, and not only by his infidelity, but by his complacence.

The ending of the story seems to have been dictated by legal considerations: one could portray almost any sort of decadence or immorality so long as virtue finally triumphed. But it may also reflect what Colette would call the "gropings of my elusive soul for its health."[14] Claudine flees Paris for her village, and recovers her innocence in nature. Renaud begs forgiveness in an abject letter, and renews his vows of love. "It's time to start it all over," she muses. "Thank God, it can all be started over. I'll tell my *cher grand:* 'I order you to dominate me.' "[15]

2

IN A FRONT-PAGE ARTICLE in *Le Journal* headlined SHOULD ONE READ IT? Jean Lorrain called *Claudine Married,* rather too kindly, "a *Liaisons dangereuses* for the twentieth century, written by a modern Laclos." Rachilde concluded that it placed Willy firmly "in the first rank of French writers," although she also considered that "he" had gone as far as he could with the character and perhaps the subject. The public was of a different mind. Willy had shrewdly judged that the serious money wasn't in publishing at all, but in the symbiotic relationship between best-sellers and the theater.[16] On January 22, 1902, he and two collaborators, the avant-garde director Lugné-Poe and the popular novelist Charles Vayre,[17] mounted a two-act stage version of *Claudine in Paris* at the Bouffes-Parisiens, with a one-act "preface" condensing *Claudine at School.* It was this play, which ran for five months, overlapping with the furor surrounding *Claudine Married,* that made Willy a household word and Claudine the most popular fictional character of the epoch.

Willy, of course, did a prodigious job of publicizing the play, and he is probably the first producer in history to have thought of marketing product spin-offs. Claudine collars, lotion, ice cream, hats, cigarettes, perfume, candies, photographic paper, and even Willy rice powder, were duly offered to the public, as were a series of twelve revoltingly coy picture postcards featuring Colette in a schoolgirl's pinafore, kneeling at Willy's feet, sketching his portrait, lifting her skirt to show a booted ankle, or playing with her bulldog, Toby. By the time the play had finished its run, every whorehouse in Paris had a resident "Claudine" and every year-end satire its Claudine parody. There was eventually even a "Claudine" murderess: a Mme Maîtrejean, who disguised herself with short hair, a white collar, a polka-dot scarf, and a hooded cape to commit her crime.

The received wisdom is that the play owed its success to the actress cast in the title role—a popular cabaret singer who spoke Parisian slang with a *pied-noir* accent and whose stage name was Polaire. Born in Algeria, Émilie-Marie

Bouchard-Zouzé had emigrated to Paris as a teenager, joining a brother already launched successfully on the comic stage. Agile, sultry, and, says Colette, "aggressive as a Hebrew insult," Polaire made her own name singing off-color songs[18] and showing her "teasing, slender ankles" and her "breathtaking wasp waist" in fantastic costumes. She was the original gamine, a prototype for Piaf and for other tiny, soulful, plebeian French *vedettes* who have penciled their brows and belted out their love songs with fists on their haunches; whose memoirs are devoted to their love of lapdogs and thugs; who have been as sentimental about respectability as they were sexually profligate; and who—having put too much trust in fame and in their managers—have died broke and disillusioned. The shrewd and sturdy old Colette would always feel a nostalgic solidarity with the type[19] but also a distinct horror for her fate. The photograph of Polaire that she chose to include in *My Apprenticeships*—an aging vamp with a bad face-lift and spent eyes—is a succinct if heartless epitaph.

Claudine, however, was Polaire's ticket to fame. Untrained in the theater but ambitious to become a comic actress, she had lobbied Jules Renard for a part in *Poil de Carotte*. Failing to get it, she set her sights on Claudine. She later claimed she had been a passionate fan of the novels, and had always felt she resembled their "vibrant and ironic modern" heroine. *"Meussier Vili, Claudine, c'est moi!"* she declared to Willy on their first meeting, to which she had come "dressed as a schoolgirl." Willy, she says, was erudite, amusing, and kind, "infinitely preferable in person to everything one said of him." Colette spoke little except to invite her guest to "plunk [her] butt down" on a chair. "But she had eloquent eyes."[20]

POLAIRE AND COLETTE were exactly the same age when the play opened—twenty-nine—although they both looked much younger, and Polaire claimed to be eighteen. Her face was a feline triangle, like Colette's, with "fathomless" eyes. Her waist, said the *Cri de Paris*, was the size of Willy's neck, seventeen inches. The role called for short hair, and Polaire cropped hers at the jawline—a style that Willy would shortly exhort Colette to copy. He went on to exploit the resemblance between his two "daughters," turning Colette and Polaire into "twins." He had identical suits and dresses made for them, and paraded them around Paris to restaurants, openings, and the races like a couple of "gussied-up animals," according to Colette, or "a pair of trained dogs," according to Polaire, creating the publicity for the sensational *ménage à trois* depicted in the novel.[21] This show disgusted Parisian society, and Rachilde would remark that Colette and Polaire resembled each other mostly in their mutual love "for the obsession of self-exhibition."[22] Colette admits that Polaire was much more sensitive than she was to their humiliation at Willy's hands: "[She] always put her whole soul into her features. It was not on mine that you would have caught such evidence of honest shame."[23]

There would be many other Claudines, including a bearded lady who had to shave before each performance. Colette herself revived and starred in the play six years later, at the Alcazar in Brussels. She was originally proprietary of her character, although in later years, happy to dissociate herself from Willy, she conceded that Polaire had brought a "profound and pure" feeling to the part of Claudine—an unjaded enthusiasm Colette didn't possess. "She gave a unique and in a sense posthumous life to a figure I had invented . . . Polaire believed in Claudine. . . . Her faith, her certainty were such that when I listened to her, I found myself secretly abdicating and I paid [her] homage. . . . There was no other 'true Claudine' but Polaire."[24]

3

As a result of the play, and to a lesser extent, of the novel, Colette became a celebrity in her own right. The ubiquitous profiles of Willy in the popular press usually now included her picture or caricature (and Polaire's). In 1904, *La Vie heureuse* devoted a feature to the décor and lifestyle of Mme Gauthier-Villars, who solemnly told the interviewer: "I have only one dream: to live in the country and there, in the solitude of the mountains, to surround myself with as many pets as possible."[25]

By now, the couple were living in the last and most luxurious of their Paris apartments, the top two floors of a mansion at 177 bis, rue de Courcelles. Willy had furnished the apartment bargain hunting at the kind of bankruptcy auction Flaubert describes in *Sentimental Education*. By most accounts, including Colette's, the results were atrocious. Polaire describes a window of green bottle glass which gave an "amusing" tint to the daylight. George Casella recalls a salon that resembled both a waiting room and a Dutch nightclub. The furniture was massive and rustic; there were heavy draperies, a copper chimney piece, and an art collection dominated by likenesses of Colette and Willy by second-rate painters. The bedroom suite of white lacquered-cane furniture upholstered in satin and decorated with fake Wedgwood was suitable, Colette thought, "for a budget-priced tart." Her only esthetic contribution was to install, in the salon, a white wood balustrade, counter height, to cordon off a dining alcove from the living area. It cut the room in two, she wrote, "crowded the table, stifled the breath of visitors," and was completely inexplicable to them. None of the visitors, however, found the "white handrail" odd enough to mention. It was Colette who was "stifling" in a "crowded" marriage, and she makes this feature of her décor into a symbol of all that was "absurd, nearly intolerable," in her life with Willy.[26]

WILLY HAD SENT his son, as Colette would send her daughter, to an English boarding school, and Jacques remembered that his elegant step-mother had "caused a sensation" among the boys when she came to visit him. By 1902, he was back in France, and he spent his vacations at the rue de Cour-celles. His parents' routine was a pleasant shock to his own austere schoolboy habits. They were out until dawn three or four nights a week. Colette rose in the late morning and spent an hour primping in the bathroom. Willy worked in his dressing gown until lunchtime. Later in the afternoon, they called for their carriage and went out, usually together, to do their errands. If Willy had appointments, Colette would take Jacques shopping, and sometimes they met up with his father for an English tea. He couldn't recall a single evening spent *en famille:* he was invariably left home to mind the pets. But at Easter, when the weather was fine, the three of them went riding in the Bois, "Colette very chic in her felt hat and divided skirt." They met their society friends in the avenue des Acacias, and "I remember," Jacques continued, "the insistence of the photographers from the glossy reviews who bombarded Colette and Willy—quintessential Parisian celebrities—the minute they caught sight of them."[27]

WILLY LIKED to work in a corner of the salon, and received his friends among the stacks of his papers and reviews. He did a great deal of business entertaining. Critics, writers, journalists, impresarios, ghostwriters, publishers, society women, gossip columnists, and hangers-on were invited to boozy dinners prepared by a *cordon bleu* named Juliette, who acquired her own modest fame.

Unlike Claudine, Colette had her reception day—Wednesday—but she was never as fond as Willy was of society. Upstairs from their living quarters was a spacious artist's studio, which she claimed as her private domain and called her garçonnière. She installed her gym equipment here—a slightly more elaborate setup than she had in the country. "All true passion has its ascetic face," she would write in *My Apprenticeships*. And her devotion to gymnastics was the ascetic face of a complex passion.

Colette was not the first woman of the century to work out, but she was one of the first amateurs. She had just turned thirty, and she had a morbid fear of succumbing to the matronly flaccidity that was the fate of the average middle-aged woman of that era. In the process of becoming fit, she discovered that exercise strengthens one's morale. *"Ô molle ardeur de la femme amoureuse"*[28]—O mushy ardor of the woman in love!—she exclaims. In the gym, she was battling that *mollesse,* and acquiring a "modern" body: hard, supple, and, from the perspective of her era, androgynous. She was also, consciously or not, training herself for the profession she would take up when her marriage ended. Colette had understood, precociously, that the true beauty of a woman's muscles is identical with their purpose, and that's self-support.

FOR THE MEN of the fin de siècle, "physical culture" already had self-defensive overtones. It came to France, as Eugen Weber notes, as a response to the defeat of 1870. The army had begun teaching its recruits gymnastics (and dancing), and physical education became compulsory in boys' schools in 1880. The new generation was beefing itself up to resist the macho Prussians—to defend its frontiers literally and spiritually.[29]

The English word "sport" had entered the French vocabulary in mid-century, but only toward the end did it cease to refer almost exclusively to horse racing and begin to signify a broader range of physical activities: skiing, tennis, cycling, boxing, swimming. By then, the interest in physical culture was motivated by something more personal than patriotism and more revolutionary than good hygiene: an "unfettered experience of [the body]." When Isadora Duncan performed in Paris, "what her dancing really symbolized," according to Alain Corbin, "was the freedom to experience the body as something no longer external to the self."[30]

Despite the pride and pleasure she took in her discipline, Colette wasn't deluded about the extent to which a contemporary woman might throw off her fetters, and her own impressions of Duncan are more astute than Corbin's. She writes of the dancer's "naive person," and what was specifically naive to Colette was the idealism of her message. It didn't escape her that the women who had come to cheer this "little naked creature in her veils" were corseted from their armpits to their knees, absurdly hatted, slaves to fashion, "heroic and bound." "I muse on how peculiar women are, watching all these ladies who applaud Isadora Duncan . . . let us not fool ourselves! They acclaim her but they don't envy her. They salute her at a distance, and they contemplate her, but as an escapee—not as a liberator."[31]

If Colette dreamed of escape, she never underestimated the difficulties posed to women by their desire to remain bound. "Reflecting on it later, it has seemed to me that I was exercising my body in the way that those prisoners who aren't concretely planning a breakout still braid a sheet, sew gold pieces into a lining, and hide chocolate under their mattresses."[32] Colette's gymnastics were flexing a will that aspired to, but wasn't yet fit for, the rigors of freedom.

4

WILLY'S FACTORY BEGAN to prefigure Warhol's. It was filled with groupies, wanna-bes, and druggies, as well as with young writers and actors of real talent. The ghosts continued to turn out the product, and Willy to orchestrate its distribution with "ecstatic articles signed by pals that I rewrote myself: a publication-day review in *Le Figaro,* a feature in *L'Écho de Paris,* an inset in *Le Journal,* a 'book of the day' in *Gil Blas,* and a few others. . . ."[33] In 1903, he was prosecuted for obscenity over a smutty novel *(La Maîtresse du Prince Jean)* about a nobleman and an actress, written for him by Léon Pas-surf.[34] (He lost.) That year and the next, there were Willy *Almanach*s, and in 1904, he posed for the illustrations of *En bombe,* a kitschy photoromance in which Maugis jumps from bed to bed, makes allusions to Colette, complains of impotence, and concludes that "life isn't worth a rabbit's fart." When Curnonsky objected that he was cheapening this character they had invested so much in, Willy replied: "I've already told you twenty times that I don't give a damn. When I need money, I'll do anything. Not that I boast of it."[35]

But celebrity brought Willy a number of satisfactions other than money. After the theatrical success of *Claudine in Paris,* he was besieged by women, nymphets, and female couples, all eager to play the schoolgirls to his profes-sor. He recruited some of them as "understudy-twins," and despite the lack of any resemblance to Colette or Polaire, "two or three dresses and as many hats did the trick, with public opinion taking up the slack."[36] When Colette was summering at Les Monts-Bouccons or staying with her mother in Châtillon or visiting Jacques in England—and even sometimes when she was at home— Willy, she says, entertained these "sinister adolescents" at the apartment. After a while, he told a friend, their "mediocre Sapphic performances turned into a deadly bore."[37] That, however, was small consolation to Colette:

> Hanging on him, cooing to him, they write: "Darling, you'll marry me when she dies, yes?" You'd better believe it! He's marrying them already, one after another. He could cull, but he prefers to collect. He thus takes on, at their own request, red-nosed, music-loving society matrons who can't spell; virgins past their prime who write a thousand neatly penned obscenities; tanned Americans with skinny thighs; and a whole series of infatuated little minors wearing flat collars and bobbed hair who come to him with lowered eyes and wiggling behinds: "Oh, Monsieur, I'm the real Claudine . . ." The real Claudine! Minors. You've got to be kidding!

And all of them wish me dead and invent lovers for me. . . . He has liberated the unscrupulous little animal in each one of them . . . they have lied, fornicated, cheated on me with the joy and fury of harpies, as much from hatred of me as for love of Him.[38]

For a long time to come, Colette would publicly affect—at great cost to her dignity—an attitude of friendly tolerance for Willy's girlizing. She posed as an "emancipated" modern wife comfortable with an open marriage. But like Claudine, what she secretly seems to have craved was an honorable, pure-hearted, mutual devotion. And the fact that Willy was constitutionally incapable of providing it didn't seem to deter her from hoping that he still might. Even as their marriage faltered and each of them went off with another partner, Colette continued to believe, touchingly and improbably, that if Willy would only renounce his other women, they could be happy.

5

THE FRIENDS WHO climbed the three flights of stairs to visit Colette's garçonnière, bypassing Willy's throne room on the second floor, were, on the whole, the kind of young men who are still attracted to the atmosphere of certain exclusive gyms: to the sensual discipline and the martial camaraderie, to the faintly sadomasochistic glamour of the equipment, to the communally practiced cult of the body. Most of them were gay.

Colette had made their acquaintance, she says, through one of Willy's secretaries, Marcel Boulestin—her model for Marcel in *Claudine in Paris*. He was, she continues, "a 'nigger' like myself, young, of good family, amusing, mischievous, whose sexual tastes were not even doubtful."[39] Willy reported that he had tried to discourage Marcel's infatuation with stocky butcher boys, and to nurture a safer passion for a "slim young ephebe," without success: Boulestin didn't like "toothpicks." Colette, he said, "observed [Marcel] with amused contempt, and picked my pockets on his behalf."[40] Forty years later, after Boulestin's death, she would write: "He must have ended as he lived, without any physical or moral pain. . . . Never in the course of his good life did [he] think of anyone but himself."[41]

But unlike Willy, Colette never underestimated the virility of her gay friends. They might be "acid-tongued," "cynical," "affected," or "childish," but they lived "like men," which is to say dangerously, and she admired that profoundly. She enjoyed their hedonism and their connoisseurship of sexual violence: "those cryptograms written on the throat with the point of a knife, or with spurs upon hard-worked thighs."[42] She admired their "intolerant" elegance, and having absorbed their lessons, at least superficially, she didn't hesitate to pose as an expert on the subject of dress, makeup, and hair to the penniless, love-struck older (female) friend she calls Marco in "The Kepi."

If her description of these "lost boys" has little warmth to spare, it also contains a good deal of gratitude, and even—rare for Colette—empathy. The same straight men, fathers and patriarchs, who framed the definition of a "real" woman in Colette's world were also the ones who decided who was and wasn't a "real" man, and she recognized the kinship of their predicament. They spoke the same language, she says, "the language of passion, betrayal, jealousy, and sometimes of despair."[43] What they shared with her was a sense of love's "gravity" and of its "barbarism."[44]

For Colette, the world of Lesbos always lacked that "barbarism," and the erotic glamour attached to it, which she idealized. "There is no Gomorrah," she declares. "Puberty, boarding schools, solitude, prisons, snobbery . . . these are fallow breeding grounds, not rich enough to nurture and develop a widespread, established vice and its essential solidarity. . . . Sodom contemplates its frail imitation from on high."[45]

Colette goes on—with a poignancy that doesn't exclude a trace of disdain—to describe the maternal solicitude and the childish dependence that she observed in the lesbian couples she had known: mannish upper-class women whose only experience of parental care and affection had come from their servants, and their younger, mostly working-class protégées. When one compares her statements about Sodom and Gomorrah, she seems to be admiring the aggressive, even sadistic component of male homosexuality while disparaging the consolatory, maternal aspects of lesbianism. Men, in other words, pursue their desire for other men with a phallic sense of purpose and a commitment to transgression, whereas women become lesbians out of frailty or by default—they sink back into the kind of regressive union of mother and child that she had gone to such lengths to escape or deny. When her own daughter admitted that she was a lesbian, Colette would disapprove.

While that disapproval seems outrageously hypocritical, it was evidence of an ambivalence that Colette articulates with great, although not always self-conscious, intelligence. As Allan Massie notes, she saw certain lesbians, like her lover Missy, as striving for an impossible, quixotic, but nevertheless noble ideal of "total fusion with the other, and self-sufficiency in a hostile world."[46] She also understood that one of the impulses that drove women into the arms of other women was a yearning for equality. Two female partners want to be individuals, and have a better chance of being accepted as such than either would with the average male. That is what the old courtesan Amalie tells her in *The Pure and the Impure:* a relationship between two women works precisely so long as one does not try to betray her nature by impersonating a man.

Colette, like Claudine, may have had her *amitiés de pensionnaire* in Saint-Sauveur and a dalliance or two in Paris, but Georgie seems to have been her first serious woman lover.[47] She would shortly take another, and these early lesbian affairs were condoned if not actively encouraged by Willy for his own entertainment. His complacence, while unusual, was far from unique in a period which finds male writers obsessed with hedonism in general and lesbian eroticism in particular, and middle-class married women in remarkable numbers having homosexual adventures. There was a chic attached to those forays in artistic and social circles at the turn of the last century, just as there is at the turn of this one.

When you first read Proust, it seems implausible that nearly everyone in Paris society, male or female, had a secret gay life, but it turns out that Proust was exaggerating only slightly. The art and literature of the period, high and low, the moralists and the libertines alike, dwelled on the subject of female homoeroticism in lavish detail. Zola had described the lesbian subculture of the great courtesans. The example of prominent women artists—George Sand and Sarah Bernhardt, to name but two—set an attractive precedent. Libertine works like Pierre Louÿs' *Chansons de Bilitis* gave harem life the stamp of "art." To the respectable married ladies who took a female lover, homosexual adultery had distinct advantages over the garden variety: there was no danger of pregnancy, almost none of venereal disease, and it was a "safe" way to satisfy their sensual curiosity or take revenge on a brutal or unfaithful husband without risking a scandalous divorce and the loss of their children or social position.

In 1901, Liane de Pougy, one of the greatest courtesans of the Belle Époque, wrote a novel called *L'Idylle sapphique,* a sensational and thinly veiled account of her affair with the American heiress Natalie Clifford Barney. Shortly after *Claudine Married* was published, Colette and Willy met the alluring and famously predatory Miss Barney in the salon of the countess de Chabanne. They had just moved into the big apartment on the rue de Courcelles, and they invited her to visit them there. She did, and Colette's gym left a deep impression. "The wild girl from Cincinnati," as a French friend called her, had spent her childhood rowing, riding, and playing tennis, but she had never considered the possibility of "methodical exercise."[48]

Natalie Barney was three years younger than Colette, and not a methodical person. She was tall and slim, with an unruly aureole of platinum hair, "sea blue eyes," by Colette's description, and "implacable teeth." She came from an extremely rich and socially prominent Midwestern family—her father was a railroad baron with connections in Washington, and her mother was a portrait artist of considerable talent, a student of Carolus-Duran and Whistler. The family had a "cottage" in Bar Harbor, a vast mansion on the coast where they spent their summers. In 1901, while Colette and Willy were in Bayreuth with Georgie, Natalie was vacationing in Maine with the new woman in her life, Pauline Tarn, who signed her poetry Renée Vivien.

Natalie and Renée, like their future friend Gertrude Stein, belonged to that pioneer generation of cultivated lesbian expatriates who, in a kind of reverse migration, embarked for the Old World to escape the intolerance of the new one, settling in Paris around 1900. Theirs were the stories of ambitious passion, self-invention, new money, and puritan vigor tempered by French decadence that Henry James and Edith Wharton could have written, but unfortunately didn't. One longs to read, for example, what James would have made of Natalie's brief engagement to Wilde's paramour Lord Alfred Douglas, or her platonic seduction of the aging and reclusive Rémy de Gourmont.

Gourmont called Natalie his "Amazon," and that was the epithet she had engraved on her tombstone. Her life spans an entire century—she died in Paris at ninety-six—and she was Colette's friend for a good part of it. "I think she was fonder of Colette than of any other woman in French society," wrote Janet Flanner.[49] And while Natalie's memoirs of that friendship are rather brief, they are more perceptive than many more detailed portraits. She possessed, as François Chapon puts it, "an objectivity toward herself and toward others that was without illusion, but also without rancor. 'To feel one must avenge oneself,' she wrote herself—'how short-sighted!' "[50]

If Natalie was unlike Colette in her distaste for vengeance, she was also, unlike Colette, a committed lesbian. Arriving in Paris shortly after her coming out (in the traditional sense), she was as enraptured by its beauties as any roguish provincial from a Balzac novel. Her delectation began at breakfast time in the Bois de Boulogne, where the great demimondaines and actresses enjoyed the morning air, descending from their carriages to take a few mincing, high-heeled steps along that inaptly named "path of virtue" which ran from the Tir aux Pigeons to the Cascade—a sport they "ridiculously" referred to, says Natalie, as "jogging." Sidelong looks were exchanged, and smiles, and it was here that Natalie was first smitten by Liane de Pougy. Here, too, she may have first glimpsed Colette, whose glance, she thought, was the loveliest of all.

Colette was there to walk her animals—a cat and dog who were shortly to acquire literary immortality in the *Dialogues de bêtes.* They had been chosen, Natalie suggests, "for their striking resemblance to their mistress. For wasn't her character composed of those two animal natures? Obedient and devoted to a master, but secretly drawing on the instinct of the wild creature who escapes from all domination."[51]

Natalie had not yet moved to the villa in Neuilly where Colette would début, three years later, as a mime in an erotic pantomime with another beautiful American, Evalina Palmer. She was living at the hotel La Pérouse, and it was probably here that her liaison with Colette began. Willy was delighted: "My husband kisses your hands," Colette told her, "and me, all the rest."[52]

Her tone in the handful of letters to Natalie which survive from the period of their affair makes it sound like a playful diversion rather than a serious romance, and Natalie, who was a scrupulous sexual bookkeeper, would later put Colette's name on the list of her "half " rather than her "full" conquests. "The adventure with Georgie," concludes Pichois, "had left Colette with a sadness and an emptiness tinged with the bitterness that provoked the business of *Claudine in Love*. Nothing of the sort with Natalie, who knew how . . . to transform their passion into a durable friendship."[53] But it was precisely the coincidence of passion and friendship that was such a revelation. Natalie was never faithful, but she prided herself as much on her erotic focus and compassion as on her prowess. And she introduced Colette to a radical new concept in sexual pleasure: privacy.

CHAPTER 15

A PHOTOGRAPH TAKEN of Colette the year she turned thirty shows an ingenue who looked, according to her admirer Claude Farrère, not more than twenty-two. She had just cut her hair, inspiring Sido's wrath and shocking her in-laws. Her new bangs are held back from her forehead with a velvet bow; she is wearing a Russian blouse with embroidery at the neck and cuffs, and her hands are clasped behind her back like a schoolgirl preparing to recite a poem.

In another photo, professionally lit, Colette perches on the edge of a desk in chiffon and pearls. An inkwell, an orchid, a mirror, a manuscript, and an ivory box lie in the foreground. She holds her pose with one arm, balancing a sheet of paper in the other and leaning her cheek against her shoulder. Here her eyes are rimmed with kohl, and she has penciled a fashionable beauty mark high on her cheekbone. Her face has the "enigmatic melancholy" typical of all her photographs, early and late: it was her policy never to smile for the camera. As she notes to her friend Louis de Robert, "I'm walking around with a morose look, which is the expression of an utter contentment."[1] A literary self-portrait written about this time captures what the camera can't: the "cinematic mobility" of a "seductive face . . . which expresses, in turn, exaltation, revolt, the ferocity of a Negress."[2]

Colette's figure, at thirty, was slim by the standards of the age, narrow-shouldered, flat in the stomach, round in the arms and haunches, trimmer than it had been when she was a bride. Through a second regime of exercise, her talent had acquired as much muscle tone as her body. But with the suppleness of prose and limb, she admits, there had also come a "hardening." She speaks of an insidious "petrification," the formation of a protective shell.³ Thirty, Colette believed, was the age of reckoning for a woman. Her emotional immune system has been tested and proved by the lovesicknesses of youth, but she must now cease the reckless dissipation of her vital forces and plan for her long-term survival. "I was," she says, "far from invulnerable, but I no longer dreamed of dying."⁴

2

THE CRITICS WERE TIRING, albeit respectfully, of "Willy's" ageless ingenue. Readers, however, were still avid for her, and that March a fourth Claudine was published. It was called *Claudine s'en va—Claudine Takes Off*— and the title was a form of notice served to both the public and her employer. Colette says that she was "awakening to a vague sense of duty toward myself: that of writing something other than the *Claudine*s."⁵

She wasn't yet ready to dismiss her husband as a collaborator and impresario, and the manuscript bears a modest though significant number of his corrections. But she could mock her indebtedness to him, and when Willy offered to "fill in the blanks" of Maugis's dialogue, she demurred. The Maugis of *Claudine Takes Off* seems to have been her creature. Willy was impressed ("coldly") by her perfect pitch for the voice of his alter ego, who is portrayed as a boozy, sentimental philanderer, "a walking wreck, unkempt and barely decent." And as if she wanted to prove that she could out-Willy him in every domain, Colette made her début that winter as a music critic for *Gil Blas*, writing a weekly column under the rubric "Claudine at the Concert Hall." Thirty-three of her arch, gossipy, and irreverent essays appeared between January and July, and they discriminate, pointedly, between her own amateur's response to music and the pedantry of "that old stickler for details the Usherette."⁶

IN SOME RESPECTS, the fourth *Claudine* obeyed a well-tried formula. It is a novel of heat, idleness, and the intrigues they breed. The first half is set at a spa called Arriège (the thermal baths in Uriage frequented by Colette and Willy). The second half takes place at the Wagner festival in Bayreuth ("the Holy City"). Parisian celebrities make guest appearances as themselves, or barely disguised.⁷ There are teasing flashbacks to places and events in the preceding novels. A parade of vain and lubricious characters engage in dangerous liaisons. There is, as usual, a settling of scores⁸—some of them Willy's, but some of them Colette's with him. One of the characters is a novelist locked up by his tyrannical wife to write best-sellers that underwrite her philandering.

But for all its frivolity, the novel marks a departure for Colette—she "takes off" in her own direction, too. Among the drafts of *Claudine Takes Off* at the Bibliothèque Nationale is one that bears, in her hand, the original title she and Willy eventually discarded: *Je m'évade,*[9] which has the double meaning of "I escape furtively" and "I free myself."

THE JANUS-LIKE WOMAN of thirty, poised between a voluptuously abject past and a solitary but liberated future, is a heroine Colette would examine in her fiction for the next five years—one who becomes, in *Claudine Takes Off,* two characters who embody different aspects of her author.

Annie Samzun, the heroine and narrator, is an overage ingenue married to a peremptory tyrant, Alain, whom she has worshiped slavishly since childhood. He leaves her on a long business trip to South America. Alone for the first time, she flounders, then begins timidly to form her own opinions, articulate her tastes and feelings, reclaim her life—discovering in the process the degree to which her marriage has been a padded cell. She also discovers that her priggish husband has been cynically unfaithful to her. An older and wiser Claudine becomes her mentor and confidante. She helps Annie to discriminate between subjection and love, to mourn her innocence, to see herself for what she is: "a battered child" cringing before a master whose "patronizing smile is devoid of goodness."[10]

Claudine's tactic is to bait Annie to anger: "I've often seen you together," she tells her. "[Alain] always seems like a ramrod and you like a wet handkerchief. He's awkward, stupid, brutal . . . it would be obvious to a child of seven. 'One doesn't do this, Annie, it isn't the fashion, one doesn't do that, Annie . . .' Me? The third time I would have answered him: 'And if I cuckold you, would that be the fashion?' "[11]

But as Michèle Sarde observes, there was still more of Colette in Annie than in the shamelessly idealized Claudine. She and Renaud have survived their affair with Rézi and are blissfully married now, and their example of mutual devotion is extremely painful to the desolated Annie. "Ah, how sad their love makes me," she says with a sigh. It clearly made Colette sad, too.

3

WHEN ANNIE BEGS CLAUDINE for advice on how to recover from the blow of her disillusionment with marriage, Claudine replies that she once sought refuge from "a bad hurt" by going home to her village, where the "divine solitude, the restful foliage, the wise blue night, the peace of the wild animals" restored her happiness.[12] She advises Annie to try the same cure.

Annie has a small estate in the country which is called Casamène and is, in all its particulars, identical with Les Monts-Bouccons. Annie flees there with her maid and the only other soul besides Claudine in whom she confides: a French bulldog named Toby. Colette's French bulldog, Toby, she told Jeanne Muhlfeld, was an adorable creature whose face looked like a frog's that had been sat upon.[13] Toby and his mistress had been photographed together for the Claudine postcards. He shared the couple's life with an angora cat[14] named Kiki-la-Doucette, who was rather more camera shy. But that summer Kiki died. To console Willy, Colette told an interviewer, she wrote a book in which Kiki and Toby exchange piquant confidences, and probably because it was too quirky and poetic to be profitable, Willy let her sign it. *Dialogues de bêtes,* written mostly at Les Monts-Bouccons, was published by the Mercure de France in March of 1904 with the dedication: "To amuse Willy."

KIKI-LA-DOUCETTE WAS also Colette's pet name for her husband, and as a couple they sometimes referred to themselves as the Doucets. Perhaps in their intimate moments they even bantered in the kind of animal baby-talk which Colette reproduced for Jeanne Muhlfeld: "Girl go bye-bye fast, forget gloves. Girl get scolded by Dog-Doucette. . . . Dog-Doucette go bye-bye today see Chicken. Girl eat din-dins all by self with Cat-Kiki. . . . Girl go beddy-bye all by self this night, can't make headsy or armsy. . . . Kaka for Chicken visit. Hugsy to the Mundos."[15]

Dialogues de bêtes was not, mercifully, composed in baby talk, although like most novels written from the point of view of talking animals, it is, in places, insufferably coy. On the other hand, it has a joyful, poetic vigor— Colette on vacation from perversity and decadence; Colette describing the kind of "normal life," the domestic life of a happy couple in the country, that she had yearned for.

"I exuded the *Dialogues de bêtes* drop by drop," Colette writes in *My Apprenticeships,* "giving myself the pleasure, not at all intense but honorable, of not speaking about love"—by which she can only mean the salacious intrigues of Bayreuth and Paris. In other respects, *Dialogues de bêtes* is a natural sequel to *Claudine Takes Off.* An eloquent, Nietzschean creature argues his superiority to a domesticated slave of love. Kiki's opinion of Toby is precisely Claudine's of Annie: "You lick the hand that strikes you. . . . My word, I'm often so ashamed for you . . . your heart is as welcoming and banal as a public garden."[16] His view of the cat is that of the "good" child alarmed by the "wild" one: "I've never understood that vanity of yours, which consists in exaggerating your very real cruelty. . . . You call me the last of the romantics, but aren't you the first of the sadists?"[17]

If Willy gave Colette permission to sign *Dialogues de bêtes,* Colette gave herself permission to open her heart in it to him. Toward the end of the volume, Toby reports the passionate tirade in which his mistress throws down a gauntlet to her master: She'll wear what she likes. She'll go where she pleases. No more premières. No more craven smiles and lowered eyes, exhausted from the effort of resisting age:

> I've had enough! . . . I want . . . I want to do what I want! . . . I want to go on the stage, to become a mime, even an actress. I want to dance naked if I feel that a leotard . . . cramps my style; I want to retire to an island . . . or spend my time in the company of women who live by their charms. . . . I want to write sad and chaste books filled only with landscapes, flowers, suffering, pride, the candor of charming beasts afraid of man. . . . I want to smile at charming faces and distance myself from ugly, dirty, bad-smelling people. I want to cherish him who loves me, and give him everything I possess in the world: my body, which revolts at being shared, my soft heart, and my freedom![18]

She goes on to lambaste "His" mistresses, and concludes: "I leave Him to them. Perhaps one day, He'll see them as I do, with their faces like greedy pigs. He'll flee, then . . . disgusted by a useless vice. . . . I insist on the term. . . . Useless, if he mistakes true love. What? . . . my life is useless, too? No, Toby-chien. . . . If only you knew how much I embellish all that I love . . ."

4

THE ORIGINAL *Dialogues de bêtes* contained four chapters. Two additional dialogues were published later that autumn, one in *La Vie parisienne,* the other in the *Mercure de France.* To these six, Colette added one more, enough new material to justify a second volume: *Sept Dialogues de bêtes* was published in May of 1905[19] with a frontispiece of Colette by Jacques-Émile Blanche and a preface by the novelist and poet Francis Jammes.

Jammes and Colette make interesting foils—the pure and the impure incarnate. They never met, although they exchanged photographs, pressed flowers, and a short, fascinating correspondence. He has been called "the Douanier Rousseau of poetry," and in a literary manifesto ("Jammism") he published in 1897, he declared that "all things are worth describing so long as they are *natural.*"[20] The style of his writing is willfully simple, and his heroines are virginal lovers of God and beauty. Jammes was, in fact, that romantic type the poet-priest, his considerable powers of seduction dedicated—privately, at least—to the salvation of fallen angels.

Colette—the Douanier Rousseau of the alcove—makes an unflattering reference to Jammes's "mumbled lullabies" in *Claudine at School,* although in *Claudine in Paris* her heroine develops "an unforeseen passion" for him because, she explains, "this absurd poet understands the country, animals, old-fashioned gardens, and the seriousness of all life's small stupidities."[21]

As *Dialogues de bêtes* was an absurdly poetic paean to animals and the country, Colette sent Jammes a review copy. He responded at the end of April 1903, avoiding all direct mention of her book and setting the tone for their subsequent correspondence, Jesus to Magdalene: "I don't at all want you to approach me from the depths of your Parisian legend, with that rather bitter grace of yours, and a spirit composed more of sobs than of laughter. . . . I'm not the rest of the world." He goes on to tell her (with that unselfconscious haughtiness of the professionally humble) that if she offers him her pages with the admiration she claims to feel, she should be careful to make the distinction: "A certain gaiety saddens me, and I only wish to see you as a corn-flower blooming in the rye field, or as a passionate meditation on the holy pallor of that leafy avenue where Kiki and Toby go dreaming your magnificent dream."[22]

THE "POET OF ORTHEZ," as he was called, was then a monkish figure of thirty-five who wore a long beard and would send Colette a photograph of himself in a Franciscan cassock. He lived a pious, solitary life in his native province, the Basses-Pyrénées, nursing an unrequited love and hinting to Colette with mysterious insistence about his "suffering." A friend of André Gide's, a mentor to the young Mauriac and Saint-John Perse, a protégé of Claudel, he converted to Catholicism the same year, 1906, that Colette went on the stage. Fearing to offend him, she tried to break off their correspondence.

But Colette refuses to be chastened by Jammes. She tests his tolerance by baiting him with her paganism: "I understand nothing of God and probably never will." She hints at her sexual captivity, calling Willy an excellent "squirrel master" who has furnished her a charming cage with squirrel toys, on which she practices her acrobatics. And it was to Jammes that she first mentions her African blood.

For his part, Jammes always refused to be shocked by Colette, and insisted on seeing her as a countrywoman, a connoisseur of nature, a virtuous wife posing unconvincingly as a decadent Parisian celebrity. "I know that, having met her in the world, certain people insist on complicating her," he writes in his preface:

> It [therefore] become necessary for me, who lives in Orthez, to teach Paris society who you are. . . .
>
> I state, therefore, that Mme Colette Willy never had short hair; that she never dressed as a man; that her cat never goes with her to the theater. . . . It is untrue that Mme Colette Willy works in a squirrel's cage and that she does tricks on the trapeze and rings of such a sort that she touches her neck with her feet.
>
> Mme Colette Willy has never ceased being the *femme bourgeoise* par excellence, rising at dawn, giving oats to the horse, corn to the chickens, cabbage to the rabbits, seed to the canary, snails to the ducks, and water to the pigs. At eight o'clock in summer as in winter, she makes her maid's café au lait and her own. . . . The apiary, the orchard, the kitchen garden, the stable, the barnyard, the greenhouse have no secrets for [her]. . . .
>
> . . . Mme Colette Willy is a living woman, a woman *in earnest,* who has dared to be natural and who resembles a village bride much more than a perverse female writer.[23]

The degree to which Colette treasured this "rehabilitation," as she calls it, suggests how much bravura went into her public posture of indifference to the gossip and scandal she both courted and endured. But she also had a simpler reason to love Francis Jammes: he saw her as a cherished character she had not yet created: Sido's daughter.

PART III

CHAPTER 16

But my darling, what are wisdom teeth doing in your mouth?
—SIDO, to Colette

1

$\mathcal{A}$ MARRIAGE MAY BE sustained by a deep complicity between two spouses long after the extinction of desire. By 1905, Colette's marriage had reached such a plateau. It is clear from *Dialogues de bêtes* that she still passionately loved Willy, but she had lost her sexual charm for him. Impotence and voyeurism are the constant themes of his fiction. Even as a young man, he had needed some strong and fresh stimulation: an intrigue, a threesome, or someone very young. And he had recently taken up with a pudgy, malleable adolescent with whom, for once, he was seriously smitten.

Marguerite Maniez, who would style herself Meg Villars, had been born in London to French parents, although having cast her lot with an anglophile, she liked to say that she was English. In 1905, she was, or claimed to be, twenty, and Willy had known her for at least four years. A photograph of Meg—one of hundreds among his papers—is dated 1901 and inscribed: "For my Daddy, his babydoll, Meg."[1] They had met, apparently, when she came to his garçonnière seeking an autograph for her copy of *Claudine at School*, and she had been among the most persistent and ingratiating of the would-be Claudines. It is not implausible that the red-haired, green-eyed Meg was drafted to make a threesome with Colette,[2] whom she claimed to revere and to find "hypnotizing."

Whether or not Willy's first wife ever shared a bed with the woman who became his second wife, Colette's image haunted Meg's career and marriage. She was still a child when she met Willy and Colette, a clinging vine who trained herself up on the trellis of another woman's character, real and fictional. For his part, Willy was a one-note Pygmalion, and perhaps that's the only kind. He had a stock scenario he was driven to replay, and his protégées were generic products. They shared certain traits: immaturity, gameness, neediness, the ambition to be the plaything of a masterful older man. You have to squint at the faces and bodies in Willy's photo albums to distinguish Colette from her copies. Meg's pictures, in particular, imitate Colette's almost comically. Like her model, Meg would go on the stage, dispense with a leotard, bare her breast, pose prone on a table and in a sailor suit, act in pantomimes with a Sapphic theme, and finally, in 1910, she published a novel "translated" by Willy, which purported to be the scandalous memoirs of a half-French bisexual ingenue in an English boarding school. Such—plus some extremely unflattering references to Colette—was *Les Imprudences de Peggy.* Its moral: all second-generation images betray the loss of sharpness and quality that results from reproduction. Meg was no exception.

2

H O W E V E R   M U C H she still loved Willy, and however much he protested his devotion, Colette had finally begun to look elsewhere for the fidelity, financial security, and sexual satisfaction he couldn't provide. Willy did his best to help her. That March, a journalist noted that the couple had attended the dinner organized to launch a glossy new literary magazine called *Le Damier,* which was published by the members of a private club on the avenue Victor Hugo. The Cercle des Arts et de la Mode, called The Farm by its habitués, was a restaurant and casino run by a déclassé Hungarian noblewoman and frequented by the Parisian demimonde and literary bohemia. According to the memoirs of the writer Armory, it was a "familial" sort of place where no one was ever asked to pay for dinner. Instead, guests were expected to lose large sums of money in the gaming room. Next to this luxurious salon with its green baize tables was a little boudoir where "the literary conversations proceeded apace while some noted pianist (often Vuillermoz) played Wagner."[3]

In addition to Willy and Colette and his collaborators Curnonsky and Toulet, other members of The Farm included Alfred Jarry; Gabriel de Lautrec, the humorist and translator of Mark Twain; Sarah Bernhardt; Jules Blois, the director of the Grand Guignol; Rachilde and her husband, Alfred Vallette; Philippe Berthelot, the statesman and writer; the novelist Victor Marguerite; Natalie Barney; and a contingent of courtesans, including Liane de Pougy and Caroline Otéro. "The soirées were brilliant," Armory remembers.

It was apparently at the launch of *Le Damier* that Colette met the marquise de Belboeuf, and their affair began shortly thereafter. Willy encouraged it, to the point, said Missy, of having "put Colette into my arms, and for that matter, completely!"[4]

SOPHIE-MATHILDE-ADÈLE-DENISE DE MORNY, Marquise de Belboeuf, called Mitzi or Missy or Uncle Max by her intimates, was a stocky, distinguished, "incurably timid" lesbian transvestite, ten years Colette's senior. "Pale," writes Colette, ". . . like certain antique Roman marbles . . . she had all the ease and good manners of a man, the restrained gestures, the virile poise of a man."[5]

Her model for manliness was the legendary royal father she had barely known. The first duke de Morny was the illegitimate son of Hortense de Beauharnais, daughter of the empress Josephine, wife of Louis Bonaparte, and queen of Holland. His father was the queen's lover Charles-Joseph, count de Flahaut. Napoleon III was thus de Morny's illegitimate half-brother. But the Flahaut blood in Missy's veins was much bluer than the Bonaparte blood: Flahaut's mother was the daughter of Talleyrand. His father was the illegitimate grandson of Louis XV.

De Morny was a soldier, an industrialist, a famous womanizer[6] and dandy, a member of Parliament, and after the coup d'état of 1851, which he helped to engineer, minister of the interior for his half-brother. He resigned after six months to resume his career in finance, but in 1856 Napoleon III appointed him ambassador to St. Petersburg. It was in Russia that de Morny received his ducal coronet and met his bride, a tyrannical and capricious Russian princess descended from the Romanovs, Sophie Troubetzkoi.

Missy was the last of her parents' four children. Her father died when she was not quite two, and her mother, who became "half deranged" with grief, and was probably crazy to begin with, cut off her hair and strewed it on her husband's coffin. This gesture, writes Colette, "heralded by the sound of horns, preserved an air of loving sacrifice. . . . 'Oh, how I wish people would shut up about my mother's sacrifice,' " Missy would grumble. " 'For two years she pestered my father to wear her hair short, and he strictly forbade it. She certainly got away with it.' "[7]

The duchess conceived "an irrational hatred" for her youngest daughter. She called Missy "the tapir" and mercilessly mocked her ugliness. The duke's biographer speaks tactfully of Mme de Morny's "slavic" attitude toward her children. She dressed them in old clothes and shoes with holes. She forced them to eat oysters for breakfast, which made them gag. When she wasn't actively humiliating them, she consigned them to the care of churlish if not sadistic servants—Breughelesque peasant maids and alcoholic grooms, a fearsome valet, a particularly cruel German governess, "the paid tormentor or the depraved ally," as Colette puts it.[8] A contemporary journalist even hinted darkly that Missy had been sexually molested by a family member. This story was confirmed to me by a collector who owns an archive of Missy's correspondence. The molester was apparently her stepfather.[9]

The duchess de Morny's second husband was a Spanish nobleman whom she looked down upon. If the duke de Sesto abused Missy, he also, according to Colette, took pity on her. But the damage was done. After Missy had contracted a bad case of typhoid from the force-fed oysters, she conceived, writes Louise Weiss, "a horror of her mother that she never overcame,"[10] a horror and, not implausibly, a profound yearning for some ideal of maternal tenderness that she sought in the arms of other women, and by impersonating the father—the virile, worldly rake—whom her mother had so passionately loved.

When Missy was eighteen, her parents arranged her marriage to the immensely rich Norman nobleman Jacques Godard, marquis de Belboeuf. He had a famous eighteenth-century château on the banks of the Seine not far from Flaubert's house at Croisset. Even then, the young marquise wore men's clothing when she went riding, and rejected her husband's sexual advances, or tried to. When she thought that she might be pregnant, she was in despair. An old footman she had brought from Spain gave her a potion to induce an abortion, and she wept while she drank it.

"With grief?" Colette asked her.

"No. I cried because, while I swallowed that horror, the old fellow tried to console me by calling me *niña* and *pobrecita,* just as he had when I was a child."[11]

Missy and de Belboeuf separated four years later and were divorced officially in 1903—an event which the marquise celebrated with a party at The Farm. If she kept her husband's name and title, it was in part to humiliate him with the notoriety she began attaching to them. She was, says Philippe Jullian, the model for Rachilde's *Marquise de Sade.* She was also, he says, the protagonist of Jean Lorrain's *Âme de boue,* a comic horror story steeped in the "odor of phenol" in which a sinister dyke poses as a corpse to inspire the pity of a former girlfriend.[12]

It is not clear whether Missy thought of herself as a lesbian or as a man. She cropped her hair and ordered her clothes from the smartest tailors in London and Paris. She wore exquisite riding breeches and boots of soft leather; impeccable evening clothes with fine white linen shirts, or sober, tightly vested morning suits with a monocle, a mauve silk handkerchief, and a white carnation in the buttonhole.[13] At the same time, she doesn't seem to have considered herself abnormal. "I don't like women who dress as men," she told Marcel Boulestin. She judged her many imitators very severely. "They raise their knees too high,"she said of women attempting to copy a man's stride; "they don't tuck in their bottoms as they should."[14] A lesbian couple, both in drag, offended her. She had a straight man's contempt for pederasty.

Missy's twenties and thirties were a period of scandal and debauchery: orgies, morphine, rapacious seduction, and the flaunting of a matching pair of carriage horses impudently named Garlic and Vanilla (*une gousse*—the word for both a clove of garlic and a vanilla bean—was the slang term for dyke). Colette describes this era more elegantly: the marquise, she says, was "sowing her wild oats like a prince."[15] And Missy's taste in lovers was nothing if not princely. She haunted the music halls of the fin de siècle, fascinated by their vulgarity. She kept a stable of young actresses and shopgirls, but she had also been pursued by more than one outraged, titled husband. Later in her life, to commemorate a love affair with a young woman who worked at the Renault factory, Missy installed a lathe in her country house, and turned tin pots on it.

In the gay culture of the time irregular morals were considered perfectly compatible with impeccable manners, and for all her flamboyance, the marquise was equally famous for her aristocratic correctness. Louise Weiss calls her "a grande dame" who would not tolerate the slightest infraction of protocol. Her house in Paris, whose décor, said Colette, "bespoke the sensual and rakish life of a bachelor," was filled with imperial furniture and artifacts, and she supposedly despised Natalie Barney for her Jewish origins and a fortune made in trade.

Depending on individual bias, her contemporaries saw Missy as a pathetic freak, an erotic altruist, a great transgressor, a decadent, an aristocrat, a class traitor, a liberator and pioneer, or an abomination. But Colette understood her better. For all the scandal she had courted—and would yet court with Colette—Missy was driven less by any sexual ideology, or even erotic exigence, than by a yearning for the mutual tenderness she had never known: "a settled sentimental attachment." She was generous and skillful as a lover but sexually frigid;[16] "the salacious expectations of women," wrote Colette, "shocked her very natural platonic tendencies, which resembled more the suppressed excitement, the diffuse emotion of an adolescent, than a woman's explicit need. Twenty years ago, she tried, with bitterness, to explain herself to me. 'I do not know anything about completeness in love,' she said"— apparently referring both to orgasm and to emotional fulfillment—" 'except the *idea* I have of it.' "[17]

3

IN APRIL 1905, a month after she met Missy, Colette contributed a "Letter from Claudine" to the second issue of *Le Damier*, "lecturing" Renaud on his jealousy:

> My own has no place here. I'm a vulgar example of it: a banal jealous woman.... There isn't one of your smiles cast toward the eyes of another woman that hasn't aroused in me the most ordinary desire to commit murder.... But your jealousy! Your tardy and awkward and retrospective jealousy! It's my glory, my hairshirt, my plaything, and my sadness.... By the simple force of your jealousy you have revived the shadow of the woman who stands between us: Rézi.... The day that you cried out to me... "You loved her!" I bent under the weight of a sudden and tiring happiness, as if for the first time you had cried, "I love you."... Know this, my nonchalant, my complacent former friend, my current tyrannical master: I will never do anything to heal your jealousy.[18]

A few weeks later, the Gauthier-Villars signed the first of two legal documents necessary for a divorce: a *séparation des biens*—the division of their communal property. On first consideration, one might suppose that Colette's affair with Missy was the motive for their separation. But she and Willy were still a couple, and would live together for another year. In fact, they remained intimate, shared hotel rooms when they traveled, wrote passionate and possessive letters to and about one another until 1908, and they were still collaborating on his fiction for a year after that. Colette said nothing to her family about a breakup. Willy continued to correspond cordially with his mother-in-law and to send her presents. Even when Colette had moved into her own apartment and he was living with Meg, they kept up the fiction of their conjugal solidarity.

No one has suggested a plausible explanation for what seems to have been, at first, a divorce of convenience. Jacques Gauthier-Villars believed that the family had pressured Willy to protect his share of an inheritance from a grandmother. But it isn't clear why Willy, after twelve years of marriage and a lifetime of defiance, should suddenly have dispossessed his wife to ingratiate himself with the Gauthier-Villars—and if he did inherit a large sum, it evaporated as quickly as every other windfall.

By 1905, Willy was nearly bankrupt. How had he managed to dissipate the royalties of at least half a million books? He gambled. He entertained lavishly. Like Colette's father and grandfather, he borrowed money to cover his imprudent speculations. He had bought two racehorses, and their maintenance and training were, alone, a serious drain on his income. In addition to the rue de Courcelles and Les Monts-Bouccons, both well staffed, he had his bachelor flat, and he kept who knows how many women.

By filing to separate his property from Colette's, he was legally exempt from the responsibility for her outstanding debts. These included a large sum owed to her couturier, Redfern, in the rue de Rivoli, who would wait another year before suing Mme Willy for the principal and interest.[19] But since her earnings couldn't now be garnisheed by *his* creditors, Colette was, in effect, in a position to launder money for Willy. She could receive the fees or royalties for their collaborations and pass them along. And this seems to have been part of their strategy.

THAT JUNE, a month after the putative separation, Natalie Barney asked Willy to "lend" her his wife for an afternoon of amateur theatricals in her Neuilly garden.[20] First there was a scene from *Pelléas*, played in drag, followed by a dance of the veils by Mata Hari, who was not yet a household word, and then the main attraction: a pastoral in which Colette played a shepherd who falls in love with a nymph—Evalina Palmer, Natalie's childhood sweetheart from Cincinnati. Eva was a ravishing pre-Raphaelite beauty with red hair to her ankles. She was shortly to marry the Greek brother-in-law of Isadora Duncan, abandon modern dress for a wardrobe of white draperies and bare feet, and devote her life to classical studies (or, as Willy might have said under the circumstances, Attitudes).

With this début, Colette embarked on the first stage of her theatrical career: amateur plays and pantomimes, most of them produced in the private clubs and salons of her rich lesbian friends. A year later, in the same garden, the same cast assembled to perform a play in verse by Pierre Louÿs: *Dialogue of the Setting Sun*. Eva was a Greek shepherdess and Colette "a perfect Daphnis" in a short silk tunic and a pair of Roman buskins. The audience on the lawn was large and fashionable, and both performers had stage fright. Eva mumbled her lines in an American accent; Colette rolled her *r*'s so nervously that she sounded Russian. "I've just had one of the most profound emotions of my life," Louÿs told the two artistes after the performance: ". . . the unforgettable impression of hearing my work recited by Mark Twain and Tolstoy."[21]

At the end of June, Parisians habitually dispersed to their spas, their islands, and their country houses, and Colette returned to Les Monts-Bouccons. It was the last season she would spend there. Polaire came for a brief visit on her way to play Claudine in the provinces. Willy went back and forth to the capital as was his wont. But as the summer faded into autumn and the autumn edged toward winter, he began to miss his wife. "Colette comes home tomorrow!" he wrote to their friend Vuillermoz. "I wasn't made to be a widower."[22]

4

ON AUGUST 12, 1905, Mme Colette celebrated her seventieth birthday. Her letters to Colette, at least those that have been gathered for publication, begin a month later. They portray an intelligent, opinionated, but supremely tender old woman, and a mother who is more domineering, but also humbler, funnier, less stoical, and more interesting than the heroine of *Sido* and *My Mother's House*. Colette would diminish her mother's ordinariness at the expense of her humanity.

The years hadn't taken the edge off Sido's temper or converted her to religion. The piety of her contemporaries never ceased to disgust her. She was ever an imaginatively morbid worrier who fretted over every boil, cold, and toothache suffered by a loved one. Her letters are also much concerned with her own maladies, the "ugliness" of old age prime among them. Her husband's coughing, her sick dog, and her own dark thoughts kept her awake, and to still them, she took Veronal. "To think that one passes one's existence in a swamp like Châtillon,"[23] sighs Sido to Colette. And one feels for this forceful and frustrated woman of the world condemned to play chess with the butcher, listen to the village chatter, and live on hundred-franc handouts from her children.

But Sido's letters also reveal how tenaciously she clung to those grown men and women, doubting their maturity, resenting her helplessness to protect them, and lamenting their distance and reticence. "All I want is your happiness," she tells Colette, and her major complaint is that her puppy doesn't write more often, and that when she does, "you hide so much from me, so many things in your life, even the big events." When she finally discovered her daughter had left her husband for a woman, she was far from being distressed: "I'm happy, my love, that you have, close to you, a female friend who cares for you so tenderly. You're so used to being spoiled that I wonder what would become of you if it ceased."[24]

BY NOW, Sido and the Captain had moved to a little house down the street from their older son. Unlike the rest of his family, Achille lived, as Flaubert might have said, *dans le vrai*. He had a useful profession, and it earned him the respect of his community. He had married a pretty, well-born girl, and they had two lively and intelligent daughters whom Sido doted on. Colette and Willy were the godparents of the elder, Colette-Claudine, who resembled the women in her father's family and her aunt's fiction, and who would even have a brief music-hall career. According to Sido, the girl had a "diabolic gaiety" and an exceptional fluency of speech. She was troublesome at school because, according to her grandmother, "she gets so bored there."[25] She suffered, as Colette had, from the "neuroses of puberty"—her self-abuse of choice was to take laxatives. And like her aunt and grandmother, she had a streak of cruelty. Listening to her father describe a particularly painful birth, she declared: " 'I'd like to know if childbirth hurts that much. I'd have a little girl to see what it's like, then I'd kill her.' When the family protested this 'ferocity,' she replied, 'Well, then I'd give her to someone.' "[26] Colette would sympathize with her fantasy.

Despite the trappings of a happy life and the proximity of a mother he adored, contentment eluded Achille. He had aged into a bitter, disappointed man who nursed his grudges and dreamed of a hermitage in the forest. Perhaps the tensions between his wife and his mother contributed to his unhappiness. There probably wasn't a woman in France whom Sido would have considered worthy of her *cher grand*—certainly not the "vain," "spendthrift," "insipid," and "flirtatious" Jane.

Léo, in the meantime, had become a gruff and ill-kempt bachelor who dressed in Missy's cast-off trousers. He worked as a clerk for the municipality of Levallois, occasionally playing the piano in hotel orchestras and ghostwriting for Willy. His musical genius had otherwise come to nothing. He had few friends, and he barely eked out a living. In love with the girlfriend of a neighbor, he listened to them panting through the wall, and baited his mother's anxiety with talk of suicide. Sido found him so "soft and lacking in initiative" that she wondered how he could be her son.[27]

As for Juliette, Sido couldn't contemplate her life without horror. She was fat, garrulous, gouty, pious, and morbidly jealous of her appalling husband, who was, she implied, molesting their daughter. "Oh, God," Sido exclaims before one of her last visits to Juliette, "and it is I who brought this child into the world!"[28]

But in spite of her trials, Sido was still a passionate woman. Her life hadn't lost its savor, which is to say she hadn't lost the ability to revel in its pleasures: Achille's devotion; Colette's talent; the lively grace of her grandchildren; the "mysterious intelligence of cats"; sunsets; literature; a traveling cinema; flowers; the "marvel that is the phonograph"; and the bleak comedy of provincial life, recounted with such charm and eloquence in her letters.

4

ON SEPTEMBER 8, Sido informs Colette somewhat too casually that her father "hasn't been as well as we might wish." After a lifetime of hard smoking, the Captain was suffering from emphysema, and his one leg no longer served him. Neither did his memory. He had lost interest in books and food, and he spoke slowly, groping for the right word. Nine days later, just short of his seventy-sixth birthday, Jules Colette was dead. He had cried out his wife's name on his deathbed: "my dear soul, he called me," Sido wrote to Juliette, and "I renounce the effort to describe to you the immensity of my grief."[29]

Colette and Willy were in Paris when they got the news, and they set off for the funeral in a rented car. But they had three flat tires and missed the church ceremony, leaving Sido to endure it "crazed with worry" that they were also lying dead on the road somewhere.[30] Two hours later, they joined the mourners at the cemetery, where the former Zouave was buried in his bullet-scarred uniform. Willy, a stickler for certain proprieties, went into mourning for his father-in-law. Colette didn't, but for the next year, her letters were written on black-bordered stationery. In a note to Natalie Barney, written from Les Monts-Bouccons shortly after the funeral, Colette describes her father "as so young, still, at seventy-six; so tenderly smitten by my mother, and loved by his children." She told her friend that she had brought home her share of the Colette patrimony: "a ribbon from the Crimea, a medal from Italy, a rosette of the Legion of Honor, and a photograph."[31] In *My Apprenticeships* she would mention another bequest: "My father left me his improvidence."

Colette says nothing of her grief to Natalie or anyone else. And thirty years would pass before she would mention the other piece of her "spiritual" inheritance: a dozen volumes which her "dextrous" father had bound in boards with spines of black linen, and which her brother had found in his library. Achille was making an inventory after the Captain's death, and while the books had been sitting there for years, no one in the family had thought, dared, or been invited to open them. Each volume had some two hundred pages of thick, cream-laid foolscap, neatly trimmed, with marble endpapers and handwritten titles: *My Campaigns; The Lessons of '70; Zouave songs (in verse)*. Achille called his sister to come and have a look, and together they discovered a "secret, so long disdained by us, accessible as it was." Except for a single page, inscribed boldly: "For my dear soul, her loving husband, Jules-Joseph Colette," the dozen volumes were entirely blank. "Imaginary works," Colette says, "the mirage of a writer's career."[32]

Achille used the luxurious paper for his prescriptions, and his daughters tore out sheets to draw on, yet the blank pages seemed inexhaustible. Of everyone in the family, Colette says, Sido attacked them with the greatest "destructive fever," using them as stationery, to line her drawers, even to make frills for her veal chops. "You don't mean to say there are still some left?" Colette has her exclaim, adding, "It wasn't derision, but piercing regret, and the painful need to obliterate this proof of an impotence."[33] But whose "destructive fever" of denial was it really?

It must come as a nasty shock to discover that the husband one has counted on to repair the wounds inflicted by one's father shares his pathology. After the Captain's death, Colette had to recognize, if only dimly, that Willy's obsessive philandering and Jules Colette's single-minded fidelity were two sides of the same coin, which left her, in both cases, feeling abandoned and desexed. The final irony was equally cruel: husband and father manifested the same secret impotence:

> I've often imagined that M. Willy suffered a kind of agoraphobia, that he had a neurotic horror of the blank page. . . . I imagine that he must have reckoned, in the throes of a pathological blackout, the courage, the solemn constancy it takes to sit down without despair at the edge of a virgin meadow . . . the raw, irresponsible, blinding, ravenous, and ungrateful white page. . . . There must have been a time when he could still believe that he was ready to write, that he was going to write, that he was writing. . . . The pen between his fingers, a pause, the swooning of his will deprived him of his illusion.[34]

Many years after her father's death, Colette consulted a clairvoyant on a question having nothing to do with her childhood.[35] The woman channeled the spirit of an old man, whom she saw sitting behind Colette's chair. She told Colette:

> "He's very much taken up with you. . . . Don't you believe it?"
> "I rather doubt it."
> "Well he is. . . . Because you represent what he would so much have liked to be when he was on earth. You are exactly what he longed to be. But he himself was never able."[36]

5

THE YEAR 1905 WAS Colette's *mezzo dell' cammin.* She had lost her father, and she was losing her husband. She had signed her first book and declared her belated adolescent revolt. Her way out of the dark wood was still obscure, but the figure of the marquise was a fitting Virgil. "The seduction emanating from a person of uncertain or dissimulated sex is powerful,"[37] writes Colette. And Missy was a child's (or a regressed adult's) dream lover: penetrating father and enveloping mother in one. About this aspect of her role, Colette was quite explicit: "If the rocking of your arms doesn't suffice to calm me, your mouth will become fiercer, your hands more amorous, and you will grant me sensual pleasure like a form of succor, like a sovereign exorcism of the demons within me: fever, rage, uncertainty. . . . You will give me pleasure bending over me, your eyes full of maternal anxiety, you who seeks in your impassioned friend the child that you don't have."[38]

By the end of the year, Colette had formally entered Lesbos on Missy's arm. "With such insignia as a pleated shirtfront, a stiff collar, sometimes a waistcoat, and always a silk pocket handkerchief, I frequented a dying society, on the margin of all societies."[39] There were discreet parties in Neuilly to which the guests wore "long trousers and tuxedos and behaved"—though not always—"with unsurpassed propriety." There were homely dinners in the smoky lesbian bistros of Montmartre, where an Algerian proprietress stood guard at a door with no sign above it. There were clubs whose specialties were fondue and dancing, and cabarets where the blue haze of cigar smoke hung over a zinc bar, and a contralto with a faint mustache sang Augusta Holmès.

Mostly, there were late nights, curtained carriages, and opera cloaks that concealed the forbidden male attire. There was cruising in the Bois between ten and noon, and on the Champs-Élysées between four and dusk. There were whispered passwords that opened the door to a high-stakes card game or a secret library of erotica. There was a code of signs and gestures: a certain glance, a certain dog—"the magnificent, fluffed-up toy poodle"[40]—and certain jewels. Missy made Colette the gift of opals.

Willy affected to accept Colette's new life as nonchalantly as he had orchestrated her affair with Georgie and winked at her liaison with Natalie. But in a novel he published in 1905, *Maugis amoureux*, there is a more complex and plaintive note—hurt, vengeful, and tender at the same time. "I don't resemble Adonis," Maugis reflects, "but I don't give a damn what women think of me, including Claudine. I know well enough what her judgment is (she's an intelligent woman), but it means nothing. . . . I eliminate it because, first of all, Claudine breaks my heart, and second, because as everyone knows, she cares very little for men—the more so because they don't at all reciprocate her indifference in kind. If she adores [Renaud], it's because he is—let us put it tactfully—more feminine than all the Rézis in the world."[41]

The novel ends with an autobiographical poem so out of character in its sincerity that it can only be read as a private love letter to Colette:

From one work
In another I find repose.
In different drawers I bury
Songs in verse
And novels in prose.
It's gay, and for twenty years,
Has been that way.
And like an old man,
Onward I go.

I would be sad, though,
If I had the time—
Time to watch the stream flow
While the trembling birch
Shines by the dawn's or the moon's glow.

And in a dream, I see myself
Close to Claudine,
She of the magic eyes
Which leave me no choice
But to forget all other music
For her voice.[42]

CHAPTER 17

1

O N DECEMBER 9, 1905, the prime minister—Émile Combes—signed legislation officially separating the French church and state. This bitterly disputed law, passed by a coalition of radicals and socialists known as the *bloc des gauches,* was the culmination of thirty years of anticlerical agitation. At a dinner party that night, Colette and Willy argued against the reforms. She saw no contradiction, and never would, between supporting conservative positions and living her life in revolt against them. At that very moment, she was making her own dramatic break with right-thinking France by taking pantomime lessons with the well-known mime Georges Wague and preparing to desert polite society by going on the stage.

Wague[1] (her Brague of *The Vagabond*) was a charismatic teacher two years younger than his new disciple. He was a short man with a dancer's physique, a head of wavy hair, and strong, expressive features. He had studied at Willy's alma mater, the Collège Stanislas, before entering the Conservatory, where he devoted himself to the art of mime. After a great vogue in the early years of the nineteenth century, pantomime had become a neglected art. It was revived in 1888 with the foundation of the Cercle Funambulesque, and respected dramatists like Mendès and Richepin began writing for it. But it was Wague "who . . . restored [the genre's] *lettres de noblesse.*"[2] He had made his début in 1898, with an actress named Clotilde Marigaux, whose stage name was Christiane Mendelys, and together they would often partner Colette.[3]

All of Colette's books about the music hall, observes Michèle Sarde, treat Wague as "a uniquely Parisian personality, kind, churlish, a hard worker, exacting with himself and others, efficient, fun-loving, fair, pitiless and unrivaled in the difficult world of . . . 'pantoche,' as Colette calls it."[4] His memoirs of Colette were equally affectionate and respectful. But their relations were not without a rivalrous current that flowed mostly from the direction of the master toward his protégée, particularly when she branched out on her own to do speaking parts. Wague was jealous, she would confess to Missy, although "he doesn't show it." But it would rankle him that she had "as much or more success. So I take care to do him, if I may say so, extravagant justice. It's rather amusing."[5]

Colette's professional début took place at the Théâtre des Mathurins, on February 6, 1906, in *L'Amour, le Désir, la Chimère,* a pantomime by Francis de Croisset, directed by the celebrated actress Georgette LeBlanc-Maeterlinck. Colette's costume was a skimpy chamois tunic fastened with thongs, and she wrote a breathless sketch of the première to accompany the production stills:

> To fit in with everyone else who's shouting, I cry: "My bow. . . . It was there! What did you do with it? And my flute? Shoot, you're stepping on it, how nice. Oh, my God! One of my horns is coming off. I'm thirsty! And the filthy audience out there is stomping. . . . Georgette, my body suit is sagging at the knees. . . . Willy! scram, go back to the hall, you'll never hold up backstage." . . . Fuming, I go to hoist myself up on the wall from which I'll spy on the nymphs when a real cry of anguish escapes me: the wall's not holding! . . . Quick, call the stagehands.[6]

Her blitheness belies the fact that this was a radical coming-out, even for a woman as reckless with her reputation as Mme Willy. Jammes might protest that she was, despite appearances, an exemplary bourgeoise, but no one except Colette took him seriously. The Gauthier-Villars family had been shocked enough when Colette cut her hair, and she'd had to lie about it, "mumbling something" about a kerosene lamp she had overturned on her dressing table. Willy's mother had died in 1904, and Colette's amoralism as a writer was eventually forgiven by the younger generation, still conventional though not so Victorian, and proud of their connection to a great writer. But in 1906, acting professionally was virtually synonymous with prostitution—a transgression of another magnitude, and for a middle-class woman, "the wife of a writer," as Caradec puts it, "a writer, moreover, who belonged to . . . the respectable, Catholic, and Polytechnical bourgeoisie,"[7] the class treason was almost worse than the imputed moral turpitude.

Willy himself was privately ambivalent about his wife's new career. He was relieved that Colette had found a way to earn a living, and he was only too eager to supply her with sketches and one-act plays. For all that it was worth, Colette had his complete moral support. In a letter from Willy to Curnonsky, who was covering the music hall for *Paris qui chante,* he told his friend that a "chic" Saturday-night audience had created a disturbance "to punish Colette for having definitively declared herself *for* professionalism, abandoning the Salons."[8] They would both be grateful, he added, if Curnonsky would show his solidarity with them by attending the next performance.[9] But in a postscript, he added: "In truth, you know, it disturbs me (and only you know how much) that C. should exhibit herself in such pieces of shit. Ah, if I had some dough, she wouldn't have to perform in such works . . . truly!"[10]

In some circles, Colette would never be forgiven. Her Gauthier-Villars relations closed their doors to her, "troubled." "Everyone has broken with Colette except me," quipped Willy shortly after their separation.[11] A few years later, the co-editor of *Le Matin* proposed to resign when Colette—"that circus performer!"—joined the paper. Her "past" threatened to sabotage the election of her second husband, Henry de Jouvenel, to the Senate. Every time her name was proposed for a decoration or a public honor, it was contested by some old statesman who recalled, with outrage, that she had once danced "naked" on a music-hall stage. She was ultimately denied a Christian funeral.

Did she care? That spring, Jammes sent Colette his new religious novel, and she told him she couldn't discuss it with him because she didn't understand anything about God. In the same letter, she excused her long silence: "I've stopped writing to you because I've started acting, and I think that this degrades me forever in your eyes. You see that I know my place. The fact of having played a faun . . . makes me arrogant with some, humble with you"— not so humble, however, that she didn't offer to send Jammes a photograph of herself in her tunic and horns, displaying her "lovely muscles."[12]

COLETTE WAS a faun again that March, in Monte Carlo, where she restaged one of the pantomimes she had performed with Eva Palmer in Natalie's garden. Willy went south with her, and they stayed with Renée Vivien in her villa Cessole, outside Nice. According to Sido, who described their visit in a letter to Juliette, it was an expensive jaunt: the villa had no glassware, so Colette and Willy had gone into town to buy some: "Pouf! Six hundred francs!" A party of their friends showed up for lunch: "Pouf! Seven hundred francs!"[13]

The "lunch" in question (for eight, "three louis a head, not counting dessert or tips"[14]) actually took place at four in the morning at a restaurant called the Cercle. It was the week of Mardi Gras, and Nice, as Colette describes it, was a bacchanal. She and Willy went to a masked ball with a crowd of courtesans, actresses, and corps de ballet members who were down from Paris, most of them part-time members of le Tout-Lesbos and friends of

Renée's—including the ubiquitous Liane de Pougy, Caroline Otéro, and Renée's sometime lover Émilienne d'Alençon. When Colette began waltzing with a "svelte, supple blonde" in a satin train, she felt an arm on her shoulder and heard the brusque voice of a bouncer advising them to "separate, if you please, ladies. It's forbidden here for women to dance with each other."[15]

Colette would come to relish the South of France, to own a house at Saint-Tropez, and to write some of her greatest books there. But in 1906, she found its beauty cloying and its famous scents banal: "Pretty, false Midi, I'd give all your roses, all your light, all your fruits—for a lukewarm and fresh February afternoon . . . in the village that I love."[16]

RENÉE VIVIEN WROTE to Natalie a week later, enclosing a poem that, she said, Colette had inspired. It was the beginning of a peculiar friendship, not only between Renée and Colette, who were shortly to become neighbors in Paris, but between Renée and Willy, whom she called "my dear uncle." He, too, became a habitué of her salon on the avenue du Bois. He had a soft spot in his snob's heart for her poetry, and the next autumn they traveled to London together, she to do research for a biography of Anne Boleyn, he to visit Jacques in college. This excursion gave Willy the occasion to reflect, in a letter to his friend Vuillermoz, on his feelings for his soon-to-be ex-wife: "[Colette] would like nothing better—I know it only too well—than to dump the Deviate [Missy] and to settle down with me somewhere. But how would we eat? How would we face the all too true-sounding gossip: 'They're living off the fortune they've stolen from la Belboeuf'? . . . And then my poor Meg, must I cast her to the waves?"[17]

Vuillermoz suggested he could keep them both, but Willy replied that he couldn't afford to, and returned to his theme, love versus money:

> Delivered from the "Minotaure," as you put it, or the Minovache, yes, it would be desirable. But remember that [Colette] hasn't saved a cent. She had to have hats from Lewis! (I don't reproach her for it, you understand, the poor little fruitcake.) Good Lord! I would never have believed that it would have been so impossible for me to do without her, vitally impossible! Oh, don't suppose it's a need for sex! But I miss her presence, her ambiguous smiles, the wild speed of her comprehension, the book she would shove under my nose, opened to exactly the right page—never a mistake— marked with a scratch; I miss her absurd fits of joy, her brief and violent rages, the talkative childishness she deployed to mask a fine, critical sensibility. I miss her moods of pensive silence. We two had incomparable silent parties. . . .

And the same month he would tell Curnonsky: "Why am I suffering? Because I'm far from the only woman I could love completely."[18]

2

AT THE END of March, Colette opened at the Théâtre-Royal in her first speaking role. The piece was a one-acter by Willy—*Aux innocents les mains plaines*—and Colette, in drag, played a little gigolo introduced to a hooker by a barman, played by Marcel Boulestin. That October, she kicked off the fall season at the new Olympia in a pantomime by Paul Franck and Édouard Mathé [19]—*La Romanichelle*. In November, at the Marigny, she had her second speaking role: as Paniska in *Pan* by Charles Van Lerberghe, directed by Lugné-Poe. This play was the Belgian Symbolist's last work; he died of a stroke that year, but not before enthusing to his director about Colette's perfection in the role: "She's right from every point of view. She's already had some experience. As for her diction, I'll take care of it. . . . To appear as Paniska in the last act, almost naked, her forehead laden with vines, dancing at the head of a bacchanalian procession, Dionysiac—it's no big deal if she has traces of a peasant accent."[20]

Pan would flop, and the critics seized on Colette's accent as a pretext to be severe with her for appearing without a leotard, and to mock the presence in the audience of her lesbian friends, "who went delirious when she lifted up her skirt." But Colette was thrilled to get the part—a lawless gypsy girl who pursues the call of her instincts, bringing down the wrath of the church, polite society, and the police. In her acceptance letter, she flattered the director with an expert mixture of modesty and hype: "a country childhood and a peaceful provincial adolescence didn't seem to destine me for the role of Paniska, but there's no love more pagan or passionate than mine for our mother Earth. . . . Pan and Lugné have desired it. I will be Paniska."[21]

Missy, astoundingly, had considered playing Pan opposite Colette, and her intention had been announced in the press. But she got cold feet at the last moment and was replaced by Wague, causing a certain consternation in the audience: "She really does look like a man,"[22] one young woman murmured when Wague appeared. The audience had come for the scandal, not the dialogue, and booed when the play got too philosophical.

By now, the marquise was such an established fixture in Colette's life that Sido's letters never fail to enclose her "fond regards." They spent that summer together at Belle Plage, Missy's villa by the sea at Le Crotoy, in Normandy. Meg and Willy were together, too, probably at Les Monts-Bouccons. Willy had already broached the subject of a definitive separation, telling the only woman he could love completely: "I am persuaded that it would be easy to organize a series of performances for you, pleasant ones—abroad. Brussels, for example, is curious about a certain sort of spectacle. . . . It would otherwise present an excellent opportunity to liquidate this deadly apartment and to find a formula more suited to a different sort of existence—oh! a bit different. . . . There's no hurry."[23]

Colette was unprepared for this unctuous and underhanded "dismissal," even though she admits that she had secretly been planning her own exit from the marriage. However inevitable it may have seemed in retrospect, she was a woman inured to betrayal who still loved her husband, and he was a man who still paid lip service to his love for her. They were more than literary partners—they were, as they would both put it, co-parents of their novels. Divorce was legal, though still rare and disgraceful in 1906. But more than that: "the spirit of contradiction is as strong in women as the instinct of possession. If all she has in the world is a sorrow, she clings to the sorrow." So, illogical though it seems, Colette was devastated. She had been "swindled of what I had been secretly plotting to relinquish."[24]

EARLY THAT NOVEMBER, Colette and Willy vacated the "deadly apartment." He moved with Meg to smaller quarters on the rue Chambiges. Colette moved in with Missy, who had a sumptuous flat on the rue Georges-Ville, but she also rented a modest pied-à-terre at 44, rue de Villejust. She and Willy continued to share the services of their maid, Francine, and custody of Toby-chien. The dog went to live with one of Willy's secretaries so his masters could take turns visiting him. Colette put a brave face on this upheaval for her mother, who replied, on November 6, greatly bewildered: "So I shall wait until you tell me when I can come to visit you.[25] I still don't have the letter that Willy's supposed to have written me. But your theories on your conjugal relations radically upset my own, even though I've always considered that it is neither proper nor fitting to sleep with one's husband. But to put streets and walls between oneself and one's husband is, all the same, a bit much."[26]

3

ACCORDING TO André Billy, the fin de siècle came to an end in 1905. Its debauches now took their toll on two of Colette's oldest friends. Marcel Schwob had died the preceding winter, and Jean Lorrain succumbed to the ravages of ether that summer. In a posthumous novel, *Maison pour dames,* published in 1908, Lorrain would satirize the ambitions and intrigues of that circle of women writers to which Colette informally belonged: Renée Vivien, Natalie Barney, and their friends Anna de Noailles and Lucie Delarue-Mardrus. She forgave him, and her cameo of Lorrain in *My Apprenticeships* is one of her small masterpieces. Despite the starkness of the light which illuminates his grotesque figure—a fawning, treacherous, doped-up queen with bloodshot eyes and a crust of powder on his veiny skin—Colette discerns, "with ease, the figure of a real man. Never, even at the end, did Jean Lorrain renounce the right and the desire to be a warrior and even a brawler." And she offers him the greatest compliment she could pay a member of the other sex: "[He] gave me pleasure."[27]

REVIEWING COLETTE'S DÉBUTS as a mime in the November 1 issue of *Fantasio,* the critic Franc-Nohain speculated publicly as to why a writer as gifted as Mme Willy should waste her time flouncing dubiously around a stage. "What's so irritating is to see her resorting to the same publicity gimmicks . . . that should be reserved for women with no talent." Sido, to whom Colette sent the clipping, rushed to concur: "You see, [he] says in his article . . . what I keep telling you in my letters."[28]

Sido concluded that Colette went on the stage only because she needed money; Franc-Nohain, because she was competitively obsessed with Polaire. They were both mistaken. Her acting career was a complex act of revolt, sexual dissidence, and self-assertion, in which the courage and idealism of a revolutionary were mixed with an adolescent's rage, glee, egotism, and puerility. She had left her marriage, she was living with a woman, and she was proud of her daring. The hypocrites were embarrassed? The prudes outraged? The bluestockings disgusted? The critics disapproved? Her mother was afraid she would catch cold? Colette's response was to engage Georges Wague for six more pantomime lessons, and to ask him if he would accept Missy as his pupil, too. The marquise, she explained, "wishes to play the Franck role [the painter in *La Romanichelle*] at the club."

This wasn't just a publicity gimmick, although it was that, too: it was also an act of provocation. Colette's social standing had been precarious to begin with, but Missy's was another matter. Early that November, a journalist named Fernand Hauser came to interview the scion of King Louis and the empress Josephine about her plans to mount the planks with Mme Willy.

Colette received him in Missy's drawing room: " 'Here's a fine busybody,' cried the author of *Dialogues de bêtes* . . . 'and what's it to you if the marquise chooses to perform with me?' "

A "man" then appeared, dressed in velvet and clutching a palette, and Hauser recognized the marquise costumed for her role. She explained politely that she would, indeed, be giving two private performances, because "it amuses me to do so. But why should you relate this to your readers?"

At this moment, Hauser continues, "the author of *Claudine at School*, Willy," entered the room, and advised the marquise that it was useless to protest: "an editor of *Le Journal* . . . will know how to make you talk."

Missy then goes on to confess her love for the theater but to insist upon her status as an amateur. She will not accept a penny, nor use her own name— she has adopted the pseudonym Yssim. Hauser wants to know if she won't change her mind and perform in public after all. "Write this: 'She/would/ not/dream/of/it,' " Colette orders him, scanning the syllables. But then the mimes invite him to watch their rehearsal. "The two artists play their parts with equal mastery," he chortles. When their act is done, Willy offers his congratulations, and Colette bats her eyes at him. " 'When Madame was married to me, she didn't give me looks like that!' " he tells her, "and they all laugh."[29]

The private performances duly took place, and on November 25, in a column entitled "Claudine Divorces," the *Cri de Paris* announced that the management of the Moulin Rouge had engaged Mme Willy for the astronomical sum of fifteen hundred francs a day to perform *La Romanichelle* with "Yssim" at their establishment. A second article in the same issue, "En Famille," offered some racy speculation about the foursome of Colette, Missy, Willy, and Meg. Colette wrote back to "assert her freedom," Claude Pichois notes, "in a tone that no other Frenchwoman of the era would have had the courage to adopt publicly." She tells the editor:

> I read your insertions with pleasure, a frequent pleasure, because for a while now you've been spoiling me. What a shame that you should have called one of your wittiest ones "En Famille." That gives to Willy, who is my friend, to the marquise and me, and to that kind and serene English dancer whom Willy calls Meg the air of a sordid commune. You have certainly hurt the feelings of three among us. Do not combine so . . . intimately in the minds of your numerous readers two couples who have arranged their lives in the most normal fashion that I can think of: according to their pleasure.[30]

On December 15, a day before the première, an anonymous article appeared in *Fantasio*, accompanied by a caricature by Sem of Missy in drag and several amorous photographs of her with Colette. It was a remarkably vicious piece of character defamation, even by the standards of the time. Whoever wrote it (and signed himself Mr. Vitriol) had intimate knowledge of Missy's life, for he speaks with authority about her childhood, even noting that "in an hour of bitterness not long ago, she claimed that the cowardly violence, the criminal advances of one intimate with her house who should have been among the first to respect her had saturated her heart and her flesh defini-tively with disgust for and revolt against the Male."[31]

The article went on to detail the scandals of Missy's youth, her depres-sions, the mauve cast of her complexion, and the trapeze she'd installed in the "love chamber" of "each of her garçonnières." It concluded:

> Today, those special guides who show rich foreigners the secret curiosities of Paris . . . never fail to point out, in the [Bois], in certain bars and certain joints . . . that desexed creature with a bloated face of soft plaster, the fixed stare of the ether addict and the day-blind, the dead lips, inevitably . . . towing a lap dog or an actress. Déclassée, fallen to the lowest . . . she'll end her days either by taking the veil or running a Lesbian bistro in Monte Carlo. . . . In the meantime, she's playing in a pantomime with a girlfriend of hers who's already famous, and tomorrow she débuts in the music hall. Poor Missy![32]

Two Christian martyrs could not have put on a braver show in the arena with the lions than did Missy and Colette on the stage of the Moulin Rouge. Their warm-up act was Footit, the famous clown, who was at first mistaken for the marquise. The audience, who had paid scalpers' prices for the tickets,[33] became impatient, and when the two mimes finally appeared, they were stomping and shouting: "Go to it, old Yssim! Take her! Go ahead, take her." And when the wanton gypsy [Colette] left the stage and the lovesick painter [Missy] collapsed in sobs, the "whole hall, in a touching burst of sympathetic solidarity, joined in her grief with an uproar of moaning and wailing. It was really very funny, and the only catcalls in the room came from the last bastions of Imperial corruption."[34]

SIDO WAS in Paris that week. It is possible she attended the performance. She definitely did go to see her son-in-law in the rue Chambiges, where he cried on her shoulder—"crocodile tears," wrote Sido two years later, "which left me cold."[35] Missy and Colette "spoiled" her so assiduously with dinners, gifts, and outings that Mme Colette would protest that they must have thought she was dying. They had no qualms about introducing her to their lesbian friends, and her acceptance of their living arrangements seems enlightened even today.

One of their dinners out was an evening at The Farm. It could not have been by coincidence that Willy and Meg were included in the party—a shock to Sido, but one she mastered with her usual aplomb. "I regarded the place . . . and its staff with a certain surprise," she told Colette years later, a surprise which "Meg and Willy mistook for the stupidity of a provincial." She slyly asked Meg to pass a dish to her "papa," and when the chance presented itself, she whispered to Willy, "You're a worthless scoundrel." To which he replied, "So I've been told."[36]

4

THE FIRST HULLABALLOO at the Moulin Rouge was the prelude to an opening-night riot in the great French tradition of *Hernani, Ubu Roi, Le Sacre du printemps,* and *Pelléas et Mélisande.* Caradec believes that either Willy and Colette were profoundly naive about the risks they were courting by "compromising the de Morny name" or, having survived so much scandal while turning it to profit in the past, they badly miscalculated the limits of public tolerance for the spectacle that they now planned. Missy, he writes, "understood it, but didn't care."[37]

The performance in question was to take place on January 3, 1907. It was a one-act pantomime for two characters entitled *Rêve d'Égypte,* written by Willy, Wague,[38] and Vuillermoz, with music by Édouard Mathé, and starring Colette and "Yssim." Colette was to play a beautiful Egyptian mummy, and "Yssim" the archeologist who discovers her. The mummy comes back to life in a jeweled bra, slowly and seductively unwinds her transparent wrappings, and at the climax of the dance, passionately embraces the archeologist.

The management of the Moulin Rouge exploited the event with a cynicism worthy of tabloid television. They posted the de Morny arms at the entrance of the theater and had them printed on the poster. Missy's brother, the duke de Morny, her ex-husband, the marquis de Belboeuf, and the leading Bonapartist, Prince Murat, rose to the bait: they bought a large block of orchestra seats and filled them with their friends from the Jockey Club and a hundred and fifty hired thugs. When Willy appeared, accompanied by Meg, this throng turned to mumble threats.

The curtain rose at ten forty-five. The stage was immediately bombarded with coins, orange peels, seat cushions, tins of candy, and cloves of garlic, while the catcalls, the blowing of noisemakers, and shouts of "Down with the dykes" drowned out an orchestra of forty musicians. None of these missiles actually struck Missy or Colette, who went ahead with the performance despite the continuing riot, and they played with such imperturbable courage that they earned the sympathy of their more impartial spectators, who stood up to applaud them.

When the archeologist took the unwrapped mummy in "his" arms to give her a lingering and unfeigned kiss, the uproar reached a fever pitch. As the curtain fell, a mob began to move on Meg and Willy, chanting, "Cuckold,

cuckold, cuckold." Willy struck out at them with his cane, Meg with her fists, and they fought their way out into the hall, she punching one man in the nose and scratching another with her ring. The police arrived to escort them from the theater, and four of their friends joined the police to do battle with the oncoming hordes, who backed off long enough for the couple to reach the manager's office and lock themselves into it.

The next day, Missy's relatives asked M. Lépine, the prefect of police, to close the show. The theater management refused, and a large crowd gathered at the Moulin Rouge on January 4 for the second performance. At the last moment, however, a producer appeared onstage to inform the audience that by order of the police, there would be certain "modifications" to the play: it had a new title, *Songe d'Orient,* and Georges Wague would replace Yssim. The performance began, and so, once again, did the riot. Stomping, whistling, and pelting the stage, the crowd never stopped shouting for the marquise. Once again, Colette was applauded for her extraordinary courage.

After the show, Paul Lagardère, a journalist for *La Semaine parisienne,* found the artiste in her dressing room with Mme de Morny and asked Colette for her "impressions":

> "My 'impressions'?" said Mme Colette Willy. . . . "I'm a bit disgusted by the cowardice of all these people who, last night and tonight, showered me with insults, and . . . if I didn't get a footstool thrown smack in my face, it's only because I dodged it in time. Very attractive, don't you think?"
>
> "Let it go, Colette," whispers the marquise de Morny. "Let it drop. . . . Sir, yesterday some gentlemen behaved like lackeys. Let's leave them in peace and go on."
>
> "On the condition that they leave us in peace," says Colette Willy, a bit nervously all the same.
>
> "You were just asking me if I had stage fright? No, it's not in my nature. Look: I'm not trembling at all. You should know for a fact that these demonstrations don't scare me, and I'll go on again unless, because of them, my engagement is broken off with tonight's performance and I'm forced to go abroad to earn my living."[39]

THERE WERE other repercussions. Missy sued the theater for violation of contract, demanding ten thousand francs in damages for breaching her "anonymity" and using her family's coat of arms. Willy wrote a letter to a provincial newspaper "rectifying" an article that had blamed him for the riot: "I'm waiting for an explanation for why you pretend to hold me responsible for the actions of Mme Colette Willy, from whom I am separated, de facto, while waiting for a court decision on our separation, de jure."[40] The January 18 edi-

Sidonie Landoy at eighteen

Mourning becomes her: Sido at thirty (1865),
engaged to Jules Colette and wearing widow's
weeds for Jules Robineau

Impossible dreamer: Captain Colette
in the garden at Châtillon, c. 1896

Minet-chéri: Colette at five

The Colette and Landoy families in 1880: Gabrielle at her parents' feet; Juliette, seated at the far left; Léo standing behind her; the handsome Achille standing second from right

*B*efore the fall: Juliette's wedding in 1885. A golden-haired Colette sits next to the bride.

*S*ido at forty-five, the year Colette, at seven, became conscious of her mother's "essential light"

*C*aptain Colette with a blank page of his "phantom opus"

The "most troubled age": Colette at thirteen, a tomboy despite appearances

A famous photograph of Colette at fifteen with braids like "whips" or "reins." She was still the "scourge" of Olympe Terrain. The next summer, she would fall in love with Willy.

*T*he Colettes *en famille* at Châtillon in 1893—the year of Colette's marriage to Willy. She is twenty; Léo, twenty-seven, on the left; Achille, thirty, on the right.

*C*olette on a bridge at Châtillon, 1893

A rare image of Willy on vacation in 1890. He was thirty-one and already courting Colette while living in Paris with Germaine Servat, the mother of his son, Jacques.

*T*he newlywed Mme Willy and her in-laws, the Gauthier-Villars, at their summer house. Willy is the image of his father, seated behind Colette.

Colette and Willy on Belle-Île the summer of her convalescence, 1895

Comme des garçons: Colette plays up her androgynous charm in the sailor suit she wore to Mme Arman's, winter of 1895–96.

The "father of the *Claudine*s" (Willy) in his trademark top hat with his "twins"—Polaire (left) and Colette, c. 1903

The age of reckoning: Colette at thirty

tion of *Le Temps* then announced that "M. Gauthier-Villars is divorcing"—a bit of news provided, no doubt, by Willy, who filed his petition only five days later, claiming desertion.[41] On January 20, a furious Sido, who had to read this news in the paper, wrote to Colette:

> You don't write to me. I can't go on like this. You don't have confidence in me, in us, I should say.
>
> Do you think all these stories leave us cold? What's this article in *Le Matin?* Why are you letting yourself get taken to this degree? . . . If my logical character serves me well, it seems that someone has pushed you into doing things so that he'll have the right to show you the door. You'll wind up poorer than I am. It seems to me you should take a hard look at all this. What will you keep of all that you possess? . . . Why are you making your-self the slave of all these people? Forgive me, dear, for speaking to you like this, but I have an absolute horror of being cheated by my inferiors, and you and I are one. . . .
>
> P.S. There's one other thing you should know: that the only person you can count on in this world is yourself. You're still young and strong, don't let yourself be cheated. . . .[42]

Considering that he had written the pantomime that caused the brawl, rehearsed it, attended it, and defended it in print, Willy's belated attempt to dissociate himself from Colette is an outrage. By now, however, he was des-perately trying to save his main source of regular income,[43] his job as the music critic of *L'Écho de Paris.* The "revulsion" against the "spectacle" of his "complacence" had been so tremendous and universal that his employers had declared that they could no longer afford to be associated with him. Meg Vil-lars broke the news—and Colette's reaction to it—to Jacques in a letter writ-ten early that February: "But the terrible part is that the scandal that Colette has caused has made papa lose his place. . . . You can guess what that means, especially since we have lost our money—Last night he told Colette! She is terribly selfish—she just said—'Oh, I am sorry' and went on talking about her own affairs, and yet she knows it is her fault, really! I am very much dis-gusted with her. Even the marquise was *gênée* [embarrassed] to see her so indifferent."[44]

COLETTE, MEANWHILE, had countersued Willy for divorce. It wasn't enough under French law for a woman to claim that her husband had been unfaithful: she had to prove that he had installed a concubine under her roof. Willy, obligingly, had done so with Meg. Colette had also gone, the morning after her second night at the Moulin Rouge, to the offices of Ollendorff to reclaim a manuscript she now declared to be her property—the last novel in the *Claudine* series. "You're no doubt aware that Willy and I are in the process of seeking a legal separation," she wrote to Mandel, the editorial director. "It is my duty to alert you that among the objects and furnishings that I am reclaiming is my share of a last novel . . . which I shall publish with the house at which I am under contract.⁴⁵ I'm aware, of course, that Willy owes you a novel, and I have no doubt that it will be forthcoming. Mine is ready, I'm taking it with me, it's a contest and I'm the winner, and that's all there is to it."⁴⁶

That was not, however, all there was to it. At the same moment that they were suing each other for divorce, airing their dirty linen, publishing farewell letters in the newspapers, and fighting over their common property, Willy and Colette were writing to each other nearly daily, negotiating—or, more accurately, renegotiating—a secret alliance. And here their relations become so byzantine that a chronology does them more justice than a narrative.⁴⁷

January 20: Colette sends Willy a letter of apology for some angry words. "When I write cruel things to you, don't hold them against me, it's only what I'm thinking at that moment. You've always told me to mistrust first impulses. Useless lesson."⁴⁸

January 31: Colette countersues for divorce.

February 13: The court hands down the judgment granting their legal separation, on the ground of "mutual wrongs." The news makes most of the Paris papers, and Willy leaves for Capri with Meg. He sends Colette vacation snapshots of Meg and Toby-chien.

February 14: Colette writes Willy a conspiratorial letter about her plans, literary and dramatic. If only someone would assure her of an income of six thousand francs, she "wouldn't be beholden to a soul alive."⁴⁹

A day or so later, in a letter now lost, Colette tells her mother that Sido's tirades against Willy do not agree with her own feelings, and asks her to write affectionately to him.

February 16: Sido replies: "You love Willy, and a lot, you say, and he's going off [to Capri] with a young and pretty woman? I assure you that we resemble each other in many ways, just as we look alike, but your ideas about your conjugal relations are far from mine, and if I judge Willy completely otherwise than you do, and if I hurt your feelings speaking of him as I do, it's because, no doubt, you don't tell me your secret thoughts."⁵⁰

Missy was as mystified as Sido by Colette's attitude toward Willy, and in a fragment of an undated letter Colette tells her: "If you don't understand it, I have nothing to add. There are things one has to grasp immediately, and without explanations, or else one can never understand them."⁵¹

February 16: Missy writes to Willy in Capri: "I don't always understand your two natures, and in the beginning, I often deplored your need to flaunt our situation (which was what you wanted) and which could have been just as free but more discreet. . . . When you put Colette in my arms—which you did completely!—I saw what you wanted, and I didn't flinch, though I could see ahead to what might happen to all three of us. I thus don't merit the reproaches of Colette, who is an impulsive child without much moral feeling, but that certainly isn't her fault! I understand that she's bored with the old, melancholy creature that I am, and I hold that against myself, but it isn't in human nature to change oneself."[52]

February 17: Colette reads Missy's description of her, and tells Willy that she is rather surprised to see the expression "moral feeling" in Missy's handwriting. This is the postscript to a letter which is one of the most confidential and intimate documents that has survived in her hand. She tells her husband that they two are more austere than common mortals; that he's been a fool for having given up the only woman in the world who suited him, just as he was the only man in the world who suited her. And she proposes a clandestine romance: they will take lodgings near but not with each other; they will renounce "other people," and he, in particular, his "dubious" other women— his "Megs and classic Claudines." She will continue to sleep with Missy, who is happy enough with their *ménage à trois.* He should take time to consider her offer, but she needs his fidelity, physical and emotional. In the meantime, she concludes, he shouldn't worry about her despair, she will never "turn the gas on. I cherish and embrace you."[53]

February 23: The Mercure de France publishes the last *Claudine,* in which Colette kills off Renaud. After considerable wrangling, Willy had "authorized" his wife to sign it, and to append a notice in which, for the first time, Colette takes partial public credit for her authorship: "For reasons which have nothing to do with literature, I have ceased to collaborate with Willy. The same readers who gave a favorable reception to our six . . . legitimate daughters, the four *Claudine*s and the two *Minne*s, will, I hope, enjoy *Retreat from Love,* and will perhaps be ready to find in this book something of what they liked in the others."

March 13–16: Meg and Willy are living in Menton, and Colette and Missy are nearby, in Nice, for a performance of *Rêve d'Égypte* (with Wague). Sido tells her daughter that she seems "enchanted" by the life she's living. She asks Colette to give Willy a hug from her if she sees him. Colette does see him: Willy tells Vuillermoz he hasn't been to the performance, but that he has visited his wife secretly at her hotel, and she has come to him secretly at Menton. "It's not my fault if I can't detest her, nor she me."[54]

March 29: Meg sends snapshots of herself to, of all people, Sido, who thanks *"la jeune Anglaise"* for the thought,[55] even though they're duplicates of a set she has been given by Colette!

April 1: Willy sends a present of expensive candy to Sido's grand-daughters: "That Willy. Whatever else one can say about him, he's always thinking about giving people pleasure."[56]

Mid-April: Jacques Gauthier-Villars is home from school for his Easter vacation. He recalls later that although Colette and Willy were officially separated, they saw each other every day, they were working on a book together, and their "day-to-day rapport seemed excellent."[57]

Colette, however, wasn't finished "raging" at Willy, as she admits to him in a letter. Apparently in response to one of her tirades, he sends her an urgent telegram:

> I thought we'd reestablished a good emotional understanding, even though we had officially broken up. But since that day, you haven't written to me once, you take an almost aggressive tone on the telephone. So what's up? Are we enemies? To think that it's Willy who must pose this question to Colette! Life is strange. However, I wasn't mistaken the other day when you told me, with that sadness of a child which I can't resist and those tears which undo me, "I don't want to live in the same city with you if we're separated. . . . I'll go to Brazil. . . ." Shaken by this little-girl anguish, I left feeling high, yes Colette, high, making great plans. They've fallen apart. So be it. But I'm going to ask you plainly what your intentions are, not the public ones, because we're of a mind, you and I, to flaunt our quarrel. But at the bottom of it, what's going on? I have the right to know, and I have, above all, the need to know. Send me a clear message. Or let me come and see you, and let's decide once and for all what will be. I can't bear any more. And don't fear any jeremiads, for Christ's sake. If you tell me it's over, we won't hold on to anything, even in secret—you don't have to fear a melodrama. I would like a prompt response by telegram for many reasons. So long as I'm in doubt, I won't abstain from sending you, perhaps for the last time, *Tendresses.*[58]

June 12: Willy confides to Sido that he is suffering from the loss of his job at *L'Écho de Paris*—not only because of the money, but because of his idleness. He tells her that he's afraid he has lost Achille's friendship, but she tells him he's mistaken. To Colette she notes sympathetically: "How I understand him! Willy no longer writing . . . isn't Willy."[59]

Summer arrives: Willy and Meg are back in Paris, where they entertain Léo Colette.

End of July: Parisians of means disperse to the mountains and the shore. Colette and Missy return to Le Crotoy, where they will live through September. Meg and Willy rent the house next door, and the two couples happily keep company. Willy photographs Meg and Colette frolicking on the beach. "I find your relations with Miss Meg fantastical," Sido admits with her usual candor. "I'm more suspicious than you are, especially of what's abnormal and illogical. I don't like complicated situations, in life: I'm too stupid to disentangle them."[60]

CHAPTER 18

1

IN 1906, Colette published nothing of substance. "I was developing strengths that had nothing to do with literature," she explains.[1] What's amazing is that she managed to keep writing throughout the maelstrom of that year. She finished the last *Claudine—Retreat from Love*—before she left the rue de Courcelles, and the novel was published by the Mercure de France in February of 1907.

In French, the novel is called *La Retraite sentimentale,* and *retraite* has the double meaning of retreat and retirement. Willy made very few corrections on the manuscript, and for the first time, Colette rejected many of his suggestions. The novel is set at Casamène (Les Monts-Bouccons), and Colette's evocations of the Franche-Comté contain some of her most sumptuous nature writing.

As the novel opens, Claudine is waiting faithfully at Casamène for the return of Renaud, then a patient in a Swiss sanatorium. Annie Samzun, divorced from Alain,[2] is keeping her company while drying out, temporarily, from her new addiction: anonymous sex with strangers, bellhops, tenors— any passing male she fancies. Claudine solicits her confessions and finds them both obscene and banal. "There's something [she] hasn't thought of," Claudine congratulates herself, and "it's love! As for me, love has made me so happy, so deeply satisfied physically, so emotionally excited . . . that I really don't know how [she] can live close to me without dying of jealousy!"[3]

Marcel arrives, more debauched than ever. He, too, is seeking refuge— from a blackmailer—and he tells Claudine about his season of glory among the pretty boys of an elite lycée. He's another "stupid glutton," in Claudine's estimation, obsessed, like Annie, with "young flesh." Imprudently, indeed somewhat heartlessly, she throws them together. It is, predictably, a humiliating disaster for them both. Marcel then leaves in disgrace.

Bedroom scenes and salacious fireside chats occupy most of the novel. At the end, Renaud returns from the hospital, aged, impotent, and terminally ill. He offers Claudine his mouth and hands, which she refuses. "Here I am, with all my strength, which has never been used to the full; here I am, young, punished, and deprived of what I secretly love with ardent fervor, and I'm naively wringing my hands at my disaster before the mutilated image of happiness. The man I used to call 'my father' as part of a filial love-game has become and will forever be my grandfather."

Renaud dies. Annie's in-laws arrive, accompanied by the drunken Maugis. Together they try to coax Claudine back to society. They fail. Chastened by death, exalted by nature, superior to their frivolity, Claudine attends to her books, her animals, her hearth, and to the estate Annie has very casually bequeathed to her. "I'm afraid of no one, not even myself," she exults in the final pages. "Temptation? I know it. I live with it. . . . Everything is possible; I'm waiting for it. It can't be terrible, desire without love."[4]

Colette may have signed *Retreat from Love*, but as Michel Mercier puts it, it was also "her last work as ghostwriter."[5] The disingenuous eroticism of Annie's confessions is pure Willy whether or not he had a hand in it, and the contrived romantic wishfulness, impure Colette. She exploits the novel to reclaim possession of what in her real life she was losing or had lost, and she repudiates her own conflicts and frailties by attributing them to characters whom she then jettisons morally.

Claudine's self-assurance, indeed her grandiosity, has a different emotional color when one remembers that Colette was sitting among the packing crates at the rue de Courcelles, rewriting the ending to her own marriage. "But tell me," Sido asks Colette, "there's no doubt, is there, that it's about you and Willy? And the end, which I find admirable, isn't at all designed to be agreeable to [him] because to call him a geezer is the last thing that would flatter him."[6]

However intense her nostalgia was, one can imagine, with Sido, that Colette had a pleasant morning writing Renaud's death scene: "I forgot myself so far as to say to the doctor: 'Oh, I beg you, give him something to make him die more quickly!' " And many years later she would reflect: "His death gave me the feeling of having attained a kind of literary puberty, a foretaste of those delights allowed to the praying mantis."[7]

2

THE EDITORS OF the Pléaide have two astute but conflicting views of *Retreat from Love,* which, considered together, give perspective not only on the novel but on Colette's life at what Pichois calls this "turning point." He discerns "an extraordinary sentiment of superiority" suggested in the early work but made explicit here. "You carry your [happiness] with a kind of pride," Annie tells Claudine, "a sort of secret superiority; one can hear that you're thinking, 'My happiness or sadness, or my sensual pleasure, and my love—they're finally better than and different from those of others.' "

The basis for this hubris, he speculates, is that sovereign vitality and attunement to nature which are also the essence, in his opinion, of Colette's greatness as a writer. This will be her bond with the fictional Sido, and with her animals. It is the excuse for Claudine's condescension toward the Renauds, Rézis, Luces, Annies, and Marcels—in short, with the decadent and fallen of the world. The pleasures of "the ego in consonance with nature,"writes Pichois, "are more important [to Colette] than the pleasures that might be provided by another person."[8]

Pichois's colleague Paul D'Hollander sees the relationship between the heroine and the author quite differently. The dialogue between Claudine and Annie is a debate, he writes, between two different "conceptions of the feminine ideal." Colette exalts Claudine's fidelity to one man, and after his death, she revels in her widow's solitude and self-sufficiency, but he wonders if "the novelist hasn't made Annie so frivolous in order to represent the risks of a life devoted so completely to sensual pleasure, and to arm herself against a temptation that is harder to resist than she admits." Annie, he concludes, "embodies the 'guilty' aspirations of the writer at a moment when emancipation was, for the first time, a real possibility for her."[9]

D'Hollander supports his argument by quoting a short magazine piece called "The Mirror." Here, for the first and only time, "Colette" confronts her doppelganger and tells Claudine (à propos of *Retreat from Love*): "It's yours alone . . . that pure renouncement of love which demands that after Renaud, your love life is finished. . . . It's yours alone, not mine, that fortress of solitude where, little by little, you consume yourself. . . . Here you have, on the heights of your soul, discovered a retreat which defies invasion. . . . So live here then, ironic and sweet, and leave me . . . my meager human portion, which has its price!"[10]

In 1908, Colette published "The Mirror" and a selection of other short prose in *Tendrils of the Vine*. The famous title piece, written before her separation in 1905, describes a nightingale who awakens one spring morning to find that his feet have been trapped by the vine's spiraling creepers. Believing he will die, he struggles to break free, and swears that he will never fall asleep again while the tendrils are climbing. "From that night on, he sang to stay awake . . . he varied his theme, embellished it, fell in love with his voice, became that mad singer, intoxicated and panting, to whom one listens with the unbearable desire to see him sing."[11] The writer identifies her fate with his.

The tone of *Tendrils* is as bittersweet as the taste of that freedom, and what makes it so is Colette's sense of the unbreachable distance between the past—"the village I have left behind"—and the present. As a contemporary critic noted astutely, the narrator is "an emancipated woman writer, artist, and rebel . . . savagely and resolutely alone" but "unconsciously still fixated on her childhood."[12] And this is her allegory for the loss of self and the dawn of vigilance, for the discovery of her voice and her gifts, and for the conflict between the drive for autonomy and the yearning for submission that will inform her work for the next forty years.

The eroticism of the most candid and intimate *Tendrils* was meant to shock, as Colette cheerfully admitted to Willy, who read the manuscript for her and made some minor corrections.[13] "Jour gris" is a feverish and melancholy reverie addressed to Missy, in which the narrator laments her lost intactness. "Nonoche" is a little paean to the siren call of male lust, for which the mother cat abandons her nursling. "Nuit blanche" celebrates Colette's gratitude to her mistress for a love so containing and steady that it feels redemptive. The writing suffers in places from an exalted and somewhat adolescent solemnity, but to read the finest of these prose poems is to enter a pagan sanctum like the Villa dei Misteri—a temple of voluptuous devotions.

3

In mid-September 1907, Colette and Missy were still at Le Crotoy. Sido wrote to them from Charny, where she had gone to visit Juliette, who was ill with a strange stomach ailment: "worrisome vomiting of a bizarre color." Léo, who had just left her, was off to London on a short vacation paid for by Willy, who was still playing the attentive son-in-law, sending Sido Colette's press clippings and reviews with his own doting comments on them.

Colette had promised her mother a visit, too, but she reneged: "You didn't come, as you said you would, but I was counting on it so little." She promised a long letter, but that also tarried. "I wanted so much to know what you are doing, what you're thinking, but that's more difficult, because you've always hidden all your pains and troubles from me. I don't worry the less because of it; on the contrary."[14]

Colette's immediate excuse was a new play: a speaking role in *Le Crin*, by Sacha Guitry, which would pay her, she told Sido, forty francs a night. It closed after a brief run, and on November 1, she and Wague opened at the Apollo in a pantomime called *La Chair* (The Flesh), which they would take on tour very profitably for the next four years. The audiences who flocked to the show in Paris and the provinces had been promised a "sensation," and they got one. *La Chair* was the original bodice-ripper. It takes place in a smugglers' hut on the Austro-Hungarian border. Wague plays the smuggler; Colette his mistress, Yulka; and Christine Kerf (in drag), Yulka's lover. The smuggler discovers them, and in a paroxysm of fury, tears Yulka's shift from shoulder to thigh. At the sight of her naked breast (the left one), he prostrates himself at Yulka's feet. She ignores his supplications. Distraught, he nails his own hand to the table with his dagger. Yulka finds him bleeding, and goes mad. "How do you dare pose practically naked?"[15] Sido wondered.

The cartoonists had a field day with *La Chair*. So did the police.[16] So did Colette herself, who wrote an amusing sketch of its dress rehearsal for *La Vie parisienne*.[17] She describes the backstage smells of plaster and ammonia, the bored musicians doping the horses in the orchestra pit, the fat producer "who bestirs himself only [to inspect] his most 'expensive numbers.' " A nasty cold has put the male principal, the mime "W," in a combative mood. The sets are too dark, the costumes aren't ready, and the female star hasn't appeared yet. Finally she arrives, cold and tired from four hours on her feet at the fitter's and yearning "from the depths of her soul for a ham sandwich, or two—or three—with mustard."[18]

4

BETWEEN HER THEATRICAL ENGAGEMENTS and her sketches for *La Vie parisienne*, Colette still found time to ghostwrite for Willy. Sido mentions their project that autumn: "So you're working for Willy? What can I tell you . . . nothing's banal in your existence." In *My Apprenticeships*, Colette would recall that after a series of "menaces and lightning storms," Willy had written to her at the rue de Villejust to propose that she do twenty pages of landscapes for his new novel, and promised her a thousand francs. "A thousand pre-war francs; a thousand post-separation francs for twenty pages, when for four volumes of 'Claudine' . . . I thought I was dreaming."[19]

The novel was published during Colette's first run in *La Chair*. It was called *Un Petit Vieux bien propre* (*A Clean Little Old Man*). There aren't twenty pages' worth of landscapes in it, but there is a five-page letter from Claudine to Maugis, which alludes to *Retreat from Love*. "I've gotten Willy's book," Sido wrote Colette. "It's always more or less the same thing: plenty of filth, very well written." It bored her, and she only finished it two months later. Claudine's letter, she told her daughter, "is what's best in the book, although it's teeming with cleverness in Willy's style. . . . Whenever there's some letter of his in the books you write, or one of yours in his, it jars so that it has the effect on me of a hair in the soup."[20]

Perhaps to flatter Curnonsky, the principal ghost of *Un Petit Vieux*, Willy minimized Colette's contribution to it. Claudine's letter, he told him, was "a mosaic cleverly composed from old notes. . . . I pasted its pieces together like a torn-up banknote."[21] But then his generosity to her would prove to be an illusion, too.

Willy was in desperate financial straits that autumn, and Colette knew it. "Willy not rich?" Sido asks, incredulous. "So the Claudines aren't selling more than ever?" And she urged Colette to have her husband acknowledge in writing that Les Monts-Bouccons belonged to her. While letters went back and forth between Achille's notary in Châtillon and Willy's in Paris, his creditors were pursuing him in the courts. One debt alone was for 20,000 francs to a lender in Besançon, and it would never be repaid. The bailiffs were knocking at his door to repossess his art and furniture, and visiting his publishers to attach his contracts. Willy quickly sold his two race horses and fired his jockey, but he never paid off his trainer. The thousand francs he gave Colette was, she would discover with horror a year later, picked from her own pocket. On September 30, 1907, without his wife's knowledge, he had sold the copyright of *Claudine Married* to Vallette, its publisher, for 2,400 francs. Three weeks later he was at the offices of Ollendorff, dumping the copyrights of *Claudine at School, Claudine in Paris,* and *Claudine Takes Off*—books which had sold at least half a million copies and are (in French) still in print today—for 5,000 francs total. That December, Colette had to cancel a lecture on "the love letters of famous women" to appear at the office of a notary in Besançon. Willy had sold Les Monts-Bouccons "by order of the court," and he needed her signature on the transfer of title.

Why, Caradec asks, did Willy forfeit the Claudine copyrights for such a pittance, but not those to his other novels? Were they worthless? No. "Did he reason that Colette's debts to Redfern [the couture house] and others we don't know about should be covered" in this fashion? But Redfern never got paid. Was it vengeance "for her appropriation of *Retreat from Love*? Did he want to make their separation final and total by severing all his bonds with her, down to the books they wrote together?"[22] Perhaps. But then how can one explain the letter he writes Curnonsky five days before he visits Vallette: "Why am I suffering? In all stupidity because I'm so far from the one woman I could love completely. . . . I thought she was happy, at least I hoped so, and I *know* now that she's not, she writes as much with no hedging: 'Let's run far away together, just the two of us.' "²³ It would seem that Willy shared Colette's "monstrous innocence."

5

COLETTE WENT on the road in 1908, but not with her husband. Her life as a vagabond was beginning. For a month early that winter, she and Wague took *La Chair* to Nice and to Monte Carlo, where Missy joined them for a brief sojourn with Renée Vivien. On the eve of their departure, Sido wrote Colette one of her saddest, most plaintive letters: "It's gray, it's cold. I don't know if it's [the weather] . . . that gives me such black thoughts, but it's true I'm sad and I shouldn't write to you in this mood, but to whom can I speak about the state of my soul if it's not to you, to you dear self of mine, who knows me and loves me? Your brother adores me and would do anything to make me happy, but he's a man. . . . I'm far away from you. I never see you. Will my life end without my seeing any more of you?"²⁴

Colette left without visiting her mother. When she got to the Côte d'Azur, she sent her a lavish gift basket of fruit and flowers, and some photographs. Sido was cheered by the thought that her puppy was "blossoming in a delicious atmosphere, in a land of dreams." She was grateful to Renée for "spoiling" Colette, and surprised to discover, from the pictures, how young and pretty the poet was: "Good! I like that."

Sido's neediness increased with her infirmity, but there are only ever two kinds of sermons in her letters: pained reproaches for her daughter's reticence or absence, and anxious opinions about her health. There's scarcely a note of moral censure or disapproval in the entire correspondence. It's true that Sido constantly regrets Colette's acting career, though rarely because of its impropriety: it distracts her precious one from writing, and exposes her to "intercourse with people who aren't clean." She's constantly thankful for the marquise, and she tells Colette: "Missy is near you to clear your path of all the thorns which wound you. How grateful I am to her!" When she's not fondly commiserating with her daughter's lover about "our spoiled child," she's counseling Colette about eating, sleeping, her teeth, her knees, her hygiene, road safety, muscle fatigue, overwork, and keeping warm. Her support is otherwise unconditional, and her only judgments esthetic. "I never imagined you had the temperament [for acting] because you were always a bit inflexible, and for the stage you need so much suppleness, physical as well as moral, and I didn't see you with those qualities. You've limbered yourself up in both senses, it's a fact."[25]

In July, Colette and Missy were back at Le Crotoy. At the end of August, Colette was in Geneva to star in *Son premier voyage,* a play by Léon Xanrof. Willy told Curnonsky that he'd sent Meg along with her as an "English nurse. They'll be back in four days. Life is bizarroid."[26] But Colette doesn't mention Meg in the letter she wrote to Wague, reporting "(with a charming modesty) that I've just had a holy success. I wasn't expecting it, because for a long time, Willy and I have been personalities much disapproved of by the Swiss. The Protestant newspapers stuck to a reproachful silence but I don't give a damn about it. The audience . . . a love! and it's said the Genevans are cold and priggish, Lord! And then, I got the two biggest box offices of my life, and that's always a pleasure."[27]

Colette's correspondence with Wague from this period was published in a volume called *Letters from the Vagabond.* It projects the voice of a female as original and modern as Claudine: the slangy, tough, self-promoting voice of a young professional on the make. The note she sent to Wague from Le Crotoy in September of 1908 is typical:

> Tell me, do you have something really *good* in the pantomime department we could fix up right away? . . . We need something striking, that hasn't been seen too much, for the two of us and a third character *who's not too expensive.* I underline expensive because the deal will only be possible for the two of us with an undemanding partner. . . . I'm being pressed by different parties to take on acting engagements in a company or on tour . . . but I'm not such a dud that I want to give up the pantomime, *which I love.* Because it's rather odd, when I'm having success in a play, I'm suddenly overcome by the need to stop talking, to express my lines in gestures, in grimaces, in the rhythm of the dance. Funny, what?[28]

The acting job Colette refers to was nothing other than the chance to play Claudine at the Alcazar in Brussels. The 1902 play was to be revived there for fifteen shows that November. Sido was dismayed when she heard about this project. She'd seen Polaire, disliked the "low and vulgar" tone of her performance, and wondered if her daughter would be able to "glide over" without "insisting" on the louche aspects of the role.[29]

The critics, on the other hand, wondered if Colette could stand comparison with her predecessor, and apparently so did she. "The real tour de force, for me," she told a reporter from *Comoedia,* "will be to succeed the charming and unforgettable creator of the role, Polaire. She lived the character with such a girlish ardor, with such a graceful oddness, so imperiously, that Willy and I didn't have the courage or even the desire to guide her imagination."[30]

Colette reworked the script by Willy, Vayre, and Lugné-Poe to make the character more consonant with her fictional "prototype" but also, no doubt, to leave more of her own imprint on the dialogue. Missy chaperoned her protégée, paid for a three-star hotel, and watched discreetly from the shadows. Willy, less discreet, attended the dress rehearsal and some of the performances, and made "smart-ass remarks" backstage. "The troupe is good," Colette told Wague, "the direction's cute, it's raining, and my nose is full of dust. . . . Excellent publicity, portraits and flyers handed out on street to pedestrians . . . like the address of a dentist's office!"[31]

6

COLETTE WAS in Lyon a month later, playing Claudine at the Scala theater. She once again had a "great success," which she detailed in a tender and gossipy letter to Missy: "I had [an audience] determined to find the least grimace of your insufferable fake child adorable. So I camped it up, which is what it takes here. The gang was delighted." Her fellow actors, she continues, are sweet to her, but "between us, old ma Borelli [who was playing Mélie] is terribly hot for me, and I pretend oh so touchingly to misunderstand her. Little Verneil is the best Marcel we've ever had, a pretty boy, chic, queer, not stupid, quick, in short, very good." She then tells Missy that she's had a night full of bad dreams. She was fighting with a man and a waitress in a restaurant, and touched the cold blade of a knife. Missy was leaving on an ocean voyage, "and I saw the boat, and you were too pale, with eyes too dark. I woke up feverish, and it left me with a migraine."[32]

The director of the theater, she concludes, was so impressed with her receipts that he came to her dressing room after the performance to pay his respects, "the first time that this bloodhound with the sinister, false eyes has bothered himself about an artist." He wanted to hold the play over for another week, but she refused: "My best excuse—the only one that counts—is at rue Torricelli, and she has ashen hair and dark brown eyes which seem almost black."[33]

NUMBER 25 rue Torricelli was Colette's new address. Her pied-à-terre on the rue de Villejust had been demolished in September, and Missy, in the meantime, had bought and renovated a spacious house near the place des Ternes. She had arranged the upper duplex for herself and had made a private apartment for her mistress on the ground floor. They consulted a lawyer together the week they moved, to plan their wills. They asked him if they could legally name each other as beneficiaries.[34]

Colette's estate, of course, was negligible, and the making of her will a gesture that was, however heartfelt, without much substance. She had a share of the house in Saint-Sauveur, some furniture in storage with her mother, and the copyrights to the three books she had signed with her own name. Missy was entailing a considerable fortune, and they both knew it. In the words of Michel del Castillo: "One trait alone renders her character. . . . Missy gives with open hands. A generosity that could be considered mad, as is everything that transcends the norm. Money, certainly, but also pictures, furniture, jewels. . . . She gives compulsively, as if, persuaded that she can never be loved for herself, she must buy love's illusion."[35]

MISSY WOULD RUIN herself for love or its illusion, and she would die destitute, by her own hand, in 1944. In the autumn of 1908, however, it was Colette who feared destitution, and while there was nothing to suggest that Missy might desert her, she had an excuse for any morbid fears she might have been harboring about her protector's untimely death. Her sister, Juliette, had committed suicide on September 9, when she and Missy were at Le Crotoy, organizing their move and Colette's autumn schedule.

Sido's letters give the sinister and tragic details. Roché, she told Willy in response to an affectionate condolence letter, had tried to pretend that his wife died of natural causes. At first it was plausible enough: Juliette had been ill for a long time, losing quantities of blood, throwing up, refusing care. She ate and drank too much, and her legs were badly swollen. It turned out, however, that she had died from an overdose of aconite, an extremely toxic plant whose roots were used as a heart medication in minute quantities. Roché vehemently denied to Sido that he'd ever prescribed aconite for Juliette, brandishing the key to his dispensary. "He's lying, alas," Sido told Colette. "Juliette wrote to me about it."[36]

In a tirade whose irony probably wasn't lost on Willy, Sido explained that her daughter had suffered and died "from not being loved by her boor of a husband. Oh, how different we were, and in her place, I would have sent [him] packing! But no, she wanted to be cherished by him."[37]

Sido begged Colette to come soon and not to forget her mourning clothes, but neither Colette, who hated funerals, nor Achille, who hated Roché, attended the burial. "I'm not ill, my treasure," she reassured her daughter on September 25, "but I'm sad all the same. Come on, she killed herself. . . . Achille is so sweet to me, but I avoid showing him my grief, and it's always been like that, for many years! I've always avoided saddening all of you with my worries on the subject of the management of our affairs by your father, and also the pain of his death. But these are repeated and painful blows to my courage, which has been weakened."[38]

7

By Christmas, Colette was settled in her new apartment. The last day of the old year, 1908, brought something rare to Paris: snow. It came down all night, and it was still falling "like a chenille veil," "crisp as taffeta underfoot," "powdery and vanilla" on the tongue, when Colette and her dogs went out to play "like three madwomen" in the deserted streets.[39]

They came in at dusk to doze by the hearth. "Here I am again," writes Colette, "facing my fire, my solitude, and myself." The snowfall and the dying of a tumultuous year made her pensive, and she gave herself over to reveries of seasons past, "the form of the years," "the winters of my childhood." When she roused herself, she found her shepherd bitch "steaming like a footbath" at her feet, the bulldog and the gray cat sleeping, and she was "astonished," she writes, "to have changed and aged while I was dreaming."

There are many suicides in Colette's work—a fact she never noticed, she told a friend in the 1930s, until it was pointed out to her by a reader. Juliette's isn't among them, but it sharpened her consciousness of mortality. Sitting by the fire that New Year's Day, she held up her hand mirror and found, in the "dark water of the glass," the first fine "claw marks" of age. What makes them so poignant to her in the French sense of the word—*poindre* means to pierce—was that she could still see beyond them to the "adorable," "velvety," "elastic," "rosy girl" who was gone forever.

"You have to get old," Colette told herself then, with more bravura than conviction, trying—as she often did—to disarm an unpleasant truth by stating it. She was three weeks shy of thirty-six: a youthful woman no longer young by the standards of her age and facing the mortality of her beauty. "Don't cry," she commands, "don't clasp your hands in prayer, don't rebel: you have to get old. Repeat the words to yourself, not as a howl of despair but as the boarding call to a necessary departure." Colette goes on to unwind the imaginary "ribbon" of a life well lived. After addressing a series of lyrical, stoic blandishments to herself—the kind of sentences that would make her wince as a more seasoned writer—she concludes: "If you haven't lost your hair, left your teeth behind you one by one, nor your spent limbs; if the dust of eternity hasn't, in the final hour, blinded your eyes to the wondrous light—and if, at the end, you hold a loved hand in your own—then lie down smiling, go to sleep, happy one, go to sleep, lucky one."[40]

Colette would die at eighty-one. At the end, her supple dancer's legs had failed her. She wore false teeth, could barely see, and she was deaf, but she held the hand of the man who loved her. As it happened, she had, practically to the final hour, kept her head, which is not, curiously enough, on her departure checklist. Braced against physical disintegration—the loss of beauty, sensual acuity, appetite, strength—Colette forgets or omits to fear the loss of her mental powers. Productive to the end, and secure in that aspect of her integrity, she would be remarkable among modern writers—perhaps the great women in particular—for a sense of self not vested in her mind.

CHAPTER 19

1

C OLETTE CELEBRATED her thirty-sixth birthday in rehearsal for a play she had written as her own star vehicle. *En camarades* opened on February 5, 1909, at the Comédie-Royale. There are fragments of an early draft in the notebooks that contain *Retreat from Love*, suggesting that the idea for the work dates from 1906. In his earliest incarnation, the hero of *En camarades* was called Renaud. In the final version, he became Max—the name her intimates gave to Missy.

En camarades was conceived as a curtain-raiser, specifically perhaps for *Claudine*, and Colette was disappointed when the producers wouldn't mount it in Brussels. This two-act bedroom farce features an insouciant Parisian couple with an open marriage. Max and Fanchette pretend to the world and to each other that they're the best of pals *(camarades)*. Their motto, Max tells his would-be mistress, a society woman named Marthe,[1] is "Do what you like, me too . . . and then at night, when we go beddy-bye, we tell each other everything."[2] While Max tries to seduce Marthe in the salon, Fanchette is next door "playing with her Kid." The Kid proves to be a strapping young *innamorato*. As the curtain falls, the two couples have both fixed rendezvous for the next day.

Fanchette has been curious to see the Kid's garçonnière, but when he makes a pass at her there, she's furious at having been so "misunderstood." The Kid reproaches her hypocrisy. "Admit that it's odd to hear you speak of Duty and Morality with capital letters! You, the child of nature, the liberated little wife . . ."

"Do you understand what I felt just now?" Fanchette replies. "A chain, a gentle chain whose weight I'd never noticed before, but which . . . presses against your flesh when you stray too far from the stake it's attached to."

"Little slave!" he exclaims.

"Voluntary slave!" she counters. "Oh, Max would understand me."

His desire frustrated and his vanity wounded, the Kid tells her that Max is meeting his mistress as they speak. He then bursts into tears. The doorbell rings—it's Max, of course—transformed into an ordinary, jealous husband. Fanchette shoves the Kid into his bedroom and opens the door to her husband. The couple trade outraged reproaches that console and reconcile them, and they leave arm in arm, she exacting a vow of love in the form most congenial to Colette: his scolding, vigilance, and domination.

2

THE REVIEWS OF *En camarades* were mixed. Léon Blum, writing in *Comoedia,* noted that the work was "wild, artless, and unpolished"—not Colette's best effort. But he took the occasion to praise her talents both as an actress and as a "true writer."[3] Sido, who hadn't seen the play, rushed to concur with Adolphe Brisson, of *Le Temps,* that Colette's diction was stilted, that she rolled her *r*'s like an actor in an old melodrama, and that her bearing was inexpressive. "Isn't that what I told you when you announced to me that you were going on the stage? Be that as it may. It's good that he notices your weaknesses: that way one pays attention to them and profits from criticism."[4]

While the comic version of Colette's marriage was ending happily every night on a Paris stage, her actual relations with Willy were deteriorating rapidly. As late as that autumn they had been making plans to collaborate on a new *Claudine*—a play Colette promised she could "bash out in two months" if he gave her an outline. Willy asked Curnonsky for the outline, but either he or Colette didn't like it. He also had an idea for a fifth *Claudine,* which he still hoped Colette might write, in which Claudine meets Willette Collie. Nothing came of it. But she did work on a play for him, *La Petite Jasmine,* which became the subject of a new dispute.

Shortly before Christmas, when Colette left Paris for Lyon to perform *Claudine* at La Scala, Willy drove her to the station, so it would appear that they were still on speaking terms. "Shit! Shit! Shit!" he wrote to Curnonsky. "I'm bored when she's not here. I don't have a cent to go with her. Meg is charming, but . . ."[5]

Meg was charming—not least because Willy was living on her earnings. But he was discovering that the feistier Colette became, the more notice her work received, the greater her resistance to his bullying, the more he clung to her. He wrote "neurotic" letters claiming he couldn't sleep, couldn't eat, "had appendicitis, meningitis, God knows what else," while she heard from his secretary that "he's eating like a hog, seeing all his women regularly, getting fatter, and is in perfect health."[6]

Willy had taken to blaming Missy for Colette's fits of rage. "She forbade my wife to see me," he would tell a friend. "Be very wary, I beg you," Colette wrote to Missy from Lyon, of *"cet individu capable de tout"*—of this individual capable of anything.[7] Her warning seems to have come in response to an angry exchange between Willy and the marquise in her drawing room, for which Willy would apologize—changing his tack, as he did periodically, from belligerence to contrition:

> My dear Max, I understand, better late than never, that you might have been hurt by the tone, which was doubtless too harsh, that I took with you, forgetting that I was speaking with a woman. . . . The next day I had, with Tétette . . . a rather painful discussion in the course of which she expressed the desire never to set eyes on me again! That is a sorrow for me that you will understand better than she does, and which adds its weight to the shitload of troubles (excuse me) already besetting me. I'm not in the habit of begging, and I'm not going to start at forty-eight. One thing, though; since she's with you, I ask you not to stir up her feelings against me. . . . Let her not be too aggressive with a man who has been crazier than wicked and whom you used to call, Your friend, Willy.[8]

But Missy was as implacable as Colette was yielding. That January, she wrote to Willy demanding that he acknowledge Colette as the true author of the *Claudine*s. He was willing, he replied, although he deplored that "in refusing to add a new book to this famous series, she deprived [me] of an excellent pretext for officially proclaiming the truth."[9]

JACQUES GAUTHIER-VILLARS, home from college for the holidays, was surprised and worried to discover that the relations between his father and stepmother had cooled so dramatically. They both avoided his questions, he told Caradec, and no one in their entourage would or could explain to him what had happened. "I didn't learn anything except that each of them accused the other of causing the rift."[10]

The cause of the rift, however, is not obscure. On February 25, Colette discovered the theft of her manuscripts that had occurred fifteen months before. "Today," she wrote to Willy, "I saw someone from Ollendorff. Is it true, is it possible, that all the *Claudine*s and the two *Minne*s are now the property of their publishers? Is it possible that all of them have been lost forever to you and to me? In the name of heaven, tell me the truth for once. Is it possible that these books, which are so dear to me, are lost forever?"[11]

Confiding this news to her friend Léon Hamel, Colette would add that, "given the conditions under which [Willy] gave away the four *Claudine*s, one has to say that he . . . wanted to assure himself that forever, even after his death, I would never regain possession of those books which are mine. I was profoundly overwhelmed, dear friend, and I told him so. He responded to my cry of despair with a cold letter, almost menacing, and I think that after the necessary elucidation which will take place after his return from Monte Carlo (day after next), everything will be finished between us."[12]

The elucidation was proffered, but the definitive break was briefly postponed. To forestall a lawsuit, Willy signed a document Colette had drafted on her own stationery, and in her own hand, which stated: "As the collaboration between Willy and Colette has ended, it becomes necessary to give each partner his due portion and to replace the single name on these volumes by the signature: Willy and Colette Willy. Reasons that are purely typographical have determined that my name be placed before that of Colette Willy, while literary and other reasons would have dictated that her name come first."[13]

That March, they submitted this document to their publishers with a note in which Colette informs Vallette that after a two-hour discussion, she and Willy had reached an agreement about the *Claudine*s which would give her the "purely honorific" advantage of adding her name to them, but from which he stood to profit "from the curiosity that the new signature might provoke."[14] Ollendorff received a similar notice.[15] At the same time, Willy wrote to the French Authors' Guild, acknowledging Colette's contributions to *La Petite Jasmine* (which had yet to be produced) and agreeing to cede her half of the eventual royalties. She'd had to extort this concession by refusing to return the manuscript until he made it.

From then on, as Caradec puts it, "things went fast." On March 5, Sido protests to Colette: "But my darling Minet, I don't remember ever advising you to *go back* to Willy! . . . You'd do well to beware of him, because I think he's capable of base behavior. Will you ask for a divorce? That's what I advised you."[16]

Sido now had two villainous sons-in-law to deplore, which she does with all the relish, bias, loyalty, and maternal ferocity native to her character.

April 3: "I fear Willy for you. He knows the value of what he's lost, and he won't resolve himself easily to not having any authority over [you]. So ask for a divorce."

June 2: "I knew from the morning after your marriage how unworthy he was of you."

July 12: "Between [Willy] and me there was always a tacit agreement not to overstep the bounds of a willed civility. I knew with whom I was dealing the morning after my visit to the rue Jacob."

July 20: "Received . . . *Claudine Married*. It has Willy's notice about your collaboration, but it's anodine. . . . You've been terribly duped by this vile and hateful creature, and I suffer for you. What I wish for, my treasure, is that you could smash him to pieces in one of your own works."[17]

That August, Willy asked Curnonsky, who was going to visit Colette's impresario, Baret, in Dieppe, "to lead the conversation, if you can, to the Willy-Colette breakup, and to find out what her version of it is."[18] He would find out soon enough. Colette, at Le Crotoy with Missy, had taken Sido's wish to heart, and on August 31, 1909, she had started to write *The Vagabond*.

3

"THE MUSIC HALL," writes Colette, " . . . made me . . . a tough and honest little businesswoman. It's a profession which the least gifted of women learns quickly, when her freedom and her life depend on it."[19] Her life as a vagabond had exposed Colette to poverty as she had never known it, and awakened her social conscience. Her sketches of music-hall life document the constant hunger of her fellow artistes, the injuries which disable them and which the impresarios won't pay for; the abortions hastily financed by passing the hat backstage and presenting it to a teenager already bleeding through the straw of her mattress in a tenement. Theirs is a realm of poignant, promiscuous, and brief youth; of abusive husbands; of bad lungs and calloused hands; of laddered stockings where a torn costume or the sickness of a child earn punitive fines. It's a "world of women where sadness rose and fell like a barometer" and happiness is to eat one's fill.

But her life as a vagabond also awakened Colette's sense of enterprise. She writes to Wague about "a very big deal" for a movie which she will not only act in, but which Missy will produce: "She'll keep the negative and sell the prints."[20] Nothing would come of it, but early in the winter of 1909, Colette embarked on another business—a surprising turn, though not so strange considering her lifelong passion for acquiring houses: she was brokering suburban real estate. Sido was concerned: "You frighten me a bit with your famous deals with the Jews,"[21] she writes. "Open your eyes! Don't let yourself be swindled by these Israelites."[22] That summer, "by a stroke of unexpected luck, and thanks to Missy's intervention," the business was concluded, and Colette told Hamel that they were at last "going to profit from our work. You would be pleased with your capitalist, your capitalists," she concludes.[23] She then left Paris for Marseille, to perform *La Chair*.

THE ONE-NIGHT STAND takes on new meaning when one considers that in the spring of 1909, Colette performed in thirty-two French cities in thirty-two days. She thrived on the bohemian camaraderie of this life, its rigor, and even its hardship. She loved the rhythm of the train and the variety of landscape and weather changing outside her window. She complained about her lodgings when they were shabby but reveled in their charm when they were rustic or grand. She slept very little and ate when she could, slugging down a cup of coffee at the station buffet before rushing off to rehearsal, or gorging on the *plat du jour* at a waterfront bistro, still open at midnight when she finished a performance. "We've been on the move since five this morning," she told her mother. "We're very valiant. It's a question of training."[24]

Colette was not yet so jaded (or so self-critical) that she wasn't thrilled by a full house or a rave review in a small-town paper, and she never tires of or disdains the enthusiasm of her provincial audiences. "They take part in the action," she wrote to Sido from Bordeaux: "They treated Wague like a scoundrel, a cuckold, and a voyeur because he wanted to harm me when he surprised me in the arms of my lover! . . . And in the love scenes, the noise of kisses echoed in the hall, and of filthy remarks shouted in lilting accents, and they made a monstrous scene the other night, but in the good sense. The sun flooded my dressing room, which didn't have a shade or a curtain, it was about a hundred degrees in there. I can't complain . . . I'm a bit beat, that's all."[25]

"Tired but content": that is the refrain that runs through the postcards she sent Sido from every town she stopped in. "More than a hundred yellowing cards," writes Michel del Castillo, "showing the most predictable of scenes, obviously chosen to inspire daydreams in a mother confined to her garden and her animals." Hundreds, too, of studio and publicity portraits, "showing [Colette] in majestic, stylized, provocative, or dubiously tasteful poses. . . . You can smile, if you like, or feel moved by these theatrical ambitions. For me," he concludes, "it's the woman I admire, her unshakable courage, her tenacious will to escape the trap. Is she mistaken about herself? It doesn't matter."[26]

4

COLETTE WROTE most of *The Vagabond* on the road: in hotel rooms, backstage between numbers, using her makeup case as a portable writing table on the train. At the beginning of 1910, she took *La Chair* to Brussels, then to Grenoble and Nice. In April, she left on the second major tour organized by Baret—another thirty cities in thirty days. Missy was with her. "Missy takes care of everything." "I'm feeling marvelous thanks to you know who." "Missy's courage? It's unflagging." "Missy put me to sleep when we got here." "Missy envelops me in that vigilant silence I find so moving." "Missy is a wonderful companion. . . . Obviously there are moments when I think it would be nice to plant lettuces with her in the morning sun, but they're rare moments."[27] And Missy invariably adds a little postscript: "Don't worry about the child. She's fine. Regards from Max."

When Missy wasn't there, Colette wrote to her almost daily. "I rest by chatting to you, my beloved." "I love you, darling. I'm nothing but a jerk, a hateful creature." "I'm not up to snuff, because of nerves, no doubt; I started crying like an idiot because I'm alone and will be for so long." "I love you, my beloved, and I am your insufferable fake child." "Happily for me, Lord! I have the luck to love you."[28] "I'm stamping the ground to make time go faster. . . . You're my Raison-d'être."[29]

But toward the end of October, a new name enters their correspondence, or rather a familiar name in an offstage context. "The Kid has just gone off," Colette tells Missy from Nice, where she's playing Claudine. "He left an *insane* letter and a basket of flowers. I can't complain about him."[30]

The Kid was Auguste Hériot, a twenty-four-year-old army officer, playboy, amateur boxer, backstage groupie, and heir to a great department store fortune, the Magasins du Louvre. He had been the lover of Polaire and Liane de Pougy before pursuing Colette. Having attended most of her performances in Paris, he had followed her tour from town to town, sending her anonymous notes and flowers. Their introduction seems to have taken place in the autumn of 1908: Colette writes to Missy from Bordeaux that the manager of the hotel where she is staying has introduced her to a man who proves to be "none other than my famous admirer": "I must say to his credit that he didn't have the gall to speak to me about the florist-messenger. He goes to the theater every night, he says, and he's a man one can chat with. I granted him half an hour of conversation—during lunch! Not after, you should know. He put his motorcar at my disposal, and I profited from it immediately by . . . going up to my room."[31]

Colette's Kid, like Fanchette's, is rich, handsome, well-bred, good-hearted, simple, smitten, and inferior; she treats him, too, with offhand affection; he also sits at her feet; his love is obsessive and adolescent—and in declaring himself, he asks for nothing better than to be treated like a "pet dog." Like so many other characters in her fiction, Colette had imagined Hériot before she met him. His is the "young flesh" Annie warns Claudine about, and which she contemplates with serene relish at the end of *Retreat from Love*.[32]

Her first much younger lover is a revelation no middle-aged woman whose senses have been numbed by rejection can ever forget. It is she who holds the power and maintains the detachment, at least in the beginning, and that novel inequality is as bracing—and as erotic—as the passion. If we believe Colette (and there's no reason to doubt her), Hériot was only the second man she had slept with, and although she never returned his love, it was a balm. His ardor and his athletic beauty were luxuries she had never known. The degree to which she prizes them in her fiction, and for the rest of her life, suggests what a potent high they were. "Ouf!" she writes in *The Vagabond.* "This big noodle of a man has turned off the blackness. It's always like that."[33] Desire is her antidote for depression.

In comparison to *The Vagabond,* the *Claudine*s are, for the most part, works of literary virtuosity, made to measure. This is literature, and it adheres to a standard of spiritual truthfulness that was new for Colette. Her first-person voice, sensuous and worldly, resounds with a radically modern independence. Renée Néré [34] is a woman trying to invent a new way of life. Acting is an escape from the claustrophobia of the self. Writing fiction assuages her melancholy: "It's only in sorrow that a woman is able to overcome her mediocrity."[35] She proudly lives hand to mouth on her music-hall wages, and becomes a realist about money in the process. She examines her addictions to men and love with amused detachment, and flirts, alternately, with abstinence and temptation. She is marvelously wry on the tonic and the toxic aspects of solitude. Is there love without complete submission and loss of identity? Is freedom worth the loneliness that pays for it? Those are the questions that Renée asks in this novel, and that, indeed, Colette explores for the rest of her life as a writer.

Renée, like her creator, is a supple and beautiful woman in her thirties who looks much younger. Like Colette, she has divorced a mendacious, tyrannical, philandering husband—the society painter Taillandy. She is no longer received in the salons of Paris except to entertain there, which she does, occasionally, because she badly needs the money.

Men throw themselves at Renée. It was said of the Comédie-Française that it was the whorehouse for the Jockey Club, and a music-hall dancer of that era was fair game for the sort of missive that Renée quotes to her reader in Part One: "Madame: I was in the first row of the orchestra. Your talents as a mime invite me to believe that you possess other talents yet more special and beguiling. Give me the pleasure of inviting you to dine."

One of these admirers is more persistent and sincere and less objectionable than the others. He has a faintly ridiculous name, Maxime Dufferein-Chautel, and Renée calls him the Big Noodle. Like Hériot, he is the heir to a department store fortune. Renée treats him with a seductive contempt and does her best to disillusion him about herself, but to no avail. He assiduously woos her,

her dog, Fossette, and her cynical music-hall comrades. " 'Tell me frankly, Renée, is it repulsive, indifferent, or vaguely agreable to you that I'm in love with you?' . . . Imitating his simplicity, I boldly respond, 'I have absolutely no idea.' "

Renée teases Maxime, and herself, with a passion she won't avow or deny. His tenderness finally overcomes her fear of surrender, and they become lovers. He proposes marriage, and she is horrified at how deliciously proprietary his love is—how bourgeois. He tells her he will wait for her to love him back. She scoffs at the clichés, but she also vacillates. She seeks wisdom from her disillusioned, bohemian friends. They don't tell her what she wants to hear, that love is rubbish and marriage the trap she has known it to be.

If *The Vagabond* is famous for Colette's refusal to romanticize sexual pleasure and call it love, it is also famous for her unsentimental though intimate portrait of the provincial music halls she toured and the troupers who worked them. It's a world of gallant narcissists—of orphans struggling to care for themselves and one another. The gaiety of the theaters and the solidarity among the performers is opposed to their sordid, hungry, sometimes violent lives and their quixotic, steamy, usually doomed loves. Her little cameos of misery are paradoxically exquisite.

On the road with her touring company, Renée writes to Maxime. Her sentiments are lavish and not entirely sincere. But her letters are as much an inconclusive dialogue with herself as with the Noodle. Does she love him? Can she love him without losing herself? The answer is no—but Renée's no, like Colette's to Hériot's importuning, is not quite what it seems. Neither the heroine nor the author admits—perhaps doesn't perceive—that she cannot love him *because* she cannot lose herself in him: he's too slavish and weak, too "inferior" to merge with. She can't transform him into a master, which is to say, into a parent.

IT HAS NEVER, I think, been noted that there was another, more shadowy model for Maxime: a rich young dandy and erotomane, this one with literary pretensions, who stalked the margins of Colette's life and who wrote a rancorous kiss-and-tell memoir of their "friendship." Sylvain Bonmariage is a bad dream of a biographer: a rejected suitor with privileged information all too eager to dish the dirt on his subject in the name of truth, unconsciously jealous of Colette's talent and fame, who believes himself to be irreproachably high-minded. As a witness, Bonmariage is pathetically easy to discredit. He was an opium and cocaine addict, a snob, a misogynist, a pornographer, a reactionary, an anti-Semite, and a lifelong partisan of Willy's. He was also, paradoxically, a naively romantic prig, easy to shock, and so blind to the contradictions in his own self-presentation (he's a vulgarian posing as a sexual philosopher and a gossip yearning for intellectual respectability) that he becomes, by accident, more engaging than any character he could ever have created by intention. "No one can contest the truth of my testimony," proclaims Bonmariage, and in a sense, he's right. His judgment is so biased that it achieves a kind of comic transparency. To enhance his own credibility, he tries to do Colette justice—allowing her strengths and virtues as he sees them— and there are some flashes of genuine insight in his writing. Ultimately, he performs a useful service to Colette and her biographers. His fixation with her acts, ironically, as a poultice on his own narrative, drawing the truth out, and with it, an impression of Colette's lucidity and her sense of humor.

Every time Bonmariage quotes one of Colette's good-natured replies to one of his long-winded soliloquies on love or morality, her charm increases. She was never interested in drugs, he tells us. Why? "Their formidable spirituality had nothing to attract this woman deprived of any spiritual feeling, who never felt any need to explore it." She asks him, however, "to define the allures of 'my vice' for her" so she could understand them. He does so in a rambling little lecture, which he reprints in its entirety, giving a nutshell history of the drug trade, "the Chinese soul," and the "sublime hours" he passes stoned, "which beautify one's thoughts." Colette reads this discourse "solemnly . . . reflects a moment," and tells him: "Words, nothing but empty words. It's a vacuum. It's for these words which correspond to nothing that you degrade yourself and constipate yourself and poison yourself and kill yourself. If I were your mother, my little kid, what a spanking you'd get!"[36]

Bonmariage was an aspiring writer when he met Willy, around 1905. His rich father disapproved of his "vocation"; Willy helped charm the old man and launch the son's career, and in the process, Bonmariage transferred his filial devotion to his mentor. With it, there was a poisonous dose of oedipal rivalry. The very title of his memoir, *Willy, Colette and Me,* is an attempt to cohabitate with this couple who obsessed him. He came as close as he could, eventually marrying Willy's last mistress and caretaker, Madeleine de Swarte, having tried and failed to carry off Colette.

Bonmariage, like Hériot and like Maxime, had proposed to "rescue" the Vagabond from her ignoble and insecure stage career, which he had nonetheless followed avidly. He never missed a performance of *Pan*, he says, and he would haunt the stage door and the backstage corridors, "intoxicated" by the "animal smell" of Colette's sweat when she returned to her dressing room. One day he barged into her flat and told her that they had to speak "seriously." She was alone and penniless, he began, while he had an independent income and "three lovely rooms near the Bois. . . . Besides which, you know I love you. Let's unite our lives. You'll leave the stage . . . we'll work. I'll watch over you. . . . I love you so much that you'll end up loving me. What do you say?"

Colette, the reader infers, was stupefied:

> She stared at me, silent, lost, without seeming to understand me. . . . I interpreted this emotion as an avowal. A twitch of her shoulders made me think that she was about to open her arms to me. I threw myself at her . . . crushing her breasts and lips to hold them tight against me with a savage frenzy. . . . I was stronger than she was . . . we fell backwards on the bed. . . . I thought that the world seemed to dissolve in vertigo. . . . We were immobile, silent, stuck together.
>
> [And then, he continues:] Colette . . . did what was necessary to assure herself of the extreme tension of the state in which I found myself. . . . The roles changed. Colette, with all her femininity, had me at her mercy. . . . "So now that you've calmed down, let's head for Marly [for dinner], and we'll have a nice evening as two friends."³⁷

Bonmariage was hard to discourage, and the funniest scene in his memoir—one of the most endearing of his would-be damning cameos—takes place in Colette's hotel room in Brussels. She is there to play Paniska. "Knowing her to be alone," he bursts in on her at nine in the morning. Only her gnarly dancer's foot protrudes from beneath the bedclothes. "I surprised myself by wondering why I wasn't resolved to assault this agile and muscled body, this hot flesh. . . . Colette seemed for that matter to have foreseen this attack. She had pulled the sheets up to her chin, and only the expressive features of her shining, ironic face emerged from the linen, along with that terrible, disappointing foot."

Suddenly, Colette declared she was getting up. "She threw the sheets back, jumped forth like a young jaguar, and rose up naked before me. I was astounded." Before she took "refuge" behind a screen, Bonmariage caught a glimpse of her "superb bust, her breasts barely fallen," but also of her "heavy thighs," her "boxer's loins," and her "enormous, flat behind." While he "assuages" his disappointment with a cigarette, the reader can hear Colette thinking fast to herself: how do I get rid of this jerk? And she finds a way.

"I jumped, suddenly, at the sound of a bursting tire. Colette laughs and announces: 'Fire one.' A new laugh and a new sound: 'Fire two.' . . . Then the same thing: 'Fire three.' Finally, in a burst of hilarity: 'It's stronger than I am. The pleasure of seeing you again! . . . Fire four.' I didn't need a fifth fart," Bonmariage concludes, "to be completely disgusted"³⁸—unfortunately, not for good.

5

FROM THE DAY she began *The Vagabond*, Colette experienced an inner resistance to the work which was new for her. "I'm not starting it without anxiety, I confess," she told Hamel, "and it makes me peevish and nervous."[39] She had contracted with Charles Saglio, editor of *La Vie parisienne*, to serialize the novel, but in February of the new year, she asked him to retract his announcement of its "imminent publication" and to postpone the first installment until May: "It's simply because I've just reread what I've done . . . and realized what's missing and what has to be changed. . . . I want to give you nothing less than a finished manuscript as worthy of you as of me."[40]

The novel began running on May 21, in twenty weekly installments. On June 4, part three was published, and Willy read, for the first time, Colette's portrait of "Taillandy." One understands why writing *The Vagabond* made her so nervous. She had to fear not only Willy's retribution—and it came soon enough—but the exposure of her own "long, cowardly, and complete complacence" in the face of his domination. One might compare those first ten pages on Taillandy to Kafka's letter to his father. They, too, are an act of parricide, inspired by abandonment, artful and subversive but passionately sincere, thrilling to read in their virtuosity, excruciating in their rawness—and they exalt the tyrant's potency even as they denigrate him.

The persuasiveness of Taillandy as a character forever castrates his avatars: the "empty bubble" of Renaud, the "indulgent papa" of the *Claudines*, the pal of *En camarades*. Colette strips the living Willy of his charm like an expert chef—too inured to weep—peeling an onion. He stands exposed to the world as the liar, the cynic, the sadist, the adulterer, the thief, and the artistic fake that Colette, in 1910 and forever after, believed him to be. "My ex-husband? You all know him." No they didn't, but now they would.

BELLE PLAGE, where Missy and Colette had spent part of every summer since 1905, was, as Herbert Lottmann cheerfully observes, "the world's ugliest" holiday villa,[41] a red and white brick box with gingerbread trim, a scrawny backyard, and an apron of rocky beach, which stood beside its equally hideous neighbors. The sea at Le Crotoy was often stormy, and the weather temperamental. Sido's letters commiserate with Colette about the rain as often as they express her envy of the "fine storms" for which she and Missy have a front-row seat: "You've inherited my tastes, beloved treasure.

You love cataclysms, the sound of the wind . . . beautiful trees, rivers, the ocean. I will die without ever being sated by so much splendor."[42]

That summer of 1910, the two lovers went "prospecting" by car for something more suitable and private, with a finer beach. By the autumn they had found it: an estate in Brittany, between Cancale and Saint-Malo; twenty acres, a "dream house" on the crest of a hill above a cove, protected by the dunes. Missy paid for Rozven but deeded it to Colette. She spent the next year making it habitable, by which time their love affair was over.

CHAPTER 20

1

*I*T OFTEN HAPPENS in Colette's life that what she writes comes to pass, and *The Vagabond* incited Willy to behave like the scoundrel she had portrayed. He immediately announced to the press that he would publish a novel called *Sidonie: or The Perverted Peasant*. Sido was anxious, Achille considered legal action, but the book was never written. That November, however, Meg signed her name to *Les Imprudences de Peggy*, "translated" by Willy.

Peggy is an English orphan raised by a nasty French aunt named Sidonie-Gabrielle-Anastasie. She describes her boarding-school love affairs to a smitten French novelist named Robert Parville, Willy's latest alter ego. He, in turn, confides in her about the ex-wife of his "poor friend Taillandy," a lesbian named Vivette Wailly. Against the advice of his friends, Taillandy tried to make an honest woman of this "intelligent and shrewd little country girl, expiring from poverty and unmarriageable in her own province since the day she decamped from her father's house to work for a music professor in Auxerre."

Vivette, he continues, tolerated Taillandy's affairs because she was afraid that childbirth would spoil her figure, and because she preferred, among other "priestesses of Sappho," "an old morphine addict who dressed like a man, the baroness de Louviers."

"Your friend divorced her, I hope?" asks Peggy.

"Not right away. The remains of a cowardly affection held him back."

"Didn't he feel contempt for her?"

"Yes, but he had always felt contempt for her, even in the days of his wildest passion."

Taillandy, Parville continues, leaves Vivette for a much younger woman, "more beloved than she ever was," and Vivette's "injured pride inspires the most ignoble revenges:

> with the help of a former secretary of her husband's, a hypocritical little bugger who wore the baroness's old suits, she stole the letters—and the furniture—of Taillandy, she accused him of having poisoned one of his mistresses, she succeeded . . . in dragging his name through the mud in a scandalous lawsuit. . . . Finally, triumphant, pacified, she retired to her château in Brittany, the gift of the ancient baroness . . . who passed the evenings with Vivette smoking cigars and getting drunk on chartreuse."
>
> "The story ends there?"
>
> "No . . . it becomes a theater piece. . . . Everyone thought the husband had resigned himself, and perhaps he thought so too, cradled by the childish tenderness of the English girl who loved him. . . . One evil morning he entered, through the front door . . . the château where the two friends were living and coldly shot each one in the head."
>
> "Was he hanged?"
>
> "Not even guillotined. He had the means, in the chamber of his revolver, to end this melodrama. The only precaution he took, before pressing the barrel to his forehead, was to move far enough away so that his body wouldn't fall on the corpses of the detested couple. He had always conserved an old drop of romanticism."[1]

Willy's fury wasn't spent yet. He published another novel of vengeance in 1911, *Lélie, the Opium Smoker,* ghostwritten by Toulet, "who had been Colette's friend and really must have needed the money," writes Pichois, "to lend himself to such a dirty piece of business."[2] *Lélie* parodies the lyricism of *Tendrils,* the patois of the *Claudine*s, and caricatures Colette (here called Gabrielle-Bastienne de Rozven-Saint-Sauveur) as a predatory dyke of forty gone to seed, with a fat behind and "a childish pout worked on assiduously in front of the mirror."[3] She was beside herself with rage, and one can only imagine how she received the "Machiavellian" letter that Willy drafted in Curnonsky's name, inviting him to remind Colette that "if [your husband] hates you to such a point, he must have loved you very much."[4]

THE GAUTHIER-VILLARS' DIVORCE became final on June 21, 1910. Colette was awarded a thousand francs a year in alimony.[5] The betrayals described in *Peggy* were unfolding, although with quite a different color from

Colette's perspective. Willy's cook and his secretary Paul Barlet did both desert him to go and live with Missy and Colette.[6] Before he left, Barlet rescued the manuscripts of *Claudine Married* and *Claudine Takes Off* from Willy's desk and returned them to their rightful owner, earning her gratitude and Willy's enmity. Colette and Willy then proceeded to quarrel bitterly over some furniture. Colette claimed she had left it with him in exchange for a monthly storage fee. He claimed he had put it in her name only to avoid its seizure, a subterfuge she had agreed to, and that she was now trying to steal it. But these accusations were petty compared to the scandal of Mme de Serres—a much graver and more sordid affair, documented by letters which Barlet may indeed have purloined from Willy, and by a dossier which Colette prepared for the plaintiff's lawyer.

Mme de Serres, Liette to her intimates, was a mistress whom Willy had discarded, having borrowed her features for the character of Marthe Payet in the *Claudine*s. She was married to his friend the composer Louis de Serres, and she had "confided" or "loaned" to Willy—the distinction would become important—a large sum of money that he was supposed to have invested in the firm of Gauthier-Villars, but which he in fact squandered elsewhere, concealing the embezzlement for a while, at least, by making interest payments on the principal.

Colette learned about this affair after their separation but while she was still on cordial, even intimate terms with her husband. According to Willy, Liette had virtually forced herself on him. Out of hatred for Colette, Willy claimed, she had invented a regiment of lovers for her rival, making such a convincing case for Colette's infidelity that he had begun to give it credence and to think seriously about divorce.

Willy seems to have dumped Liette definitely in 1908, and she promptly demanded the repayment of her principal. Willy was desperate: he had committed a serious fraud, and if she still had their correspondence, it could send him to prison. He had, according to Colette's deposition, tried to enlist her help, seductively at first, then menacingly, in blackmailing Mme de Serres. He had shown her Liette's love letters, which were not, she adds, particularly incriminating,[7] but warm enough to be extremely embarrassing. Willy wanted Colette to feign a betrayed spouse's rage and threaten Mme de Serres that she would take the letters to her husband.

Colette was, she admits, "extremely irritated" with the lady.[8] But she didn't like blackmail or fraud, she told the lawyer. What she did promise Willy was to beg Mme de Serres "to have pity on a man she had once loved." This plea was delivered by telegram in May of 1909, and for a while, says Colette, it did the trick. Mme de Serres was persuaded that Willy was about to commit suicide, and she backed off. As for Colette, she "resolved to resist all his [future] demands. . . . I no longer wished to be exploited, and I even wanted to sign the future editions of [the *Claudines*], from which [Willy] had, up until then, taken all the honor and the profit."

But then Mme de Serres reconsidered. Returning to Paris, Colette continues, "on this subject, [Willy and] I had stormy meetings, threats, supplications, bargaining, and when he found me unbending, he asked me in the most urgent manner to remain *allied* with him . . . and to take his part against you know who."[9]

Mme de Serres filed a civil suit against Willy, forgoing the criminal charges she might rightfully have brought. She attached his royalties, and his estate would still owe her five thousand francs at the time of his death. In December of 1910, Colette brought her own civil suit against Willy—for the furniture—and she summoned Marcel Boulestin as a witness, paying his fare from London. Willy intercepted Boulestin on the courthouse steps and threatened to have him arrested in the courtroom: "You know I have the goods." Boulestin fled to Calais, probably fearing an accusation of pederasty, "and Colette was out of pocket [for his ticket]. I've often wondered what revelations he was afraid of, because I didn't have anything on him."[10]

There is one last point of contention we should consider—the blackest: Colette's accusation that Willy had murdered the mother of his son. And despite her "dislike" of blackmail, it appears that she was not above it. In November of 1909, probably in response to the "threats" Willy was making, Colette let him know that she had "evidence" to suggest that in 1892, a year before their marriage, he had killed Germaine Servat. This "evidence" was Achille's recollection that during a visit to Châtillon before Germaine's death, Willy had asked him what a fatal dose of morphine would be. Achille said he didn't know, but when he unlocked his dispensary after Willy's departure, he found his vial of morphine missing. "He will go to Paris if it's necessary," Sido writes, "to give his testimony. I imagine that Achille has weighed the gravity of his words, but it will be best to reflect before going to such extremes, for the consequences of all this are so heavy."[11]

Achille would never bring formal charges against his ex-brother-in-law, and it seems improbable that he would have helped marry his sister to a wife killer, then invited that criminal to become his daughter's godfather. Perhaps the story of the morphine vial was prompted by the death of Juliette, and her family's suspicions that Roché had supplied her with a fatal overdose of aconite. Perhaps Colette had convinced herself that since Willy was capable of character assassination, he was also capable of murder. That, in any case, was the rumor she began to circulate. "Recently," Willy told a lawyer in February of 1910, "a woman of letters who has much more talent than good sense has been spreading the story that I killed one of my mistresses, perhaps two (she wasn't absolutely certain). I considered these charges tainted by a regrettable exaggeration, but I didn't, however, refer them to the courts."[12]

MURDER, BLACKMAIL, FRAUD, intimidation, lawsuits, character defamation—what bitter dregs. "Watch your back," writes Sido to her daughter in 1910, and indeed she was afraid, as were Colette and Missy, that "the vile and hateful bastard" would make good on his threats of violence.

Capable de tout: capable of anything. It is the phrase that Willy and Colette both use like a leitmotif, referring to each other. "There's nothing here that ennobles Colette, and nothing that rehabilitates Willy," writes Pichois of these last scenes from their marriage. ". . . The modern and model couple were washing their dirty linen in the public square."[13] Caradec concurs, but with somewhat more sympathy for both parties. When you read the documents, he writes, "you are totally convinced that Colette and Willy were both acting in bad faith. But isn't that the common fate of such litigants . . . when two beings rend each other limb from limb because neither can forgive himself for having loved the other?"[14]

Jacques Gauthier-Villars was back in France at the end of 1910 to sort out his military service. Neither Willy nor Colette nor anyone in their entourages mentioned the "murder" charge to him. His father, he told Caradec, "seemed cheerful as always, and he was quite 'himself.' " He was living with Meg in Monte Carlo, beyond the reach of his creditors, and he had two new ingenues in his harem.

> Suddenly, in a casual tone, he told me that his relations with Colette were no longer strained—they were broken.
> "*Tant pis,* " I replied, impassively but devastated.
> "Yes, so much the worse," said Willy. "For her and for me."[15]

2

COLETTE WAS in Naples, enjoying a ten-day vacation on the Amalfi Coast with Auguste Hériot, when *The Vagabond* was published.[16] They made the whole "Cook's tour," visiting Pompeii, the gardens of Procida, the convent of Camaldoli, and the Blue Grotto. It rained in Herculaneum, and while its marbles left Colette "cold," she loved Nero's temple and the "trip one makes through [the Sybil's cave], in the water, in the darkness, on the shoulders of a half-naked guide, with the delicious odor of smoking torches."[17]

From Capri, Colette sent Léo and Missy—who was supervising the renovations at Rozven—the same bland and cheerful postcards. "One can see

Fersen's villa from here," she writes her mistress from a restaurant terrace.[18] (Fersen d'Adelwart was a famous homosexual dandy of the Belle Époque.) "I wouldn't want it, not for thirty-nine francs, because it's as unsaleable as it is inaccessible. . . . I embrace you with all my heart." And Hériot adds: "And with my big one, too."[19] To her friend Hamel, Colette was more discursive and revealing. "My little companion is a sweet child when he's alone with me," she told him, "but he'll never be happy. He is built on a foundation of sadness."[20]

Missy had accepted Hériot with the same stoicism Colette had once shown toward Willy's mistresses, and for a year they co-existed peacefully. She had long understood that her "insufferable fake child" would eventually tire of her "old melancholy person," and she had never resented this disposition toward restlessness. Colette did her best to reassure her lover that "all comparisons only serve your cause. A providential irony murmurs to me, 'This isn't worth Missy.' "[21]

EVERY DIVORCE FORCES a triage of the ex-couple's friendships, particularly when their parting is as bitter as Colette's from Willy. She had already been dropped by their more proper acquaintances when she went on the stage. The society woman she calls "my friend Valentine" in a number of sketches[22] continues to frequent and defend her, but discreetly. She disapproves of the bare-breasted pantomimes, the louche company Colette keeps—the dykes, queens, and hustlers mothered by the proprietor of the "Semiramis" bar[23]—and she reminds her, with innocent condescension, that the rules are different for *"nous autres"* (women in good standing like us). Colette then tells the reader what she thinks of her "friend Valentine":

> You holy little busybody! I sometimes have moments of weakness when I'd like to make you understand me, pulling you by that golden hair—some of it real, some fake . . . and boxing your ears to shake up all the prejudices, the stumps of ideas, the debris of principles that, put together, make such an immoral little package. . . .
>
> Yes, immoral, you little trollop. . . . You'll never know all I really think of you, all the ill I think of you, who consider that in ceasing to have a husband I've contracted an embarrassing disease, hard to conceal, hard to confess. You would laugh as at a facile paradox if I tried to explain that the state of matrimony seems absurd and rather abnormal to me.[24]

Colette was a fallen woman, but her somewhat campy, epicene charm had earned her a cult following among gay men, as both a writer and a performer.

Robert de Montesquiou, the grand duke of Sodom himself, was one of her admirers.[25] Montesquiou, a contemporary of Willy's, was "allied," as he never tired of reminding one, "to the greater part of the European aristocracy." In his youth, he had modeled for Huysmans's esthete Des Esseintes. By the turn of the century, he aspired to being taken seriously as a poet, and to this end, he befriended Mallarmé, Edmond de Goncourt, and Proust and condescended to frequent the salon of Mme Arman, where he read his work in a high-pitched voice, leaning languorously against the chimneypiece. Colette would have met him there when she first came to Paris.

The count shared Willy's love of puns, the crueler the better, and his talent for making enemies with them. Their circles overlapped, for among Montesquiou's protégés were the composers Fauré and d'Indy and the artists Boldoni and Jacques-Émile Blanche, Willy's cousin, both of whom had painted Colette. Willy, still on cordial terms with the count at the time of his financial troubles, wrote him unctuous letters (although his unction was always cut with the acid of his resentments), and in 1907, Montesquiou tried to help him raise some desperately needed cash by buying Boldoni's portrait of Colette.

Perhaps her image hanging in his Pavillon des Muses helped to pique his interest in her, and perhaps he was intrigued that she was living with the great-great-great-granddaughter of Louis XV. Whatever the reason, from 1907, Montesquiou took an interest in Colette's career, which he discussed with his fellow gay esthetes. "I don't think I told you," writes the painter Georges Barbier to the count, "how much I loved the poses struck by Mme Colette Willy in a very simple pantomime where she played, with all the robust and svelte grace of her pretty legs, a young faun disappointed in love. It is rare to have a day of art at the theater, but I must confess that I was given one by . . . the animal grace of Mme Willy. . . . The author of *Dialogues de bêtes* is a hybrid creature—refined and troubling."[26]

Such a refined and troubling hybrid creature could only be congenial to Proust's principal model for Charlus. And despite his famous snobbery (or perhaps because of it—he hated to conform), Montesquiou took up Colette. She had sent him *Retreat from Love*, and he wrote to thank her for her "curious work," noting the "strange resemblances" between her characters and those of Beardsley: "the same ingenuity in perversion; the same manner of obtaining, through their grace, absolution for what one was going to reproach them."[27]

In exchange, Montesquiou sent Colette his essay on Beardsley. She ignored the gift—she was in the middle of her separation—although such a lapse of manners, even at a moment of turmoil, was unusual for her. By the time she did reply, in her best high style, she had moved to the rue de Villejust:

It's true, Monsieur, I never answered you this summer. Your letter, so utterly flattering, found me on my little beach, far from everything, and the languor of July, the moral and physical malaise of a rather . . . transitory state, made me forget the most elementary social duties. The dispatch of my book was a timid excuse; you liked it, so I am content.

I have read your study of Beardsley, for whom I have an almost guilty passion, at least three times, so much do the designs of this very young man, who is a bit mad, correspond to my inner secrets. . . . I would like to know the name of the Lady [sic] who so liked the Faun. I have so few friends, Monsieur. This isn't a complaint, certainly not! But I live, I am assured, in an uncommon manner, and I know that I am condemned for doing so. I am condemned so much above all because I haven't sufficiently explained my reasons for breaking with nearly all that is proper or passes for proper. But I assure you that I am not base, and that there is not a single low motive to my conduct! You couldn't care less, but I do not like to be misunderstood, not by a certain quality of person.

I have contrived a pretty, slow dance for myself. If it would please you, once, to see the ex-faun with the beautiful muscles dance before a shadowy little idol, beneath veils the color of night, I would be happy to place myself at your service, to thank you for having liked my book. Be assured, dear monsieur, of the true sympathy of Colette Willy.[28]

Colette was generally so reticent about her "inner secrets" and secret affinities that when this letter was to be auctioned, in the 1920s, with other papers from the Montesquiou estate, she threatened a lawsuit to forestall its sale. She was not alone: there were letters of protest from other literary figures, scandalized by the "impropriety" of auctioning an author's private correspondence. Paul Bourget, for one, defended the absolute separation of art and life, to which the writer of the preface to the sale catalogue responded that what Bourget referred to as the "regressive" propensity to seek the truth of a work of art in a writer's life *("la manie du document")* was really a refusal to plumb the circumstances under which a work was created, the methods by which an author had "formed and fashioned his material. To judge," he concludes, "must one not first understand?"[29]

The sale took place, and the Montesquiou archives are now kept at the Bibliothèque Nationale. There is nothing as comparably frank or intimate in the rest of his correspondence with Colette. When she began to publish *Tendrils of the Vine* in *La Vie parisienne,* the count, who was timid, as are so many of the most flamboyant souls, conveyed his admiration for these essays to her publisher. "Saglio tells me that you like [my work]," Colette wrote to him in mauve ink. "I know through others that you speak of me with benevolence. I sometimes forget an insult, but never a kindness." She invited him to lunch with her at the rue Torricelli—calling it a "campsite," but promising him a decent meal.[30]

IF THE GREAT ESTHETES of the Belle Époque found Colette compelling, it was partly because her style, despite its much vaunted "nudity"— like her persona, for all its seeming naturalness—owed them a considerable debt. She is never as transparent or as spontaneous as she seems—quite the contrary. The estheticism of Proust, Wilde, Huysmans, Beardsley, Schwob, and Montesquiou are more useful in understanding her than the philosophy of Rousseau.

It is true that most of these men were closeted transgressors, while Colette played out her revolt in public. They were secretly attracted by her vital force. Their languor and formality were alien to her—but not their fetish worship of human beauty. She penetrated their exotic habitats—visited their opium dens, dined at their clubs, performed in their private temples, studied their perversions—and wrote about them like an anthropologist, a good one, though she wasn't always aware of her own bias. The work that best reveals Colette's complex relations with this demimonde is her portrait of Renée Vivien.

Renée, who had died in 1909, was born Pauline Tarn to an English father and an American mother. She was an ethereal blond four years Colette's junior, and part of that community of literary Anglo-Saxon lesbians who had settled in Paris at the turn of the century. Natalie Barney did the honors of Renée's initiation, and the two women had a long, tempestuous affair with many breakups and reunions. They were designed to frustrate one another: Natalie was, like Colette, one of life's gourmands, robust and lucid, a great seductress, and incapable of fidelity. Renée was bookish, morbid, puerile, frail, "famished for transcendence"—and Natalie needed all her erotic skill and patience to awaken, in this self-described "Puritan," her capacity for passion. Renée's poems, written in French (a language she spoke with a lisping English accent), are, for the most part, pastiches of her two idols, Baudelaire and Sappho. They are filled with "love and anguish," with moonlight and the scent of dying lilies, with trembling hearts and lips, and they were already démodé when they were written. Colette was grateful that Renée never wanted to "talk shop" with her.

When Colette moved to the rue de Villejust, she and Renée became neighbors: their apartments communicated through a series of back gardens to which a "corruptible" old concierge had the key. Renée and Natalie were living separately by then. They had been to Lesbos (the real Greek island) and back, their brief idyll and their dream of founding a colony for women poets cut short by a letter from Renée's imperious "master," a Rothschild heiress, the immensely rich, sexually rapacious Baroness Van Zuylen. She summoned Renée home to France, dictated a letter in which Renée told Natalie she could henceforth see her only with her "master's" permission, and installed her in a sumptuous and gloomy apartment on the avenue du Bois.

Renée—rich in her own right—was a generous patron to Colette in her early days as a performer. She and Willy, then she and Missy, were Renée's guests in Nice, and she often invited Colette, "in a professional capacity"— always insisting she should name her terms—to dance at her soirées in Paris. These late suppers of sushi and foie gras, well irrigated by dry champagne and strange alcohols, were served on plates of jade or lacquer by Renée's Chinese "slave," to a select company of ladies[31] and the occasional sympathetic male. Colette found these evenings stilted and tedious. Renée's windows, she discovered, were nailed shut. The air was heavy with a "nauseating" bouquet of clashing perfumes: sweet tobaccos, overripe fruit, funereal flowers, and incense burning at the altars of the priceless Buddhas that were part of Renée's "unstable" decor. The tables and divans were low, and the light was so dim that Colette—"wickedly intolerant" of so much affected unwholesomeness—once brought her own oil lamp to a dinner party. "Renée wept big tears over this, like a child."[32]

Colette's intolerance was more than the simple distaste of a frank and energetic realist for a romantic dreamer. The back way through the garden door that led through the locked gates to connect their two ground-floor apartments is an image for an emotional proximity Colette couldn't avow, although it can't be a coincidence that the heroine of *The Vagabond* is also called Renée.

"If I were to publish the correspondence of this poet . . . it would astound only because of its childishness. . . . I stress this very particular childish quality. . . . There is not a single feature of her youthful face that I do not vividly recall. . . . Renée's gay laughter, her liveliness, the faint halo of light trembling in her golden hair all combined to sadden me, as does the happiness of blind children." *Childish, childlike, youthful:* it's a musical refrain: "At Renée Vivien's I could have wished to be younger, so I could be a little fearful."

Colette was a recovering masochist when she met Renée, and here was an eternally "trembling" slave of love who would abruptly desert her dinner guests after the entrée to obey a "summons" from her absent master. Twenty years later, when Colette recalls this public spectacle of self-abasement in *The Pure and the Impure,* she finds it offensive. But in 1910, her own Renée "trembles" with the same weakness of will every time her lover calls her "my beloved child." She trembles with the fear of a fragile creature who sees a potential parent in every lover, and who braces herself against the powerful undertow of regression that ebbs and flows throughout the novel.

"I live in danger," says Renée Vivien. Her master might kill her, she declares, and how? "In four words she explained how she might perish. Four words of a frankness to make you blink." One can imagine what the four words are, and Colette makes it clear that Renée is dishonest, that she longs for just such a death—the voluptuous obliteration of the self. But here is Colette's own Renée of 1910:

Escape. How to accomplish it? Everything is against me. The first obstacle is this woman's body barring my way, a voluptuous body with closed eyes, voluntarily blind, stretched out full, ready to perish. . . . I'm she, this woman, this brute beast so stubborn in her pleasure. "You are your own worst enemy." My God, do I know it! Will I also vanquish—a hundred times more dangerous than the greedy beast—the abandoned child who trembles within me, weak, nervous, ready to stretch her arms out and implore: "Don't leave me alone!" It is she who fears the dark, solitude, sickness, and death.[33]

The actress who flaunted her sexuality in vulgar melodramas listened to the drawing-room exhibitionist flaunting her love affairs in vulgar language and was appalled. Renée's "way of talking about physical love was rather like that of little girls brought up for a life of debauchery: both innocent and crude," writes Colette. ". . . And when, beyond the poet who praised the pallor of her Lesbian loves, their sobbing in desolate dawns, I caught a glimpse of 'Madame How-many-times, counting on her fingers, mentioning by name things and gestures, I put an end to the indiscretion . . . and not very tactfully."[34]

The only confrontation mentioned in their letters was not over Renée's sexual escapades or profanity; it was about her drinking. Colette had called her an alcoholic to her face, in front of their assembled friends, and Renée was understandably humiliated and furious.[35] Their mutual confidant, Léon Hamel, played the mediator, and Renée sent Colette a peace offering—an "all-purpose" Japanese porcelain bowl "you can use as a basin, a water bowl, a bidet, or anything." For her part, Colette suppressed the outrage and anxiety Renée inspired in her: "The friendship one has given to a human being who is already going to pieces, is already headed toward her own downfall, does not obey the dictates of pride."

But Renée wasn't only drinking herself to death: she was terminally anorexic. Colette is probably the first writer to describe a modern case of the disease—compulsive fasting motivated not by any religious aceticism but by an obsession with thinness. Colette is famous for her love of food, and for a comfort with her flesh that resists all modern dictates about what makes a woman's body lovely or desirable. Self-starvation was a form of female martyrdom that she abhorred morally and esthetically, and at a time when dieting was only just becoming fashionable, Renée was already a vision of things to come. She was tall—five foot seven—and her "ideal" weight was one hundred and three pounds. When she discovered, one day, that she had gained ten pounds, she disappeared for a week to lose them by walking in the woods and living on tea.

Colette describes how this fast began. She goes with Renée to a costume house to rent clothes for a masked ball. Renée mistakenly puts Colette's coat on, and discovers that she can't button it. "It almost fits you," Colette tells her, laughing. "It almost fits me?" Renée repeats, aghast. "It's a great misfortune you have just announced to me."[36]

"In that period I was a pleasant little cob pony of a person," Colette explains cheerfully. But when she wrote her memoir of Renée, she weighed nearly a hundred and eighty pounds. And while she jokes about her obesity in letters, she never laments it, or at least not sincerely. As the years pass, she proudly consolidates her flesh and her power.

IT IS EASY ENOUGH to appreciate from Renée's letters why Colette found her so exasperating. They show her languid and spoiled, and are full of coy innuendos and poetic exaltation. She calls Colette "my child" and jokes about the "serviceable Missy" and the big bed she'll have ready for them when they come to Nice. There's a presumption of sexual complicity—one lesbian to another—which Colette, wary of intimacy, disdainful of identity politics, and indeed deeply ambivalent about lesbianism, could only find obnoxious.

"The alcohol . . . the thinness . . . the poetry. . . . What is the dark origin of all this nonsense?" Colette asks herself. When she discovers that the nonsense is in fact not simply faddish or feigned depravity, but a form of mental illness, her sympathy conquers her repugnance. She can never approve of Renée, or really like her, but she tries to understand her own antipathy: "Like all those who never use their strength to the limit, I am hostile to those who let life burn them out."[37]

There are certain rare men and women, and Colette was one, whose confidence and equanimity seem to wax with age. They outgrow or disavow the terror of loss and abandonment. Life makes them the sternest judges of dissipation. Renée Vivien offends Colette deeply when she sheds her substance and flings herself "with a great display of frenzy" into an abyss. "An abyss she imagined?"[38] asks the corpulent and secure great writer in the late 1920s. She has forgotten her own Renée of 1910: "I'm suffering. I can't attach myself to what I see. . . . I am clinging and listing like a tree which has grown up at the edge of an abyss; in the fullness of its bloom, it inclines ever more toward its loss. I go on resisting, and who knows if I shall succeed?"[39]

3

COLETTE HERSELF THOUGHT it "worth remarking" that the intimate friends of her years as a vagabond, "the true and faithful ones," were all "luckless and irremediably sad." She considered that it might be "the solidarity of unhappiness that unites us" but decided that it wasn't. She "attracted and retained the depressives, the solitaires," she reasoned, because they were simply fellow misfits, unencumbered by families or convention, and "dedicated to a life of seclusion or wandering, as I am."[40]

Missy, Hériot, Renée, Léon Hamel—the Hamond of *The Vagabond*—certainly belong in this category. Sido mentions Hamel for the first time in August of 1908, and Colette's first extant letter to him is dated that July. He was a frequent houseguest of Missy and Colette at Belle Plage and Rozven, and one of the *Tendrils*—"Fishing Party"—is dedicated to him. He, in turn, seems to have advised Colette not only on matters of the heart, but on her money: "I thank you once again," she tells him wryly, "for taking such good care of my *vast* capital."[41]

Colette confided in Léon Hamel more openly than to any other correspondent whose archives have survived. His letters to her have vanished, and he destroyed hers to him, though not before recopying them in his delicate handwriting. He was so reticent that little is known about him. Colette urged him to speak about himself to her, "because you could forget to."

Pichois gives a brief sketch of Hamel's life in his introduction to *Letters from the Vagabond*. He was a man of Willy's age, although physically his opposite: "tall, thin, very distinguished-looking," and athletic. His military family had left him a private fortune, and he was "a dilettante by vocation" who collected butterflies, appreciated literature, and loved to travel. He had lived in China, and for more than fifteen years in Egypt, where he helped to manage the affairs of the viceroy Ismail Pasha. He took an avuncular interest in Renée Vivien, and was one of the few men welcome in Lesbos. It would be surprising if this tender and secretive bachelor, so much at home in the culture of North Africa, hadn't also been gay.

But Hamel was not the only man in whom the Vagabond confided. He had a rival who has not figured very prominently in any of Colette's biographies, probably because their letters, with one exception, have never been published.

Louis de Robert was Colette's contemporary. He had written three well-received novels about the chagrins of love, and Colette thought highly of them. "How often you must hear that your 'sensibility' is 'completely feminine,' " she tells him.[42] Colette might have been introduced to Robert in the early years of her marriage, although there is no record of their meeting. He contributed to *L'Écho de Paris* when Willy was its music critic, and he had also frequented the salon of Mme Arman, where he became friends with Marcel Proust. The two young *sensibles,* both ardent Dreyfusards, had attended Zola's trial together. A chronic illness ruined Robert's health and curtailed his pursuit of love, and by the time Colette began writing to him, he had become an invalid and a recluse in the village of Sannois, just north of Paris. The autobiographical novel Colette refers to, *Roman du malade,* published in 1911, told the story of his afflictions and his acceptance of them, and made him famous. When Proust read it, he decided to renew their friendship. "I've written a long book which I call a novel because it hasn't the casual element of memoirs,"[43] he told Robert, with dazzling understatement, remarking on the similarities between their work and fates.

Proust had, by then, drafted the first two parts of his great novel. He hoped to have them serialized in a good journal before publishing them in book form, but the advances he had made to a number of influential editors had produced nothing but silence, broken promises, or rude rebuffs. As *Roman du malade* had done extremely well both critically and financially, Proust thought Robert might help him.

Unlike Gide, who had rejected *Remembrance of Things Past* on behalf of *La Nouvelle Revue française* without reading more than a few pages (and would regret his stupidity ever after), Robert recognized it as a work of genius, and was confident that others would do likewise. He urged Proust to send the novel to a number of influential writers, including Colette. Proust explained that he hadn't seen Mme Willy since her quarrel with Mme Arman in 1896, and while he had continued to "admire" her, he didn't feel it would be proper to renew their acquaintance by asking for a favor.[44] In the meantime, Robert tried to place *Remembrance* with his own publisher, Fasquelle, who rejected the manuscript, and then with his friend Humblot, the director of Ollendorff, who told him: "My dear fellow, I may perhaps be dead from the neck up, but rack my brains as I may, I can't see why a chap should need thirty pages to describe how he turns over in bed before going to sleep."[45]

Proust was living secretly with the tormented love for his chauffeur that would inspire *The Captive.* When Louis de Robert confessed that he, too, was suffering from an unrequited passion, Proust offered to intercede: "I, who have been so unhappy in love . . . yes I, so impotent to move the hearts I would join to my own, when I am not concerned, dear friend, I have the powers of a magician that you ought to employ. . . . I have not only reconciled friends, but lovers, and spouses. I have given an unhappy lover prestige in the eyes of the courtesan who disdained him. Oh, dear friend, friend, if I could do something for you . . . you have only to speak."

"Touched by this letter," Robert confided certain details of the affair to Proust, including his feelings of decrepitude and hopelessness, without, however, revealing his beloved's name. Proust pressed him to do so. He would go to see the lady; his eloquence would vanquish her reluctance; he would make her fear to lose him and feel "lucky to love you. . . . I have realized, my friend, that the most insurmountable difficulties don't exist."[46]

But they do exist. Louis de Robert had entered Colette's confidence by posing as a successor to Francis Jammes: an ideal reader living in monkish seclusion and "impatient for the almost painful pleasure" her pages give him; a fatherly critic able to chasten her spiritual faults; and an ardent platonic correspondent to whom she could reveal herself from a safe distance. "Yes," he tells her when *The Vagabond* is published, "I sense that the best of you, the summit, the flame, the soul of your being, is in your books; it's far from you that I enjoy them. And that is why I can go for so long without seeing you if I have something of yours to read."[47]

Robert, however, was deluding himself. He lived for Colette's letters, and importuned her to come and see him in a tone that had to have reminded her of Sido's, and to have engaged the same guilt and resistance. She would promise to visit him in Sannois, then put off her trip, or cancel it. She would let months pass without answering him: "The ill one can do me with an unkept promise, by keeping me waiting—you know them. . . . But what is baser, more wicked than doing me ill is taking I don't know what perverse pleasure in depriving me of the illusion that you are good."[48] This tense, epistolary friendship would take a surprising turn.

CHAPTER 21

1

$\mathcal{J}$N THE FIRST ten years of her literary career, Colette had published
not only eleven volumes of prose and two plays, but a considerable
body of criticism and reportage. Even if she had never written another
novel, she would still be remembered as one of the most prolific and original
French journalists of the century. Her focus was intimate, but her range was
wide. She would be one of the first women to report from the front lines of
World War I, and to go up in an airship and an aeroplane. One of her specialties would be crime, particularly domestic violence, and criminal psychology,
and she would cover some of the great trials of the century. Her film and theater criticism fills several volumes, and while she never lost what the Buddhists
call her "beginner's eye"—her unjaded freshness of perception—she brought
a lifetime of experience as an actress and a practical knowledge of stagecraft
to her task. For several years she would be the literary editor of a major Paris
daily. She wrote about fashion with a knowledgeable irreverence that still
sounds provocative today. She penned advice columns on love, food, gardening, motherhood, exercise, decorating, and other traditional women's-page
subjects, but she was eloquent and often scathing about the plight of divorcées
and the unemployed, of women in brutal marriages and marginal jobs.

Colette's fiction, as Dominique Aury would contend, and justly, "has no
past, is outside castes and nations, protected from any contamination by society (there is no society in Colette), protected from the fear and temptation of
God (there is no God) and from the anguish of death."[1] But the work of the
journalist should be read as the temporal companion to the timeless work of

the novelist, and as another aspect of the dialectic between the pure and the impure.

IN DECEMBER OF 1910, after several months of negotiation, Colette signed a contract with *Le Matin* to write a regular bimonthly column, which was to become weekly after a trial period. Her first articles were published anonymously under the headline "Tales from the Thousand and One Mornings." "Today's story," wrote the editors on December 2, 1910, "is signed with a mask. It conceals, capriciously, a woman writer of the first rank . . . whose intimate talent, a mixture of exquisite sentiment, keen observation, and impious fantasy, has once more been confirmed in a love story that is today's best-selling novel." A month later, Colette lifted the mask. "It's me," she proclaimed, "Colette Willy."

She had initially agreed to suppress her identity because the management of the paper was concerned that her scandalous reputation might offend its "chaste" subscribers. The "management," however, was not of one mind on the subject. There was a permanent editorial director and two rotating editors in chief, each of whom worked a two-week shift, in part because of the long hours and late nights the job demanded. One of these editors, on learning that Colette was to become his colleague, threatened to resign: "If this person joins" the paper, declared Stéphane Lauzanne to his boss, Charles Sauerwein, "I'm leaving straight away."

> "Straight away seems to me very emphatic," retorted Charles Sauerwein. "Do you know her?" . . .
> "I! I know that circus performer, that . . ."
> Charles Sauerwein, who was well-disposed towards me, held out his hand to Lauzanne:
> "Goodbye, old friend, I say goodbye because Colette's first short story appears tomorrow. . . ."[2]

2

SIDO WAS TROUBLED by Colette's new job: "Minet-Chéri, you're taking on a heavy commitment to *Le Matin*. That's a lot of work, and I don't approve because journalism is the death of the novelist, and it's a pity you're doing it. Don't waste your talent, my darling, be sparing of it, it's worth saving."[3]

Colette would not, in fact, publish a new novel for two years. But if her fiction suffered, her stage career did not. Early that January, she and Wague revived the ever popular *La Chair* for a two-week run in Paris. "Celebrity takes one over, as you see," wrote Sido, lamenting a long period with no letters from her daughter.[4]

A month later, Colette was on the road again—off to Nice to dance in Richepin's *Xantho*. This time it was Hériot, not Missy, who acted as her *cavaliere servante*. The couple stopped at Beaulieu, then at Monte Carlo for a few days of recreation before checking into the Hotel Majestic in Nice. Here they were joined for their meals and excursions—and in their bed—by a young beauty named Lily de Rême.

Colette would later use Lily as her model for the character of May in *The Shackle*, a Holly Golightly for 1913: rootless, profligate, sexy, and radiating a "perishable freshness with no character."[5] She is an outmoded type, still common, though, in fiction and the entertainment business. Many first novels have a Lily, and a young hero fatally smitten with her. "She doesn't sleep, forgets lunch, smokes and drinks, and likes cocaine."[6] There is generally a sensible female confidante who looks upon her—and the suckers she enchants—with incredulity. How can anyone, she wonders naively, fall for such a bimbo?

Lily was in her early twenties when Colette met her, and she couldn't imagine turning thirty. She was ditzy, illiterate, capricious, chatty, and seductive toward both sexes. Like May, she dressed eccentrically, "exaggerating fashions that were already insane," and she liked high heels, bright silk, lace stockings, kimonos, folk embroidery, and short skirts. Her bohemian style had its worldly glamour, but she was also full of vulgar prejudices that she expressed in a loud voice, confident of their charm.

"We make a trio which would interest you," Colette told Hamel. "These two children in love with me are remarkable—for the sole reason that they love me. I force-feed them and make them sleep. My egotism is satisfied maternally by their appetite and their fresh complexions. But I'm not happy with the little Hériot. How many times have I hesitated to speak about him with you. . . . The die is cast, and it's from you that I'll seek secrecy and advice, for the affair seems grave above all for him, I'm not morally in danger."[7]

As the affair with Hériot progressed, Sido couldn't help cheering in his corner. "The wealth of your friend? I've contributed a bit to it, for I have been a client of the Magasins du Louvre since they opened, and—by an amazing coincidence—the piece of handiwork I just laid down so I could write to you is the remnant of a black silk dress which papa ordered from the Magasins du Louvre for the day of your birth. . . . How indulged you are!" she concludes, "how loved! But you have always been so, since your childhood, excluding those years you passed with the 'phenomenon,' which, however, helped give wings to the talent that was within you."[8]

MISSY, MEANWHILE, was at Rozven, working on the renovations in her overalls and feeling, despite her stoicism, abandoned. Without forgoing any of the pleasures supplied by Hériot and Lily, Colette tried to assuage her lover's wounded pride. "I can see the light of [Rozven]," she wrote to her from Nice. "I hear the sounds of morning and of your voice." She recounted the praise she was receiving for *The Vagabond,* and imagined—forgetting that her lover was not, after all, a selfless and doting mother—that it would make Missy happier than it made her.[9]

Colette could not, however, have failed to appreciate that the novel's scenes of passion must have made painful reading for the marquise, or that where Renée describes the second-class love, "the bitter happiness" of "two women intertwined," and "the melancholy and touching image of two weaknesses,"[10] she was repudiating that weakness in their relations. "I think," she offers Missy, obliquely apologetic, "that it's because I pass my time doing things I regret that I feel them so vividly and that I write about them in a rather personal way. People who are perfectly sane and happy don't make good literature, alas."[11]

THE GUILTY PLAYGIRL made the long train journey back to Rozven for a few days at the end of February. Missy had apparently argued that such a short stay did not warrant such a grueling trip. "I don't give a damn about exhausting myself to come see you," Colette protested. "Go on, don't be so strict with me. When your vagabond will have spent the 'vertigo' of her *âge dangereux,*[12] as the Danish lady calls it, you'll see that she stays home with you. For the home is yours, darling, everything about it bears your imprint and the mark of your care."[13]

But her vertigo wasn't spent yet. After a few days of being "scolded, cared for, and warmed up" by Missy, Colette was off again with the Kid and Lily, this time to North Africa. Somewhere between the ruins of Carthage and the souks of Tunis, she dumped Hériot "very coldly." She wasn't willing, she told her mother, "to be his slave."[14] He rushed back to France—to lick his wounds at Rozven. The house was still in chaos, but Missy fixed up a room for him, and his presence gave her an outlet for that maternal (or avuncular) solicitude which, in Colette's absence, lacked an object. "The little noodle is making puppy eyes at Missy," Colette told Hamel. "Perhaps he's planning your conversion,"[15] she cracked to the marquise, not kindly.

Hériot and Missy make a touching pair. They were both as rich and idle as they were incurably sad. They were both attracted to temperamental and prestigious women. They tried to buy love while secretly hoping that their devotion would inspire a true attachment. They belong to the Belle Époque, which they outlived, ruined and lonely. One can't help imagining what Jean Lorrain would have made of them as a couple: a transvestite Madonna of the Sorrows, selfless and noble; and a mustachioed Child with an innocent gaze and an erection.

Lily, in the meantime, was being "impossible," her specialty. "She carries on in a Moslem country," Colette told Missy from Tunis, where she was performing in *Claudine,* "as if she were in a Montmartre bar, singing in the street, mocking the natives, whom I find much better brought up than she is."[16] She wanted to visit a harem with a male friend disguised as a woman; she wanted to caress the beautiful daughter of a Jewish family about whom Colette wrote an article for *Le Matin;* she wanted Colette to go on with her to India ("I'd rather drop dead," she told Hamel).[17] Hériot was a better traveling companion. "First of all because I'm the one who gives the orders, and second because he almost never makes any noise."[18]

3

COLETTE SPENT the first month of the spring at Rozven with Missy and Paul Barlet. She cleaned out the wells and waxed the floors. On April 10, she wrote to inform Louis de Robert she was returning to Paris. "I'm finally recovering from my fit of vulgarity," she assures him. "I've taken hold of myself and left the false Midi and those companions [Lily and Hériot] who so much resemble that impossible place. I regard them from afar with severity, as if I had never known them. How are you, my friend? I'm always afraid, when I reread your book, that you are actually suffering as I read you. It's idiotic but affectionate."[19]

Colette now kept her promise to pay the importunate Robert a visit. She asked Hériot to drive her to Sannois, but since he had been so recently repudiated for his vulgarity, he had to wait "like a good boy" in the car. Fortunately for him, he did not have to wait long. Colette reemerged a short while later, "horrified, revolted, filled with pity, too, and a bit overwhelmed. . . . This man with the dead hands," she explained to Missy,

> the sickly breath, the fever sores on his mouth, who desires me absolutely, tried to bar my way, sobbing desperately. . . . You know what a terrible thing physical disgust is, you know one can't compromise with it, I contained my fury and when he begged me to kiss him, I nearly beat him up. . . .
>
> One doesn't give oneself out of pity. One gives oneself, in the begin-

ning, out of love. One can also give oneself for the sake of appetite, gaily, as one satisfies a thirst or hunger, and that's not very serious, but to give one-self for pity—and to a man—you know perfectly well one can't do it, when disgust is the cause of the refusal.[20]

After this distressing scene, Colette wrote to Robert: "I don't want it, I don't want it, and I can't do it. I wanted to give you the best of me, and you insisted stubbornly on desiring the rest. . . . This diminishes your stature in my eyes—to want me! So you see I have no pity for you, on the contrary. I'm angry with you, and with myself. How do you expect me to *take refuge in you* if you want me?"[21]

Robert did not accept his rejection calmly. He poured out his confused and bitter fantasies to her, and it was perhaps on Proust's advice that he took an aggressive tone. ("You've been too good," Proust had told him. "And when kindness doesn't succeed, one must do the contrary, cease to be kind.")[22] He had, Robert told Colette, entered her life at the moment she was losing her beauty, and that "consoled" him. If he'd wanted to see her naked body, he would have paid five francs for an orchestra seat at one of her performances, like the rabble. She had a virile soul that seemed "willfully neuter" to him. He wanted to be her tender friend, and something more than a friend, but not a lover. They were two sad, lonely creatures meant for each other. He wasn't a beggar: if she couldn't appreciate the precious gifts of his friendship and devotion, she wasn't worthy of them. And finally: "you have more of a hold on me through your letters than by your presence. There's always something in your presence that disappoints me."[23]

Their friendship did not recover, although as they aged they showed each other, in their memoirs, a wary mutual respect. Robert fell in love with, and later married, the telegraph operator in his village, and wrote to ask Colette for his letters back. " 'Dear friend,' " he began, " 'do you happen to have in your possession a letter of mine. . . . Its rapturous tone, if my memory serves me right, worries me in case it might fall into hands less affectionate than your own. . . .' I recall," writes Colette, "that I felt offended by so much caution and that, from sheer mischief, I kept the letter. . . . Less young, I should have shown myself less susceptible to the punctilious, refined, and fragile author of the *Roman du malade*."[24]

4

PHYSICAL DISGUST can't be compromised with, but neither can its opposite, the *coup de foudre*. A woman still privately shuddering at an unwelcome sexual advance is all the more susceptible to an electric mutual attraction. It burns out the distressing image of dead hands and fever sores, and its current scorching the nerves short-circuits their memory of repulsion.

Colette spent the last two weeks of April baring her left breast in *La Chair* at the Gaîté-Montparnasse. If she brought fresh ardor—or perhaps self-conscious modesty—to this familiar exhibition, it was for the benefit of a certain prestigious and rapt spectator stroking his fine mustache in a house seat. He was Colette's colleague and Lauzanne's co-editor at *Le Matin,* Henry de Jouvenel.

HENRY BERTRAND LÉON ROBERT, baron de Jouvenel des Ursins, was born on April 2, 1876.[25] He was thus three years Colette's junior. She called him Sidi—Arabic for Pasha—which suited both his physique and his sensual, lordly temperament. Sidi had those heroically romantic good looks that Willy had once yearned for. "Physically," wrote his son, Renaud,

> he was quite a tall man, with a tendency to stoutness; he had a proud glance, an aquiline nose, of which there are many in central and south-western France since the Arabs passed that way. He had a generous mouth and proud moustaches he was to shorten later. He had undeniable presence; he had what people call a dashing air. He had a "tone of voice" (the expression is his own) . . . which had a great effect on women and on senators. He used it. A tyrannical father and friend, he was irascible, suddenly stung into terrifying rages. Deep down, he was a sensitive, indeed a weak man who hid his weakness under a crusty manner. . . . He was a real spendthrift, he led a life which was nearly always magnificent. He has been compared to a Florentine nobleman of the Renaissance. In my opinion he was also, perhaps above all, a Rastignac.[26]

Henry's grandfather, Léon de Jouvenel, may actually have served as one of Balzac's models.[27] Léon, like Rastignac, was a brilliant upstart and opportunist. He was the son of a provincial surveyor, well-bred but poor, who went to Paris to make his fortune, charmed his way into society, made an advantageous marriage with the daughter of a general, and acquired, like his father-in-law, a Second Empire title. It was Léon who embellished that title with the ancient and noble name of "des Ursins," claiming to descend from the Orsinis of Rome and the Juvénal des Ursins who fought with Joan of Arc and became Archbishop of Rheims—a connection that has been disputed.

In 1844, Léon de Jouvenel bought the château of Castel-Novel, in the Corrèze, and brought his old father home to die there in baronial splendor. He ran for parliament as a royalist in 1848, was defeated, switched his allegiance to the Republic, and served briefly as a deputy under the Second Empire. His influence helped to secure a lavish sinecure for his only son, Raoul—Henry's father—who became the youngest prefect of the Third Republic. In 1874, Raoul married Marie-Juliette-Émilie Dolle, the daughter of a rich landowner, related on her mother's side to the banking and political dynasty of the Casimir-Periers. He retired from politics to Castel-Novel in 1876, the year that Henry, his first child, was born.

The diminutive baroness Marie—Mamita to her children and to Colette—gave birth to a second son, Robert, five years later. Her husband mistreated her so egregiously that she left him for another man, Chevandier de Valdrôme, with whom she had a daughter, Edith. According to the family archives, the baron and baroness legally dissolved their marriage in 1901. According to the family, this divorce never took place. "My grandmother departed," writes Bertrand de Jouvenel, Henry's son by his first marriage: "One didn't divorce in that era, one went off. This was very well illustrated by Colette in [a short sketch]. She pictures herself at the movies with her daughter. . . . Who asks her: 'Tell me, mommy, what does it mean, to live one's life? Does it mean to go off with the gentleman?' And her mother replies, 'Yes, you have understood very well, it's to go off with the gentleman.' "28

Henry spent his childhood in the country with his mother and his younger brother. At seventeen, he moved to Paris to live with his father, who enrolled him in Willy's and Wague's alma mater, the Collège Stanislas. Henry's best friend there—and forever after—was another young aristocrat, the future senator and cabinet minister Anatole de Monzie. Monzie recalled Jouvenel as a fastidious student and a brilliant orator who "could not help being our Prince Charming. All the women ran after him. . . . He was torn between his taste for pleasure and his taste for love, between caprice and lyricism, adventure and passion."29

The elder baron de Jouvenel was a reactionary and an anti-Semite, and the proud, hot-tempered son rebelled by entering politics on the left and marrying a Jew. Anatole and Henry both outraged their families by supporting the cause of Dreyfus, Zola, the anticlericals, and the League for the Defense of the Rights of Man.30 They were arrested together at a pro-Dreyfus student demonstration, and they would both remain ardent democrats and republicans.

Jouvenel went on to earn a degree in philosophy at the Sorbonne. He worked as a volunteer in the government of Waldeck-Rousseau. He gave speeches at the Cercle Républicain. His eloquence impressed Alfred Boas, a rich and influential Jewish industrialist, who helped to secure him an appointment in the government formed by Combes when Waldeck resigned. Jouvenel became chief secretary to the minister of justice, while his friend Monzie occupied the same office at the Ministry of Education.

This was the era of the *bloc des gauches* and the rise of radicalism. During the Occupation, *Le Matin* would become a collaborationist paper (still under the direction of Lauzanne), but at the fin de siècle it supported a coalition of slightly left-of-center reformers who also had close ties to the world of big business and the press. Believing, at this stage, that his true calling was political commentary rather than politics, Jouvenel was eager to write for *Le Matin*. "What he liked about journalism," wrote Monzie, "was the daily opportunity to squander his nobility."[31] Henry explained his attraction to the life of a newspaperman with more modesty. It gave him, he wrote, "the chance to play host to the happy diversity of minds. . . . Many hypotheses are needed to make a science and many discussions to achieve an average of truth."[32]

Once again, Alfred Boas opened doors for his protégé. He introduced Jouvenel to *Le Matin*'s publisher, Maurice Bunau-Varilla, who offered him a part-time job at a generous salary. This helped to underwrite his work at the ministry, and it also helped to underwrite his marriage to Boas's daughter, the beautiful and ambitious Claire. They were wed in 1902, in a civil ceremony, and their son was born the following year. Bertrand de Jouvenel would remember the dim light of the family's high-ceilinged rooms in a Left Bank mansion, leaded-glass windows, a massive banister, ornate woodwork, and the studded leather armchairs of his father's library.

Of his father, however, he had only a vague childhood memory. In 1906, Henry de Jouvenel left his family and went to live with his mistress in a charming wooden "country house" on the rue Cortambert. Isabelle de Comminges, Colette's immediate predecessor, was known as the Panther.[33] She was a ferocious and "unstable" Amazon with bronze eyes and Titian hair who rode her stallion side-saddle in the Bois and told her lover he sat his horse so badly he should "buy a buggy." Her mother was a Polish princess, and her father came from one of the oldest noble families in France. They had no money, which is to say no serious money, and the count de Comminges had married his daughter to a rich Parisian banker, Count Pillet-Will. His title, Isabelle liked to point out, was even more recent than that of the Jouvenels ("She was always ready to throw her genealogy at you," wrote her son). But a dubious pedigree was not the poor parvenu's only liability. Pillet-Will had a psychotic breakdown. He thought he was a dog. He shot his wife's Great Dane. His family committed him to an asylum, where he spent the remainder of his life barking.

The countess took her maiden name again, moved in with Jouvenel, and in

1907 gave birth to his second child—Renaud. She waited twenty years to legitimate her son, Jouvenel having done so, grudgingly, only a few years before. The boy was treated so harshly by both parents that his chronic sadness evoked Colette's hard-to-win maternal sympathies.

"A great lord," writes Pichois; "that's the epithet that recurs constantly in descriptions of [de Jouvenel]."[34] Says his son Renaud,

> An aristocrat who was somewhat infatuated by nobility, and a radical social-ist of the old school—sincerely democratic [who] hardly ever swerved, to my knowledge, from his haughtiness or his bourgeois prejudices, because one can be both a bourgeois and an aristocrat. . . . He had a lofty idea of his duties as a statesman, as an ambassador for his country. . . . He was of such a different race [from Colette] that I cannot make out what attracted him, contemporary esthetics apart, in this literary debutante [sic]. . . . Perhaps he had repressed plebeian instincts, as my mother, the countess, used to tell him to his face.[35]

5

IT IS SO OBVIOUS that Colette would be irresistible to a man like Jou-venel that only a critical and jealous son could have been mystified by her allure. The rebel was attracted by her notoriety; the sexual predator, by her danger; the sensualist, by her voluptuous beauty; the intellectual, by her talent. The tension between them—two partners matched in vitality and worldliness—must have been exquisite. For once Colette had met a peer, not a parent or a child. Henry did more than desire her, he recognized her, and one of the most revealing statements that she would ever make about their romance is this one to Sido: "I receive letters from de Jouvenel that are truly worthy . . . of me, if I dare to say so!" To which Sido responded, "You deserve to inspire them, my dear."[36]

A note from Colette to Wague, posted at the beginning of May 1911, gives the first glimpse of this disruptive new emotion in her life. She had just arrived back at Rozven. "It's too beautiful here," she tells him; "it's that delicious, incomparable and fragile instant of the year." And then in a "private" post-script she confesses: "Oh, my little one, what a homecoming. It's tough—arrangeable, but tough. I'll tell you the story. Write to ask me what I can do about rehearsals. Tell me that Pimply Q. is free to rehearse *La Chair* from May 25 to June 2."[37]

The fact that Colette was "seriously worried about Missy's mental health," as she told Wague's wife, Christiane Mendelys, suggests that she had confessed the truth, or some of it, or that Missy had guessed it. Hériot,

conveniently abroad for a few weeks, was, in the meantime, sending Colette
urgent telegrams begging her to marry him. "If he wants to make you his wife
so badly, let him pay court to Missy and win you from her?" suggested Sido
playfully,[38] still ignorant of Jouvenel.

THE BARON BROUGHT Colette home with him for the first time one
night in June. The moon was full, and the acacias were in bloom. They drove
to Passy in Jouvenel's open car, and he opened the massive gate of his porte
cochère. Lamps with red silk shades were glowing behind the drawn curtains
of a Swiss cottage trimmed with vines and gingerbread, set in an immense
garden of old trees. "I stopped at the edge of this trap, this excess of charm,
this ambush. Perhaps there was still time to turn back? But the host was
already coming toward me."[39]

It is late, too, that night in *The Shackle,* when Renée Néré first goes home
with her lover Jean. He lights a fire for her in the salon. They sit in the dark
room cross-legged on the carpet, drinking sweet wine and eating grapes. She
watches the flames and inhales the scent of woodsmoke with "the trembling
audacity of a woman about to fall, watching herself fall." Then Jean pours
himself a glass of water, wipes his fingers, and sighs, " 'Ah!' with the meaning
of: 'Now we have to decide something!'

> And I suddenly realize that he, too, may be feeling intimidated and unde-
> cided, that his reserve, since the kiss he gave me, owes more to hesitation
> than to diplomacy. . . . In the same instant that I was about to lose even the
> appearance of aplomb, a providential malice restored it to me. I repeat
> "Ah!" in the same tone he used, and I add:
> "It's the transitional phrase that I was looking for. It leads us naturally
> to the one that follows, which is 'Eh! eh!' In every language, that translates:
> 'Already past midnight!' "

The fire burns down into embers, the shadows grow, and Renée sees Jean's
silver eyes "glowing with an almost Negro ferocity." He asks her if she wants
to leave, and she says no. He pins her to the floor, and she begins to struggle,
murmuring, "This is stupid." And then she utters the "sentimental female's
indignant cry: 'But you don't even love me!' " To which he replies, "And what
about you, then?"

> After two minutes of resistance, I give him to myself like a respite. How
> sweet the naked mouth is, the full lips. . . . How sweet it is to lose oneself to
> the point of thinking, "Here I am, freed from the care of thinking. . . . But

this mouth belongs to an enemy made savage by a kiss, who knows me weakened, and who spares me nothing."[40]

TOWARDS THE END of June, Colette and Wague left for a ten-day Swiss engagement of *La Chair*. On reaching Geneva, Colette found a letter from her mother, wondering who was with her. Hériot suspected something was amiss, and he cabled Colette that he was coming to Switzerland. She was not yet ready to face his jealousy—or perhaps not yet confident enough of the Man to dismiss the Kid—and she put him off with a series of "frantic, deceitful, and contradictory" dispatches. "Your life's not a bed of roses because you're being loved too much," Sido told her. "I'm afraid of a catastrophe if these two gentlemen cross paths but I'm more worried that it's you who'll be the victim, and if Chérubin [Hériot] discovers your pious lies, he'll be furious."[41]

Hériot stayed in Paris, "prowling around" Colette's apartment and interrogating her maid. On June 27, the play moved to Lausanne, by which time Colette could no longer contain her ecstasy: "Jouvenel has cabled me to say that he'll be here tomorrow, wounded, because he can't bear to live without my company! Men are terrible. Women, too."[42]

CHAPTER 22

I'm the male of my species. I lead the restless life of all those whom
love creates for his hard labors. . . . I fight as I eat, with a methodical
appetite. . . .

It's that savage season of love which weans us from all other joys
and multiplies, diabolically, in the gardens, our rangy females. . . .
I want them all without either preferring or recognizing any one of
them. Once she has submitted to my cruel embrace, I no longer hear
her sob. . . . There is no lover inaccessible to me.

— COLETTE
describing a tomcat named Sidi,
La Paix chez les bêtes

1

S IDI ARRIVED in Lausanne with a dueling wound that he had incurred
defending the honor of *Le Matin* against a slur from its rival, *Le
Journal*. With his arm in a sling, the warrior cut a dashing figure—
especially, no doubt, to the Captain's daughter. He repeated in person what he
had told Colette in his letters: that he "couldn't and wouldn't live without"
her.[1] The lovers spent a few passionate days at the Hôtel du Château ("It's all
going . . . too well," Colette confides to Christiane Mendelys)[2] and returned to
Paris after her last performance.

The baron then hastened to inform Mme de Comminges that he was leaving her for another woman. She told him she would kill her rival. Colette
reports to Hamel:

A desperate Jouvenel conveys this threat to me. . . . I go to her and tell the Panther, "I'm the woman." Whereupon she falls apart and begs me. A brief fit of weakness, because two days later she announces to Jouvenel that she plans to murder me. Re-desperate, Jouvenel has me picked up by Sauerwein in the car, and comes with me . . . to Rozven, where we find Missy icy and disgusted, having already been informed of the affair by the Panther. Then my two bodyguards leave me and Paul Barlet mounts guard, clutching a revolver. Missy, still icy and disgusted, f—— off to Honfleur. . . . Three days later, Jouvenel summons me back. . . . The Panther is on the prowl for me, also armed with a revolver. Here begins a period of semi-sequestration in Paris, where I am guarded like a precious reliquary by the detective squad. . . . This period has only just ended, brought to a close by an unexpected, providential, and magnificent event! . . . M. Hériot and Mme la Panthère have just embarked together on [his yacht] the Esmerald for a six-week cruise, having shocked Le Havre, their home port, with their drunken orgies. Isn't it nice? Isn't it theater? A bit too much so, no?[3]

Missy had been so anxious to keep Colette on any terms that, accepting Hériot as the lesser evil, she had installed him at Rozven, and "she imagined," writes Colette, "that she could impose him on me quasi-conjugally. It was enough to disgust me forever with that young man."[4] Now Missy refused to answer Colette's letters—or those of Sido, who imagined that "she must be sorely tried, and she has good reason."[5]

Unlike her mother, Colette couldn't seem to appreciate either Missy's need for or her entitlement to some detachment. "My dear Missy," she writes on receipt of an anguished letter. "If you knew the pain that caused me, I don't think you would have written it."[6] She writes to Hamel, too, about her own "pain, necessary to pay for happiness (touch wood), yes, or something that resembles happiness, and whose glimmer is so close to my grasp."[7]

But she can't break the habit of confiding in the woman who had mothered her for so many years: "My dear, I persist in writing to you despite your silence," she tells the marquise. "I am being guarded . . . like an escaping monarch. It's not pleasant but it's reassuring. The Panther is spreading hateful rumors about her ex-lover." And she concludes: "I don't know if you're very interested in what I'm writing to you. Too bad, I'm giving in to the need to tell you."[8]

Definitively rejected yet stoical as usual, Missy had relinquished Rozven to Colette, but kept most of the furniture (hers to begin with), which she moved to a new villa—the Primrose—two miles away. "She's still icy and disgusted," Colette tells Hamel, "and whatever I do, I can't get a rational word out of her. I promise you, it's not meanness on my part. It pains me."[9] But to

Christiane Mendelys she wrote meanly: "You want news of Missy? I don't have any, and she continues to detain all my possessions. I always like to be treated like a special case, and I will be the first person ever to have seen 'the marquise' ask for money from a woman whom she's leaving [sic]."[10]

Neither Hamel nor Sido heard anything from Colette during the month she had spent hiding out in Paris. Upon reaching Rozven on July 30, she apologized to her friend for the worry she had caused him, "and for that matter, caused my mother."[11] Sido was indeed frantic. "What's keeping you from writing to me? . . . If you haven't written when you receive this letter, send me a telegram. . . . Would you at least like news of my health?" And a few days later: "You don't write anymore. You're too busy, you're too hot? . . . Is your life being threatened? Are you pregnant? Are you sick? Write to me truthfully."[12] And finally: "Ah! You've given yourself a master!! You poor little darling."

On August 3, the poor little darling motored off with her lover to the Corrèze, to meet *his* mother. From the road, she sent a postcard: "Write to me at Castel-Novel. Everything's fine. I'm happy." At Castel-Novel, among her new "in-laws"—the cigar-smoking Mamita and the docile Edith—she forgot Sido's seventy-sixth birthday, but sent some impressive snapshots of the château.

2

IT WAS an abnormally hot, rainless summer. The animals were dying of thirst, and so were the vines. Sido worried about the "burning highways" and the danger of flat tires. The Limousin was drier than Provence in August, and at sunset, the towers of Castel-Novel were black against the cloudless sky. Colette was enchanted by the dark, crumbling, romantic castle, with its unpruned roses and its gleaming silver. She slept with the doors and windows open to catch a breeze, and bats "flitted . . . between the pillars of the four-poster bed. I was, for more than one reason, dazzled."[13]

When Colette and Jouvenel returned to Paris, she had, she told Hamel, "a new heart"—quickened by love but also lightened of its old burdens. Missy had apparently taken up with a pretty fat lady who "praised her to the skies"; Hériot and the Panther were busy quarreling in Morocco; Willy had finally married Meg. That autumn, Colette and Henry ran into the Gauthier-Villars at the theater. The "most embarrassed" member of the foursome, Sido speculated, must have been Willy, because, she told her daughter, "men are always jealous of the woman who has given them her virginity, and I rejoice in Willy's fury."[14]

Jouvenel had gone back to his grueling schedule of "twenty-one-day 'two-week' shifts" at the paper, working early into the morning, and Colette opened in a new pantomime at the Ba-Ta-Clan. There was no time for rehearsals, and she improvised her choreography "with a gall," she told Christiane Mendelys, "that she doesn't get from her mother."[15] "Come see me," she urges a writer friend. "I'll be ridiculous and charming."[16]

Those stalwart troupers Wague and Mendelys had, in the meantime, spent their August holidays working out daily on the beach. When Christiane boasted about her muscles and her suntan, and accused Colette, teasingly, of having forsaken the parallel bars for the bedsprings, Colette riposted: "And anyway, who tells you I'm neglecting my gymnastics? I just have a new method, that's all. The Sidi method. Excellent. No public classes. Private lessons—damn private!"[17]

Jouvenel's liaison with a music-hall actress was a constant source of gossip and disapproval, to which he paid no attention, and of envy, which he enjoyed. He never asked Colette to stop working. She loved the stage, and in any case, they needed the money. She could no longer live downstairs from Missy, and had taken a room at the Hôtel Meurice, on the rue de Rivoli. Jouvenel, in the meantime, began renovating his house for her—the ceiling leaked, the bathtub was a drinking trough for the dogs, the roof slates were falling—and the faster the workmen tried to plug its cracks and repair its plumbing, the more it seemed to crumble.

It was October when Colette moved to the rue Cortambert. According to the unwritten *"code de collage"*[18] that governed such love affairs, Jouvenel was now officially her protector. "He doesn't have a fortune," Colette told Hamel, "he has *Le Matin* (forty thousand francs a year), and as I earn a good living, we'll make out.[19] Must I add that I love this man who is tender, jealous, unsociable, and incurably honest? It's not worth the trouble."[20]

But Colette had little leisure to spend in her new "lair." Later that autumn, she revived *La Chair* at Le Havre, and then again in Paris. She started rehearsing a new play with Wague—*L'Oiseau de nuit* (*The Night Bird*)—which opened in December. After Christmas, she spent a few days in Grenoble with Hamel. On January 28, she celebrated her thirty-ninth birthday. Her mother, who observed that "one reaches forty without realizing it,"[21] worried that Colette was working too hard, living too fast, doing too much at once, that she needed rest, adding ominously, "my repose depends on yours, as my health does."[22] It was precisely this naive and loving but terrible insistence on confusing their fates, bodies, and souls that had driven Colette away.

3

SIDO'S OLD NIGHTMARE about Colette's abduction by a handsome stranger had once again come true. A year had passed since the affair had begun, and she had not yet met this Jouvenel, whom she refers to, sarcastically, as "Your marvel." She never asks to be remembered fondly to him, as she did to Missy and Willy, but sends her regards, abstractly, "to those who love you."

Colette had always lied to her mother about her suffering, but she was just as reticent about her happiness. She spoke of bringing Sido to Paris but didn't fix a date. "Hurry up if you want to see me," Sido wrote—the bad weather was setting in—"and arrange for M. de Jouvenel to be there. But perhaps I've been so nasty to him in my letters that he wants to escape my visit? I want my full of hearing your voice and contemplating you, because . . . who knows, I'm really old."[23]

It was probably in response to this letter that the baron wrote to Mme Colette, inviting her formally to visit them on the rue Cortambert. His handwriting, noted Sido, was "diabolical." "You have my daughter," she told him, "you have that happiness, but I will say nothing more—mothers sound so stupid when they praise their daughters to the skies . . . but admit that Willy was a right imbecile for not knowing how to keep her."[24]

A year before Colette's death, and long before the publication of her mother's correspondence, *Le Figaro* printed Sido's formal response to Jouvenel's invitation, unfortunately not dated. It was a version—a significantly different version—of the letter Colette cites on the first page of *Break of Day*.[25] *Le Figaro*'s version:

> Monsieur de Jouvenel,
>   I have decided to accept your gracious invitation for many reasons, among them one I can never resist, to see the beloved face of my daughter and to hear her voice. And finally to know you, and to judge as far as is possible why she has, with such great enthusiasm, kicked over the traces for you. But I will be abandoning, for several days, the beings who only have me to count on: la Minne (her cat) . . . and a magnificent sedum about to flower. . . . They will suffer without me, but my daughter-in-law promises to take care of them. She will . . . be only too happy to get rid of her mother-in-law for a few days. Until soon, then, I think, but tell Gabri that I'm waiting for her to write to me. Do you know who Gabri is? It's even worse: she's called Gabrielle. Did you know? My name is Sidonie Colette.[26]

Sido never made the trip, and it is not certain she ever set eyes on Jouvenel. Her instincts told her she was dying, and they were right. She had survived two mastectomies, but her heart was failing. Achille put her on a spartan diet and prescribed arsenic and digitalis, which alleviated her fits of suffocation but couldn't, as she well knew, cure them. "My sacred heart? Done for, my darling. Used up." Her vanity suffered as much as her flesh did: "I'm losing weight"; "I'm becoming as ugly as possible. Nothing can be done about it." "I can sometimes remember I used to be a woman."[27]

Sido couldn't even leave the house anymore, although she hoped that when spring came, she would be able to take a short walk in the warm air. Achille insisted that his maid, Adelaide, sleep at his mother's. She hated to have someone always there, "watching me live." But at least, she tells Colette, Adelaide was a natural-born "woman of the world."

Colette responded only erratically, even to her mother's most poignant and frightened letters. She came in January for two nights—her first visit in six months—and Sido complained that she only ever saw her flash by "like a meteor." "How deprived I am of your presence! How much I miss your arm to lean on." And she asked Colette not to take on any engagements, or if she had to, to provide for an emergency leave of absence.

On her good days, the old mother was chipper, forgiving, ironic, and philosophical. "It's true that you've forgotten me, but I chalk that up to your numerous occupations, and . . . to your honeymoon. All the same, it's annoying to have children for nothing more than the benefit of others."[28] On her bad days, which were increasingly frequent, Sido was frankly disconsolate: "You couldn't have received the letter in which I tell you how sick I am . . . or else I don't know you anymore."[29] Colette didn't fathom, couldn't bear to admit, or chose to ignore the seriousness of her mother's condition—even when her brother spelled it out for her. "Maman is suffering from a weakness of her cardiac muscle which is somewhat sclerosed by age, without, however, any internal lesions, but it comes to the same thing as if there were." He then begged his sister to "write to mother, even when you have absolutely nothing to say. She loves your letters so much. Pointless to tell you that a visit would be a thousand times more agreeable."[30]

The season turned. Colette promised and canceled several more two-day visits to Châtillon, although she sent Sido and her nieces a steady stream of expensive gifts and delicacies: straw hats, chocolates from Hédiard, and a basket of oranges from Provence, where she and Jouvenel had gone that March. Sido rejoiced vicariously in their imagined pleasure: "What a fine voyage you two have embarked on, remember it well. You have everything: communion of thoughts, youth, intelligence, and . . . pocket money, for the moment. . . . You're happy, you're footloose, and you're eating well? Perfect! One needs such good moments in life to think back upon when one gets old."[31]

But her own condition was steadily weakening. There were longer spaces between her letters, which she wrote in pencil now, in a spidery hand, from her bed. "It's true that mother has really been suffering," Achille informed his sister. ". . . Now she's feeling a little better thanks to the digitalis, but it is possible, it's *even probable,* that this improvement can't be maintained for long. So don't fail to come on Saturday. I told her that you said you were coming . . . if the situation gets worse before then, I'll cable you."[32]

Colette fatuously blamed Jouvenel and his jealousy for keeping her from Châtillon. He would only give her a "two-day leave" at most, she told Hamel, and when she returned from a weekend at the end of March, she found him "depressed," she told Sido—who had the strength to retort: "that's what he gets for cultivating such rare flowers."[33]

It was an unseasonably warm and early spring. Sido was awake at four in the morning of April 6 when she heard a "delicious chirping" outside her window and realized that the swallows had returned to their breeding grounds: "We're old friends, as you know." But by now she couldn't leave her bed, except for her armchair. Colette began rehearsals for a new pantomime, aptly named *La Chatte amoureuse* (*The Cat in Love*). She sent her mother a photograph of herself in a cat suit, wearing cat ears and painted whiskers, and Sido teased her about her behind. She tried valiantly to banter and to gossip. "How stupid everything I have to say sounds, and I would like to be the young mother whom you listen to sweetly, and who makes everything better with kisses, books, and bonbons. *Tendresses,* dear treasure."[34]

4

COLETTE CONTINUED WRITING her weekly column for *Le Matin*. She covered the boxing match between the great white hope of the French, Georges Carpentier, and the American champion "Kid" Lewis. She visited the salon of an avant-garde couturier and was outraged by his "misogyny."[35] She reported on the final laps of the Tour de France. She went up in the dirigible *Clément-Bayard* and felt a "joy without shadow, joy without age."[36]

In late April, she was driven to a grimy suburb where, in a garage on the rue Ordener, the police had cornered a notorious gang of anarchist bank robbers. The crowd behind the barricades with her was "as gay as at a suburban fair," men and women stomping and shouting for the bandits' death. The police dynamited the garage. Colette was blinded by dust and smoke and could see nothing of the final assault. She was pummeled, nearly to death, by knees and elbows, and disgusted by the spectacle of mass bloodlust.

COLETTE'S COLUMN, "The Thousand and One Mornings," was a mixture of short fiction and reportage. The previous August (1911), she had introduced a morbid, sniffling young man with Hériot's ruinous taste in women and Bonmariage's for opium. By January of 1912, she was disgusted with him, and he metamorphosed into a handsome young gigolo named Chéri, in love with an aging courtesan. But Chéri was still only a passing fancy. In June, the paper sent her to Angers to cover an important air race, conducted in high winds and won by the pioneer of aviation Roland Garros. A week later she was in Tours, to write about a crime of passion. The defendant confessed to having "killed for love." The femme fatale was a defiant Juno in black veils: "Once again, I cry to myself, what a solid thing is woman."[37]

Between assignments, Colette returned to the rue Cortambert, where she now kept a menagerie and where she led, as she would say later, "and not without amazement, 'the life of a real woman.' "[38] But all the "real women" in Colette's novels are the patient victims of deceitful men, and she was no exception. Her letters to Hamel imply that Jouvenel's infidelities were the cause of "sinister weeks and hours," "singular crises," and "stormy scenes." His "egotism," she writes, "is so naive and so childish that I feel like laughing and crying at the same time." Could it last? "I am not so mad as to hope for it, dear Hamel. But I give in to an ephemeral, animal happiness which damn well has its price; you know what it's worth . . . the presence of the *necessary* being."[39]

By now, however, Colette had learned the lesson that clinging is fatal, and that tearful pleading is tactically never worth a show of strength and indifference. From Tours that June, she reproduced one of their quarrels for Hamel in a page of dialogue:

J: We have to separate.
C: Yes!
J: Life together
C: . . . is impossible.
J: That doesn't prevent us from remaining good friends!
C: On the contrary!
J: So we're going to leave each other!
C: Right away!
J: Oh, there's no hurry.

(That was Willy's famous line, but now she had the aplomb to parry it.)

C: Yes there is, yes, it's absolutely urgent.
J: Absolutely is not the word . . .
C: Absolutely. July 1: big breakup, each one takes off on his own, and if . . .
    I meet someone beddable and congenial, simple loyalty demands
    that I . . .
J: Certainly, but in the meantime . . .
C: I'm out of here. To [Barlet's house].
J: That's useless, even stupid. You're better off here.

C: No. Goodnight, Sidi.

J: But . . . where are you going?

C: Where is my own business. You yourself said . . .

J: Oh, what I said doesn't matter. Shall we play a game of bezique? . . .
Would it revolt you to dine under the stars at Laurent's? It's lovely out,
and I do so want to stay with you! etc. etc. . . .

"I'm giving you the comic side, dear Hamel," Colette concluded. "Unfortunately, there are others. But . . . I don't despair of treating him as lightly as Hériot."[40]

BY THE END of July 1912, Colette was disgusted enough to consider leaving Jouvenel, but she realized that she couldn't yet afford to do so. After she paid her bills, she would have fifteen hundred francs left. She could expect another thousand from Henry, who paid her a monthly allowance; fourteen hundred from the Ba-Ta-Clan; and a little more from the publication of a luxury edition of her essays that Paul Barlet had planned for the next year. "There's not enough for moving out, renting something else, or traveling," she told Hamel. "So until things change, I'm still living with Jouvenel. We're on 'good terms.' On his part (I tell you everything), there is even a rather unique carnal tenacity. As I am subject to the same tyranny, I've concluded that there are five good minutes and fifteen bad ones. It can't last long, and I'll keep you posted on my progress, as on my backsliding, very dear Hamel."[41]

Jouvenel went off alone to Brive, near Castel-Novel, for a week of flying lessons, and Colette stayed in Paris. He asked her to supervise the interior decoration of his house as if, she says, "I were supposed to spend the rest of my days there." In the meantime, she was "fomenting" a secret escape plan (which sounds like a love affair[42]) and raising some cash to "assure myself of the freedom to leave in two hours if I wanted to." The only person who could furnish her discreetly with a "nice, round sum" was, she told Hamel, Auguste Hériot, who agreed to accept her pearl necklace—the Claudine pearls—as collateral, and with it, perhaps, the promise of her return.[43]

Jouvenel had been telling his side of the story to his friends Sapène and Sauerwein, who were, like Hamel, mystified and somewhat indignant that the couple, for all their mutual recriminations, continued to live under the same roof. But when the baron returned to Paris at the end of August, a jubilant Colette reported to Wague that she was a "screwed-up animal" with a stupid smile, and to Hamel that the reconciliation was "so complete, and at the same time so bizarre and motivated, that the story will surely interest you." In the meantime, she was leaving for Châtillon, "where my sainted mother is insufferable, not that she's more gravely ill, but having a fit of 'I want to see my daughter.' Sidi gives me three days—maximum."[44]

5

WAS IT SIDO or death that was "insufferable" to Colette? She hated death's protocols; it aroused all her instincts for impiety; she refused to observe the bourgeois conventions that governed mourning; she was always happy to contribute money for an abortion, but never for a funeral; when an animal "dies on you," she told the horrified Paul Léautaud, "you should throw its body into the sewer."[45] "I sometimes try to make myself think about [death]," she writes at fifty, "to convince myself that the second half of my life will bring me a bit of gravity, a bit of consideration for what comes *after*. . . . It's a brief illusion. Death doesn't interest me. Not even my own."[46]

Sido was, under the circumstances, heroically understanding. "Remember how long you took to understand about papa?" she reminds Colette, attempting discreetly to breach the wall of her denial. She now had her shroud ready, and she wanted her daughter to hear about it. She only regretted that she couldn't be laid to rest in the fine coffin of black ebony and silver that her brother's friend Victor Considérant had given to her sister-in-law, Caroline— who had been so horrified by the present that she'd passed it along to her maid "instead of to me! You see how lovely I would look in such a niche? . . . Don't be shocked. . . . It's as it should be."[47]

Sido's final published letter to her daughter is dated July 11. "You see how my hand trembles? It's just weakness, because my old heart isn't too agitated."[48] But some ten years later, Colette would open a drawer in her desk, looking for some money, and a sheet of writing paper would fall out of it. "It was a letter from my mother," she told Marguerite Moreno, "one of the last, written in pencil, with the words unfinished, and already filled with her departure. . . . How strange it is: you resist your tears victoriously, you hold on perfectly well at the hardest moments. Then someone gives you a friendly little sign from behind a glass . . . a letter falls from a drawer, and everything crumbles with it."[49]

In *Break of Day*, she would add:

In writing [the last letter], my mother no doubt wanted to assure me that she had already renounced the obligation to use our language. Two penciled pages bear nothing other than signs that seem joyful, arrows starting from a half-sketched word, little rays, two 'yes, yesses' and a very clear 'she danced.' Farther down, she also wrote: 'my love'—she called me thus when our separations were long and she was yearning for me. But this time I feel a scruple in claiming such a burning word for me alone. It takes its place among the . . . messages of a hand that was trying to transmit a new alphabet to me, or the sketch of a place glimpsed at dawn by the light of rays which would never reach the gloomy zenith.[50]

ON AUGUST 28, Colette left for Châtillon, promising Hamel she'd be home by the weekend to give him "the excellent news" about her reconciliation with Sidi. From Achille's house she wrote to Christiane Mendelys, repeating that she was only at her mother's for two days—"Sidi considers that a very sufficient leave of absence, a fact which in itself should illuminate our current relations." Christiane's brother had just died. Colette had not yet had the time to write a proper condolence letter, but she adds: "I think you endure your grief in your own way, which means by saying nothing, and betraying nothing by your expression, which is the manner of courageous people for whom grief is not a new acquaintance. . . . Mother isn't wonderful," she adds, "but she can still hold out for a while, and that's all one asks of her." And finally, she tells her friend to "think of me, to wish for me that this will last," by which she means her happiness, and not her mother's life.[51]

On September 18, Colette opened in *The Night Bird*. On September 25, Sido died in Châtillon. Her daughter didn't cancel her performance to attend the funeral. "I don't want to go," she told Hamel, without explanation. She didn't wear black, and later she claimed it was Sido's wish.[52] Her life went on, the death not mourned or even acknowledged publicly, and "right now," she told her confidant, "things are going pretty well. But I'm tormented by the stupid thought that I can't write to Mother anymore, the way I used to so often do."[53]

Colette spoke of her grief "practically to no one." But she suffered one of those mysterious and violent pelvic "inflammations" which afflicted her, she told Hamel, "when a pain is major enough. . . . De Jouvenel tends to my sorrow . . . in a loving and delicate manner."[54] She doesn't elaborate, but she doesn't have to. Jouvenel nursed her in his fashion, and Colette mourned Sido in hers. "Accidentally," she says, they conceived a child.[55]

PART IV

CHAPTER 23

If, exceptionally, when I was young I busied myself with some needlework, Sido would shake her divinatory brow: "You'll never look like anything but a boy sewing." Had she not said to me: "You'll never be more than a writer who has produced a child"?

—COLETTE,
The Evening Star

1

SIDO AND THE Belle Époque died together. In 1913, the year that a motherless and pregnant Colette would embark on her new life, Diaghilev produced Stravinsky's *Rite of Spring,* with choreography by Nijinsky. Copeau opened the avant-garde Théâtre du Vieux-Colombier. Alain-Fournier published *Le Grand Meaulnes;* Apollinaire, *Alcools* and his treatise on cubism; and Proust, *Swann's Way*—of which Louis de Robert sent Colette a copy. It was, she would say, "everything one would have wished to write, everything one neither dared nor knew how to write."[1]

By then, Dreyfus was a memory, but nationalism resurgent. Charles Péguy, the ardent socialist, was born again as a devout Catholic, and he began to argue that the two evil idols of modernity, money and technology, were embodied in Germany. He wrote a verse play about Joan of Arc, which his old adversary and Colette's former patron Maurice Barrès used as a vehicle for his pro-church and -army propaganda.

The playwright Jean Richepin, who had cast Colette in *Xantho,* founded the League for the Defense of French Culture. Gide, who was just finishing *Les Caves du Vatican,* joined it. It called for a revival of traditional French values in art and religion to correct the imbalance of German "scientism." "Our young people," Richepin proclaimed, "are showing a taste for heroism and glory, inspired by the triumph of recent French inventions [the airplane and the car]."[2] Technology, apparently, was godless only when it wasn't French.

Further to the right, Charles Maurras and Léon Daudet of *L'Action française* were hammering away at their twin hatreds: "Germany and bad Frenchmen." Four of the era's most prominent women poets, all of them Colette's friends—Lucie Delarue-Mardrus, Natalie Barney, Renée Vivien, and Anna de Noailles—belonged, according to Maurras, in the category of bad Frenchmen. Their work, in his view, was polluted by foreign influences, their souls by a "barbarous" Romanticism alien to "the classicism that is France."[3]

Lucie, a Norman, had polluted herself by marrying the Orientalist Dr. Joseph-Charles Mardrus, famous for his fin de siècle translation of *The Thousand and One Nights*. Their wedding, in 1900, caused a minor scandal when the bride appeared at the ceremony in a cycling outfit. She was a prolific poet, novelist, playwright, biographer, and sculptor, famous for her love of cats and her affairs with women—Colette, it has been said, among them—and she considered *Dialogues de bêtes* "an eternal masterpiece." Colette, in turn, paid Lucie the supreme compliment of calling her "a man of letters."[4] The correspondence of their youth attests to a mutual fondness, resemblance, and admiration, though something short of intimacy: it was not until the late 1920s that they began using the familiar *tu*. After her divorce, in 1914, Lucie lived in Normandy with her lover, Germaine de Castro, and her "only flaw," Colette told her, "is that you never come to see me."[5] But as they aged, the chagrins of love, a passion for animals, and the agonies of arthritis were commonalities that intensified their bond.

Anna de Noailles, like Natalie and Renée, was foreign-born—a Romanian princess of feverish dark beauty who had married a French count. Her poetry would often be compared, in its "majestic," "instinctive," feeling for nature and childhood and its melancholy view of love, to the prose of Colette. They had once been voted first and third, respectively, in a poll to determine which women writers might be worthy of ascension to the Académie Française, and in 1935, two years after Anna's death, Colette would succeed to her chair in the Académie Royale of Belgium. From the fin de siècle, and intermittently for some thirty years thereafter, the two women maintained an amiably rivalrous friendship that produced an unctuous correspondence.[6] Colette's flattery of the countess was always a bit backhanded. She calls her work "an ardent formula in which the pain of loving responds to nothing but the happiness of suffering," and she defines Anna's "humility" as "that of a creature who recognizes no peer."[7]

If the poet of the (self-proclaimed) "boundless heart" was, as Colette suggests, a conceited neurasthenic, her opinion of her own genius was largely shared by her contemporaries.[8] Anna was no less convinced of her spiritual sublimity, and she had long been searching for a creed worthy of her faith. Francis Jammes wrote an essay on her spiritual evolution, while Abbé Mugnier ministered to her "ever suffering soul." But, as she told Jean Cocteau, "if God were to exist, I should be the first to be informed." So instead of becoming a Catholic, the countess converted to the nationalism of her lover, Maurice Barrès, and to the cult of Joan of Arc, whom she revered less as a saint than as a militant: "a heroic soldier, rallying her people in a time of danger, and finally giving her life for *la patrie*."[9]

Colette, for her part, listened with detachment to that "heroic buzz, contained, though perceptible . . . murmured by a thousand half-closed mouths: *Mourir pour la patrie*."[10] While reviewing the great military parade staged for the visit of the English sovereigns in April of 1914, she wrote: "My eyes are bad, I don't have a lorgnette—so the spectacle is even finer for me." And it was with that same ironic myopia that she would always regard the spectacle of her times. She goes to hear Aristide Briand speak, and what she notices is "the game of arms, now crossed with power, now sweeping and chafing invisible things." She listens to Jean Jaurès—the old Quixote of the left[11]—and laughs at this "*vomiter* of the word. He lifts his voice in lamentations worthy of a prophet: 'Listen to me, all of you . . . I will speak the truth, even if it costs me my life.' " (It did.)[12] There was not an idea that could carry Colette away, or a sensation that couldn't.

2

AFTER SIDO'S DEATH, Colette had another week in *The Night Bird,* and she played out her contract. When the play closed, on September 30, she and Jouvenel went for some rest to Castel-Novel. She had a bad cold, and the entire household was agreeably solicitous about her health. "Everyone is charming to me," Colette tells Hamel. "My mother-in-law, as Sidi calls her, is youth itself, and gaiety."[13]

Mme de Jouvenel was indeed youthful—only three years older than Colette's sister would have been. She had married at seventeen, given birth to Henry at nineteen, and when Colette met her, she was fifty-seven. She shared with Mme Colette a fierce maternal devotion and an indifference to bourgeois convention. Despite her snobbery, Mamita accepted her notorious new "daughter-in-law" with the same aplomb she had shown when her son brought home a Jewish wife and later fathered a bastard son. Edith, the fruit of her own adulterous liaison, was now a teenager whom Colette describes as "gigantic and sweet." And perhaps this vigorous noblewoman who smoked cigars, played tennis, and swigged brandy like a soldier helped to banish the other, more distressing maternal image—the affront of Sido's mortality and of the wasted old body Colette had refused to see.

SHE WASN'T YET certain of her condition, but when Colette returned to Paris in mid-October, she went to the doctor. "You're indeed pregnant, Madame," he told her. "Very good. Now you will oblige me by forgetting about it. . . . I have no other advice to give you. Of course, four or five months hence, it would be better not to fall down stairs, bellyflop, or go riding. Apart from that . . . go ahead, lead your normal life."[14]

"I remember welcoming the certainty of this late child," writes an admirably candid Colette, ". . . with a considered mistrust, and keeping quiet about it. It was myself that I mistrusted. It wasn't a matter of physical apprehension. I was worried about my maturity, my possible inaptitude for loving, understanding, absorption. Love—so I thought—had already served me ill in monopolizing me for twenty years in its exclusive servitude."[15]

So she did continue to lead her "normal" life, telling almost no one about the baby, and she was deeply flattered by Charles Sauerwein's remark that she was having "a man's pregnancy." No sooner had she returned to Paris than she was off to Geneva with Wague and Kerf to perform *The Night Bird,* "with its arranged fights, blows with a pitchfork, the hand-to-hands on the table. . . . A man's pregnancy?" she gloats. "A champion's pregnancy, rather. . . . And the flat, muscled belly of a gymnast."[16]

Her partners, however, could not help noticing that Colette seemed to have acquired an "involuntary smirk," which alternated with sudden fits of sleepiness and depression. She finally confessed her secret on their first Sunday off, after a boat tour of Lake Leman. Wague was much moved, "pretended that he wasn't, called me a broody wood-owl," and warned her about "the cravings." They moved her to the best suite at the hotel, and the next morning they brought her a breakfast tray with fresh coffee brewed in their own rooms, to spare her the "hotel piss." "Good companions!" she reflects.

Those performances in Geneva were her last as a mime, and "every evening I said a small farewell to one of the good periods of my life. I was well aware that I should regret it. But the cheerfulness, the purring, the euphoria submerged everything."[17]

LIKE MANY WOMEN, Colette felt "most pregnant" in the evening. She ate methodically, and was gaining weight "slowly but surely," but it distressed her to have lost that keystone of her well-being, a good appetite. Her doctor "wasn't happy" with her urinalysis or her blood test and diagnosed anemia. He ordered a special diet and prescribed a strychnine tonic.[18] "I have to make a proper, well-formed child, good Lord!" Colette tells Wague.[19] By the beginning of her third month she had weathered her nausea and outgrown her fitted clothes. The child "needs space," she told Christiane Mendelys, "he'll break everything. You see that he already resembles his father."[20]

Henry was not yet divorced from Claire Boas. According to their son, Bertrand, the first baroness was exceptionally gracious, under the circumstances, about facilitating the legalities "in the interest of the child."[21] By the end of November, Jouvenel was a free man, and the banns were published for his wedding to Mme Willy. It was an "utterly simple" civil ceremony, which took place on December 19, 1912, at four-thirty, in the *mairie* of the sixteenth arrondissement. The bride's witness was Léon Hamel. Mamita was in Paris for the occasion, but there is no mention of Colette's brothers, Léo and Achille. The festivities were organized by the couple's colleagues at *Le Matin*, who passed them from "table to table," and they concluded a weeklong gastronomic "orgy" by carousing until dawn. "If this child isn't the lowest of high-livers," sighs Colette proudly, "I give up!"[22]

3

MADAME COLETTE WILLY, woman of letters, notorious lesbian, bare-breasted music-hall star, and social pariah, was now the baroness de Jouvenel des Ursins, and the wife of one of Paris's most influential political journalists. A week before her fortieth birthday, she and Jouvenel were at Versailles to report on the presidential elections. The centrist, Poincaré, handily defeated the radical, Jules Pams, but his real rival was the minister of finance, Joseph Caillaux. A self-made millionaire, Caillaux had risen meteorically from a back bench in the Chamber of Deputies to become premier in 1911. He was hated by the rich (he had proposed an income tax) and by the nationalists (he'd opposed the draft and favored an accommodation with Germany), but his charisma was acknowledged even by his enemies. "No one else," writes Edward Berenson, ". . . dressed with such flair, flaunted women so openly, or displayed a combination of intellectual power and financial acumen such as his."[23] Jaurès had called Caillaux "a dandy straight out of Balzac." Anatole de

Monzie admired his intellect and his principles. So, with reservations, did Henry de Jouvenel. The Jouvenels and Caillaux were cousins, and photographs of Henry and Joseph suggest a family resemblance. They were both ardent republicans, realists, and reformers, and unafraid of controversial marriages: Caillaux had scandalized his peers by marrying two divorcées in a row, the second of whom—Henriette Claretie—was shortly to become the most notorious woman in France, and the protagonist of the "trial (or at least another one) of the century."

4

COLETTE DE JOUVENEL, as she proudly signed herself, now turned back to fiction. She was working on *The Shackle,* a sequel to *The Vagabond* and her first new novel in three years. It "tortured" her, she told Wague. "I'd like to see all my characters in a hundred feet of ... [shit]."[24] And she was only a chapter or two ahead of the weekly installments that, in March, began running in *La Vie parisienne.*

Yet the pressure both of her deadlines and of her pregnancy don't show until the last third of this almost great novel. Renée Néré is Balzac's *femme de trente ans* in 1913, which is to say, she's almost forty (just as she's now almost fifty), childless and single, wary of love but not done with men, and living alone on a small inheritance. The old vagabond still has no fixed address and spends her idle days in some of the provincial towns where she once performed. One afternoon, on the Promenade des Anglais in Nice, she catches a glimpse of the man she didn't marry, the man whose love was too proprietary and conventional and perhaps too generous. Maxime Dufferein-Chautel is strolling with his new wife and their baby, and he doesn't notice Renée. But "the revelation" of seeing him as a family man gives her a "shock": the intimation of her own fragility.

At her hotel, Renée falls in with three equally idle companions. May is an exasperating young beauty modeled on Lily de Rême. Her lover, Jean, is a rich and well-born Parisian who resembles Jouvenel.[25] Jean's dissolute but serviceable sidekick, Masseau, like his model, Paul Masson, is either "capriciously *wired* or completely prostrated" by drugs.[26] Renée amuses herself by charming this eccentric trio, and they entertain her in spite of her disdain for them, arousing "that old pride of the ex-bluestocking who smiles with irony and pity" at Masseau's weakness, May's mispronunciations, and Jean's vanity.[27]

When Renée steals Jean from May and they become lovers, she has a second revelation. Taillandy was a tyrant, Maxime a patsy, but this time she has met an "equal," a "fine adversary" who sees through her:

"Your gimmick, forgive the word, is reticence, a flash from lowered eyes, from a stealthy smile, from a hand withdrawn—it's theatrical method, my dear friend. . . . And now you can crush me with your superior silence, but I won't retract a word."

"But Jean, on the contrary, I'm listening, I'm astonished, I'm even full of admiration. It's not at all stupid, what you're saying."

"And you don't hide your astonishment. What a miracle! He can talk! What joy! He's mistreating me a little."[28]

The curious young virgin whom Colette describes in *My Apprenticeships* eagerly "puts her hand into the velvet paw" of a mature seducer but wonders afterwards: "Is this all?"[29] The mature heroine of *The Shackle* is tired of hearing "cocksure young women declare, 'My motto in love is, All or nothing.' Well," Renée concludes, having slept with Jean, "a nice little nothing, well presented, is already something." And a little further she concedes: "I've never known this—the intelligent joy of the flesh."[30] Then she puts on her clothes and goes back to a hotel room paid for by her own money to savor her "gluttonous" memories. "Is this all?" she asks. "But of course this is all. And who wouldn't be content with it?"[31]

Embarking on her adventure with Jean, Renée believes that she has "weaned herself from love."[32] It's a revealing phrase, the more so from a woman pregnant with her first child, who has just lost her mother. Love, for Colette, is mother's milk, and the infant's hunger for it. It is also a form of poison, for to fall in love is to want and to need everything necessary for survival from one all-powerful and barely differentiated Other. Renée is safe so long as she and Jean remain "two friends walking parallel, side by side, on opposite sides of a glass wall, ignorant of what separates us." He complains, jokingly, as will the rake in *The Tender Shoot,* that he sometimes has the feeling that "you don't love me, but that you're using me." What he doesn't know, and what Renée can't tell him—because Colette doesn't know it yet, either— is that their civil and discreet mutual exploitation constitutes more intimacy than a man and a woman in her fiction usually achieve.

A year before she began *The Shackle,* Colette had remarked to Hamel, of Jouvenel: "I don't despair of treating him as lightly as Hériot."[33] And for most of the novel, Renée struggles to maintain that lightness with Jean. The moral of the story is clear enough: feign detachment, treat passion with wariness, and stay separate. But like her author, Renée can't. It's not the man who is so powerful and beguiling, but the old temptation to give herself a master. When she finally loses herself, it's to love, not to Jean, and one of the paradoxes of Colette's fiction is that men always dissolve as characters the minute their women surrender to them. For better or worse, desire obliterates the individuality of its object. Renée doesn't know how it happens, and perhaps neither does Colette, but one day the man is no longer her "succulent prey" but the thing that is more necessary to her "than air or water" and to which she prefers "those fragile possessions which a woman calls her dignity and her self-esteem." "Alas," thinks Renée, of Jean, "I don't see you anymore."[34]

5

THIS WAS THE WORK that occupied Colette for the last trimester of her pregnancy. The first roses bloomed, the first strawberries ripened on the vine, and by the end of June, she was back in Paris from Castel-Novel. "The child and the novel," she wrote, drove her on. She was tired all the time, and she had the "look of a rat dragging a stolen egg." When she felt the first contractions, she put down her pen and gave her garden a thorough watering. That morning, she would remember, was cloudless. "The imperious child, on its way towards its second life, ill-treated a body, no less impatient than itself, which resisted."[35]

Two days later, on July 3, the infant was born. "I have a little Rat, and I paid the price for it," Colette told Wague: "thirty hours with *no* relief, chloroform and forceps."[36] When she came to from the anesthesia, the room was silent, and she realized she had stopped screaming. Her husband told her that they had a little girl. Colette asked to see her, but her "true desire was to postpone the moment when she would have nothing more to wonder about her work. In a moment she would know if the child was ugly or deformed, she would know if she did or didn't love her, everything would be irreparable."[37]

The nurse helped her to sit up and put the swaddled infant in her arms. Colette saw that she was a shapely female with a full head of hair, but she didn't feel that "famous rush" of maternal feeling, and she wondered whether she was "a monster." Her husband sat beside her, radiant with the "joy that had been promised her" and which she didn't feel. She examined the newborn hands, the sleeping face, the eyebrows, the mouth, and cried out to Jouvenel: "But it's you, *c'est toi!*" And in that moment, she says, she was inflamed with the revelation of "a love, of love, period"—but for her man. "O little creature," she asks herself, ". . . when will I love you purely for your self alone?"[38]

The baby would not be christened, because her father wanted her to make her own religious choices when she was mature enough to do so. But she was, of course, named: Colette Renée—for her mother and her mother's alter ego. To complete this trinity, she was given her mother's nickname: Bel-Gazou. *"Toi, c'est moi."* That is how Sido defined her relation to Colette, and perhaps Colette expected to be reborn—*renée*—in this child, who saw light exactly nine months from the day of Sido's death.[39] The baby's "astonishing" resemblance to her father, however, only waxed with the years. This was a disillusionment, and there were others, but would maternity have come more naturally to Colette with a child who was her mirror image? "The outcome [of labor] is of no importance," she would write: ". . . The outcome is sleep and appetite, selfish and restorative. But it's also, once, the attempt to creep towards me of my little swaddled larva which had been put down for a moment on my bed. Animal perfection! She divined, scented, the presence of my forbidden milk,[40] strove towards my stopped-up source. Never have I wept with so rebellious a heart. What is the suffering of asking in vain compared with the pain of denial?"[41]

And the mother's denial would never waver in its resolve.

IF THE ENJOYMENT of an exciting sex life has never been incompatible with the production of a distinguished oeuvre, motherhood is a different matter. For the last two centuries, a striking number of literary women—among them the greatest ones—have been childless.[42] Some were celibate, others were homosexual. Poverty, spinsterhood, infertility, chronic illness, or emotional fragility determined the circumstances of others. The unhappy or sacrificial examples of their own mothers were often discouraging. And no one who has tried both to mother and to write can honestly say they are not, at times, conflicting vocations.

Physically and materially, Colette's life presented fewer impediments to raising a child than did the lives of most of her literary sisters. She also had the example of a mother whose success in living fully she idealized. Thus her own rejection of any real responsibility for her daughter can seem harder to fathom. She defines the second sex as the strong one; she challenges the received ideas about the incapacity of females for work, pleasure, autonomy, and aggression; she rises to the challenge of becoming both a person and a woman. But she also demurs to the conventional assumption of an absolute choice between being a sovereign artist and a good enough mother, and shakes herself free—often brutally—of what she calls "the maternal yoke."

"My strain of virility," Colette writes with pride, "saved me from the danger which threatens the writer, elevated to a happy and tender parent, of becoming a mediocre author. . . . Beneath the still young woman that I was, an old boy of forty saw to the wellbeing of a possibly precious part of myself."[43] But not only would there never be any contest; there would never be any balance between her own well-being and that of her child. Colette and her daughter only lived under the same roof for the odd month in summer. Bel-Gazou was raised at Castel-Novel by her English nanny, and sometimes half a year would pass without a parental visit. The wild and lonely little girl was sent to boarding school at eight, and when she reached adolescence, farmed out to various women friends who acted as Colette's surrogates. "All weakness was forbidden to her," writes a friend, "and above all, that of . . . asking for love. . . . She learned never to complain of solitude or abandonment."[44]

When the old Colette insists in memoirs and interviews on her "born passivity," it comes as a surprise and seems to jibe very little with the evidence of her drive to dominate. But passivity marks her relations with Bel-Gazou. She describes how she listens from the landing outside her daughter's bedroom door while a toddler afraid of the dark talks herself to sleep, and she never even seems to consider going in to comfort her. She rejects her nanny's invitation to tussle with the baby on the carpet, explaining that she's "too busy" watching her "live." When the grown daughter rushes to her side after an accident, she rebuffs her coldly: she doesn't want any "upsetting" filial tenderness. Occasionally, her repressed passion overwhelms her: "How little one knows oneself," she confides to Hamel in one of her most poignant letters: "I arrive serenely [at Castel-Novel], I find the little one in the salon—and I burst into tears."[45] She bursts into tears again, years later, when her teenage daughter comes home late from an outing, and she squeezes the flesh of the child's arms and shoulders to assure herself that "my fruit is [still] nice and firm."[46] But most of the time she is candid about her own "inaptitude" as a mother: "I have not forgotten how I used to take a child every year to the sea, as to a maternal element better fitted than I to teach, ripen, and perfect the mind and body which I had merely rough-hewn."[47]

Colette wrote fondly, at times ecstatically, about her daughter. The vigor and beauty of the girl, the teenager, and the young woman inspired the same meticulous contemplation that she had lavished (in prose) on the baby. She claims that she eventually became an "ordinary"—which is to say a besotted—mother, but she also calls this conversion a "violation." The picture of mother and child that emerges from her collected works is of two proud and discreet strangers, "sparing of words" and "containing their emotion," which they are unable to express. Her letters offer an even sadder contrast: between a supremely vivid and powerful Colette who is by turns possessive and detached; and a Bel-Gazou who is by turns effaced and rebellious, and who extorts a reflection—makes herself exist for her mother the only way she can: by becoming her greatest disappointment.

CHAPTER 24

l

COLETTE HAD BEEN terrified that childbirth would compromise her physical and erotic fitness—that it would slacken her irreparably. Now she was elated that it hadn't: "I've repaired myself as if by magic,"[1] she boasts to Hamel. A month later, she tells Sacha Guitry's wife, Charlotte Lysès, that "it's really so sweet to feel light, flat, fit for tennis and driving, and to discover that one has suffered not the slightest damage."[2]

She went back to writing with the same energy, and finished *The Shackle* by the first week in September, working, at the end, eleven-hour days. But the novel, unlike her body, never recovered "from the blows inflicted by the feeble and triumphant creature."[3] "I despise [the book]," she told Hamel. "I vomit it up." Her memoirs apologize to her readers for "the fine but empty tone of an ending in which [her characters] do not believe."[4] She tried to rewrite it, but didn't succeed, and she took the loss of this "contest" as a warning, which she never forgot.

PRESIDENT POINCARÉ WAS in Brive that week to convene with the mayors of central France. Colette and Jouvenel gave an official dinner for him, his wife (a cat lover), and eighty-seven guests. Then Hamel arrived to stay at Castel-Novel for a few days, and after his departure, Bel-Gazou's wet nurse lost her milk. The baby was weaned to a bottle, and Colette had to rush back to Paris to recruit a "dry" replacement. "My life," she told her confidant, "has been spent in nanny bureaus. . . . I promise you it was horrible. I've suffered anguish, anxiety, boredom, and I've been thoroughly pissed off."[5] She finally hired an "ugly, providential" Englishwoman named Miss Draper, a "harsh, cross-grained, grumbling foreigner hard on others and on herself, [who] exiled herself voluntarily to the country alone with a small child."[6] She is known to Colette's readers as "Nursie-dear," and in her conversations with Colette she referred to her charge as "my baby." Renaud de Jouvenel would recall her as a "nasty old witch." Bertrand de Jouvenel protested to Colette that Miss Draper not only locked his sister up but beat her.[7] Bel-Gazou, said an old friend, grew up "in terror" of her.[8]

Having solved her child-care problem ("whew! . . . I'm wiping my brow"), Colette went back to writing her weekly column for *Le Matin.* The baby became a frequent subject. The first anniversary of Sido's death came and went, unnoted by Colette in any extant documents. Georgie Raoul-Duval died on November 2. Now Achille lay dying, too. He couldn't mistake his symptoms—he had written his doctoral thesis about them—and cancer of the liver killed him on the last day of the year. He was only fifty. Colette was silent to all of her usual correspondents about the death of this "big brother with no rival." Achille's widow has been blamed for destroying all of Colette's letters to Sido, but Achille may well have burned them himself before he died, with his grief for his mother and his sister's negligence of her still so fresh. "You know Achille," wrote Sido to her Minet-Chéri, "He never pardons any insult, and he never forgets one.[9]

2

COLETTE'S CALENDAR that winter was typically overcharged. She introduced a performance of *L'École des femmes* at the Théâtre Fémina with a well-received lecture on Molière, explaining that while he satisfied her intelligence, he disappointed her feelings, and she could happily live without him. "Shit for Molière!" she tells Moreno.[10] At the Café Excelsior in Tournai, she gave a reading from her new collection of animal portraits.[11] She covered an air show and described a film set. She wrote as insouciantly about parliamentary debates as she did about getting her hair done. Her columns were preoccupied with spoiled children, abused wives, bubble-headed lady lecturegoers, fashion victims, and exercise fanatics. "Physical culture, physical culture!" she exclaims with a certain proprietary contempt for the dilettantes who were taking up the fad. "They rush for it . . . with their bull-terrier enthusiasm," and "they all do it, not for very long."[12]

The Jouvenels went constantly to the theater, and Natalie Barney, who had moved from Neuilly to what was to become her legendary apartment on the rue Jacob, gave a dinner for them in her new, all-white salon. Among the guests was Robert d'Humières, Colette's former neighbor and an avid fan of *Dialogues de bêtes*. As she had passed his garden window on her way to visit Renée Vivien, he would offer her "an armful of snow"—his cat, Lanka—saying, "To you I entrust my most precious possession."[13]

Viscount d'Humières was an anglophile, the author of a history of Great Britain and a translator of Conrad and Kipling. He had also helped Proust translate Ruskin, and had lent certain of his own features to Saint-Loup. The man and the character would both die in the First World War. D'Humières's death on the battlefield was a heroic suicide, his friends believed, committed to escape an impending scandal exposing his homosexual activities. The viscount was married and had a daughter, but his preferences were well-known, and George Painter speculates that d'Humières "was the invert to whom, as Proust later remarked to Paul Morand, 'love of men brought virility and virility brought glory.' "[14] Something about this tender, secretive, and melancholy figure—an officer in the Zouaves—reminded Colette of her father.

3

AT THE END of February 1914, Colette made a quick trip to Belgium, where she was proclaimed "the most beautiful novelist in France and one of the two or three great prose writers of our time."[15] In March, she spent three days at Castel-Novel visiting her child, and she was still in the country when she heard the news that Mme Joseph Caillaux had gone to the office of Gaston Calmette, editor of *Le Figaro,* and shot him dead, point blank, with a little Browning revolver she had bought earlier that day.

Calmette had been waging a virulent smear campaign against Caillaux, and had not only attacked his patriotism but exposed his sex life, publishing a series of love letters that Caillaux had written to his first wife while they were both still married to others. The crime captured headlines in every major daily and obsessed the capital for the next six months. On March 17, Colette rushed back to Paris, where the Chamber of Deputies was meeting in extraordinary session. Jouvenel was covering the crisis for *Le Matin,* and Colette waited up for him with the wives of several other political journalists and deputies, all invited for a late supper at the home of a minister.

Although she never wrote explicitly about the Caillaux affair, she did describe that dinner party, and her column, published on March 26, makes an interesting footnote to the social history arising from the trial, which has been analyzed with great lucidity by Edward Berenson. The defense, he explains, hoped to have Mme Caillaux acquitted by proving she had committed a crime of passion. The prosecution hoped to prove she had acted rationally in her own self-interest. The issue was her femininity: was she a real woman or a New Woman? Was she weak, passive, and emotional, or steely and calculating? As the trial progressed, every aspect of Mme Caillaux's character, comportment, domestic life, and sexual history was examined by the court and in the press. If she could be portrayed as a feminist acting rationally and decisively, she might be found guilty of premeditated murder. If it could be proved that she was a distraught wife acting impulsively to preserve her husband's honor, she might be exonerated. "Because no controversy existed over whether or not Henriette Caillaux had killed Gaston Calmette, she would be judged in large part through the meanings and associations suggested by those two words. . . . Femininity and feminism."[16]

Colette's article in *Le Matin* reveals the entrenched conservatism that coexisted in her character with the better-known radical non-conformity. Without naming the murderess, she damns her implicitly by comparing her to the devoted "real women" who had gathered that night to succor their tired warriors: "The freshly adorned women seem to be entertaining exhausted paladins who demand cool water, a basin and ewer, and perfumes. A slender hand slips into the large hand of a man; another secretly strokes a balding forehead to examine and cool a fever." The women at the supper party are indignant at the crime, even violently so, but they sublimate their own feelings to the feminine task at hand, and the men's "strength and laughter" respond to their ministrations. "The guests remember that there are women present who are their wives, attentive to their role, and filled with silent devotion . . . they simply become men again, beneath the tender and, as it were, rewarded gaze of their good females."[17]

There is no irony to this little sketch, and there is no sense that Colette is conscious of any paradox in writing it—that the same bad girl who divorces, goes on the stage, wears men's clothes, earns her own money, lives openly as a lesbian, and mocks the decorous, bourgeois hypocrisies of her friend Valentine should now be the champion and member of the good-wives' club. Armand Lanoux explains that Colette "wanted it all: to conserve the sexual prestige of the child-woman and the privileges of independence."[18] One might also say that she was exercising the hallowed privilege of a "real woman" to be thoroughly erratic.

Mme Caillaux's trial began on July 20. On July 23, almost a month after Archduke Ferdinand was assassinated in Sarajevo, Austria-Hungary delivered an ultimatum to Serbia which made war in the Balkans inevitable. The Austrians and their German allies had timed it carefully: Poincaré and his premier, Viviani, were at sea, returning from a strategic conference in Russia, and with no ship-to-shore radio, they were incommunicado for six days. Stéphane Lauzanne was with them, so Jouvenel was running *Le Matin*. Like the other

Paris dailies, it was fixated on the trial and carried remarkably subdued news of the international crisis.

On July 28, Austria declared war against Serbia, and the Caillaux trial went to the jury (she would be acquitted). Colette was vacationing at Rozven with a young friend, a showgirl turned silent-film actress named Jeanne Roques, whose stage name was Musidora. "The Caillaux Affair?" Colette writes to Hamel. ". . . I have a thousand opinions about it which I will restrain myself from putting into writing, because four out of five of Sidi's letters to me get here opened. . . . The baby is superb, golden brown as a piecrust," she continues, Musidora is "showing her ass," and she is patiently working out her old muscles with housework and swimming.[19]

On July 31, the leader of the German social democrats arrived in Paris to meet with Jaurès, hoping for some miraculous last-minute negotiation that might avert the spread of the Balkans war. He was met with the news that the pacifist had been assassinated in a café on the rue du Croissant. That evening, Sidi wrote to tell Colette that he "still believed in peace." The following afternoon, he cabled to say that "grave things were happening."[20] Viviani had issued the order for a general mobilization, and Henry would be called up to fight for his country with every other able-bodied man in France. "The war of 1914," wrote Bertrand de Jouvenel, "came to pass exactly as Jaurès had foreseen in 1909."[21]

4

LATE THAT AFTERNOON—August 1, 1914—Colette and Musidora drove to Saint-Malo to hear more news. The sea was green under an overcast sky as they approached the golden ramparts of the old town. On the beach, the children were packing up their sand toys and going home for tea. Colette told her readers she would "never forget that hour." They drove through narrow streets as clogged with people as the air was thick with drumrolls, tocsins, and weeping. In the town square, a crowd had gathered around the crier, who was reading the mobilization edict. Their car was quickly engulfed by a sea of sobbing women and young men with the stunned air of "sleepwalkers," who climbed on their hood and roof to get a better view.

As in a dream, writes Colette, they made their way home through fields ripe for harvest. The cliffs were purple, the sea was dead calm, but the country resounded with alarm bells. They packed their bags, and the next morning, leaving Bel-Gazou and Miss Draper at Rozven, they drove to Paris without a stop, arriving at dusk. The streets of the capital were deserted. Most bourgeois families were still in the country for the August holidays, and vans, taxis, and cars had been requisitioned by or volunteered to the military. The heat and humidity were suffocating, and there was a strange plague of flies. Searchlights raked a night sky as "heavy as a pot cover," and in the days that followed, everyone got a smallpox vaccination. Fresh vegetables were still cheap and plentiful, but the elderly remembered the famine of 1870, and Parisians were gorging "as a precautionary measure." Panicked housewives frantically shopped for provisions, hoarding what they could find. There was no veal in the butcher shops, bakers were forbidden to make "luxury bread," and the sale of absinthe was forbidden, too. All of the chic boutiques were closed, "but the cocottes of Paris, in diamonds and pearls, were busy making tricolor rosettes and selling them for the Red Cross."[22]

Jouvenel joined the infantry as a sergeant,[23] and on August 12, he left for Verdun. "Couldn't see you," he wrote to Monzie. "I'm off. I'm counting on coming back. But one never knows. If by chance I stay there, I ask you to take care of my family."[24] That day, Marguerite Moreno noted in her journal that Colette's husband was equipped for battle with a jerry can and a saber, and that he departed "quite joyfully. [Colette] feigns a lightheartedness that is painful for her friends. As soon as he put on his uniform, he was miles away from [his wife] and everything else. This brusque transformation of a civilian into a soldier changes the way one thinks about and loves [them]."[25]

After Marcel Schwob's death, Moreno had remarried, emigrated to Argentina, founded a national conservatory of theater arts, and divorced, and she had recently returned to France to revive her stage career. She was living with a new husband, the actor Jean Daragon, in a ground-floor apartment on the rue Jean-de-Boulogne, not far from Colette's chalet on the rue Cortambert. Daragon was obese and suffered from emphysema, thus was exempt from military service. When war broke out, all the theaters of Paris were closed, and Moreno's income was drastically reduced. Without Sidi's salary from *Le Matin*, so was Colette's. She was still writing her own column for the paper ("One has to live," she told Christiane Mendelys), but with the Battle of the Marne raging and the capital threatened by an invasion—the Germans were boasting they would be there by the 15th of September—the government had moved south to Bordeaux, and she feared that the papers might soon cease to publish.

Colette dismissed her servants and, for the first time in her life, kept house for herself. Miss Draper refused to accept a salary and eventually moved with Bel-Gazou to Castel-Novel, where food was plentiful—the estate had its own farm—and Mamita footed the bills. Colette and Moreno decided to pool some of their resources. Musidora joined this commune as "she was broke, too," and so did a fourth friend and neighbor in the sixteenth arrondissement, Annie de Pène.

"Musi" was then in her middle twenties—an exotic beauty with the eyes of a Keane waif and the same exaggerated pallor. A decade earlier, she had been one of the "infatuated little minors" who, like Meg Villars, had thrown themselves at Willy. He became, she says, her "protector," and through him she had approached Colette, sending her some amateur sketches of "a naked and prettified Claudine" enclosed in a mash note. Mme Willy responded in a gracious letter, declining the offer of "your life . . . and the rest. Through it all, I am a prudent woman . . . not old yet but losing her youth, which I don't try to hide, and I would be very happy to shake your hand."[26]

In 1910, Musidora had embarked on her own stage career, but she was also writing theater criticism. An "ecstatic review" of a lecture by Colette earned her an invitation to lunch with her idol, and from that day, wrote Musi, "I clung to her." They both performed at the Ba-Ta-Clan, and after Musi had displayed her charms in an "erotic" adaptation of *Paul et Virginie* at the Folies-Bergère, Gaumont approached her to make films. She was extremely photogenic, and with her coltish legs, Cleopatra bob, and kohl-rimmed eyes, she wouldn't have looked out of place as the heroine of a modern cult horror film. Indeed, she pioneered the genre, playing Irma Vep in the twelve episodes of Louis Feuillade's *Les Vampires*, which made her a star and the pinup girl of the Surrealists.

Musi was not yet as rich as her film career was to make her, and she was renting a modest studio on the rue Decamps, around the corner from Colette. But when the Zeppelin bombing raids started, she began sleeping on an iron cot at the rue Cortambert. It seems likely they were sharing something more piquant than their fear and solitude. Musi's weakness for nasty, unfaithful men—indeed, for thugs—did not preclude the occasional dalliance with a woman, and it is said that she had such a fling with Colette.[27]

The fourth communard, Annie de Pène, was a journalist and novelist who lived in a cottage on the "countrified" impasse Herrent.[28] She became, with Hamel, Colette's closest confidante of the period. The two women shared the same brusque style of speech, love of food, hatred of sentiment and prudery, and physical vigor. Annie's daughter, Germaine Beaumont, was shocked at how casually her mother spoke of her famous friend, but the absence of awe is probably the key to their intimacy. "You write me the things I would like to write you," Colette told Annie. "I'm never afraid that you'll disillusion me, and I'm not saving any nasty surprises for you."[29]

Like Moreno, Annie was that rare exception in Colette's circle of women acolytes and protégées, a true peer. But she was also something Moreno wasn't: a professional writer. They had so much in common that Musidora would refer to Annie as "a second Colette" and Colette made Annie an honorary "friend from childhood."

Colette's "phalanstery of women" was not quite the testosterone-free zone she describes. Annie's lover, Gustave Téry,[30] came for dinner almost every night. Moreno had Daragon to care for, and for a month or so, Musi "recovered" some long-lost boyfriend. But the friends kept house together and shared those evenings that weren't otherwise taken. Musi shopped and cooked while Colette gardened, cleaned, and did the laundry. Annie scouted the provisions—it was she who could rustle up a blood sausage or a farm chicken—and when she got lucky, she made them one of her famous Norman dishes. Moreno's role was chief comic, sage, gossipmonger, whip, and morale booster. With "a cigarette between her lips, [she] would sprinkle our domestic tasks with the beneficent dew of news, true or false, anecdotes, and prognostications."[31]

A MONTH INTO the war, the Germans were at the gates of Paris. "On windless nights," the women could hear "the belch of the howitzers,"[32] and Moreno once danced a tango to the rhythm of the explosions. A bomb fell in Isabelle de Comminges's garden. The Battle of the Marne now began to take its ghastly toll. Péguy and Alain-Fournier were among the first writers to die. Robert de Jouvenel was badly wounded, and Henry survived a barrage of fire which killed the comrade fighting beside him. In a "brief and tender note" from the front, he told his wife how much he loved her. She was, writes Moreno, "exultant."[33] "This isn't the moment for me to lose my courage," she remarks to Hamel. And she asks him to proclaim Sidi's glory at the Primrose—Missy's villa near Rozven.[34]

In mid-October, Colette volunteered as a night nurse at the Lycée Janson-de-Sailly, which had been converted into a hospital. It was a shift nobody wanted. She says that she worked for thirteen hours, from seven in the evening to eight in the morning, and had eight critically wounded soldiers under her care. One had lost his jaw and eye, another his leg; a third had walked six miles with half his face blown off, having left his tongue and all his teeth in a trench, and he didn't consider himself so badly wounded. When she wasn't changing their bandages, making them tea, administering anesthetics, or tending the hot-water furnace, she sat with them and talked about her father. They wanted to know where he had been amputated. "Higher than me? And he could still walk? . . . and he married all the same? What was his wife like? Tell us."[35]

Colette toiled through the night for about a week, then was transferred to the day shift. By now, she told Hamel, she hadn't seen her husband for two months. A few weeks later—no longer able to bear the separation—she decided to join him at the front, and left Paris under a false name (Anna Godé), with borrowed papers, on a train bound for Verdun. The worst "perils" she faced en route were those of being recognized by three friends on the same train. The horizon had a red glow from the fighting, and the ground shook with a "sumptuous thunder." It took thirteen hours to cover about a hundred miles, and what made them so long, says Colette, was not her anxiety but her impatience to arrive.

In Verdun she went into hiding in the apartment of a French officer and his wife, the Lamarques. The worst of it, she told Musidora, was that she had forgotten her shower cap and her makeup kit, and she described herself as "nothing but a sort of rag, limp with love."[36] Her months at the front were among the happiest in her life, in part, surely, because she had no rivals for Henry's heart, ardor, or gratitude. She kept her shutters closed during the day, exercised, wrote, painted, scrubbed floors, and studied chess—the "ultimate proof of love" that she could give her husband.[37] Only after dark did she go out for a nightly walk, in stealth, along the Meuse. "I divine the river, the hospital, and the citadel," she told Hamel. "From the height of a bridge, I glimpse the furious water of the barrage. That's all, but it's enough. At night, Sidi returns to his harem."[38] He's *"le maître de tout,"* she confides to Annie, and she has nothing more to say except that "his presence relieves me from all care of thought . . . and from doing anything but arranging our bedroom or my face."[39]

CHAPTER 25

1

COLETTE STAYED at Verdun through February. Once, through her closed shutters, she observed a parade of German prisoners. They were jaundiced with fatigue, but they looked "relieved." Twice a day, the punctual enemy made his bombing raids. Every night, she took her "hygienic" walk. Sometimes she brushed against another "cloistered female prisoner," veiled, like herself, and living "an oriental life." Occasionally she ventured out in daylight, for an excursion with Mme Lamarque along the canal, past the deserted pleasure gardens of the suburbs. They witnessed an air battle and took refuge under a bridge. Another day, with Sidi, she visited the bombarded villages in the surrounding countryside. She was surprised to find so many children among the ruins. They slept in cellars and chanted their lessons in roofless classrooms: *"Mourir pour la patrie/C'est le sort le plus beau, le plus digne d'envie."*[1] The noise of their games mingled with "the basso of the cannon, as steady, since this morning, as the sound of the wind or the pounding of the surf." She recalled the words of a Greek friend: "There is no condition one adjusts to so quickly as a state of war."[2]

Back in Paris, the chief of police banned all forms of "necromancy"— unscrupulous fortune-tellers and mediums were exploiting the anxiety of soldiers' families. A fire destroyed the Moulin Rouge. The Germans bombarded Dunkirk, sank the *Lusitania,* and gassed the battlefield at Flanders. Auguste Hériot was wounded and received the first of several decorations for valor. Gaston Arman de Caillavet was killed in the Dordogne. Robert d'Humières, posted to the front lines, "took the first opportunity of charging to his death."[3] "I haven't had the courage to reread his charming letters," Colette told his editor. "He was the only person who used to call me Bel-Gazou, as my father called me, and as I call my daughter."[4]

She had returned to her commune on the rue Cortambert, but only briefly, for she was back in Verdun by mid-May. A week later, on the twenty-third, Italy declared war on Austria. "My thoughts turn to a former captain in the first Zouave regiment," wrote Colette in *Le Matin*. "He could still be alive, he would only be eighty-six. He lost his left leg in Italy, amputated at the groin. The year was 1859, at Melegnano. . . . He came home radiant with a crutch and a cane."[5] It was the first time that the "old boy of forty," intoxicated as boys are with war, could celebrate her father as a hero.

COLETTE'S WAR REPORTAGE is full of the Captain's "radiance." It thrums, too, with Sido's "love of cataclysms." The violence as she describes it is as sensual and as picturesque as that of a medieval tapestry. There is not a single corpse in any of her dispatches. There is anxiety but no despair, hunger but no starvation. She is the rare writer of her stature who never revolts against the horror, the folly, and the arrogance of World War I, and whose view of human nature is not profoundly blackened by her experience. She describes, with pride and tenderness, how the old men on the home front knit socks for the boys, and how nobly the women left behind accept their privations. The soldiers she encounters are all gallant and indefatigable; the children play "happily" in the ruins; there are no "neurasthenics" among the wounded, or among the nurses in her ward at the hospital. "I've never seen any sadness," she writes. "The majority of these young Frenchmen, who have escaped death at the price of a limb, get better and bloom like a pruned tree."[6] The worst atrocity she can find to mention at Ozéville, a village outside Verdun, is that a German officer has stolen two clocks, a trousseau, and the best books in the house: "The villain knew how to read."[7] From Clermont-en-Argonne, a village obliterated by bombardments, she writes about a dinner on New Year's Day: "the gaiety, the serenity are those of an elegant table in the middle of Paris." In one of her dispatches from Verdun, she describes "the beauty of the air chase" and the "white bouquets" of the exploding flak. Even in her letters, she experiences and describes the war with a lyrical exuberance. "What a fine cannonade, Annie! It's . . . beautiful to see from so close at hand the source of the pink glow and the circular aurora borealis. . . . The noise is magnificent and as varied as the noise of a storm."[8]

It is likely that Colette "feigns lightheartedness" out of patriotism and to keep up the morale of her readers. "Lighthearted" is always a supreme compliment for her. She equates weakness with dishonor, mourning with indiscretion, and weeping with incontinence. She's an old-fashioned stoic. But it's useful to compare her accounts with, to give one example, those of Henri Barbusse, who was also at Verdun, and whose novel *Le Feu* won the Prix Goncourt in 1916. "This book," wrote Colette's stepson Bertrand de Jouvenel, "bore witness to the worst horrors of trench life."[9] And there is no passage in her surviving letters comparable to the words her husband wrote her at the end of that year:

> My dear love:
>   I've taken up riding again, and fencing. I'm searching for something wholesome. . . . There are times when one shouldn't despise living in a daze, because it alone makes life bearable. . . . Oh, happy are the beasts these days! This parade of women and sobbing mothers, of fathers who come to ask for their sons' bodies, and to whom one can't give those bodies, these letters from refugees begging to be sent home to their village, even though it's being shelled, and whom I'm forbidden to help. All this makes for a horrible atmosphere. My dear love, you're always there, aren't you? You still love me? Happily, there's that. And then Belgazou . . ."[10]

2

IN JUNE OF 1915, *Le Matin* sent Colette to Rome as a reporter. Count Primoli, Missy's Bonaparte cousin, entertained her at a lavish, "awful" eight-course lunch in his palace, whose décor she describes as an "Italian salad." He introduced her to a bishop who recited her *Dialogues de bêtes* and confessed that he slept with his cats. She was also introduced to the novelist and journalist Sibilla Aleramo, who had defended Colette's work against its Italian critics,[11] and together they would visit the gardens of the Knights of Malta. The French establishment—embassy and academy—received her cordially, and she was generally treated as an official emissary, which perhaps she was. Italy had not yet joined the Allies (it would do so that August), and from the tone of Colette's dispatches,[12] she may have had a discreet diplomatic mission attached to her journalistic one: to help inspire a visceral sense of fraternity between the French and the Italians.

But the baroness de Jouvenel had a rude surprise when she checked into the Excelsior, on the via Veneto. The manager looked suspiciously at her passport and her letters of introduction, then refused her a room. He treated her as an "adventuress," she told Hamel. It turned out that Claire Boas had only recently stayed at the same hotel under "that name which she loves so well," as Colette puts it, adding that "this may be too much for my forgiving nature."[13] The baroness Colette took her revenge on the baroness Claire by nagging her husband to deny his first wife the use of his name and title—a struggle which ended five years later when Claire, with fatal imprudence, sent Bertrand to plead her cause.

Claire and Colette had their beauty, ambition, egotism, and strength of character in common. But the first Mme de Jouvenel was, like her husband, a political animal, who styled herself in the mold of the Enlightenment *salonnières*. Her house was a meeting place for the men who would change the map of Europe. During the war, despite the rationing, she gave sumptuous dinners, made important introductions, and acted as a lobbyist for her chosen cause, the independence of Czechoslovakia. After the war, she was still, as Bertrand puts it, "young, beautiful, rich, and free," and she would be "the queen of the Peace Conference."[14] In her drawing room, foreign delegates, journalists, and writers met their French counterparts, and it was here that Bertrand conceived his own passionate political enthusiasms and opinions.

In May of 1915, a month before Colette arrived in Rome, Claire had traveled in a private railroad car through northern Italy with her old friend (and Henry's) Gabriele d'Annunzio, prince of Monte Nevoso. The flamboyant Italian poet, novelist, playwright, dandy, soldier, satyr, and nationalist was waging his own campaign to persuade Italy to join the Allies. "Whenever the train stopped," writes Geneviève Dormann, "they were acclaimed by crowds who showered them with lilies of the valley . . . it is not, then, difficult to understand why Colette was greeted with suspicion when she claimed to be the baroness de Jouvenel."[15]

Colette checked into the Hotel Regina/Carlton, across the street from the Excelsior. D'Annunzio, ironically, had the suite next door. They had already met several times in Paris: at the fin de siècle, he had embellished Mme Arman's salon, and he had fled to France again in 1911 to escape his creditors. Colette, however, found him "much more agreeable in Rome." They explored the ruins of the Forum and the trattorias of Trastevere, and exchanged books. For *Dialogues de bêtes,* he gave her two volumes of his poetry, one inscribed to "my adorable ally" and the other "to my sister in Saint Francis of the Animals."[16]

There's no reason to suppose that d'Annunzio and Claire weren't lovers, and the famously predatory prince apparently also tried his best to bed Colette. At a dinner given by Violet Trefusis twelve years later, she told her fellow guests that she'd had to make it clear that "he could expect nothing more" than friendship from her, but that said, he became "the most delicious" of companions.[17] At a different dinner, d'Annunzio recalled that Colette had pulled her daughter's photograph from her handbag at least four times, asking each time, "Don't you know my lovely baby?"[18] He found this insistence curiously sentimental. He didn't recognize it as one of the world's oldest and most reliable ploys for discouraging a masher: waxing maternal.

Abbé Mugnier, who recorded the Trefusis party conversation for posterity, added that he would have loved to see d'Annunzio and "the future creator of Chéri wandering through the Eternal City in the footsteps of Goethe, Chateaubriand, and Lamartine."[19] But if Colette was a vagabond, she was not, like her predecessors, a great urban explorer, and her "Impressions of Italy" are sketchy and touristic. She admired the gardens, the fountains, the flower market, the Colosseum by moonlight, Shelley's grave, the cats in the Forum (of course), the music of the language, and especially the *bambini*— "more beautiful than one can say." But she had no interest in architecture, no knowledge of Italian art, and no religious awe, and while one can adore Italy without them, they help. "I'm vomiting basilicas," she grouses to Hamel.

Colette actually suffered more than most people from a French malaise for which there is no precise translation: *dépaysment*. Her sense of self didn't travel. She always did her best writing *en pays connu*. And after her first few days in Rome, she confesses to feeling "the unease of being nothing more than a Frenchwoman detached from France."[20]

IN JULY OF 1915, Colette spent a few days at Rozven with Bel-Gazou, who had just turned two. She apparently hadn't seen her child since January, and the little girl had never known a world without war. A plane flew overhead, and she would exclaim, "*Taube*. Boom. Shoot." Told that it is a French plane, "the word unleashes [her] ready chauvinism: '*A mon ʒafa de la patr-i-e!*' That's the extent of her 'Marseillaise.' " She had an enormous map of Europe on her bedroom wall, and "every day," writes Colette, "she points to where her relatives are fighting: 'Papa here . . . uncle there . . . not hesitating to oblige the French general staff to camp in Sicily, at the same time providing our infantry with a highly advantageous staging area in the north of Denmark."[21] Her experience of her parents was as exotic, exciting, and abstract to her as that of the war.

A week later, Colette was back with her husband at Verdun, describing the "magnificent racket" to Annie. There were periods of intense fighting, but the seven-month siege of 1916, which made the name Verdun a synonym for the obscene futility and carnage of World War I, was half a year away. At the beginning of August, Jouvenel was sent home on leave, and they both returned to Paris.

Colette had written to Annie that "Sidi dreams of a harem [the commune] . . . And as fate grants him everything he desires . . ."[22] The sultan of Verdun, however, could not resist the temptations of that vaster harem that was Paris without its men. D'Annunzio had remarked on Colette's "adoration of a cruel husband" without being more specific, but Paul Léautaud confided to his journal that "the Jouvenel marriage, it seems, isn't going very well. [Georges] Pioch . . . who sees them often, reports that Jouvenel tells Colette, in front of everybody, things like this: 'You! At your age, and with the kind of life you've led, you don't even know how to fuck.' He still has great admiration for her writing, but the passion is spent, and he doesn't hesitate to distract himself elsewhere."[23]

Natalie Barney describes another of Colette's public humiliations. The two friends were chatting in Colette's office at *Le Matin* when Jouvenel came in, "apparently in the best of humor."

After greeting me cordially, he addressed Colette in a detached and conceited tone:
  "Don't expect me for dinner tonight."
  "But you'll be home right after? . . ."
  "No, I'm afraid that I'll be late. Above all, don't wait up for me."
  Having delivered his blow, [he seemed] pleased to demonstrate, in the face of Colette's heartbroken silence, how much she cared for him. . . .
  In spite of certain common tastes, the table and the bed among them, in spite of their . . . shared duties at *Le Matin,* nothing assured me that this union, which seemed happy enough, could survive. There must, however, be happy marriages, but why are they never ones we have heard of? In any event, this handsome dark-haired man in the prime of his life, vain and intelligent, so attractive to women—who were so attractive to him—how could he be tied down to one woman, even if she was Colette?[24]

Moreno's opinion of Jouvenel agreed with Natalie's, and Colette's best friends perceived, as she refused to, that her marriage was doomed by Henry's infidelity, and by the streak of sadism that he jokingly called "my natural barbarity."[25] Until the very end of their life as a couple, Colette was always ready to excuse him. Sidi, she tells Annie, is "a questionable spouse (not for me!), a troubling lover (except for me!), and a friend equal to any trial."[26] And however one analyzes her enthrallment, one feels its heat steaming through her letters.

THE FOLLOWING JULY, the couple had a brief reunion at Castel-Novel, and that autumn of 1916, while Henry was stationed in Milan, Colette wangled a commission to write some articles on Italy for *La Vie parisienne.* They arranged to meet at the Villa d'Este, on Lake Como, where they were joined by Robert de Jouvenel and his girlfriend Zou. Colette would spend two months there.

This luxurious hotbed, a prototype for other white hotels and magic mountains, was crowded with aristocratic foreigners sitting out the war. The air was mild and the landscape lush, with fruit and flowers on the same bough. The hotel guests, most of them women, changed their clothes four times a day. Colette reports on the frenzy which greeted a trunk show of French couture. She also gleefully describes how a catty Russian countess entertains them by mocking the German royals. An obese empress who wears orange gloves and a crown prince who carries a watch chain made of hair are, she declares, "capable of anything."[27]

Colette professes to be charmed by all the gallant and idle female narcissists at the Villa d'Este, even as she condescends to them from the heights of her professionalism and vitality. This "very Catholic harem," she concludes, "observes the rituals of an oriental morality: fill the weeks of the lord's absence, increase in beauty and good humor, and display yourself for him when he returns. Never mind if some of them slip, a bit, into the puerility, the greed, of an Islamic harem: these are the games that good wives play."[28]

She, too, was waiting for her lord's return. Henry's commander was apparently generous with passes. Both Jouvenel brothers enjoyed the smorgasbord of women at the hotel, and the eternal parties of bezique. Colette mocked them to Annie, but halfheartedly. "Everything is beautiful," she exults. "And it's all so easy with this great devil of a Sidi so optimistic and so young."[29]

When he went back to war, Colette consoled herself in her own fashion—not with clothes, cards, gossip, or a casual affair, but with the blue mountains, the wild storms which reminded her of Le Crotoy, the figs, the blooming sage, the smell of earth, and by learning to row. After two weeks she could cross Lake Como with Zou as if it were "a puddle . . . and that means three hours at the oars. . . . My strong arms are just what is needed."[30]

3

AT THE BEGINNING of November 1916, Colette returned to Paris to go house hunting. She had noticed what seemed to be a leak in her bathroom ceiling, but she took a better look and discovered a pile of bricks and beams lying in her garden. A corner of her house had just collapsed, the sound of the fall muffled by a thunderstorm. Living in the chalet had given Colette a taste "for a tiny, private universe where I wouldn't meet people in the stairway." A FOR RENT sign outside a house in Auteuil, on the boulevard Suchet, "beckoned" to her. It faced the "soiled, luxuriant, overgrown moat" of the old fortifications, and just beyond them were the Bois de Boulogne. When Colette knocked at the door, she discovered that the tenant was an old friend, the great Belle Époque actress Ève Lavallière.

*R*enée Vivien (standing) as a Directoire dandy, with her lover, Natalie Barney, in a costume of the same period

*F*auning: Colette and Willy in a publicity still for her début as a mime in *L'Amour, le Désir, la Chimère*, February 1906

*C*olette in drag, c. 1910:
the cigarette is a prop—
she didn't smoke much.

*P*hysical culture:
Colette working out on her
portable gym with Missy
as her spotter outside the
Villa Belle-Plage in
Normandy, c. 1907.
Willy wrote the caption:
"dislocated aristocrats."

*C*olette and Missy (center)
flanked by lady friends

*C*olette's grand entrance at a theatrical fête, 1908

*C*olette baring her lovely
left breast in *La Chair,* first
performed in 1907 and
revived profitably for the
next four years

*C*olette at thirty-four in a publicity still for the sensational *Rêve d'Égypte.*
Her "mummy" costume owed quite a bit to fin de siècle iconography of Salomé.

The great cat lover about the time she wrote *The Vagabond* in a publicity portrait by Reutlinger

The mummy and the scholar (Missy) moments before their climactic kiss in *Rêve d'Égypte*

*C*olette with Missy (left, headless) and their dogs on the beach at Le Crotoy

*C*olette, her bulldog ,Toby-Chien; and Willy's mistress, Meg Villars (right) at Le Crotoy

Colette in her dressing room at the Ba-Ta-Clan, April 1912, where she was playing in *La Chatte amoureuse*. Musidora was starring in a different act of the same revue.

Missy and Colette in her flat on the rue de Villejust, March 1910

A rare photograph of the young marquise de Morny dressed (sort of) as a woman

*C*olette as a reporter for *Le Matin* before a flight in the Caudron airbus, 1912

Lavallière, nearly blind from an accident, was moving to a pied-à-terre on the Champs-Élysées. She gave Colette a disheartening house tour. The bedroom walls were black and ocher; there was a black and white faux-marble carpet in the salon and a daybed covered in tarnished gold lace. "Nowhere did I see a luxurious or even simply solid material, a carpet of honest quality, a mattress both elastic and firm, a decent coat of paint." And "because times were hard," Colette concludes, "I respected what she left me."[31] The house was in fact neither tiny nor sordid. In most of what she writes about her real-estate transactions and her domestic life, Colette exaggerates the modesty of her circumstances. She's embarrassed to be caught living grandly, or on unearned income, and she insists on being perceived as a working artist who struggles to survive. "Dispossessed once again," she writes about the rigors of moving, "did I lose my courage? No. You lose patience and courage if you move only two times in half a century. Migrants of my sort don't bother about . . . decorative paint jobs. . . . We're in and settled in two days."[32]

Not exactly. Her early days of austere living in a phalanstery were by now over, and when Colette left the rue Cortambert, she had two groaning moving wagons filled with antiques, carpets, mirrors, paintings, glassware, leather armchairs, china, her piano, and the wood paneling from her old dining room. This hoard was professionally packed for her by two servants—a chambermaid and a cook—and by a crew of four movers, who worked for three days before loading the wagons.[33]

No sooner had she unpacked than Colette was off again to Italy. This trip fulfilled a wish she'd made in Rome two years before, inspired by the voluptuous beauty of a "steaming" garden: to return with Sidi.[34] Poincaré had named Jouvenel a delegate to a summit of the Allies. The Germans had proposed a negotiated peace, and the meeting had been convened to consider this possibility.

Colette arrived from Paris on New Year's Eve, after a strenuous journey. Jouvenel had just come from Udine. They checked into the Palace Hotel and threw themselves at each other: "What do fatigue or even sleep count for?" Colette asks Annie.[35] Then they spent the next day atoning for their excesses by listening to the "monstrously insincere" child preachers at the Church of the Ara Coeli.

The Jouvenels had a suite with a balcony, and the weather was so balmy that Colette could sunbathe in the nude. Food was rationed (there were "only" two courses per meal), but she set out to enrich their diet. She found a place to buy fresh mozzarella in little pots and sampled a "sublime" dessert of muscat grapes rolled in green chestnut leaves and baked in the sun. She raved to Annie about the grilled spring lamb, and confessed to gorging on fritters and raw artichokes from the market. With a young artist named Caterina

(Katja) Barjansky—a friend of d'Annunzio's—she discovered a coach stop on the via Appia where they would go to eat pasta, prosciutto, and *carciofi* omelettes.

If the bed and the table were her chief pleasures, Colette also found time to walk her dog, Gamelle, in the Borghese gardens, to watch the sunset from the Palatine Hill, and to edit her war reportage "with a lazy pair of scissors" for the volume which became *Les Heures longues* (*The Long Hours*). One evening, she read from *Dialogues de bêtes* at the British Embassy to benefit an "animal lovers' society," and the "luminous, free, intelligent" English children made her miss Bel-Gazou. She told Annie she was "seeing a lot of people" but trying not to be "invaded." Annie also got and saved a postcard of the famous hermaphrodite at the Museo Borghese. The figure had a pensive air. "What," wrote Colette, "could s/he possibly dream of that would be better than what s/he has?"[36]

4

ROME WAS the center of the fledgling film industry, and Colette was one of the first writers of the century to take the new art seriously. In 1914, she had described a "movie factory" and the making of a documentary on the Scott Expedition. In 1916, *L'Ingénue libertine* (a condensation of the two *Minne* novels) had been adapted for the silent screen by Jacques de Baroncelli, with Musidora in the title role. In Rome, she was impressed by how "mad" the Italians were for the movies. She went to see Thomas Ince's *Civilization,* and reviewed it astutely for the French weekly *Film.* Her earliest movie reviews date from that spring. "Colette," writes Pichois, "was able to recognize, in an art which was too often content with filming the stage, the originality and the greatness of Ince, Griffith, and Abel Gance."[37]

The cinema appealed to Colette for another reason: producers were willing to pay royally for suitable properties. "I absolutely have to negotiate a film," she told Annie that January, "or else I'm a goose."[38] By the spring, she had a contract for *The Vagabond* and was writing a shooting script from her own screenplay.[39] "I'm more than a little proud to be one of the first writers who will have created, unaided, a film purely 'in images.' It has absolutely nothing to do with literature . . . but it's an astonishing gymnastic exercise, and you ought to learn how to do it, it could be useful to you. . . . I am doing what would normally be done by a professional director after the writer (me) has supplied the story. You would find it fun."[40]

After trying out "a thousand actresses . . . each one more stupid and gauche than the next," Colette and the producers managed to disentangle

Musi from a pimp boyfriend and some prior commitments, and she was to play Renée Néré.

WHEN THE SUMMIT ended and Jouvenel returned to Paris, Colette stayed on in Rome. Miss Draper wrote to say that Bel-Gazou was thriving and "had the look of a boy," complicitous with the pride which Colette always took in her daughter's androgynous beauty. Colette reported the good news to Hamel, and invited him to Castel-Novel. She had heard through the Roman grapevine that he had been ill for a few days, and hoped that he was better. But Hamel was not better. He died on April 20. Colette stared "numbly" at the letter announcing the news. She couldn't yet "feel" the loss, she told Annie. "He was a transparent and fragile friend who seemed to need only life's bare necessities. How intolerable it is . . . to sow people behind you."[41] And to a relative of Hamel's she confessed: "I'm thinking sadly of all the hours I must henceforth pass without him. You can see clearly that I'm grieving, because I'm thinking only of myself!"[42]

CHAPTER 26

1

 N JULY OF 1917, Jouvenel won a brief reprieve from the perils of
active service. His friend Anatole de Monzie, a deputy from the Lot,
had just been named under-minister for the merchant marine, and
he appointed Henry his private secretary. With her husband "tied down"
to the capital by his new duties, and probably by a new mistress, Colette—
"rusticating" at Castel-Novel—was the kind of weekend wife she had once
been to Willy at Les Monts-Bouccons. She put a brave face on her privation of
the "necessary being." "This house without a man was made for you," she
tells Annie. "No stockings, shoes, curlers. They're bringing in the hay, and
the byres are full. . . . The stud bulls look so beautiful with their curly fore-
locks. And beautiful countryside all around us."[1]

Colette hadn't seen her daughter in six months, and Bel-Gazou, at four,
had become a delicious creature with plump cheeks, calloused hands, sturdy
legs, and hair cut in a pageboy, who spoke a comical peasant patois. She may
have looked like her father, but she had her mother's "bossy" temperament,
and she knew her way around the woods and fields of her domain "like a barefoot princess." One day, Colette writes, the two of them went walking, hand
in hand:

> A blindworm, slow and swollen, crosses the road.
> "Ay! Look out!" Bel-Gazou exclaims with the voice of a carter, giving it
> a nudge with her foot. Then she flashes me a sidelong glance. She knows
> that I am preoccupied with itemizing on her everything that six months
> have brought in my absence. . . . She knows that I am containing my emo-

tion, she knows that I admire her and will not tell her so. But I am truly afraid that, thanks to her fresh instinct and her savage-keen senses, Bel-Gazou must know me better than I know her.[2]

Colette told Annie that if "there were no damned pig love" in her life, she would never return to Paris. It was hard to write when there was butter to churn, a windfall apple harvest to sell, and a dog to bathe in the river. But "a crisis, oh! very ordinary" (and very familiar)—"being broke"—confined her to her study. Her anticipated royalties from *The Long Hours* (which would be published that winter) had long since been spent. She stopped writing reviews for *Film* because the journal didn't pay enough, but she took on new work for half a dozen richer reviews. And late that summer, she started the novella which became *Mitsou*—her first sustained piece of fiction since the war began.

THE ALLIES LOST the murderous Battle of the Somme but took the offensive in Flanders. The tsar of Russia abdicated his throne. Diaghilev produced *Parade,* Cocteau's controversial modern ballet, with music by Willy's old nemesis Erik Satie and sets by Picasso. Paris was filled with General Pershing's troops on their way to the front. Early in September, Colette came to town to deliver an article and collect a check. She must have been extremely distracted—perhaps by her "crisis," perhaps by a more intimate preoccupation—because she lost a manuscript in the Métro for which she didn't have a first draft.[3] That evening, she told Wague, Sidi found her trembling under her bedclothes with a hot water bottle, despite the summer heat. The next day "I hitched myself up to the most vomitous task that I've ever done, starting something already finished. It's over now, all retyped. You see by this piquant story that I'm working—and nothing but."[4]

Also that autumn, the twenty-three-year-old French flying ace Guynemer was shot down. There were mutinies in the trenches, draconian rationing was imposed, and shop workers threatened to strike. Mata Hari was tried for espionage and executed in October. Lenin seized power in Russia, and in December, signed an armistice with Germany. Ribot had succeeded Briand as premier, and he was replaced by Painlevé, who was replaced, in November, by the seventy-six-year-old Clemenceau, who was determined to fight through to an unconditional German surrender. His election was bad news for Monzie and Jouvenel, who both favored a negotiated peace. Monzie lost his cabinet post. Jouvenel lost his temporary exemption from active service, and was shipped to the Eastern Front.

It was the last winter of the war, but that fact wasn't obvious to the combatants. The Germans bombed Paris mercilessly, and having gained ground in Picardy, fired on the capital with the infamous long-range cannon known as Big Bertha. Colette's old wooden house "shook like an empty barrel." One night when the alarms sounded, she and Marcel Proust were caught in the place Vendôme. He had an asthma attack, and they took shelter in the Ritz. At the all-clear, Proust "hurried out, breathless but animated by a well-bred grace," to find Colette a taxi—"as if there were taxis in Paris at two o'clock in the morning. I took my leave of him, walking toward Auteil. Beyond the Concorde, Paris dissolved in a massive blackness. I took off my shoes and stockings and walked on . . . reassured by the feel of my bare feet groping the path."[5]

Jouvenel's unit, Colette told Wague, was in the thick of the fighting, and she was having some "hard days—and nights."[6] "My love," she wrote to her husband, "you're not getting my letters either. We're nothing but poor beasts."[7] In April 1918, he was promoted, and two months later, he was cited for valor. "I thought it would mean a lot to you," he told Colette, "being the daughter of a soldier."[8]

It did mean a lot to her, and Colette rushed to share the news with Wague and Musidora. Thanks to Jouvenel, who had used his influence with the minister of arts, Wague had been appointed to teach a newly created class in pantomime at the Conservatory. Musi had by now made more than fifty silent films and was one of the leading stars of the screen. She managed her fortune shrewdly and produced most of her own work, and that autumn, she offered Colette ten thousand francs to write her an original screenplay, *La Flamme cachée.*[9] Shooting began in October, but Colette declined an invitation to participate. Jouvenel had a two-week furlough coming, and she went to the Corrèze "on farm leave" to spend it *en famille.*

A tender snapshot from that vacation captures the parents and child embracing on a parterre at the castle, but thirty years later, a grown-up Bel-Gazou would share a more somber memory with a journalist. She and her mother, she recalled, had been waiting anxiously for Henry to arrive, and she had been dressed up to greet her father. While running down a flight of stone steps, she tripped, took a bad fall, headfirst, and scraped her face. Colette rushed over, but not to offer comfort. "Her irritation expressed itself with a pair of slaps and this sentence: 'I'll teach you to ruin what I've made!' "[10]

Jouvenel went back to war, but Colette was still in the country when she received the news, on October 14, that Annie de Pène had died—a victim of the great Spanish flu pandemic which claimed more victims than the war. Writing to Annie from Verdun at the end of 1914, Colette had used an unusually charged image to express how much she missed her: "Time never fills that void which a solid friendship leaves behind."[11] Let this line stand as an epitaph for her "better than best" friend, "one of the most lively of the living,"[12] for Colette was otherwise laconic and even resentful about the loss. "What an idiotic death," she grumbled to Wague. "She forgot to eat lunch or dinner, or skipped meals so as not to get fat, and the flu took her with her defenses down, which is to say on an empty stomach."[13]

Gourmandise had been a great bond between Annie and Colette, who were eating partners the way some friends are drinking partners. In her memoirs, Colette recalls that Annie shared her own outrage at the anorexia of Renée Vivien: "Finished at thirty, what stupidity!" Annie exclaims. "Renée Vivien would have done better to eat my stuffed chicken or my creamed haddock."[14] But Annie had apparently deserted Colette by going on the wagon—succumbing to that "dreadful neurosis about being slim."[15] And perhaps Colette blamed Annie's dieting for her death to convince herself that her own accumulating flesh was a kind of life insurance. She had been gaining weight steadily since she had stopped exercising professionally, and had lost her figure. "Colette paid for her greed," writes Dormann, "with liver trouble . . . violent indigestion, and kidney problems." She was prone to bingeing, and she once bet a friend that she could eat four hundred hazelnuts between lunch and dinner. Recovering from a violent case of food poisoning caused by some contaminated mussels, she "provoked a slight but well-merited relapse" by eating a "delicious stuffed cabbage with cider and currant tart."[16]

Having skipped Annie's funeral, Colette called on her daughter, Germaine Beaumont, who was herself recovering from the flu. She offered no consolation except to lay a bunch of grapes on the bed and to ask how Germaine was feeling. When the young woman burst into tears, Colette "refused to weep with [her]," but she did observe "that physical pleasure could overcome even the worst grief, and to prove her point, she immediately took Germaine to Prunier's and ordered a dish of prawns."[17]

It seems far-fetched to suppose that Annie really succumbed to the flu because she forgot the odd meal. Food, however, was Colette's own first defense against emotional pain. Liane de Pougy would leave a harsh but plausible recollection of her "swollen with fat," "dancing and guzzling, with the corpse of a woman she loved lying in the room next door, shouting at the top of her voice: 'That's how we'll all end, the dead mustn't depress the living!' . . . Colette," concludes the ex-courtesan, "fears neither sin nor death."[18]

But Colette's "disgust" for mortal frailty, and her response to it—eat and thrive—is a symptom of her intolerable anxiety about all forms of hunger. She utterly abhors a vacuum, and her famous insatiability is proportional to her exaggerated terror of any vital insufficiency—of love, nourishment, or money. That *horror vacui* was also the form that the pain of writing took for her: "Then, suddenly, a mental block, emptiness, annihilation, exactly resembling, or so I feel, what must be the approach to death."[19]

2

IN NOVEMBER, the Great War ended, and the survivors—one out of five French soldiers had perished—came home.[20] Jouvenel went back to *Le Matin,* and Colette now joined the management of the paper as its literary editor. It was an onerous job that might have distracted a less disciplined writer from her own work, but Colette was prodigious, especially when she needed, or felt she needed, money. She recruited Germaine Beaumont as her secretary, and while Germaine didn't get a salary, she considered the relationship its own reward. Colette was an inspiring mentor, and her protégée repaid this spiritual investment by achieving distinction as a novelist and a journalist. Their correspondence reveals Colette at her most generous and maternal— she always calls Germaine "my daughter"—and reading it, one cannot help but feel a vicarious pang of jealousy on behalf of Bel-Gazou.

Henry's chauffeur drove Colette to her office on the boulevard Poissonnière every afternoon at four or five, and she stayed until dinner. She made phone calls, worked on her proofs and her correspondence, vetted submissions, stuffed herself with chocolates, and used her prestige and charm to solicit stories from well-known writers for her old column, "The Thousand and One Mornings." On Fridays, she presided over an informal literary salon. She was now in a position to make reputations and confer favors, and she enjoyed helping to promote the talents of a rising generation, including Georges Simenon, Tristan Bernard, Francis de Miomandre, Henri Duvernois, Marion Gilbert, and two young men who were to play an important role in her life, Léopold Marchand and Francis Carco.

Carco was thirteen years Colette's junior. He had done a stint in Willy's workshops and ghostwritten two novels for him. Willy had always told him that Colette wasn't easy to get along with: "She had an old grudge to settle with the male sex, which seemed to put her eternally on guard."[21] Carco, however, never found Colette's love grudging or guarded. "Dear friend," she wrote him in 1918, shortly after Annie de Pène had introduced them, "I so like to get your letters. . . . The warmth of a young friendship like yours is so pleasant. I don't have the courage to deprive myself of it."[22]

Carco was still in his twenties when he published a famously sensational first novel, *Jésus la Caille,* that was written almost entirely in slang. He was, as Pichois puts it, one of those "Parisian myths: the bad boy with the heart of gold," whose tough talk and precocious worldliness concealed a tender, depressive nature. Colette, wrote Carco, liked sadness in general and his own in particular. She told him that when she was young, she had wanted to write a book called "Nothing Without Pain."[23]

Colette helped to get Carco's *Scènes de la vie de Montmartre* published by her friend Téry, and she solicited his work for *Le Matin*. He sent her a nostalgic memoir of his provincial childhood, which she rejected for reasons that suggest her shrewdness as an editor and literary impresario—another aspect of her debt to Willy. "[Your] name and reputation," she told him, "already, and with good reason, have a certain flavor attached to them." For his own sake as well as for hers, she wanted him to make his début with a piece that was more in character with the tough, Parisian Carco—the brand name—"that the public knows."[24]

JOUVENEL AND COLETTE were living increasingly separate lives. His brief stint as Monzie's private secretary had given him a taste for political office, and he began courting the power brokers in preparation for a run for Parliament. An outspoken woman with a scandalous past who holds politics in contempt doesn't make a model wife for an aspiring statesman. "It is a dangerous period that the public man embarks on when he emerges from his initial obscurity," writes Colette. It was dangerous, at least, for his marriage. "The Commission's luncheon, the weekly dinner of the Group, the monthly banquet of the Left of the Vivarais . . . I only glimpsed these feasts, no one wanted my presence there."[25]

On the nights when her husband was thus engaged, Colette often went slumming with Carco. At least once she left one of her own semi-official dinners after dessert and before coffee and cigars, telling her guests that she was going out on the town with a man who "knows how to talk to a woman."[26] Carco, a romantic about lowlife, remembered that they strolled through the dark streets of the worst neighborhoods in Paris and sought "new sensations" in "the basest company." He introduced Colette to those picturesque little clubs of the place Pigalle where pimps, thugs, and their molls danced the java to accordion music, and where the tables were bolted to the floor so that they couldn't be smashed up in the nightly brawls. Once, says Carco, he took Colette to a dive in the rue de Lappe owned by Marcel Proust's former valet. When the police made their usual entrance, swinging fists and nightsticks, the baroness de Jouvenel climbed on a table and shouted: "Hooray! At last, a bit of fantasy!"[27]

Colette and Carco had something in common besides a voracious appetite for backstreet adventures. They were both workhorses. "Copy, little Carco! Copy!" Colette exhorts him, and he always got it to her on time. Her own ability to write under pressure had never been more essential. The deadlines were relentless, and "even when I was young," she would write, "I was never able to adapt my slow rhythm to the pace of the great dailies. The obsession with overdue copy . . . has for long held the same place in my dreams as the 'examination [nightmare].' "[28]

3

SIDO HAD BEEN right about Henry de Jouvenel: he was bad for Colette's fiction, at least for as long as she was happy with him. Six years had passed between the appearance of *The Shackle* and the novella-length *Mitsou,* which was published in February of 1919. *Mitsou* is a wartime love story written half in dialogue and half as the letters between a working-class cabaret star and a well-born young soldier. The principal characters were modeled on Henry's brother, Robert de Jouvenel, and his mistress, Zou,[29] although in Mitsou's letters one can also hear the distant echo of a very young Gabrielle Colette, "full of dangerous simplicity, unanswerable sincerity,"[30] writing to the cultivated and blasé Henry Gauthiers-Villars.

The story begins backstage. Two lieutenants on leave are visiting a chorus girl named Piece-of-Fluff, whose contribution to the war effort consists of sleeping her way through the French army. She'll be fined if the stage manager finds the soldiers in her dressing room, so she asks her friend Mitsou—the star—to hide them for her. Mitsou obliges unwillingly. She's expecting a visit from the elderly tradesman who keeps her, and she doesn't want a scene.

The officers flirt with Mitsou, who teases them expertly. She makes them hide in her armoire while she dresses for her next number. When she can't find her wardrobe assistant, the "blue" lieutenant (his friend wears the khaki of a different regiment) is impressed to lace up her corset. They play a farcical set piece when the old lover arrives. "They're not mine," Mitsou tells him. "They're Fluff's." The next day, the blue lieutenant sends Mitsou a gallant note and some pretty dressing table bottles in gratitude for her "forced" hospitality.

Then he's off to the war, perhaps to his death. Mitsou goes back to her routine of starlet and kept woman, but she can't forget him. She writes to him at the front, and her letters are marvels of artless eloquence, charm, candor, and self-revelation. They astound and seduce their recipient, who tells her that there are few women who "could boast as you can of so many essentials in fifteen lines of handwriting: irony, the knowledge of what is correct, a mystery." As this epistolary courtship continues, the blue lieutenant falls in love with the mysteriously rich, even noble, character Mitsou reveals herself to be.

When they meet again in Paris and consummate their affair, it's she who has the revelation. She has never slept with so young a man, or felt lust, tenderness, and respect for the same person. He, however, is disillusioned by her vulgarity. Mitsou is not *sortable*. She's too loud and eager; her taste in furniture is appalling; she has no table manners. He realizes that she is only the "rough draft" of the woman he will one day love and marry. So he stands her up for their next date, and brushes her off with a contrived letter that doesn't delude her.[31]

Mitsou's reply contrasts the generosity of her spirit with the callowness of his, and it was this letter which made Proust weep, he confessed famously to Colette, although he also chided her for a certain incongruous "preciousness" in the tone. And he was right: Mitsou has too much crude life to play Griselda, aspiring to be "worthy" of a snob's embrace, and Colette should never have left the door open for a happy reunion. But that is what she was doing in her own marriage.

The novella was received respectfully by the critics, and it was a great success with a public avid for something light and hopeful. But Colette always knew, as she put it, "where my best work as a writer is to be found."[32] During the Occupation, she sent a copy of *Mitsou* to her old friend Richard Anacréon with the following dedication:

"This makes an operetta, a 'great war of 14–18' dressed—or rather shrunken—for the music hall, isn't that so, dear Richard? But it's because I was eking out my livelihood at *La Vie parisienne,* that 'pink market' of the old war. . . . Put away this little souvenir in the drawer of our friendship."[33]

4

THE DEMANDS OF her career after the war left Colette little time for her daughter, and she was endlessly grateful to the indispensable Miss Draper. Nanny and mother shared a stern pedagogical philosophy: both had an implacable horror of scenes and tears, which they regarded as a form of "blackmail." When Bel-Gazou was only two, Miss Draper had scolded her: "Cry! Are you not ashamed to cry in front of me and in front of your mama? You should no more cry in front of anyone than do your business with the door open!"[34] In her "intimate talks" with Colette, Miss Draper prided herself as much on the "well-deserved punishments" she meted out to her charge as on the little girl's "virtues."

Sometime in 1918, Colette brought Bel-Gazou up to Paris for three weeks, or, as she curiously puts it: "On one special occasion I had to take my daughter up from La Corrèze." The little girl stayed with her grandmother in Passy, "and with her fresh complexion and boy's knickers she enjoyed in Paris the success that was her due." She had apparently never been separated from her nanny or alone with her mother before. Miss Draper had relinquished her quite unwillingly, says Colette, although the child gave no sign of missing her except, perhaps, for the fact that she was unusually quiet and "rather distant."

When the special occasion came to an end, Colette accompanied her daughter back to the Corrèze. As their train neared the station, she caught sight of Miss Draper on the platform and pointed her out to Bel-Gazou: "Now mind you say how d'you do to her nicely." But, Colette continues, "there was no question of her saying how d'you do nicely! I had beside me a small creature who had just burst into a flood of tears. . . . So shaken with emotion was she that she never dreamed of getting down from the train and could only sob 'Nursie-dear, ooh-ooh-ooh! Nursie-dear! Nursie!'

"There and then," concludes Colette, "I learnt that a very small child can weep for joy in just the same way as a lovesick maid. As for Miss Draper! Never have I seen a gendarme at a country station weep so unashamedly."[35]

Perhaps the mothers of Colette's class and generation simply did not experience the rivalry, the guilt, and the regret that modern working women so often do when they entrust their child to a nanny. If Colette ever felt her rightful place had been usurped by Miss Draper, she never admits it. But it is interesting that a woman as proprietary as Colette, and such a connoisseur of jealousy, should be so immune to this intense form of it.

ON BASTILLE DAY, July 14, the Allied troops marched triumphantly through Paris, and a cheering crowd of millions lined the streets from the Porte Maillot to the place de la République. That August, well-to-do French families took their normal vacations for the first time in five years. Colette left for Rozven with Germaine Beaumont and was joined there by a ghost from the past—Meg Villars.

There was physically nothing very ghostly about the fat and fetching Miss Meg, a veteran of the music hall, who was now thirty-four. She had dumped Willy in 1913, running off to America with an elderly Belgian nobleman, and she was currently engaged to another man of letters, Charles Catusse, whom she would marry when her long-delayed divorce from Willy became final. She had also just embarked on a new career: writing a "Letter from Paris" for *The Tatler* of London. From the rather forbearing hints Colette drops in her letters, one gathers that Meg's character had matured less than her figure: she was still petulant, self-dramatizing, and treacherous. And if the gossip is true, she apparently could not resist testing Colette's bedsprings with Henry de Jouvenel.

From Rozven, Colette apologized to Carco for not keeping up her end of their correspondence. "My physical life consumes everything," she told him.[36] Not quite everything, because she also mentions that she has transformed a one-act play she had been working on into a novel, and that she has written forty-three pages of it. The novel was *Chéri*.

CHAPTER 27

It's as if I stripped myself of my secret jewels, the better to esteem them: as they shine on you, I weep to see them so precious.

—COLETTE,
The Shackle

1

THE CHARACTER OF a beautiful bad boy living with a courtesan old enough to be his mother had his origins in eight short stories that Colette wrote for *Le Matin* before the war. In three of them, her protagonist is called Chéri, and he appears much as he would in the novel of 1919. In five others, where he is called Clouk, he is a more pathetic figure: a would-be playboy with bad skin and a perpetual sniffle, addicted to cocaine and to abusive mistresses. "When I gave birth to him, he was ugly, a bit of an abortion," Colette admitted, ". . . and I felt obscurely that I couldn't become attached to this almost scrofulous child."[1] Sido, one might recall, was also biased against ugly and weak offspring.

When the barely post-adolescent Clouk/Chéri first catches sight of Léa at a restaurant, she isn't the mature beauty of the novel, but a plump old lady with white hair, gorging and laughing with three similarly uncorseted old friends, and he longs to crawl under the table and lose himself in her soft and, as he imagines it, benevolent maternal flesh. Colette was thirty-nine when she imagined this scene. Her models for Clouk—Auguste Hériot and the cocaine-snorting Bonmariage—were younger, but not quite enough to be her sons, and her lover of the moment, Jouvenel, was a contemporary. Willy's sullen schoolgirl bride and Missy's "insufferable fake child" was not, of course, a stranger to incestuous love, but Léa was a projection—a vision of her future, perhaps—not a self-portrait.

There was no dearth of models for the affair in French literature,[2] although, as Pichois puts it, "the fact that the sources are so numerous simply proves that there is no source."[3] There was also no dearth of Léas among Colette's friends. Most of the great fin de siècle cocottes had at one time kept much younger men. Liane de Pougy—who was, like Léa, famous for her pearls—had, in 1910, married a Romanian prince twenty years her junior. Suzanne Derval, a leonine blond enjoying a comeback on the stage, had a nubile young lover, and they are probably the couple Colette describes in her preface to the 1949 Le Fleuron edition of the novel.[4] She was also well acquainted with the German-born Baroness Deslandes—the writer Ossit— who was more admired for her sexual conquests than for her novels. She had been married to three noblemen, including a royal prince, and had been the mistress of Barrès, d'Annunzio, Forain, and Boni de Castellane, among many others. When Colette ran into the fifty-something baroness again in Rome in 1915, she regaled Annie de Pène with that indefatigable lady's latest triumph. Posing as a virgin of twenty-five, "Old Ma Deslandes" had managed to seduce a Roman duke of seventeen and a half:

> She calls him "my little page" and drives him crazy (the job was already half done). Intrigues, moonlight strolls, letters, bribed servants. Old Galese [the duke's father] learns everything; he packs the kid off to a monastery. . . . The sweet fiancée demands justice, pours out her grief . . . to the Count of Cossato, a sinister old Roman. . . . Old Cossato listens, glowers under his white eyebrows, says nothing. Then he explodes: "You've come to tell me that? You've come to find out what I think? I think Galese should have given his son a hundred sous twice a week, a hundred sous, you hear, to visit the whores. . . . At least he would have learned what a woman is and wouldn't have fallen into the clutches of a mad old thing like you. A mad old thing. . . ." It's even better in Italian [Colette concludes], you can hear the clinking of the coins— *"cinque lire, cinque lire."* And he went on shouting at her like that in the stairwell. . . . It's a pretty story, isn't it?[5]

The "pretty story" found its way into *Chéri* virtually unchanged, except for the names. The sordid, gaga old Lili and her semi-catatonic princeling are presented as a grotesque parody of Chéri and Léa—and a foreshadowing of what their love affair might become.

There was, however, another incestuous couple whom Colette knew more intimately than Ossit and her Roman prince, or Suzanne Derval and her "genteely born" young gigolo. Léa's obsession with Chéri's diet ("Stick out your tongue!"), the high standards of her housekeeping, her benevolent tyranny, her candor, her provincial common sense, her repugnance for ugliness and old age, all have echoes in Colette's descriptions of her mother, and in Sido's letters.

The "chaste" old mother and the lascivious courtesan seem at first glance to have little in common. Sido considered love frivolous and men suspect—but then *sons* weren't in the same negligible category for her as mere *men*. Achille, not the Captain, was Colette's true rival in the family, and she had observed his romance with their mother vigilantly and jealously all her life.

Colette's handsome older brother was thirty-five when he married, but his well-brought-up wife, like Chéri's Edmée, was a pale and ineffectual rival to the queenly mother who remained, as she boasted, "first in his heart." Colette knew how inseparable Achille and Sido really were, how mutually dependent, and what "least admitted secrets of the flesh" were dissembled by an otherwise exemplary devotion. "My brother in the provinces is going to be very unhappy,"[6] she writes laconically after her mother's death, and so it was: he outlived her by only a year. Like Léa, Sido had made a man of her *cher grand* in every respect except the most essential one: his ability to survive without her.

2

FOUR MONTHS INTO the composition of *Chéri,* Colette accepted yet another demanding job at *Le Matin.* While retaining the post of literary editor, she now became the chief drama critic, which meant that in addition to recruiting, reading, editing, and often writing material for "The Thousand and One Mornings," she was also reviewing a play, and sometimes two, each week. "My old force," she told her new friend Hélène Picard, ". . . is still pretty great."[7]

Hélène had entered Colette's service as her second secretary at *Le Matin* that May and had quickly joined the little circle of intimates who vacationed at Rozven. She was a gifted poet—Colette calls her a "genius"—who had won the Prix Fémina in 1907 for an early work, *L'Instant éternel,* and enjoyed a brief period of celebrity before becoming obscure and poor again. A dreamer, a recluse, a provincial—she was born in Toulouse—Hélène was, from the early 1920s until her death in 1945, one of Colette's closest confidantes.

The two women were the same age, and Hélène spoke French with the southern accent of Colette's father. She lived in a fourth-floor walkup on the rue D'Alleray, an address important to Colette for other reasons, which we shall revisit. It was an aerie painted and hung in shades of blue and furnished with eccentric objects from the flea market. Hélène collected milk glass, oil lamps, painted chairs, embroideries, scraps of lace, and "pious images." She also kept two blue parakeets in a cage. Here she lived "a nun's life," as Colette calls it, while writing her "unbridled but chaste" books. Her last collection and "masterpiece," according to Colette, was a volume of "scandalous" love poems entitled *For a Bad Boy* and inspired by her obsessive though unrequited love for Francis Carco: "A life as pure as hers can't fail to seem mysterious."[8]

Hélène the Pure loved Colette the Impure with a ferocious loyalty that Colette reciprocated. She sincerely revered the "secret incandescence" of Hélène's work, and used her influence to find an appreciative audience for it. When Hélène fell ill with the excruciating bone disease that eventually crippled and deformed her, Colette discreetly helped to defray her medical expenses. Her letters to Hélène are exceptionally tender and fraternal,[9] and Hélène's to Colette were filled with "trenchant" criticism.

But a willing sexual martyr like Hélène, ethereal and submissive, who belongs to the tribe of Renée Viviens and Luces, could also not fail to arouse Colette's *méchanceté,* her impatience with exaltation, her instinct to dominate, even to oppress. One day at Rozven, not long into their friendship, Colette sneaked up behind Hélène with a pair of scissors. Hélène still wore her hair in two thick, conch-shaped coils over her ears. Before she could protest, Colette chopped off the hair. "The sacrifice of her mane . . . cost her qualms, regrets, even tears," Colette continues blithely, without mentioning her own role in that sacrifice, "but she acquired a charming bohemian air and a profuse foliage of curls."[10]

A photo taken about this time suggests Hélène's uncanny resemblance, after the haircut, to Colette. They have the same muscular neck, strong nose, firm mouth, stubborn chin, sensuous eyes. And they were both approaching "that age of authority" that so often coincides, according to Colette, "with the stage of erotic exigence."[11]

3

IT IS A cruel trick of fate that the stage of erotic exigence—the last few years before a woman begins menopause—also coincides with the diminishment of her sexual allure. Colette was losing or had lost hers for Henry. He was infatuated with a younger woman who would be his mistress on and off for ten years, and Colette was, in her own way, infatuated with her, too. Germaine Patat was what the French call *une femme douce,* an angel in looks and temperament. She owned and ran a very successful small couture house which catered to an American clientele, but her youth, her delicate blond beauty, and her gentle manners belied her professional competence. She was a frequent guest at Rozven, and Colette found her presence nurturing despite the discomfort it must also have caused her. She confided in Germaine, missed her "cruelly" when they were apart, and wrote her letters whose warmth verged on seduction. In this way she attempted, as she had with Lotte, Georgie, Meg, Musi, and various other women in her life, to join forces with a rival she couldn't unseat.

An angel, by definition, is easy to impose on. Germaine Patat would later pay for Hélène Picard's private nurses. She helped care for both Bertrand and Renaud de Jouvenel, and she would become, in effect, Bel-Gazou's foster mother, taking the girl under her wing when Colette lost patience with her. In addition to the Jouvenels, Germaine had her own "heavy" family to support, and Colette, apparently unconscious of the irony, liked to warn Germaine about the perils of altruism: "Be an egotist! Egotists don't get exploited!"[12]

Happily for Colette, Germaine didn't take this advice. She loaned Colette significant sums of money, provided her with clothes, and most important, suffered with and for her. "Your little face is the symbol of tenderness and good luck for me," Colette would tell her. And elsewhere: "You are such a sensitive little being." And elsewhere: "I embrace you, my child. And I give to that word, embrace, its ancient meaning, when it concerns you. . . . I take you in open arms, physically and emotionally."[13]

SOME OF THE growing marital tension between Henry and Colette surfaced in their discussions of *Chéri*. One day, she recalled, when she was having trouble with the novel, he gave her a little lecture on the necessity of making an outline. He even offered to make the outline for her, so that she could see how it was done. He set to work on it, and soon presented her with a neatly typed and detailed plan for twenty-two chapters. "I haven't forgotten it," she told the interviewer André Parinaud. "I don't know what my stupid reaction was when I was confronted by an outline which I hadn't conceived myself, but I remember that I couldn't stop myself from bursting into tears."[14] As Colette often noted elsewhere, she despised tears, and had been raised since early childhood never to shed them, so her chagrin at being patronized must have been as exceptional as the outburst.

Elsewhere in the same interview, she admitted that "M. de Jouvenel did not like Chéri very much. There was no great sympathy between those two men." Her husband wanted her to write something more serious, worthier, and more compatible with his own tastes—the story, say, "of a great, honest man, because he found that great honest people were missing from my literary production."[15] In *Break of Day*, she relates Jouvenel's complaints more specifically: " 'But can't you write a book that isn't about love, adultery, semi-incestuous couplings, and separation? Aren't there other things in life?' If, pressed for time, he hadn't always been rushing off to an assignation—for he was charming and handsome—he might perhaps have taught me what can take the place of love in a novel or out of one."[16]

4

THE HEROINE OF *Chéri* is also reaching the stage of authority, erotic exigence—and forced retirement. Léonie Vallon, professionally known as Léa de Lonval, is forty-nine when the novel opens—in 1912—and her lover is twenty-four. Their liaison has lasted for six years. What makes it uncommon is less their age difference than the fact that Chéri is, in his own right, a millionaire. He has been able to put aside most of his income because it is a point of pride with Léa to keep her "wicked nursling" in the grand style she has always enjoyed as a kept woman. It is also a point of pride with her never to have "soiled her hands or mouth on a decrepit creature." "Radiant youths and fragile adolescents" have been her specialty.

"Chéri"—Fred Peloux—is the only child of Charlotte Peloux, a retired courtesan and Léa's best friend, or what passes for a best friend in the demi-monde, which Colette understands to be as inbred and treacherous as any other cloister or harem. " 'Marie Antoinette's nose!' Chéri's mother was in the habit of saying, without ever forgetting to add: 'and in another two years our Léa will have a chin like Louis XVI.' "

Charlotte is a shrill little harpy long gone to seed, but still tightly corseted and proud of her small feet. Fred's anonymous father has left him a princely fortune, which Charlotte has invested for him in the booming fin de siècle stock market. She has not, however, been willing to devote the same daily vigilance to her son's upbringing. Fred has had the "old-fashioned" childhood of a fallen woman's son. He has been raised by servants, haphazardly schooled, exposed to every vice and caprice of his mother's dissolute and campy world—doted upon or just as extravagantly neglected. In that respect he is a brother to the other precociously corrupt, sexually ambiguous, and damaged orphans-with-a-living-parent in Colette's fiction—and life.

Chéri's beauty, like his character, is all black and white: raven hair and pearly teeth, a perfect mouth and an ugly laugh, an angel's grace and a "dago's" taste in ties. He is both childlike and degenerate. Léa pretends to find him impossible, but she is secretly proud of their liaison, which she "sometimes, in her weakness for the truth," refers to as "an adoption," and she enjoys him best at his most insolent, for then she can, like Sido, exercise her "maternal, which is to say humiliating," power to dominate him.

The "baroness" de Lonval, a Norman, like Annie de Pène, is at the end of a "richly paid career." One of her proudest trophies is a rope of pearls, forty-nine in all, the number of her years, each priceless. When the novel opens, she is lying in her flesh-pink bedroom, in her enormous wrought-iron bed, watching with "voluptuous condescension" as the naked Chéri plays covetously with her necklace. She no longer wears it to sleep, aware that its luster might, in the morning light, draw unwelcome attention to her neck. Léa is still magnificent, but only at the cost of constant vigilance. Her incipient jowls and graying hair are skillfully dissembled. Like her author, she is as critical of her own flaws as she is indulgent of her taste for luxury, order, and "young flesh."

While Léa is confident that her "high-slung breasts" will hold out "till well after Chéri's wedding," she has not reckoned on that event taking place in the near future. But in the opening chapters of the novel, Chéri confesses that Charlotte has arranged his marriage to the daughter of another mutual "friend," a successful and still ravishing cocotte named Marie-Laure. Their negotiations, as he relates them to Léa, are an exquisite parody of the mating rituals conducted by bourgeois families like the Gauthier-Villars. It will be a merging of two compatible clans, two fortunes of the same vintage and provenance, and two only children equal in rank. Indeed, the parallels between the demimonde and society—the symmetry of their conventions—is one of Colette's favorite themes.

When Léa stops laughing at Chéri's imitations of his mother and future mother-in-law, she professes to be appalled on behalf of the prospective fiancée: "Marriage for Chéri! It's not possible, it's not . . . human . . . you can't give an innocent girl to Chéri. . . . People don't know what Chéri is." He is touchingly unprepared for and wounded by her nonchalance, which is her intent. "Do you expect me to . . . pine away? To stop dyeing my hair? . . . Is that what you want?" But that is precisely what Chéri wants: "I don't give a single damn that I wasn't your first lover. What I should have liked, or rather what would have been . . . fitting . . . decent, . . . is to be your last."

Léa is, for once, less than candid when she pretends—to herself as much as to Chéri—that she's relieved to be getting rid of him. He is uncharacteristically naive when he thinks he can exchange her for a young wife the same way he has replaced his stable of horses with a garage of motorcars. Each tries to forget the other, to no avail. Léa leaves Paris on an extended pleasure trip with an imaginary lover invented for the benefit of Charlotte. She has a brief last fling with a gigolo, then returns home determined to renounce the pleasures of *la chair fraîche.* "Let's go out and buy playing cards, good wine, bridge-scorers, knitting needles—all the paraphernalia to fill a gaping void, all that's required to disguise that monster, an old woman."

Chéri, in the meantime, also returns home, depressed, from his Italian honeymoon. The newlyweds move in with his mother while he procrastinates over the décor of their new mansion.[17] He occasionally condescends to feel a vaguely fraternal affection for his bride and fellow "orphan," but otherwise she bores him. "Nineteen years old, white skin, hair that smells of vanilla; and then, in bed, closed eyes and limp arms. That's all very pretty, but is there anything unusual about it?" "How could you know?" she retorts courageously.

Marie-Laure's daughter is no stranger to the cruel games of love. She plays her weak hand with aplomb, and she has hidden reserves of mettle. She can't help but feel that her bed is haunted by Léa's ghost, but she is in love with Chéri despite his indifference, and despite her refined disgust for his manners, which she tells him are those of a tart. "When it comes to judging such matters," he replies with magnificently unselfconscious vulgarity, "there's no greater authority than young Peloux. I'm a connoisseur of 'cocottes,' as you call them. . . . A 'cocotte' is a lady who generally manages to receive more than she gives."

By this definition, however, his liaison with Léa has nothing in common with other voluptuous and mercenary arrangements between older women and younger men, a revelation that will dawn on both of them, but first on Léa. "My poor Chéri," she reflects, "it's a strange thought that the two of us—you by losing your worn old mistress, and I by losing my scandalous young lover—have each been deprived of the most honorable possession we had upon this earth!"

Without understanding that he is punishing Edmée for not being Léa, Chéri leaves her. He hooks up with his former friend and parasite, the penniless Viscount Desmond. They make the rounds of the clubs, dives, and opium dens, although Chéri abstains from drugs and women. The one new obsessive habit he does acquire is that of taking solitary nocturnal walks through the city, which lead him inexorably to Léa's door. She is still out of town, and the villa remains shuttered and empty. This "monotonous existence" continues until the night that he finally sees a light streaming through the rose draperies of her bedroom. "Ah!" he whispers to himself, "so this is what they call happiness. I never knew."

Chéri now buys his wife a sapphire bandeau and, in excellent spirits, goes home to her. The exemplary Edmée accepts him without reproach. Léa revisits Madame Peloux, and Chéri's mother gloats sadistically over the newlyweds' happiness. "Far be it from me to reproach you, Léa dear, but as you'll be the first to admit, from eighteen to twenty-five he really never had the time to lead the life of a bachelor."

One night, however, at midnight, Léa, already undressed, hears footsteps on the stairs, and Chéri bursts into her bedroom, announcing that he has left his wife again and come back to her. She mistreats him just long enough to reassert her dignity: "Wicked creature . . . heartless little devil . . . you great slut!" He looks at her in craven gratitude. "That's right . . . go on, bad-mouth me. Ah, Nounoune." Then he confesses his love, and they fall into each other's arms. "A strangled little laugh that she couldn't repress alerted Léa that she was about to abandon herself to the most terrible joy of her life."

And so for the first time in their affair, and perhaps for the first time ever, Léa lets herself go. In doing so, she loses Chéri. For the unspoken pact between incestuous lovers is that the master-parent will hold on for both of them. Léa's submission, if only to her own hope for happiness, violates the deal.

While the best contemporary critics would recognize *Chéri* as the master-piece that it is, others would describe it as "soulless," "vulgar," "immoral," and "perverse." Colette herself understood that it was esthetically the finest and emotionally the most generous book she had ever written. Heroism may take many forms, and Chéri's is to transcend his narcissism, if only briefly, in order to console Léa for her loss of him. Her last words are heroic in their own way, too. They are the confession—and in that sense the edict of liberation—that spoiled children, wicked nurslings, and slaves of love yearn to hear: "Had I really been *la plus chic,* I should have made a man of you, and not thought only of the pleasures of your body and my own happiness. . . . Oh, no, my darling . . . I am to blame for everything you lack."[18]

5

Chéri WAS BEING serialized in *La Vie parisienne* and about half of it had been published when Claire Boas sent her son, Bertrand, alone to the boule-vard Suchet. He had never before been permitted to meet Colette. It was early in the spring of 1920. Bertrand de Jouvenel was sixteen. He was preparing for his baccalaureates in math and philosophy and boarding in Versailles, near his lycée, with an elderly Protestant spinster.

Bertrand describes himself at that age as timid, bookish, and immature. His greatest pleasure, he writes, was his father's library, and his worst night-mare his mother's balls. Snapshots of him taken that summer at Rozven show an extremely good-looking young man with a runner's body—it was his best sport[19]—all sinews and lank. He had strong features and cheekbones, Henry's irresistible cleft chin, and stylishly cut straight hair streaked by the sun. His eyes, he notes, were the same color as Colette's, sometimes gray, sometimes green, changeable like the sea, which the French call *les yeux pers.* "We were," he told Geneviève Dormann, "going to form a club for people with sea-colored eyes."[20]

Colette wasn't home when Bertrand arrived, and the maid ushered him into the shadowy salon, overlooking the garden, where he cowered behind the piano with his bouquet of flowers. "My trembling," he writes, "wasn't, like so many others', that of a literary fan, but of a frightened child. My father's wife had an intimidating reputation, and I had been sent on a mission to her."[21]

Claire Boas was in fact using her son as a *bouc émissaire,* to encourage Colette to persuade Henry to let her keep using her married name and title. She was then much in the news as an influential hostess and unofficial lobbyist to the peace conference. Henry, egged on by his wife, was becoming "increasingly irritated" by what he considered Claire's exploitation of his prestige to promote her own political activities, however praiseworthy.

Either Claire's strategy was remarkably cynical or it was mythically unconscious. Beauty's father acted in the same way when he sent his daughter to the Beast's mansion. He didn't deliberately set out to pimp her, just to get his debts paid. One has to wonder if Claire was reading the installments of *Chéri,* and more to the point, if Bertrand was. He was certainly not ignorant of the erotic legend attached to his stepmother's name.

The boy's position was fraught but thrilling. It was an intensely theatrical situation, and according to Bertrand, both he and Colette sensed it:

> The door to the antechamber opened abruptly, almost violently, and a woman walked very briskly toward the French doors. Not seeing anyone, she blinked. "Where is this child?" she muttered, turned around, and saw me.
>
> Small, stocky, quick, powerful—that was my first impression, based only on her movements. As she came toward me, however, she tilted her head back, the better to inspect me, no doubt, for I was taller than she was; and that gesture bared her brow of the curls with which she always covered it. It would require greater art than I possess to express the majesty of Colette's nose and head. The superb convex line of a large, high forehead extended to the brows, which were noble and imperious. The line of the nose was long and narrow, and very slightly concave. When she bent her head back, as she often did because she was short, one was struck by the perfect triangles formed by her nostrils. Her liberal use of kohl and lipstick, both thickly applied, attracted attention to her eyes, which were beautiful and slanted, and to her mouth, which was fine and lively; she thus distracted attention from the stronger architectural elements of her face. When those were not camouflaged by her hair, and when her face wasn't softened by her invariably coquettish smile, with its double promise of tenderness and mockery, Colette's natural aura was extraordinarily imposing. . . .
>
> My primary impression was of power, and a power whose shock was sweet to me. I was a relatively docile child, accustomed to the greatest

possible inner freedom; I didn't let anyone impose opinions or friendships on me, and I never felt that need, so common among adolescents, to follow the pack. But with my first glance at her, I do believe that I surrendered to that protective influence that Colette promised me with her first glance.[22]

6

BERTRAND'S MISSION WAS successful, so much so that Claire and Colette decided it was time they should meet, and "in the space of twenty minutes," Colette told Moreno "we established an old friendship."[23] Colette was leaving to spend Easter at Castel-Novel, and Claire briefly considered joining the family party, but she changed her mind, "entrusting her charming son" to her new old friend. Mamita came along, as did Robert and Zou, and Meg Villars, who played tennis with Bertrand and the twelve-year-old Renaud—"a terrible, seductive, savage, tender, utterly astonishing destroyer," according to Colette.[24] Renaud, however, would later protest that he didn't recognize himself in her letters—that "she saw human beings through a loupe which enlarged, distorted, and . . . idealized them, carried away by the heat of her own temperament and the need to transform everything into literature."[25] Sidi "hover[ed] over the group with a Mohammedan serenity" but left, typically, after spending only one night. She enjoined Moreno to anticipate a juicy debriefing session when she got home.

Bertrand returned to his studies, and to a fledgling romance: he was in love with an English girl of his own age, the sister of a school friend. They were both virgins, and their long liaison remained, as he takes honorable pains to insist, chaste. Bertrand confided the details of this romance to Colette, who acted as a conduit for their love letters and would use their story as the basis for *The Ripening Seed*. In 1920, the fifteen-year-old Pamela had no inkling that the poignant stirrings of her first passion would be the subject of a controversial novel.[26]

Colette went back to *Le Matin* and to *Chéri*, which she kept revising, even through its serial publication. "It's not just that it has to be finished," she told Hélène Picard; "it has to be polished."[27] That June, she could report to Hélène that Sidi had read and approved it, that she was celebrating her deliverance by pruning the rosebushes and giving herself over to an exquisite mental laziness: "I just can't get over the fact that it's done."[28] Her amazement and pleasure were heightened because "for the first time in my life I felt morally certain of having written a novel for which I need neither blush nor doubt."[29]

CHAPTER 28

The perversity necessary to satiate an adolescent lover doesn't devastate a woman sufficiently; on the contrary. Giving becomes a kind of neurosis, of ferocity, an egotistical frenzy.

—COLETTE,
Break of Day

l

COLETTE GENERALLY LEFT Paris for the Breton coast as soon as the hot weather set in. That summer, she brought Bertrand with her. Claire had reservations about letting him accept the invitation, but Henry insisted, telling his ex-wife that he wanted Bertrand "at his side." After a few nights, he went back to someone else's side in Paris, leaving the boy with Colette.[1]

There was a constant flow of houseguests between the city and Rozven. As there were a limited number of guest bedrooms, the schedule of arrivals and departures was a complex affair. Germaine Patat sometimes arrived with Henry, but Colette was even happier to have her on her own. The elegant Germaine may have had consumption, for Colette describes her extreme pallor and sudden flushes, her chronic high temperatures in the evening, and her battle against losing weight. "Come to me nice and pink and heavier by a kilo. I demand only one kilo!"[2]

Renaud also came to be fattened up, bullied, and consoled. His father had been supporting him, but he legally recognized him for the first time only that year. His mother wouldn't do so until 1928. He had spent his childhood in boarding schools. Like so many of Colette's characters, he was an orphan with living parents, and she was moved by his ferocity and isolation. "Defend yourself against the cockroach of depression," she tells him in a typical letter. "It's a creature one shouldn't let live in clean places."[3]

Renaud, however, was never warmed by the affection of his "Tante Colette," which he evidently considered superficial, and his mature recollections of her were bitter. She belonged, he wrote,

> to the race of demanding parents. . . . I still hear her voice calling the children to dinner, a bit the way she summoned the dogs, though in comparison to us, they always had certain advantages. They were served their meals with delicacy and invited to enjoy them, while we had to behave, eat what we were given down to the last crumb, and do as we were told. . . . As everyone knows, children never give satisfaction, and their existence troubles the peace of their parents, even when they don't have the bad taste to disturb the animals, as Bel-Gazou did at a meal the day she was bitten by a wasp. Aunt Colette reproached her sharply for having excited the creature—well known for its passivity—by her frightened movements.[4]

Francis Carco and his wife, Germaine, alternated and sometimes overlapped with Léopold Marchand and his mistress, Misz Hertz, and with Meg Villars and her new husband, Charles Catusse. "When a woman is earning money," Colette joked jealously to Carco, who was by then back in Paris, "has pretty clothes, a man to fuck her, another begging to fuck her, a third—a superb and smitten gigolo making the same proposition—and when this woman is sad and yellow, there's something wrong with her."[5] She then somewhat sheepishly tells him to destroy the letter.

When the couples left, Colette settled into a quiet routine, not unlike that of her old wartime phalanstery, with the children, Hélène Picard, and Germaine Beaumont. With Colette's encouragement and help, Germaine had graduated to her own career at *Le Matin*. She wasn't writing fiction yet, but she edited a letters column, the women's page, and later, the literary section of the Sunday magazine. She also wrote a regular chronicle, which she signed "Rosine," in honor of her mother.

Both friends were expert needlewomen, and Hélène began to teach the six-year-old Bel-Gazou to embroider. Colette, as usual, took pleasure watching her child "live," but from a distance. Bertrand retained a vivid memory of his rosy, robust little half-sister, trailed by the out-of-breath Miss Draper, but he found it strange that he had no recollection at all of Bel-Gazou together with Colette. "Their images were totally detached,"[6] he writes, which is probably a polite way of implying that Colette ignored her daughter.

She did not, however, ignore her "adopted" son: "She had apparently decided to educate me." His education began with the contemporary fiction in her library, which was, for the most part, a collection of novels by her old friends. He discovered Marcel Schwob, Jammes, Jean de Tinan, and Proust, whom Colette vaunted as a "modern Balzac."[7] Bertrand read him reverently but was, understandably, more riveted by *Chéri*. Colette gave him one of the first editions and inscribed it to "my CHERIshed son Bertrand de Jouvenel." "This was," he writes solemnly, "unexpected. I wasn't her son, I barely knew her, but she already had me in her thrall."[8]

Colette taught Bertrand to swim. He was a quick study. They fished for shrimp together in the little tide pools that formed between the crevices of the rocks. She fattened him on lobster and crème fraîche, and keeping his weight up became one of her great obsessions. He even learned to relish their shopping trips to the antiques shops and flea markets of Saint-Malo, where Colette, an avid thrifter, added to her collection of old faience. These distractions were a revelation to the studious and repressed boy. "My sensibility became in some ways a parasite of hers, feeding on her pleasures. . . . She understood this phenomenon very well and found it amusing but also touching."[9]

One day, Bertrand was coming back from his regular training run on the beach when he realized Colette had been watching him. She was wearing her bathing costume—one of those tight-fitting black jersey tank suits of the 1920s—and it clung to a body which by modern standards would be called obese. But fat women, when they are fit, are often much sexier half-naked than dressed, and Colette was still limber and superbly muscled, with Venusian breasts and the biceps of a discus thrower. "She passed her arm around my waist," he wrote. He trembled "uncontrollably."[10]

Colette's gesture was a question too delicate or too indecent to be spoken. Bertrand's flesh gave her the response of which his voice would have been incapable. She rephrased it a few nights later when she intercepted him on the stairs as he was going up to bed. He offered his cheek for a goodnight kiss, but she insisted on his mouth. Again he shook violently and almost dropped a kerosene lamp he was carrying. Colette said nothing except "Hold [it] steady."[11]

The sixteen-year-old virgin was now, for a while at least, the lone male at Rozven with three sexually avid older women. Colette describes how they would sit companionably, gossiping and sewing homemade nightgowns of the silk and cotton remnants they bought from a draper in the neighboring village. Each of these crude shifts had two side seams, a lopsided hem, and a hole for the head: they were evidently not designed for seduction.

Hélène, for her part, had been tantalized by the presence of Carco. Germaine was having an affair with a married man whom she saw infrequently. Colette was still, if not more than ever, attracted by her husband, but she had only the occasional night every few weeks with him, and his libido was engaged elsewhere. Bertrand had begun to notice that his stepmother and her two friends were often in a huddle over their sewing, whispering and laughing over some plot or secret. He says he avoided this coven out of discretion, but he must have sensed that he was the subject of their "confabulations." Finally, he writes, Colette took him aside and asked him which one of the two women he "preferred." He had no idea what she was suggesting. So she put it bluntly: "It's time for you to become a man."

Bertrand now found himself in the delicate position of another princeling—Paris—invited to choose his goddess. When he balked, his stepmother decided for him. Germaine was the youngest by two decades, so perhaps Colette, feeling a last scruple, or making some obscure gesture of obeisance toward propriety, delegated her to have the first go at his innocence. That night, or soon afterwards, Germaine took Bertrand to her bedroom. It's hardly surprising that she failed to deflower him, for by his own admission he had already "surrendered" emotionally to Colette. When he "emerged, depressed and unhappy in the middle of the night," he found his stepmother waiting on the landing. He would later tell a friend that it took "all of her skills to complete his initiation," but he would also say that she had been a "demanding, voracious, expert, and rewarding" professor of desire.[12]

By autumn, when he returned to Paris, Bertrand de Jouvenel was deeply in love with his father's wife, but she would wait until their affair was almost over—nearly five years later—to tell the boy explicitly that she loved *him*. In the interim, she contented herself with a famous citation from Oscar Wilde: " 'Whatever one writes, comes to pass.' Perhaps she wanted," Bertrand concludes, somewhat too modestly, "to live what she had written."[13]

2

ABOUT THE TIME Bertrand met Colette, his father engaged a young secretary named René Aujol, who would serve Jouvenel for the next eight years and then go off to pursue a distinguished legal career. I called on Maître Aujol at his pleasant suburban villa in 1991. He was then a frail though cordial and lucid man in his early nineties. Although he was slightly older than Bertrand, they were to become intimate friends, and there was always a fraternal dimension to their friendship: " 'You're the true son of our father,' Bertrand told me wistfully one day. By that time he and Henry were estranged, and perhaps he thought I was getting the filial affection that he surely wasn't. But Henry never showed me much tenderness. He wasn't a tender man."

As her husband's protégé, Aujol, of course, also saw a good deal of Colette, and his acquaintance with her outlasted her marriage to Jouvenel.

She called me *tu,* although I, of course, said *vous* to her. I never liked that famous, and to me false, familiar style of hers. But I do believe she felt a maternal affection for me. She was always hospitable, smiling, ironic, never biting, as she could be to others, although I also never found her endearing. In later years, she continued to receive me, I think, to have the luxury of speaking—which is to say speaking ill—of Henry.[14] She was by then terribly bitter, and still passionately jealous, which is why I believe she really loved him, though she would deny it. It was she, of course, who seduced Bertrand.

Why? I asked him.

There was the thrill of incest, a bit of that. Her whole life was a theater piece, you know, and Phèdre is a classic French role. There was also the thrill of vengeance against an unfaithful husband. Then you must also understand that Colette was a *provocatrice.* She belonged to the first generation of twentieth-century sexual revolutionaries. That revolution was as much if not more intellectual than it was erotic. The more fundamental a taboo, the better to defy it. But in a way, all this is too psychological. Psychologizing is not that useful in understanding Colette. She herself was not a good psychologist. She was easily misled about her own emotions, and misread those of others. And one must not underestimate the carnality, the very genuine and passionate physical attraction, between the two of them.

I told Maître Aujol that I could easily understand Colette's attraction for Bertrand, but what, I asked bluntly, did a beautiful boy of sixteen see in a fat and domineering woman of fifty, however charming she might be? He laughed, though not unkindly, at my naiveté, and replied exactly as Colette might have—she who was accurate about the aging process in women not to the year, but to the minute: "*Attention, Madame!* Forty-seven is not fifty! And Colette was desirable, oh, extremely! One could easily imagine sleeping with her. She had a powerfully seductive aura that's not obvious from her photographs."

But here some dark, private thought tempered his enthusiasm. "Without all of that ever making her, you understand, a real woman. A real woman is good. Colette was not good. A real woman is one who forgives. Colette did not forgive."[15]

IT IS TEMPTING but too facile to see Colette as a sexual predator and to underestimate Bertrand's active, even aggressive (or at least passively aggressive), complicity in the affair. "There was a great vacancy, a void of affection in Bertrand's life," said a close friend of his, "and Colette filled it. That's why their relationship was so intense and so durable. But there was also a great void in her life, and he filled it for her."[16]

The boy experienced his own thrill of incest and the perhaps even more voluptuous thrill of vengeance. The incest was, after all, a technicality. The vengeance was a complex act of revolt against a brilliant but overbearing and neglectful father, and a dazzling but vain and seductive mother who had disingenuously, to say the least, thrown him into Colette's arms. An unusual capacity for transgression in a conscientious personality seems to be prerequisite for those who, like Bertrand de Jouvenel, achieve some form of greatness. Bertrand's old friend puts it more simply: "He was a *faux faible* [a false weakling]. All of his women were, in fact, dragons. He always gave the impression of capitulating. In fact, he did just as he pleased."[17]

WHEN CLAIRE CAME to reclaim her son that September, she was alarmed to find him "changed," and she complained to Henry that their child had been "corrupted." Bertrand was through with boarding school, so his mother took him home to her sumptuous apartment on the boulevard Saint-Germain. He would be entering the university and was ready for some finishing in the real world.

According to Colette, who was no longer Claire's "old friend," Bertrand was "in despair from the moment he was carried off. He had never enjoyed a frivolous vacation, and he can't get over it. Things will work out."[18] Things would not work out immediately, because for the next ten months, Claire "took pains" to keep Bertrand from seeing Colette alone. Now and then, on a Sunday, he would lunch at boulevard Suchet, but these visits were sanctioned by Claire, writes Bertrand, for the sake of "my political education by my father and my Uncle Robert."[19]

Their formal and chaperoned encounters gave both lovers the opportunity to have second thoughts about their liaison and its dangers. Colette was cool and reticent with him, says Bertrand, which may well have been a strategy for discouraging his love, or at least imposing discretion on it in close quarters. But he was seeing his stepmother in a different light—with her "Paris face"—and he found her "impoverished" of her beguiling summer radiance. He was also "estranged" by her utter lack of any political or intellectual idealism. The frivolity that had felt so liberating in the country now seemed "affected" to him, and he began to compare Colette's friends and interests unfavorably to his mother's.

3

Chéri WAS A commercial success. By the autumn, it had sold some thirty thousand copies. It was, on the whole, also extremely well received by the literary establishment, although, as Colette notes, it "massed my partisans and my adversaries around me."[20]

An adversary weighed in first. In the July 22 issue of *Le Temps,* Paul Souday found the affair between "this old warden and this gigolo" unlikely and uninspiring. "There is no poetry and no music between them, and their love, if it can be called love, has nothing interesting for us and nothing terrible for them." He couldn't believe that Léa, with her "admitted gluttony for fresh meat," wouldn't simply replace Chéri, or that he, "whose true passion was greed, wouldn't trade on his fatal beauty more methodically."[21]

Colette's old friend Jean de Pierrefeu took up the same theme that October in the *Journal des débats.* Her characters, he charged, were soulless; her novel was too facile: it demanded neither erudition nor refinement of its reader. Indeed, Colette's "art of sensation," he continued apocalyptically, paved the way for "the night of the intellect, the end of all culture, the definitive impoverishment of the human character reduced to the level of an animal." The mission of art, he concluded, was to exalt the spirit, and he called upon Colette to forsake those "strange and vulgar milieus of no interest where she seems to enjoy herself. It's time for her to find some new characters. She has too much genius, doesn't she? to continue to debase herself."[22]

Colette had known Pierrefeu for a long time, and she was more amused than angry at his jeremiad. "What's the matter with you, dear Pierrefeu and others, that you want to regenerate me? Is it so vile to examine the lives of the poor? For Léa, and Chéri even more than she, are the poorest of the poor. You see, I just can't get that into my head. And it seems to me that I've never written anything as moral as *Chéri.* Shake your despairing head but also my affectionate hand. For I love you a great deal and I thank you for your fine piece in *Débats.*"[23]

By then, however, Colette had heard Henry Bataille call *Chéri* an exemplary modern masterpiece, Henry de Régnier praise the candor and sureness of her style, and Fernand Vandérem consider the novel one of the most faithful and profound portraits of the demimonde ever written. André Billy echoed the theme of *Chéri*'s "extreme rarity" and Colette's "exceptional talent." Early in December, Benjamin Crémieux saluted, which is to say consecrated, Colette's achievement in the most important and influential of all French literary journals, *La Nouvelle Revue française:* "Here Colette's talent reaches the very height of perfection. Everything in this novel serves as a model: the composition . . . the exposition of the subject in the first twenty pages, the character studies, the true ring of the dialogue, the quality of the style. Colette . . . dominates her gifts, rather than surrendering herself to them. She is writing in the manner of the classics . . . her material is not still coalescing but is hard and polished. . . . Let us salute this regeneration of Colette's, which promises such happy surprises."[24]

It was this review, apparently, which inspired André Gide to read *Chéri*, and to write his famous fan letter:

> Madame:
>   I will bet that the one rave you never expected to receive was mine. I am myself completely astonished to be writing to you, completely astonished by the great pleasure I've had in reading you. I devoured *Chéri* in a single breath. What an admirable subject you have chosen! and with what intelligence, what mastery, what understanding of those least admitted secrets of the flesh!

He did complain about Chéri's "disappointing" final tirade—he would have preferred silence—before concluding that what he loved best in the novel was its "nudity." "I already want to reread it, and I'm afraid to. Suppose I liked it less? Quick, let me post this letter before I throw it into a drawer."[25]

4

ON SEPTEMBER 25, Colette's "regeneration" was officially celebrated by the Third Republic, which made her a Chevalier of the Legion of Honor. Anna de Noailles received her decoration in the same ceremony. But their recognition, writes Pichois, had certainly been retarded by the misogyny of the establishment. "What is most distinctive about the crosses awarded to Mme Colette and Mme de Noailles," wrote Vandérem, "is not the fact of their attribution, but that of the obstacles they encountered en route to their recipients."[26]

So many letters of congratulation poured in to the boulevard Suchet that Renaud de Jouvenel was assigned to catalogue them. "Everyone is buying me drinks and feeding me," Colette exults to Carco. Sapène, her boss at *Le Matin,* gave a banquet in her honor, Sarah Bernhardt sent a telegram, and at Castel-Novel the Jouvenel kids and their father requisitioned the castle's armor and staged a parade. They also tied red ribbons to all of Colette's pens.

Colette jubilated with them. She gratefully accepted the decoration and the respectability it conferred without any bohemian cynicism, and without any resentment for the years she had been treated as a fallen woman. Pichois makes the point that she needed such reassurance because a "real writer is always in search of her identity" and can never be sure of her "true path."[27] Despite appearances, Colette was even less sure of her identity and of her true path than many of her peers. When André Parinaud asked her, at the end of her life, about her own sense of her "value as a writer," she exclaimed, "My value as a writer! Now there's a disagreeable notion that will oblige me to speak to you about a certain inferiority complex which has often obstructed my writing life."[28]

The timing of Colette's decoration was auspicious for another reason. Parliamentary elections were to be held early in the new year, and Henry remained in the Corrèze to wrap up his campaign for the Senate. His wife had graced his table at the occasional official dinner or reception, but she had not taken any part in the day-to-day electioneering, partly because it bored her, but partly because her past was a potential source of bad publicity and embarrassment. "In the department," said René Aujol, "Colette was a liability to Jouvenel. The mayors and the local politicians and the middle-class electors were aware of her reputation and offended by it. The peasants, of course, didn't care. They were too busy sleeping with their daughters. But they also didn't vote."[29]

Henry, says Aujol, "still admired his wife profoundly," and he treated her with what Colette so shrewdly calls "that graceful, complimentary manner of unfaithful husbands."[30] Despite the fact that their worlds had diverged, that they spent very little time under the same roof, that he tortured her with his infidelities, and that she had betrayed him with his own son, Colette was still passionately in love with him. He didn't keep her letters—according to Aujol, he did not keep most of his correspondence—but he made an exception for the one addressed to "Mon amour chéri" on October 28:

> . . . I found your note when I came in. I understand, of course, that you're running around like crazy, and that's why I've deprived myself of writing to you. . . . If only you knew how I am always with you. If only you knew how much I love you and how much I've suffered from the fear of losing you this year. . . . Don't prevent me from coming down there at the end of your work and at the moment (touch wood) of your success, which everyone says is probable. . . .
>
> I'll spare you my thousand and one stories and my thousand little bits of gossip. Just look at this portrait, which is sweet, of your Sido[31] and her new friend, Bâa-Tou. She's a panther from Chad, a ravishing, terrible creature which Philippe Berthelot has given me. She's a year and a half old, and fat like a beautiful dog. . . . Bâa-Tou is pure of all civilization, which is to say

she is without treachery and fears nothing. Despite her power, I'm not in any danger, for she *understands* admirably, and I'm as comfortable with her as with a cat. What great smacks I've given her! . . .

The illness of Germaine Beaumont has me drowning in paperwork. My little Léo [Marchand] is working on a new screenplay. . . . He is so kind, and it is quite a touching experience to see yourself instinctively understood so truly, and so delicately for that matter, when you're sad and you think you're hiding it. What can you do? That's happened to me. And you know very well that I can only be very sad or very happy because of you. Léo knows it, too. This is too long a letter, and you have so little time. But I'm so glad to write it. You know my desire. I only have one. It has your face and your form and the term of my own life.[32]

CHAPTER 29

A woman doesn't give herself to a boy. At the most, she helps him to take her.

—COLETTE,
to Sylvain Bonmariage

1

AROUND THE TIME *Chéri* was serialized, the young Pierre Drieu La Rochelle was strolling in the seventh arrondissement with his friend Maurice Martin du Gard, editor of a literary review called *Écrits nouveaux,* a showcase for upcoming writers. They had been discussing, indeed dissecting, Colette because Martin du Gard wanted to solicit a story from her. Drieu teased him: "Are you trying to make us look older, or her look younger?" At that moment, they saw a stocky woman in a tailored suit emerge from a building on the rue Saint-Senoch. She had kohl-rimmed eyes and was leading a small dog. "It's the Vagabond!" Drieu exclaimed. Colette didn't notice them—her myopia had gotten worse—and he remarked on "her pensive allure, which bespoke solitude and the anguish of getting old."[1]

Drieu had picked up the first installment of *Chéri* at his barbershop and hadn't been impressed. He didn't like "whores in literature," and he found the writing "flabby."[2] Compared to the original of Chéri, whom Drieu claimed to have known (having served in the war with Hériot), he judged "her gigolo of no interest," and he reproached Colette for having transformed "a great, hardworking bourgeois family into a bunch of old queens, harlots, and boxers." He then turned to the subject of Colette's marriage. Jouvenel had the potential to become the president of the Republic, but he laughed with *horreur* at the image of Colette presiding over dinners at the Élysée.[3]

The baron's "potential" had long been nurtured by Monzie, who liked to say that he was more ambitious for his friend—and for France—than Henry was for himself.[4] But as an editor of *Le Matin* (and in that capacity, a lobbyist of great influence), Jouvenel had already made his mark as an analyst of foreign policy, a champion of syndicalism, and an advocate of "organized democracy." In 1920, he had endeared himself to patriots and veterans by waging a successful press campaign to have an unknown soldier buried beneath the Arc de Triomphe. In the months preceding his campaign, he had founded the Confederation of Intellectual Workers, an umbrella group which reconciled the fractious unions representing journalists, actors, engineers, teachers, scientists, and musicians.[5] He was no Captain Colette.

On January 9, 1921, Jouvenel—running as an independent leftist—was elected to the Senate on the first round of voting. His wife was in the South of France, staying with the Carcos. Earlier that week, she was supposed to have attended a Paris dinner party hosted by Jacques Porel, though she sent regrets at the last minute. "We were expecting Picasso and Colette," a disappointed Abbé Mugnier reported to his journal, "but Picasso is expecting a baby, and Colette is having a face-lift."[6]

Léa would deal with the "anguish of aging" by accepting it, but her creator wasn't ready to. A month after the brutal and rather crude operation that a face-lift was in the early 1920s, she was back in Paris for some painful dental work. ("Why can't one simply have one's teeth all pulled and replace them with green jade?"[7]) A few months later, she had another harsh, experimental operation, this time on her hair. The celebrity coiffeur Desfossée had begun giving permanents, and Colette was one of his first clients to try one. She adored the results: "What a brilliant invention!"[8] And she wore her hair permed for the next thirty years, in an aureole of mauvish frizz which became her trademark and—consciously or not—suggested an affinity to her mother's Caribbean ancestors.

COLETTE HAD the blessing of a body that healed quickly. She was soon back "drowning in work" at *Le Matin*. Early that winter, she published two collections of short prose.[9] She was also adapting *Chéri* for the stage and *The Vagabond* for the screen. Léo Marchand was her partner on both projects, and it was a happy collaboration, the first of many. Colette wrote most of the dialogue while Léo—who became a distinguished dramatist and director in his own right—grappled with the structure. She invariably addresses him as "my little Léo," "my child Léo," or "my dear son Léo" and his fiancée as "Ma-Misz."

Léo and Misz Hertz, who was Jewish and would perish during the Second World War, planned to marry that April and to spend part of their honeymoon at Rozven. They had already set up house together in an apartment on the rue d'Aumale. But as fond as she was of the couple, Colette was depressed by their settled domesticity. "Oh! To rationalize oneself into matrimony," she sighs to Germaine Beaumont. "Oh! to decide something so grave in life 'after mature consideration'! Choose the color of a dress after a thousand hesitations, but for God's sake, get married without reflecting on it! That's the grace I wish for you. May you even be so distracted that day that you walk past the registry office without remembering to stop there."[10]

2

WHEN THE SUMMER CAME, Colette returned to Rozven, and without any unduly mature consideration, resumed her love affair with Bertrand. She was acting on a principle she would enunciate to Moreno: "Content yourself, I urge you, with a passing temptation, and satisfy it. What more can one be sure of than that which one holds in one's arms, at the moment one holds it in one's arms? We have so few chances to be proprietary."[11]

Bertrand had been working unofficially for his father, who was by now a member of the Senate foreign affairs committee. He read academic and professional journals in English and French and compiled a dossier of extracts for Jouvenel's committee meetings. It was an excellent exercise not only for Bertrand, an eminent political historian in the making, but for the rapport between father and son. This was the leverage Henry used on Claire to win her grudging consent for another summer at Rozven.

The house was a hotbed of Chekhovian drama. Bel-Gazou, at eight, understood more than she let on about the intrigues around her, and it made her secretive, which irritated her mother. The infertile Carcos were desperately trying to conceive a child. Miss Draper lorded it over the resentful local servants, particularly a young maid from the Corrèze—Pauline Vérine—who had entered Colette's service in 1916, became her faithful housekeeper, and served her for the next thirty years. Germaine Patat was the confidante, and perhaps something more, of her lover's wife. Hélène was lovesick for Francis, and Germaine Beaumont was breaking up with one married man and conducting a clandestine love affair with another, both of whom tortured her. Meg Villars was again exploiting Colette's hospitality while she fixed up a pied-à-terre in Paris. Renaud was going through the bleakest, most mutinous years of his adolescence. Now that she was on the outs with Claire, Colette had befriended Isabelle de Comminges and found rooms nearby for her, explaining to Germaine Beaumont that her old rival was "alone, ill, extremely sad, and down on her luck," and that she was "looking for a little spot where she could see her son from time to time. . . . The little Comminges is dying for it."[12]

At first, Bertrand felt awkward with Colette, not knowing what to expect. He preferred the company of Carco or Marchand, who were happy enough to "play war" with him. It wasn't long, however, before Colette resumed her lessons of the previous summer.[13] One day, he recounts, he and his stepmother were watching Bel-Gazou skip rope behind the house when the little girl suddenly paused in mid-jump, "visibly" struck by the scent coming from the privet hedge. "It happened that Colette's eyes and mine, drawn to her at that moment, reached an understanding, which made us smile with a communal sense of pleasure." After that, says Bertrand, "everything began again, and we were allied as before."[14] He doesn't elaborate about their communal pleasures, but they were apparently quite consuming. "My dear soul," Colette sighs to Moreno toward the summer's end: "I don't see any way of writing to you. . . . Not only am I gaga and living only by my body, but I'm still surrounded by a terrible horde. . . . There's also Bertrand de Jouvenel, whom his mother has consigned to me for his hygiene and his unhappiness. I give him rubdowns, force-feed him, buff him in the sand, and brown him in the sun."[15]

Colette also continued Bertrand's literary education. She encouraged him to try his hand at fiction. He did so, and she considered one of his stories good enough to publish in *Le Matin,* although he signed it with a pseudonym—"Bertrand Degy"—so as not to "alarm" his mother. They had long discussions about Balzac, and she reminisced to him about her own Balzacian childhood. He found her stories deeply moving and seized on them as a pretext to give Colette some lessons of his own. "I became progressively more bold," he writes, in criticizing her work. His reservations echoed his father's, and to a certain extent, Jean de Pierrefeu's. The louche milieu of *Chéri* and the *Claudines,* writes Bertrand, "got on my nerves."

How exquisitely French: this serious boy, not yet of voting age, who dabbed spots of iodine on his infected pimples, and who was honing his sexual technique on his stepmother's body, objected to the absence of any moral perspective in her writing! Eventually, he "dared to ask her why she depicted characters who had, to my eyes, so little interest when at the same time she spoke so willingly about Saint-Sauveur, her mother, and a childhood which were so [compelling] in such a different fashion."[16]

Colette was evidently not unmoved by the insistent desire of so many high minds to rehabilitate her. Writing to thank Anna de Noailles for a book of poems, and taking the self-deprecating tone she liked to use with the countess, she promised to send her a copy of *Chéri* "if you really want it. But I'm afraid you won't like it. It's a little novel about sad people who are almost unworthy to suffer."[17]

3

ONE CAN'T WRITE a great elegy for one's childhood until one has enough distance to comprehend the scope of one's loss. Colette had considered a memoir as early as 1913, but she was still mining the material for her fiction. Nor was she, at forty, quite old enough to look back. She aged at what might be called a modern rate: her adolescence was prolonged into her thirties, and until she wrote *Chéri*, as she told Proust, her characters were all "vagabonds and assorted 'shackles' always a bit vaguely resembling claudines."[18] Whatever their real ages—seventeen, thirty-five—they are the kind of children who, like Colette, yearn for total fusion as much as they fear it; who overvalue detachment but are terrified of abandonment, and for whom there is never any secure middle ground of mutuality.

Léa, however, is the transitional figure in Colette's life and work. Her deep but clandestine resemblance to Sido reconciles Colette with her mother and helps her both to face her maturity and to contemplate her past. The seduction of Bertrand completes the process begun by the novel. It is by impersonating Léa that Colette accepts maternity for the first time, however perversely, and graduates from being the slave of love to the master, and from the child to the parent. That autumn, she and Bertrand drove to Saint-Sauveur together, so that she could show him the places she had described and refresh her own memory of them for the memoir she now began to write, which would become one of the most enduring works in her canon.

Colette began composing *My Mother's House*[19] quickly, surely, and without any of her usual anguish. She had no plan for a book yet, although she was confident, as she told Martin du Gard in an interview that August, that the sketches and anecdotes she was writing—"the bits and pieces"—would coalesce into one. In it she would discover "her childhood, the real one; her adolescence, the reality of it, . . . and then her mother. She would rediscover her, but this time it would be the good one."[20]

4

THE COLETTE-MARCHAND ADAPTATION of *Chéri* opened at the Théâtre Michel in Paris on December 13. The play is charming and well made, but it has nothing of the novel's modernity, and is a work of much lesser quality, as the contemporary critics were quick to point out. It had, however, a very respectable commercial run, toured the provinces, and was revived several times, most notably in 1949 with Valentine Tessier as Léa and Jean Marais as Chéri. "It was my dream role," Marais told me in 1991. "I worried that I was too blond and too old to play it, but Colette approved of me anyway: 'After all,' she said, 'who wrote it?' "[21]

Perhaps it was in the same proprietary spirit that Colette asked the theater management if she could assume the role of Léa for the play's one-hundredth performance. They were happy to oblige her, the more so because attendance had been flagging. On February 26, she mounted the stage again for the first time in ten years.

Colette spent the New Year's holidays at Castel-Novel with the children. She was trying to lose a little weight, but the weather was not cooperating with her virtuous intentions. It hadn't stopped raining, she told Léo, and "I drink to console myself, I eat to forget about it, I sleep to defy it, and the rest of the time, my daughter recites me the fables of La Fontaine."[22]

Henry was in Paris, where Parliament was trying to push the budget through before the first of January. She reported on Bertrand's health to Claire, describing him as "a good companion of, for the most part, wonderful intelligence."[23] To Léo, however, she confides that "the cuckoo's egg" (Bertrand) had been ill and was suffering from "a chronic *emmerdite* that he's caught from his mother."[24] By the time the rain stopped, Bertrand had recovered from his motheritis, and they went out riding. Colette took a bad fall and was trampled by her horse. The boy was more shaken by the accident than she was.

It was, she told Hélène, "a pure life," and she let herself live it, although she kept working. They stuffed themselves with garlic sausage and drank mulled wine every night at five. The chimonanthus bloomed, and Colette was ravished by its scent. The children were much preoccupied with a ghost in the attic. One night, Colette stayed up to keep watch with them and discovered not a spirit but a great horned owl roosting in the rafters. She used the story in *My Mother's House*.

After their return to Paris, Bertrand, to his mother's dismay, saw his stepmother more frequently. She began taking him to opening nights, and when they were out late, she sometimes brought him home to sleep at boulevard Suchet. This gave him, he recalls, "the opportunity to watch her work early in the morning. Wrapped up in a blanket, she attacked the blue pages she always wrote on. It was a great lesson for me, for she would fill four or five pages easily, then throw away the fifth, and so on in this manner until she was tired."[25]

Colette was, in fact, very tired. She was overworking prodigiously. In addition to the sketches for *My Mother's House,* she had begun a new novel, which was tentatively called *The Double.*[26] Early in March, she left thirty pages of it, for which she had no other draft, in a taxi, along with the story of the week for *Le Matin* and a "hundred other papers." The loss "poisoned" her life. She was still back and forth to the dentist, although she had a beautiful new capped tooth to show for it. And finally there was the ongoing drama "at the house of the cuckoo's egg." His mother made "a scene of the first water to Sidi,"[27] who was not yet ready to admit any of Claire's suspicions about Bertrand's increasing intimacy with Colette. That April, the boy and his step-mother left for two weeks in Algeria.

ALONE FOR THE first time, and journeying through a torrid and erotic landscape, mother and son enjoyed what was, in effect, their honeymoon. They crossed the desert, which Colette found as inspiring as the ocean. At night, they listened to the Berber drums and admired the enormity of the sky. They reached the oasis of Bou-Saada, "an explosion of green in the sand" whose mud walls were "the color of excited flesh." They drank mint tea in the bazaar and went to see the dancer Zorah, who was dressed only in her "brown flesh and a silver girdle."

At Tipasa, they stayed with Colette's friends the prince and princess de Polignac, who had a villa by the sea and a garden filled with orange trees and blue cineraria. They visited the forest of Bainem. They admired the vineyards which produced an intense white wine from a Sauternes grape "that recalled its noble origins: the child that a prince makes with a beautiful shepherdess."[28]

Arriving in Algiers, they found that the French president, Millerand, and a large official delegation were staying at their hotel. Colette complained about the endless round of activities to which she, as the wife of a senator, was invited. She did go to the great ball at the summer palace, held on the lawn and lit by a thousand green lanterns. An Algerian policeman later took her and Bertrand to the Casbah to see La Belle Fatma and her dancers.

Her stepson was not, Colette told Germaine Patat, a good traveler. His habits were too set, and he "finds our life too civilized." But he "amused him-self " all the same. *"Je vous embrasse, "* Colette concludes, "and my big boy, too. He is sitting at another table, next to the fire, a blanket wrapped around his legs."[29]

5

BACK IN PARIS at the end of June, Abbé Mugnier cashed his rain check to meet Colette at the Porels'. Paul Valéry, Henry's friend and admirer,[30] was among the guests, and the earnest priest, who buttonholed Valéry on the staircase, questioned him about his conception of morality. "He was rather embarrassed" by the question, and complained that Christianity had played two dirty tricks on mankind: first, suppressing polygamy, and second, insisting on forgiveness. "It would be better," declared Valéry, "if we repaid one wrong with another."[31]

Neither the poet nor the priest had any notion of how apt Valéry's Christian revisionism was to the situation of M. and Mme de Jouvenel. The abbé— a Correzian like Henry—was immediately fascinated by the latter. "It's Colette," he continues, "the ex–Colette Willy, who absorbed my interest." She was wearing a dress of white Moroccan crêpe, and she had "the air of a child who hasn't been well brought up, who doesn't know how to behave, completely lacks reserve, and is amusing all the same, and perhaps at heart, a good girl. She called her husband . . . 'mon chéri.' "[32]

Colette regaled the company with stories of her recent trip to the desert and spoke to the abbé about her new novel. She and her husband invited him to baptize their daughter, apparently having changed their minds about giving her religious freedom of choice. After dinner, chatting with the wife of the playwright Henry Bernstein, Colette fondly patted her breasts and complimented her on her good health. "What a funny person!" the priest concludes. "If her husband's a stickler for decorum, I pity him."[33]

Ten days later, the Jouvenels returned the Porels' hospitality, inviting them and Abbé Mugnier to an "abundant, well-irrigated" lunch at the boulevard Suchet. Their other guests were André Maginot, then minister of war; Colette's Algerian hosts, the Polignacs; and the beautiful Romanian princess and writer Marthe Bibesco, of whom we shall hear more. After lunch, Colette gathered a basket of petals from her garden—roses, tuberoses, absinthe, mint, and melissa—and the abbé took some home to press. "M. de Jouvenel didn't shine," he concludes. "He seems anxious. There is something in Colette's face—I don't know what—that is hard and closed."[34]

CHAPTER 30

1

W HEN C OLETTE SAT DOWN to write *My Mother's House,* she was
the matriarch of a household whose three children were spaced in age
exactly like Sido's:[1] Bertrand was eighteen, Renaud fifteen, and Bel-
Gazou just turning eight. Colette is an eight-year-old herself when she makes
her own first appearance in the narrative, in the sketch called "The Little
One." Here "the personage of my mother—the personage who has dominated all the rest of my work"—is placed at the heart of it.

This is the chapter in which the village girls on their Thursday off from
school get together to gossip, curse, argue, cheat at cards, gorge themselves on
bread and honey, and, when they get bored, play the game of "what shall we
be when we grow up?" After her friends leave, "The Little One," exhausted,
remains alone in her garden. Her dreams of travel and freedom are a screen
for "the desire to be a boy and to wear trousers and a blue beret." The wind
comes up, the light falls, and "the garden, grown suddenly hostile, menaces a
now sobered little girl with the cold leaves of its laurels." She "keeps her eyes
fixed on the lamp" which has just been lit in the sitting room:

> A hand is passed in front of the flame, a hand wearing a shining thimble. At
> the mere sight of this hand the Little One starts to her feet, pale, gentle now,
> trembling slightly as a child must who for the first time ceases to be the
> happy little vampire that unconsciously drains the maternal heart; trem-
> bling slightly at the conscious realization that this hand and this flame, and
> the bent, anxious head beside the lamp, are the center and the secret

birthplace whence radiate in ripples ever less perceptible, in circles ever more and more remote from the essential light and its vibrations, the warm sitting-room with its flora of cut branches and its fauna of peaceful creatures; the echoing house, dry, warm and crackling as a newly baked loaf; the garden, the village. . . . Beyond all these is danger, all is loneliness.[2]

Age, loneliness, and betrayal had sobered Colette as she had once been sobered by that remote dusk. The would-be sailor boy had tasted the thrills and dangers of androgyny, and they had briefly afforded her a sense of freedom, but she had ultimately not escaped the confines, both social and biological, of her woman's body. There was no maternal heart left to drain, except hers, and it wasn't her own Little One who was given leave to drain it.

When Colette was the age of the girl-child in her sketch, and learning to knit, she was obliged, she says, "to go back and rip out rows and rows of stitches until I found the little overlooked flaw—the dropped stitch, which, at school, we called *une manque*."[3] Literature offers writers, as motherhood offers women, a similar opportunity: to recover and repair the *manques*—the lacks or deficiencies—of their childhood by creating an experience of wholeness for their readers or their children, and ultimately for themselves. Writing *My Mother's House* was a reparative act for Colette, but it is one of her life's saddest ironies that she acknowledges her ancient need for her mother's "essential light" at the very moment that Bel-Gazou first becomes conscious of the maternal void in her own life, and begins to rebel.

In *La Chambre éclairée* (*The Lighted Room*) Colette describes how she had once tried to forge a bond with Bel-Gazou by telling her some of those stories from her own childhood which Bertrand, a few years later, would find so enthralling. She had wanted her to know that as females, provincials, tomboys, and daughters, they had much in common. One of the stories concerned an imaginary playmate named Marie, who refused to wear anything but a checked apron. At bedtime, the little Colette made over to Marie most of her iron cot: " 'But what fad is this,' my mother cried, 'sleeping on the edge of her bed!' "[4] As Bel-Gazou also had an imaginary playmate—a blond brother in England—it seemed to Colette "that this confidence would raise me very high in her esteem. It seemed to me she would finally understand that we are of the same blood, that we are the same. But I quickly renounce it out of fear of the look she has when I tell her stories from my childhood, a timid look in which the good manners she has learned temper her incredulity."[5]

Bel-Gazou was perhaps more suspicious of her mother's motives, and resentful of her sudden and uncharacteristic wish to be intimate, than she was incredulous of the stories. The perceptive little girl of eight must have suffered from her mother's preference for and mysterious complicity with a handsome, much older half-brother—as indeed, Colette had suffered from Sido's romance with Achille.

Miss Draper left the Jouvenels' employ sometime that year. Her departure coincides with Bel-Gazou's increasing wildness, and as Colette describes it, her "insufferable independence." The girl had mixed feelings about her nanny, but this was the woman who had raised her from the age of five months, and from whom she had virtually never been parted. If the separation was welcome and liberating in some respects, it must have been extremely painful and disorienting in others, particularly as no one discussed it openly or with any sympathy. Perhaps Bel-Gazou had hoped that in losing a harsh hired guardian, she would magically recover an attentive mother, but this was not to be. Colette de Jouvenel has said very little on the subject of her early estrangement from Colette, except to admit that she "was like the mother cat who, after a certain time, tells her little one to shift for herself."[6]

IT DIDN'T HELP that her mother was depressed and ill for most of that summer, that her father, as usual, was absent and elusive, or that the weather at Rozven was unusually cold and rainy. Colette had one of her mysterious pelvic inflammations. "I was more afflicted than I knew," she tells Léo Marchand on July 12, "and I measure my diminution by the difference between the me of this year and the me of last year. Imagine . . . that for a whole week I have tried neither to swim nor to go walking! An old woman, what? Bring a lorgnette."[7]

Bertrand had exams to prepare for, and after the Bastille Day holiday, he returned to Paris, where he could study without distraction. Colette wondered if her "little leopard," "her great whippet of a boy"—her images of him are mostly of a highly raced animal—would come back. "Share my heart" with him, she tells Hélène, who had been deputized to "take care of him."[8]

He did come back for a brief stay in August, along with his father, his uncle Robert, the two Germaines, and the Carcos and Marchands, but when they decamped, Colette was more melancholy than usual. "You've left me with a feeling of 'not enough,' " she tells Germaine Patat, "and I had a crazy desire to leave with you. Those who depart never realize how much they take away with them."[9]

But Colette could not acknowledge the similarity of her daughter's predicament: the "feeling of not enough" made her less rather than more tolerant of Bel-Gazou's awkward and even savage attempts to protest her own sense of abandonment. She tells Moreno that the girl was "insolent" and "uncontrollable," that she "defied all parental laws" and would be "interned" that autumn in a boarding school. She repeats this threat in various forms to all of her friends. To Hélène: "My daughter is . . . a holy terror who is tempting me to intern her, I promise you."[10] To Germaine Beaumont: "My daughter has succeeded me brilliantly in the role of loose cannon."[11] To Léo: "What will I do with her? A few good slaps—you know my wicked temper."[12] And finally, most candidly, to Germaine Patat: "I've quickly acquired, with you, that special tone of unjust nastiness which I reserve for those whom I love. I've become as difficult with you as I am with my monster of a daughter, to whom I say: 'You'll never be too good-looking, or too intelligent. . . .' With you, though, I would never know how to demand that you be more intelligent or lovelier to look at than you are. But I pinch your arm with a menacing look, and if you cough I cast my awful glance at you." And she signed herself "Your insufferable Miss Draper, Colette de Jouvenel."[13]

Germaine Patat was mature enough to understand Colette's need to find a scapegoat for her troubles. Bel-Gazou was not. There were moments of respite, even of calm and tenderness between them, although Colette found them almost intolerably poignant. If she never ceased to celebrate her daughter's vigor, her expressiveness, her "taut, shining cheeks," and her "sailor boy's" muscles, the "admiration" she felt was mostly "for myself, for having done such fine work."[14]

2

THIS DEPRESSING SUMMER was remarkably productive. Emotional hardships and physical disabilities always aroused Colette's fighting spirit: "that will-to-survive vested in every female of the species, and the imperious instinct to wallow in calamity while at the same time working it like a mine rich in precious ore."[15]

She kept ahead of her deadlines, worked on the dramatic adaptation of *The Vagabond,* and at the end of July, *Le Matin* began to serialize her new novel, *The Ripening Seed,* which was set among the dunes and cliffs of Rozven and based on the story of Bertrand's concurrent romances with her and with Pamela.[16]

By 1923, the novel of adolescence was, as Pichois points out in his excellent introduction to *The Ripening Seed,* a crowded and successful genre. There were fifteen works on the subject that year alone, including one by an actual adolescent, Raymond Radiguet's *Le Diable au corps,* as well as Cocteau's *Thomas l'imposteur* and Carco's *Rien qu'une femme.* Nor is a young man's seduction by an older woman and the ensuing conflict between his loyalties to her and to a young girl a new subject in French literature. What is original in *The Ripening Seed* is the attention Colette pays to the woman and the girl.

Phil, sixteen, and Vinca, fifteen, have spent every summer since infancy at a beach house that their families share on the Breton coast. The families belong to the Parisian bourgeoisie, and they would ask for nothing better than to see their offspring marry—eventually, when he has finished his education and she has served her domestic apprenticeship. As the novel begins, their intimacy is on the threshold of becoming something more than the secretive, ardent, sometimes brutal complicity of a sister and brother. The waiting time ahead of them seems unbearable and endless. In the natural course of things, they would endure it—he would lose his innocence to a prostitute, and she would meet him as a virgin at the altar of a fashionable church.

One day that summer, however, Phil encounters an older woman on the beach road. Mme Dalleray[17] has taken a wrong turn in her car and asks him directions. Their conversation is, from the first, erotically charged. They meet again as he is on his way to the village with a telegram. He passes her villa, stops to rest, and she invites him in for a fateful orangeade.

Phil's older woman is twenty years younger than Chéri's or Bertrand's—Colette's little concession to propriety, or perhaps to vanity. We learn little about the lady's circumstances and less about her feelings, although extreme discretion flags some of the most self-revealing passages in Colette's writing. She describes Camille Dalleray as "a beguiling and hypocritical pedagogue, dedicated to the delicacies of kidnapping, gifted with a genius for spoliation, and with a passionate implacability."[18] "I only like needy people and beggars," Mme Dalleray tells Phil in a cold fury when he returns to her villa a second time, with a bouquet of wild thistles, to repay her for her "hospitality." "So if you do come back, come with your hand held out."[19]

Phil, of course, does come back with his hand held out, and Mme Dalleray becomes his mistress "and sometimes his master." Her voice is both "sweet" and "virile," in keeping with the ambiguity of her name (that of a famous fallen woman and romantic victim, but also quite commonly, as Colette remarks, that of a man). Her soft flesh dissembles her strong muscles. She has an imperturbable manner. The boy is too young to see through the woman's pose of absolute self-possession, which is the pose Colette struck with Bertrand. She may ask for nothing, but she's needier than she allows. She resents her marginal role as his erotic whetstone, and she envies his romantic devotion to Vinca. "Thus burdened" (by her feelings of age and exclusion), Mme Dalleray carries Phil off to bed and "towards the confines of the shadowy realm where she, in her pride, could interpret a moan as an avowal of grief, and where beggars for favors of her kind drink in the illusion of generosity."[20]

At the beginning of the novel, Vinca still has the "rough dignity of a child," but she's about to lose it. "Maybe next year," writes Colette, "she'll fall at [Phil's] feet and speak a woman's words to him: 'Phil! don't be cruel . . . I love you, Phil, do what you want with me.' " And had Mme Dalleray not intervened, Vinca might have enjoyed a year's reprieve from the humiliations that await girls of sixteen in Colette's fiction. But she is "telepathically" attuned to Phil, and she understands that he has both robbed and betrayed her. This knowledge arouses a savagery in her that Phil, in his innocence, couldn't have suspected. He's even afraid that she might throw herself off the cliff. But submission, guile, passion, vigilance, and above all jealousy have made Vinca a woman. She hasn't the slightest intention of dying. Calming down— exercising the "will to survive that is the lot of the female of the species"— she offers herself, and thus repossesses him.

The Ripening Seed is Colette's most sensuously written novel, and its beauty, typically, distracts the reader from its emotional austerity. It is also one of her most lucid and impartial attempts to compare the first sexual experiences of a man and a woman. She is uncharacteristically evenhanded with her sympathy, but she rejects the received wisdom about what the "loss" of their virginity means to women. It is Phil and not Vinca who feels the most profoundly possessed, violated, and transformed by his initiation.

Much has been written about the shallowness of Colette's male characters, and by her own admission, they do indeed receive short shrift in many novels. The paradox, however, is that she sees men as both the nobler and the weaker sex. Here one should recall what she had once written on that subject to Louis de Robert: "It's one of those clichés that make me furious—feminine delicacy in literature. Except for three or four women writers, their [women's] vulgarity, their sentimental brutality, has all that it takes to make any man whatsoever feel wounded and embarrassed. . . . Only a man could express [as you have] that fragility of the young lover who is scorched by everything."[21]

There are, of course, innumerable contradictions and exceptions to the case Colette makes, in *The Ripening Seed,* for the power that the mature woman and the crafty girl exercise over the young man who is diminished at their expense—and her own life is full of them. But perhaps the erotic prestige of the French woman not only *chez elle* but everywhere in the world has its roots in the attitudes she articulates in this novel. At least since the Puritan revolution, and probably since the reign of the first Elizabeth, ambitious Anglo-Saxon daughters have been taught that their greatest worldy leverage—the route to influence in art, politics, or anywhere in the public sphere—resides in abstention. Despite misogynistic laws and traditions, French culture ultimately prizes and respects sexual appetite and daring in women and, as these women age, values their prowess and wisdom—one reason Colette would become a national treasure.

She later told the journalist Frédéric Lefèbre that she had first imagined *The Ripening Seed* as a one-act play for the Comédie-Française: "The curtain rises. The stage is dark; two invisible characters talk about love, with considerable knowledge and experience. Toward the close of their dialogue, the lights go up and the surprised audience discovers that the characters are fifteen and sixteen years old. By this I wanted to signify that passionate love has no age."[22]

The loss of innocence, that other great subject in Colette's fiction, has no age, either. One has the sense that she so fiercely protects her own to have the virginal privilege of losing it over and over.

3

COLETTE SENT Bel-Gazou to stay with family friends for part of August and September, and reveled to Germaine Patat about the return of peace to Rozven. On October 1, the little girl was to start boarding school in Saint-Germain-en-Laye, and she went shopping with Colette for her new school "trousseau." Her brother Renaud was already unhappily ensconced at a Jesuit college in Pau. When he wrote Colette a plaintive letter, she refused to console him except to note that his sister would "also be locked up on Sunday" and that "everybody here below has his 'cell,' my dear boy. It's not his fault if your father owes himself to Europe more than to his family. Don't torment yourself. . . . And don't show your weaknesses—at least not to anyone but me."[23]

She is referring to the fact that Poincaré had appointed Jouvenel the chief French delegate to the League of Nations, which meant he was in Geneva, participating in the debates on disarmament and reparations. He hadn't written, and Colette got her news of him from *Le Matin:* "If the buggers don't make him king of France after this!"[24] she exclaims proudly to Léo, having read the reports of September 22. Jouvenel was indeed playing a central role in a historic but brief moment of European unity.[25] When he returned from Switzerland, he recounted his triumph to Colette and Bertrand over dinner at Prunier's. "He was full of enthusiasm, and with good reason," writes his son. "He had worked hard for peace and for France."[26]

4

A FEW DAYS BEFORE the end of 1922, Colette received a letter from Pierre Blanchar, an actor she had often praised in her reviews. He had discovered an old essay from *Tendrils of the Vine*—"New Year's Reverie"—which had recently been republished. Though he was only twenty-six, he had been deeply moved by Colette's courage in imagining her own decline. She replied promptly: "But that's such an old thing, this New Year's Reverie! I was a young woman when I wrote it. A young woman knows very well how to preach the necessity of aging. Later on, it gives her rather more trouble, and she forgets the lesson that the young woman taught. . . . Your letter is charming, and I count it as a benefice of my ripe age."[27] A month later, she turned fifty.

The half-century mark is an occasion for retirement, mourning, spiritual conversions, even suicide for the beauties in Colette's essays and fiction.[28] While she deplores their weakness and lack of pride, she also sympathizes profoundly with their sense of invisibility. There are, she notes wryly, all sorts of consolations and occupations for a fifty-year-old who has been deposed from the throne of youth: gluttony, malice, greed, gossip, family, and "the love-affairs of others."

But Colette was not yet ready to abdicate her power as a woman. Years of vigilance had kept her fit. Her glance was smoldering and expressive. Her energy was tremendous. Getting fat had its rewards: her complexion was unlined. Even the cranky Léautaud admits to his journal that "she is, in effect, still extremely pretty—and pretty is not the right word. What one should say is that she emanates love, passion, sensuality, sexual power, along with a depth of sadness."[29]

There were some signs of age, however, that not even Colette could dissemble. She had begun menopause. When she'd missed "a visit from cousin Pauline" the preceding spring, she had thought that she might be pregnant.[30] The Jouvenel family doctor, M. Trognon, disabused her: "having poked two fingers into the place of mystery, he told me: I don't find anything. . . . It's possible that [your] period won't come back."[31]

THE FIRST MONTHS of 1923 were devoted to theater projects. The script of *Chéri* was published, *The Vagabond* was in rehearsal, and Colette had contracted to play Léa on a March road tour in Provence. Her letters to Léo have all the verve and toughness of the Vagabond's youthful correspondence with Georges Wague: "Yeah, have the big scene typed up. [The actor to play]

Brague? Don't know yet. . . . Falconetti [a potential Renée] is a pain in the ass. She's doing her Duse number. No makeup, a horrible old neck. . . . Let her drop dead. She's now asking a thousand francs for a rehearsal. She must be a sordid old jewess who never washes. . . . Fifty performances, as far as I know. But as you know, I don't know anything."[32]

The Vagabond had its première on February 2. Colette had taken an active part in every aspect of the production: the script, the casting, the scenery, and even the direction. When the drama critic Albert Flament visited the theater, he found her onstage, demonstrating one of the male roles. She seemed extremely cheerful and lively, but she told him she wasn't getting enough sleep—rehearsals started after lunch and continued until three in the morning. She was compensating for this deprivation by eating like a "monster."

Colette enjoyed herself in the South of France, playing Léa in Nice, Cannes, and Menton. Even a little pang of stage fright couldn't spoil the nostalgic pleasure of hotel rooms, footlights, greasepaint, and applause. But when she came home and stepped on the scale at Castel-Novel, she was dismayed to find that she now weighed nearly one hundred eighty pounds. She joked about her weight regularly in her letters, and while she carried it with aplomb, Bertrand de Jouvenel told Geneviève Dormann that Colette never let him see her naked.[33]

WITH BEL-GAZOU in an expensive boarding school and Henry living like a potentate, Colette was always interested in new ways to make money. She accepted several lecturing engagements, as well as an offer from Ferenczi to edit a line of twenty new novels by relatively unknown writers. It was called the Colette Collection, and the publisher was buying not only her prestige and her fine instincts as a talent scout and editor but, as Lottmann notes, her connections to the reviewers as well. She took the opportunity to promote Hélène Picard, who contributed her novel *Sabbat* to the series.

Hélène was becoming increasingly disabled by a lesion of the bone and a detached lung, the results of a bad fall. She had stubbornly refused to see a doctor, and by the end of the summer, she was bedridden, coughing up blood, and suffering from severe depression. Colette coaxed her into a clinic and helped mobilize their mutual friends to visit her (although she never went herself). She also had Ferenczi transfer money secretly from her own royalty account to Hélène's.

5

HENRY DE JOUVENEL HAD a serious new love—Marthe Bibesco—and he made only the most perfunctory attempts to hide his romance from Colette. The Romanian princess, née Lahovary, was thirty-four, unhappily married, pious,[34] the mother of a nubile daughter, and the author of several novels that were slighter in talent than in ambition. Marthe was a famous beauty with soulful eyes, much envied for her elegance, connected to most of the royal houses of Europe and to the highest society in France. She was a salonnière with her own entourage of distinguished men—historians, writers, esthetes, ministers, ambassadors, even kings—most of them elderly. Like Claire Boas, Marthe had a passion for politics, which is to say, for power. "Her will," writes her biographer, "had many goals, of equal interest in her eyes: to be the great writer of the century, to make history through the mediation of great men, and then, when the age of love and loveliness had passed, to write the history she had contributed to making." She thought of herself as "the Nymph Europa."[35]

Men found Marthe Bibesco irresistible, but she had never experienced a consuming sexual passion. "Making love isn't what I do best," she would say later. "Her senses, rarely aroused, counted for little. . . . She always seemed to project a perfect self-control"[36]—always, that is, until she met Henry de Jouvenel. That spring, he pursued her with all the reckless, predatory ardor he had once lavished on Colette. The princess struggled with, then abandoned, her religious scruples (and concealed her transgressions from the abbé). The couple "promised each other eternal love and divorces on both sides,"[37] although Marthe also told Henry that they would have to wait until her daughter, Valentine, was respectably married.

In the meantime, Henry continued to dally with Germaine Patat and postponed a confrontation with his wife. "From the minute they're smitten," wrote an undeluded Colette to Germaine, "all men are dishonest."[38] She was at Rozven, where the frogs were "as big as my behind" and the sea and sand "acted as a poultice for all one's physical and spiritual wounds."[39] Her husband eventually showed up for two nights before leaving for Paris, bound from there for Romania to attend a session of the Petite Entente and to visit the princess in her native country.

Bertrand was in Switzerland, spending a few weeks at Saint Moritz with his mother. When he arrived at Rozven at the end of August, Colette complained bitterly about his condition. "Nothing is new here," she told Moreno, "except for a child who has been returned to me ruined by the excessive altitude, tennis, dancing, costume balls—in short, everything that the most baneful maternal presence has encouraged. Compared with [Claire], all the mamitas of the world are so many sugar beets."[40]

Her daughter was at Rozven, too. A year at school had both chastened and matured her. "She has been, if anything, too sweet with me," Colette told Germaine. "This causes me a great, poignant pleasure and moves me terribly. I don't want such emotions," she concludes, ". . . neither for her, nor for me."[41]

6

THAT OCTOBER, Colette drove her daughter back to "prison," alighted briefly in Paris, and avoided her office as much as possible, complaining to her confidantes that she was tired of the grind. "I don't want to deplete myself with weekly stories," she tells Germaine Patat. "Suppose I tried a novel about a married Chéri, would you approve of me?"[42]

She then proceeded to quarrel with the management of *Le Matin* about her salary, which wasn't, she felt, commensurate with her workload. They haggled with her, so she decided to take a leave until they came round to her terms. To supplement her income, Colette now accepted an engagement for a series of lectures in the South of France. Her choice of subject was to prove unfortunate: "The Problems of Living as a Couple." Jouvenel was at the League of Nations, "in the process of governing the people of Central Europe" and of romancing Marthe Bibesco. "He has too much to do to write to me," Colette allows philosophically, "but I look forward to every post. That's what is most reasonable about my nature: hope."[43]

When he returned, he dispatched Colette "in a great haste" to Castel-Novel, telling her he was dying for a vacation. He didn't mention that he planned to vacation with his new love. So she took the car, believing he would follow on the train. He never arrived, but his forwarded mail revealed that he had left Paris for an unknown destination. "Amour, amour . . . Anagram of amour: rouma. Add a 'nia,' " she tells Moreno, "and . . . you find a lady with the bones of a horse who hatches two-volume novels. He doesn't have any luck, our Sidi. . . . I expect him from hour to hour, from day to day, from week to week."[44] In the meantime, she consoled herself with Bertrand, and by sharing her "intimate little miseries" with Germaine. "I have to write them to someone. To Sidi, you would say? I wouldn't ask for anything better, but where do I write?"[45]

AT THE END of October 1923, Bertrand de Jouvenel turned twenty. He celebrated his birthday at Castel-Novel with his parents. Colette was pointedly not invited. Claire and Henry discussed their son's future, and she insisted that he separate the young man from his stepmother. Together they arranged a political internship for Bertrand in Prague, as the private secretary and apprentice to Edvard Beneš, the Czech foreign minister, and a family friend. Back in Paris, Henry announced this decision to his wife. "No," said Colette. "What do you mean, no?" answered Henry. "Bertrand will stay with me," said Colette. "I don't want him to go away." The discussion "took a violent turn." Colette admitted the affair, and Henry stormed out. This, at least, was Bertrand's version.[46]

There is another version, which seems somewhat too literal, in which Henry surprised Bertrand and Colette in bed. The admission of the affair would have been a sufficient outrage. In any event, the baron returned to boulevard Suchet the next morning, packed some belongings, and moved to his mother's. Colette left Paris for her speaking tour in the south. "Work is poisoning my life," she told Moreno. "Having painfully hatched thirty pages" of her lecture, she threw them out and spoke, instead, on her experiences as an actress, fighting off a depression "with a methodical appetite directed primarily toward seafood."[47]

BERTRAND DE JOUVENEL "was horrified to see myself, or to believe myself, the cause of this drama."[48] Defying both parents, he traveled south to meet Colette at her hotel in Marseille. "He has shown himself to be someone who is worthy of my gratitude. For you understand, my child"—Colette was again writing to Germaine Patat—"everything I'm not speaking of in this letter. . . . Distance and reflexion have been working on me, and I am obliged to observe that I've been brought to this place by a *well-prepared* train of events, which horrifies me. I also know that the house I shall return to will be empty."

Did Colette actually believe that Henry had conspired to force a separation for which she bore no responsibility? It appears that she did. In a remarkable letter which supports his judgment of her "monstrous innocence," Colette tells Germaine: "If one must be punished for loving, for loving too simply and too diversely at the same time, I will be thus punished. Nothing remains to me except to be someone who has never acted in her own best interest, and who has never known a greedy passion except one: to cherish."[49]

CHAPTER 31

Poor over-loved sons! Preening under feminine glances, wantonly nuzzled by the female who carried you, favorites from the deep night of the womb, beautiful cherished young males, whatever you do you can't help betraying when you pass from one mother to another.

—COLETTE,
Break of Day

1

F JOUVENEL HADN'T been actively "plotting" to get rid of his wife, as she believed, he accepted fate's invitation and took steps to divorce. Anatole de Monzie offered his legal services to Colette, partly, no doubt, to ensure that the proceedings would be handled with the maximum discretion. Jouvenel, Monzie told her, was willing to let her file as the aggrieved party. She declined the offer: "Try to make Sidi understand that I am not being hostile when I refuse to open hostilities. But I simply refuse to become the type of woman who takes legal action against her husband. If he thinks he has enough grounds to turn the separation into a divorce, he can do so."[1]

The "type of woman" Colette alludes to is the aggressive New Woman, and once again she expresses her unlikely solidarity with the "real women" and conservative men who despise her. But she was also, by now, a master of the marital endgame, and her letter to Monzie was, in part, a defensive stratagem. In order for Jouvenel to file as the plaintiff in a divorce suit, he would have to accuse Colette of adultery. She knew he would never do so, if only out of consideration for their daughter. She was worried about her income, and by insisting on the long separation which was necessary for a no-fault dissolution of the marriage, she was probably hoping for a more favorable settlement—and perhaps secretly, and against all odds, as she had with Willy, for a reconciliation.[2]

When she returned to Paris from her lecture tour, it was only briefly, because she left almost immediately for a ski vacation in Gstaad, with Bertrand. She was following her own often repeated dictum that physical pleasure can overcome the worst grief. They stayed at the Winter Palace, and Colette exulted to all her usual correspondents about the amenities of the hotel and the glories of the Alpine landscape.

At fifty, she was experiencing the "miracle" of the snow and learning to ski for the first time. "As soon as I got here," she told Moreno in an elated letter, "I realized that I would not be able to stop myself from living physically with a great intensity."[3] She stood neither on her middle-aged dignity nor, for very long, on her skis, and she depended on strangers to haul her out of the drifts. "They find me . . . on my back, like a beetle, my legs and arms flailing."[4]

Bertrand took "tender care" of her when they skied together, but he was much more proficient and preferred going out with the guides. Colette was intent on "moderating" his activity, and in her best Miss Draper mode, she weighed him daily and checked his temperature morning and night. This obsession with the boy's bodily functions was, in part, an aspect of her ferocious rivalry with Claire, who had very different notions of what was salutary for her son. Bertrand had come to Gstaad straight from Claire's even more snobbish and luxurious hotel at Mégève in the French Alps, carrying a "pharmacopia" with which his mother had been "dosing" him. "[She] wants to obtain the maximum effect in the minimum of time," Colette complained to Germaine Patat: "the tonics, the injections, the bazaar of drugs—as if the child needed more than pure air, rest, and food."[5]

Colette was cheerful about the low exchange rate and the "ruinous" expense of the Winter Palace and all the "cream teas and raw ham" she felt were necessary for Bertrand's nutrition. At the same time, she was feeling poorer than ever. Germaine Patat was seeking a new partner for her couture business, and Colette proposed herself as a righthand woman: "How many times have I been ready to tell you: make use of me . . . my physical solidity, my good head, which isn't crazy, my desire for work, my good old bourgeois work ethic, which compels me to succeed at whatever task is entrusted to me."[6]

Nothing came of this impetuous offer, although it expresses the longing which so many writers feel to do something worldlier, more thrilling and lucrative than slaving at a desk. Colette would reactivate her entrepreneurial ambitions more seriously in a few years, when she embarked on a career in the beauty business.

In the meantime, it was obvious she could no longer continue working for *Le Matin*. In a strained telephone conversation with Henry, one of their last, she asked him to make overtures on her behalf to the other leading Paris daily, *Le Journal*. Apparently he did so, and *Le Journal* offered her a lucrative contract to write two weekly front-page columns and a monthly short story, and to publish the installments of her next novel. For ethical reasons, she was obliged to wait three months before beginning to work for a rival newspaper, and so she appealed to Monzie to secure her some interim support from Henry, reminding her lawyer that she hadn't saved a penny during her marriage and was "almost broke." "Jouvenel could and should help her, she insisted. Once he had promised her a car; now he wasn't even speaking to her. Was he counting on her committing suicide?"[7]

Henry de Jouvenel had many defects of character, but he was still no Willy. He continued to pay his wife's rent, furnished her with an allowance, and the new car—a Renault—eventually did materialize. Colette, who had always had a chauffeur, now took driving lessons, thrilled by the challenge of acquiring yet another skill. She was also not so broke as to deprive herself of a second ski vacation, this time at Montreux, again accompanied by her young lover.

2

IN DEFIANCE OF his parents, Bertrand moved into the boulevard Suchet. "I was so accustomed to living in Colette's shadow," he writes, "that I couldn't detach myself from her. One might well judge it monstrous that I continued to frequent [the house] once my father had deserted it. I justified myself by saying, as I told my uncle Robert, that having been the cause of a rupture between my father and Colette, I couldn't abandon her."[8]

Colette-Bertrand sightings were now the sport of Paris. They drew stares and inspired snickers at the opera. They were gossiped about by all those diligent journal writers who recorded the conversation at literary dinners. Élisabeth de Gramont recalled meeting Colette and a certain "tall young man" walking the dog early one morning in the Bois. Willy—delighted by the turn his ex-wife's fortunes had taken—was moved to make one of his most inspired puns: *"Colette, cette bonne à tout Phèdre."*[9]

She braved the scandal as she had in the days of Missy. Abbé Mugnier met her at a dinner, dressed in red, with bare arms, voluble and greedy, entertaining the guests with her recipes for bouillon and truffles. She "wasn't meant to write books," she told them, "she was meant to do nothing, ride horseback, swim and sunbathe."[10] And yet, as always, Colette found solace in her productivity. "I'm working from 8:30 in the morning until one at night," she tells Hélène Picard. She and Léo had begun a new screenplay. She contacted her old friend the playwright Robert de Flers, who was also the literary director of *Le Figaro,* and he engaged her to write four chronicles a month for the front page of the Sunday paper. She collected her short stories from *Le Matin* for a volume, *La Femme cachée* (*The Hidden Woman*), which was published in the spring. She agreed to write a children's book, and she mentions to various correspondents that she was also working on one, and perhaps two, new novels. Writing fiction was the real test of her courage: "It's terrible to think," she told Carco, "as I do every time I start a book, that I no longer have, I have never had, any talent. Does it happen to you?"[11]

Only occasionally do Colette's letters betray the effort it took, in the months after her separation from Jouvenel, to conceal her heartache and humiliation. When Christiane Mendelys reported that her husband was having an affair with a young woman, Colette replied: "If it's true that one is only happy by comparison, be happy, at least in comparison to me."[12] And writing to Germaine Patat from Montreux, she admitted, "I've had yet another taste of the horror inherent to a state of physical ill-being, complicated by a loss of morale, a fall into bitterness, anxiety, and regret. . . . It's not amusing. Avoid everything that has the power to negate you."[13]

3

ON JULY 2, 1924, Robert de Jouvenel, aged forty-two, had a sudden and fatal heart attack. Colette told Moreno that she'd had a premonition of his demise. She had awakened to what sounded, in her sleep, like Henry's voice, and when she checked the clock, it was precisely two in the morning—twenty-four hours to the minute before Robert's death. Henry, she reported, had been at his brother's bedside constantly for the final hours: "[Robert] was, alas, the *only* great and deep love of [Henry's] life."[14]

Colette was for once willing to attend a funeral, although as she told Moreno, "they've all distanced me, so I'm staying [in Paris]." She phoned her mother-in-law, who refused to speak to her, and wrote a condolence letter to the family, even though she anticipated (correctly) that they would return it unopened. She had been expecting Bertrand home from Prague, but he was, for the moment, needed by his father. Colette had been furious at him for leaving her for three months to oblige his parents by accepting Beneš's offer of an apprenticeship, and she was even more furious to learn, a few weeks later, that a beautiful young girl, the daughter of a family friend, had been included in the funeral party as a "provision" for Bertrand.

As usual, Colette concealed her own sense of abandonment behind a stoical, even surly façade. But her dream suggests how mystically attuned she felt to Henry, and also how much she must have suffered from the loss not only of a husband, but of a family.

4

IT WAS THE MOMENT of the year Colette returned, as always, to Rozven. A local pharmacist with a large family of noisy children had erected a "hideous" new villa near her property, and after a series of tense negotiations, she had managed to option enough of the surrounding terrain to protect herself from any further such encroachments. "Rozven is my refuge," she told Germaine Patat in a fairly hysterical letter, "my empire, the fountain of youth where I restore myself."[15] And she asked Germaine to lend her the considerable sum—thirty thousand francs—necessary for the purchase of the land. The check was immediately forthcoming.

Colette was accompanied to the sea by a new young secretary named Claude Chauvière. They had met through Monzie, who had perhaps decided that an intelligent acolyte with a slavish temperament was just what Colette needed in her present state of disarray. Chauvière was an aspiring novelist who had no real secretarial skills, and she took the job because she wanted to write Colette's biography. Her book, which appeared in 1931, is part hagiography and partly the memoir of her own education by the great writer. The author intersperses reverent first-hand observations with quotes from Colette's work, eulogistic reviews, fan notes from famous writers, snatches of biography, and some fascinating unpublished letters to Bel-Gazou. But the woman it portrays, and whom we are invited to worship, is "larger than life" in an irritating, noisy way, and Chauvière's biography suggests how damaging to its object undiluted awe invariably is. In the attempt to pay homage, the book betrays the egotism and condescension of the master, who, unaware of being viewed through more critical eyes (those of the reader), preened shamelessly for her disciple.

The two women were alone for a fortnight before the annual influx of houseguests. They took long walks on the beach and in the dunes, gorged on seafood, and went antiquing. At meals, Colette corrected Chauvière's table manners. After a siesta, each worked alone in her corner, and in the evenings, Colette held forth about her life and work while Chauvière "received with devotion the manna of her experience."[16] Eventually Colette noticed that her secretary hadn't said anything for days. "You're always silent, *ma petite* Claude." "That's because, Madame, my privileged hours of listening to you are numbered."[17]

WHILE COLETTE AND HENRY negotiated their divorce and fought over Bertrand, Bel-Gazou was, as usual, relegated to the shadows. Unsurprisingly, she was failing at school and growing more and more rebellious and morose. Colette attributed her "bad grades, her laziness and contrary humor," to precocious puberty. "It would be too much to be harsh with her," she told Germaine Patat, "but bad to be too forgiving." Perhaps a change of air was all she needed. Colette considered dispatching Bel-Gazou to Castel-Novel with her maid, Pauline, but the young peasant woman of twenty had no authority over the autocratic ten-year-old. Then there was the family of Bel-Gazou's best friend, but they were "very low, clever little Jews" and wouldn't "do," particularly, perhaps, because Bel-Gazou had expressed an interest in converting to Judaism, explaining to her mother that "Jewish parents loved their children and often came to visit them at school."[18] "This business of arranging a holiday" was difficult, Colette concluded, the more so as her daughter was, "by virtue of her independence, her initiative, and her slyness, already a considerable personality."[19]

At the end of July, Bertrand and Bel-Gazou were briefly reunited at Rozven. Colette was kept busy deploying scale and thermometer. She includes her daughter's temperatures along with her stepson's in her bulletins to Germaine Patat, whose weight gains were also duly noted and celebrated. Everyone's health had improved—indeed, the little Colette was, at ninety pounds, quite fat—"She resembles me, at least on the platform of a scale!"— and Bertrand's cheeks were "filling out nicely," although he had balked (one can only imagine the scene) at being weighed on a public scale in Saint-Malo. Bel-Gazou was now old enough to be a companion, or at least a mascot, for her half brother, and Colette notes that they were, for the first time, "very complicitous," which enraged her, and which seems to mean that they banded together to resist their mother's bullying. But she forgave them whenever she "saw them eat."

BY THE AUTUMN, Bertrand was back in Geneva with Beneš.[20] He had spent most of the summer organizing a youth congress, giving speeches, meeting with "a rabble of young democrats," writing articles, and fielding offers from as far away as the United States to give lectures. Colette the mentor retailed his accomplishments to all her friends. Colette the mother worried obsessively about his health and complained, with echoes of Sido, that "the imbecile" was "compromising my work."[21] Colette the lover suffered the familiar pangs of jealousy and abandonment: "To the devil with all useless tenderness, and that beating of wings which surrounds a bird hatched from a cuckoo's egg!"[22]

"The pleasures she gave me," wrote Bertrand de Jouvenel, as an old man, "were all those which open a window on the world, which I owe entirely to her."[23] But as Pichois notes, the world he was then entering owed nothing to Colette and everything to his parents. Sensing their advantage, they pressed it on every front. They introduced him to a marriageable young heiress named Mlle de Ricqlès, and he acquiesced to the arrangement. Henry made the ceremonial visit to ask, on his son's behalf, for the lady's hand. The wedding was set for the end of December.

> You'll say it's my fault [Colette told Moreno,] when you learn that in an exasperated moment I threw him out. Those around him were only waiting for their chance, and the young lady in question has been waiting for it, with the patience of a virgin, for a long time. I haven't seen him for eight days. He was here yesterday. But I see him as seriously trapped. And even admitting that he might extricate himself, or delay, he can't do so except at the price of a scandal. I haven't written a word to you for all these days. And I add nothing now. Don't keep this letter, which has no interest other than as a not very pretty [wedding] invitation.[24]

But Colette had never balked at paying the price of a scandal, or at asking her partner to split the tab, and she did not do so now. On the day of the engagement dinner, Bertrand came to see her. He told her, a bit belatedly to be quite believable, that he "didn't desire the honor" that was being bestowed upon him. "Why go, then?" Colette exclaimed. "Don't go!" "All the same," he continues, "I decided to go, and I was leaving [the garden] when from the window a piece of paper drifted down to me. 'I love you,' it said. Which Colette had never told me. And I went back up to her."[25]

5

JUST AS PARENTHESES qualify and sometimes subvert the meaning of a sentence, the two books Colette published in 1924—one at the beginning of the year, one at the end—illuminate, as her letters don't, the dark period of intense creative torment and personal suffering which they contain.

The Hidden Woman is the collection of twenty-three short stories written for *Le Matin*. They are brief, shapely, bleak, and cruel and have often been compared to the work of Maupassant. In the title story, a woman trapped in an unhappy marriage goes alone, in disguise, to the Opera Ball. She thinks her husband is out of town on business, but he has followed her secretly, expecting to surprise her with a lover. She throws herself into the orgy of masked revelers. As he watches from the shadows, she yields to the embraces of a naked wrestler; a Turk; fondles a Dutch girl; then seizes the "panting, half-open mouth" of a handsome young man. Instead of rushing forward to tear them apart, the husband disappears into the crowd. He has discovered a more intimate and disturbing secret than simple infidelity: her "monstrous pleasure" in "being alone, free, honest, in her native brutality, of being the one who is unknown, forever solitary and without shame, whom a little mask and a hermetic costume had restored to her irremediable solitude and her immodest innocence."[26]

The other stories are nearly all what Claude Pichois and Alain Brunet so aptly call "black idylls." On her wedding night, a young bride is revolted by the sight of her husband's murderous thumb. Another bride, married to a divorced man, discovers her regret when they meet his ex-wife at a restaurant and she finds herself envying the single woman's freedom. Two rivals for the same man both come to despise him. A lover casually receives the news that his mistress is dead: it's preferable to her desertion. A sleepless man abandoned by his wife—"the surgical suddenness of their break had left him stupefied"—tries to recall the happy memories of his youth, but they turn "mean and bitter" on him. A middle-aged woman is talked into a new hairstyle by a sadistic coiffeur; her young butler stares at her with "an indescribable expression of horror and shame," and she suddenly perceives how hideous she has become.

The characters in *The Hidden Woman* are naifs and romantics. They are men and women whose true natures are hidden from themselves and others. They seek in passion or marriage (and only in passion or marriage) that magical mirror which reflects the elusive wholeness of a fractured self and the possibility of complete union. But the images that are held up to them are broken, ugly, brutal, hopeless, banal, and pathetic. They are all, as Colette now felt herself to be, "irremediably alone."

Everyday Adventures (*Aventures quotidiennes*) is the non-fiction companion to *The Hidden Woman*. It contains the essays that Colette wrote between April and September for *Le Figaro* under the rubric "A Woman's Opinion." There is enough beauty in ten of her lines to content a lesser writer for a lifetime. Yet they were just Colette's "bread and butter." A partial inventory of her "quotidian" subjects: rape, flowers, abortion, serial murder, vampirism, motherhood, birds, poverty, suicide, child abuse, boarding schools, disfigurement, animals, sadism, and the cinema. Her one great theme, as in *The Hidden*

Woman, is the loss of humanity's "immodest innocence." In "Wings" she describes how it feels in her dreams to fly and to do serene battle-to-the-death with mythical animals. In comparison with the birds, she concludes, we are tormented creatures "crucified" on the earth, and the only "complete being" is the fetus ready for birth but still swimming in the womb.

In the essay called "Assassins," she describes a "calm, dark, unfathomable eye . . . devoid of language, tenderness, and melancholy." It could belong "to a bird" but is, instead, the organ of the infamous murderer Landru. She had covered his trial for *Le Matin* in 1922, and after his conviction, Landru, noticing Colette in the courtroom, had asked for her autograph. There was a bond between them which she won't deny.

The murderer's eye, like Colette's when she is writing at the height of her powers, is unblinkered by the morality of the socialized, whom, like Nietzsche, she despises. It is "created to see, to spy, to diminish, to conceal emotion, to weigh up every passerby and every spectacle. An eye as serene as that of the first men, an eye that contemplated bloodshed, death, and pain without blinking a lid—as very small children do, as our ancestors did before they invented pusillanimity, when they still enjoyed the blood freed from its fleshly prison, the water springing out of the ground, milk spurting from the udder, and the juice of crushed grapes."[27]

The assassin, the dreamer, the bird of prey, and the pre-conscious child understand the Dionysian "pleasure of killing, the charity of bestowing death like a caress."[28] Animal purity, the absolute freedom of instinct—sociopathy in a civilized society and even in an uncivilized one—is, of course, that old and discredited ideal of the Romantics. It is Colette's ideal, too, although she is not a Romantic. Her dream of flying is a metaphor for an impossible, lost state of autonomy in which there are no bonds of need, rage, guilt, or dependence and no yearnings that shackle one creature to another: two lovers of whatever age or sex, the tamed beast and its master, parent and child. In the implacably tragic and primitive view of life Colette sets forth in these essays, and so gallantly dissembles by the intoxicating beauty of her prose—as she dissembles it in her life by her Olympian vitality—love is the Fall.

PART V

CHAPTER 32

From where do I return, and on what wings, that I should accept, so slowly, humiliated and exiled, to be myself?

— COLETTE,
The Vagabond

I

B
Y 1924, Colette and Marguerite Moreno had been friends for thirty years. *Soeur-âme*—Soul sister—Colette calls her; *"mon ami,"* using the masculine as a transcendent compliment; *"mon cher moi-même,"* which one could translate as dear twin, dear double, or simply as dear me. Sido had used the same expression, but between Colette and Moreno there was never any competition for a shared identity.

After the war, Moreno's career had languished. She took character roles and turned from the classics to melodrama. Her income declined and her pride suffered, but not her vitality, her sense of humor, or her libido. Liane de Pougy tells a charming anecdote about Moreno in her *Blue Notebooks*. They were guests at a country house for the weekend, but the weather was bad and the company confined indoors. "What shall we do?" asked one of the restless *convives*. "Fornicate," drawled Moreno.[1]

Her husband Jean Daragon had died in 1923, but there was an old lover waiting in the wings. "I was admiring you in Paris for being so yourself," Colette told her a few months later, "while I was descending into a moral and physical abyss." She counseled her friend to cease mourning and take up the lover. "It doesn't wound you that I say so? But then I can't imagine what we could ever do to hurt each other."[2]

About this time, Moreno retired to an old farmhouse in her native province, the Lot. Here she fell in love with a cousin some thirty years her junior, Pierre Moreno-Boyou. Moreno referred to him in private as her *petit serviteur,* and in public as her nephew. Their love affair was not as scandalous as Colette's with Bertrand, but there were many parallels. When her confidence faltered, Colette could offer Moreno some advice: "One should neither play nor engage in discourse during the approach of 'a something' which destiny is either fashioning in the shape of a good meal, to be digested promptly, or in the form of a solid, mystical engagement. . . . So your province, which has done so much for you in the past few weeks, had another gift to give. Take it. It's not light. It's worth all your solicitude and your mistrust. And write to me."[3]

Moreno always did,[4] and their letters from that autumn were taken up with their plans to act together in a revival of *Chéri,* as Léa and Charlotte. The play was scheduled to open early in January, but the theater was pre-empted by a production of two short comedies by Colette's friend Henri de Rothschild. Her producer assured her that the plays—a vehicle for the author's mistress—would bomb after three days, but the critics thought differently, and the opening night of *Chéri* was postponed until February 5. In the meantime, Colette turned fifty-two.

2

ON AN OFF NIGHT early in the run, Moreno was invited to dinner by some rich society friends, Andrée and Bernard Bloch-Levalois. She asked if she might bring Colette, aware, perhaps, that among the other guests she would meet a regular of the house, its resident extra man. He was a stylish, cultivated Jewish bachelor of thirty-five—"exactly the age of the Eiffel Tower"[5]—and his name was Maurice Goudeket.

Goudeket had the white satin skin and black hair of his age-mate Chéri. His manner was reserved, with a subdued fire that bored matrons in general and Mme Bloch-Levalois in particular found beguiling. This was a distinct asset to his business—selling pearls—which was, before the widespread marketing of the cultured product, very lucrative if one possessed, in addition to a good eye and some capital, a courtly temperament. Goudeket dressed impeccably, spoke well, wrote poetry, owned an expensive chauffeured car and a fancy pied-à-terre in the sixteenth arrondissement.

Colette's first act upon entering the Bloch-Levalois' drawing room was to commandeer a sofa and stretch out on it "like a great cat," leaning her tousled head on her bare arms. This breach of decorum displeased the fastidious Goudeket, who noted to himself that she was "a bit too fat" but that she had lovely shoulders, a fine profile, and a penetrating "voice of bronze." At dinner, he was placed beside her. She immediately seized an apple from the centerpiece and took a toothy bite, confirming his impression that she was "acting her own character," and he was put off. They exchanged "banalities," and she held herself aloof from the conversation—an exchange of "general ideas"—except to interject one brusque and deflating *"pourquoi?"* When Goudeket refilled her glass, however, Colette thanked him with a "midnight blue glance, ironic and interrogatory." He didn't have the presence of mind, at least not yet, to interpret its question.

"There was something rustic and wholesome about [Colette's] aura,"[6] Goudeket remembered many years later. There was nothing either rustic or wholesome about his own. Maurice was a little too young to have frequented the salons of the fin de siècle, but their hothouse atmosphere might have bred him and his malaise. He was a self-invented and artificial man, a misfit and outsider hungry for acceptance and distinction.

Goudeket had been born in Paris to a French mother and a Dutch father in the diamond business. Although he held French citizenship and had served in the French army during World War I, he was often described as Colette's "Dutchman." After living in Amsterdam for thirteen years, the Goudekets had returned to Paris in 1900. Maurice and his older brother were sent to the prestigious Lycée Condorcet, where they both excelled, although in the beginning their excessively polite French and provincial straightness isolated them from the other students. It was the height of the Dreyfus Affair, but Goudeket could never remember any incidents of anti-Semitism. "The reserve," he recalls, "came from us" and from his father, who discouraged his sons from any intimacy with their gentile school friends.

M. Goudeket *père* was a passionate francophile and a Jewish patriarch of the old school, demanding respect and formality from his children. Maurice admits that he inherited his father's starchiness of speech and manner. He yearned for some paternal tenderness but never got it. His mother didn't fill the void. She was a vain, volatile little woman whose closest relations were with her dressmaker, her upholsterer, and her coiffeur. She had a morbid fear of the country and of the elements, disapproved of sport and exercise, made terrible scenes with her husband, enjoyed them, overworked her servants, boasted of it, and took the same sort of pride in dominating her children. "A few slaps on the cheek are one thing," wrote Maurice. "When one also had to lower one's arm and proffer one's face for them, it was no longer a punishment, but an outrage."[7]

The family was prosperous, or kept up the appearance of being so. Mme Goudeket, by her son's description, was a downmarket Mme Verdurin with a penchant for collecting second-rate antiques and dinner invitations. Her own table was as mediocre and pretentious as the guests she gathered at it—fake countesses, amateur poets, and senescent generals—and as neither of the hosts drank, there was never enough wine to lubricate an evening. This little touch of barbarity galled the observant, sensitive Parisian sons "out of all proportion."

It was during his lonely years as a student at the Condorcet and as a silent, resentful fixture at his mother's dinners that Maurice Goudeket discovered the early work of Colette. It was for him, as for so many sexually seething young bourgeois readers, a call to freedom and revolt. He claimed to hear in it the voice of a "soulmate," and he even declared to his parents, quite preposterously, that he would one day marry Colette.

Unlike his idol, however, the young Maurice had grandiose dreams of intellectual or literary "glory" which, he admits, he did little to advance. He was, by his own account, depressive, puerile, and inhibited. He had published a "little book" of poems that was received politely, "but this wasn't glory," and he subsequently (though not permanently) renounced writing for publication. Thus he passed from a "wildly imaginative childhood" into a successful but boring life as a broker of pearls and extra man without quite knowing how the transformation—the degradation—had taken place.

Chéri RAN FOR six weeks at the Théâtre Daunou, then moved to the Renaissance for another six weeks. The public loved it. The critics were of several minds about Colette's performance. Her friend Marie de Régnier, who wrote under the name Gérard d'Houville, proclaimed that "Colette doesn't act, she lives, she breathes, she fears, she lies, she protects, she suffers." Albert Flament admired her expressive flesh—"the image of a Renoir"—and the "painful humanity" she brought to the role, "in spite of so much . . . exuberance." *Fantasio,* on the other hand, advised her not to quit her day job, and the review was accompanied by Vertes' caricature of an elephantine and blowsy Colette. "Léa," wrote its reviewer, "must be played by an elegant and beautiful woman, without which Chéri becomes utterly ignoble." Colette's old friend André Rouveyre, writing in the *Mercure de France,* concurred with more solemnity if not more tact: "In these willful attempts of hers," she is "completely inferior to herself. . . . May [she] not be deceived: the spectators come only out of curiosity" to see the famous writer.[8]

3

COLETTE MAY HAVE been an actress and dancer with more verve than talent, and she was, like so many other great novelists infatuated with the theater, a mediocre dramatist. She did, however, write one masterpiece for the stage, and that was her libretto for Ravel's opera *L'Enfant et les sortilèges.* This "lyric fantasy in two acts," as it was billed, had its première in March of 1925 in Monte Carlo. The orchestra was conducted by Victor de Sabata. The production was choreographed and directed by George Balanchine. Colette took a few days off from *Chéri* to attend it.

She was hearing the music for the first time, but it was ten years since she had written her libretto. In 1915, Jacques Rouché, the director of the Paris Opéra, had commissioned Colette to create a "fantasy ballet" for his company. He had an intimidating and powerful competitor to reckon with in Diaghilev, whose five seasons at the Théâtre du Châtelet had given the French public a ravenous appetite for all that was pagan, exotic, and revolutionary in dance and music.

Colette readily agreed to write the ballet, and she was ecstatic when Rouché proposed Ravel as a composer. In the last years of the nineteenth century the two had often crossed paths at the musical soirées of Mme de Saint-Marceaux and of Misia Natanson, who was one of Ravel's early champions. Colette would remember the Ravel of those years as an aloof little man with delicate hands, flashy ties, a flamboyant mustache, and the bright, darting glance of a squirrel. His outsize head of wild hair crowned a tiny body, and he carried himself with that faintly comical and off-putting hauteur sometimes affected by short men. "While seeking attention, he feared criticism," she writes, "and that of Henry Gauthier-Villars was cruel to him."[9]

Willy's distaste was shared by the conservative critics who judged the Prix de Rome. They had steadfastly refused to award Ravel the Grand Prize, and in 1905 they went so far as to reject his application, so incensing Misia—by then Mme Edwards, the wife of the immensely rich and powerful proprietor of *Le Matin*—that she made his rejection a cause célèbre in her husband's paper. "Other newspapers," write Misia's biographers, "took up the issue, and Ravel's public identity was established."[10] The director of the Conservatoire was forced to resign, and Fauré named to his place, inaugurating a "forward-looking era" in French music.

Colette had apparently never shared Willy's prejudices. She had always been "attracted" by Ravel's music, and her original curiosity about it was amplified by "the light malaise of surprise" and the "sensual and malicious charms of a new art form."[11] They achieved stardom at about the same pace.

By the time *L'Enfant* had its première, Ravel was considered a greater artist than his master, Fauré, or his rival, Debussy.

IN 1915, Ravel was at the front driving an ambulance. He accepted Rouché's commission, but other projects and distractions postponed his work on *L'Enfant* until 1920. By then it was a two-act opera. Rouché had warned Colette that the composer worked "with a slow frenzy, and in hermetic seclusion," and during its very long gestation period, says Colette, she "lost the habit of thinking about *L'Enfant et les sortilèges*." Even when the music was almost ready, there was very little correspondence between the two collaborators: "He didn't treat me as a privileged person."[12]

Ravel and Colette, however, shared a private wavelength. They were close contemporaries (he was two years younger) attracted by the same Romantic subjects—the mysteries of nature, animals, childhood, and adolescence[13]—to which they brought a modern sensibility. In 1904, the year Colette published *Dialogues de bêtes*, Ravel set Jules Renard's *Histoires naturelles* to music. They both reworked the fable of Daphnis and Chloe. They both outgrew the provocative carnal opulence of their early style without forsaking the "sensual and malicious" iconoclasm which informed it. "There's intellectual music," Ravel once told a friend. ". . . And then there's the music of the feelings and the instincts: mine."[14]

Both Ravel and Colette were laconic about "the feelings and the instincts" from which they drew their inspiration. That evening in Monte Carlo, she was silent and apparently expressionless throughout most of the performance. Ravel, sitting beside her, was silent, too. Finally he turned to whisper, "Isn't it amusing?" But she couldn't reply: "I had a lump of tears in my throat."[15]

L'Enfant et les sortilèges is unlike Colette's other work on many counts, the first of which is that she wrote it so quickly—"in fewer than eight days"—and without any of her usual "slowness and pain."[16] She could never explain this feat to herself. But perhaps the speed of its composition accounts for the uncensored, dreamlike symbolism of the writing, and for that magisterial sureness and economy—utterly pure of pedantry—with which Colette dramatizes the crisis of her protagonist.[17]

The curtain rises on a room in a Norman farmhouse, opening to a garden. The walls are hung with an old-fashioned toile depicting shepherds and shepherdesses in a bucolic landscape. There are two deep armchairs and a grandfather clock. A cage hangs by the window, holding a captive squirrel. A kettle is humming over the embers of the hearth, and the cat is purring with it.

A furious child of "six or seven" sits at a table, balking at his homework: "Feel like going for a walk. Feel like eating all the cakes in the world. Feel like pulling the cat's tail, cutting off the squirrel's. Feel like scolding the whole world. Feel like putting Mama in the corner."

Mama enters, carrying his tea tray. "Has Baby been sage? Has he finished his page?" From the child's perspective, she is a terrifying giantess. All he perceives is an expanse of skirt, a rustling apron, a pair of scissors hanging ominously from a steel chain. When she notices the blank notebook and the carpet stained with ink, Mama turns severe: "Do you promise to work? Will you beg my pardon?" Baby replies by sticking out his tongue. The skirt backs off a little. The hand sets down the tray:

"Here's the snack of a bad child: dry bread, black tea with no sugar! You can stay here alone until dinner! Think about your offense! Think about your homework! Think, think, above all, about Mama's grief."

In these few singsong lines, Colette sets forth a primal dilemma. The child is wild with frustration at the mother and the discipline which oppress him. His rage knows no bounds. He wants to burst forth from the tidy, civilized cage in which he has been imprisoned. He soils the floor. He has sadistic fantasies. And his retribution comes in the form of a disembodied skirt with a pair of scissors dangling from her bosom.

Colette's Mama is a figure of myth, an omnipotent source of nourishment who flaunts her powers of denial and castration. She uses the threat of abandonment, verbal and physical, to enforce her will. At "six or seven" the child is still her Baby, yet it's she who demands gratification: he must think of and write for her.

When the door closes on him, the child is seized "by a frenzy of perversity. . . . I'd rather be alone! I don't love a soul! I'm very bad! Bad! Bad! Bad!" And he begins to rampage, breaks the teacup and saucer, stabs the squirrel with his pen, overturns the kettle, rips the wallpaper to shreds, opens the clock and pulls out its pendulum, trashes his books and papers, "drunk with destruction" and shouting, "Hooray! I'm free, free, bad and free!"

The familiar objects that were once a source of comfort to the child retaliate for his abuse. They come to life and cry: "Away with the child!" The chairs deny him their arms. The teapot and cup speak Chinese. The fire chases him: "I warm the good but I burn the bad." The figures of the wallpaper sing a heartrending lament: they have watched over him, and he has torn them apart. Here Colette specifies "a ballet of little figures who express, in their dance, the grief of being unable to unite."

Now the beautiful princess from the storybook which the child has ripped to shreds emerges to reproach him: "You sought me in the heart of the rose and the perfume of the white lily. You sought me, little lover, and I was your beloved. . . . What will happen to me?" The child is "anxious," then "desperate." "If only I had a sword, I would know how to defend you!" He clings to her hair and veils, but she is swallowed up by "dream and night."

Searching in vain for her in the scattered pages of the fairy tale, the child finds only "arid" schoolbooks filled with "bitter and dry" lessons. As he kicks them viciously, the numbers from his math book come to life. They are led by a hunchbacked automaton, old "Arithmetic," brandishing a ruler, and together they chant a robotic chorus of sums and figures which make no sense—"Three times nine thirty three/Two times six twenty-seven/Four and four eighteen." The numbers and old Arithmetic encircle the child and drag him into their "mad rondelay." Shuddering with fear, weeping and desolate, he collapses. His cat, grown "great and terrible," plays with his head like a ball of yarn.

Act Two takes place in the garden, where the child seeks refuge but finds only more terror and reproach. "Our wounds, our wounds," cry the trees, "the ones you made with your knife." He is attacked by all the creatures he has injured. A bat reminds him that he killed his mate and orphaned his little ones. The squirrel he stabbed, and who has escaped, speaks poignantly about his imprisonment and warns the thoughtless boy: *"You will have my fate."*

Then, suddenly forgetting him, all the creatures—cats, frogs, bats, squirrels, insects, and birds—abruptly begin to mate. The garden becomes "a tender paradise" from which the child is excluded. "They love each other. They are happy, they've forgotten me," he cries. "They love each other. They've forgotten me. I'm alone." At this moment, "despite himself," he calls out the word *Mama*.

But she has forsaken him, too, and now the creatures mass for an attack. "It's the child with the knife! It's the child with the stick! Who loves no one. Whom no one loves. . . . Unite! Unite!" They fall upon him, though soon their fury turns to a fierce rivalry among themselves for the privilege of inflicting the child's punishment. They throw him to a corner of the stage. The little squirrel, wounded in the fray, crawls close to him, and the child spontaneously takes off his kerchief and binds its bleeding paw. "There is a general stupor among the beasts," then silence, then an astonished and repentant cry: "He's binding the wound. He's bandaged the paw. . . . He knows how to heal. We have wounded him, what shall we do?"

One beast points toward the house: "Help is there! Let's carry him to his nest! They have to hear the word, the word he cried. Let's try to cry that word . . . Mama . . . Mama!"

"A light appears in the windows. . . . At the same moment the moon emerges from the clouds, and dawn, pink and gold, floods the garden with a pure light." The creatures, who have helped the child to his feet, escort him to the door and leave him standing with arms outstretched "towards [the one] they have called Mama!" As they retreat, they chant: "He is good . . . so good . . . he is wise, he is good, so good, so good."[18]

COLETTE YEARNED TO love and to believe in love, but always had the greatest trouble doing so. She was dominated too early and for too long by exploitative masters—first her mother, then her husband—both of whom lend certain features to Mama. She had split her own mother into two mythical figures, a beautiful, seductive "princess" whom she loved romantically, and a powerful, phallic virago whom she feared. She believed this sorceress could read her thoughts, and so she armed herself—and much of her writing—with an inscrutable exterior.

The rivalry bred of her primitive anxieties—her father's indifference, her mother's romance with Achille, her feelings of exclusion—was one of Colette's strongest passions, if not her predominant one; and she couldn't avoid, indeed actively, perversely sought to reconstitute, the original love triangles of her childhood in most of her adult relationships and everywhere in her fiction. It is no wonder that she calls love "that hair shirt which sticks to the skin where love is born and tightens its grip as it grows."[19] And she acknowledges that the greatest obstacle to her escape from the torture of the hair shirt—"a hundred times more dangerous than the greedy beast [of lust] is the abandoned child who trembles inside of me, weak, nervous, *ready to stretch out her arms and beg: 'Don't leave me alone!'* "[20]

In 1915, when she wrote *L'Enfant,* Colette was still the slave of her childhood privations. She continued to vacillate between her terror of abandonment and denial of that terror, between reckless surrender and furious repudiation. She tried to obliterate the solitude, and the self that suffered it, with the intoxicant she calls love, a violent poison whose antidote is so often— and particularly in the case of her own daughter—ruthless detachment. As a mother herself, Colette was, in the self-accusing words of *L'Enfant,* "bad, bad and free."

By the late 1920s, she had begun to bind her own wounds. "Love, one of the great commonplaces of existence, is slowly withdrawing from mine," she writes in *Break of Day,* her finest novel from this period. "The maternal instinct is another great commonplace. Once we've left these behind, we find that all the rest is gay and varied, and that there is plenty of it. But one doesn't leave all that behind when or as one chooses."[21]

Her critics and biographers have objected that when Colette wrote these lines, she was, on the contrary, embarking on a new affair—with Goudeket—which led to a new marriage, the most enduring and serene relationship of her life. This is a polite way of implying that she's fooling, even lying to, her readers. But their charge is mistaken in the sense that Colette's new love would not ultimately prove to be the violent and destructive passion she evokes in *L'Enfant* and had, all her life, called *amour*.

CHAPTER 33

A woman reaches an age when the only thing left to her is to enrich
her own self.

—COLETTE,
Break of Day

1

AURICE GOUDEKET HADN'T seen Colette again except
briefly, backstage, after a performance of *Chéri*. He was having an
affair with Andrée Bloch-Levalois, but it wasn't curing his
depression. "Not much gave me pleasure. I felt my life was at an impasse." He
made plans to visit Italy for a few days that Easter, but lost interest and canceled the trip.

The Bloch-Levalois were spending the holidays on the Riviera, at the
Hotel Eden Cap-d'Ail. Goudeket and Moreno decided to join them, and his
chauffeur drove them down from Paris. After a few days at the Eden, Moreno
announced that her "nephew" would be arriving with Colette. "Ah!" said
Goudeket. "And we were so peaceful!" His three friends gave him a strange
look, and he realized that he had just made a confession. Colette had left a
more troubling impression than he'd wanted to admit, and "I so habitually
curbed my natural inclinations that I'd put myself on the defensive."[1]

Goudeket believed that Colette and Moreno hadn't previously organized
this reunion, but he was wrong—they had cooked up the whole thing. At the
end of March, Colette told Misz Marchand, who had gone south without Léo,
that "I have a hope of meeting you . . . in a few days. We'll see. And perhaps
I'll be at the Eden Cap-d'Ail."[2] When the party of six was fully assembled, it

must have made an intriguing erotic puzzle for their fellow guests: two grandes dames famous for their transgressions; a pretty boy; an affable bourgeois; his petite, garrulous wife; and an attractive, unattached man. Who belonged to whom?

Colette played her hand with discretion. She spent her mornings secluded in her hotel room and her afternoons visiting other friends. After dinner, the little clan took their seats at the card table for a game called Taminti (*t'as menti*, i.e., you lied). "Colette laughed freely, surrendered to her own vivacity, to her playfulness. As for me," Goudeket continues, "I grew more and more reserved, to the point that one of the players—since the game consisted of discovering who was lying—remarked: 'Oh with Maurice, it's difficult. He is always calm, calm like . . .' " And Colette finished the simile: "Like a covered flame."[3]

It was love, it was France, so everybody was lying. Colette had more than one motive to fall in with Moreno's plan. Bertrand had been sent to Cannes by his mother earlier that winter "with the pretext" that he needed the warm weather for his health, but really, he says, to distance him from Colette. He had still managed to see her once, at the end of November, when she was lecturing in Marseille, but only, he says, to kiss her hand.

Claire was still trying to arrange Bertrand's marriage, and she'd installed her new white hope in the hotel next to his. This young lady was Marcelle Prat, the niece of the distinguished dramatist Maurice Maeterlinck, and Bertrand says that for once Claire had made "a good choice." Marcelle "was very intelligent and very good company." They had become engaged and were to be married the following December.

Not, however, before Colette tried one last time to repossess her *fils chéri*. While she was at Cap-d'Ail, she invited him to lunch. He came alone, but she brought Goudeket, perhaps hoping to make Bertrand jealous. At the very least she succeeded in making him uncomfortable, for Bertrand told Geneviève Dormann that "for some reason he found the lunch difficult," that Goudeket "irritated him," and that Colette looked like a "sly cat."[4]

As they were leaving the restaurant, Colette took Bertrand aside and invited him to visit her at the Eden. It was to be their last night together. At some moment between midnight and dawn, Colette asked her stepson "gravely" if he wanted to resume living with her, and he told Dormann that he was, indeed, "ready to spend my life with her."[5] By morning, they had "agreed that it was impossible."[6] Perhaps Bertrand's body betrayed that impossibility. Or perhaps it was Colette's.

He never received the letter she wrote him that Marcelle Prat intercepted and destroyed, though not before she'd memorized its contents. When she admitted the theft years later, she could still recite Colette's parting words.

One would love to know them. Were they as generous as Léa's to Chéri? Bertrand was silent on the subject except to ask: "Are there any beautiful separations?"[7]

Goudeket, meanwhile, received an urgent telegram recalling him to Paris, and decided to leave the same night, by the express train from Monte Carlo. The Bloch-Levalois and the Morenos had already made their travel plans, so he offered his empty car and idle chauffeur to Colette, who "accepted with joy, liking nothing better than a leisurely road trip."

Goudeket claims he had come to the conclusion that there was "nothing either possible or desirable" between him and Colette. A thank-you note for the use of his car would be accompanied by an inscribed book, and "our relations would stop there. It was all for the best." He then goes to elaborate lengths to explain that he returned to Cap-d'Ail that night only after having diligently, even heroically, tried and failed to secure a berth on the night train. When he asked Colette solemnly if she would grant him the favor of a passage to Paris in his own car—a favor "which you are perfectly free to refuse"—she laughed in his face, and they left the next morning.

2

COLETTE SET OUT for Paris more hopeful about the immediate romantic future than her companion. "What tumult in my damned existence!" she told Hélène Picard on the eve of her departure. Goudeket was apparently already "something" to her, although whether that something was, as she had put it to Moreno, "a good meal . . . or a solid, mystical engagement," she couldn't yet say.

Maurice did receive an inscribed book—*The Vagabond*—but with it an invitation to lunch. He came for the meal and stayed for the engagement. "I was quick," says Colette. They both were. It is easy to see what a passive, rootless, secretive, aloof, disappointed man like Goudeket, who yet had so much untapped passion, would admire in Colette. Paul Valéry thought he had defined the affair when he christened Maurice Mr. Goodcock (a play, in franglais, on the name Goudeket—good *quéquette*). But the lovers' disparities tend to obscure their great point of resemblance. At thirty-five, Maurice had managed to preserve himself from any meaningful attachments while "saving himself " for a "unique love in which, at the depths of my being, I no longer believed."[8] So, at fifty-two, had Colette.

IT WAS an unseasonably hot spring. "There's a satyr behind every leaf," writes Colette. To cool off mind and body, she went rowing on the lake in the

Bois. "O healthy exercise, distract me from such thoughts that might unsettle a sturdy creature of my kind!"[9] The lovers went about their separate lives during the day, meeting late and talking through the night. Colette describes "orgies of mineral water, oranges, grapefruit, and cigarettes," but there were ecstasies, naturally, of another kind. She began to describe Goudeket as her "Satan" and asks Moreno to fill in the ellipses of her letters. Yet the letters are plain enough: "The boy is exquisite . . . what masculine grace there is in a certain softness, and how one is touched to see the interior fire melt its containing envelope."[10]

However humble Goudeket was before the great writer he had loved since childhood, he was worldly enough to play at being masterful with the woman. "Don't you think," asks a smitten Colette, "that there are very few men who know, without raising their voice or changing their tone, to say . . . what has to be said?"[11] It was a meeting of two profoundly proud, suspicious people. Colette felt Goudeket listening to her, feeling her out with "his antennae." That image of fragility guarded by hypervigilance suits both of them.

Colette's vigilance, however, was short-lived. Toward the end of June, Moreno received a manic letter which confirmed all her fears: "Ah! la la, and again, ah! la la! And never enough la la! She's in a fine fix, your friend . . . up to the eyes, up to the lips, up further than that! Oh, the satanism of quiet people—I say that for the kid Maurice. You want to know what the kid Maurice is? He's a bastard, a so-and-so, a cool guy, and a skin of satin. That's where I'm at . . ."[12]

This was not the state of affairs which the matchmaker had intended. "Great!" she replied by return post.

> What a mess! Lovely!
> You've pulled your finger out of the dike!
> You can't know peace, you miserable woman!
> One gives you a servant, and you make him a master![13]

IN APRIL OF 1925, Colette's divorce became final, and she ceased using a married name. "Behold," she wrote, "that legally, familiarly, and in literature I have only one name, which is my own. Did it not take thirty years of my life to reach that point—to return there? I'll end up believing it wasn't too much to pay."[14]

Early that June, she returned to Saint-Sauveur, where, thanks to Anatole de Monzie, a plaque celebrating her one name was affixed to her birthplace. "My ex-scourge must be dreaming that she's Georges Sand, Sarah Bernhardt . . . and Sacha Guitry, too," wrote a scornful Olympe Terrain to

Jean Larnac.[15] The local people snubbed Colette, her entourage, and the cere-mony: "Did she expect an ovation? If she did, she was disappointed. Even though we're not prudes here, her charms are considered less than edifying. 'It's the triumph of pornography,' say the villagers, who in literary matters are more sensitive to the substance than to the form."[16]

By now, Bertrand had also vanished from her horizon. Colette hadn't heard from him since they'd parted at the Eden. "Indignation," she told Moreno, "is an excellent tonic." When the landlord of his apartment on the rue d'Alleray sent her a bill for the next quarter's rent, she "serenely" dis-patched it to Claire Boas.

There was one more Jouvenel left to dispatch, and that was her daughter. When summer came, Colette made what would prove to be a definitive break with Rozven, its landscape, and its memories. She went south with Goudeket, who had rented a villa in the Var, consigning her rebellious child to the care of Germaine Patat, who showered her with new clothes and solicitude, for which Colette was grateful, if a little envious. "I gave you this little girl you love with the feeling of having deposited her in a safe place," Colette wrote to Germaine. "After that I was able to play my hand of the moment—this year's game. . . . I had a great need to unburden myself. I speak simply to you because I am, no doubt, so 'monstrously simple,' as Jouvenel used to say. And because I'm making friends with a simple creature who has nothing monstrous."[17]

COLETTE HAD NEVER much liked what she had once called "the pretty, false Midi." As recently as that April, she'd told Hélène Picard, on a postcard from Cap-d'Ail, "This isn't any country for me." That summer, she under-went a radical conversion. "What a country!" she exults to Carco only three months later. "I don't want any other. No kidding, Francis!"[18]

Goudeket had taken a two-week lease on a pink villa—"a chic campsite" called La Bergerie, surrounded by vineyards and fruit trees. The Mediter-ranean was at the foot of the garden. By day, the heat was torrid, bleaching the sky and sea and melting the resin of the pine trees. The couple gaily braved sunstroke to go touring in their open car, stopping to bathe on deserted beaches. Colette assured Hélène Picard that she was "becoming very south-ern. Measure all that has changed in me by this detail: I haven't once eaten meat since my [arrival]."[19] To Moreno she was more confiding: the sand and the sea were her "native element, and love too."[20]

The nights were so fine and clear that the lovers dragged their mattresses onto the terrace and slept under a light cover, awakening to the setting moon and the "somber, dark orange dawn." Colette felt so well rested she didn't need a siesta. Her companion was more spent by his exertions. "One always feels a little guilty writing beside a sleeping creature," Colette told Moreno one afternoon, "even when it's to confess, in a few lines, that he is charming and that one loves him. Wasn't it last winter that you told me I would meet, during a voyage, a man who would change my life?"[21]

The nearest village to La Bergerie was Sainte-Maxime, which had already been colonized by the denizens of the French theater world. Colette and Maurice saw her old friend Sacha Guitry and his latest wife, the Belgian actor Jules Berry, and the beautiful model-turned-actress Exiane—but "just long enough for a lemonade." They preferred their own company, and when they wanted some nightlife, they drove to Saint-Tropez, across the gulf. In 1925, Saint-Trop was still a sleepy port with no traffic and a few rustic piano bars frequented by the local fishermen and a handful of adventurous artists. "I'd love to bring you [here] to drink white wine at the fishermen's ball," Colette told Anna de Noailles, "because I love you, and because you'd so enjoy seeing such beautiful boys dancing together."[22]

If Colette was particularly fond of Anna at that moment, it was because Anna was so willing to be charmed by Maurice. She was in a minority, for as Colette would note in *Break of Day,* "my true friends always gave me this supreme proof of attachment: a spontaneous aversion to the man I loved."[23] More galling was the snobbery Maurice had to endure as an obscure Jewish upstart who sold jewelry and aspired to the place in Colette's life once filled by the brilliant Willy, the noble Missy, and the powerful Jouvenel.[24]

Anna, however, had made a friendly point of gushing to Colette about Maurice in a flurry of letters, and had asked him to write privately to her. They'd even spoken of having the countess join them at La Bergerie. It is a measure of the trust Colette placed in her new lover—of an atypical lack of possessiveness—that she accepted the homage as his due, and without alarm. It seemed "absolutely natural" that Anna should be "crazy" about him. As for her, she told Moreno, she wasn't "crazy" at all. "It's much worse than that."[25]

Their two-week idyll in the south so utterly "seduced" Colette that before she left, she decided to sell Rozven and buy a property near Saint-Tropez. ("You see," she told Moreno, "I'm accepting to speak about next year.") She mobilized her friends in the region to find her a farmhouse which she could renovate. They promptly turned up Tamaris les Pins, a peasant *mas* with four small rooms. There was no plumbing or electricity, but the well was deep and full, and there was a charming terrace which faced north and was shaded by an old wisteria. The house stood on about two and a half acres of land planted with vines and fig trees. Beyond the garden was a stand of old pines and a little path which led directly from the house to a deserted beach.

Colette immediately began to plan improvements and to settle down in her imagination. "Just as she could never start a book without having a title," notes Goudeket, she wanted to give the house a name, even before she had signed the contract. Tamaris les Pins sounded to her like a train station. When the owner pointed out the ancient muscat vine encircling the well, Colette made her mind up: "Good. We'll call it La Treille Muscate." To the fastidious and incurably bourgeois Goudeket, it would never be "really beautiful or really comfortable," although Colette would give it—"magically"—as she had given all her Edens, the illusion of being so.

THAT AUGUST, with Maurice in tow, Colette went on the road with *Chéri*. It was a strenuous tour for a woman of fifty-two, made more so by the heat. She played at sixteen casino-hotels in as many days, informing all her usual correspondents by postcard about her triumphs, her receipts, the crowds, and what was, in spite of all, "a lovely voyage with Satan."[26]

In September, Maurice left on a business trip to London, and she spent a few days at Rozven with Bel-Gazou. Colette hadn't heard from her all summer and had written to Germaine Patat from La Bergerie to ask playfully what she had "done" with "their" daughter. Germaine had, in fact, taken the twelve-year-old to spend part of the vacation with Jouvenel. Colette always maintained that Henry "spoiled" her, but to Bel-Gazou, his indulgence was a balm for what Pichois calls her mother's "sudden fits of authority."

Her parents' acrimonious divorce, followed immediately by Colette's immersion in a new affair and her abrupt defection from Rozven, had naturally been overwhelming for Bel-Gazou. She would never accept or like Goudeket, whom she called "the crocodile" and who was wary and reserved with her. After Colette's death, they would spend years fighting bitterly, in and out of court. But no settlement could indemnify Colette de Jouvenel for that just portion of maternal love of which she had been cheated.

4

IN OCTOBER, Bel-Gazou was sent abroad, to an English boarding school, and after a trip to Brussels—to play Léa—Colette took up the novel she had been working on for at least a year. *The Last of Chéri* had started out, as Colette told Germaine Patat, "as the story of Chéri's marriage." Most of her sequels were inferior in power and artistry to their originals, but this was an exception: a bleak and ambitious masterpiece. For the first time in her fiction, Colette ventures into the realm of social history. With the adjustment of some minor details, the characters in *Chéri* might have lived anytime from 1880 to 1913, but *The Last of Chéri* takes place at the moment it was written—1925— and the keen eye of the reporter, adept at compression, is very evident. Writing from Chéri's perspective and never violating the limits—indeed, the claustrophobia—of his view, Colette is able to suggest the revolution in manners, the shift in sex roles, the breakdown of hierarchies, the speeding up of time, and the alternating currents of greed, euphoria, and despair that defined postwar Paris. The effect is a modern version of a Renaissance portrait: a prince, splendid and sullen, sits in the foreground; through an open window behind him, one glimpses a glittering, embattled city.

Colette worked on *The Last of Chéri* with the kind of single-mindedness she had not devoted to a novel since the first *Claudine*. She refused to take on any journalistic assignments, and put her lecturing and acting careers on hold. "If I attempted any short-term jobs at this moment," she told Germaine Patat, "my novel would suffer, and I don't want it to. It won't be a fun sort of book, maybe no one will like it, but I promise you it won't be emotionless."[27]

To Moreno she speaks of the "nudity" of her style, and of an "aversion to adornment which surprises even me."[28] The author's esthetic repugnance for excess mirrors her view of Chéri's revolt against the frantic materialism of his old friends, and the "virile" purposefulness of his wife and mother. Charlotte Peloux has become a patron of charity, a speculator in real estate, and a crony of the pols on the city council. The war has transformed Edmée from a subservient little *femme d'intérieur* into a superb manager who runs the household, manages the stock portfolio, and occupies her minutely scheduled days visiting the wounded at the hospital she has endowed, and with whose chief doctor she is having an affair. Chéri inhabits her décor and lives in her shadow.

The Last of Chéri is the work of a deeply, even radically conservative writer, and it allies Colette to novelists like Drieu la Rochelle, Georges Bernanos, and Maurice Barrès. Chéri's idleness, passivity, weakness, puerility, and inability to adapt—none of which she contests—constitute, in her view, a kind of noble revolt against modernity. Once he was a heartless gigolo. Here he is a man who "backs away, with an unspeakable repugnance, from the idea of living . . . in a world no longer ruled by love."[29]

Scourged by the war, spiritually homeless, filled with inarticulate yearning, Chéri has come to represent the yin principle in a clockwork yang world where even the women—especially the women—have become too tough and competent. They have seized the whip and abandoned the harem where Chéri stays on as a voluntary last holdout.

"Perhaps I wrote *The Last of Chéri*," Colette told Parinaud, "to create a sort of justification for him, to endow him, vis-à-vis the public, with a kind of innocence. What would you like Chéri to do in life? He wasn't going to become an industrialist! . . . [That idea] produced such a sinister effect on me that I almost burst into tears, and I killed him. . . . Yes, Chéri's purity! You must excuse me, but I believe it existed, if only in my will and my imagination."[30]

If Chéri embodies a new *mal du siècle,* he also evokes a much older and familiar figure. Colette's father was another wounded and decorated veteran who came home from war humiliated to have survived. He, too, was a useless man, frivolous and depressed, married to a woman who had all the aptitude for life and for survival. Sido considered her husband's doting, indeed his life, entirely "frivolous" without understanding, as Colette did, that love was all the dignity and idealism that were left for him.

"Endowed with patience, and often subtle, Edmée neglected to note that the female lust to possess tends to emasculate all its living conquests and can reduce a male, magnificent and inferior, to the function of a courtesan."[31] In "justifying" Chéri, Colette finally honors and mourns her father.

THE SCENE OF Chéri's abortive reunion with Léa is probably the greatest Colette ever wrote. The catastrophe of the war and the catastrophe of losing her are inseparably linked for him. "The two together," he reflects, "have driven me outside the times I live in."[32] Without ever ceasing to dream of her, he realizes one morning, with a terrible shock, that he hasn't seen her since the war began. He counts the years on his fingers, calculates that she must be sixty, and a page later, faints.

That day, he goes to an address on the rue Raynouard, supplied by his mother. A maid admits him to the salon. There are two ladies there, but he doesn't recognize either of them and wonders what they've done with Léa. He hears a familiar laugh, resonant and grave—which plunges him into the "torment of memories." Slowly he realizes that the laugh is coming from the throat of one of the two women, the one with the coarse gray hair and the fat red neck: "She wasn't monstrous, but huge, and loaded with exuberant buttresses of fat in every part of her body. Her arms, like rounded thighs, stood out from her hips on plump cushions of flesh just below her armpits. The plain skirt and the nondescript long jacket proclaimed that the wearer had abdicated, was no longer concerned to be a woman, and had acquired a kind of sexless dignity."[33]

Léa and the lady named Valérie (who, one surmises, is a former cocotte, although she bears an "authentic" royal name) appraise Chéri at their leisure, "sparing him neither goodwill nor curiosity." They chat, like expert judges at a cattle fair, about another young man, the latest prize of a friend. "Speaking of proportions," says Léa with spectacular and deliberate vulgarity, "you'll never come across anything to touch Chéri." Her friend remarks that Chéri hasn't changed much and reminds Léa how proud she was of him. "No," says Léa "with perfect calm. 'I was in love with him. . . . It's true, I was in love with you. Very much in love, too.' "

Léa's complacence shocks Chéri as much as her obesity, or the uncoiffed gray hair, the ruddy cheeks, the bloodshot eyes, the charmless suit, and the "jovial air of an old gentleman," all of which she flaunts with the same incomprehensible serenity, declaring, "I love my present. I'm not ashamed of what I've had, and I'm not sad because I have it no longer."

Valérie departs, and Léa makes petty small talk about money, real estate, and the help. She tells a horrified Chéri that he should have his urine tested and gain ten pounds, offering to give him the address of an undiscovered little bistro where the owner still does the cooking. Without an interruption—for he is incapable of speaking a word, and closes his eyes to help detach the sound of the beloved voice from the colossal figure in the armchair—he hears her attribute the "disease of his generation" to its "neurasthenia" and self-pity, and to chide him for presuming to think himself unique: " 'A certain kind of sickness of the soul, my child, of disillusion, is just a question of stomach. Yes, yes, you may laugh!' He was not laughing but she might well think he was. 'The whole lot, simply stomach. Love itself! If one wished to be perfectly sincere, one would have to admit there are two kinds of love—well-fed and ill-fed. The rest is pure fiction.' "[34]

Chéri fights the impulse to "cry out loud, 'Stop! Show me your real self! Throw off your disguise!' " And Colette permits Léa to betray just enough valiance and distress, just enough dissembled coquetry—a flash or two of her old feline cruelty—to leave the reader doubting, with Chéri, the sincerity of her performance.

There are forty pages left to the novel, at the end of which Chéri shoots himself. But by the time he leaves Léa's apartment, she has already "drained" what "lifeblood" there was left in him. "The privilege which Colette accords woman," writes Yannick Resch, "is to regenerate herself " at the expense of the weaker male.[35] The privilege she accords man is tragedy.

Colette had formed this Darwinian theory about the dominance of the female principle by observing nature and her parents' marriage, and her own life would bear it out. She had survived her first husband, but "the late Willy" declined into oblivion without her. Missy, more man than woman, floundered and diminished, and would eventually meet Chéri's end. Jouvenel would die prematurely, and despite his real distinction as a statesman, he would be best remembered as her second husband. Maurice became Monsieur Colette. The paradox, however, is that the price of triumph and detachment for Colette's New Woman is her female form. She devours man and incorporates his powers. And in *The Last of Chéri,* one hears the voice of Old Man—of all those misogynists of the fin de siècle, subtle and crude, gay and straight, all of them confused, angry, terrified, and fascinated—incorporated by Colette.

CHAPTER 34

To become young again, no. To become younger than I ever was, yes!
—COLETTE,
to Dr. Helan Jaworski,
author of *How to Rejuvenate*

1

OLETTE KILLS OFF Chéri at the moment she makes one of those radical breaks with her own past that she calls a rebirth. Like so much of her fiction, *The Last of Chéri* explores the dead ends and close calls—the alternative fates—she manages to escape. Chéri and Léa embody two dangerous extremes—of detachment and surrender, respectively—in her own character. He is the child yearning for an impossible lost state of fusion. She has bought her self-mastery at the price of being denatured and desexed.

Goudeket's memoirs hint that he suffered from Chéri's malaise,[1] and his letters to Colette suggest he might have succumbed to it had her vitality not rescued him.[2] But then his ardor also rescued her. She is explicit enough when she writes, in *The Break of Day,* "I invented Léa as a premonition."[3]

Léa is also a self-caricature, crueler than any cartoonist or critic had ever drawn. But Colette is never more evasive than when she's being revealing, and all of her self-portraits are diversionary acts. The closer they approach the truth, the more anxiety one feels in the text, as if a powerful magnet wielded by a curious child were now straining, now compressing, the syntax.

The Last of Chéri was published in March of 1926. With her readers and

356

critics riveted by the spectacle of an elephantine Léa baring her veinous face to Chéri's gaze and "cheerfully inviting [him] to sit in judgment of her appearance," Colette was rehearsing a new role. She was preparing to play the romantic lead—the thirtysomething Renée Néré—in her own adaptation of *The Vagabond*.

2

THE YEAR 1926 was one of vagabondage for Colette, as strenuous as 1908. She went on tour with *Chéri* in January, revived the play in Paris a month later and again that autumn, in Bordeaux. In October, she played Renée in Brussels. In November, she was in Switzerland, lecturing on her experience of the music hall in six cities. At the end of the year, she took *The Vagabond* to Nice, Cannes, Saint-Raphael, Toulon, Menton, and Monte Carlo, with Paul Poiret, the couturier, playing Brague to her Renée.

These separations were excruciating for Maurice, who wrote her extravagant letters in which the ecstasy of "young love" alternated with an equally florid despair. "What cannibalism on my part," she told Moreno, "to accept them." Yet if his excesses pained the stylist, they moved the woman; her feelings—humility, mistrust, in short, love—seep through the cracks of her reticence: "I write to you about such ordinary things . . . dark little things which are like the grains in a mortice which bind the solid volumes. . . . Look at me, abashed to write that I love you. I'm going off to hide my embarrassment in a hot bath."[4]

Between her engagements, she and Maurice found time for a New Year's holiday in Saint-Tropez and a sumptuous idyll in Morocco, where they were guests of Al-Glâwi, the pasha of Marrakesh. "I wish to contemplate something dazzling under a Moroccan sky before becoming a completely old lady," she told Renaud de Jouvenel in her best false-Léa mode.[5]

She had her wish. The pasha was a sybarite like Haroun al-Raschid himself, with the same "sunken, almost fearful eyes of a dreamer" and a "small capricious chin of unrestrained violence."[6] His eighty cooks produced banquets that were "a poem in a hundred courses." He put his limousine at Colette's service, and his palace in Fez, along with an army of slaves— "negresses glossier than any fruit" and "Chleuhs the color of barely tinted ivory." The walls of the palace were made of colored tiles, the stairways of mosaic, and "the night wind and chafed the troubling perfumes"—jasmine, roses, mint, honeysuckle—of the scent garden.[7]

In her journal Colette wrote: "Illusion of having reached a goal. . . . 'I've come to the very end . . .' The end of what? Life? Desire? Movement?

Love? . . . For today, for two previous days, the illusion has lasted."8
But Colette's susceptibility to illusion is invariably as intense as it is
ephemeral.

SHE MOVED TWICE that year, and each move was a major upheaval. In
July, she returned to Rozven, which she had put up for sale, to supervise the
shipment of her furniture to Saint-Tropez. When the crates were safely
loaded into the vans, she and Maurice drove south to wait for them. The *mas*
was still without beds or running water, so Colette began to drive the construction crew "like galley slaves." "I succeeded," she told Hélène Picard.
They finished installing the windows, the shutters, the patio, and the plumbing. Bel-Gazou arrived with a school friend, and they were immediately put to
work in the garden. Pauline returned from a brief vacation just in time to help
unload the crates that had finally arrived from Rozven. Forty-eight hours
later, Colette boasted to Léo, "we've set up a *pretty* house that looks as if it has
been lived in for ten years. . . . If I don't leave four kilos behind me here,
there's no just God."9

Even before they left for the south, Colette and Maurice had discussed the
possibility of her renting out the house on the boulevard Suchet, and of finding "a more manageable" place to live in Paris. Maurice worried, she told
Moreno, "that such a change would make me melancholy, but what an error!
He doesn't know how much creatures like us are enriched every time they
can change a country, a house, a skin, provided they take with them what's
necessary—necessary to them!"10

It was just as difficult to find a decent cheap apartment in Paris after World
War I as it is today, but Colette's entourage had lately acquired a resident
miracle-worker. Alba Crosbie, a rich English expatriate, was one of those
smitten fans who often have stifled literary aspirations of their own and attach
themselves to a great older writer as a companion, secretary, translator, nanny,
life manager. Alba enters Colette's letters in 1925 as a "providential little person" who visits her on tour in Brussels, and later that year in Nice, where she
"cares for me like a race horse."11

Once Colette decided to rent the house, Alba went looking for a tenant
and found an "honest American (no joking!)"12 who was willing to put up a
large deposit. By the date he was ready to take possession, Colette had still not
found a suitable apartment, so Alba again came to her rescue—vacating her
own pied-à-terre in the Palais-Royal. It was a cramped and lightless entresol
(mezzanine) on the second floor under the arches, and they both believed it
would be a temporary sublet. Colette—who moved in November—stayed for
three years.

THE ANCIENT AND HISTORIC Palais-Royal, which lies just north of the Louvre on the Right Bank, was built by Cardinal Richelieu in the seventeenth century. No sooner had the new palace been finished than Richelieu offered it to the king, who died almost immediately, leaving it to his widow, Anne of Austria, and his infant son, Louis XIV. In 1692, it passed to the king's brother, Philippe d'Orléans, then to *his* son, Philippe II, who held famous orgies there. During his regency, the Palais-Royal acquired the licentious reputation it kept well into this century.

Fire destroyed most of the Palais-Royal in the mid-1700s, and it was rebuilt by the future Philippe-Égalité as a low, three-sided palace with an extremely fine columned arcade that enclosed a public park. The galleries on the ground floor were rented as shops; the low-ceilinged entresols—where Colette would live—housed servants, while the prince and his entourage occupied the upper stories.

In July of 1789, Camille Desmoulins organized a demonstration in the Palais-Royal which was the prelude to the storming of the Bastille. The fashionable ladies and gentlemen who had once cruised the garden subsequently lost their heads, and by 1791, when the southern side of the quadrangle was enclosed, the galleries had become a trysting place for prostitutes, gamblers, rakes, pedophiles, moneylenders, abortionists, spies, black marketeers, pornographers, and hustlers of all kinds. The Palais-Royal then began to figure in French literature as the City of Light's heart of darkness.

By the time Colette moved to 9, rue de Beaujolais, on the north side of the gardens, the royal suites had long been broken up into apartments with eccentric floor plans, grand moldings, and splendid views, many of them occupied by the theater people attached to the Comédie-Française, next door. "But the *entresols?*" she writes. "Am I the only one who defends or will defend these lairs huddled under the arches, squeezed between the first floor and the shops beneath?"[13] Colette was happy enough to have a cheap rent and a roof over her head, even if she could touch the ceiling with her hand. ("Don't jump for joy," a friend told her, "or you'll fracture your skull.") She would jump for joy, she replied, when the tenant immediately above her moved out and leased her his apartment. For this, however, she would have to wait until 1938.

In the meantime, she "ceased to envy that sunny floor, [and] took a liking to the sombre level where I could hang curtains and pictures without needing a step-ladder." By day, she lived by the "footlight glow" of the sun reflected by the paving stones of the arcade, with the cooing of the pigeons, the barking of dogs, the footsteps of pedestrians, and the "throbbing" of the printing press in the shop below. The nights were somewhat more tranquil, thanks to the patrols of the vice police. But "repose of mind and body," Colette concludes, "is not dependent on silence. . . . My 'tunnel,' haunted by footfalls and voices, cradled a unique peace."[14]

3

EARLY IN 1927, a literary historian named Jean Larnac published the first biography of Colette. He had researched her childhood and interviewed Olympe Terrain, who showed him Colette's letters. In making a case for her greatness, Larnac daringly compares Colette to Corneille, Racine, La Bruyère, Constant, and Rousseau (but also to Paul Bourget). He defends her against the argument—still common—that her amoral characters have no inner lives, and that her view of human nature is a debased one: "Morality? No. Psychology. In focusing with such constancy on the instincts which drive us, Colette has enriched our self-knowledge; she has exposed the unknown forces hidden in our subconscious. . . . Stripping the human being of those sentiments that envelop him like Jupiter his cloud, she describes . . . the essential mechanism that we hide under the hood of convention. Behind the intelligence, which is so often faulty, behind the emotions—that unreal blue sky—Colette shows us the one true spring . . . instinct."[15]

At the end of the century, there is more to say about instinct than Larnac, or even Freud, could say in the early 1920s. Later theorists of human nature, like D. W. Winnicott and his heirs, are perhaps a better guide to the behavior of Colette's body-bound characters, who are struggling to preserve "the capacity for excited love" in the face of inhibitions from without, and fears of ruthlessness and aggression toward the beloved object from within.

It is not that Colette's characters lack an inner life: they suffer, if anything, from having too much interiority. Her work preserves the legacy of a child's earliest thinking about self and other—self and mother in particular— whether the mother is absent, like Claudine's, or all too present, like Léa and Sido. Whatever the story, and however frivolous or anecdotal its surface, Colette reminds us of that lost age at which we had not yet categorized desire into good and bad, male and female, real and imagined, passive and aggressive. She writes from the point of view not of the analytic adult but of the child first "sorting out" her paradoxical instincts and experience.[16]

Larnac's biography and Colette's new novel were both still being reviewed when she dined with François Mauriac, André Maurois, their wives, and several other guests at the home of the playwright Henry Bernstein. Mauriac had just considered *The Last of Chéri* in an essay on contemporary fiction, which Larnac had quoted to persuade his readers that if such a pious Catholic and unimpeachable moral authority could appreciate Colette, then so could they.

The subject of Mauriac's essay was the place of God in the modern novel, and he insisted that even if a writer were "absolutely devoid of religious feeling, he still describes, whether he will or no, what Pascal called the wretchedness of man without a savior. . . .

> No one has succeeded better in this than a great living writer, a woman writer—and one who, unless I am much mistaken, is quite indifferent to religious questions. I am talking about Colette. A great many of you have read her last two books, *Chéri* and *The Last of Chéri*. If you have read them, you know that it is difficult to imagine poorer, more deprived, more squalid people than the ones we find there. . . . And yet it is not enough to say that these two wonderful books do not abase us, do not soil us; the last page does not leave us with anything like the nausea . . . we suffer when we read licentious books. With her old courtesans, her handsome, animal, miserable young man, Colette moves us to our very depths. She shows us to the point of horror the ephemeral miracle of youth, obliges us to feel the tragedy of the poor lives that stake everything upon a love as perishable, as corruptible, as its very object: the flesh. So it is that these books recall the sewers of great cities that still flow into the river and mingle with its waters, and reach the sea. This pagan, this woman of the flesh, leads us irresistibly to God.[17]

That evening, the abbé Mugnier was on hand to record the conversation. While a Mme Bainville defended L'Action Française and Maurois deplored the pope's latest "pitiless" admonitions to modern youth, Colette, oblique and mischievous, teased Mauriac as she had once baited another priestly figure offering unsolicited absolution for her sins of the flesh, Francis Jammes. "She talked cooking, Château d'Yquem, and the dishes one should serve with it. She brings everything down to gourmandise: the greed for food, the greed for sensual pleasure. She kept repeating that purity is a temptation like the others, and not a nobler one."[18]

4

WHEN THE good abbé asked Colette if she would ever write something he could read, she replied that she would give him a book that would be a veritable "orgy of virtue."[19] She would keep her promise, in her own fashion, when she wrote *Sido* in 1929. In the meantime, she paid another visit to Saint-Sauveur.

Achille's heirs—Jane and her daughters—had recently sold the Robineau house, and the buyer, a Dr. Delorme, had offered it to Colette for whatever use she wished to make of it in her lifetime. "Thirty-three years! Think about it, thirty-three years," she exulted to Germaine Patat, "since I've seen the inside of the house or the garden. What a great emotion! What a feeling of obliterated time!"[20] She briefly considered using the house for occasional visits, but need triumphed over sentiment, and she installed a tenant.

She had also finally found a buyer for Rozven. Her profits went straight into the renovation of La Treille Muscate, where she was adding a little outbuilding to serve as both guesthouse and garage. For the next ten years, she would spend every summer on the Côte d'Azur, and often a month at Christmas, lamenting her separations from Maurice, who could only ever take off a few weeks.

The pearl business was already beginning to feel the advance shocks of the coming crash. The pound was falling, many speculators had gone bankrupt, and Maurice, who financed his inventory with borrowed money, was grappling with a "crisis" about which his correspondence gives few specific details. But Colette hoped that Paris would be "profitable" for him because "we're luxurious creatures who need bulldogs that cost seventy-five thousand francs and prize cats and comfortable cars."[21]

In August, with Maurice away, her daughter came for a long stay. Colette II, as Colette I now called her, had left her English boarding school after six months and been sent to a college at Versailles, where the headmistress complained about her indifferent work and her "unspeakable" attitude. Colette attributed her daughter's failures to a "facile self-satisfaction which implies a lack of respect for others." Her parents and teachers could influence her education, her health, and her well-being, but they couldn't do anything for a heart that was "too small, insouciant, and ungrateful." It wasn't anger, it was sadness, Colette claimed, that prompted this judgment.[22]

In another letter, Colette scolds her daughter for being arrogant with her teachers and fellow students. She reminds Bel-Gazou that she herself had not had the privilege of a fancy education. She had gone to a humble village school with the daughters of peasants, but even so, she hadn't made the mistake of exalting herself above them. "It's thanks to my scruples that I have been able to make a name for myself in literature, darling."[23]

One is somewhat surprised to see the word "scruples" in Colette's handwriting, but then a fourteen-year-old girl in the throes of puberty has the magical power to make a pompous bourgeois of even the most liberated and indulgent parent. Colette couldn't stop herself. All summer, she raged on about Colette II in long letters to Germaine Patat, returning to the theme of her own adolescent humility and virtue: "At twelve years old, in the one-room school of a village with 1,300 inhabitants, I knew more than this child, who has been taught everything, never deprived of a book, a play, or a museum. . . . I'm horrified by her grades, and by the commentaries that go with them. Weak character, vanity, Poouah! Everything that wounds me most in the world. *Mediocre, Passing-fair, good enough, lacks candor, amateurish*. All gray, all murky, all never-mind what." And she would much rather see her in a trade school, learning something useful—like home economics. "I swear to you," Colette concludes, "that from this day hence, I would prefer that she didn't call herself either Jouvenel or Colette's daughter. What a disastrous thing to be the daughter of two somebodies. She has a damned good need to call herself Durand, my daughter does."[24]

Perhaps because she really did share Léa's belief that "it's all stomach," Colette put Bel-Gazou on a diet to lose some weight: "She's too heavy for her age, and a lot of her laziness must come from that." What is particularly odd, apart from the fact that Colette considered dieting a perversion, is that a picture of Colette II from that summer, on horseback, in a bathing suit, shows a magnificent young goddess with budding breasts and a swimmer's body—not really fat, just juicy and well developed. Perhaps it was the "arrogance," "ingratitude," and "insouciance" of Colette II's youth and beauty, as much as of her character, that were arousing so much maternal animosity. And perhaps the diet was meant to reduce and control more than her daughter's weight. Colette's doctor made an interesting diagnosis, prompted by her own complaints about palpitations and a racing pulse: "Take care of your heart," he told her. "You must have had to dominate many emotions in your life in the effort to conceal them from those around you."[25]

5

COLETTE DID Maurice the honor of attributing her heart troubles to his departure. She told him that she slept badly without his body next to hers, dreaming of "being stung by a spider, then badly burned on my left hand . . . the amputation of a leg, etc. etc." If her letters sounded self-obsessed, she said, talking about herself was the only way she found of "being with" him.[26]

Her letters to other friends give a rather more cheerful picture of her solitude at La Treille Muscate. She went swimming at least twice a day. She ate huge quantities of garlic and raw onions, shopped for old pottery in the Provençale hill towns above the coast, and explored the ruins of their ancient settlements. In the morning, before the sun was too hot, she worked in her garden, digging an irrigation ditch for her tangerine trees and mulching them with the heaps of seaweed she carried home from the beach and rinsed in well water. "When you open up the earth . . . you always feel like the first man, the master, the husband with no rivals."[27]

Her daughter left for the Limousin, the Marchands came for a visit, and so did Germaine Beaumont. The bohemian colony of Saint-Tropez[28] claimed her for picnics under the stars and for dancing under the bare lightbulb at Pastecchi's bar. She often shared an impromptu supper with her closest neighbors, a "peaceful" young couple named Vera and Julio van den Henst. "The protocol of the season demands that a sudden unanimous whim, rather than friendly planning, should regulate our relations."[29]

Occasionally, Colette transgressed this protocol to enjoy a grander, more impure repast at Cap-d'Ail with the Bloch-Levalois, at Beauvallon with the poet Paul Géraldy, or on the yacht of Lucien Lelong and his new wife, the Russian princess Nathalie Paley. To Germaine Patat she gossiped about the sex parties given by "the snobs of vice" in their lavish villas along the coast. "Lend me your wife," she overheard one married guest ask another, who replied: ". . . If you'll lend me your eldest son."[30]

And then there was literature. Colette had promised a new novel to the publisher Flammarion, and before she left Paris, she had an idea for it. "I'm doing nothing else but finishing a moving piece of work," she told Moreno that July, "rereading all Mama's letters and extracting the gems."[31] Those gems formed the kernel of an intensely personal narrative which immediately began to cause her the usual "pain" and "humility." "The further I get," she told Christiane Mendelys, "the more completely inferior I feel."[32]

By mid-September, after two months of steady labor, she had finished only thirty-five pages. With a certain relief, she stopped writing and helped the farmhands bring in that year's meager harvest of exceptionally "fiery" and sweet grapes. When the new wine was in its casks, she closed up the house and went back to the arms of her famished lover, who had told her to "prepare the body I have chosen for the celebrations given a returning exile."[33]

"Autumn," she wrote in *Break of Day*, "is the only vintage time. Perhaps that is true in love, too. It is the season for sensual affection, a time of truce in the monotonous succession of struggles between equals, the perfect time for resting on a summit where two slopes meet"[34]—the slope of two lives, one waxing, one in decline.

CHAPTER 35

I felt stirring at the root of my being the one who now inhabits me,
lighter on my heart than I was once in her womb.

—COLETTE,
Break of Day

I

COLETTE'S LATE FIFTIES were probably the happiest and certainly the most fecund years of her life. Pichois likens this period to a second youth, but she was more resilient than she'd ever been as a young woman. "Try not to regret the past too much," she advised Germaine Patat, suggesting her own method for gaining buoyance by dumping ballast. "Most often, the past drops away from you because it's ripe. . . . There's a ripeness to events, a ripeness to places, a ripeness to relations. All of them disconnect . . . like a child ready to be born. The child . . . bruises us too, yet it *must* fall."[1]

John Updike once observed "that in the prize ring of life few of us would have lasted ten rounds with Colette."[2] "I have no sporting qualities," she herself admitted. She compared her own character to tempered steel, "sharpened and hardened" by her sufferings. Her benevolence had a truculent edge, and even a pious vestal like Chauvière remarked on her "cruelty": "I put on a healthy air for her because Colette loathed the poor, the sad, the ugly, the sick, the unhappy, just as she dreaded the mad and the unlucky."[3]

She continued both to live and to work like an Olympian, and as must all champions, she kept in training. She walked and swam vigorously. She smoked and drank very little. She kept her muscles toned with massage. She and Maurice apparently had an athletic sex life.[4] During the summers, she adopted a frugal diet and began losing weight.[5] Back in Paris, she consulted a fashionable quack who gave her blood transfusions—the donor was an attractive young woman—and these, she claimed, improved her vision and increased her vitality.[6] But perhaps her most essential beauty secret was to surround herself with a circle of younger friends, male and female, whose hunger for life helped to recharge her own. "The pleasure I take in contemplating lives on the ascendant reassures me about myself," she told Germaine Patat. "I see so many people who, as they age, find joy only in . . . their diminution!"[7]

The greatest work of this period, and perhaps of her oeuvre, *Break of Day,* is shaped by Colette's intimate contact with two ascending lives. If she isn't conscious of her own failure as a mother, her conflict with Bel-Gazou seems to make her ever more grateful for the privileges she enjoyed as a child. Her love for Goudeket is a profoundly reparative experience. His constancy gradually disarms her mistrust. He enjoys her bullying, but they make a game of it—becoming partners and playmates rather than victim and oppressor. His virile devotion, which is unconditional, contains her, and the security she experiences for the first time in a relationship that is emotionally as well as sexually intimate helps her both to separate from Sido the tyrant and to embrace Sido the lifegiver, distinguishing her mother's menace from her blessings.

Claude Pichois views this process of repossession as a ruthless conquest. "Sidonie Landoy became Sido, a harmless character, dominated by her author." Elsewhere he writes: "In creating Sido, Colette abolishes Sidonie, the real mother. . . . Sido becomes her reflection. She assimilates her mother, who becomes her idealized double. Filial love? No, self-love."[8]

Pichois is a judicious reader who has devoted decades to illuminating Colette, and is understandably impatient with the tiresome received view of Sido and Colette as the exemplary mother-daughter couple. But his mistake is to insist on giving Colette only one motive, her old one: to "master." His reading, like those of the sentimentalists, screens out the paradoxical aspects of Colette's portrait of mother and daughter, and these are precisely what make it so profound.

Break of Day would better be translated *Birth of Day,* as it is in French *(La Naissance du jour),* because it evokes the relation of a mother and daughter at a juncture critical for them both: the birth of the self, the moment a child begins to detach herself from a mother's psyche. The mother of the novel is a spirit restless and interminably pregnant with urgent, revolutionary wisdom she has been waiting a lifetime to deliver. The child is a woman who, as Colette puts it to Germaine Patat, is finally ripe to "fall": to accept her existential solitude.

And here, perhaps, one should juxtapose the description Sido gives her daughter in *My Mother's House* of Colette's reluctant, original fall: "They do say that children like you, who have been carried so high in the womb and have taken so long to come down into the daylight, are always the children that are most loved, because they have lain so near their mother's heart and have been so unwilling to leave her."[9]

In 1923, writing from Rozven, Colette told Moreno how she had come upon a cache of Sido's last letters: they "fell" from a desk drawer where she had been looking for some money (and it is worth noting that money is precious to Colette, both symbolically and literally, as the currency of independence). "What is so curious," she observes, "is that one resists tears victoriously at the most difficult moments . . . and then someone gives you a friendly signal from behind a glass—one discovers a flower in bloom that was still furled the night before—a letter falls from a drawer—and everything falls with it."[10] This account prefigures the story she would tell in *My Apprenticeships* some ten years later of yet another birth—that of her writer's life—when Willy, also searching his desk drawers for money or something convertible to money, discovers the notebooks in which she had drafted the first *Claudine*.

In the opening pages of *Break of Day*, a narrator who calls herself Colette defines herself as the daughter of a woman named Sido, who is the author of a dozen marvelous letters that appear at intervals throughout the text. For the narrator, these letters—Sido's musings on love, age, motherhood, men, nature, and village life—serve as objects of meditation, a reflective surface, though not quite a mirror, in which she seeks her mother's image, comparing it self-deprecatingly with her own.[11] At the same time, she is careful to remind us that while her own prose is a reflective surface, it is not quite a mirror, and we are not to seek the real Colette either here or elsewhere in her novels. She reserves the privilege of hiding herself—like Poe's purloined letter—in plain sight. And it's here, too, that she posts her famous caution: "Am I portraying myself? Have patience, this is only my model."[12]

Colette suggests (though not, I think, consciously) that a perfect mirror makes narcissism too inviting, and this conclusion anticipates some of the most lucid contemporary research on the mother-child dynamic.[13] A woman too fragile, anxious, or frustrated in her own life to recognize her child as a separate being—who insists on merging their two identities—presents the same danger: what originally looks and perhaps even feels like harmony is in fact domination. The bliss of oneness and the dread of maternal omnipotence are conflated, and a child who carries such a predicament into adult life may adopt the defensive extremes of misogyny (a self-protective repudiation of all that is woman and mother, therefore engulfing) or masochism (surrender to an idealized master—a father figure counted on to confer the self's missing boundaries). Where this model of mothering is common, it translates into a sexually polarized society that exalts virile detachment and rationality as the antidotes to female power, and it seeks to disarm women by shackling them to a set of rigid expectations about their purity, dependence, and self-sacrifice. Throughout her life, Colette struggles nobly with the circumstances, particular and social, that have forged her identity as a woman, but she can't transcend them. Her fears about women and maternal power are voiced by the conservative writer and "old boy" who deeply mistrusts change and champions "real" femininity, while her drive for self-sovereignty is expressed by the iconoclast who challenges received ideas and asserts her freedom.

Break of Day deserves to be read not only as a great work of literature but as a daring, even avant-garde, psychological experiment in novel form. Colette attempts to locate or to imagine—and she purposely blurs the distinction—her "good" mother, which is to say a woman who is able to help her daughter negotiate the task of separation, find peace and autonomy in her adversarial (and paradoxical) relations with men, and provide a steadfast example of mutual love. By mirroring both their differences and their likenesses, the narrator's mother enables her daughter to entertain the possibility of closeness without engulfment and of solitude that is not felt as abandonment. Is this ruthless revisionism, as Pichois contends? Is it simply the wishful fantasy of a dominated child? If art were child's play, the answer might be yes, but art is not only qualitatively more nuanced than fantasy; it's humbler about loss and limitation. *Break of Day* celebrates "Sido" the good mother, but it is also a work of mourning: Colette's projection of a "model" mother and daughter as they might have been in a family and a culture that afforded both of them more latitude, and where each woman had been able to repair the *manques* of her own childhood.

The Sido of *Break of Day* is a provincial housewife who has managed, miraculously, to become a sovereign individual attuned to nature and to reality, rather than merely a slave to her maternal and wifely roles. The novel is her daughter's sustained homage to and reverie on this feat, and a poetic account of how "Colette" emerges from the long night of her own filial and feminine subservience to achieve autonomy in her own way. Yet as her title suggests, the moment of first light, of revelations, of consciousness, of day birth—*la naissance du jour*—is ultimately ephemeral. The diurnal cycle is a metaphor for the oscillations between growth and regression, blindness and lucidity, wholeness and fragmentation, that continue throughout a lifetime, because in a fallen world there are no perfect reparations of one's primal wounds, and neither identity nor gender can ever be "a final achievement" or a "cohesive stable system."[14]

Break of Day is as experimental and as viscerally personal in its style as in its substance, employing techniques that seventy-five years later are called post-modern. There is a complex tension—an interplay of dissonance and resemblance—not only between the actual and imaginary mother and daughter, but between fiction and reality. Colette ignores or deliberately flouts the conventions of narrative: she invites real friends to mingle with her invented characters; she speaks in, but repudiates, the authenticity of her first person; there is more digression and philosophy, more dreaming aloud, than there is plot; her prose is like quicksilver, dense, fluid, shimmery, and difficult to capture.

Yet there is a solid enough story, set at La Treille Muscate. It takes up where *The Vagabond* and *The Shackle* leave off. Colette has, she claims, finally begun to enjoy the calm and solitude of middle age. On the evenings when there is no other place setting at her dinner table, "I am simply alone, and not abandoned." Her life as a "militant is finished."

Friends, however, and especially young ones—artists—are drawn to the serenity of her house and the flame of her charisma. One of them is a decorator of Maurice's age and temperament, named Valère Vial. Another is a painter named Hélène Clément. They are both too solemn and intense, although Colette likes them—Vial especially—and she decides to play the matchmaker. These virtuous intentions backfire. Hélène believes that Vial won't have her because he loves Colette, and she is right. Colette declares to Vial that she won't have him because, for the first time since she was sixteen, "I'm going to have to live—or die—without my life depending on love. It's so extraordinary. . . . It's so prodigious. . . . Sometimes women who have just given birth awake from the first sleep of their deliverance and reflexively begin to scream again. I still have, imagine it, the reflex of love; I forget that I've pushed out my fruit. . . . Sometimes I cry internally: 'Oh, God, please let Him still be there,' and sometimes, 'Oh, God, please let Him be gone.' "

Vial and Colette are the mortal youth and the mature goddess, he scorched by her power, she forced by his heroic presumption in wanting her to show her human face. In the end, they part without ever consummating their amorous friendship. She insists on her independence, and he leaves her to it. But Colette also reminds the reader that this is an old trick of hers: imagining an unsatisfying ending so that she doesn't have to live it.

Maurice always denied, implausibly, that he was Colette's model for Vial, but the tone of his own prose scotches any doubt. Vial's stilted eloquence, his ferocious pride, his stifled passion, his faintly comic formality, his "horrible" sadness, and most of all, the purity of his attachment to Colette are all to be found in Goudeket's memoirs. Vial's portrait in *Break of Day* is Colette's public avowal of a love that her friends considered a comedown, her daughter resented, the snobs laughed at, and which may have embarrassed even her. "So you're astonished?" she asks the reader. "What, you say, this little man, you dare to compare him to . . . Well it can't be discussed." And elsewhere: "Love recognizes no caste." And finally: "I've had the best. I've had Vial."

2

DESPERATE TO FINISH *Break of Day,* Colette drove south the week before Christmas 1926 with Pauline and the cats and opened La Treille Muscate. "The novel torments me," she told Moreno, and "I don't really see what I'm doing." They fired up the stoves, in part with the pages she kept tearing up, and ate large quantities of fish and garlic. But it rained steadily, and the house was so damp and cold that Colette moved to a hotel, where she was briefly joined by Maurice. She couldn't sleep, she rewrote one scene eight times, but by early January the worst was over: "I'm working with a rigor which may not produce abundant results, but which lets me preserve a sort of self-esteem."[15]

On January 11, *La Revue de Paris* began to publish the novel in installments. A few days later, Colette left for Saint-Moritz, where she spent her birthday skiing with Alba Crosbie. She neither consulted nor invited Maurice, who complained bitterly about her desertion. He told her that he would never have done the same thing to her—and that, of course, was part of his great allure.

Back home again, she immediately began a new novel. "Yes. You can't believe your eyes?" she asked Moreno. "I want to get into the habit of writing novels." She promised her editor he could have it by June, which was a little optimistic, even for a writer on such a tremendous roll. Having promptly written eighty pages, she scrapped forty of them. In April, she took the manuscript, which she was calling *The Double,* to La Treille Muscate, where she posed for a portrait by her new friend André Dunoyer de Segonzac.[16]

But the novel was going badly, and she was much more enthusiastic about a newly discovered talent of a different kind: "I'm a dowser!" she exulted to Germaine Patat, ". . . no matter where, with no matter what sort of forked branch."[17] She was so thrilled that she related this miracle to most of her correspondents, musing (typically) that perhaps she could turn it to profit—supplementing her income by divining wells for her wealthy neighbors.

When her deadline for *The Double* passed, Colette cheerfully set herself a new one: the end of September. She spent a fortune on a prize bulldog bitch, which she aptly named Souci. Then early that summer, at Angers, she performed an unlikely spiritual office for Claude Chauvière. The former secretary had decided to become a Catholic, and she was baptized on July 2, 1928, with Colette standing at the font as her godmother. "Toward the altar, toward that which is above the altar," she wrote, "[the convert] lifted her great eyes, on the point of tears." But this epiphany was short-lived. Two years later, Colette observed to Maurice that Claude had relapsed into her chronic depression. "Is the Catholic fantasy already beginning to pale? One doesn't manufacture a believer from a weak young woman discontented with her profane life."[18]

A week after the baptism, Colette was camping at La Treille Muscate, which was undergoing yet another radical renovation: "To do up a house is nothing; to redo it when the workmen have undone it is a nightmare."[19] Her daughter arrived for a monthlong stay, cheerfully helped with all the dirty work, and jived in patois with the Italian masons. Bel-Gazou had just turned fifteen, had finally settled down to studying for her baccalaureate, and had become "miraculously" lovable. "What a charming creature!" Colette told Moreno. "I don't wrangle with her anymore."[20]

Maurice joined them for a week's respite from his increasingly unprofitable business, and by the time he left, the nights were cold and the mornings smelled of fall. Colette brought in the grape harvest and swore to Moreno, as she had to Annie from Rozven, that if it weren't for love, she would never return to Paris.

She did return, of course, to find Alba embroiled in a nasty dispute with the owner of the apartment at 9, rue de Beaujolais. Colette moved to a hotel while lawyers and plumbers sorted out the damages. On November 7, she was able to console herself by pinning a precious flower to her lapel: the rosette which signified her promotion to the rank of Officer in the Legion of Honor. There was, as usual, some opposition to the honor in official circles, but Colette had a powerful advocate in her old friend Louis Barthou, then minister of justice. "They should have given you a belly band instead of a ribbon," joked Anna de Noailles. "You mean a G-string," replied Colette.[21]

The Double—rechristened *La Seconde* (*The Other One*)—continued to make her "ill." The hubbub of Paris was never conducive to finishing a book, so she and Maurice bundled manuscript and animals into the car and drove eleven hours through a pea-soup fog to a gloomy château-hotel on the Belgian side of the Ardennes. Here they spent a solitary Christmas, walking off the heavy Flemish meals in a forest blanketed by snow. It was so silent, Colette told Moreno, she could hear the blood running in her veins. "It's good for me, because I'm sweating out all my fatigue."[22] She also managed to sweat out her last chapters, finishing the novel as the clock struck midnight on New Year's Eve.

The Other One is a short book and, compared to *Break of Day,* a conventional, melancholy, and airless one. It's one of Colette's harem novels, in which a wife, Fanny, discovers that her most intimate relationship is really with her husband's mistress, Jane. The husband is a selfish, sexually charismatic playwright named Farou. His two resident houris (there are other women on the side) devote their lives to his welfare and glory, although he's clearly not worth their sacrifice. Each woman recognizes the superiority of her rival to the master they both serve, but neither rebels. They accept their subservience and resign themselves to living in his shadow, with the consolation of each other.

Colette was drawing on her own experience with Jouvenel and Germaine Patat, and the characters have many of their features. The mistress is slim, blond, practical—she's the husband's secretary—and a natural caretaker. She's had a string of lovers and takes a modern single woman's disillusioned view of the asymmetry between the sexes. It is woman's lot to feel lonely and unsatisfied with a man, she reminds Fanny: "A man isn't so important: he isn't eternal! A man is . . . a man is only a man! Do you really believe that you meet a man, on his own, just like that, alone, free, quite ready to devote his life to you? A man is never alone, Fanny—and indeed it's rather horrible that he should always have a woman, another mistress, a mother, a maid, a secretary, a relation, a female of some sort. If you only knew the various types of woman I've found around a lover! It's horrible—the word is not too strong."[23]

Jane reproaches Fanny for her complacence toward Farou's faithlessness, but Colette reminds us that Fanny has simply always lived by an "ancient [wifely, oriental] code." She gives Fanny her own most fetching feminine weaknesses, much idealized. Fanny's an endomorph: small and fleshy. She likes her creature comforts. She's a tender stepmother to Farou's teenage son (who's in love with Jane), and a domestic goddess who inspires worship. But her best feature, the one Colette dotes upon most lovingly, is her sumptuous, "old-fashioned" hair, and one suspects that Fanny is Colette's fantasy of the "real" woman she might have been had she never been forced to earn a living and never cut her own old-fashioned braid—the cord of her voluptuous and "natural" feminine dependence.

3

The Other One began running in serial form in *Les Annales* on January 1, 1929. "It's a novel-novel," Colette told André Billy, "and I'm a little worried about it."[24] Billy reassured her, in the form of a glowing review, that her influence on French prose was as important as Flaubert's, Rousseau's, and Chateaubriand's.

Just before her fifty-sixth birthday, Colette fell seriously ill with a bout of influenza, which confined her to bed for two weeks. Her doctor blamed the dampness of the entresol for weakening her lungs, and strongly advised her to move. When she was out of bed again, she went house hunting. In the meantime, she received a visit from the future writer and fascist Robert Brasillach, who was still a student at the École Normale.

Joanna Richardson recounts their meeting: "It was traditional for normaliens to invite writers and artists to [the faculty on] the rue d'Ulm." Brasillach had paid a preliminary visit to the rue de Beaujolais, where he found a convalescent Colette looking dumpy and wearing too much makeup. She was "very amusing," however, and they arranged their tea. On the day, she brought her bulldog, whom the students plied with banana sandwiches. They were ecstatic to meet her, Brasillach told his aunt, and "we took her all round the École (not on the roofs, she is too fat) and sang her the really spicy songs from the École revue." As they walked through the garden she "referred to all the trees by their names, which we didn't know, as if they were friends."[25]

Colette enjoyed that innocent afternoon among those impious young men who were so reverent to her. But her relations with Brasillach would one day compromise her, and embitter him.

BEFORE COLETTE and Maurice left on an Easter trip to Spain and Morocco, she found an unfinished ground-floor apartment near the Quai d'Orsay and signed a lease for it. When the renovations were finished, she didn't like the results and refused to move in, assuaging her disappointment by renting a weekend house near Montfort-l'Amaury, twenty miles west of Paris. She told Hélène Picard that she was looking forward to furnishing the house with fifteen hundred francs' worth of camping equipment, and of giving her profligate daughter a lesson in decorating on the cheap.

The lesson never took, for Colette de Jouvenel had her father's taste for princely splendor, which she would indulge impetuously all her life, spending her windfalls as they came. That year, she had just inherited a little money from a paternal aunt, and in September, she arrived at La Treille Muscate after a summer of "ruinous and marvelous" travels, showing off an expensive new portable phonograph. Colette was only a little more scandalized (or jealous) to hear from Germaine Patat that "their" daughter had a teenage boyfriend named Paul, whom she had vowed to marry. Everyone urged her to wait, and in the meantime, Bel-Gazou danced all night, slept until noon, wore boys' shirts, borrowed the car and drove it like a demon, swam underwater "like a shark," flaunted the "breasts of a young negress," and in general, overflowed with life.

COLETTE'S OWN TRAVELS were never ruinous, either because they were underwritten by rich hosts like Alba Crosbie, the Glâwi, or Henri de Rothschild, or because, like Willy, she contrived to get well paid for writing about them. In June, a publisher commissioned her to visit and describe the wild animals at the Anvers zoo for a luxurious limited edition illustrated by Paul Jouve.[26] In October, she was invited to Berlin by the Franco-German Society for several days of lectures and banquets. She was back in Berlin with Maurice the following February to visit the famous Sarrasani circus. That summer, she, Maurice, and the Marchands spent a month cruising the Norwegian fjords on Rothschild's yacht the *Eros*. In 1931, she lectured very profitably in Vienna, Bucharest, and six cities of North Africa.

The Vagabond was eternally game for the glimpse of an unknown landscape. The old trouper was ever eager to meet her fans. The hedonist could always be ravished by a new pleasure. Until the end of her life, Colette retained her village girl's delight at the munificence with which she was received. "One couldn't have dreamed of a warmer welcome," she told Moreno from Berlin. "I'm as happy as can be. As tired, too."[27]

4

DESPITE HER TRIPS, her reportage, her renovations, her house hunting, the composition of several short texts she describes as "pretexts" for their illustrations,[28] and a brief stint as the drama critic for *La Revue de Paris*, Colette found time, in the course of 1929, to write *Sido*. A first edition was published in November, and an expanded edition—the definitive one—the following May. Colette bound the manuscript with a piece of faded linen salvaged from a dress that Sido had worn as a young bride. "I don't repent of having taken a scissors to it," she wrote, "because its pale blue, flowered with white, now clothes, as of old—clothes ever and for always—my dearly beloved Sido."[29]

Sido is constructed in three long sections which form the kind of triptych, richly detailed and human, which adorns the altarpiece of a stylized Madonna. One section is devoted to Colette's mother, one to her father, and one to her siblings. Colette's letters give very few details about the book's composition. She says herself that in the seven years between the publication of *My Mother's House* and *Sido,* she had "continually laid aside, then taken up again," the short chapters which they contain, and that in this way, she "remained in touch with . . . the personage of my mother. It haunts me still. The reasons for this prevailing presence are not far to seek: any writer whose existence is long drawn out turns in the end toward his past, either to revile it or to rejoice in it."[30]

What's striking about this explanation is the starkness of the choice—the triage—as Colette sees it, that the aging writer makes among her memories of childhood: to revile or to rejoice. The tone of her prose is elegiac and the scenes are suffused with a mellow, sentimental light. The memoir fulfills Colette's promise to the abbé Mugnier to write a book that would be a veritable "orgy of virtue," and in 1930, the critic Pierre Scize called *Sido* "the most pious monument ever erected to a mother."[31]

Pious monuments, however, are often raised by the survivors of a great disaster to propitiate an angry deity who has seen fit to spare them. It is easy enough for the tourists who admire their beauty, even the late-born natives who worship at them, to forget the loss and suffering that they commemorate. Colette was the sole survivor in a family, of a family whose other members had failed to escape ruin or disappointment. Survivor's guilt, belated mourning and the tenderness born of her own maturity and happiness all color the romantic portrait she gives of her characters.

But the truth has its place in *Sido,* too, and it would not be the persuasive, enduring work it is without those fleeting shadows of ambiguity and failure. Juliette submits to the foul husband. Léo lives pathetically in the past. Achille falls prey to his increasing "fits of misanthropy," and in the last lines of the book is remembered as a "captive" in the "prison yard" of his life. The Captain conceals his sadness and works on his phantom opus. He is "misunderstood" and "unappreciated": "a man banished from the elements which once sustained him." Even Sido betrays, by the sudden flicker of "wild gaiety" in her all-seeing gray eyes, "an urge to escape from everyone and everything." "To look happy," Colette writes of her family, "was the highest compliment we paid one another."[32] And that is the compliment which, in this memoir filled with pride and felicity, she pays them.

5

THE AMERICAN STOCK MARKET crashed on October 24, 1929, two weeks before *Sido* was published. The financial crisis didn't hit Europe immediately, and Maurice chose to ignore this ominous portent for his already failing business. In his letters to Colette, he speaks of having ambitious plans for a new career, something more interesting than selling pearls, and perhaps to convince himself that his dreams were solid, he recklessly bought a weekend house near the little property that Colette had been renting in Montfort-l'Amaury.

La Gerbière was a modest villa with two stories, built on a hill. Its charm was its closeness to Paris and its situation. One side of the house faced the valley and had a panoramic view of the landscape and the sky. The other side faced a rose garden, and beyond it a lawn, and beyond that a little park of old trees which sloped down toward the road. "It satisfied Colette's taste for limited horizons," wrote Goudeket, "for houses built on a human scale, and also her need for great, airy spaces."[33] It was here Colette finished the expanded version of *Sido*. And here she enjoyed the proximity of Germaine Beaumont, who lived nearby, and of two new friends—an artistic couple, both passionate cat lovers—whom she had met in Saint-Tropez.

Luc-Albert Moreau, who owned an old house called La Maison des Vignes, was a painter and lithographer. He began his career as a Cubist, but after the war, badly wounded and profoundly traumatized, he turned back to realism and painted the horrors he had survived. His work mellowed with time, and his meticulous life studies, luminous Provençale landscapes, and illustrations—including those he engraved for an edition of *Break of Day*—enjoyed a great vogue in the 1930s.

Moreau's companion and future wife, Hélène Jourdan-Morhange, was a violinist. As a prodigy of ten, she had entered the Conservatory, and at fourteen, she had taken first prize at the annual competitions. Ravel was her great love, and she became one of his favorite interpreters. The composer also lived at Montfort-l'Amaury, and while he shunned society and worked in almost total seclusion, he made an exception for the company of this brilliant young musician who understood his art so well. Ravel would dedicate his *Sonata for Violin and Piano* to Hélène, and it was he who gave her the nickname Moune, which Colette adopted.

When Moune's hands were crippled by "violinist's cramp," she had to abandon her budding career as a soloist, and she subsisted, for a while, by giving lessons. Colette encouraged her to write, and Moune became a distinguished music critic, specializing in Ravel and "The Six"—Milhaud, Durey, Auric, Honegger, Poulenc, and Tailleferre. Moune kept every letter Colette sent her. This extremely affectionate if somewhat dull correspondence, filled with cat talk, gossip, weather, gourmandise, bulletins about Colette's health and work, as well as generous encouragement for her friends, spans a quarter of a century. Moune and "Toutounet"—her nickname for Luc-Albert—were part of that nucleus of younger people who reassured Colette about her own vitality, and her own goodness. Their devotion would help to buffer the shocks and losses of her declining years.

WHEN COLETTE AND Maurice returned from their Norwegian cruise on the *Eros,* they drove straight to La Treille Muscate. Her neighbors, the van den Hensts, had warned her that Saint-Tropez had become "uninhabitable." An explosion of development had crowded the coastline with new villas, and the unsullied little port had been taken over by the "sort of people photographed by *Vogue.*" Colette (who was, as Joanna Richardson notes, also photographed by *Vogue*) was disgusted by the spectacle of Hispano-Suizas and Bugattis triple-parked in front of the little shop where she bought her toilet paper, and by the crowds of movie stars, moguls, and titled ladies wearing overalls and beach pajamas. One morning, she found a horde of curious tourists waiting for her outside the stationer's. "I didn't hide what I thought of them," she told Moreno.[34]

As the season progressed, things got only more frenetic. There were no more cheap suppers of bouillabaisse and rosé with her artist friends, or fishermen's balls with the unspoiled local boys. The bistros had become nightclubs, and the restaurants were charging Deauville prices. "No enticement or constraint could make me dine in the port this season," Colette protested, exaggerating just a little. She still enjoyed the occasional night out with Francis Carco and his theater friends or the odd dinner with a duchess. And she did attend the "Noodle Ball," to which the guests wore hats and costumes "amusingly" decorated with dried pasta by an "inspired" former actress turned society milliner.

Fortunately, La Treille Muscate "was still peaceful and sufficiently out of the fray." Colette got up at sunrise to weed her tomatoes and to wander in the silent woods, trailed by her cats, returning with her espadrilles soaked in dew. She breakfasted on the wild figs she had picked—or stolen—and she joyfully described their variety to Misz Marchand: "green ones with yellow flesh, white ones with red flesh, black ones with red flesh, violet ones with pink flesh, mauve rather than violet, with a fine skin."[35] Twice a day, early and late, she swam in a coppery sea. The air was miraculously light and swarming with butterflies, and the only other bodies sunning on the white sand of her beach were the lizards.

La Treille was never quite the bed-and-breakfast resort Rozven had been, but Colette welcomed select visitors. Alba Crosbie and her husband came with their new adopted baby; Renaud de Jouvenel drove down from the Pyrenees to pick up his sister; Moreau and Dunoyer de Segonzac sometimes painted in her garden; and André Billy, invited for lunch and an interview, arrived from Paris.

While Pauline fetched the wine bottles up from the well and laid out a meal of melons, vegetables, and grilled fish, Colette gave them her house and garden tour. She started with her workroom, one of the additions which had caused her so many headaches. It was a simple concrete cube whose thick walls retained the cool even at midday. The furnishings were spare: there was a handsome Breton cupboard filled with books, a huge divan swagged with mosquito netting, a big writing table, and a collection of pottery whose "vegetal green" stood out against the milky whitewash of the plaster. Billy noted two stacks of blue paper on the desk, one pristine, one "covered with the famous writing, firm and upright." He also noted the balled and crumpled wads strewn over the floor. "What a penance," exclaimed Colette, "to shut oneself in here for fifteen hours a day when it's so beautiful outside."[36] She was just starting that most difficult, strange, and favorite of all her books, *The Pure and the Impure.*

It had barely advanced by the time she came home to Paris. Maurice had preceded her, but Colette stayed only long enough to change suitcases. Pauline was taking her annual vacation, and without Pauline, she couldn't manage her four pets and the housekeeping. So she took her menagerie and her manuscript to La Gerbière. "The animals, the forest, and my work," she wrote to Carco—"that's enough to shorten the days. The forest above all." It had no scent in summer, but "it grows fragrant as it starts rotting." She was eating wild mushrooms and making beds. Maurice drove out most weeknights to dine and sleep with her. After resisting her book all summer, she would "try to rehabilitate myself, in my own eyes, by working."[37]

CHAPTER 36

1

B Y THE END of 1930, Maurice was bankrupt. He gave up his expensive flat and chauffeured Talbot and sold La Gerbière. The new owner—Coco Chanel—didn't plan on decorating with fifteen hundred francs' worth of camping equipment. She had grand designs, and she wanted to start work on them at once. Maurice and Colette had to move out in a hurry.

They spent Christmas at Saint-Tropez, then returned to new quarters in Paris. Colette was still hoping to take over Gustave Quinson's apartment one flight up in the Palais-Royal, but his lease had two years to run, and her doctor didn't think her lungs would wait—she had been suffering almost continuously from bronchitis. In the meantime, she moved into a suite at the Claridge, a luxury hotel on the Champs-Élysées. Colette's friend the Glâwi of Marrakesh stayed at the Claridge when he came to Paris. Before his fabulous frauds were exposed and he committed suicide, so did the financier Alexandre Stavisky, who lived with his family in a suite and nodded to Colette in the restaurant or the elevator. The pasha and the crook (who was fascinated by Colette and eventually invited her to dine) no doubt paid full price for their accommodations. But she had struck a deal with the management for "two small connecting rooms under the roof, a bathtub, two small twin balconies at the edge of the rain pipe, red geraniums and strawberry plants in pots, most of my own furniture, and all my books on the walls."[1] A large closet was converted to a kitchenette where Pauline could boil an egg or a bowl of pasta. Otherwise, Colette lived happily on the *plats garni* sent up by room service.

Maurice had adjoining rooms on the same floor. As they weren't married, he explained with his usual public primness, "it was necessary to preserve appearances. We took great care to do so, installing separate bells ... and telephone lines, all of this at no little cost."[2]

Their friends predicted the Claridge experiment would last two weeks. Colette and Maurice stayed for four years, leaving only when the bankrupt hotel closed its doors. "A writer can work well in a hotel," the old vagabond observed. She relished "the silence of great height and a surprising peace." By day she had the light and sky, and at night, leaning over her balcony, she watched the birds moving more swiftly than the traffic. She also had the benefit of a staff without the expense of one. The floor waiter and the chambermaid, she said, offered proofs of devotion, even love, and the management loyally protected her from intrusion. "There is warmth everywhere," she concluded, "if only we hold out our hands to it, fan it with our breath. I've received such gifts, even in the midst of one of those places we consider heartless."[3]

2

IN THE SPRING of 1930, Paul Léautaud paid a visit to his old crony and passionate fellow anti-vivisectionist Rachilde, who had just turned seventy and was not only decrepit, he noted in his journal with typical malicious relish, but a bit mad. Nevertheless, he enjoyed gossiping with her, and one of their favorite subjects was Colette. Publicly, Rachilde stood by her original judgment of Colette, and considered her the only woman writer (or the only *other* woman writer) in France worthy of esteem. In private, she called Colette "the worst piece of trash" she had ever known.[4]

This was the voice of a has-been, as famous for the violence as for the inconsistency of her opinions. Rachilde's chief distinction was as a critic, and while her enthusiasms were erratic, her reviews in the *Mercure de France* were often eloquent and perceptive. But she'd given up her column in 1925, when declining health made the burden of the deadline pressures too onerous.

Rachilde's fiction, on the other hand, had suffered the same fate as Willy's. They were both relics from the age of decadence. He was still writing about rakes and schoolgirls, she about drugged artists, well-born nymphomaniacs, sex slaves, perverted noblemen, transsexuals, thugs, rats, and orgies staged amid sumptuous Ottoman décor. They had lost their audience. Serious readers were disappointed by the mediocrity of the books, and thrill seekers by their failure to deliver the goods promised by titillating titles.

In spite of her advanced age—and she had twenty more years to live—Rachilde enjoyed playing the enfant terrible. She worried her friends by going nightclubbing in flamboyant dress with a band of beautiful and predominantly gay young protégés who resembled the characters in her novels. "All kinds of perverse behavior was attributed to her," writes her biographer, "though it is unlikely that she was guilty of it."[5]

There is something quixotic and therefore both pathetic and noble about the figure she cut, a fierce old lady in warpaint jousting with taboos that no longer existed. Rachilde might have been honored as a valiant battle horse of the fin de siècle gender wars had her reactionary pronouncements not alienated the younger generation. She was a rabid chauvinist and anti-Semite.[6] The scandalous author and geriatric clubrat could sound like Saint Paul on the subject of women. She had always been a misogynist, but she became an increasingly entrenched one. In 1928, she had published a polemical pamphlet entitled "Why I Am Not a Feminist," explaining in her preface that "I have never had any confidence in women, the eternal feminine having betrayed me from the outset in the guise of my mother."[7] That was succinct enough.

Rachilde reserved her supreme contempt for the women writers and intellectuals she considered her inferiors, though she had always excepted Colette from her tirades. Colette's "virile" genius, she held, justified the excesses of her life. "Let us give her the complete freedom of her actions," Rachilde exclaimed. "She is one of those who would shake the stars while falling from the skies into the mud of our poor earth."[8]

If the honest critic refused to retract her admiration, the bitter woman couldn't forgive Colette for her glory and, as Rachilde saw it, her base ingratitude to the champion who had done so much to advance it. Colette, she complained to Léautaud, had never bothered to write three lines about her. Colette's promotions in the ranks of the Legion of Honor particularly rankled the undecorated Rachilde. "It's a pretty [little ribbon]," she sniped to Léautaud in 1920, "with all those prostitutes they give it to." (She got her own red ribbon in 1924.) Eight years later, when Colette got her rosette, Rachilde was livid. Replying to a young woman writer who asked her for career advice, she told her to copy Colette and become a whore.

When Léautaud went to see her that June, Rachilde had just published a collection of essays called *Portraits of Men*, devoting an admiring chapter to Willy. They were exactly the same age; they had their politics, their misogyny, and the world's neglect in common; and in their letters they bad-mouthed Colette like two friends jilted by the same femme fatale. Willy, wrote Rachilde in her essay, "was the sweetest and most naive of men. The guilty premeditate while the innocent edit . . . the dangerous works of others."

She goes on to describe Willy's kindness to her, his Parisian charm, his impeccable manners, his musical ear, his "heart of crystal," and to praise his talents, shrewdly enough, as a "clown of literature."[9] The essay doesn't mention Colette, except as that "provincial plant [he] forced to bloom in a greenhouse so that she would yield double flowers." But Rachilde concludes her portrait with the image of a "tragic" Willy, choking back his tears and "keeping the true secret of his heart—a sincere love, never avowed, even to himself, for . . . someone much stronger than he is, and much more cruel."[10]

As Colette had once told Robert de Montesquiou: "I sometimes forget an insult, but never a kindness." This principle apparently guided her behavior toward Rachilde. She ignored *Portraits of Men,* and if she heard about Rachilde's vicious insults—she probably did—she ignored them, too. They were cordial in public. They often met at Natalie Barney's luncheon parties, and occasionally at the Tuesday receptions which the Vallettes still hosted at the *Mercure.* Colette made sure Rachilde received copies of her books, at least the bestiaries: "I boast, dear Rachilde, of being worthy to 'talk animals' with you," she told her in a letter written during the Second World War, concluding: "I am ever taken by so much firmness, by an insolence full of grandeur, those reactions of a wild creature which were always yours."[11]

WILLY, HOWEVER, couldn't be forgiven. Several times during the 1920s, he and Colette had quarreled in print about his contributions to the *Claudines,* she vehemently protesting to several interviewers that he had made only minor corrections to the work, and he or his friends hotly disputing her assertions.

"The sweetest and most naive of men" had been living in Monaco to avoid his creditors, but the dry heat of the south aggravated his migraines, and he returned to Paris, settling into a fifteen-franc-a-night hotel room on the avenue Suffren, where he was cared for by his last Claudine—the future Mme Sylvain Bonmariage, Madeleine de Swarte.[12]

Madeleine and Willy occasionally saw Léo Colette, now sixty-four, "a fat, red-faced, shabby man," according to Bonmariage, "given to profanity,"[13] who was still a clerk in Levallois and living there in a tenement. Léo, recalled Jacques Gauthier-Villars, was a "Peter Pan" who "still [affected to] believe in Santa Claus," and he showed them a book Colette had just sent him dedicated "to Léo, when he turns twelve." Madeleine and Willy saved their stamps for Léo—his great passion was philately—and over a welcome free meal and several beers, he might consent to talk about his sister, whom he still referred to, in his thick Burgundian accent, as "la barrronne de Jouvenel."[14]

Colette only rarely saw her first ex-husband, never by design. They crossed paths once in 1923, just after she had dropped his name from her fiction. He told a friend that she now "had an ass as big as a stagecoach, which doesn't tempt me to take a ride."[15] A few years later, they met at a press banquet to which Charles Catusse and Meg Villars were also invited. Catusse shook Willy's hand, but according to Willy's old secretary Pierre Varenne, Colette—who arrived late—merely scowled in his direction and left before dessert. "She should have stayed for this chocolate pudding," Willy whispered to Varenne, "what a treat! I feel like writing to let her know what she missed."[16]

Willy had been calling Colette "my widow" for a long time and referring to himself as "the late Willy." It was an epithet all the more exquisite for being so exact. "The new society," wrote J. H. Rosny, "was interring him before his time."[17] He continued to publish ghostwritten novels—*The End of Vice, The Story of a Manicurist,* and *Green Fruit* were among his last—and the occasional rambling memoir in which he rehashed old jokes and obscure vendettas. But he was finished: "No one is interested in a seventy-year-old usherette," he told an actress friend in 1927, thanking her "in advance" for sending him some money. "I've helped out so many friends, and here I am alone, and abandoned to real destitution."[18]

His poverty wasn't quite as dire as he pretended. He had the devoted Madeleine; his son, Jacques, hadn't abandoned him; and in 1928 a group of old friends and fans from the theater world planned a benefit at which several famous actors promised to perform. It never took place, but the subscription its organizers circulated raised four thousand francs. Colette declined to make a contribution. She also politely declined to hear the arguments of a well-meaning mutual acquaintance who tried to reconcile them: "I feel like telling you, as I would my daughter, 'You're much too kind, you can't understand.' "[19]

By the end of the 1920s, Willy's health was extremely fragile. A lifetime of dissipation had taken its inevitable toll. "His ravaged face, with red blotches, his faded blue eyes were pitiful," wrote Rosny.[20] He was suffering from rheumatism, arteriosclerosis, and perhaps from syphilis.[21] He was almost blind; he staggered like a drunk—a symptom, he said, of his arterial disease—and he had been hit twice by cars as he crossed the street. After the second accident, he had a mild stroke, despite which he remained lucid enough to scrawl a few last letters in his minute, spidery hand, reread his books, and dictate corrections to Madeleine. "If I've survived this long," he told Pierre Varenne, "it's thanks to [her] incessant care."[22]

Willy spent the next two years living with Madeleine and her sister. A friend tried unsuccessfully to reconvert him to the Church. He passed the days in an armchair by the window, listening to records—"not Wagner," says Caradec, "but Franz Lehár." Besides those waltzes, which the great tastemaker had once held in contempt, Rachilde's essay was one of his last satisfactions.

"The final word on Willy as a writer won't be said until he's gone," said Louis Barthou, Colette's friend, but Willy's too, who was both the minister of culture and a member of the Académie Française. Willy died on January 12, 1931, and three thousand mourners, including representatives from every major French literary institution, followed his casket to the Montparnasse cemetery. Léautaud asked Vallette if the ex–Madame Willy was among them. He laughed: "Her? She must have said: 'Not a moment too soon.' "[23]

There were important obituaries in most of the major papers and reviews, but Colette wrote nothing about Willy's death to any of her friends. She would wait four years to have her own last words in *My Apprenticeships*.

3

COLETTE HAD just turned fifty-eight. Her lover was struggling to make a living—he would shortly take a job selling used washing machines and a tool to unclog toilets—so she shouldered the burden of supporting them. Early in February, she revised her screenplay for *The Vagabond,* noting to Hélène Picard that they'd had a "terrible" year and that she'd long since "eaten" the advance. Shooting started immediately under the direction of the twenty-two-year-old Solange Bussi, the first woman to direct a "talkie." Colette got her daughter a job on the set as a script girl.

The young Colette was now a beauty of seventeen. She and her boyfriend Paul were engaged, although it was apparently a stormy romance. Colette's sympathies were with the young man, who was doing his military service and "couldn't easily write [letters]. So my daughter, pinched and haughty, waits. My God, how great is human folly, and young folly above all. My beautiful child doesn't understand a thing about what she's squandering."[24]

Her book about "old love stuff, with unisexual love mixed into it,"[25] was driving her crazy, and she "hated" it. She took a brief ski vacation in Mégève with Maurice and Moune; then a series of lucrative invitations to lecture abroad gave her another excuse to escape, at least until the summer. In Vienna she was received with great pomp by her Austrian hosts and the French ambassador, gave twenty interviews, signed autographs for fans who had been waiting on line at her hotel for hours, then left by train for Bucharest. She came home to Paris "prostrate" with fatigue, spent four days in bed, then departed for another performance in Cahors, after which she had a few days off before repacking for a lecture tour of six cities in Algeria. "I'm not made to be on show for sixteen hours out of twenty-four," she told Hélène.

But no experience, familiar or exotic, was ever wasted on Colette. Like a good provincial housewife, she always made something exquisite of her left-overs. The gardens of Algeria; the despots and their dancing girls; the craggy splendors of the fjords; the desert and its flowers; reptiles; captive leopard cubs; perfumed dishes; the landscapes of Provence; depressed lions; heat and wind; magicians; roses; hidden springs; young wine; millionaires; white nights; beggars; the scent of dung and lilies; the smell of baked potatoes—such were the souvenirs of Colette's travels. She dashed them off as quickly as she repacked her clothes, and they fill many volumes. But the title she gave to a collection of these poetic sketches, published in 1932, suggests their significance, at least for her. It is called *Prisons and Paradises.* The discipline of work sharpens the savor of pleasure. The bondage of art contains her violence and sanctions her freedom with more authority than any of her other masters. And the escapee always returns voluntarily to her cell because "the rewards and the anguish are inseparable, they revolve together . . . driven by an ancient pride."[26]

4

IN JUNE, Colette was back in her aerie at the Claridge, negotiating for a film, an illustrated book, more lectures, foreign editions—all to help shore up her finances. The telephone, wrote Claude Chauvière, never stopped ringing, and visitors "came and went" as if the apartment "were a mill." These distractions continued to interrupt Colette's work on *The Pure and the Impure.* But in the meantime, she received a visitor who figures prominently in its conception: Missy.

After their rupture and the nasty quarrel over their communal property, Colette had quietly resumed contact with her old lover. The surviving fragments of their correspondence suggest that it was a regular and sustained dialogue. Colette's letters are suffused with sweetness and devotion. She sends Missy news of her cats, her garden, her travels, her health, the weather—taking that tone of the good child writing dutiful but unrevealing bulletins to a slightly gaga old mother, a tone that had once infuriated Sido.

Missy apparently did not ask for more than the privilege of being allowed to worry, maternally, about her old "fake child." When Colette went abroad, the marquise sometimes cared for her animals, and regularly showered her with small gifts—chocolate, flowers, and that June, "a marvelous clip-on lamp." She could no longer afford opals or villas, having been ruined, or nearly so, by a series of rapacious lovers. The bravado of her youth was spent, too, and the insecurity bred of unhappiness in love, the loss of wealth, the fragility of age, and the knowledge that she was—to all but a few old friends—a pathetic and grotesque figure had made her ever more diffident and self-effacing. When she stayed with Colette and Maurice at La Treille Muscate, Colette invited a "little clan of friends" to join them, but not without reassuring Missy beforehand that they were "all [people] whom you know."[27] And one evening when Missy arrived unannounced at the Claridge and found Colette's flat swarming with "ladies," she fled "terrified," into a rainstorm.

COLETTE HAD DEFECTED from Lesbos without ever severing her ties to its society. That society gravitated, in the late 1920s, to the sumptuous white salon of Natalie Barney on the rue Jacob, and to her villa at Beauvallon, not far from Saint-Tropez. Colette was a member of Natalie's informal Academy of Women, a frequent houseguest on the Côte d'Azur, and a regular at the Amazon's all-women lunches in Paris, as were Moreno, Germaine Beaumont, Rachilde, Marie Laurencin, Lucie Delarue-Mardrus, Romaine Brooks, Gertrude Stein, Princess Edmond (Winnie) de Polignac, and Élisabeth (Lily) de Gramont.[28] It was here that Colette met a distinguished circle of somewhat younger lesbian writers and artists, most of them English or American, including Djuna Barnes, Janet Flanner, Mina Loy, Noelle Murphy, Sylvia Beach, Radclyffe Hall, and Lady Una Troubridge, who became one of her best translators.

The Amazon was something of a legend to this new generation. She figures as a profane "saint" in Barnes's satiric *Ladies Almanack* and as a pioneer of freedom in Hall's *Well of Loneliness:* Natalie, alias "Valérie [Seymour], calm and assured, created an atmosphere of courage," writes Hall. "Everyone felt normal and brave when we convened in [her] salon. This charming and cultivated woman was like a sort of beacon in a storm-swept sea."[29]

Colette admired Hall's controversial novel about a mannish young woman isolated and tormented by her homosexuality, although with serious reservations. She thought the landscapes and the descriptions of a melancholy childhood were "incomparable." But when it came to the sex scenes and the psychology that informed them, she was quite "shocked" and, worse, irritated by their improbability. She didn't believe that a truly homosexual woman would feel so "abnormal" or would accept the world's definition of her abnormality with such abject self-hatred. "It's all terribly adolescent," she told Troubridge. "Obscenity is such a narrow domain. One immediately begins to suffocate there, and to feel bored."[30]

There is an interesting gulf of both culture and temperament between Colette and "John" Hall. Colette's literary judgment of *The Well of Loneliness* is fair and lucid. But sometimes worldliness can be provincial, and her incomprehension of Hall's alienation reflects the narrowness of her own perspective. Colette is privileged by the paradox of her own nature and talent, which permit her to live as an erotic "militant" while holding conservative social views. Her personal success at defiance, her sense of entitlement to pleasure, and not least, her experience as a Frenchwoman coming of age sexually in a milieu that was tolerant of lesbianism, blinded her to the sufferings of a more introspective and susceptible character raised among Puritans and conformists.

UNLIKE THE ARISTOCRATIC LESBIANS and their working-class girlfriends who had once gathered in Missy's Empire salon, Natalie's friends were, for the most part, educated upper-middle-class women who took lovers from their own world and were, in the twenties, beginning to protest their marginalization. In her Neuilly garden during the war, Natalie had hosted pacifist rallies for prominent women. Some were feminists; some were lesbians; some were both; some, like Rachilde, were neither, but they shared a repugnance for the bloodlust of men that had fueled an obscene war. "I neither like nor dislike men," Natalie wrote at the time. "I resent them for having done so much evil to women. They are political adversaries I enjoy insulting for the needs of the [pacifist and feminist] cause. Beyond the battlefield of ideas, they are strangers to me."

Natalie was a gynocrat at home in her shapely and well-exercised woman's body. She possessed fine jewels, dressed only in the best couture, and disapproved of female transvestites on both political and esthetic grounds. If men were "heartbreaking" spectacles of "insufficiency" enslaved to their "mediocre" needs and obsessions, then how much more heartbreaking were the women who impersonated them?

One might object that Natalie's appetite for conquest—she once admitted to making eighteen rendezvous for the same night—and the trail of broken hearts and marriages she left in her wake were those of any Don Juan racking up his score. She never would have agreed. "Man tears woman apart without decoding her," she asserted. Women, she believed, wasted their lives waiting for a love of which men were incapable. Her own desire, she claimed, was never anonymous or "mechanical" like a man's, never uniquely physical, but focused on the "being" of a beloved in its "entirety." And even an astute former lover like Lucie Delarue-Mardrus—who calls a fictional character based on Natalie "perverse, dissolvent, egotistical, unjust, stubborn, sometimes miserly, often an actress, most of the time irritating . . . a Monster"— recognized her as a "revolutionary who awakens others to revolt. . . . You are capable—and it's your only fidelity—of loving a person for that which she is. . . . For that I esteem you."[31]

If any happy and faithful heterosexual couples existed in Natalie's Paris, she does not seem to have noticed them. If a woman felt the duty to reproduce herself, Natalie considered that, having fulfilled it, she ought to have the sense to become a lesbian. Women, she wrote, did not yet "know how to be free." Freedom, by her definition, meant "exploiting" one's individual capacities to their highest degree, and never consenting to be shackled by a monogamous domestic life. Long before Sartre and de Beauvoir set their dubious example of a free union of equals, Natalie and her chief consort, Romaine Brooks, had separate apartments in Paris and separate wings at their villa in Beauvallon, which was called, appositely, the Trait d'Union (the Hyphen).

Like Sartre, too, Natalie dictated and revised the terms of her affairs and insisted on a freedom that was generally one-sided. She was indifferent to the suffering she caused, and to jealousy among her lovers, which was often extreme. Dolly Wilde, Oscar's niece, who was, with Romaine, a long-term lover of Natalie's, usually locked herself into a hotel room with a supply of razor blades, alcohol, and cocaine each time the Amazon went off with another young beauty. But Natalie left the job of consoling Dolly to her faithful housekeeper, Berthe, and pursued the adventure of the moment.

MISSY AND NATALIE had never found each other congenial. Colette avoided taking sides, except, perhaps, in *The Pure and the Impure,* where she states "my conviction that sapphic libertinage is the only unacceptable one."[32] Missy's great failed ambition, writes Colette, was "to establish a real and lasting affair with a woman." Natalie made a cult of her promiscuity. Missy called Natalie, disparagingly, "the pope of Lesbos," yet worried to Colette that Natalie didn't like her.[33] Natalie—famously guiltless and lucid, rapacious and cruel, endowed with self-described "nerves of steel," author of admired memoirs and aphorisms, muse to dozens of important writers, master of an inexhaustible fortune and a harem of fleshy beauties (like Colette, she despised thinness)—had the sovereign self-assurance which Missy had never known. "I love my life," wrote the blithe Natalie. "I never act except according to my pleasure. . . . After all, one cannot judge an existence except according to what it makes of us and we of it. If life should be an expression and not a suppression of the self, have I not fully filled and succeeded at my own?"[34]

"I often reflect that nothing has come to me from you," Colette told Natalie, "great or small, that has not been good."[35] Janet Flanner, interviewed by Natalie's biographer, George Wickes, said she believed that "Colette must have been more satisfactory [to Natalie] than almost anyone else in her life."[36] Satisfactory, perhaps, but ultimately elusive. "Apart from those meetings at which Colette excelled in playing and in being Colette," wrote Natalie in her memoir "The Colette I Have Known"—"beyond that lazy intimacy through which we saw each other so often and so badly, what were our real encounters? Did I have, with Colette, any of those flash moments of illumination when the mysterious nature of a being is suddenly revealed to you? But a tender friendship like ours doesn't need violent revelations."[37]

5

THAT SUMMER, Colette went back to *The Pure and the Impure*. John Hall and Una Troubridge were helping her with the documentation.[38] She was also polishing *Prisons and Paradises*, although in a letter to Moreno she makes a slip, which she laughs at, calling it *Prisons and Solitudes*. The kind of solitude Colette associates with paradise is a state of erotic detachment enjoyed by someone like Natalie. She had always envied her friend's mysterious sexual aplomb, and in *Claudine Takes Off*, she had written: "There is no serenity crueler than yours, Amazon. It's not your bite . . . that astonishes me. It's your serenity, falling from high upon us. Just enough love, just enough contempt for love." For her part, Natalie would always admire Colette's "joyous authority" while deploring her slavishness to men: "Torn between the desires of her two contrary natures: to have a master and not to have one, she always opted for the first solution."[39] And that predicament is Colette's subject in *The Pure and the Impure*.

This key work is commonly read as a study of misogyny, of homosexuality, of the ancient enmity between the sexes, or according to Colette's own instruction, as her "personal contribution to the sum total of our knowledge of the senses." It is all of that, but something deeper, too: a meditation on the way human beings eroticize their first bonds.

The popular Colette, the daughter of Sido/Ceres, is our guide to the earthly paradise. But in *The Pure and the Impure* she takes us on the tour of a realm with which she, like Proserpine, is on intimate terms. This erotic underworld has no glamour for her, and she knows the prisoners to be quite ordinary poor devils: "phantoms I seem always to be losing and finding again, restless ghosts unrecovered from wounds sustained in the past when they crashed headlong or sidelong against that barrier reef, mysterious and incomprehensible, the human body."

As these ghosts confide the secrets of their flesh ("always the flesh") to Colette, a pattern begins to emerge from their confessions. All of them have lived their lives starved for an essential nutrient and unable to renounce the fantasy of meeting the Provider who will fill the "void" once and for all.[40] The sex act tantalizes them with a fleeting taste of completeness, but they blame the deficiencies of their partners for their inevitable relapse into the void—and so move on to the next warm body. Colette looks closely at the different strategies by which these famished ghosts seek to master their voracity. The strong take the offense: they attempt to recover an illusion of wholeness through domination, and they become the sadists and seducers of both sexes. The weak experiment with some form of defensive self-starvation:

asceticism, celibacy, anorexia, but most commonly masochistic submission. This voluntary privation feels superior to the original hunger of the infant, which was suffered helplessly.

Colette's resistance to and anxiety about this subject show in the baroque syntax and in the ubiquity of suspension points, of obscure references, and of contradictions that make the text, in places, an exasperating experience for the casual reader.[41] Even a judicious Colette biographer like Joanna Richardson complains about its "incoherence." Yet Colette considered *The Pure and the Impure* her best book, and the one most likely to endure. It certainly represents her greatest risk as a writer, and the cryptic prose serves the ironic purpose of teasing the reader—viscerally and intellectually—like an unsatisfied desire. She will conclude that "the word 'pure' "—understood fulfilled—"has never revealed an intelligible meaning to me."

The Pure and the Impure opens sensationally enough, with the description of a faked orgasm. This act takes place in the reddish gloom of a "big, glass-roofed" studio somewhere in Paris, which has been converted by its owners into an opium den. There are mattresses on the floor and cheap Chinese embroideries draped over the balcony. The nameless guests exchange their street clothes for kimonos. Colette tells us she is there "on a professional assignment," and throughout the unfolding of her story, she draws out her informants like the skillful journalist she was, or as she puts it to Carco: "a contemplator, lucid and moved." Yet she also admits that she has come "in a spirit of bravado" and that she has brought with her "a well-concealed grief " and "a frightful passivity of the senses." This admission hints at her complicity with the "restless ghosts" whose stories she elicits in succeeding chapters, and who use sex the way the habitués of the opium den use drugs: to dull their concealed griefs even as it heightens their passive senses.

Colette declines to smoke the pipe, but the scent of the smoke, a "black, appetizing aroma of fresh truffles or burnt cocoa bestowed upon me patience, optimism, a vague hunger." Hunger is the form in which a human child first knows suspense, and it is the narrative experience in its most primal form. Hunger and thirst, which are inseparable for the infant, drive all the ravenous lovers in Colette's narrative, and the author herself, writing from a place (or a pose) of denial and abstention.

As she settles down chastely on her mattress, "quite expecting to be bored," Colette listens to a young woman "making a faint sucking sound" as she chews on her opium pellets, "an animal sound like an infant at its mother's breast." Later, the husky voice of a woman drifts down from an alcove off the balcony. "Is that you, Charlotte?" asks one of the opium eaters. "Sing some more." But Charlotte's lover shouts back angrily that she "didn't come here to sing," and later still, Colette hears the same husky voice "trying hard to delay her pleasure and in doing so . . . hurrying toward its climax and destruction."[42]

Colette and Charlotte meet on the staircase as they are both leaving, and twice after, the last time back at the opium den. Colette learns that this lovely woman in her forties has staged her "almost public display of pleasure" for the benefit of the "boy" she loves—a desperate and needy young man with bad lungs. "Isn't it funny," she asks Colette, "that in such a couple it's the older one . . . who happens to be obliged to lie? I'm devoted to that boy, with all my heart. But what is the heart, madame? It's worth less than people think. It's quite accommodating, it accepts anything. You give it whatever you have, it's not very particular. But the body . . . Ha! That's something else again."[43]

The selfless and, in Colette's view, heroic Charlotte "expects nothing" from her lover, but the boy understands instinctively that her body is lying to him, and "he flies into senseless rages." What makes him so angry is the feeling of jealousy and impotence that afflicts the infant of either sex—the budding misogynist—proprietary of a mother he is too weak to dominate and too small to satisfy. And this couple is exemplary of the lovers in *The Pure and the Impure,* who give pleasure but can't receive it, or take it but can't give it, who are mismatched in age, appetite, egotism, and experience—who all feel obscurely cheated.

Their elusive grail is an ideal of parity which Colette defines principally by its exclusion from her otherwise exhaustive catalogue of erotic possibilities: the bonds between lovers and rivals of both sexes in every combination, between adults and children, masters and animals. She impartially surveys all forms of desire, discerning the sadist's honor, the parasite's vitality, and the pervert's heroism, along with their pathos, complacence, folly, and delusion.

"What memory," Colette asks the woman-hating Don Juan she calls Damien, "do you believe you left with the women, with most of them?" "Why, without a doubt, a feeling of not having had quite enough." A little later in one of the paradoxes typical of the text but also of the love affairs she is describing, Damien exclaims: "By what right did they always get more out of it than I did? . . . They allow us to be their master in the sex act, but never their equal. That is what I cannot forgive them."[44] And Damien's last words to Colette—the distillation of his wisdom—are "give nothing, take nothing."

A perfect union, Colette suggests, would be one in which both partners could give and take mutual satisfaction. But her exhaustive quest turns up no equals. There are stoical givers like Charlotte and La Chevalière (Missy). There are boastful and greedy takers like Renée Vivien or Amalia X, counting their conquests on their fingers. There is Lady Eleanor Butler of Llangollen, who, for fifty years, keeps a diary that records the "perfect bliss" of a life spent in forced reclusion with her "Well-Beloved," Sarah Ponsonby. But after reading her with "a friendly and comprehending emotion," Colette concludes: "What I would like to have is the diary that would reveal the victim . . ."[45]

Eros, in the impure realm Colette visits here, is a struggle to the death, and if you're not the predator, you're the prey. The alternative to being drafted into sexual combat is the form of conscientious objection suggested by her friend Carco: " 'Ah,' he sighs in moments of simplicity and gloom, 'a man should never go to bed with a woman he loves, that spoils everything.' "[46]

The Pure and the Impure comes closer than any other of Colette's books, memoir or fiction, to revealing the "mysterious nature of [her] being," as Natalie calls it, which she guarded so fiercely, even from her intimates. She explores her own sensual torments, admits her failures, flaunts her powers, confesses her weaknesses, and toward the end of her journey, sums up the three kinds of passionate attachments she has known. The first is with those on whom she "lavishes" her gifts, and these include children, animals, and sexual rivals. The second is with those whose "riches" she still has the strength to "plunder."

> But apart from those individuals who hurriedly let themselves be filled by me, leaving me empty and drawn, and apart from the superabundant ones, still worse, whose indigestible contributions I quickly reject, there spreads a zone where I can disport with my equals. . . . They are usually just emerging from the worst kind of youth, the second childhood. They have lost their solemnity and have acquired a sane notion of what is incurable and what is curable—for instance, love. Ingeniously, they fill each day from one dawn to the next, and they have an adventurous spirit. They perceive, as I do, the pernicious element in daily work. . . . In short, they are frivolous, as have been hundreds of heroes. They have become frivolous the hard way. And they secrete from one day to the next their own ethics, which makes them even more understandable to me. . . .
>
> The thing we all have in common is a certain diffidence: we never dare to show openly that we need each other. Such reserve acts as a code of behavior and constitues what I call our "etiquette of survivors." Cast upon a rocky coast by their dismasted vessel, should not the survivors of the shipwreck be the most considerate of messmates?[47]

"It is only when one is better that one discovers one wasn't very well," Colette once told Maurice.[48] And *The Pure and the Impure,* her great ode to emptiness, was written by a woman who felt full. She faces the void—was perhaps only capable of facing it—with the support of a "considerate messmate" she both slept with and loved. Their devotion wasn't pure, and it certainly wasn't equal, but it was mutual. And for the last twenty-five years of her life, Colette paid Maurice Goudeket the honor, which he earned "the hard way," of calling him "my best friend."

CHAPTER 37

1

THE SUMMER OF 1931 was unusually lovely. The grapes were bursting with sugar, and the dew, Colette told Moreno, "makes them as blue as lavender." She was living alone at La Treille Muscate, working "like an ant" on *The Pure and the Impure* while Maurice was in Paris "to look after his crumb—crust is too opulent a word."[1]

He joined her in September, and on the morning of the fifth, they set off by car to swim from the pristine Plage des Salins, a mile from the house. The road narrowed to a dirt path, and while Maurice backed up, Colette got down to open a grille, giving him more room to maneuver. The hinge stuck, so she pushed hard, lost her balance, and her leg sank into a deep trench that had been concealed by foliage. It was instantly obvious that something was broken, because Colette was howling with agony. Maurice left her with the dog and ran to the beach, where he found Moune and Moreau. They managed to get her to the clinic in Saint-Tropez, and Dr. Frichement, who set the break, told her that it could have been much worse.

A vacationing Parisian specialist advised Colette to go home immediately. She bought her ticket and worried that her pregnant cat would give birth on the train. In the meantime, however, she was in such pain from two sores underneath the plaster that Frichement decided to remove the cast several weeks prematurely. It took him an hour, aided by Pauline, using two pairs of hedge clippers and a pruning shears.

Back at the Claridge, Colette finished her book, "as usual, in nights and days of despair." Having heard about the accident, Bel-Gazou rushed to her mother's side, but made the error of showing her own anxiety and was coldly repulsed. "My daughter . . . was very emotional," Colette told Moune, "but I soon put an end to her outbursts. . . . I have not been mithridatized against every emotion—I mean every manifestation of emotion—and I am less afraid of catching the itch than of showing how dreadfully weak I am."[2] Her leg was bandaged and painful, but by October she could walk a hundred yards on crutches. Maurice Martin du Gard noted that the injury obliged her to wear flat heels, and she began going barefoot in a pair of "Spartacus" sandals made by a shoemaker in Saint-Tropez—a style which henceforth became her trademark. The bone healed faster than the ligaments, and she accepted, sadly, that she would have a long convalescence. But perhaps, she told Maurice, the accident was an omen of "the end of the bad patch."

2

MAURICE SPECULATES that this injury, which seemed minor at the time, probably contributed to Colette's physical decline, leaving her vulnerable to the excruciating arthritis of the hip that would eventually immobilize her. But that autumn, she was full of hope for a new project that would make their fortune and give her a respite from the lonely anguish of writing books. She and Maurice planned to manufacture and sell beauty products under Colette's name. She would concoct the formulas and do the public relations. He would oversee the business.

Renaud de Jouvenel claimed that this "baroque idea" came from Maurice. Colette claimed that it came from her old friend André Maginot,[3] although she couldn't have entirely forgotten the success of Willy's Claudine face powders and lotions. Maurice pretended he had done his best to discourage this dubious second career, warning Colette that it risked "tarnishing her glory." But Colette, he said, wasn't worried about her glory. She felt a need "to renew her contact with those unknown, ordinary people who had always been her true characters," and the idea of demonstrating her products in department stores—even doing facials and makeovers—appealed to what she liked to think of as her idealism. She would save "naive" women "childishly ignorant of what suited their faces" from their lapses of taste and their terror of aging.[4]

That autumn, while Maurice courted investors, Colette did research and development. She asked Moreno "to steal some Max Factor for me. . . . It's for the lab, of course." (At the time it was available only through theatrical wholesalers.)[5] She had her eye on an elegant apothecary shop that belonged to the duchess Sforza, and she asked Germaine Beaumont to enquire discreetly if it might be for sale.[6] By the end of November, she told Hélène that she had one perfume ready and two tonics for different skin types. "The other poisons, lipstick, creams, are late. And I have to lunch and dine with backers. . . . I crawl away dead. But we *have* to succeed."[7]

The business was incorporated in March of 1932, with 750,000 francs in seed money from several rich friends: Winnie de Polignac; Simone Berriau, the actress and director; Léon Bailby, the publisher; the Glâwi of Marrakesh; and the banker Daniel Dreyfus. The partners found a suitable site for a beauty institute at 6, rue de Miromesnil, and Colette supervised the renovations. The Art Deco interior would be stylishly clinical: mirrored walls, chrome and leather armchairs, nickel and glass counters, white shelves on simple brackets that displayed Colette's potions in chic black pots. She drew her own profile for the labels, and their logo was her signature.

The press was fascinated by the announcement that Colette was going into the beauty business. "Whether I like it or not," she told Léo Marchand, "[the eager journalists] have already given me 50,000 francs' worth of publicity. I'm beginning to believe it can work."[8] Yet not all the response was friendly. Shocked fans of her work stopped her in the street to ask if the news was true, and Colette was deluged with letters, some of the writers pleading for "salvation" from their wrinkles, but many outraged. She found herself defending this act of nerve as she had once defended her decision to go on the stage. No, she hadn't "sold" her name: she was an authentic makeup expert. For more than thirty years, she had been making beauty products—cold cream, quince water, "a certain pomade of lanolin"—from her own secret recipes. She "adored . . . changing the hairdos [of her friends]—taking the scissors to them, not even sparing the visiting stranger."[9] So why shouldn't she exploit these gifts and get paid for them?

Colette's beauty institute opened that June with a blaze of flashbulbs and a crush of celebrities vying for a turn in the chair where Colette, in a white lab coat, was doing makeovers. Liane de Pougy recalled her own entrance. The patron exclaimed, " 'My fortune is made—here is . . . beautiful Liane!' And she threw herself into my arms. I reeled—she is no mean weight—and let her sell me everything she wanted. . . . A few friends approve of what she is doing, but most people blame her." Not, however, the courtesan-turned-princess: "No work is disreputable," she noted in her journal, as well she might: "one thing will advance the other."[10]

That August, Colette opened a branch in Saint-Tropez and another in Nantes. She spent a good part of the next year on the road, giving exhibitions of her products at provincial trade fairs and in department stores. Her clients inevitably brought books for her to inscribe, and she often finished her long days as a beautician lecturing on her writing in the town halls. Maurice, in the meantime, was putting all his "passion," "fury," and "vigilance" into the business. "It's my one horizon," he told Colette,[11] his letters contradicting the passive version of his role that he gives in his memoirs.[12] He was always find-ing a "soulful" dimension to the work and "a mysterious radiance" to the products which "people seem to perceive." He swears by his good name that he'll succeed, and admits his guilt about her "fatigue," promising that "very soon" or "in a few months" or as "the business develops" she'll be able to go back to writing.

Colette wrote to him faithfully from all her provincial outposts, grousing about the food, the importunate fans and reporters, and the "thirty-year-old lightbulbs." His absence made her *"méchante"*—bad-tempered—and her bad temper becomes a refrain. "I'm not sure if you are, as you say, 'useful,' " she told Maurice from Strasbourg, "but I'm sure you're very inconvenient for me, because I find five days very long without you."[13]

The venture was a disaster for its investors and a waste of time for Colette. Neither her fame nor Maurice's "passion" could save it. By the middle of 1933 it was obvious that they needed a large infusion of new capital, and a commit-ment, on Colette's part, of several more years spent "resting" from her true work. It wasn't easy to launch any new enterprise in the depths of the Depres-sion, but perhaps Colette's misjudgment of her own talents—and her own motives—had something to do with the failure: "I find the women beautiful as they emerge from beneath my writer's fingers, and I enjoy touching the liv-ing flesh, heightening its colors, concealing its defects with my impartial fin-gers, inspired by a kind of benevolent, maternal feeling. And then . . . I know so well what one ought to spread upon a terrified female face, so full of hope in its decline. I have stared so often at that great landscape, the human face, that I don't hesitate to tramp across it."[14]

Benevolence? Maternal feelings? Impartial fingers? Natalie Barney met Bel-Gazou as she emerged from the shop in Saint-Tropez "slathered with livid pink and blue makeup": her mother had transformed "a wild child" into a "streetwalker." The celebrated actress Cécile Sorel fared even worse: she came out looking "twice as old" as when she went in.[15]

3

BETWEEN 1933 AND 1939, Colette published three short novels—*The Cat, Duo,* and its sequel, *The Toutounier.* Their views of love's pathos and of the hopeless incompatibility of men and women were quarried directly from *The Pure and the Impure,* but instead of treating special cases—gays, addicts, outcasts, Don Juans—Colette examined the behavior of ordinary, bourgeois couples.

The Cat is the first and best known of these three novels. It took its title from the name of the superb pearl gray Chartreuse Colette bought at a cat show in 1926 and who also figures in *Break of Day*. The crimes and love affairs of The Cat fill Colette's correspondence to Maurice from Saint-Tropez, and she lived until 1939, adored by her masters, who could not bear, thereafter, to replace her. In this novel of which a cat is the romantic heroine, Colette's prose is particularly feline—both detached and voluptuous, minutely obser-vant of those pleasures and irritants of the flesh which are lost on grosser human senses.

Saha, also a Chartreuse, belongs to Alain, a young man who worships her. Alain and his mother live in a crumbling suburban villa with an idyllic garden, served by their old retainers. His father, now deceased, was a silk mer-chant. Alain still works in the firm, whose fortunes are in decline. As the novel opens, he is engaged to Camille—"the little Malmert girl," as his mother calls her. Both mother and son accept that Alain is marrying down: Camille's family has made its embarrassingly new money selling washing machines.

Alain is as reserved and secretive as Saha. He goes through the motions of his engagement and marriage with an occasional rush of enthusiasm for Camille's body, but mostly rather annoyed, as a cat would be, by her intru-siveness and lack of subtlety. Whenever possible, he seeks refuge in the gar-den, his childhood "kingdom," to be alone with Saha. They have the perfect understanding he will never share with another member of his own species— and certainly not with the fastidious mother who doesn't want her own gray fur ruffled by his upsetting confidences.

After Alain has performed a nightly "ceremony of adulation appropri-ate to the graces and virtues" of his beloved, master and cat sleep together in the childhood bed he is loath to exchange for a double one with Camille. Saha's touch on Alain's chest arouses "a disquieting pleasure," which is the same sen-sation these faintly perverse love scenes arouse in the reader.

Snobbery is an element of Alain's love for Saha, whom he describes as a "perfect specimen of her race."[16] But so is Camille a perfect specimen. She's a modern girl of the middle class with well-muscled buttocks, bossy and a little vulgar. She smokes too much, she drives too fast, her voice is loud, and she's full of false confidence. If she were an animal, she'd be a big, rambunctious black Lab, jumping on the guests and leaving paw marks on the silk uphol-stery. After their marriage Alain discovers with dismay that she's quite com-monplace in bed, too, and "immoderately" greedy.

There is no suspense about the marriage—it's doomed from the beginning by Alain's contempt and by Camille's jealousy, which he does nothing to assuage, although it would take little enough. Out of bed, his young wife bores him, and in bed, her lust shocks him: "Who taught her to outstrip me like this?" And he takes his revenge by cynically "making use of her—body-to-body."[17]

The newlyweds are living in a borrowed high-rise apartment while Alain's house is being fixed up for them, at Camille's father's expense. One morning, as Alain is going off to visit Saha on the pretext of inspecting the renovations, Camille confronts him: " 'Confess that you're going to see my rival!' " " 'Saha isn't your rival . . .' 'How could she be your rival?' he went on to himself. 'You can't compete with the pure; your rivals have to be among the impure.' "[18]

It is then only a matter of time until Camille pushes Saha off the ninth-floor balcony of the apartment.[19] During the interval, Colette entertains us with exquisite descriptions of a Parisian summer and of the scents and flesh tones of two young bodies, one cruel and selfish, the other insensitive and banal. While she treats Alain and Camille impartially, she ultimately disdains both of them, and she constructs the narrative so that only the sublime Saha merits our anxiety.

Saha has an unfair advantage: the benefit of her animal mystery. She also has the benefit of an awning on the fifth floor, which breaks her fall. She survives intact, and the guileless would-be killer admits her guilt. Alain couldn't be happier: he has an excuse to go home to his mother, carrying Saha in the cook's market basket. The next morning, Camille bravely comes to see him, hoping for forgiveness or at least some sign that in time his outrage will subside. But the poor thing has made the error of getting dolled up like a "shopgirl," and what's worse, of keeping her gloves on, calling Alain's attention to her hands: "A little, innocent animal as blue as the best dreams, a little soul. . . . Faithful, capable of dying exquisitely if she loses what she loves. . . . That is what you held in your hands above empty space, and you opened your hands. . . . You are a monster! I do not want to live with a monster!"

Camille protests that her jealousy was only human, and what's monstrous is for a man to prefer his cat to his wife. Then she goes off, a little mollified because Alain permits her to keep their convertible. When she looks back one last time, she glimpses her husband ensconced in the deep shade of his garden, caressing Saha, who is "following Camille's departure with the expression of a human being."

The Cat was published in May of 1933, and Colette's daughter, who turned twenty that July, had unknowingly modeled for her age-mate Camille. Bel-Gazou had just quit or been fired from a film company, apparently because she'd been impolitic on the set and her nasty remarks about the producer had been repeated to him. Colette then wangled her a job as a production assistant on *Lac aux Dames,* a film directed by Marc Allégret and produced by Philippe de Rothschild, who had commissioned Colette to adapt the screenplay from

Vicki Baum's novel *Ladies' Lake*. That spring, Rothschild, Allégret and their crew rented the suite directly beneath Colette's at the Claridge, and they came upstairs every afternoon at two, lolling around her sitting room in their pajamas, ordering room service, and hashing out the plot and dialogue until well past midnight. Colette complained, but enjoyed herself.

She was also pleased to see her profligate daughter gainfully employed, and even more relieved that she had broken off her engagement. According to Renaud de Jouvenel, who loved his sister well though never uncritically, Bel-Gazou had been desperate to marry for the wrong reasons. She was impatient to be "the absolute mistress" of her own establishment, and she'd fixed on Paul more out of "vanity" than love. He observed that a girl who was "defiant and despotic at the same time" would always be "difficult to marry."[20]

BY NOW, Henry de Jouvenel had abandoned both Marthe Bibesco and Germaine Patat, and married for a third time. His new wife, Germaine-Sarah, was a woman of his own age and the widow of an extremely rich Jewish industrialist, Charles Louis-Dreyfus. Their union, writes Jouvenel's biographer, "passed for being little else" than expedient, which is how Colette would depict it in *Julie de Carneilhan*. The couple's intimate friends, however— André Maurois among them—had never seen Henry "so serene or happy."[21]

The Jouvenels settled in a mansion on the rue Férou that had once belonged to Talleyrand, and renovated Castel-Novel, although they had little leisure to enjoy country life. In 1924, Poincaré appointed Jouvenel to his cabinet, and the following year, he became the High Commissioner in Syria, where he would incur the wrath of right-wing nationalists for seeming to collude with the British, France's rival power in the Middle East. When his mission ended, the baron devoted his energies to the League of Nations and, with Lord Robert Cecil, organized an International Peace Congress, which was disrupted by rioters from L'Action Française. in 1932, Jouvenel was named ambassador to Italy. Hitler had just come to power, and France could not afford an Italo-German alliance. Jouvenel's delicate mission was to cultivate a strategic friendship with Mussolini. While they were in Rome, his wife undertook to renovate the embassy—housed in the historic Palazzo Farnese—at her own expense.

Renaud de Jouvenel had, in the meanwhile, fallen in love with his new stepsister, Arlette Louis-Dreyfus, who was exactly the age of Bel-Gazou. The young women both had rooms in the mansion on the rue Férou and had become devoted friends. Renaud lodged a few streets away but took his meals with them. All three were rebels who felt superfluous to parents absorbed by their own loves and careers, and when the Jouvenels were away, the children threw bohemian dinners for "forbidden friends"—and were grateful to the servants for their discretion.[22]

The second former Mme de Jouvenel was apparently one of the people Arlette was forbidden to frequent, but Bel-Gazou introduced—or reintroduced—them anyway.[23] Colette was touched by this "round, suave little Jewess with beautiful, long-lashed eyes, the hair of Salomé, and the complexion of a peach."[24] And she was sympathetic—as Henry and Germaine certainly were not—to Arlette's romance with Renaud, cheering when they defied their parents to elope. "All is well that ends in marriage," Colette told Hélène Picard. "Arlette is a delicious girl and will perhaps make Renaud into less of an agitated wild creature."[25]

When the newlyweds came to visit her in Saint-Tropez, she observed to Maurice that marriage had not improved Arlette's looks and that she had made a fatal mistake in cutting her hair, but was a lovable girl who had acted with "patience and courage."[26] Arlette, however, would always resent Colette on Bel-Gazou's behalf. "Little Colette was the sister I always wanted. I thought her magnificent. Her gift for writing particularly enchanted me. . . . On the other hand, she was always a bit intimidated and silent with her mother . . . I would even dare say . . . awestruck . . . and that irritated me, because I wanted her to be more critical."[27]

Colette continued to find relations with her daughter the disappointment they had always been. She felt herself forced into the role of "an ageing adversary, faced with a child in whom, the better to wound her, there flourishes all that got the better of her."[28] Bel-Gazou was undoubtedly reckless and brash, although her arrogance dissembled her insecurity. Like Camille, she was, in Colette's view, too "modern," which is to say ungrateful and rebellious. She smoked hard, drove fast,[29] stayed out late, left the cap off the toothpaste, dirtied all the towels, slammed doors, scattered her clothes on the floor, and had no scruples about the extra work she caused Pauline. Colette was forever shooing predatory older men away from her, perhaps reflecting, as Alain does, "who taught her to outstrip me like this?"

"I should by rights be her grandmother," she sighed to Maurice in an atypically philosophic moment. He played Saha's role in their domestic triangle, and he often signed himself "the feline" or "Tomcat." Bel-Gazou resented him deeply: "a child doesn't easily accept sharing her mother," she would tell a journalist,"[30] unwittingly echoing Colette. When the three of them were alone in Saint-Tropez, there was some of the same tension in the house—the sense of an intruder's unsubtle presence—that Camille imports to Alain's paradise.

4

THE CÔTE D'AZUR that summer of 1933 was "as hot as Indochina." Maurice fired the director of the Société Colette and was kept in Paris running the business on his own. Colette minded the shop in Saint-Tropez. She gossiped to Moreno about Chanel's rumored engagement to the "demonic" Paul Iribe, admired the face-lift of Lady Mendl, dined with the Greek princess and psychoanalyst Marie Bonaparte,[31] and lunched with Jean-Michel Franck, the designer. Nadine Hwang, a "piratical" Asian beauty and Natalie's sometime girlfriend, tried to seduce her, but Colette remained (she says) "loyal" to Natalie. The Amazon herself, accompanied by Romaine Brooks, came for a swim. Colette noted to Maurice with "malicious" pleasure that they were both now fatter than she was.

Because she "hated" spending lonely evenings, she often dined with her neighbors, Vera and Julio van den Henst. Julio was a Guatemalan-born dentist of Dutch descent "with an amazing heart," and one of Maurice's closest friends. The lovely Vera was the daughter of a Russian doctor attached to the Ballets Russes, and she had danced with Diaghilev. She doted on her little girl, Hélène, universally called Nouchette. Colette also found the toddler enchanting—"She sees and retains everything"—but nevertheless, couldn't help disapproving of all the coddling and praise the baby got. "They let her eat too much," she told Maurice, and "Vera is spoiling [Nouchette] with her unbridled admiration."[32] In Colette's view, "the extravagant desire to give all, poisons motherhood, as if to punish it for its passionate origins."[33]

THE "VANDERS" KEPT the kind of Chekhovian open house Rozven had once been. Vera was always happy to whip up a rustic supper for twenty, or to improvise a masquerade. They treated Colette as a member of the family, and she reciprocated their loyal and uncomplicated affection. As is often the case, this nurturing, secure couple attracted wild, unstable friends, and Colette enjoyed keeping Maurice abreast of their partying and their romantic intrigues. But she didn't tell him about an intrigue of her own.

Among the mutual friends of the Vanders and the Goudekets were Georges and Joseph (Jef) Kessel. They, like Vera, were Russian Jews whose parents had immigrated to France after the Revolution—the Kessels by way of Argentina—where their three sons were born. They settled in Nice, and the brothers received a French education while continuing to study Yiddish and Russian culture. They were all expected to excel and to repay with distinction the sacrifices that their parents made for them.

The eldest Kessel brother, Lazare, called Lola by the family and Siber in the theater world, excelled brilliantly, though not in a manner pleasing to his austere father. He was the most promising young actor of his day, and a protégé of Colette's great friend Édouard de Max.[34] In 1920, he took first prize for tragedy in the annual competitions held by the Conservatory. Colette was a member of the jury, and the next day, in *Le Matin*, she called Kessel's performance—the fourth act of *Ruy Blas*—"gigantic, fiery, and magnificent."[35]

Six weeks later, in the middle of rehearsals for a new play, Lola Kessel shot himself in a Left Bank hotel. He left his family a note that did not explain his death. But his "fame was so fresh and so great," writes Jef's biographer, "that his suicide became the symbol" of all that was morbid and vitiated in the spirit of his generation—the generation of Maurice Goudeket, and of Fred Peloux.[36]

The right-wing press picked up the story of Lola's suicide and, in a series of editorials that made up for in viciousness what they lacked in evidence, attacked his character. Lola was accused of winning his prize high on cocaine, of using morphine, of alcoholism, homosexuality, and a degenerate estheticism. "Everything that's against nature pleases these young neurotics," wrote *La France du Nord*. "We shouldn't send them to The Odéon but to a mental hospital."[37]

Colette never publicly referred to Lola Kessel, his suicide, or the scandal surrounding it when she discussed *The Last of Chéri*, but she was typically reticent about her sources. Léa's indictment of Chéri and of his generation could have come straight from the anti-Lola tirade in *Le Journal*, which spoke about "a veritable epidemic of strange symptoms" affected by "young people too avid for originality who indulge in puerile depravities."[38] Her paradoxical view of Chéri's "purity"—and Chéri's own expression of his worldweariness—echo those reported by Kessel's most eloquent defender, Henri Jeanson:

Siber was an exquisite being. . . . To live, he often said, to live in order to pursue a desire and not attain it—what's the use? Siber had the rare privilege of understanding, at twenty, the futility of existence, and he put an end to his *nights* because he esteemed that this society, which will be eternally dominated by ugliness for the simple reason that it's so ubiquitous, wasn't worthy of the beauty that he offered it. I remember that one day at the Comédie-Française, he took a long look at the spectators. A fat tear rolled down his cheek, and he cried: "God, but these creatures are stupid!"[39]

Lola Kessel may or may not have taken drugs, but Georges and Jef abused them famously. The mythically virile Jef had an appetite for dope of every kind, as well as for combat, drama, alcohol, gambling, sex, vagabondage, and transgression which made even Colette seem prim by comparison. He learned to fly and explored the globe from the pampas to the steppes. He became one of the great political reporters of his age, and one of the most acclaimed novelists, pioneering a genre, "the literature of action and of manly brotherhood [later] elaborated by Malraux and Saint-Exupéry."[40] He lived like a pasha, dividing his favors among a long-suffering wife and several grateful mistresses, each with her own establishment.

"What couldn't one forgive in such a man?" asks his biographer. "But Kessel didn't forgive himself anything. . . . His masochism, his taste for remorse—an essential thread in his life and work—judged all the positive aspects of his experience as negligible."[41] He particularly could not forgive himself for having been blind to the depressive anguish of his older brother, Lola, and for overshadowing his younger brother, Georges, seducing him by his own dangerous example into a life of dissolution for which Georges didn't have his stamina.

Georges Kessel was a wit, an idler, a pretty boy, and a dandy. He had married very young and well, his wife's income supporting his passion for gambling. He dabbled in fiction and worked briefly as the private secretary to Gaston Gallimard, who was impressed by his decadent charm. But at twenty-four, unexpectedly, Georges shook off his dilettante's torpor and became the editor in chief of a weekly magazine devoted to crime stories, called *Détective*, to which Jef was a prime contributor. The venture was underwritten by Gallimard, who paid Georges an enormous salary. He earned it, but he also began embezzling large sums from his patron, in the form of advances to fictitious authors, to pay for his cocaine habit and his debts at the track.

The theft was discovered in 1931, while both Kessel brothers were recuperating from the injuries they had suffered a few months earlier in a devastating car crash. Georges had been driving his Talbot high on cocaine after a night of orgiastic partying. His feet were burned and his leg was so badly fractured that it had to be amputated. His wife, Marise, was partially scalped when she was thrown from the passenger seat, and Jef, who had crushed two vertebrae, was encased from head to foot in a cast.

Jef rebounded quickly, and so did Marise, but Georges, already prone to addiction, got hooked on the morphine he was taking as an anesthetic. His wife left him, Jef forced Georges into a detox clinic in Grasse, and for a while he kept clean. But by the summer of 1933, he was still unemployed, living on Jef's charity, and, as Colette put it, back to "fighting with his poison."[42]

Colette was recovering from her own car accident when she heard about her friends', and she joked to Renaud that she had broken her leg to "demonstrate that without great expense, screeching metal, or level crossings, I could . . . one-up all the Kessels."[43] She also knew Georges and his habits well enough to have given him his nom de plume—"Smoke." It is easy to understand why she might be susceptible to his charms. He resembled Chéri. He also fits Pichois's description of Jules Colette: "a droll man with the melancholy gaiety of amputees and southerners, attentive, gallant, fervent"—a list of adjectives to which one could add empty, voracious, and utterly broken. Georges, indeed, was one of those "alluring voids" whom Colette describes to Carco, and who inspired *The Pure and the Impure.*

That summer, while Jef was staying in a hotel at Le Lavandou writing a new novel—*Les Enfants de la chance*—and avoiding the temptations of Saint-Trop nightlife, Georges was recovering from an opium binge. As the story of what happened between him and Colette comes primarily from her letters to Maurice, there are many omissions. The Vanders' house, she told him, was overcrowded and their well was low, so she agreed to "share" Georges with them. But the Vanders' daughter, Nouchette, remembered events a little differently. Her mother, she said, couldn't stand Georges, and she doubted there had been any "sharing."[44] In any case, he needed a nanny, because a one-legged, suicidally depressed drug addict couldn't be trusted on his own. So Colette took him in.

Colette's houseguests generally stayed in the little annex next to the garage, but she put up Georges Kessel on the divan where Maurice slept when he wasn't sharing her bed. Did Georges stay on the divan? Vera van den Henst didn't think so, and neither did Maurice. Someone informed him of the situation, and he fired off an angry, jealous letter. Here is Colette's reply, almost in its entirety. It is probably the most spontaneous and unretouched self-portrait of her that exists. There are very few corrections on the manuscript. Colette apparently sent it as it was written:

> I immediately sent you a telegram, my love. I would have liked my letter to go as quickly. In yours, there is only one word that counts, that you're suffering. The rest I must brutally, yes brutally, not respond to. No, yes, I must. Perhaps I owe you an accounting for the divan? And for the breakfast? These are images that distance, jealousy—excuse the word—distort. If Léo Marchand had come to stay, he would have slept on the divan. . . . Carco? No, no longer. Before I lend your bed, certain conditions are necessary, and they are the same ones that . . . [determine] the people in whose company I can work or can't work. It happens that Kessel's "heaviness" doesn't bother me at all—attention, mashoo, my well-beloved, my mis-

treated one—I write to you without any order, as I would speak to you—attention, you're about to accuse me of [the fault for which] Jouvenel reserved his strongest reproach, you're going to speak to me about my "monstrous innocence"! But naturally I didn't tell you that Kessel was sleeping on the divan. I would have told you [in Paris], as certainly as I love you. But I'm a prudent woman, my darling, where you're concerned. Do you remember in *Sapho* [the novel by Daudet] when the young man wants to read one of those bundles of love letters that Fanny wants to burn? She tells him . . . "I'm very willing, but you're going to hurt yourself again." To me, you can say anything without scorching me too badly, the essential thing being that you're there. I'm not ignorant of the places where I can wound you. So I didn't tell you, "Kessel is sleeping on the divan, your divan."

Another thing. The "what will people say" thing that's on your mind. The truth is also in what I've written to you: La Golyade [the Vanders' house] and La Treille are sharing Kessel. . . . For [his] material needs, I told Pauline: "I'm abandoning him to you, see to his care so that I never have to worry about it." She has acquitted herself all the better because the boy arrived in an extraordinary state of Ukrainian abandon, without shirts, without money, without anything, green and pearl gray from opium and other filth. Here we touch, my darling, on what is *my* sensuality: total authority: "Eat this, drink, go to sleep, shut your trap, look healthy or I'll kick you out". . . . You recognize me in that. It doesn't displease me to get paid in results, and even in fervor. If I weren't, the boy would be the worst of scoundrels. And it is also *my* sensuality to be the guest at a physical and moral repast, I am not for nothing the daughter of my mother, and blast it, mashoo, I've had nothing to chew on this summer, I can't even brutalize and torment you for your own good!

As for accusing me of "friendship," you go too far. It requires, to forge a bond like ours, a little series of miracles which I don't feel I have the force to re-create, nor the desire. . . . "You are free." No, I am not free. It isn't because you write it that I would be, where you're concerned. . . . At the most, you have succeeded in getting a string of curses out of me, a long string of "shits," a tender contempt for so much stupidity, my gratitude for so much love. . . .

You're suffering, I'm making you suffer, and at the same time, I ask myself: "What does it matter that he should suffer? I owe it to him, he's getting repaid for the nine years of melancholy insouciance that he stole from me. 'To break the pact of friendship which, of friendship that . . .' " If I go on, you're going to make me angry. It's idiotic, it's idiotic. And you have, of course, "a great respect for the freedom of others." Yes. Not mine. . . . And do I have any respect for your freedom? Not the least. What else? What else can I discuss, defend, explain, excuse? . . .

But naturally Kessel thinks I've "saved" him. But naturally he also has a fine soul, and he says that he wants to ask Maurice Goudeket for his "permission" not to lose the sound of my voice, my scoldings, and my tales from the barracks, and my "radiance." All of you to the Devil! Except you, of course. I'm so stupid! I'm trembling with rage, my darling. You could so easily not have written that letter. . . . Oh, well, it's done . . .[45]

CHAPTER 38

1

IN MAY OF 1933, Colette went to see her favorite psychic, the celebrated Mme Fraya, who had once channeled the ghost of Jules
Colette. Fraya told her she was doing too much at once and that she
should give up the world of business: "it will only bring you heartbreak."[1]
Colette and Maurice dissolved their company that year, but rather than enjoy
her freedom, she accepted two new and extremely demanding jobs. She promised a daily article to *La République*,[2] and she signed on as chief drama critic
for *Le Journal*, beginning that October.

Consider for a moment what this meant. In addition to her fiction, her
journalism, and her work on film scripts,[3] this sixty-year-old was going to four
or five opening nights a week, sixteen to twenty plays a month, two or three of
them critiqued every week in a Sunday column of some two thousand words.
And the Paris stage of the 1930s wasn't Broadway. The richness and variety of
the offerings were almost dizzying: Anouilh, Duhamel, Guitry; Claudel, the
Catholic mystic, and Joe Jackson, the Jewish clown; Shakespeare, Dumas,
Goethe, and Giraudoux; Drieu La Rochelle and Rip; Henry Bernstein and
Noël Coward; Stefan Zweig and Lugné-Poe; Josephine Baker, Jacques Tati,
Mistinguett, Chevalier, and the Grand Guignol; Molière, Goldoni, Racine,
and Ibsen; Cocteau, Pirandello, and Artaud.

Between 1934 and 1938, Colette's collected columns were published in
four dense volumes under the title *La Jumelle noire* (*The Black Opera Glasses*).
Each review is a shapely literary essay. Their range and fluency are tremendous, and they're informed by a breadth of culture—a grounding in the classics of European theater and a familiarity with the avant-garde—that isn't

obvious from her novels. To all of this Colette brought an intimate knowledge of stagecraft and acting, and a freshness exempt from the vanities of the pedant or the academic. She judges the theater, as Robert Brasillach puts it, "as she would judge real life: from her experience; with her rough, illuminating wisdom."[4]

2

THAT WINTER, Colette also began writing *Duo,* a shorter and darker variation on the theme of *The Cat.* In the first novel, the male is the feline egotist and the female the mortal lover, rival, and loser. In *Duo* the roles are reversed. A wife's casual fling—a "stupid caprice" she would like to forget—leads to her husband's suicide. He discovers an old love letter she has imprudently left in her blotter, and its contents torment him. She considers that he ought to have the strength of character to forgive her and resume what has been a happy enough marriage. But her nonchalance only fuels his self-destructive jealousy, which in turn arouses her contempt, and in the lucid words of the critic Michel Mercier, the couple trap themselves in a "false combat which is also an unequal combat. All [the husband] has . . . is his love and his pride." The wife has the benefit of her well-honed instinct for self-preservation. "She refuses to expose what is vulnerable in her and prefers, toughly, to resent someone rather than to understand him too well."[5]

Duo, like *The Last of Chéri* and *Break of Day,* is one of those novels in which Colette imagines an alternative fate: a loss averted, a tragedy that didn't happen, a renunciation she had the sanity not to make. When she alludes to Daudet's *Sapho* in her letter to Maurice, she suggests her source for the device of the love letter, and the premise of the novel was clearly inspired by the challenge of a betrayal—the Kessel affair—which both she and Maurice, unlike their fictional counterparts, rose to meet. Colette, the stronger and guilty party, offers the compassion to her fragile mate which Alice can't summon in a comparable situation. She reproaches Maurice both for the impertinence of his jealousy and its "imbecility," but she chooses to receive it as a proof of love, rather than of weakness.

Maurice, in turn, refused to let his hurt pride or his sense of inferiority sabotage their life together. He had dedicated his life to a "wounded" woman who, when they met, "no longer believed in love except as a brief flame which soon enough had to go out, leaving nothing but ashes." His mission, as he saw it, was to "demonstrate [to Colette] that constancy isn't a vain word." And he wasn't boasting when he writes that "from year to year her reassurance grew, and her last books are evidence of a serenity which she wouldn't otherwise have acquired."[6] Without Maurice, wrote Jean Cocteau, "Colette would have been the victim of her heart."[7]

3

COLETTE WAS NOW, as Pichois puts it, "at the height of her glory." In March of 1935, she was elected to the Belgian Royal Academy of French Language and Literature.[8] In a poll of French writers taken that year, she was named the greatest living master of French prose. Edmond Jaloux, reviewing *Duo* in *Les Nouvelles littéraires,* spoke of her "classical transparency," and Henry de Montherlant called her "our greatest natural writer." Colette, he continued grandly and not without condescension, "writes as she thinks, as she feels, as she speaks. Between what we read and what she has thought, felt, spoken, *there is nothing.*"[9]

Nothing? "One has only to examine the manuscripts . . . laden with corrections," writes Marie-Christine Bellosta, "to understand the price [Colette] paid, line after line, for the density of expression, the precision of detail, that transparency . . . that give us the illusion of naturalness."[10] And to a young woman writer who sought her advice, Colette replied: "When you are capable of certifying that today's work is equal to yesterday's, you will have earned your stripes. For I am convinced that talent is nothing other than the possibility of resembling oneself from one day to the next, whatever else befalls you."[11]

PICHOIS ALSO RECORDS one of the rare discordant notes in the "chorus of praises" that greeted almost every book Colette published from *Chéri* on. It came from a left-wing critic named Marc Bernard, who complained of her "uninterrupted procession" of petit-bourgeois characters with their petty loves and hates. He implied that her work could be summed up in the title she gave to a collection of essays: *Le Voyage égoïste* (*Journey for Myself*).[12]

Considering Colette's lifelong indifference to politics, it is no surprise that her work of the 1930s neglects the grave crises of those years: Hitler's ascension to power in Germany, four hundred thousand unemployed workers in France, fuel rationing, the proliferation of strikes and violent demonstrations, the flight of capital and the devaluation of the franc, the consolidation of power on the left and the increasingly explicit fascism of the right. When Colette took an interest in current events, they were inevitably crimes of passion; she found a local ax murder in Saint-Tropez, a parricide like Violette Nozières, a serial killer like Eugène Weidmann, or a Moroccan madam on trial for the torture-slayings of five child prostitutes infinitely more interesting than the rise of a peculiar little tyrant in Munich who didn't eat meat and didn't seem "to like fucking anybody, not even men."[13]

To say that Colette's life was a *voyage égoïste* is not to underestimate its perils, or the courage and stamina required by such a solitary expedition. But she is troubled by the storms of history only when her own vessel is in imminent danger from them. War, politics, and metaphysics are the follies of men. The female self struggling with the bonds of love remains her subject, and whether they are adventurous vagabonds or docile homebodies, Colette's women are always cloistered behind the walls of instinct.

"No one has ever built so well in the realm of imagination," writes Dominique Aury, who observes that each of Colette's heroines is furnished with a house, a boudoir, a bath, sometimes a kitchen, always a garden, set in a landscape that even in Paris "isolates it like a sea of which one can hear only the murmur."[14]

But there was enough violence in that confined, earthbound domain, enough truth and mystery behind those guarded walls, to occupy the inner lives of their inhabitants and of their author. And here one might consider how Natalie Barney defends Colette against "those critics who reproach [her] for 'too narrow a view.' Does one reproach someone for her myopia if that myopia is a sort of natural microscope that . . . details . . . all that she observes closer and better than anyone else?"[15] "She has no other care than this," concludes Aury: "to adjust herself to living."

4

IN 1935, the Claridge went bankrupt. Colette and Maurice moved a few blocks up the Champs-Élysées to a new apartment house on the corner of the rue Marignan, where they took adjoining flats on a high floor. The building had been thrown up fast, and the roof leaked, the plaster cracked when a door slammed, a summer hailstorm "wrenched the window sashes from their frames." Colette consoled herself with the view from an immense rooftop terrace, from which she could watch "the horizon stir and . . . the clouds gesticulate." From this vantage point, she could also observe the funerals and riots that now regularly took place on the Champs-Élysées and which "hardly seemed more real to me than a dream."[16]

After the debacle of the beauty business and his brief stint selling deluxe plungers, Maurice had "taken refuge" in journalism. He and the Kessel brothers briefly edited a magazine called *Confessions,* and he was contributing short articles to *Paris-Soir,* happy, he says, to be fulfilling his old ambition to write. That spring, he and Colette were invited by their respective papers to cover the maiden voyage of the *Normandie* from Le Havre to New York, where they would spend four days on shore before sailing home. They knew, writes Maurice, that American hotels would not consent to lodge an unmarried couple in the same room, but " 'if we got married,' I said jokingly, 'there wouldn't be a problem.' Colette looked at me in such a way that I suddenly understood all that this cementation of our relations meant to her."[17]

The seventeen-minute civil ceremony took place on the morning of April 3, at the town hall of the eighth arrondissement. The groom was forty-five, and the bride sixty-two. Their witnesses and only wedding guests were the van den Hensts and the Moreaus, and afterwards the bridal party drove to a country inn, where they feasted on pork knuckles and pancakes.

The afternoon was seasonably warm, but on the way home, there was a spring snowstorm. Colette asked her "old friend, and new husband," to stop the car so she could "hear" the flakes, which were falling "like a burst eiderdown." Their sound—"the quiet praying of a crowd," "the diligent turning of silky pages"—was her most treasured wedding-day souvenir.[18]

Colette announced her marriage to her closest friends only after the fact, in a sentence to Hélène, an aside to Germaine Patat, and a parenthesis to Germaine Beaumont. The newlyweds spent Easter in Saint-Tropez, embarking on their transatlantic honeymoon on the twenty-ninth of May. Colette's passport bore the name Mme Goudeket, and Lucien Lelong had furnished her with a trousseau of new coats and dresses.

The crossing took five days and set a record. Bertrand de Jouvenel was, coincidentally, one of the journalists on board. He planned to spend several months reporting from the States and to visit his lover of those years, the brilliant young American writer and future war correspondent Martha Gellhorn. Colette, who had resumed cordial if infrequent contact with her stepson, had recently been introduced to Gellhorn—a lovely blond with an acerbic wit, who was then in her late twenties—and Gellhorn recalled their encounter with ferocious amusement.

> She was a terrible woman. Absolute, utter hell. She hated me on first sight, that was obvious. She was lying on a chaise longue like an odalisque, with green shadow on her cat's eyes and a mean, bitter little mouth. She kept touching her frizzy hair, which was tinted with henna. . . . Having looked me over maliciously, she insisted that I pencil in my eyebrows—which were so blond as to be nonexistent, like the White Rabbit's—using a black crayon, so that the lines almost met in the middle. Well, I did it. Why? Because she told me to. And it was three days before some kind, candid friend said to me: "My dear, what dreadful thing have you done to your face?" She was jealous of me. . . . And Bertrand just adored her all his life. He never understood when he was in the presence of evil.[19]

Neither Maurice nor Colette mentions Bertrand's presence, but she does say that she was very sorry not to have the boat to herself, and she rose before dawn to enjoy the illusion of solitude in the winter garden, the sumptuous exercise rooms, and the labyrinth of corridors. As it was a press junket, the meals were exemplary and the accommodations, for a star of Colette's prestige, lavish. She worked in her stateroom, avoided the gossip columnists, and traded detective novels with her old friend Claude Farrère.

When the silhouette of Manhattan came into view, blurred by the dawn fog, the skyscrapers looked to Colette "like a Gothic bouquet," and she had an "almost religious seizure." The boat was met by a crowd of American journalists who had no idea who this small and stocky woman might be but were impressed by her bare feet and scarlet toenails—she was wearing her trademark sandals. The Goudekets were "disappointed" by the chaos at the customs house, having expected a display of "American efficiency." After several hours, they gave up trying to clear their luggage and taxied to their suite at the Waldorf.

Maurice and Colette quickly made "two important resolutions": to avoid the official ceremonies organized for their group and to visit New York like two young honeymooners "from Detroit or Pittsburgh." So they went to the observation deck of the Empire State Building and had their picture taken. They saw a Mae West film from two of the six thousand seats at the Roxy, and enjoyed the chorus line. They lost themselves in the streets and in Central Park, stopping for a dish of American ice cream that tasted of "prussic acid" and was decorated by a sprig of parsley.

Colette was a devotee of Parker pens—she never wrote with any others—so they made a pilgrimage to the Parker headquarters. What she saved on replenishing her supply at the source, she spent on taxis. Maurice was appalled, in fact, at how much time they were wasting in the shops ("and what shops!"), but Colette, the inveterate thrifter, fell ecstatically in love with Woolworth's and couldn't be pried loose from the bins of cheap—and, in Maurice's view, "useless"—trinkets.

One afternoon, the couple toured Harlem, which struck them as "sad and gray." On the fourth and last evening of their honeymoon, they went back to sample the nightlife. They took in the show at the Cotton Club, then the dancing and jazz at the Savoy. Colette had been expecting a scene of "frenzy" and was disappointed. But she praised the "innate art" of the dancers, the "genius" of the musicians, and she noted the difference in quality between the Negro spectacles that were packaged so slickly for Europe and the real thing. "Harlem," she wrote, "has more restraint and at the same time more fire than the nostalgic Harlem for export."[20]

Colette and Henry de
Jouvenel in Rome, 1917

Colette and Henry de
Jouvenel in the garden of
their house on the boulevard
Suchet with two dogs and
a cat. She was living the life
of a "real woman."
He was growing tired
of their "menagerie."

*C*olette's daughter, Bel-Gazou, at about three. The caption was written (in faulty French) by her English nanny, Miss Draper.

Bonjour mama chéri

*C*olette and Bel-Gazou at Castel-Novel during one of Henry de Jouvenel's home leaves from World War I

*C*olette at Rozven in the early 1920s: to her right, Francis Carco; to her left, Hélène Picard; on the step, Germaine Carco and Bertrand de Jouvenel

"Fils chéri": Colette's stepson and lover Bertrand de Jouvenel

Colette tobogganing at Gstaad during her vacations there with Bertrand in January of 1924. She had just learned to ski—a week before her fifty-first birthday.

*S*oul sisters: Colette and Marguerite Moreno in Nice, 1926, where they were performing as Léa and Charlotte in *Chéri*. On the right is Léopold Marchand.

*T*he honeymooners: Colette and Maurice Goudeket on the observation deck of the Empire State Building in New York, 1935

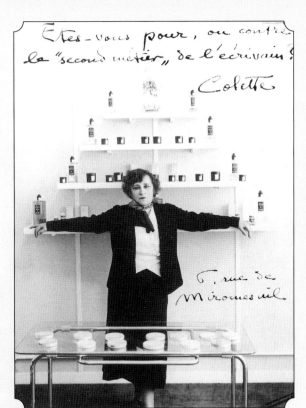

Étes-vous pour, ou contre le "second métier" de l'écrivain?

Colette

rue de Miromesnil

A svelte Colette poses in her flagship beauty salon, rue de Miromesnil, 1932. Her handwritten caption asks: "Are you for or against the writer's 'second career'?"

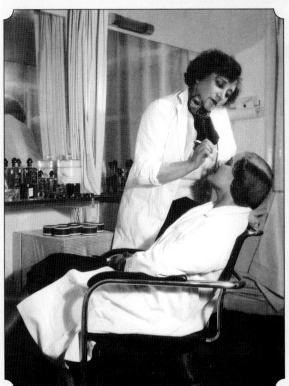

*C*olette's last fling, Georges Kessel

*M*aternal makeover: Colette demonstrates her beauty products and technique on the face of her nineteen-year-old daughter, 1932.

Colette and The Cat

Colette I and Colette II in Nice, spring 1940

Colette and Maurice in her bedroom at the Palais-Royal with the "blue lantern" behind them

*C*olette with Audrey Hepburn, who played the role of Gigi on Broadway

*C*olette and friend in the arcade of the Palais-Royal. She is wearing her trademark sandals.

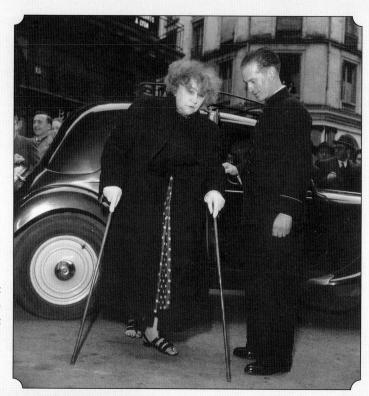

*C*olette arrives at Drouant in 1949 for the Goncourt Prize ceremony. She was seventy-six.

*T*he Great Colette and her housekeeper, Pauline, in a famous photograph by Henri Cartier-Bresson

It is a shame, however, that Colette's impressions of the black community are expressed in clichés—albeit enthusiastic ones—about its "animal vitality" and "physical aristocracy." One might object that from her this was fraternal praise, but she no longer mentioned her own African ancestry. Maurice's brother had a Haitian wife, and while Colette admired her elegance and spirit—and helped feed her during the war—she would also write: "She's not one of us, she's . . . a 'colored woman.' Her courage, like her weaknesses, is different from ours."[21]

5

COLETTE II WAS STILL determined to marry, perhaps more so since her mother had beat her to the altar. That July, she brought a new fiancé to Saint-Tropez. Camille Dausse was a surprising choice for the restless and bohemian Bel-Gazou. He was a pompous provincial doctor of thirty-two whose beard and glasses aged him prematurely. Renaud, invited to witness the introduction, disliked Dausse intensely, suspecting him of being a fortune hunter and, worse, a "cretin" and a prig.[22] The doctor discussed Colette's aches and pains with her and brought her a potted orange tree. He was probably trying to be poetic when he noted, "It's so like your daughter."[23]

A little later that summer, Colette sent a dry little note to Bel-Gazou, regretting that she hadn't heard from her, "but as my old friend Lady Westamcott wrote to me yesterday, 'I have so much to forgive you that I don't know where to begin.'. . . I didn't win anything in the last lottery—I who was counting on it to give you a dowry."[24]

On August 7, Bel-Gazou announced to her mother that she was marrying Dausse four days later at Castel-Novel. Henry de Jouvenel had arranged a picturesque country wedding for the couple, which Colette would not attend. It isn't clear whether she was excluded from the festivities or chose to forgo them, but she took moral credit for her absence, telling her daughter that while she wouldn't be there to worry over the dress or to give her "the timeless, ordinary advice of all mothers," it was "better" this way. Why? Because "nerves get old, even mine." And because Bel-Gazou had such a "charming face" and Castel-Novel so many memories, she was afraid that she wouldn't be able to master "the most evident signs of emotion."[25]

A few weeks after the wedding, the newlyweds visited Colette in Saint-Tropez. She thought that they seemed "good" together, neither too nervous nor too ecstatic. "Above all, they have the air of having known each other well, and for a long time. Insh'Allah!"[26] They actually knew each other so superficially that the marriage didn't survive the honeymoon. Bel-Gazou later told Renaud that she had probably married Dausse "because I wanted to normalize myself." "She must have begun very early," he told Richardson, "to have relations with girls or women."[27]

It also isn't clear how much of her predicament she explained to Colette, who announced the separation tersely to Hélène Picard: "Definitive motive: physical repulsion. One can't argue with it."[28] She asked her friend to keep it confidential. But for once, Bel-Gazou had her mother's sympathy. "You're twenty-two, dearest *chou*. I don't want you to be unhappy at twenty-two. When you're forty-two, you undoubtedly won't be able to help it. One never escapes it, and perhaps that's good. Now go to your father and tell him the oracle has spoken." Henry was equally understanding. The problem with Dausse, he told Bel-Gazou, was that he was a pedant who had bored her—and him, too. "Being bored by someone can make you think of murder. I left many women because of that. Rid me of this gentleman and never forget, as Montesquieu says, that solemnity is the shield of fools."[29]

Jouvenel promised his daughter he would help her to divorce, presumably by making her a generous allowance. But he didn't live to keep his word. On October 3, 1935, Mussolini invaded Abyssinia. This was a blow to Europe, and to Henry personally. In 1923, it was Jouvenel who had introduced the motion to admit Abyssinia to the League of Nations. He had served as ambassador to Rome until 1934, cultivating Mussolini's goodwill—and his personal friendship—on behalf of a military alliance which France deemed strategically urgent, and which was meant to fortify both countries against Hitler's menace to the Balkans and his threat to reunite Germany and Austria.

On the afternoon of the fifth, the baron was at home on the rue Férou, collecting his thoughts about the crisis. He received his elder son, with whom he was now reconciled. Bertrand had since become a prominent political journalist, impassioned, like his father, by the ideals of the League of Nations. As he had just returned from America, father and son discussed the New Deal and Roosevelt's foreign policy. Henry then told Bertrand that in the wake of the invasion, Premier Pierre Laval had asked him to head the Foreign Ministry in his rightist government. France needed someone respected by the English—Laval wasn't—and trusted by Mussolini. But Jouvenel hadn't yet decided whether to accept.

That evening, Henry took his wife to the automobile show at the Grand-Palais, then sent her home with their chauffeur and went for a late-night constitutional on the Champs-Élysées. Around midnight, two policemen saw a "well-built gentleman" collapse on the sidewalk and rushed him to a hospital. Henry died that night of a massive embolism. He was fifty-nine.

Colette hadn't seen her second husband in twelve years, and she had been shocked when someone showed her a recent photograph: "He's finished!" she exclaimed. Told that Jouvenel's heart had killed him, she was said to have retorted, "No kidding." She may also have spoken callously about his death to Bel-Gazou. According to Michel del Castillo, Colette de Jouvenel had suffered through her mother's tirades—delivered with "the crudity and disgust of an unextinguished hatred"—about Henry's adventures with women, including the rumor that he had died in the company of a streetwalker.[30]

As soon as she got the news, Colette wrote to Renaud: "You can imagine that I didn't learn about this death without feeling a great, sudden chill. Let me be a bit egotistical, in my fashion, which is to worry that it should happen just as Jouvenel was giving some useful support to [his daughter], who's going through a rough period, and taking her nasty adventure [marriage] too seriously."[31] She also wrote a condolence letter, not, certainly, to the devastated widow, but to Germaine Patat. "I think that this death will revive deep memories for you, and there's no emotion of yours that isn't mine." And she repeated her irritation at the bad timing of Henry's demise.[32]

6

EVERY SECTOR OF the French economy was suffering from the Depression. Colette's work continued to sell—both *Duo* and *The Cat* had initial print runs of forty thousand copies—but the Goudekets were, or felt themselves to be, living on the edge. Having written her own ads for the beauty business, Colette now lent her name and pen to other companies, writing promotional material for Lucky Strike cigarettes, Ford cars, Perrier water, a chain of wine shops, a line of mattresses, and a silk manufacturer.

Maurice conceived a plan to make some money from Colette's vast backlog of unpublished manuscripts. He founded a private book club called The Friends of Colette.[33] For a thousand francs, each subscriber was to receive four luxuriously printed, limited editions of Colette's *Notebooks* that would not be for sale on the open market. Maurice chose the texts, and Colette's artist friends—Dignimont, Segonzac, Daragnès, and Moreau—did the illustrations. But the project was a failure—there weren't enough subscriptions—and Colette never took much interest in it. Today, the *Notebooks* are collector's items.[34]

Colette didn't have time to rummage through her archives because she was too busy generating new work. She wrote the screenplay for Max Ophüls's film *Divine*, which was based on her *Music Hall Sidelights*, and she took part in the production. She was also writing *My Apprenticeships*, which was published in 1936. As I have discussed the memoir at length in earlier chapters, it remains only to ask why Colette should choose this moment to resurrect and rebury Willy.

Shortly after his death, an obscure magazine called *Sur le Riviera* had published two pieces of "Willyana," which consisted of notes on his collaboration with Colette. "I'm reading a ravishing article," Colette told her old friend Vuillermoz, "composed of extracts from M. Willy's correspondence, where he says, complaining sweetly about my laziness, that for *Minne* I practically let him labor on his own. One of these days I'll get angry, sweetly."[35]

She took no immediate action except to ask Vallette for copies of his contracts with Willy,[36] perhaps hoping to find something she could use to contest them. As it turned out, there was no remedy either for the new or the old perfidy except to continue, as she always had, vilifying her ex-husband with gusto whenever his name was mentioned in her presence. Liane de Pougy was only one of the many celebrity diarists who recorded Colette's dinner-table rants with shock (shock!) and with relish.

In the mid-thirties, as Jacques Dupont observes, the Belle Époque was enjoying a nostalgic revival, thanks in part to recent memoirs of their apprenticeships by Paul Morand, Polaire, and Jean Cocteau. Polaire and Cocteau briefly evoked the young Colette, and they probably also inspired her—great rival and fierce competitor that she was—to think that she could do herself and the period better justice. Dupont agrees with the contemporary reviewers that her portrait of the era—"the most authentic and animated documentary that we have on the first years of the century"—is what is finest in *My Apprenticeships*.[37]

She had never before written anything so explicitly confessional, at least not in the form of a memoir. If she needed a provocation to do so, she got one that year, when Albin Michel, who owned the copyright to *Claudine at School*, sold the film rights to a producer named Jacques Hail.[38] Colette noted to Claude Chauvière that the publisher had volunteered to give her a small cut of the sale, but hardly the sum that would have been her due, and there were three other novels in the series, each a potential windfall that she couldn't touch.[39]

The Claudine books, as Colette had so often said, were her children. By now they were grown children who should have been helping to support their mother in her old age. Thanks to Willy, she was still condemned to "forced labor"[40] at the age of sixty-two. This combination of financial stress and freshly revived outrage was inflammatory.

"Insight—the titillating knack for hurting!" exclaims Colette in *The Pure and the Impure*, and it makes a concise enough epigraph for *My Apprenticeships*. She worked fast, with none of her usual complaints, avenging her impotence with a thrilling display of virtuosity. What sweeter recompense for the frauds perpetrated by a hack than to make him the villain of a masterpiece?

There were critics who remarked justly on the memoir's "sobriety and power" and on the "passionate coldness" of "a portrait more imposing than cruel."[41] Most, however, judged Colette severely for it. " 'Aunt Colette, you have done a bad deed," said Willy's niece, Paulette Gauthier-Villars. "My child," Colette replied, "I know it."[42]

7

IN THE SPRING of 1936, the Popular Front won the parliamentary elections, and a general strike that began among auto and aviation workers before spreading to almost every other industry paralyzed the country. In June, Léon Blum became the premier of a left-wing government, backed by a coalition of radicals, socialists, and communists. He took immediate steps to alleviate the hardships of the working class, sponsoring legislation that raised salaries and mandated paid sick leaves and a forty-hour workweek. He also created an under-ministry for the protection of women and children, which was headed by Suzanne Lacore, the first woman in a French cabinet.

Colette was apparently willing to lend her name to this effort, for among the papers of Louise Weiss, an activist for women's rights, is a short, rather perfunctory public statement "applauding everything that women . . . will attempt, individually or in groups, in favor of public health, the physical and moral protection of childhood, and with the goal of improving their own condition. I wish them all good luck. As for courage, they don't lack it."[43]

She was more enthusiastic when it came to championing women in the arts, and in 1937, she ventured a protest against the sexism of the theater world. Alice Cocéa had just taken over the direction of the Théâtre des Champs-Élysées, and Colette reviewed her first production, Musset's *On ne badine pas avec l'amour:*

> This steely young woman has already, in six or eight weeks, recruited a company with discernment, chosen the sets, directed the rehearsals night and day, overseen the production of the costumes—and here I am only speaking about her practical tasks. No one dreams of quibbling about her courage and, at the moment, her success. My feminism, which is very subdued, simply observes that regarding the revival of a charming theater, the praise and admiration would be less discreet if the labor, the independence of spirit, the success were those of a man and not of a woman who doesn't weigh more than a lamb.[44]

It had been twenty-five years since Colette declared that feminists deserved the whip and the harem. In 1927, she had discussed her views on the women's movement with Walter Benjamin, who interviewed her at the

Palais-Royal for *Die literarische Welt*. Women, she told the great Marxist critic, should never participate actively in public life. Politics could only encourage the native "brutality of the feminine character" and whet women's recently discovered "taste for power," which she pegged to the "fashion for dieting." Slimness was "masculinizing" them, she declared. In twenty years, "women will be as flat as boards." She also added that even those women— and she knew some—who were "well-balanced" and "intelligent" enough to serve on a jury or a commission still experienced "monthly" bouts of moodiness and irritability that rendered them unfit to make important decisions.[45]

Over the years, however, she had done her part, both privately and in public, to champion women's writing. She had served on the jury of the Prix Fémina and had been a generous mentor to Germaine Beaumont, Claude Chauvière, Hélène Mourhange, Hélène Picard, and others. Her insistence on being fairly remunerated set a salutary precedent, and when an editor of *Nouvelles littéraires* protested that André Gide accepted a quarter of what she asked for an article, she replied: "André Gide is wrong. If famous writers act as he does, what will the starving ones be able to get?"[46]

In *Bella-Vista*, a collection of three novellas and a short story she published that year, Colette distills her indignation at the exploitation of women—and of a dark-skinned male servant who does women's work. The title piece, she told Hélène Picard, was the "meager fruit of my vacation (?)," composed at Saint-Tropez, where it is set, during the summer of 1936. She wrote "The Patriarch" ("Le Sieur Binard") that autumn, "Gribiche" and "The Rendezvous" between May and October of 1937. The novella, observes Goudeket, was "henceforth her preferred genre. It represented neither an impoverishment nor a loss of patience, but a willed divestment."[47]

Maurice is right, and readers searching for Colette at her purest will find her in the late novellas. It's as if she were adjusting her style, like a diet, to a more sedentary and less flamboyant life. Gone is the acrobatic syntax of *The Pure and the Impure* and the linguistic gourmandise still evident in *The Cat*. As she aged, wrote Goudeket, "Colette increasingly refused what came most easily to her," and when, one evening, he found her tearing up the day's work, she explained that she had caught herself in the act of "doing Colette."[48]

In an essay on the novel, published as she was finishing *Bella-Vista*, Colette declared: "I am certain of never having written a novel—a real one— a work of pure imagination, free from the alluvia of memory and egotism. . . . What I call real novels are the ones I read, not the ones I write."[49] But this is too modest. "Pure fiction" is a prosecutorial expression. It suits an alibi better than a work of art.

Three of the impure fictions in *Bella-Vista* are narrated in the first person, and they purport to be remembered rather than invented. All of the stories concern "a guilty secret," as Marie-Christine Bellosta puts it, which is sexual in nature. The "lesbian" proprietors of the hotel in "Bella-Vista" are, in fact, a man and a woman, he a fugitive from the law. Their client, M. Daste, is a sadist who tortures birds. Mme Saure in "Gribiche" is a backstreet abortionist who lets her daughter bleed to death. The peasant father in "The Patriarch" considers it his right to deflower and impregnate his daughters, the youngest not fifteen. Bernard, the French architect in "The Rendezvous," obsesses about a woman until the moment he is forced to choose between sleeping with her and saving the life of Ahmed, the wounded Moroccan boy: "One doesn't easily find a child in the shape of a man, hurt enough, unknown enough, precious enough to sacrifice some hours of one's life to him, not to mention the jacket of a suit and a night of love."[50]

Bernard's sacrifice at the end of "The Rendezvous" is rare if not unique in Colette's oeuvre. Its ambiguity is what makes it credible: he isn't risking much when he saves Ahmed—the selfish and vulgar Rose wasn't worth keeping—and Colette suggests that there is a homoerotic undertow to his compassion. But her own embrace of compassion is the real revelation of *Bella-Vista*.

The narrator, "Colette," figures as a sheltered girl, a bourgeoise slumming in the music hall, a well-fixed woman writer preoccupied with doing up her country house and with "the shameless necessity of speaking of love in my own name." This woman considers herself worldly, someone who knows hard work and suffering, but in every story her eyes are opened to a reality more brutish than she has imagined. After visiting Gribiche in her tenement and seeing the effects of her botched abortion, Colette goes home to "dream about anxieties which had never, until then, been my lot." They will never be her lot; her feeling of solidarity is ephemeral. She implicates herself in the crimes that she witnesses but does nothing to prevent them, and that's partly the point of the book. "I was born under the sign of passivity," she writes in her essay on the novel, which is a more far-reaching admission than it seems. But she also has the decency never to forget that she's a cherished daughter, a well-paid professional, and a curious tourist just passing time in the lower depths between engagements, brushing against but not sharing the squalid reality of the condemned: fragile creatures like the chorus girls in "Gribiche," the abused children in "The Patriarch," the pregnant housemaid and symbolic birds in "Bella-Vista"—all doomed to be preyed on.

There are many guilty secrets in *Bella-Vista,* collective and personal, and the narrator's self-absorption is one of them. Colette is too much of a pagan to judge the fallen for their sins, and too conservative to believe that human nature is capable of reform. What she does here for the first time outside her journalism is to bear witness to poverty, incest, racism, and exploitation, and—because she is writing as an artist, not a journalist—to mistrust the witness that she bears.

The social conscience Colette manifests in *Bella-Vista* was not lost on the critics, at least the more discriminating ones. The Catholic press savaged the book, and the reviewer for *Le Figaro* entirely missed its point, deploring her "nauseating" characters and taking the conventional view of her "primitive" morality and the coincidence of "an impoverished soul in a rich nature." But André Thérive compares her achievement to the "social portraiture" of Gorky, and Bellosta comments that by "examining what is most inadmissible and atrocious about the female condition," Colette expresses a sense of sisterhood which links her to future generations.[51]

THE IMPASSIONED ACTIVISM of the era may have inspired Colette's solidarity with exploited women and colonized men, and her outrage at those fin de siècle laws that still, in 1937, encouraged a high birthrate—the production of cannon fodder—by denying women access to safe abortion. It may have stirred her to examine her own privilege and complacence—but not to the point of refusing to publish "The Patriarch" and "The Rendezvous" in *Candide*, an organ of L'Action Française, and "Bella-Vista" and "Gribiche" in the rabidly anti-Semitic and pro-fascist weekly *Gringoire*.

The publisher of *Gringoire* was Horace de Carbuccia, a rich Corsican with whom Colette had a casual social relationship, mostly in Saint-Tropez. In the late twenties, Carbuccia's politics and those of the weekly were anti-Marxist but center-left, and Joseph Kessel was the literary editor. Kessel recruited his writer friends, Colette among them, and *Gringoire* had a distinguished roster of contributors. By the mid-thirties, however, Carbuccia had become an apologist for Hitler, and an outraged Kessel had departed.

In 1931, Colette had sold Kessel the serial rights to *Ces Plaisirs . . . (The Pure and the Impure)*, but after running three installments—about half the book—Carbuccia intervened and suspended its publication. He didn't alert Colette beforehand; he simply cut off her text mid-sentence with the word *Fin*. Some readers, he explained lamely, had objected to her subject matter. It was an astounding insult to so eminent a writer, and Colette was furious.[52] But five years later, she either found it in her heart to forgive Carbuccia or, what is likelier, swallowed her pride: "funds were low," as Willy used to say, and *Gringoire*, which paid extremely well, had a circulation of some 650,000 readers.

Bella-Vista began running in *Gringoire* on September 18, 1936. The contents of the issue gave the irony of the title a new dimension. There was a glowing report from Carbuccia's man in Nuremberg on the annual Nazi rally; a front-page exposé on the "non-French" (i.e., Jewish) background of Léon Blum; a cartoon showing Jewish and other anti-fascist refugees from Germany stuffed into trash cans and captioned "France, the garbage dump of Europe"; and a vicious article, one of a series, smearing Roger Salengro, Blum's minister of the interior and the architect of his labor reforms.

The campaign against Salengro was based on the false claim that he had deserted from the front during the First World War. It was orchestrated by a man Colette calls "that stout, gallant Henri Béraud"[53] (referring, however, not to his politics, but to his kindness in cheering up a depressed Claude Chauvière). Her friend Béraud was a writer and critic who had won the Prix Goncourt in 1922 but by the mid-thirties had abandoned literature to write polemics for Carbuccia. Salengro gassed himself to death a few weeks after Béraud's series—and Colette's novella—had finished running. And it wasn't the last piece of fiction she would publish in *Gringoire*.

CHAPTER 39

1

I N N O V E M B E R O F 1 9 3 7, Colette gave an interview to a journalist from *Paris-midi* who had heard that she was once again changing her address. The Goudekets were fed up with their jerry-built aerie on the rue Marignan and had found an apartment—a wreck with a fine view—in the place Vendôme. Colette coyly pretended that her legendary love of moving was a "lie": "First of all, I've moved only fourteen times, each time forced to do so by an absolute necessity."[1] She would never have left the Palais-Royal, she continued, if she had managed to get the apartment that she had always coveted, one flight above her old cave on the mezzanine. The day after the interview appeared, Colette received a letter from the occupant of that apartment. He had just read that she "lusted" after it, so he was "ceding" it to her. "There's sunlight, the gardens . . . the air! Everything!" she exulted to a new protégée, Renée Hamon.[2]

Colette's triumphant homecoming to the first floor of 9, rue de Beaujolais, her final and most famous abode, was delayed by a mover's strike, but she was settled in by the beginning of the new year. By then, Renée Hamon was back from a twenty-month voyage to Tahiti, and Colette gave her "little corsair" the house tour: in the front, two elegant, high-ceilinged rooms looking out on the quadrangle; a small adjoining salon opening to a dining room with a leaky stained-glass ceiling; in the back, a bedroom for Pauline with a window on the street. It was "her" Palais-Royal, Colette told Renée—a provincial village in the heart of Paris. Everyone recognized her: the bookseller in the arcade, the friendly hookers, the man who sold crêpes on the corner, the neighbors who shouted greetings from their open windows. The tenants downstairs were a cultivated Russian émigrée and her daughter, with whom Colette formed a deep attachment. The concierge was a deaf erotomane prematurely wasted by her passionate exertions, which had "recently driven her husband to his grave."[3]

Colette paused briefly to sympathize with Renée about an article on her travels which had been crudely abbreviated by its editors at *L'Intransigeant* ("They always cut, little one!"), then told her to "get lost: When you see me in a dressing gown like this, it means I'm working."[4]

Colette and Renée Hamon had been acquainted for twelve years, but their intimacy was recent. At thirty-eight, Renée was still small and lithe, with the head of a sailorboy on the body of a waif; and like Claudine, of whom she was an echo, she was attracted to fatherly men and sensual women. At three, she'd been abandoned by her mother, and she had been raised by her Breton grand-parents. By her mid-twenties, she had been married and divorced and had lost her only child. A wartime love affair with an American officer lured her to New York, but when the romance foundered, Renée supported herself by teaching French, returning after eighteen months with the short hair and skirts of a flapper.

According to Goudeket, Renée "was truly possessed by the demon of adventure." In the port city of Nantes, she entered a beauty contest that she didn't win, but one of the judges brought her to Paris. When they parted, Renée lived on her charms, doing a little modeling, a little painting—she spe-cialized in seascapes—and auditioning for minor roles in the movies. She was photogenic but she couldn't act or paint, so she went looking for a job in fash-ion, and in 1925, she met Paul Poiret, who was, writes Pichois, "seduced by her wit." Poiret introduced her to Colette when they were performing together in *The Vagabond*.

Renée was then twenty-seven, Colette fifty-one. A courtship ensued, Renée taking the aggressive role. "It's easy to meet Beings who excite you," she wrote, "but beings who bowl you over . . ." She wooed Colette with rare and expensive flowers, which she paid for with her grocery money. Colette replied with brief thank-you notes and occasional invitations, although, as Pichois remarks, "there's nothing [in this correspondence] between 1925 and 1932 that presages a great friendship."[5]

In 1928, Renée married a Swedish translator named Harald Heyman, who was thirty years her senior. In 1933, she left him in Europe, embarking on a round-the-world bicycle trip which lasted for three years. This adventure did nothing to dampen what Maurice calls Renée's "burning" ambition to be "intimate" with Colette. Upon her return, she began dispatching her "discreet emissaries"—a dwarf azalea, a rare camellia, the fragrant daphnes of her native province—and by April of 1936, Colette was saying *tu* to her.

Renée would live out Colette's tomboy fantasies of running off to sea, and she was already planning her Tahitian journey. Her aim was to follow in Gauguin's footsteps and "to reconstruct his life in the solitude of the Pacific." An influential friend arranged free passage for her on a French research ship, and *L'Intransigeant* commissioned a series of articles. She also planned to make a documentary and considered the possibility that Bel-Gazou, who had some experience in film, might go along as her assistant. Colette was skeptical: "Don't count on my daughter. She is resolute only in words. She's a charming child whom I adore, but she 'consumes' time without employing it."[6]

While Colette wrote *Bella-Vista,* Renée explored the "isles of light"— Tahiti, Tuamotu, and the Marquesas. Her husband joined her there, staying behind to become a beach bum. Her reportage, writes Pichois, was "courageously" critical of the "negligent" colonials who had used Gauguin's sculptures for firewood and imported squalor and disease to the Tahitian paradise. Renée eventually turned her articles into a book, for which Colette helped her find a publisher. It wasn't a work of literature, so the mentor hesitated when the protégée asked for a preface to endorse it as such. She writes, instead, about Renée's vocation as a vagabond, her "hard little Breton head," her "human pity," and her "chaste friendship with young island women devoid of malice or virtue."

If Colette's preface is evasive about Renée's talents as a writer, it is revealing about her attractions as a minion—a *mignonne,* in the old French sense of the word: a royal favorite, privy to the monarch's confidences, outfitted in her image, petted, protected, and, just as fondly, mistreated. "She whom I call the little corsair," writes Colette, ". . . stands before me looking like a timid schoolgirl. It's doubtless because I have a nasty air." And she goes on to describe how she instills confidence in Renée, who doesn't think that she can write:

> Two years ago, while she was getting ready to go off again, I wanted to put the notion into her head that the best witnesses to a voyage . . . are not photographs, straw mats, sarongs, songs, seashells . . . or even a piece of living wood cut by Gauguin's knife. I dug my spurs into her silence, which is that of an authentic vagabond. In short, I aspired to compel her to recount, in black and white, what she would have seen and done, and which serves us who are sedentary as a substitute egoist's voyage. . . . I didn't succeed on the first try. As with children, I had to threaten and manipulate. This corsair with the little foot reacted in a puerile fashion, and even whimpered, repeating: "But I don't know how to make a book.". . . Renée Hamon went off as if I'd beaten her[7]

Colette always liked to have her bullying "repaid with results," and the corsair came back with a manuscript, the first of many which Colette used her contacts to promote. Renée venerated Colette and gratified her need to dominate, but what was more essential, she fulfilled the promise Colette had seen in her. She wasn't a dilettante like Bel-Gazou, a martyr like Claude Chauvière, or a self-destroyer like "Smoke" Kessel, and her mobility, spiritual and literal, helped rejuvenate Colette as her own vigor was undermined by age and debility. "Bit by bit," writes Maurice, "they tied the knot of one of the most moving bonds of friendship that adorned Colette's life."[8]

Like so many royal favorites, Renée was also something of a spy, and Colette discovered that she was secretly keeping notes on their conversations, which she intended to publish in a book called *Colette and Friendship*. As Colette's prime requisite for a confidante was discretion, this discovery gave both Goudekets pause, and particularly the possessive Maurice. By then, however, Renée was suffering from the uterine cancer that would kill her at forty-six, and Colette didn't have the heart to reproach her for what was a well-meant, but in her own view misguided, betrayal of trust.

Renée's journal and her correspondence with Colette were eventually published, somewhat bowdlerized. They are illuminating but less incisive, in their sum, than a press clipping that I found in a small file of the corsair's papers belonging to a passionate collector of Colettiana, and which eloquently suggests the challenge of being Colette's friend, or her biographer: "Colette's art is that of the lie, but the great game she plays with us is, precisely, to stuff her best lies with great flashes of truth. To read her with pleasure thus consists of disentangling, with a deft pair of tweezers, the true from the false. I have enjoyed this game of patience for a very long time. One must fatigue oneself . . . as much as she has done in surrendering to the shocks of her fate, in order to love her with that hard-won justice."[9]

2

IN MARCH 1938, the Nazi Blackshirts and their tanks paraded through Vienna past cheering crowds, and the *Anschluss* began. In April, Léon Blum resigned and Daladier formed a new right-wing French government. In June, Colette quit *Le Journal*, then immediately began contributing to *Paris-Soir*. Earlier that month, Bel-Gazou had an emergency appendectomy. The operation was performed by Henri Mondor, the celebrated surgeon, historian, and biographer of Mallarmé, who had also treated the Kessels after their accident and consulted on Colette's broken leg. He forbade her to visit the hospital—perhaps at Bel-Gazou's request—but Colette "disobeyed." She later told Mondor that her daughter had cried like a small child.

Bel-Gazou now lived a somewhat aimless and spendthrift life, vacationing with friends in Gstaad, taking and leaving jobs, occasionally bouncing checks. She made very little effort to stay in touch with her mother, who she knew disapproved. She had long since come to depend on Renaud de Jouvenel for the support, material and emotional, that her parents couldn't or wouldn't give her. Colette and Henry had "found it quite simple," he told Richardson, "that I should replace them."[10]

After Jouvenel's death, Renaud's wife, Arlette, bought Castel-Novel, and he gave Bel-Gazou the neighboring estate of Curemonte, which he had inherited from his uncle Robert. Colette was always grateful for Renaud's generosity to Bel-Gazou, and it was mainly through him that she kept abreast of her daughter's movements. "I would be so foolish as to worry about her," she tells him in a typical letter from Saint-Tropez, "had passing friends [Bertrand and Carbuccia] not seen her in good health in Paris."[11]

COLETTE SPENT WHAT WAS to be her last summer on the Riviera working on *The Toutounier*, which was published in March of 1939. This sequel to *Duo* is one of Colette's least appreciated novellas. It is told from the perspective of the widowed Alice, who returns, sobered and deepened by Michel's death—and as this is a Colette story, enriched by his life insurance—to the dingy Left Bank artist's studio where she and her three sisters grew up. Two of them, Hermine and Colombe, still live there, eking out a living and suffering the humiliations of love affairs with married men. The destiny of the youngest and most beautiful, Bizoute, is played out offstage. She has thrown herself away on a worthless filmmaker, and she's off starving with him in the Marquesas. Her character is a little homage to Renée Hamon. Like so many of Colette's heroines (and friends), the Eude sisters are *orphelines de mère* who have been raised by their musician father. They belong to that strata of Parisian society that Colette best loves and understands, the bohemian working class, and she describes their milieu and their struggles to escape its claustrophobia with a precision of detail worthy of Balzac.

The Toutounier is the family reunion of three women whom we see simultaneously as types and as individuals. Each one of them represents a "different, inevitable stage," as Michel Mercier puts it, of innocence and disillusion. Hermine, desperate to land her married lover, tries to kill his wife. Colombe, fearful of surrender, examines her platonic attachment to a conductor who has just been offered a good job in the provinces. Alice, both liberated and abandoned by the husband who has killed himself, reflects on death, autonomy, and desire.

The title of the novella refers to an enormous old leather sofa, an inanimate family mascot, that is the centerpiece of the studio, and where, in the last scene, the sisters sleep entwined in one another's arms. Had Colette wanted to be more ironic and less modest, she might have called her novella *Woman's Fate*. It's her version of the grander epics about the solidarity among warriors told by writers like Malraux, Kessel, and Saint-Exupéry. The studio is an exclusive, single-sex commune like any trench or encampment. Its inmates smoke and drink hard, dissemble their fierce mutual tenderness with tough talk, devour a good meal when they can, and live cheerfully in their squalor. While they fantasize about escape, they will discover, later, that a life of comfort in the world seems insipid by comparison.

Like warriors, too, the Eude girls observe a stoical code of silence about their hardships. Colette's feeling for them is like that of a general for his troops. She loves them from a distance, safe herself and aware that she can't spare them risks or pain. They fight as naively as do young soldiers for the ideal of a decent life, but she knows that the conflict is impure at its core, and that its outcome will be disillusioning.

Hermine and Colombe are still innocent enough to have a romantic notion of victory, which is, by the conventions governing the wars between men and women, the bourgeois marriage. Alice, the bloodied veteran, knows better. Her sisters will leave the chaste *toutounier* for their dubious men, as Bizoute has, and maybe one day Alice will go off with a stranger, too. "We can never resist a man," she thinks. "It's only in death that we don't follow him." But she also understands that they will never be better cherished and known than they are, in their virginal redoubt, by one another.

3

BY MID-SEPTEMBER, Colette was back in Paris, dining with Georges Kessel at the rue de Beaujolais. Hitler had announced his designs on the Sudetenland, and France had called up a million men. A new war now seemed inevitable, and the Goudekets, like all citizens with a private car, received a letter informing them that their vehicle might be requisitioned by the military. Colette told Moune, who was still in Saint-Tropez, that she and Maurice were both negotiating to write for *Paris-Soir* and that "everything would be splendid if human folly weren't hovering about our heads." The evening news, she continued, "was terribly black. Aren't you thinking of coming back before the cat gives birth? We'll see the war begin together, and make our plans."[12]

Later that month, however, Mussolini, Chamberlain, and Daladier met with the German chancellor in Munich and negotiated the treaty they believed would forestall any further annexations of territory in Central Europe. In November, with peace provisionally assured, Colette and Maurice went abroad. *Paris-Soir* had dispatched them to Fez to cover the sensational murder trial of one Oum-El-Hassen, known professionally as Moulay, a Moroccan prostitute who had operated a famous whorehouse for French officers outside Meknès.

During the colonial uprisings of 1912 and 1925, Moulay had hidden some of her clients, barring her door to the mob with her own body. She'd killed an attacker and received a bullet wound. Her grateful protégés took up a collection and proposed her for the Legion of Honor, which—Rachilde would have been pleased to note—at least this one whore didn't receive. But "Moulay's unbound spirit," wrote Colette, "escaped the passivity that ambushes women . . . enslaved to men."

Moulay didn't, however, escape the ravages of age, or of an addiction to hashish or to that "bloody and joyful cruelty" which, Colette tells us, "had been her lot since childhood." In 1936, some urchins playing in an overgrown lot behind her house found a coffin stuffed with a dismembered body. The madam "condescended" to allow that the corpse had been one of her girls. As they were interrogating her, the police heard a faint scratching behind a wall, and when they broke it down, they found four more teenage girls and a thirteen-year-old boy barely alive—all had been tortured with knives and rope. Of the fourteen child prostitutes in Moulay's establishment, four were dead, three were missing, and seven had been irreparably crippled.

Moulay never admitted and never seemed to understand her guilt. "What words or images can we use to make Oum-El-Hassen understand what we mean by cruelty," asks Colette, "and how could the accused murderer and torturer communicate to us her conviction that she is innocent? What we call cruelty was ordinary life to her. . . . Everything that bruised, wounded, or dessicated was from the beginning her fate as an adventurous girl. Where would she have learned that the punishment one inflicts on women, which is to say on beings who have, properly speaking, no value at all, has any limits?"[13]

As the toothless madam in her immaculate white veils listened impassively to the evidence of her victims and her accomplice—a debauched old slave who eagerly demonstrated his garrotting technique for the court—another army-loving murderer with a patriotic bent was preparing to purge the European continent of the beings he, too, considered subhuman. On September 1, 1939, Hitler invaded Poland. On September 3, France and England declared war on Germany.

The Goudekets had spent the last weeks of August vacationing in Dieppe with the Marchands. Maurice had traveled north from Saint-Tropez with a mass exodus of English tourists. The weather, Colette told Renée Hamon, was as beautiful as it had been in 1914, when she and Musidora had driven through a Breton landscape thrumming with bells to reach Paris. Much against Maurice's wishes—"he begged me to stay here," she told Hélène Picard—they returned to the capital.

Maurice was fifty, so he wasn't called up for active duty, although he was on standby for service in the reserves. On night three of the war, Paris had its first air-raid alert. He convinced Colette that she should "set an example" and go down to the cellar with her neighbors. After two nights of sharing the damp and sinister seventeenth-century vaults of the Palais-Royal with the deaf countess, the sex-crazed concierge, Pierre Lazareff (her editor at *Paris-soir*) and his family, who lived next door, and various other neighbors, all of whom behaved with impeccable aplomb, she refused ever to return—even, notes Maurice, during the intense bombing raids of 1944.

The overcrowding didn't bother her; it was the lack of air—she declared that she would rather brave the bombs than suffocate. So when the sirens sounded, as they did unpredictably, Colette opened her windows to spare the glass, propped her elbows on the sill, and contemplated the blacked-out expanse of Richelieu's great quadrangle. "I would never have believed," she told her old friend Hélène, "that the human race would come to this point once again."[14]

4

THE OUTBREAK OF WAR overshadowed a series of poignant deaths and significant displacements in Colette's private life. In February of 1939, The Cat, riddled with cancer, had to be put down, and Souci the bulldog expired of epilepsy a month later. Colette vowed never to replace them, and their deaths initiated her into an unfamiliar and particularly austere form of solitude: living without an animal.

That April, Claude Chauvière died. Colette wrote a moving obituary for her. In June, she sold La Treille Muscate with all its furnishings to the actor Charles Vanel, thus ending her long romance with the Côte d'Azur. Mussolini, she told Hélène Picard, was to blame for the bad bargain she made—he had just signed his "pact of steel" with Hitler, and Saint-Tropez was a short skip from the Italian border.

Maurice was annoyed that his wife had, as usual, accepted the first offer from the first prospective buyer without haggling, "afraid that he'd change his mind." He wasn't anxious about the impact of fascism on coastal real estate, although he readily admitted that Colette's celebrity had made the resort uninhabitable for them. Their house was only eighteen hundred yards from the village, and tourists trooped past the gate, picked the lock, rang the bell, invaded the beach, picnicked in the garden, gawked at Colette when she did her shopping, and importuned her for autographs and dedications. She had been particularly outraged when she discovered that a local stationer was selling picture postcards of the property, captioned "Villa de Collette [sic]."

After clearing their mortgage, they had enough money left to buy and renovate a very pretty country property called Le Parc in the village of Méré, near Montfort-l'Amaury, though they didn't get much use of it in the first months of the war: their construction crew was drafted, and then the army requisitioned Le Parc as a barracks. Colette was bitter about it: "You'll never make me understand," she complained to her friend in Toulon, Alice Bénard-Fleury, "why our military so urgently needs a doll's house."[15]

COLETTE TOLD Denise Tual, her neighbor at the Palais-Royal, that she liked spending her wars in Paris. Her friends in the provinces—Alice in the Var, Renée Hamon in Brittany, and Yvonne Brochard and Thérèse Sourisse, two pious fans who lived in Normandy, outside Nantes, and whom Colette addressed fondly as her "little farmers"[16]—all kept her well provisioned. When she discovered that her concierge was starving and that the unemployed former shopgirl who lived in one of the maids' rooms didn't have a cent, she fed them. The Russian countess and her daughter were eking out a meager living doing knitting, and Colette got Germaine Patat to commission their handiwork. She took up embroidery herself, to pass the time—"it's a vice I manage to satisfy only in wartime"—and made tapestry seat covers for herself and friends. Literature, she noted, had "suppressed" her vocation as a needlewoman, but war evoked another true calling: as a hoarder. By the end of October, Colette's coal cellar was full, and her stores would see her through the bitter winter of '41.

Polaire had died two weeks before. By then, Léo Colette—"the only brother left to me"—lay dying, too. He had collapsed in the stairwell of his tenement in the first few days of the war, and Colette and Maurice had managed to find enough gasoline to evacuate him to the safety of a clinic near the house of their niece Geneviève, in Bléneau, not far from Saint-Sauveur. "A strange and efficacious chasm has always stood between him and reality," Colette reflected to Charles Saglio, who had just lost his own brother. "But . . . he will take away with him our common childhood, and an irreplaceable cache of memories."[17]

Léo held out until March, but Colette admitted to Alice Bénard-Fleury that as he deteriorated, she had nothing left to wish for him but an end to his suffering. She could not yet know that she had already begun serving her own life sentence of crippling pain, of futile and mostly misguided treatments for it, and of progressive immobility that would, in time, become absolute. For a year she had been feeling pangs and stiffness in her legs which occasionally left her unable to walk, forcing her to cancel an outing or an engagement. But when they abated, she attributed them to the old broken fibula and forgot them. Then in December, an X-ray revealed rheumatoid arthritis in both hips. "I'm entirely disgusted," she told her fellow invalid Hélène. "As my mother used to cry, 'O hideous old age!' "[18]

PART VI

CHAPTER 40

*I always obey a kind of asceticism at the core of my being that con-
sists of denying myself what I love. I don't know where the impulse
comes from.*

—COLETTE,
Lettres aux petites fermières

ι

COLETTE'S WAR YEARS are richly documented by her correspondence. The uncertainty of fate, the forced separations from friends,
and the "smallness" of a life reduced in scope by privations and her
increasing frailty made the writing and receipt of letters one of her greatest
luxuries. If those letters contain no outrage, and indeed very little apparent
cognizance of the war's horrors, it is partly because, as she tells Moune, "these
aren't, in fact, things one puts into a letter."[1] Colette steadfastly practices what
she likes to call *"le sage repliement sur soi"*[2]—the wise retreat into her private
bastion, which also translates, less poetically, as lying low. Prudence, as she
saw it, was the better part of valor. And what may strike a reader today as
indifference, passivity, myopia, opportunism, or simply naiveté in the presence of an overwhelming evil was also her ancient—and guiltless—instinct
for survival.

In her actions as in some of her work under the Occupation, Colette sets
an example of old-fashioned female stoicism and resourcefulness. She keeps
her hands busy with knitting and needlework and penning distractions—
articles about cuisine, fashion, and décor; about the reckless coquetry of the
war-weary; about animals and childrearing. The Paris she observes from her

windows at the Palais-Royal is peopled by a race of beasts and humans with her own virtues, and when the sirens sound or the ground shakes, the young people in the garden beneath her don't look up from the old review or yellowed novel they are reading, or the infant they are rocking in a makeshift cradle. Her voice is firm, and her prose has its old lushness. In these sugarless years, she extracts the sweetness of life, like some tireless old bee, and offers it as a gift to her readers. If optimism is a "contagious" form of resistance, as Colette claims it to be, then she, however modestly and at little risk, affirms herself a *résistante*. She even imagines that a French art of the future is being "incubated" in the prison camps, and that the visionaries among the "two million prisoners of war"—"lucid in the bosom of their suffering"—will come home to bring forth a new art "saturated with the virtues of the free air and the recovered light."[3]

As all books or articles published under the Occupation required a stamp of approval from the Nazi censors, every writer who published his work became, technically, a "collaborator." Most simply needed to earn a living, but a courageous few refused, or wrote for the underground. Colette was not among them. She publishes her writing, moreover, in some of the most repellent organs of the pro-Vichy and pro-German press, and maintains cordial relations with their editors.

Her daughter, her stepson Renaud, and some close friends were risking their lives in the Resistance; others were working happily under if not directly for the enemy. Sacha Guitry scintillates not only on the stage, but at dinners given by the consul general, Schleier, who commandeered one of the Rothschild mansions, and at the German embassy. Alice Cocéa "can't" refuse the occasional invitation to attend them either. Dunoyer de Segonzac tours Germany and Austria with a party of French painters. Maurice Chevalier enthusiastically supports Pétain and also entertains in Germany; in September of 1942, Colette decides to recall their first meeting and youthful camaraderie as music-hall artistes in an article for *Comoedia*. Renée Hamon, inexplicably, writes some of her journal on stationery from the Commissariat Général aux Questions Juives, and Colette helps to get her work published in *Gringoire*, where she continues to publish her own fiction.

When Moune asks Colette to sign a petition protesting the arrest of Julien Cain, the Jewish director of the Bibliothèque Nationale, she declines on the ground that her name will call attention to Maurice.[4] Yet the Goudekets socialize openly with *le tout Paris* of the Occupation. Among their hosts are the artist and architect José-María Sert—Franco's ambassador to the Vatican—and the American art patron Florence Gould. Mme Gould mixes her guests with a certain flair. "An American, a German, a Russian, four French people, counting us—and the Carbuccias!" Colette relates to Moune. "An electric atmosphere. Maurice suddenly became imprudently magnificent, and there was no further conversation between him and the German."[5]

Colette's powers of denial were tremendous, or as she puts it herself: "a credulity, a forgetful exhaustion endowed me with delusion."[6] In the same letter that describes the German bombardments of the roads around Méré, she exults about the nightingales in her woods, and the solitude, and her respite from cerebral labors. She is obsessed by food, like most of her compatriots, although she is rather more clever—she's miraculously clever—at keeping her larder stocked. She and Pauline, she notes wryly, are the only Parisians who don't lose forty pounds in the terrible winter of 1942.

When the Nazi race laws exclude Maurice from commerce or journalism, she tells her "little farmers": "as long as that's the extent of the sanctions, we'll be consoled."[7] She likes to call her husband "the Jew who doesn't know he's one."[8] "He knows he's one" definitively on the day the Gestapo knock at his door, but until then, Maurice seems only slightly less oblivious than Colette to the danger he is courting by living openly in Paris. He spends six weeks in the detention camp at Compiègne, and when he is released, he speaks of returning to "normal life."[9] Perhaps they both assumed that her prestige would protect him, and to some extent, this assumption had some merit. "Celebrity," write Gilles and Jean-Robert Ragache, "creates an exceptional situation which doesn't reserve the same fate for the simple Jewish artisan and the famous writer."[10]

Some of the Goudekets' closest Jewish friends had no such illusions. Misz Marchand would commit suicide. The van den Hensts would escape to Guatemala. Winnie de Polignac was in England. Alba Crosbie and her husband fled to New York, where Alba scrubbed floors and studied hairdressing. The Kessel brothers also took their families to America, although Jef returned to fight with de Gaulle. Pierre Lazareff left with the Kessels.

Colette evokes her "departed" friends, who have made no provision to return, in an essay from the summer of 1940. She muses on their sudden disappearances in summer coats, leaving their worldly possessions at the railroad station or on the quai. "It's easier for us to believe that these 'departed' have gone off with their old habits, their everyday playthings, the insignia of ease. I think the truth is elsewhere. A terrible blow between the shoulders has made them spit up a bloody truth that shortened their breath, and it's thus unburdened they have departed."[11]

A year later, however—does she swallow the truth hard first?—she is willing to let Carbuccia serialize her only novel from the war years, *Julie de Carneilhan,* in the ever more stridently pro-Vichy, anti-English, and Jew-hating *Gringoire* and to let Fayard publish it in book form with the advertisement for a work by Hitler on the back cover. *Julie*'s greatest virtue, she claims, is that it "doesn't speak about the war—or so little!"[12] That remains to be seen.

Throughout the war, Colette insists, as she had all her life, on "a close surveillance" of her emotions. "Pity is the worst danger," she tells Renée. "We must refuse ourselves affectionate words and tumultuous good tears."[13] There is emotion, however, and some intelligence of her duty in the volume of portraits and short memoirs she published in January of 1941. Much of this *Journal à rebours* (*Looking Backwards*) was written during the summer of 1940, from her refuge at Bel-Gazou's château in the Corrèze. "All spectacles," she writes on the first page, "inspire an identical sense of responsibility, which is perhaps only a temptation: to write, to portray. I have not seen any of this war's violence by the glow of its conflagrations. To every writer falls a task which is dictated by his faculties, by fate, by the decline or vigor of his powers."[14]

Colette's task as a writer, she suggests, is like that of the Correzian peasants who have seen invading armies come and go, and who milk the cows and bring in the harvest. It is like that of the village innkeeper she calls Providence—a divine conjuror who nourishes their little band of shipwrecked Parisians on the provisions—a sausage, a dozen eggs, a rabbit—she nets in her dawn raids on the countryside. And we also come to understand that Colette's stance as a writer is modeled on the attitude her mother takes during the Franco-Prussian War. Sido is laconic about her memories and annoyed with the young Colette for asking about them. "Was it terrible?" "Why terrible. My God, this child is ordinary." She does recall that her husband hobbled out on his crutches to meet the Germans, made a heroic speech, and that this might have forestalled the sack of the village. She also recalls having herself encountered one ghostly Prussian with a rifle. "What did you do?" asks Colette. "I went home and buried the good wine," Sido answers, "not without pride. The wine that dated from my first husband. Château larose, château lafite, some chambertin, château d'Yquem . . ."[15] This is Colette's impulse, too: leave the heroics to the heroes, and don't excite the children. But safeguard that part of one's inheritance that is most irreplaceable, most fragile, most sacredly French—the savor of the past.

2

IN THE EARLY MONTHS of what was called "the phony war"—before the Germans invaded France—the Goudekets both did live broadcasts to America for the French radio's international program. They had been recruited by Jean Giraudoux, who had just been named the minister of information. Colette, says Maurice, thought of Giraudoux as an unlikely candidate for the job. He was a writer who "proceeded by negation to define things and people by what they were not."[16]

They were glad, however, to lend their voices to a program of genteel propaganda aimed at inspiring a sense of solidarity with and appreciation for French culture in the neutral American audience tuned to the station. Maurice, speaking fluent English, would introduce the classics of French theater, after which the station aired recordings of the plays. Colette gave a few words of greeting in her broken English, after which an announcer read a short text in translation. She reminisced to her listeners about her childhood and about the last war, and informed "the women of America of what we're like in October of 1939, who we are, and how we are fighting against everything that could engender discouragement, sadness, and cowardice, even if we're not directly involved in combat."[17]

As the broadcasts were live, the Goudekets went on the air between midnight and four in the morning. Once a week, on Sunday night, they drove through an eerie autumnal fog that made the blacked-out city seem even darker, to the radio station on the rue de Grenelle, which was pulsing with activity and light. What Colette loved best about this brief patriotic service was the camaraderie of the canteen, and to watch the dawn reflected in the waters of the Seine as they drove home.

THE DAMP AND then the cold of that exceptionally frigid winter made her hip worse, and she submitted to a series of X-ray "treatments" which did not, unsurprisingly, seem to help. Between the hip, her teeth—two healthy ones and two rotten ones were extracted to make room for a bridge—and a tenacious case of bronchitis, she was in almost constant physical distress, although it didn't slow down her writing. She was working on a novella—*Chambre d'hôtel*—and on a series of articles on beauty and fashion for the women's magazine *Marie-Claire*, where, for a while, she also wrote a charmingly bossy advice column.

In February of 1940, on the recommendation of her doctors, Colette went south to convalesce, staying at the Hôtel Ruhl in Nice with Maurice and her daughter. The garlic, the oranges, and the flower market restored her a little, and she reminisced to Moune about their last sojourn there, when they were mugged on the Promenade des Anglais.[18] She also won five hundred francs in the national lottery and treated her German translator, Erna Redtenbacher— a refugee from the Nazis—and Erna's lover, Christiane, to a big seafood lunch.

This idyll was obviously not to last. On May 10, Hitler launched his blitzkrieg against Holland and Belgium. The advancing German forces encircled the French army and cut it in two, stranding one half along with the entire British Expeditionary Force on the promontory of Dunkirk. Jef Kessel was the only French reporter who made it through to the front lines, and he described the "hallucinatory," "hellish" "beauty" of the spectacle for the two million readers of *Paris-Soir*. By June 2, the French soldiers finally received permission to follow their British comrades into the boats. By the fourth, the Germans had overrun the ruins, taken their prisoners, and begun their march on Paris.

Toward the end of May 1940, Colette received a letter from the little farmers begging her, "under the tragic circumstances," to advocate the patriotic gesture of draping Sacré-Coeur with the French flag. "I won't do anything of the sort," she replied. "To communicate a thought warmly, fruitfully, you must have it solidly within you. My entire career . . . has been devoted to things, people, and feelings that are familiar to me, and I have never been able to speak of what I don't know."[19]

By now, she had taken refuge at Méré. With a great show of indignation and the help of the local mayor, Maurice had managed to oust a detachment of Moroccans who were billeted there with fifteen horses. After installing his wife and Pauline comfortably in their pretty house, he went back to Paris. There was such a shortage of manpower that in addition to writing for *Paris-soir* he had, much to Colette's amusement, become the literary editor of *Marie-Claire*.

Erna's lover, Christiane, arrived to spend a few days with Colette while she waited "like a frightened bird" to hear about Erna's fate. Despite her status as an anti-Nazi refugee, Erna had been rounded up in a sweep of enemy aliens and interned in a camp somewhere in the Basses-Pyrénées. But there was good news from another quarter: the Goudekets' friend Raymond Leibovici, who had been fighting at Dunkirk, had made it onto one of the last boats and was coming home.

The roads around Montfort-l'Amaury were now being bombarded by the advancing Germans. One of Colette's neighbors lost a leg, and another was decapitated when she sought refuge under an apple tree. On June 9, the French government fled the capital, first to the Touraine and later to Bordeaux. Their retreat precipitated a mass exodus of civilians. Colette, Maurice, and Pauline loaded their car with all the provisions and gas it could carry, and at four in the morning of June 12, headed south for the Corrèze.

CUREMONTE WAS a medieval hamlet, partly abandoned. Bel-Gazou's château, which lay mostly in ruins, had high stone walls that enclosed a courtyard blooming with flowers, and she was trying to grow vegetables in an ambitious kitchen garden. Renaud and Arlette had restored part of the ancient cloister, which had three bedrooms and an elegantly furnished salon with an immense stone fireplace where the "shipwrecked" Parisians boiled their laundry and cooked their meals on an iron tripod.

The sense of relative security that they had living in this quaint redoubt did not reconcile Colette to her isolation, or to her discomfort at being beholden to Bel-Gazou. She called Curemonte "a green tomb." No sounds rose up from the village, except for the cries of swallows nesting in the towers of the ancient fortress. There were floods after a storm, and it was difficult to keep warm between the walls of stone. When they ran out of logs, they threw painted Renaissance beams and Louis XV paneling onto the fire. Bel-Gazou insisted on supplementing their meager rations with her own inedible concoctions—root vegetables pickled in vinegar for three days, and sugarless fruits steeped in eau-de-vie. Valuing her life, as Colette put it to Germaine Beaumont, she refused to taste them.

The enforced intimacy, particularly between Colette's daughter and husband, was a strain on the household. Their worst privation, however, was the absence of any news from the outside world. There was no electricity, so their radio was useless. The mails had been disrupted, so there were no letters or telegrams, and they were afraid to use any of their "precious and unobtainable" gasoline even to go as far as Castel-Novel, fifteen miles away, where Renaud and Arlette were harboring a houseful of her Jewish relatives and Bertrand was waiting to join up with a local regiment.

Finally, after five weeks of excruciating suspense, they drove into Clermont-Ferrand, which was jammed with refugees. There they learned that the French government had surrendered, and that a new regime, headed by Maréchal Pétain and Pierre Laval, had been installed at Vichy. The country was divided into two zones, one controlled by the Germans and the other by the collaborationists. Paris was intact, but occupied and sealed off to any travelers from the non-occupied zone, and the Corrèze was part of the non-occupied zone.

By mid-July, the postal service had begun to function again. They now learned that Germaine Beaumont had spent three weeks on the roads, camping in the open fields, and had been slightly wounded in a bombing raid. Maurice's brother, an amputee with tuberculosis, hadn't budged from Paris. He and his Haitian wife were hungry but surviving. The Kessels and Lazareffs were en route to America. The van den Hensts were still in Saint-Tropez, which was bloated with refugees desperate for lodging at any price. In one of the first letters to get through—from Renée Hamon—they heard that Christiane had succeeded, through bribery, in rescuing Erna from captivity, but that on the eve of the Nazi invasion, they had both committed suicide. "Our quiet life," wrote Maurice, "seemed guilty, and our euphoria was tinged with anguish."[20]

Wanting passionately to be back in Paris—"the only village where one can possibly live during a war"—but finding her way barred, Colette took up her journal, *Looking Backwards*. In one of her sketches, set in Curemonte, she describes a boy of thirteen who won't listen to the village radio; who tunes out his father's recitation of all the new prohibitions; and who, to his mother's irritation—"are you from the moon? are you deaf? are you a barbarian?"—doesn't seem to appreciate what the "armistice" really means and that it's "terrible."

Colette sometimes sees this dreamy boy wandering alone along the river-bank outside the hamlet or through the woods, usually talking to himself. "He's a child poet," she thinks. "Being without sin or malice, he is mysterious, like everything empty." And one afternoon, she overhears him behind a hayrick, pretending to be the voice of Radio Corrèze:

> We hereby make it known to our listeners that the armistice isn't true, and that, on the contrary, everything is going fine. It's not true either that the Arnoux boy has been killed. . . . The sale of chocolate, heretofore restricted, has been declared free . . . and the sugar ration augmented from fifty-five grams to three kilos. By relay from Radio Toulouse, we have learned from an informed source that all cattle requisitioned by the cavalry will be returned to its owners. To compensate for the inconvenience, each horse will come back with a new cart.

She concludes that she was right about him, and we conclude that she is comparing him to herself. "Solitary, exalted, Tonin was giving himself over completely to the mission of the poet: to forget reality, to promise the world miracles, to sing of victory, and to deny death."[21]

COLETTE ALWAYS "denies death" by eating, and "bread and butter" (or a butter substitute) were, she says, the Goudekets' foremost concern. Having heard that *Paris-Soir* might regroup in Saint-Tropez, they considered going south. They would have friends and, potentially, some income. But housing would be a problem, and they couldn't possibly save up enough gas for the trip. Late in July, they made it to Lyon, hoping to obtain there the travel documents that would permit them—even though the borders of the occupied zone were closed to Jews (as well as foreigners and people of color)—to reach Paris.

While living at a seedy hotel on the banks of the Rhône, Colette wrote articles for Charles Maurras's exteme right-wing *Candide.* She also visited her old friend and Jouvenel's Édouard Herriot, who until the surrender had been president of the Chamber of Deputies, and was mayor of Lyon. He used his influence to procure the Goudekets a laissez-passer, but when they reached the frontier, a German soldier looked at the frizzy-haired Colette and said: "You, Jew." Upon receiving her terse denial, he scrutinized the swarthy Pauline: "You surely Jew." Goudeket writes that he was so disgusted he told the guard in his own language that *he* was the Jew.[22] "Alas, I married an honest man," Colette sighed to a friend.[23]

They were sent back to Lyon, where they tried to pull other strings— including, writes Lottmann, giving an actress friend a letter to Otto Abetz, the German ambassador. It was finally the Swedish consulate that provided their papers. They crossed the border to the sound of "clicking heels" and without being searched, which was lucky, because Colette had stowed a loaded revolver in the glove compartment. They reached the Palais-Royal on the night of September 11.

3

THE TERRIBLE COLD of that winter set in precociously, and with it, "the constant hunt for fuel and food." Colette had begun to accept that her hip would never be better. Her only means of transport was the Métro—their car had been confiscated—but the steps were excruciating, so she stayed put and worked on a volume of novellas—*Chance Acquaintances*—which Fayard would publish in December.

The Germans had immediately begun to censor (and to subsidize) the press. Abetz published a list of proscribed writers—Jews, Gaullists, nationalists, and decadents—which included Colette's friends Carco (a decadent), Kessel (a Jew), Roland Dorgelès (a nationalist), Rachilde (a mistake),[24] and Henri Béraud, who, despite his virulent anti-Semitism, was banned as anti-German.

Bertrand's unrepentant pro-Nazi friend Drieu La Rochelle became editor in chief of *La Nouvelle Revue française,* replacing Jean Paulhan, who went underground to publish the literary review of the Resistance, *Les Lettres françaises.* Brasillach, who had converted to Nazism heart and soul, was denouncing Jews and bad Frenchmen in *Je suis partout.* Bunau-Varilla's *Le Matin,* which had veered toward the extreme right even before the war, enthusiastically embraced "the new order." So did the new pro-German management of *Paris-Soir,* who used the familiar masthead and typeface to publish a "fake" Paris edition of the paper while the "authentic" *Paris-Soir,* edited by Hervé Mille, was still alive in Lyon. The occupiers hoped that readers in the capital, with no access to any information from the unoccupied zone, just might not notice.

Le Petit Parisien, under Paul Dupuy, struggled briefly to retain some measure of independence. Colette began writing for *"P.P."* as soon as she returned to Paris and continued to do so even after January of 1941, when the editor in chief—Dupuy's Jewish wife—was ousted. The entire staff then quit in protest, taking all the copy for several issues with them—"including my last article," Colette lamented. She expected to be "unemployed," she told Moune, but a new management was recruited from *Le Matin*. Colette would concede that the work she was doing was *"moche"* (ugly).[25] If she found the editorials *moches,* she doesn't say.

Patrice Blank, a hero of the Resistance and a close friend of Bertrand de Jouvenel's, believed that Colette's willingness to write for *P.P., Gringoire,* and even the pro-Nazi *La Gerbe* reflected

> an unconsciousness shared by a large number of French artists. It was very widespread, and the excuse one heard most often was that the theater should function "normally" and the "voice" of French culture should not be stifled. There were very few, and I underline very few, true *résistants.* . . . As Pascal put it, "I believe only in witnesses who have had their throats cut." Colette belonged to that herd of passive collaborationists who were legion. As the balance of the war began to shift, so did the proportion of those who actively supported the Allies and the Free French forces. But they changed their allegiance out of prudence, because Germany was losing, and not from conviction.[26]

THE NAZIS HAD moved quickly to Aryanize the publishing industry. Max Fisher, Colette's Jewish editor at Flammarion, was replaced by René d'Uckermann. The Calmann-Lévys had fled to safety, and their publishing house was taken over by its former literary director, Louis Thomas, who rechristened it Aux Armes de France. He courted Colette assiduously and would publish three of her titles. The Jewish proprietors of Ferenczi, who owned a backlist of twelve titles by Colette and the contract for a new volume, had also left Paris when the war began, arranging to sell their business to Hachette, with a secret understanding that it would be returned to them after the war. But the Nazis were not duped. The house was acquired "like a simple armchair," as Colette puts it, by a German consortium, and an amenable Frenchman was appointed to run it. He was an old friend of Willy's—Jean de la Hire. Colette went to see him and reported to Germaine Beaumont that he had received her graciously.

In September of 1940, the association of French publishers had signed an agreement with the occupying powers to establish what was, in essence, a system of "self-censorship."[27] In exchange for suppressing the voices of Jews or subversives, Ambassador Abetz gave the publishers a margin of discretion in deciding what works to publish and what passages should be cut from them. Every house that remained active under the Occupation was to some degree compromised, although, as the Ragaches point out, there were nuances of collaboration and some striking anomalies. Louis Aragon and Elsa Triolet, for example, both published novels with Denoël, who had willingly taken on a German partner. Their fiction was thus in the company of not only Céline, but a fascist of much less talent and more virulence, Lucien Rebatet. Gallimard supported Drieu's *Nouvelle Revue française* but also secretly financed Paulhan's *Lettres françaises,* and he would manage to slip Camus's *The Stranger* and Saint-Exupéry's *Pilote de guerre* past the censor.[28]

THE GERMANS HAD NOT gone to the trouble of occupying Paris only to deprive themselves of its pleasures, and the Parisians themselves were desperate for distraction. The theaters, the opera, the cinemas, the music halls, the cabarets, and the brothels all began to reopen. Mistinguett was performing at the Casino de Paris, where a sign was posted at the artists' entrance prohibiting its use by "dogs and jews." The Gypsy jazz composer-guitarist Django Reinhardt was enjoying a huge vogue at the Hot Club de France despite the fact that, as the Ragaches put it, "from a Nazi perspective, his future wasn't bright."

The cafés were full, and so, despite the strict rationing, were the great restaurants—Maxim's, Drouant, Le Tour d'Argent—where celebrities, black marketeers, the newly rich, and the anciently noble rubbed elbows with the "tourists." Everyone, however grand, was obliged to catch the last Métro, except for those hardy revelers who circumvented the eleven-o'clock curfew by staying in the clubs all night. Colette reports to Moune that their friend, the composer and member of Les Six Georges Auric—out on the town with the countess Marie-Laure de Noailles and a German officer—had his leg crushed: "nightclub, two in the morning, champagne, accident."[29] She also reports gaily that a playwright friend has invited her to a "sumptuous" lunch at the Café de Paris, and that oysters are a "cheap luxury." At the same moment, she begs Renée Hamon to send her onions and potatoes.

Occupied Paris was almost as famished for books as for entertainment or food. "Standing up, shackled to a trance, the youth of Paris read passionately," Colette wrote. "They read and contemplate works of entomology, odd collections of art books, a good old novel by Alphonse Daudet, annals of medicine with missing pages, manuals of practical science, and the memoirs of an eighteenth-century traveler."[30] On the black market, copies of *Gone with the Wind* sold as briskly as chickens or nylons. "For the first time in France," write the Ragaches, "demand exceeded the supply. New or old, everything was selling."[31] Maurice was among the many amateur bibliophiles trying to earn some money trading in used and rare editions.

Colette, always eager to feed the hungry, worked more prodigiously than at any other period of her life. Her confinement focused her powers, and in the course of the four French war years, this invalid entering her seventies produced eight books, if one includes the revision of *The Pure and the Impure* and *Belles Saisons,* published in 1945, but composed during the Occupation. This spectacular final flowering would exhaust the reservoir of her fiction, but not before she had written some of her best-loved novellas.

CHAPTER 41

T HE FIRST CHRISTMAS of the war was a bleak holiday. The Goudekets spent it "in silence and reclusion." On New Year's Day 1941 the snow fell for six hours. Fuel was extremely scarce, and some of the most fragile Parisians succumbed to the cold. "It hurts in one's heart," Colette told Renée, "to think of freezing children."[1]

She celebrated her sixty-eighth birthday in bed, suffering from a severe case of flu and a relapse of bronchitis, but working with "an unaccustomed speed" on a new work of fiction that she calls a *"semble-roman."*[2] "I don't know what to think of it," she admits. Years later, she would tell André Parinaud that she clung to the "perhaps absurd" conviction that *Julie de Carneilhan* was one of her "best conceived" works of art.[3]

Bel-Gazou had decided to brave the winter at Curemonte, although when the temperature dropped below zero, she decamped to Saint-Tropez. Colette complained that she heard from her only rarely. "My daughter is . . . rather secretive," she told the little farmers. "I've encouraged that, by the way. Her instinct is to keep silent about her depths. I don't very much like those young people who leak from every side like a colander."[4]

She suffered from her daughter's silence all the same. To Germaine Beaumont, who was living at Montfort-l'Amaury and working on a novel, Colette notes wryly that under similar circumstances, Mme de Sévigné would certainly have expired. But her own correspondence with Germaine was fitful, and the younger woman was feeling neglected. Colette protests fondly: "Let's not be idiots, you and I, in our aristocracy of the heart: she doesn't write, she doesn't want to write to me, she's forgotten me. . . . I think that you couldn't forget me any more than I could neglect my solicitude for you. All it takes for us to feel as if we had never parted is to meet once again."[5]

That spring, her other "daughter," Renée Hamon, came down from Brittany for a brief visit, observing that a lunch of creamed cauliflower and roast chicken at the rue de Beaujolais "reconciled one to wartime shortages."[6] The little farmers were doing a valiant job of keeping Colette supplied with the first radishes, a small leg of lamb, chestnuts, brussels sprouts, salad, and, as the season progressed, strawberries, camellias, and roses. Her letters testify to a gratitude that, as their editor, Marie-Thérèse Colleaux-Chaurang observes, is both filial and maternal. She calls the couple "my little daughters who are my little mothers at the same time"; she describes herself as their "nursling"; and she is afraid of becoming, like all voracious infants, a "vampire."[7] Not so afraid, however, that she doesn't sometimes scold her "angels" for the state in which their care packages arrive: a melon crushes some eggs, spoiling a rabbit, and in the future, they must remember to degut the chickens.

A little bit of Renée went a long way. Adulation was tiring. "It's been a long time," Colette told Germaine Beaumont, "since I've been able to stand an entourage."[8] When one of the farmers—Yvonne—came from Nantes to see her, Colette sent her away and discouraged any further visits. She admired the couple's purity and took vicarious pleasure in their passionate gardening and husbandry and a superstitious comfort from the religious medals they sent her—which she wore—but to preserve its "ideal" character, writes Colleaux-Chaurang, "the relationship had to remain"—as it had with Francis Jammes and should have with Louis de Robert—"epistolary."

Contemporaries and old friends fell into a different category. She welcomed the visits of Luc and Moune, of Musidora, and particularly of Georges Wague, who would bring his tool kit, repair her broken chairs and knick-knacks, and even patch her upholstery. She lunched with Lily de Gramont and dined with Henri Mondor, Georges Duhamel, and Léon Barthou in a private room at the Café de Paris, where they feasted on contraband steak and lobster. She kept in touch with Missy, Rachilde, Misia Sert, and Lucie Delarue-Mardrus, who was living in the country crippled by rheumatism.

Jean Cocteau was Colette's neighbor in the Palais-Royal, and the war cemented their friendship. He lived on the rue Montpensier in an "enchanting" mezzanine flat furnished like the set for one of his plays. He had known both Goudekets for forty years—Colette from the salons of the fin de siècle, Maurice since their schooldays at the Lycée Condorcet.

In 1941, Colette describes Cocteau to Moune as "worried, charming, and tormented by money problems."[9] His status as a homosexual and a decadent made him an obvious target for the Germans and the Vichyists. While his plays were licensed for production during the Occupation, they were reviled by the press, and performances of *Les Parents terribles* and *La Machine à écrire* had been halted by thugs throwing stink bombs and shouting obscenities at Cocteau and his lover, Jean Marais.

Early in the war, Cocteau had published a courageous address to young writers, urging them to defy the book burnings and the witch-hunters and "to defend, against your unworthy fellow countrymen, the domains of the spirit."[10] Yet he also cultivated a circle of German friends, published a volume of his own poetry written in German, and an article in *Comoedia* acclaiming the work of Hitler's favorite sculptor, Arno Becker. "During the four-year period," writes Francis Steegmuller, "he displayed his usual ambivalences in heightened form, his usual affinity for paradox, his usual insecurity concerning his 'position'; and despite the official clearance [by the purge tribunals] he emerged from the Occupation more seared by inward guilt than ever before."[11]

Cocteau was middle-aged now, and Colette was old, but one has the impression from his memoirs that when they were alone they played at being two enfants terribles: bringing out their secret stash of crimes, cruelties, and truths which they traded like precious marbles. "We've never needed many words," Colette told him. "Nothing about my attachment escapes you. You are my young brother, who is in everything, magically, my elder."[12] Cocteau would describe Colette's extreme old age without pity, which is perhaps as she—who loathed pity—would have wanted it. When the war ended, she would be swamped with honors, and in death with pious eulogies. He paid her the loyal tribute of refuting the sentimental views of her work and of her character. "Everything in art is monstrous," he wrote succinctly, and "Madame Colette does not escape this rule."[13]

2

THE HOUSE AT Méré had been empty since the first days of the war, and without a car, it was a useless luxury. The Goudekets put it on the market that June. They found a buyer immediately but then got an "enormously" better offer. The formalities of the transfer were complicated by the many new bureaucratic regulations, but by October it was sold, and for the first time in more than forty years, Colette was without a foothold in the country. She was now and henceforth definitively a Parisian.

That summer, she received a copy of Germaine Beaumont's latest novel, *L'Harpe irlandaise*. She had always encouraged the career of Annie de Pène's daughter, and her success aroused the unqualified maternal pride which she could never vouchsafe to Bel-Gazou. She addressed Germaine by Flaubert's epithet for George Sand, *"mon cher maître,"* and told her she was the only contemporary gothic novelist worthy of the name. "In all my life, I would never have known how to write a novel whose characters are a ghost, a fallen apple, a ruined house, water, and a moth. Maybe what I lack is reverie, or a sense of the fantastic."[14]

IT WAS AN EXCEPTIONALLY hot summer. The fountains of the Palais-Royal were dry. On July 14, Bastille Day, a German orchestra in tailcoats gave a Mozart concert in the Cour d'Honneur. Colette enjoyed this night music, but by day, the children playing war games—blowing their whistles and shooting off their toy pistols under her windows—drove her crazy and inspired a cranky tirade in the *Petit Parisien.* "Although I have no penchant whatever to embrace a late career as a reformer, and am persuaded that I will have no success if I propose to orient our young citizens toward games which don't make any noise, I propose it all the same."[15]

Most of the great couture houses were still open, and Colette covered the collections for a glossy fashion magazine, *L'Officiel de la couture.* The evening gowns of white silk jersey and pink lamé were as fantastical as the lobsters at the Café de Paris. She was also writing three comic sketches (one entitled "The Return of Claudine") which were to be performed by Yvonne de Bray and Parisys that September at the Théâtre Michel. This entertainment inspired a piece of hate mail from a lady named Georgette Mayer who hadn't seen it but had read the reviews: "We've had enough of your decadent literature. We don't want any more of these *Claudine*s, these *Ingénues libertines.* . . . No more *Perversities* by Francis Carco and stories of pederasty by André Gide. . . . All that is *jewish* art![16] Thank heavens, the national Revolution is changing it all."

IN NOVEMBER OF 1941, Aux Armes de France brought out the definitive edition of *The Pure and the Impure.* The editor's unsigned preface, presumably written by Louis Thomas, seems to anticipate objections like those of Mme Mayer to the subject's "decadence": "Whatever the judgment of posterity must be of this work, which beneath its apparent lightness confronts with exemplary lucidity the difficult problem of the sexes, it is certain that Colette has a decided preference for it. 'One will perhaps eventually perceive,' she willingly says herself, 'that it's my best book.' She has manifested her predilection . . . in making changes and additions important enough for the present edition to be considered, in part, original."[17]

One small but telling change comes in the final paragraph. In the original edition—*Ces Plaisirs . . .*—Colette admits that she doesn't understand the meaning of the word "pure," "but within it, in the pictures it evokes, I construct a refuge for myself." She goes on to explain that these images of lightness and transparency are the substitutes for "isolated" places—childhood, innocence, wholeness—beyond her reach. In the wartime revision, the "refuge" is gone and the "isolated" places are not just remote, they've become "imaginary."

3

THAT SAME NOVEMBER, Fayard published *Julie de Carneilhan,* Colette's last novel. Her critics have been indulgent in their judgment of *Julie.* My own pronounced distaste for this work isn't on account of the prose: by now Colette could beat an old carpet and make it shed gold dust. By now, too, she had a long history of using fiction as an instrument of revenge, and here she raises the ghost of her second husband to accuse him of treachery, but also to enjoy one last poisonous taste of his charms. *Julie* is far from the masterpiece that is *My Apprenticeships,* and one could pass over it lightly were it not for the fact that in its context, Colette's rancor is inflammatory and her personal vendetta becomes political.

The story takes place on the eve of war in the late thirties. The eponymous heroine—one of the rare thin leading ladies in Colette's fiction—is modeled loosely on Isabelle de Comminges. She is a beautiful countess of forty-five, twice married and divorced. Her title is ancient, but her family has lost its money. Her father still works the land and camps in his crumbling château, while her rugged brother Léon ekes out a living training racehorses. It's a milieu Colette knows only secondhand, and throughout the novel she dotes on Julie to the point of mistaking her selfishness and vulgarity for an aristocrat's insouciance and candor.

The countess, she tells us, "had lived a great deal among lies before plumping for a small life of her own, a sincere and restricted life from which all pretense, even in matters sensual, was banished."[18] Julie may knit her own gloves and skip the odd meal, but it's a life of idleness all the same, marked by her contempt for those who share it. She has a puppyish young lover named Coco Vatard—a *fils à papa* who works in the family business, cleaning and dyeing. Her best friend is a pea-brained little nightclub cashier and pianist. They are socially her inferiors, and Julie treats them that way. Then there is Toni, the teenage stepson of her second husband, Herbert d'Espivant. Toni adores her, but he's not her type. She tells his father that she imagines he has two mauve nipples "and a dismal little—." When he tries to kill himself for her sake, Julie is amused.

Early in the novel, Julie hears from her brother that Espivant has suffered a heart attack in the street and may be dying. He summons Julie to his bedside, and when she sees him, she has the same reaction Colette does to Henry's photograph: "He's done for." Espivant is a politician, an unctuous parvenu with "effeminate" features, and has recently married a rich widow. He has bought his seat in Parliament with her money. Marianne, the exotically beautiful new Mme d'Espivant, is Jewish, like both the first and third *baronnes* de Jouvenel, and Colette devotes a long passage to describing her bottomless foreign fortune. "It's a labyrinth," she concludes.

Espivant pours on the charm for Julie, plays on their old sensual complicity, and seduces her. "He's never more irresistible," she reflects, "than when he wants something for entirely selfish reasons!" What he wants is to dump his wife, but he can't afford to. He knows that Julie has kept an old promissory note for a million francs which he signed, partly in jest, at the time of their divorce. If she gives it back to him, he can reclaim that sum from Marianne, who "doesn't like debts." Julie agrees in the vain hope that, once extricated from his marriage of convenience, Herbert—"my greatest love of all, happiest part of my life, and my greatest sorrow"—will return to her. But she also expects to split the proceeds of their scam.

The countess has given herself a fresh manicure, and despite the fact that Herbert is supposed to be on his deathbed, she is waiting hotly for his knock on her door when his wife turns up instead. This lady wears too many diamonds and too much scent. She looks to her rival like a woman "made up entirely of precious materials—jade, green-spangled quartz, ivory, amethyst." Julie is amazed that Marianne can speak French, yet admits grudgingly that she behaves with dignity.

Marianne has come, in part, to see what kind of monster would blackmail a dying man she once loved. Blackmail? It takes Julie a moment to understand how cynically Herbert has betrayed them both. He has manipulated Marianne into giving him the means to leave her, and Julie into accepting the blame and the humiliation. He counts on love being all Julie knows of honor, and he's right. She bursts into tears and backs up his story. Marianne is moved, and offers her absolution. She also leaves an envelope on the hall table. The envelope is from Herbert, and Marianne hasn't noticed its lightness, but Julie does. It proves to contain not half a million, but a hundred thousand francs—a ten percent cut—and that without a thank-you. "That's the commission of a middle man or a rental agent," the countess exclaims bitterly.

In the last scene, Julie takes down her riding boots and begins to polish them. Léon has just sold his stable—it was failing anyway—and he is going home to wait for the war at Carneilhan. He will be riding his beloved mare, Hirondelle, and he asks Julie to ride her old mount, Tullia. She reluctantly agrees. She hasn't had another word from Herbert, and it is obvious she has nothing more to hope for than a frugal life in the country with her old father. The parvenu Paris of the d'Espivants and Vatards is finally no place for the Carneilhans.

AMONG THE QUALITIES missing from *Julie* is that sense of humor about greed, lust, vulgarity, and pretension which relieves *Chéri* and *My Apprenticeships* and makes a comic masterpiece of *Gigi*. Colette doesn't have enough distance from her subject, or from her malice. Infatuated with her heroine's nobility and determined to smear her ex-husband's character, she presents this contrived story as a romantic drama rather than as the black comedy about false high-mindedness that it wants to be.

Before the war, *Julie* could have been read as a minor novel dashed off by a great writer with a bad case of the flu and a personal score to settle, but 1941 is a treacherous moment, morally, to be writing about "bottomless" Jewish money, crooked Third Republic politicians, and exploited members of the *petite noblesse*. To appreciate Julie's significance as a gesture of collaboration, or at least a passive gesture, one must read the virulent polemics of the period—not just the reportage or the editorials, but the book and theater reviews, obsessed with rooting out the Jewish corruption—*the enjuivement*— of French culture. Colette would condemn this "crude propaganda" in *The Evening Star* and associate herself with those who "mocked" it. On the other hand, Renée Hamon was prompted to note in her journal of April 1943—after an Easter lunch at the Palais-Royal—that "Colette is a born anti-Semite, especially toward Jewish women."[19] Did she not realize how ingratiating the characters of Espivant and Marianne would be to the rabid nationalists and anti-Semites of *Je suis partout, Gringoire, La Gerbe*, or *L'Action française*? As a couple, they are, precisely, the fascists' bugaboos: the effete and whorish democrat dependent on the shadowy billions of international Jewish capital. D'Espivant's pure-blooded victim and her family are, moreover, the standard-bearers of old France, relics of that feudal aristocracy of the sword that has supposedly been defrauded and marginalized by the ruling cabal of corrupt materialists.[20]

Julie had been serialized in *Gringoire* that summer.[21] In the same issues, the journal blames the hunger of the French on Jews and other foreigners who are eating their food. It attacks the "crimes" of England, the venality and selfishness of America, and the "lies" of the Free French radio (broadcast, it claims, by Jews). It rallies behind Pétain and Darlan and defends "the new Europe," which will "respect" the national identities of its member states "while not making the error of confounding them with the exorbitant pretensions of . . .

ethnic groups." A political gossip column ticks off the names of "traitors" who have fled abroad, and who have Jewish wives. Adolf Hitler is never mentioned. The Occupation seems to have nothing to do with Germany. The war is the product of a conspiracy among "the four Internationals: Jews, communists, freemasons, and financiers."[22]

Monzie had heard rumors about *Julie de Carneilhan* months before he got his hands on a copy. When he finally read the book, he was outraged: "As if there weren't enough filth in the atmosphere of Paris, this adds to the pestilences of our miserable lives!"[23] Then he continues in a calmer vein. He tells Colette that he didn't "feel" there was a resemblance between Espivant and Jouvenel, but his love for Henry compelled him to ask her—"tell me the truth, dear Colette, yes or no"—whether she had purposely "slimed the face" of her daughter's father.

Colette wrote back to Monzie, furious. If he didn't recognize his friend, that was because he wasn't there. Who better to make that discernment? Monzie had always told her that they were the only two people in the world who really knew Jouvenel. As for herself, "I have scarcely been more than one of his 'abused widows.' " But she assured him that her enmity was "short of breath and shorter of memory. . . . And I am not contained, whole, of a piece, with the best and worst of me, in the books where your anxiety searches so severely for this old friend of yours."[24]

4

ON JUNE 22, 1941, Hitler broke his pact with Stalin and attacked the Soviet Union. Maurice could not contain his "natural optimism." "The war is over!" he exclaimed to Colette. "It might still last three or four years more, but for me, secure in the absolute, Hitler has already disappeared and the German soldiers you see passing by at this moment are nothing but phantoms."[25] She told him he was crazy.

On December 8, the United States entered the war. The Resistance began its first acts of armed subversion, and the Nazis retaliated by arresting a thousand prominent Jewish Parisians. Before dawn on the morning of December 12, the Gestapo came for Maurice. While he dressed, Pauline woke Colette. She helped her husband pack a small valise and walked him to the stairwell. They were both aware they might be parting forever. The effort they made to control their feelings was, he writes, "the greatest proof of love" either could imagine.[26]

"[Maurice] left very calmly for I don't know where," Colette told Hélène, "charged with the crime of being a Jew, of having served voluntarily in the last war, and of having been decorated."[27] She learned quickly that the prisoners had been taken to the detention camp at Compiègne, northeast of Paris, and she immediately launched a campaign to free him. "There was no effort and no humiliation she wasn't willing to undertake," says Maurice. "She saw collaborators and she saw Germans."[28] She was, she said herself, "given hope."[29]

Maurice was to spend seven weeks in detention. The inmates slept on vermin-infested straw, thirty-six to a hut. They were fed a bowl of soup at midday and half a pound of bread at dinner. These conditions, he writes, while "crude and depressing," were endurable for the fit, and apart from two daily roll calls, their warders left them more or less in peace.

The absence of letters, Colette told her friends, was her worst privation, although Maurice managed to smuggle out a few notes begging for food, books—one of her anthologies—and, curiously, old neckties. He hoped, writes Lottmann, "that their friends were helping her" and that she was working for his release. Through the same clandestine channels, she was able to send him at least some of the provisions that he had asked for.[30] In the meantime, she turned sixty-nine. She had stopped sleeping, lived in a constant torment of anxiety, and sometimes she felt her "persistence, credulity, and patience" giving out. "Luckily," she told the little farmers, "I don't let it show too much."[31]

Maurice Goudeket was released on February 6, 1942, about eighteen pounds thinner but otherwise unharmed. The order to free him apparently came from Otto Abetz, the German ambassador, to oblige his French wife, Suzanne. Frau Abetz had been introduced to Colette by mutual friends[32] and had taken up her cause. Ten days later, she would send Colette a thank-you note for a bouquet of flowers and express pleasure at her "happiness," obviously alluding to the captive's return. Later that spring, Frau Abetz invited Colette and her husband to tea. "Imagine it," writes Lottmann, "tea at the German embassy for Maurice Goudeket, only sixty days before the historic roundup of the Jews that signaled the commencement of the death-camp deportations." With the invitation, which was delivered by her chauffeur, Suzanne Abetz sent some books for Colette to autograph. There was another card at Christmas, addressing Mme Goudeket as "My Colette" and "my dear protégée."[33]

Colette was at her beauty parlor on the rue Saint-Honoré when Maurice reached the Palais-Royal. Pauline phoned her, and she asked a friend who was also having her hair done to "stay with me a little. I don't dare go back. I'm afraid." They were both afraid, says Maurice. "Having prided myself on the firmness we had shown when I departed, I must confess to this moment of shared cowardice in the face of joy."[34]

5

FOR A BRIEF MOMENT, Colette felt "cured of everything."[35] Then her elation gave way to a profound fatigue, which, she told friends, she treated as a luxury. She hadn't worked for weeks, except on her embroidery, and she found it difficult to begin writing. In April, she submitted to more X-ray therapy for her arthritis. A careless technician badly burned her stomach and thighs. Then a doctor famous for his success with arthritis—he had cured Sert—gave her intravenous injections of sulfur and iodine, which killed her appetite. "I am capable of losing weight," she joked to Renée Hamon, "as incredible as that might seem."[36] In June, she bought a motorized wheelchair.

Sacha Guitry came to see her that spring, to promote his latest literary project. He was planning to celebrate "the glory of France" in a volume of essays entitled *From Joan of Arc to Philippe Pétain.* Paul Valéry, Georges Duhamel, and other contemporary masters of French prose were each to commemorate a great predecessor. He asked Colette to write the Balzac chapter, and she accepted.

On June 10, the Jews of France were obliged to begin wearing yellow stars. Colette makes light of this event in her letters, telling Germaine Beaumont that Maurice seemed perfectly "serene" and observing to the little farmers that "only those who don't want to wear [the star] expose themselves to unpleasantness."[37] The mass deportations of French Jews began a month later. Almost eighty thousand men, women, and children—all native-born citizens of the Republic—were sent to the camps. The Vichy authorities rounded up forty thousand more foreign Jewish refugees and handed them, too, to the Germans. Only a tiny percentage of these deportees would return. About thirty thousand Jews were saved by courageous French citizens who risked and sometimes lost their own lives in doing so, and among those partisans were Renaud and Colette de Jouvenel. Misz Marchand, who had lost her entire family in Poland, committed suicide on July 27, apparently to spare her husband the attentions of the Gestapo. Having overdosed on barbiturates, she lingered in a coma for four days. "I have lost an irreplaceable friend," Colette told the little farmers. "Hunted, or believing herself hunted for racial reasons, she left this life voluntarily. We had been close since 1914. Pray for Micheline, who had such a pure soul."[38]

After the deportations, Maurice and Colette began to worry that, despite the protection of influential friends, Paris was too dangerous for him. A young shop assistant who lived upstairs in one of the maids' rooms volunteered to hide him—in her bed, if necessary. The antiquarian bookseller in the arcades of the Palais-Royal fixed up a secret hole behind his shelves. But Maurice wrote later that he strongly felt Colette needed a "respite" from her anxiety, and that he could best give her one by leaving for the free zone. She, in turn, told the little farmers that she "sent him away" for "his health." In either case, he traveled south on forged papers, slipped across the border, and spent the next few months living with the van den Hensts in Saint-Tropez.[39]

6

IN HERBERT LOTTMANN'S OPINION, Colette "could not now do more for the collaboration than she had done before, but she could also not do less."[40] Perhaps she believed that the copy she continued to furnish for the Occupation and Vichy presses was a form of credit she could draw on later, to ransom Maurice. Perhaps, unlike her husband, she had her doubts about an Allied victory. Renée Hamon had been taking German lessons, and Colette had encouraged these "useful" studies, telling her: "One has to think of future voyages."[41]

Yet Colette's reluctance to take any sort of stand, even privately, or to voice any sentiment of outrage at the persecutions, even in her letters, is a symptom of that moral lethargy she admits so candidly in "Bella-Vista," where the narrator bears witness to crimes she does nothing to stop. "I was born under the sign of passivity," she writes then. And she writes, now, to Renée: "Save your aggression for your work. For the rest of your day-to-day life, passivity suffices."[42]

She followed her own advice. By November she had finished the five novellas which would be published in 1943: *Gigi*, "The Kepi," "The Tender Shoot," "Green Sealing Wax," and "Armande."[43] She had them typed and submitted them to the censor. "At the end of two weeks," she explained to Renée, "one of the lady members of this thing [the censorship committee] calls up to tell me that I have her best wishes and that she 'hopes' to give me some good news soon. She's twenty-four years old. It's the Europe of the future. Best not to say anything. Best just to wait."[44]

In the meantime, Louis Thomas published *From My Window*, a collection of Colette's articles from *Le Petit Parisien*. She chose a dictée for the schoolchildren of France, on the theme of "solidarity," which was published in the Vichyite *La Semaine*.[45] In late October, she gave *Gigi* to *Présent*, another pro-Vichy journal, noting that she was happy enough never to have seen a copy. She also sold an article to Joseph Darnand, editor of *Combats*, the journal of the murderous Vichy militia. It was entitled, one hopes subversively, "Fanatiques."[46] In November she contributed "My Poor Burgundy" to *La Gerbe*, sharing a page devoted to her native province with a writer from the Propaganda-Staffel. He took up a subject which she had once tackled herself, as a twelve-year-old sitting for her primary-school exams: "Germany's ancient claim to Burgundy." Mme Viellard's best writer scored only a three out of ten because the assignment was so obscure. Her failure was public then, and her shame was public now. *Les Lettres françaises* reproached her in an article entitled "Colette, Burgundy, and Mr. Goebbels": "In giving to the Occupation-controlled press even the slightest fragment of an article, and even an article untouched by politics, a writer sounds his note in the concert of enemy propaganda orchestrated by Goebbels. And it is painful to see the name of Colette, respected until now, serving such a task."[47]

7

NEVER ARE COLETTE'S "powers of denial" greater than in her last works of fiction, and never is she more endearing or accessible. Perhaps that is why the old sinner who narrates these tales, and who, like Gigi's Aunt Alicia, is so rich in erotic wisdom, has been the writer most widely read, revered, and remembered. She escapes from old age, and from a time, as Monzie calls it, of filth and pestilence, to an innocent and lighthearted past. The tone of these novellas is elegiac, and they are suffused with greenness. There are touches of the green of poison, the green of acid, the green of bile, but the verdancy of youth is their antidote. Colette is generous and tender to her young lovers. In *Gigi* and "Armande," true love is tested, but it triumphs. The worst that happens in any of these tales is that a feverish dreamer who has been naively contriving an apotheosis—of romance in "The Kepi," of death in "The Sick Child" and "The Photographer's Wife," of pleasure in "The Tender Shoot"—is safely disillusioned.

In her novellas from the war years, Colette reveals the smiling face she begrudged to the camera throughout her life, and the maternal benevolence that she feared so terribly to show her child. They signal a sickbed conversion of sorts. It's not quite to a solid faith in love, in lasting happiness, or in redemption—she was too inveterate an unbeliever and too vigilant an artist to let herself go so far. But she allows that in a marriage or an affair there may be no victims, except, perhaps, of vanity, and that lust is not invariably predatory or destructive: it may coexist with devotion.

Toward the beginning of *Gigi*, Aunt Alicia, the retired courtesan, gives her niece a lesson in gemology. She opens her jewel box and asks Gigi to identify the stones. When she mistakes a yellow diamond for a topaz, the old woman is scandalized. "A topaz among my jewels? Why not an aquamarine or a chrysolite?" And she goes on to instruct the girl that one must never wear either semi-precious or "artistic" baubles, such as "an Egyptian scarab. A large engraved amethyst. . . . A studded tortoise." Cameos fall into the same sentimental trash heap. "There are precious stones and pearls," she concludes. "There are white, yellow, blue, blue-white, or pink diamonds. . . . Then there are rubies—when you can be sure of them; sapphires when they come from Kashmir; emeralds, provided they have no fatal flaw."[48]

It's a sublimely charming little lecture about professional pride that applies equally well to the gem of a story Colette is telling, and to the jewel box of her prose, which contains, at this late stage, nothing flawed, nothing showily "artistic," nothing unworthy. Colette's style is never purer than at the end of her career in fiction, and her artistic feat inspires the same hushed admiration that Gigi feels for the large square-cut emerald her aunt got from a king, and which she slips onto Gigi's finger with the observation that "only the most beautiful emeralds contain that miracle of elusive blue."

Alicia knows, as Gigi doesn't, how much labor, intrigue, squalor, degradation, and also how much passion have been endured in order to pay for such an untainted miracle, and it's an image for Colette's unlikely trajectory in life and for her gift—mined from an obscure bed in the earth, acquired cheaply by a speculator with a canny eye, and polished by love's abrasions.

CHAPTER 42

1

ON NOVEMBER 7, 1942, the Allies landed in North Africa, and the Germans moved to occupy the whole of France. One of their first concerns was to purge the formerly free zone of the Jews who had escaped internment by Pétain. Maurice fled Saint-Tropez and went into hiding with friends in the Tarn, but stayed there only briefly. By early December, after several close calls with a French roadblock and a German border patrol, he had managed to regain Paris. For the next eighteen months, he spent the hours between midnight and nine in the morning sleeping in a maid's room in the Palais-Royal. He admitted later this was probably a ruse worthy of an "ostrich," but explained that he and Colette had decided "a bit arbitrarily" that if the Gestapo hadn't come for him by dawn, he was safe for another day.

If Maurice's behavior is evidence of a puerile wishfulness, it was also exceptionally gallant. He had survived Compiègne, he had worn the yellow star, and he must have, by now, come to understand the scope of the Nazi persecutions. But he also understood that Colette couldn't live without him. "You know that I'm an animal who hides herself when she feels unworthy to face the daylight," she tells Renée while her husband is living with the van den Hensts. "At this moment, I'm paying, with a secret weakness, for my three consecutive years in Paris. I'm losing air, physically and morally. Maurice writes to me every day, I write to him every day. But so many days go by, and I feel so old."[1] So he risked his life to relieve her solitude and her anxiety. "Maurice is fine," she tells Pierre Moreno after her husband's return to the Palais-Royal. "His strength of character never deserts him. I can't tell you that we're 'tranquil,' but he's so good at substituting serenity for security that I'm often fooled."[2]

PERHAPS IT WAS an ostrichlike impulse of her own that inspired Colette—a lifelong agnostic—to begin flirting with religion, or at least with a particularly seductive and eloquent emissary of the Church, François Mauriac. Goudeket recounts that in the spring of 1943, Colette received a series of bedside visits from Mauriac, who had decided that it was his personal mission to "lead Colette to God." They had long discussions about grace, exchanged letters, and Colette began reading the Bible, particularly the epistles of Saint Paul, and "other pious works." She told Mauriac that she would like to have a "humble black missal" like the one she used as a girl to prepare for her First Communion, and by a "miraculous" coincidence, a humble black missal arrived at her door. It hadn't come from the great writer, as Colette initially supposed, but from a very ill lady admirer to whom Colette had appeared in a dream, asking for just such a gift. On the first page, the lady had inscribed a line from Saint John: "For if our heart condemns us, God is greater than our heart."[3]

Colette's heart had any number of its own reasons to contemplate atonement and forgiveness, and Mauriac, writes Goudeket, believed that he was close to effecting her conversion. She had just turned seventy, she was incurably crippled, and she frequently wondered aloud if she would live through the war. Two of her closest friends—Hélène and Renée—were terminally ill, and Renée, in the care of nuns, was receiving the sacraments. Colette encouraged her devotions, and she lit candles at her parish church not only for Renée but for other imperiled friends.

Goudeket, however, took a more skeptical view of his wife's motives. They were "complex," he allows, "but . . . the hope that [her "spiritual flirtation" with Mauriac] might give me some immunity in a moment of great danger was certainly paramount among them."[4] Mauriac had tremendous influence in Church circles, and when Colette asked him to help obtain Maurice's baptism, he did what he could. If her own protestation of faith would make her husband's more convincing, she was game. "I feel a savage about so many things," she told her mentor, "but without the least bad will, on the contrary. Maurice Goudeket is beginning to learn how to plant little candles on the altar of Nôtre Dame des Victoires, next door. . . . [He] is so well worth knowing. More than me."[5]

In the end, the Jesuit father to whom Mauriac recommended Goudeket "frigidly" rejected his rationale for becoming a Catholic. Asked why, at the age of fifty-five, he suddenly wanted to convert, Maurice improvised a little speech about "desiring to embrace the religion of my country." The religious imperative, he continued, was to seek perfection, so it really shouldn't matter whether God existed or whether man had created him.[6] Colette, "alas," had married an honest man who couldn't lie to a Nazi or a priest.

Mauriac takes on the project of Colette's conversion at the same time he is engaged, in his writings for the underground, with exhorting his countrymen to examine their consciences and reject collaboration. There's an ironic symmetry to their perspectives on honor and salvation: his are large, spiritual, and austere; hers are focused on the survival of one essential being, and she would collaborate with anyone—God or the devil—who might help her keep him.

One afternoon in mid-April, having written to announce a visit, Mauriac arrived at Colette's apartment to be told that she wouldn't see him. She may just have been feeling too low and *méchante* to receive visitors—she turned many close friends away for that reason—but he wrote her a hurt letter noting that "certain rumors" led him to believe that she had "slammed her door" on him because she judged his friendship too "compromising."[7]

This letter stung Colette to the quick:

> "Compromising!" Dear, dear Mauriac, it's a word that suits you as badly as it does me. How could you have written it? I'll reproach you for it a very long time.
>
> Sometimes your plump bee falls beneath herself. The moment you recall to me was a vile moment. A bad, somber, hopeless moment when I was trembling for the one I love the most. So I hide myself. I don't feel myself to be honorable.
>
> I am still trembling. But where to find reassurance? . . . Dear Mauriac, tell me that there is no cloud between us.[8]

2

COLETTE'S LETTERS FROM 1943 begin to resemble Sido's. They are a long, mostly wry catalogue of village gossip and petty woes, her own and others'. She started a course of acupuncture for her arthritis, which brought no relief. She lost her best pen. Her friend Tonton was mugged.[9] Fashion was taking an alarming turn: adapting to the shortage of cloth, the women of Paris were wearing oddly cut short skirts which flaunted their thighs.

In July, Colette had contracted what she thought was a case of violent food poisoning or enteritis, but it proved to be an exotic and extremely stubborn South American protozoan. "Where could I have got such a bug?" she wonders to Moreno. "I've traveled so little!" The bug ravaged her intestinal tract for five months, and by the autumn she was taking large doses of "poison," including laudanum, in an attempt to kill it.

At the end of October, "after two years of torture," Renée Hamon died of cancer. She had no family, but a devoted friend had arranged for her care, and it was he who informed Colette of her death. "You and I will be, I think, very calm when we meet again," she told him. "I have always worked like a dog not to admit [my grief], and most of the time I've succeeded. But I can't refuse myself the sad pleasure of telling you that I'm in pain. If, by chance, you bring back [from Brittany] any possessions you feel obliged to give me, please be kind enough to keep them for a while. I don't need them at the moment. I don't even need to see them at the moment."[10]

THE PRECEDING SPRING, Colette had finished several minor prose "concoctions" which she wrote for her "daily bread" and which were published in luxury editions.[11] Her long illness interrupted her work, but by the end of the year, she was feeling strong enough to begin the short story which was to be her last work of fiction. The Proustian hero of "The Sick Child" is a fastidious boy of about twelve, bedridden by a nameless malady that we infer to be polio, for it comes with a high fever and paralysis. Jean's secret is that he is not at all unhappy to be sick. He is enjoying his privilege as an invalid and only child to conduct an intense romance with his mother, and Colette describes him as the "lord of her sorrow and joys." His maid and his books provide all the other companionship and adventure he requires. While his two houris take turns at his bedside, he escapes from the body that is fighting off death into a dreamworld that is so vivid and intoxicating he is loath to leave it. But when his crisis passes, so do his visions: "A time comes when one is forced to concentrate on living. A time comes when one has to renounce dying in full flight. With a wave of his hand, Jean said farewell to his angel-haired reflection. The other returned his greeting from the depths of an earthly night shorn of all marvels, the only night allowed to children whom death releases and who fall asleep, assenting, cured, and disappointed."[12]

It is one of the great ironies of her career that her own farewell story should be a song of innocence, a poetic fugue in which Colette disavows the pleasures of the flesh, pays tribute to the seductions of books, language, and death, and gives free rein to that "dangerous" lyricism she had tried for fifty years to suppress. Critics have called its style "surreal" or "experimental," but Colette's real experiment, in "The Sick Child," is with letting life go.

3

COLETTE WRESTLED with her last story for three months, living in seclusion. When it was finished, a few days before her seventy-first birthday, she celebrated by attending a matinée of Claudel's new play, *Le Soulier de satin*, at the Comédie-Française. She almost never left her apartment anymore, and she had been worried about sitting through the five-hour performance. Managing to enjoy it was a proud feat.

The spring of 1944 was one of rumors, terror, roundups, executions, blackouts, and extreme shortages of fuel and food. France, writes Philippe Burrin, "was a virtual militia-state." Pierre Moreno, an active member of the Touzac Resistance, had been arrested in February, and Colette wrote almost daily to Marguerite, commiserating with her grief and impotence. "God keeps me from recounting to you everything that's happening around us, very close, too close," she told her old friend. "What sustains us if not a fatalism that is content to be more and more blind?"[13]

Refugees from the south were arriving in Paris with no money and no place to stay—among them the van den Hensts. Colette found them a temporary refuge at the Palais-Royal, and a month later, they "miraculously" made their way to Portugal, and from there to Guatemala.[14] Renaud arrived from the Corrèze to report that the militia had requisitioned Castel-Novel. Monzie was helping him to recover his property, and he suggested that Moreno ask the former deputy, who had considerable influence with the Vichy authorities, to help free Pierre. "Naturally, if I can do anything at all between you and him, use me," Colette urged her. She also offered, more reluctantly, to approach Sacha Guitry.

The Allies were bombing strategic German targets inside France, and on April 23, their planes hit the La Chappelle staging grounds in Paris, subjecting the capital to an intensity of firepower it hadn't yet suffered. "You know the Palais-Royal enough," Colette told Moreno, "to imagine what a bombardment (the first of this sort) can produce in the way of noise and vibration on a charming but crumbling edifice. I won't insist." Like most of their compatriots, the Goudekets were waiting impatiently for "the pretty little communiqué" that would announce an Allied landing on French soil. When D-Day came—on June 6—Colette mentions her "excitement" only briefly. She had been toiling on a volume of her essays for a Swiss publisher,[15] and "under what conditions!"

The news of the Normandy invasion reached Colette at the same moment she learned that Missy had tried to commit suicide in "something like a harakiri." She had been out of touch with the marquise for two years, she told Moreno, as the result of a quarrel which Colette put down to "one of those childish whims (81 years old) which [Missy] always had. She *signified* to me that she wouldn't see me again, and I took good care not to protest. She proceeded to lose more and more of her memory, and couldn't find her way around Paris, even with little notes to remind her of where she was going. There is nothing gay about the end of her life. . . . Maurice was full of pity and astonishment in the face of this unfinished creature."[16]

If she herself felt any pity for her old friend, she doesn't voice it. Missy made a second suicide attempt on June 29—this time with gas—and succeeded. André de Fouquières reported in his memoirs that she had outlived most of her relations, and that there were only about a dozen faithful friends at her funeral. Sacha Guitry was her chief mourner.[17]

4

BY THE MIDDLE of August, there were twilight traffic jams in the streets of Paris as Germans and collaborators fled the advancing Allied forces. Small crowds of citizens stopped to jeer at their vehicles, many of which were laden with the spoils of last-minute looting. Abetz ordered the evacuation of Pétain and his administration to Belfort, on the German border, and from there to Sigmaringen, on the Danube. So many staff members of *Je suis partout* had joined the exodus that the paper had been rechristened *Je suis parti*.

Hitler had instructed the military commander of Paris, General von Cholitz, to defend the city to his last man, then reduce it to rubble. The general fortified his strongholds—the Senate and Parliament buildings in the Luxembourg and Bourbon palaces, the École Militaire, the Invalides, and Nazi headquarters in the Hôtel Majestic. He later protested that he'd had no desire to go down in history as the barbarian who sacked Paris, but that all he could do was to hope the Allies arrived before the Luftwaffe.

Eisenhower hadn't planned to march on the capital for another two weeks, giving Patton the opportunity to pursue the retreating Germans across northern France. De Gaulle and Leclerc, the head of the Free French Forces, begged him to reconsider, afraid, in part, of a communist takeover of the city if they hesitated. On August 22, the Americans changed their minds and told Leclerc he could advance, which—to "exultant yells of *Mouvement sur Paris!*"[18]—he did at dawn the next morning.

The communist Free French had, in the meantime, mounted barricades in the student and working-class neighborhoods. The police refused to arrest demonstrators or to help the Germans restore order, and went on strike. The

Resistance radio began broadcasting the "Marseillaise," and all over the city, citizens played the anthem at full volume from their open windows. Bands of partisans armed with Molotov cocktails ambushed German convoys, and the Germans fought back with tanks and machine guns. There were heavy casualties.

Maurice was almost among them. He went out on the eighteenth to breathe the air of insurrection, and crossing the Tuileries near the place de la Concorde, he stopped—"out of curiosity"—to witness an exchange of fire between the Germans and some undercover French policemen. When the Germans set up a machine-gun nest and began rounding up pedestrians, he hid in a bomb shelter beneath the gardens, and when they locked the gates of the Tuileries, he was trapped there for three days. Colette, frantic with anxiety, sent friends to search for him in the hospitals, morgues, and impromptu medical stations around the city, and when he arrived home to recount his idiotic misadventure, she cursed him roundly.

On the last night of the Occupation, a terrible air battle raged over Paris. Colette and several neighbors took refuge in her foyer, all having refused to descend into the shelters. By the next day, the partisans could hear the Allied cannons in the suburbs, and a great crowd began to gather at the Porte de Saint-Cloud. Cyclists spread the news that Captain Dronne and his tank regiment were approaching the Pont d'Austerlitz. For the first time in four years, the great bells of Nôtre-Dame began tolling over the Seine. Improvised tricolors appeared at windows around the city—making them a target for the German snipers and the militia. Women made themselves beautiful for their liberators. "Most planned on wearing the tricolor in some form or other, in panels on their skirt or even on earrings. Others sewed flags out of old clothes to greet their French and American liberators the next morning."[19]

Colette and Maurice turned on the radio to hear a choked voice announce the liberation of Paris, but the sound was drowned out by the fusillade from a German tank shelling the buildings on the rue des Petits-Champs just behind them. At two that afternoon, Cholitz met Leclerc at the Prefecture of Police and signed the surrender. At eight, General de Gaulle greeted the leaders of the Resistance at the Hôtel de Ville, and from its balcony, he raised his gangly arms in the sign of victory to a tremendous weeping and cheering throng. For France, the war was over.

Colette could see only as far as the thicket of ragged red, white, and blue flags "waving like foliage along the rue Vivienne." But looking eastward, she glimpsed the blaze of torchlights, like an aurora, at the Hôtel de Ville. It was still early on that mild summer evening, and the victory celebrations—the "orgy of fraternity," as de Beauvoir puts it—would go on through a night in which Venus, incarnate in a million women, paid homage to Mars. How poignant that night must have been to the aching old women of Paris, kept awake, as Colette was, by their memories and their insomnia. It was a long time, a lifetime, since she had taken the virile body of a young stranger into her bed. "Happy were those, that night, who did not restrain their frenzy," she wrote. "Happy those who were beside themselves!"[20]

CHAPTER 43

To be a grown-up person . . . is the one thing none of us can ever be.
— COLETTE,
to Truman Capote

l

OLETTE HAD ten years left. She spent most of them in her bedroom
at the Palais-Royal, on the daybed that she called her "raft" and where
she worked and slept. Her reading lamp had a blue bulb and an improvised shade made of her blue writing paper. At night, it marked her window to
anyone passing through the gardens. She would call her last memoir *The Blue
Lantern*.

The daybed-raft was pushed up against the window, and when the weather
was warm and dry, Colette would, as she put it, "go to sleep outdoors." But
the damp was killing to her arthritis, and she was, as the French say, *frileuse*—
a born shiverer who suffered inordinately from the cold. For most of the year,
she wrapped her pain-crippled legs in a fur throw and kept her room at the
temperature of a hothouse. It was a real old lady's boudoir, rosy, scented, and
overstuffed. There were boxes of chocolate and bowls of fruit by her bedside,
and jugs and vases of flowers—the tributes of her admirers or bribes from
journalists, producers, and autograph seekers hoping for an interview. The
well-ordered drawers of her bureaus were filled with photographs: Colette
Willy in a lion skin and a tuxedo; the last Cat; her brood of Jouvenels at
Rozven. She spent the hours when she was too ill or distracted to work poring
through them.

Colette had a passion for crystal paperweights, and her collection crowded the mantel. Her own needlework adorned several of the chairs. Winnie de Polignac had given her an antique writing table that she had modified, adding wheels and raising the top. She could draw this lap desk up to her bedside by hooking it with her cane, the same method she used to retrieve books, the phone, her little American radio, or the thermometer, and which she called "fishing from the raft." A blue jar on the table held her "bouquet" of pens.

The walls and ceiling of this lair were papered in Colette's favorite color, red, and hung with her mounted butterflies and her paintings. She had once asked Francis Carco to help her acquire a collection of modern art, and she could, he writes, "have bought a dozen Mondrians for a thousand francs."[1] But he quickly saw that her sentimental taste for watercolors, landscapes, drawings by literary friends, and pictures of fruit and flowers was unshakable. She did, however, own a fine Derain and a little portrait by Marie Laurencin. Otherwise, she had "banished" all representations of the human face.[2]

Even close friends could never be assured that Colette would receive them. She instinctively hid her fragility and her fatigue, as indeed she always had. Her husband and Pauline protected her fiercely. "Monsters need their tamers, and without them, they figure out their power and eat us," wrote Cocteau. "Maurice Goudeket has always been the tamer of his wife's monsters, and of that delicious monster she was herself."[3] But when she did consent to receive a visitor, she knotted a scarf around her wizened neck and called for her makeup and her hand mirror. She still permed and hennaed her hair, which she likens to a "bird's nest." Cocteau, more grandiosely, compares it to the tawny mane of "a captive lioness" amused by the human spectators admitted to her cage ("my mousetrap," says Colette). She regarded them, he continues, "with the gaze of a pensive wild animal . . . and as these persons, once their curiosity had been satisfied, didn't know what to say, the roles were reversed, and it was the lioness who threw them the tidbits of a few words, until Maurice . . . appeared and showed them to the door."[4]

In the first book Colette published after the war, her memoir *The Evening Star* (1946), she wonders if she can learn how not to write. She couldn't. In the late forties, her Swiss publisher, Mermod, had the inspired idea of sending her a bouquet of flowers once or twice a week for a year, and of harvesting her literary portraits of them in a little volume which she called *Pour un herbier* (1948). *The Blue Lantern* was published the next year. That stoical and serene memoir was her last original piece of writing, but she wasn't yet finished with her labors. She wrote the dialogue for the (French) film version of *Gigi*. She undertook to reedit, preface, and, where necessary, revise her entire oeuvre for a fifteen-volume *Collected Works*. At seventy-nine, two years before her death, Colette tried, for the first time in her life, to keep a diary:

I should indeed like . . .

1) to begin again . . .
2) to begin again . . .
3) to begin again . . .[5]

2

COLETTE'S HABITS AND constitution had promised her a vigorous old age, and she had always imagined she would, like her mother and their old mare, "die in her traces." Her infirmity was a cruel, a never-endingly cruel, surprise. "Old age is an uncomfortable piece of furniture," she told the little farmers.[6] Crippled, corpulent—it would take two strong men to carry her wheelchair up and down the stairs—she was, in the last years, as immobile as an old Chinese empress with bound feet. "I miss so much," she wrote, "with such obstinate strength and intolerance, a sky, a countryside, and unbounded and inalienable possession."[7] Yet she proudly refused narcotics or sleeping pills and even aspirin, which, she protested, "changes the color of my thoughts."[8] She showed an athlete's disdain for physical suffering: pain was, as passion had once been, her "gymnasium for the will."[9]

Every time Colette was tempted by self-pity, she recalled that morning in December when her husband had been taken from her, and she consoled herself with the thought that the greatest calamity that could befall her had already happened and had been survived. The date of his arrest became a mantra. Maurice is an ever vigilant, discreet presence in her last writings and letters. "One senses their loving tact to each other," writes Richardson. "She is maintaining the pretense that she is not in pain, and he is pretending to believe it."[10] To Natalie Barney, Colette describes her husband as "the pearl— the diamond—of houseguests. Present and absent just as one desires. He's the man I should have adopted twenty years ago . . . but then we'd probably have created a scandal."[11]

Maurice, approaching sixty, was not quite young enough to be her son, but he was still a healthy male, vain of his fitness, fond of society, who would remarry after Colette's death and father a son of his own. "Poor Maurice," writes Colette to Moune, "I burden him with cares. He has a charming manner of asking, apropos of everything, 'You don't need me?' with a detached—and revealing—air."[12] When she didn't need him for anything, he pursued his own pleasures beyond the confines of his wife's sickroom, and he had an erotic life about which Colette had no illusions. In 1939, when Renée Hamon had asked her for the secret of her marital happiness, Colette had answered candidly: "What binds me to Maurice and him to me? It's my virility. I shock him sometimes, but it's only with me that he can live. When he feels like fucking, he chooses a very feminine woman; he likes to surround himself with that kind of woman, but he would never know how to live with them."[13] In *The Evening Star* (*L'Étoile vesper*), which she dedicates to Venus—Vesper's other name—Colette suggests that the impulse to scourge her rivals is still alive in her, that jealousy "remains one of my mysterious recreations as an old woman."[14]

CHRONIC PAIN DULLED but never completely extinguished Colette's wanderlust. She describes her last writings as "a promenade, an aimless unplanned contemplation," but only on the page could she "direct [her] steps in an unforeseen direction." What bothered her most—the verb "bother" having become her euphemism for any more "tragic" expression of distress— was the loss of access to the impromptu, and the ability to satisfy the little craving of the moment: tucking into a platter of oysters on the terrace of a café, browsing among the dusty wares in an antiques shop. Like the movements of an old empress, all her excursions had to be elaborately choreographed and attended. "I'm deposited on the plane like the inert parcel that I am," she tells Germaine Patat cheerfully in the early 1950s, en route to Monte Carlo.[15]

Colette's last decade was, nevertheless, relieved by visits to friends with comfortable houses, sojourns at four-star hotels, and excursions to provincial and foreign spas, where she was always game to try some new miracle treatment for her arthritis. She submitted to electric shocks, to hot baths, to X-rays, to painful massage, to injections of hormones, novocaine, and thermal waters—excruciating shots into her neck, her knees, her spine. "There are so many ways of being cured," she muses optimistically. "Perhaps I shall invent one."[16]

DURING THE SPRING of 1945, the Allied forces were advancing on Berlin and liberating the camps as they moved deeper into Germany. The first *déportés* began to reach Paris.[17] "France," write Beevor and Cooper, "had been partially shielded from the appalling truth," and few were prepared for the condition of the survivors. They descended from trains at the Gare de l'Est or the Gare de Lyon like skeletons from an old French *danse macabre*, some in rags, others in prison uniforms or in borrowed camouflage many sizes too large. Their skin was gray; their eyes were hollow and unseeing, their heads shaved or bald from malnutrition. "Those who could [remain upright] stood to attention in front of the welcoming committee and began to sing the 'Marseillaise' in cracked voices. The audience was devastated."[18]

De Gaulle, meanwhile, was staging a series of pre-victory celebrations and military parades to rally a citizenry heartened but also shaken by the reports from Germany, politically restive and still hungry. Early in April, the Goudekets were invited to a banquet for a hundred guests held in conjunction with one of the parades. Colette left the oppressively crowded party toward one in the morning, though Maurice stayed behind. The streets were impassable, so the young military chauffeur who was driving her home stopped at l'Étoile and helped her from the car. The entire avenue, she told the little farmers, "was a block of incandescent silver, sparkling with balls of fire, and because of the flags that lined its vault, the interior of the Arc de Triomphe was the color of lavender blossoms and mauve clematis. . . . At that hour, I was content . . . submerged in the crowd and the noise, to enjoy the sounds and the spectacle with a feeling of solitude, alone with a young French gentleman, anonymous and happy, a pure grain of France."[19]

LATER THAT MONTH, and again that summer, the Goudekets stayed with Simone Berriau[20] at Hyères, where Colette worked on *The Evening Star*. They had a ground-floor room with a private terrace and a view of the salt marshes. The beauty of her surroundings consoled Colette, though not entirely, for the hectic rhythm of the establishment and the "alarming" exuberance of their hostess, who thought nothing of inviting twenty stray celebrities home for dinner. Among them was Jean-Paul Sartre, who "loved and admired" Colette's writing.[21] She, according to Berriau (who would produce most of Sartre's plays at her Théâtre Antoine), was somewhat awed by the existentialist's formidable intelligence and "cold passion."[22] Their hostess, however, would recall that they played canasta together, and she would arrange a more stimulating encounter for them three years hence.

While the Goudekets were in Provence, Bel-Gazou was in Germany as a correspondent for the left-wing review of culture and politics *Fraternité*, and she was one of the first French journalists to report from the camps. "She signs herself Colette de Jouvenel," Colette observes strangely to the little farmers—it was, after all, her name. But she was impressed by her daughter's courage and "tone," which were "so like her father's."[23] "The *authentic* accounts of the torture camps," she concluded, "create an unbreathable atmosphere. What imagination will ever equal that of the executioners?"[24]

ON MAY 2, 1945, Colette received a singular honor: she was elected to the Académie Goncourt. The academy and its annual prize for the year's best novel—the most prestigious literary award in France—had been established by Edmond de Goncourt upon his death in 1896. By the terms of his will, women, Jews, poets, and members of the Académie-Française were excluded from the ten chairs that he had endowed. An exception had been made only once, in 1910, for Judith Gautier.[25]

Colette's election was attended by a barrage of publicity, which exhausted her, and by the delivery of a boxcarload of new fiction to read, which she did assiduously, her labors rewarded by the monthly Goncourt lunch at Drouant. Here she joined her friends Francis Carco, Roland Dorgelès, Léo Larguier, and André Billy, who were mere striplings compared to Lucien Descaves, eighty-four, and J. H. Rosny the Younger, one of the academy's original members, still flirtatious (not to mention ambulatory) at eighty-six. When Descaves died, in 1949, the academicians would choose Colette as their president. "We are diverse, we are fiercely unalike, we are rebels against cohesion," she wrote. And: "It is no good my posing as an old buck, for I still thoroughly enjoy the intensely feminine pleasure of being the only woman at the Goncourt Lunches. . . . They have the air, one and all, of remembering the woman I was once."[26]

The purge trials—*l'épuration*—were in full swing by the beginning of 1945. There were new blacklists and book burnings. Many collaborators who had been questioned and released, or only briefly imprisoned, like Chanel and Georges Simenon, received death threats and left the country or went into hiding. Arletty's head was shaved. Maillot's studio was sacked. Drieu La Rochelle committed suicide. Charles Maurras was imprisoned for life. "It's the revenge of Dreyfus!" he shouted as he was led back to his cell.[27] Henri Béraud, the editor of *Gringoire,* was condemned to death, although de Gaulle commuted his sentence to life on the ground that he had never actively provided the enemy with intelligence. Brasillach, who was tried for treason a few days later, received a death sentence the same day. The speed of these proceedings and the ferocity of the oratory that enveloped them alarmed a number of the most eminent literary *résistants,* including Paulhan, who kept his distance from the hard-liners at *Les Lettres françaises;* Camus, who called for justice without hatred; and Mauriac, who sympathized with the rage and grief of those who had been tortured or lost members of their family, but who begged his fellow citizens to resist, "at all cost, walking in the boots of the Nazis."[28]

The enthusiasm which greeted Colette's election to the Goncourt is one measure of how unscathed her reputation was by her contributions to the Occupation press. She owed her seat to the resignation of Jean de la Varende, compromised by his staunch support for Pétain, and the academy subsequently voted to expel three other tainted confrères, among them Sacha Guitry, who was one of the first Occupation celebrities to be arrested—on August 23, in his dressing gown and slippers.

Colette deplored the *épuration* in much stronger language than she had ever used against the Occupation: the trials were *dégueulasses* (vomitous), she told Lucio Saglio. "I use this word, which is itself ignoble, on purpose."[29] Yet when Brasillach's attorney, Jacques Isorni, solicited her name for the petition he was circulating among eminent writers, imploring de Gaulle to commute his client's death sentence to life in prison, she refused to sign it. She told Isorni:

> I don't know the Robert Brasillach of *Je suis partout*. I knew the young writer, the novelist who began his career so brilliantly. I cannot and shall not speak of any other. During the war, he asked to see me at least once. He knew that I was the wife of a man who had suffered the horrors of a concentration camp in winter, then the necessity of living hidden and being hunted for interminable months, in short, one of those men for whom *Je suis partout* never ceased to demand the worst treatment. However, I received Robert Brasillach . . . we agreed to observe the truce of a conversation that tried in every possible way to faithfully reproduce the tone of our former meetings, when Brasillach was so happily embarking on his literary career and I watched him, with pleasure, progress in it. . . . Brasillach had nothing to ask of me, and I had nothing to implore of those whom he believed to be all-powerful. His work? It is for time to judge. I have often written him to praise his novels and to rejoice in his gifts.[30]

Brasillach was indignant. "When I think that Colette signed her letters 'your old friend' and that she wrote, 'I am happy that I watched you grow up . . .' That was during the Occupation; she knew quite well what I was doing; I haven't changed since then. . . . Better just to shrug our shoulders!"[31]

Cocteau finally persuaded Colette to change her mind, and she lent her name to the appeal, which de Gaulle rejected. There were no nuances to Brasillach's case under the law: he had committed treason; he had worked for the enemy and traveled to Germany; he had written propaganda and delivered pro-Nazi speeches; he had advocated the execution of Resistance members and argued passionately for ridding France of its Jews, even the "little ones." On February 6, 1945, he was executed by a firing squad.

Perhaps Colette's stance toward Brasillach was also influenced by her daughter, who had run a clandestine hospital for the Maquis (Resistance guerrilla fighters), founded a relief organization in the Corrèze immediately following the liberation, and worked tirelessly to feed the starving and relieve the misery of the dispossessed. That November, Bel-Gazou had moved back to

Paris and was helping to edit *Fraternité*. In her own articles, she took a fierce stand in favor of the *épuration* and against the "indulgence" being shown to collaborators less controversial than Brasillach. The gravity of their crimes was not abstract to her. Some of her closest friends in the Resistance had been deported to Buchenwald, and almost none of them had returned. Colette describes a couple of these rare survivors to Moreno: mute women with dead eyes who, outside a café in the place des Ternes, "raised their skirts to show their legs, devoured up to the groin by the camp dogs."[32]

3

A DAY BEFORE her seventy-second birthday, Colette received a letter from a stranger who had found Hélène Picard—unrecognizable and near death—in the communal ward of a Paris hospital. Hélène died a few days later, clutching a last telegram from Colette, unopened, in her hand. She died like a poet, Colette would write, "a poet of 1830," starving, tubercular, and by her own choice—she wanted no one to see her as the "unrecognizable dwarf "[33] she had become—utterly alone. Her aerie on the rue d'Alleray was a shambles. It had been years since the once impeccable housekeeper had laundered her tulle curtains or put up her jam. She had renounced meat, and human contact. There was five hundred francs' worth of locks and bolts on her door. She believed that she was being spied on by the same nameless persecutors who were supposedly diverting her mail.

Colette had been out of touch with her old friend for a while—their last published exchange of letters is dated 1942—believing she had left Paris to live with her sister in the Ariège. "It was [Hélène]," she writes, "who decided that our friendship had grown to become a bond which separation stretches but does not break, which is tested by its strength in absence, and which forms its judgments with uncompromising freedom."[34]

"If I thought Colette would ever see me living like this, I'd commit suicide," Hélène told a neighbor who sometimes looked in on her, the only living soul besides a local doctor and a delivery boy from the dairy shop for whom she unlocked her door. The neighbor and the doctor arranged the funeral. Colette sent violets. Later, she asked for Hélène's papers, hoping to salvage enough new work for a volume. There were reams of unfinished poems and some letters to Colette that had never been mailed. "You penetrated her, you vivified her," wrote the neighbor, "to the point that she was living through your life. [You two were] so alike and so different!" Colette, she concluded, was "the authentic being of which Hélène Picard was only a reflection."[35]

Colette made no comment on this awestruck and morbid homage, although she thanked the neighbor graciously for her acts of kindness. Her own mourning took the form of a magnificent obituary that detaches Hélène from the shadows of her subservience, her misanthropy, her failures. The strange and ferocious woman who emerges from this portrait existed for Colette—penetrated *her* reticence—as few people did. "How many friends have passed away whom I can call friends? Very few. Very few, thank God. How can one gauge friendship, save by its jewel-like rarity? When death intervenes, with its constancy of regret and its illumination, we can think: 'I loved truly.' "[36]

4

MORENO WAS NOW Colette's only remaining intimate of her own generation. In the autumn of 1945, she was rehearsing her title role in Giraudoux's *The Madwoman of Chaillot*, which opened in December and ran through May. The brilliance of the production blinded the audience, although not the more discerning critics, including Colette, to the contrivances of the text. It was, however, an unqualified triumph for Moreno, whose lunatic radiance as Aurélie consolidated her reputation as France's greatest comic actress.

The *Madwoman* was the hottest ticket in Paris. Colette went to the fifth performance. "The end of the play as you act it," she told Moreno, "grabs the heart. . . . It confirms your infinite possibilities—which you underestimate."[37] And she began signing her letters to Moreno as Sido had always concluded hers: *"Je t'embrasse comme je t'aime."*

The Evening Star was published on Bastille Day, 1945. Paris was deserted, and the book received very little publicity. Colette herself was not at home. At the urging of her physician and friend, Marthe Lamy, she was taking a cure at a spa-hotel in Uriage, close to the resort where she had stayed as a bride. She was suffering "night and day," she told Moreno, and the medical director of the establishment cautioned her not to expect results for two months. Maurice had never seen her so discouraged.

Hoping to revive her spirits in that southern climate that had nurtured their early love and some of her best work, Maurice took her to spend ten days with their friends Charles and Pata de Polignac, who had rented a villa south of Grasse. Charles was Winnie's nephew, and a kinsman to Prince Pierre of Monaco—a Polignac before his marriage to the hereditary Princess Charlotte. Pata became Colette's last confidante and one of "the two or three people in the world" from whom she made no attempt to conceal the true extent of her pain. The countess visited Colette regularly in Paris, and Colette "surrendered to her friend's authoritarian solicitude,"[38] which no doubt reminded her of her own—and Sido's. She pined for Pata when they were separated, begged humbly for letters, and apologized for her own "epistolary incontinence." They traded gossip, beauty and decorating secrets. The countess was Colette's designated shopper, entrusted to find pearl buttons, a pepper mill, silk embroidery thread, rouge, and upholstery fabric. But what was most beguiling to Colette about these cultivated aristocrats was their harmonious married life. It is "astonishing," Colette admits, to meet a couple "in which neither of the two is overshadowed by the other."[39]

5

THE GREAT EVENT of that autumn was the marriage of Colette's housekeeper, Pauline Verine, to a man named Julien Tissandier, who worked in Les Halles and whose existence she had long kept secret from her employers. Pauline had entered Colette's service in 1916, as a thirteen-year-old girl. She came from that Correzian peasant stock Colette admires, in *Looking Backwards,* for its stoicism, its ferocity, its gourmandise, and its fidelity to the French soil. The "moody" and "wild" little serving maid, writes Maurice, had long since become the competent and resourceful life manager Colette counted on "day and night." For thirty years, her devotion was the oil that lubricated the great engine that generated the nearly eighty volumes of Colette's oeuvre. Pauline "had no other horizon" beyond her service to "Madame" and "had never, would never, serve another master."[40] She was nearly past the age of childbearing when she finally confessed her desire to marry, asking Colette's permission like a feudal vassal or a dutiful daughter. Perhaps she felt that a child of her own would have divided her loyalties. A "placid" middle-aged husband was a manageable diversion.

Colette was Pauline's witness. After the church ceremony, the Goudekets and Bel-Gazou joined the family for the wedding breakfast, which was held in a bakehouse in Clichy owned by the groom's sister. Strict rationing was still in effect, but the couple's numerous relations, most of whom had come to Paris from the provinces, supplied the lambs, the racks of venison, the braces of game, the poultry, the sumptuous harvest vegetables, fruits, cakes, old wines and brandies, for an orgiastic feast that "no middle-class, princely, or royal house" could have provided, asserts Maurice. The Goudekets left after six hours, satiated and exhausted, just as the guests were preparing to take a little nap at their tables before resetting them for dinner.[41]

6

EARLY IN the new year, Colette's pains had become intolerable, and at Maurice's urging, she consulted a Swiss doctor named Menkès, known for his success with arthritis. After a bout of flu, she developed rheumatism in her right shoulder, which kept her from writing. It was a winter of "physical dread," and when she left that April for Geneva—where Menkès was to undertake her treatment—all she could hope for was "the return of some of my strength, or rather of some of my optimism—the two are really one and the same—if not the decisive killing of my pain."[42]

For the next six weeks, she lived in a corner room at the Hotel Richmond, with a view of Lac Léman and the mountain "of solid silver" behind it. A flock of sparrows nested on her balcony. She gorged on the wholesome delicacies that were still scarce in Paris, particularly fresh milk. Every morning, she put on a pretty dressing gown for the benefit of the "cherubic" doctor who arrived punctually to torture her for two hours, and afterward they flirted a little, like two lovers resting from their exertions on the bed. Menkès brought her lilacs and seemed desperate, she told Moune, "for me to get better. I keep wanting to lie to him: 'Yes, yes, I'm all healed . . .' or else to tell him: 'To hell with my leg, let's forge a friendship. It would be more of a success than any physical cure.' "[43]

Colette had concluded even before she left Paris that her case was hopeless, but to make both Maurice and the doctor happy, she pretended to feel a little better. Menkès suggested that her troubles were due in part to her liver and her intestines, and he put her on a spa diet. Gradually, despite her skepticism, she did feel better. She and Maurice took slow drives through the city to savor the "hesitant spring," the "military elegance" of the roses in the public gardens, and the neat shops stocked with goods that were, to Parisian eyes, fantastical in their pristine abundance. She was particularly impressed by the "luxurious" cleanliness of the Swiss children, girls in starched pinafores

> boldly [wending] their way through the peak-hour crowds, their hair a torch, their bare knees like glazed, crackling fruit skins.
>
> I admire, I rejoice, I get about, I come into contact with all these long-legged Atalantas whose praises I sing—oh no, a thousand times no, don't run away with the idea that I am jealous, or sad! Do me the honour of believing that I do know how to make the most of what is left me of my part, do know how to bear lightly what would have seemed heavy in days gone by, and derive from the flaw by which metaphorically I am ploughed and furrowed a certain . . . yes I shall say it . . . a certain nobleness of spirit.[44]

7

THAT SUMMER Colette received a surprise visit from two old friends: Natalie Barney and Lily de Gramont. Natalie had only recently returned to France, having sat out the war comfortably ensconced with Romaine Brooks in a villa overlooking Florence, and just as comfortably having adopted the views of her friend Ezra Pound toward fascism and the Jews. When the Germans had tried to requisition her apartment on the rue Jacob, Natalie's housekeeper had protested that Madame couldn't possibly be a Jew—she was a friend of Mussolini—and they had desisted.[45] Natalie remained in Italy until order had been restored to Paris, but when she finally quit her "egoist's paradise," the French authorities refused to grant her a residence permit. Colette sent her to a friend at the Foreign Ministry,[46] and the problem was ultimately resolved.

The Amazon would live for twenty-five more years, all but the last of them on the rue Jacob. She resumed her Wednesday luncheons, wrote her memoirs, traveled extensively. She had a last great love. "She incarnates that phrase of Radiguet's," wrote her biographer, " 'every age bears its fruits, it's all in knowing how to harvest them.' " Colette would have agreed, although probably not with Natalie's blithe conclusion: "the last fruits are the best."[47]

Colette had always envied Natalie's freedom from the bonds of love, and she continued to admire her vitality, just as she enjoyed Lily's flamboyant chic and the marvelous fitness of the ninety-one-year-old Elsie de Wolfe—now Lady Mendl—with whom she dined that summer. Elsie was, Colette told Moreno, "as slim as a girl," and in a dress of white muslin, with a choker of sapphires at her throat, she gave Colette, Maurice, and Prince Pierre of Monaco a tour of her fantastical topiary garden in Versailles.

Recalling the Lesbos of her youth, which was also Natalie's, Lily's, Elsie's, and Colette's, Liane de Pougy would write: "We were passionate rebels against a woman's lot, voluptuous and cerebral, little apostles, rather poetical, fond of illusions and dreams. We loved long hair, pretty breasts, simper, charm, grace, not boyishness. 'Why try to resemble our enemies?' Natalie-Flossie used to murmur in her nasal voice."[48] And these game old ladies in couture frocks, who had all shared something of Claudine's erotic recklessness, were congenial to Colette as the younger generation—her daughter, and the "self-infatuated" daughters and granddaughters of her friends—were not. "I find our young French girls to be lively and ambitious," she wrote, "but troubled in mind. Their self-confidence is merely a façade. They are mettlesome but quickly discouraged, like draught-horses that are not properly fed. They bear the traces of an inner conflict that has barely troubled their conscience, as if it were a painless wound."[49]

Perhaps every generation of sexual iconoclasts feels both slighted and "intimidated"—Colette's word—by the arrogance or laziness of its heirs, who take for granted the hard-won and tenuous freedoms that they suffered for. In the section of *The Blue Lantern* where Colette describes one of those modern ingrates—"a fresh-cheeked girl, sophisticated, hard as nails, courageous"—her opportunism arouses Colette's indignation as "an old warrior." She also looks forward, not without pity but also not without sadistic relish, to the day when the girl will return to visit her, humbled by "the hand, the mouth, the body" of her first man.[50]

8

COLETTE'S SEVENTY-FIFTH BIRTHDAY, on January 28, 1948, was the occasion for an outpouring of public homage. The newspapers, she wrote, were "splashed with affectionately possessive references to 'Our Colette'!"[51] Maurice gave her a gold bracelet, Bel-Gazou a stem of orchids. Her apartment overflowed with telegrams and tributes, and the birthday dinner was accompanied by a jeroboam of champagne and a bottle of Burgundy from 1873, her birth year, which, she noted, had, "like me . . . retained something of its fire and colour."

From the red hothouse in the heart of Paris and the fur-covered bed laden with offerings of love, Colette would recall another twenty-eighth of January, in another room. "There was very little of charm or comfort" in the chamber where she was born, or that is how she chooses to recall it. She commemorates her birthday by evoking, first of all, the cold, then an ugly wardrobe, her parents' chaste twin beds, the distraction of the midwives attending the woman in the agony of labor: "I caused my mother much pain in her travail. For close on forty-eight hours, she struggled as only women in the pangs of childbirth know how to fight. The women about her lost their heads and forgot to feed the fire in the grate. By dint of her cries and anguish my mother drove me from her womb, but since I had entered the world blue and silent, nobody thought it worth while to bother about me."[52]

This loaded passage pure of embellishment is Colette's account of the violent, primal separation that would forever color her experience of love. With her own birth is born her struggle for a sense of worth, and the mesmerizing paradox of her feelings—vengeful and reverent—for the wonderful, terrible mother who, having driven her from the womb, wouldn't let her go. Intimacy, thereafter, was oppressive to her, but more so was solitude. Her innate vitality was as sovereign as her "born" passivity was deep. She became a young woman with a weakness for bondage and an old woman with a genius for domination. Insatiable and untrusting, she sees to her own nourishment and becomes a glutton for but also an inspired dispenser of warmth, fullness, beauty, and pleasure. As Laforgue wrote so lucidly of Baudelaire: "Neither a great heart nor a great mind; and yet what plaintive nerves, what nostrils open to everything, what a magic voice."[53]

It is Colette's ambivalence toward daughterhood, then toward maternity, that fuels her drive for detachment, of which that masterful, magic voice is one expression and her resolute narcissism another. Her wariness of a potentially intrusive, too meaningful other—mother, lover, child—is, as she suggests to Germaine Patat, her defense against being "negated." Behind that shield a fugitive creature resists being captured and possessed.

"She succeeded in subduing events, people, and words," writes Margaret Crosland, who entitles her biography of Colette *The Difficulty of Loving*. "After long and almost invisible aggression she achieved, in the end, a smooth-running life and a literary style of apparent ease."[54] Yet no one I have ever met, no writer I have ever tried to read, is as elusive or ultimately as self-suspicious. As she warns us herself, she is always hiding in plain sight. "Her extreme modesty," wrote Bel-Gazou, "keeps her from playing the modest woman."[55] Even in her letters, often in her memoirs, the character she exposes to most of her friends and readers has been confused with—"subdued" by— the genial persona the newspapers hailed that day in January as "Our Colette."

CHAPTER 44

I often think I'd like to live among a race other than the human race.
— COLETTE,
Lettres aux petites fermières

ℓ

THE FIFTEEN-VOLUME EDITION of Colette's collected works
began appearing in 1948, published by Maurice's new company, Le
Fleuron. It was a costly production—two million words on seven
thousand pages of quality paper—for which the Goudekets had put up part of
the capital, more than a million francs, the rest coming from friends.[1] The corporation also bought the Palais-Royal apartment, possibly to shelter part of
Colette's estate. In the will she drafted in 1945, she left half of her assets to her
daughter and half to her husband, whom she named her literary executor.
Perhaps anticipating the bitter litigation between Maurice and Bel-Gazou that
did, in fact, ensue, she stipulated that if her daughter contested the will, she
would be disinherited.[2]

As Colette reread, corrected, and prefaced her texts, Maurice sometimes had to prevent her taking "a too hasty pair of scissors" to the earliest of
them. It was "idiotic" work, she complained to Moreno. Yet the range and
richness—and the sheer volume of her achievement—finally impressed even
her. "Have I really written all that? Is it possible, Maurice, that I've written all
that?" she asked. And "sometimes she was emboldened enough to offer the
opinion that 'it's not badly done.' "[3]

Colette never outgrew her terror of poverty, and she had always been secretive about her income. She may have been a good haggler, but she was an incompetent bookkeeper, and she had more than once paid hefty—and, as she admitted herself, "deserved"—fines for neglecting her taxes. "She believes there are a few banknotes in her bureau drawer," Cocteau told his diary. "Her savings account has always been that drawer, which she filled by writing articles and emptied to pay Pauline. Judging by the estimated taxes that Maurice admitted they owed, she must have earned very large sums."[4]

Maurice's main concern, as her powers declined, was to consolidate both her reputation and her fortune. He renegotiated her foreign contracts and arranged for new translations in England, America, and Germany. He also vigorously pursued the exploitation of her film rights. Between 1947 and the year of her death, 1954, six of her novels were brought to the screen; and even before Vincente Minnelli adapted *Gigi* for Hollywood, Colette's work was in the process of being discovered by a vast and heterogeneous new audience.[5]

Colette, of course, was not a newcomer to the film business. From the First World War through the 1930s, she not only wrote screenplays, trenchant film criticism, and—when "talkies" were introduced—dialogue; she also actively collaborated on the films drawn from her novels. This firsthand experience made her an initiate of on-the-set politics and a connoisseur of the art as well as of the artisanship that goes into a film—the set and costume design, the lighting and editing.[6] She was one of the first critics to discern the mythical allure of the action hero, and to observe the "monomaniacal" process by which a studio's publicity machine turns a pretty teenager into a star whose "overblown features" are forever "engraved on one's memory."

As a former mime, Colette had a nostalgic bias for the silent film, and as a Frenchwoman, a patriotic concern with the imperial ambitions of Hollywood. "French commerce, French art, the French economy itself," she writes prophetically in 1916, "will have something to worry about and suffer from after the war because of the progress the American cinema is making."[7]

The film historians Alain and Odette Virmaux speak of Colette's "discoverer's eye," and in 1951, as Maurice was wheeling her through the lobby of the Hôtel de Paris in Monte Carlo, where a film was being made, Colette noticed a bewitching young actress switching fluently from French to English. Without hesitation, she announced to Maurice that she had found "our Gigi for America." The young actress was Audrey Hepburn.

Colette chose, however, to exclude most of her writing for and about film from the Fleuron edition, a scruple which the Virmaux explain by noting that in the late forties "the history of the cinema was not yet being studied in any organized fashion" and screenplays were generally treated as literary ephemera. But Colette, they insist justly, was a pioneer of the medium whose formative years coincide with her own, and who contributed to the creation of its language: "To the extent that it offered her the diverse image of an animated, changing, multiple, and constantly renewing universe, it suited perfectly her insatiable appetite for discovery and sensation."[8]

ON MARCH 5, 1948, Simone Berriau reunited Sartre and Colette. His play *Mains sales* was then in rehearsal at the Théâtre Antoine, and Berriau gave a dinner party to which she also invited Cocteau, who was directing the production, and Sartre's consort, Simone de Beauvoir. De Beauvoir described the evening in a letter to her American lover, Nelson Algren:

> I think you heard of Colette: she is the only really great woman writer in France, a really great writer. She was once the most beautiful woman. She danced in music-halls, slept with a lot of men, wrote pornographic novels and then good novels. She loved country, flowers, beasts, and making love, and then she loved too the most sophisticated life; she slept with women too. . . . Now she is seventy-five years old and has still the most fascinating eyes and a nice triangular cat face; she is very fat, impotent, a little deaf, but she can tell stories and smile and laugh in such a way nobody would think of looking at younger, finer women . . . I hope I shall see her again. I was in love with her, through her books, when I was a girl, so it meant something to me to see her. It is strange an old woman when she has lived so much, so feverishly, so freely, when she knows so much and does not care for anything anymore because now everything is over for her.[9]

De Beauvoir was finishing *The Second Sex* when she met Colette, but it wouldn't be published until 1949, so she was not yet a literary star in her own right. Her memoirs, composed much later, give a different version of their first encounter. Berriau, she writes, had brought her to visit the great old writer at the Palais-Royal:

> I had been told that she was not very cordial toward [younger] women and she received me coldly. "Do you like animals?" "No," I say. She looks me over with an Olympian eye. I didn't care. I hadn't been counting on any real contact between us. It was enough for me just to contemplate her. Arthritic, wild-haired, violently made-up, age gave her sharp face and her blue eyes an electric brilliance: between her collection of paperweights and the gardens framed by her windows, she appeared, paralyzed and sovereign, like a formidable Mother-Goddess. When we dined with her and Cocteau at Simone Berriau's, Sartre also had the impression of facing a "sacred mon-

ster." She had made the effort to come, in large part out of curiosity to see [Sartre], and knowing that for him she was the principal attraction of the evening. . . . The Burgundian fullness of her voice didn't blunt the acuity of her words. Her speech flowed from a natural source, and . . . Cocteau's brilliance seemed contrived in comparison.[10]

EACH HAVING FOLLOWED her own crooked path to glory, Colette and Moreno had become, at seventy-five and seventy-seven, respectively, national treasures. After her success in *Madwoman,* Moreno was in great demand as a comedienne, and she even mounted a one-woman cabaret act—reciting poetry at Tonton's Liberty's Bar. Her show ended well after midnight, but knowing that the insomniac Colette would be awake, she sometimes came to unwind with her old friend by the light of the blue lantern. "I hope that we haven't finished exchanging 'stories,' " Colette told her, "which have some worth because it's you and because it's me."[11]

Colette's last letters to Moreno are filled with the pride she takes in her friend's "magnificent ubiquity" and with lively interest in Pierre Moreno's new baby—Marguerite's grandniece—Françoise. She begged the new parents to "furnish her museum of Françoises" with updated photographs, but she was also prompt with her typically opinionated advice. They must repress the "infantile neurosis" of scratching; they mustn't spoil or even handle her too much. "I'd so much love to consort with her in my favorite way," she concludes. "When my daughter was little but already walking and she played on the terrace at Castel-Novel, I liked to install myself [in an armchair] without moving, until such time as she forgot me. It's a good way of observing them. They are so dissembling, so affected, in our presence."[12]

On July 8, 1948, Colette received a dictated reply to this letter, informing her that Moreno was "out of danger." Colette hadn't known her old friend to be *in* danger, but a week later, Moreno was dead. She had caught a bad cold after giving a benefit performance in Cahors, and it had developed into pleurisy. "I have never thought so much about Marguerite," Colette told Pierre. "What pure bitterness and tenderness mixed together in a loyalty as involuntary as ours. I have deeply missed the great poet who was Hélène Picard. . . . But nothing in the losses I have suffered is like the shock that I feel every time I think of Marguerite. . . . At my age, there's no getting used to it."[13]

2

COLETTE AND MAURICE spent the rest of that summer in the South of France, first with Simone Berriau and then with the Polignacs, who had Prince Pierre as a houseguest. Colette concealed the fact that the heat which she used to love was "devastating" both to her energy and to her arthritis. Maurice and her hosts, she explained to Moune, were all "drunk on the sea, the air, and their adventures," and she wanted him to enjoy himself. Work gave her a "pretext for solitude," and she was writing articles, working on *The Blue Lantern* and on an "anecdotal" memoir of Moreno which would not, she hoped, be "unworthy of her and of me." One night at dinner, however, surrounded by her fit, suntanned companions and her "exultant" husband, she couldn't help railing against the life of an invalid writer: "It's frightful, it's idiotic, it shouldn't be allowed. It's a horror, it's disgusting, it's impossible!"[14] Yet there was nothing for it, and in the last pages of *The Blue Lantern* she describes the futility of her revolt: "I can feel stirring within me—apart from the twisting pain, as if under the heavy screw of a winepress—a far less constant turnscrew than pain, an insurrection of the spirit which in the course of my long life I have often rejected, later outwitted, only to accept it in the end, for writing leads only to writing."[15]

At the end of August, the Goudekets flew back to Paris, where Colette corrected the "interminable" proofs for her collected works and finished the essay on Moreno. She also wrote the preface for her friend's posthumously published memoirs. "I keep colliding with [her] absence," she told Pierre, "and it hurts me badly."[16] In September, the new director of the Théâtre de la Madeleine proposed to revive *Chéri* with Jean Marais and Valentine Tessier, a project haunted by Moreno's ghost and by Colette's constant regret that Marguerite had not survived long enough "to re-create Mme Peloux at a theater and with a troupe worthy of her."[17]

The revival, however, didn't get under way until the fall, and the early months of the new year were a period of fatigue and reclusion. Colette almost never left her room and suffered from a "great nostalgia" for the country. "One has to accept . . . the many forms of resignation," she told the little farmers, adding that at least she had a fire, and the sunlight, and "they don't deprive me of toys."[18]

One of the few letters that survive from that winter was to Germaine Beaumont, who was struggling with a serious depression. She had destroyed a manuscript and resolved never to write again. Colette scolded her lovingly, and she advised Germaine to follow her own method for exorcising an evil spirit: find a scapegoat and "eliminate" her or him from one's life.[19]

THAT SUMMER, the Goudekets returned to the Polignacs' villa in Grasse, where Maurice luxuriated and Colette suffered. She flew home to find "the sweet little face of my daughter waiting on the stairs." Bel-Gazou was now thirty-six. She had her father's powerful features and her mother's stocky physique. Her smile was dimpled like a baby's. She dressed liked a squire. Her intimates were women of her own aristocratic background and artistic affinities. A male friend who was part of their circle observed to me that these rather temperamental women

> were products of the caste system that still operated in the France of their youth, and lesbianism was both a refuge and a gesture of revolt against the inexorable social pressure exercised by their families. When they traveled, it was to places like Capri or Casablanca, where there was an established homosexual society—a high society. Colette [de Jouvenel] was bohemian, but there was a strong element of *arrivisme* to her character. She was wild, litigious, lordly, secretive, impecunious, sarcastic, and she had her mother's instinct to dominate. But she could never dominate the overbearing image of her mother.[20]

"There are few things that excite young Colette's irascibility more than being introduced as Madame Colette's daughter," wrote another friend, Monica Stirling, in a discreet but revealing profile for American *Vogue*. "Not that she wishes to repudiate her mother; she adores her. But an immense reserve and an immoderate inferiority complex have committed her to the supposition that her mother is her only title to interest. This attitude has funereal consequences upon her writing—since it combines with her laziness (the latter quality . . . in no way inherited) to prevent her working steadily."[21]

Bel-Gazou was still contributing to *Fraternité* when the *Vogue* profile was published. But she abandoned journalism abruptly one day when Colette told her, "I like this article less than the others."[22] She wrote poetry but refused to let Colette read it. "The maternal monster," explained Cocteau, "intimidated her daughter to the point of preventing her from writing. As the reason for this timidity complex escaped [Colette], I always saw mother and daughter calling each other from a distance, groping toward each other as if in a loving game of hide and seek, or blindman's buff."[23]

In describing her own life, which she did with extreme brevity and reticence, Colette de Jouvenel took a fatalistic view of her contradictions, attributing them less to her upbringing, or her lack of one, than to her genes. "It seems that I've always known that in conceiving me, my parents surrendered to an illusion they never mastered. In that, they resembled all parents, but others know how to correct, by what is conventionally called education, the effects of farcically distilled chromosomes." Colette and Henry, she continued, didn't make a child who contained "the essence of what was finest" in them. Instead, they endowed her with all that was weakest and least admirable in their "chromosomes": the Captain's "incurable dreaminess" and inaptitude, Léo's waifish sadness and futility, Mamita's greed for frivolous pleasure, Raoul de Jouvenel's nonchalance and detachment.[24]

Michel del Castillo and other friends of Bel-Gazou were less philosophical and forgiving. They agreed that Colette had disapproved of her daughter's homosexuality. One said she had simply refused to acknowledge it. "Perhaps she just wanted her to have a more secure life," offered another—although del Castillo didn't think so. "Colette," he told me, "constantly spoke ill to her daughter of the father whom she had adored, and she liked to compare Henry's promiscuity to [Bel-Gazou's] lesbianism. To be gay, in her view, showed a kind of 'sexual irresponsibility.' That," he shrugged, "was one of the enormous contradictions in Colette's character."[25]

In the mid-1940s, Bel-Gazou sold Curemonte and opened an antiques shop on the rue Bonaparte in Paris. It floundered, and she lost interest. Later she would write songs, produce films, and decorate houses, but she could never commit herself to a profession or an art. Her friends considered her a woman of great gifts who had squandered them, of great qualities that she deprecated, and someone with a "vastly underachieved destiny." Toward the end of her life she wrote: "Today one understands—finally!—that there are no truly lazy individuals. There are only mad perfectionists who wait, paralyzed and riveted, for the eruption of a volcano of beauty."[26]

By then, however, Colette de Jouvenel had found an enterprise in which to invest her vital force and her rage. After years of litigation with Maurice, she had regained control of her mother's copyrights. She became, writes del Castillo, her mother's "priestess," taking the oeuvre as her "Bible," and she was determined to make herself "worthy" of this mantle she had wrested "so painfully" from her rival.[27] As all the books were, in her view, equal in virtue and importance, she contested any perceived slur, slight, or criticism—even those she herself had once made. At the age of sixty, eight years before her death, Colette de Jouvenel recalled her mother as the font of a "tenderness and warmth that made me radiant with happiness. And nothing that later came to torment or frustrate me could tarnish that magic."[28]

3

IN THE AUTUMN OF 1948, the cast of *Chéri* came to rehearse in Colette's bedroom—"I mean on my bed!" she told Pierre Moreno. Jean Marais, she said, "balked at the role like a horse before a snake," and she argued with the set designer, Jean Wall, whom she wouldn't forgive "for always being right." On the evening of the dress rehearsal, Cocteau, who had served as her unofficial go-between with the cast, took the stage to pay her homage: "She has joined no literary school, and she has charmed them all," he told the audience.[29]

Colette had just received the first of a series of experimental male-hormone injections in the days before the première. "These poor doctors can't figure out what . . . to feed my behind," she joked to Pata, confessing that she was suffering from not only her arthritis but a bad case of stage fright and "something unexpected and bizarre . . . aching nipples! Damn it . . . a person of seventy-seven has no more right to breasts. Let's hide them."[30]

When she took her seat in a stage box at the Théâtre de la Madeleine on the evening of October 30, all that the audience could see of her was a "nimbus of radiant hair." After the performance, she received a standing ovation "from the three generations of *le tout Paris*."[31] Among them, surely, was at least one ancient dandy with tears in his eyes who remembered those perfect breasts she had once so insolently and proudly bared.

IN MAY OF 1950, Maurice and Colette made the first of what were to become annual trips to Monte Carlo, where they stayed, as guests of Prince Rainier, in a ground-floor suite with a private garden at the Hôtel de Paris. She regaled Pata with descriptions of the appallingly inelegant foreign tourists and indulged in a little name-dropping. The ruling monarch, she told the countess, had "put his principality at my disposal." Prince Pierre invited them to dine. The hotel was crowded with assorted millionaires and minor royalty. Cocteau and Jean Marais arrived with a film crew. Ferenczi sent her two hundred copies of *En pays connu* (*In Familiar Country*), a new anthology of her previously uncollected essays, to autograph in the sun. A sculptor wanted to do a bust of her, an abbé asked for nothing in particular, her daughter came to visit, and Léo Marchand arrived to collaborate with both Goudekets on a play adapted from *The Other One*, which was produced very successfully the next year.

Meanwhile, yet another doctor—this time an Englishman—tried his luck with Colette's arthritis and had no more success than his predecessors.

Admitting to Pata that her agony had never been worse, she asked her touchingly: "What do you think of Anacin?"[32]

COLETTE FINISHED the play script of *The Other One* that August in Versailles. Maurice had installed her and Pauline at the Trianon Palace hotel to escape the worst heat of Paris. He and Léo Marchand commuted from the city, where they were organizing the production. In the autumn, the cast came to rehearse at the Palais-Royal. Colette was still inquisitive and vivacious, although for increasingly short periods. Her dentist made house calls, and the Académie Goncourt held meetings at her bedside. Gérard Bauer, who first met her in the days of her marriage to Willy, was now one of her confrères. "I have known Claudine," he wrote. "I find her again in this face which speaks to me, in this shock of hair which is hardly gray, in the rather singsong tone of the voice, sometimes mocking to feign surprise. But the pantheism of youth has turned into a grave acceptance of life, a profound dignity that always knows how to lavish the delicacies of friendship."[33]

WHEN COLETTE CRAVED a grander or more festive meal than Pauline could provide, she was carried downstairs to Le Grand Véfour. The great two-hundred-year-old restaurant in the arcade of the rue de Beaujolais had recently been revivified by its new owner, Raymond Oliver. He made Colette's favorite dishes—cassoulet, *blanquette à l'ancienne, coulibiac* of salmon—and he would often have a portion of something special, such as a lark pie or a pot of apricot jam, sent up to her. On dark winter afternoons, in the lull between lunch and dinner, Oliver himself would come to visit, uncorking a bottle of old champagne and a store of equally sparkling fresh gossip.

In 1951, when a flash fire broke out on the mezzanine directly under her apartment, the restaurateur rushed over to help evacuate Colette, having groped his way up a stairwell filled with dense smoke. A crowd had gathered under her window and was urging her to jump. Knowing they would never make it through the flames with her wheelchair, Maurice, Pauline, Oliver, and Bel-Gazou—who happened to be visiting—struggled to conceal their panic. "All the same," they heard Colette protest over the din of the shouts and the breaking glass, "there's no reason not to have some coffee."[34]

"I MARRIED a saint," Colette told a friend that winter. It was a frequent refrain. Maurice claims that he didn't mind receiving mail addressed to

Monsieur Colette. "Am I going to die?" she'd sometimes ask him. "Not until I give you permission," he'd reply.[35]

He thought of moving Colette to a ground-floor flat but realized that she couldn't stand the shock of the uprooting. He vetted her guests and timed their visits. The première of *The Other One* was, he felt, too great an exertion for her, despite the charge she got from the adulation of the crowd. He bought her a television set, which sat on a bookshelf facing her raft, and it became, he writes, her main lifeline to the real world. Monte Carlo, where they spent increasingly long periods every spring, and Deauville, their resort of choice for the summer, were stage sets peopled with decrepit characters from a Belle Époque operetta. Colette enjoyed the air in her wheelchair, the occasional movie, the sumptuous meals, but the life of grand hotels and their "fake cosmopolitan" society were more to Maurice's taste than to her own. "We're cared for very nicely here," she writes to Moune from Monaco, "but . . . it's hardly a normal life. *Rien ne nous manque, tout nous fait défaut*"[36]—we want for nothing, we lack everything.

4

WHEN PIERRE MORENO HAD suggested, in 1949, that Colette try a pilgrimage to Lourdes to cure her arthritis, she didn't laugh at him. Perhaps she might, she replied: "The day comes when one abandons oneself." There are many forms of self-abandonment. Her dependence on Maurice was one, and the valiance it took, on her side, to conceal the humiliation was matched only by the gallantry, on his, to conceal the burden.

Colette resigned herself—another form of abandonment—to being the detached spectator of her daughter's life. An occasional visit, a display of "reserved affection," a breathless postcard from Morocco—such was their intercourse. "I am happy," said Colette, "that her friends give her what I cannot."[37]

Colette also abandoned herself to the lenses of certain great photographers, who took her portrait in extreme old age. Cartier-Bresson captures the wariness and the challenge of her gaze; Ora, its limpid and ferocious animal beauty; Gisèle Freund, a faintly comic, quizzical sagacity. Irving Penn, who photographed her on her eightieth birthday, produced an image of Colette that "stupefied" even Maurice:

> It shows only the torso, isolating Colette from her décor, her legend, stripping her for posterity. The head rises above a jumble of fabric and fur . . . supported by a clenched fist. The expression of the face is severe, taut,

intense. The forehead offers itself almost entirely naked, enormous, significant, magisterial: it's a striking image but also a betrayal, a theft of conscience. It reveals all that Colette wished to dissemble, and certainly all that
she didn't know about herself. One cannot say that the picture resembles
her. It is sexless, while Colette remained feminine to her last breath. . . . It is,
in truth, the photograph of The Other, of the hidden being each of us carries in himself and who alone was capable of writing certain pages of
Colette.[38]

But the ultimate abandonment of self was to stop writing. "I'm happy
you're working well," Colette tells Moune in June of 1951 from Monte Carlo.
"Not me. But I don't push myself. It's doubtless because I have nothing—
nothing more—to say."[39] This wasn't strictly true, because until she fell silent
in the last months of her life, she wrote lucid and tender letters to her friends,
and she pushed herself just a little. Maurice saved her last notes. She imagined
a final story about an untold love: "If I had omitted from what the Le Fleuron
edition calls my 'Complete Works' the account of an amorous adventure,
what to do, now, with this commodity. . . . Where, henceforth, to lie? Where
to confess?"[40] *To lie, to confess.* Colette's "least admitted secrets of the flesh"
repose between those two temptations, as in the arms of a lover.

CHAPTER 45

It is true enough that in her vital days, she eagerly picked the fruits of the earth without discriminating those which were forbidden—but this is only the lesser part of the story. Love has two faces, agape *and* Eros, *a deep understanding and appreciation of the lovable, and a petulant willfulness to seize it. It is not easy to divorce them. Colette was immensely rich in the former, and therein resides her greatness; for the latter, she suffered ample retribution.*

—BERTRAND DE JOUVENEL

1

*J*N 1951, a young woman named Yannick Bellon made a documentary about Colette, filmed at the Palais-Royal. It captures the intensely feminine charm and coquetry of her presence that are absent from Penn's photograph. The film is an homage, as one would expect and as is fitting. It opens with Colette and Maurice having breakfast, he perched decorously on her bed. Pauline enters to discuss the day's menus. Cocteau drops in to banter affectionately. When Colette smiles for the camera, one glimpses the timidity that her writing and her acting belie. In one of the most poignant scenes, she reminisces about the mother whom "I never loved well enough." At the film's première, she remarked to a journalist: "What a beautiful life I've had. It's a pity I didn't notice it sooner."[1]

The child whom Colette loved too well had finally returned to France from Switzerland, where he had been living since the last years of the war. That spring, Colette wrote to Bertrand de Jouvenel: "You have a pretty house? Children you're proud of? I am a bit responsible for these many blessings; show them to me, if only on a postcard. I can't take a step. In five days, Maurice is taking me, as he did last year, to Monte Carlo. When I come home, my mirror will tell me if I can call you. But will you still be young enough? I embrace you, my boy, from the heart."[2]

She now addressed an equally moving last letter to Germaine Beaumont. There had been some "misunderstanding" between them. Perhaps there was one of those typical lapses in their correspondence which the sensitive and adoring younger woman perceived as a rejection: "How can you forget, or cease to feel, that I love you as I love no one else? Within you is everything that comes to you and to me from Annie. I was mistaken, too, I was afraid you loved me less. Miserable beloved creature, give me back everything I've missed in you, that I came close to losing. . . . Above all, don't stop loving me. The friend that I've been, that I am, where would you find such another?"[3]

A SUMMER AND an autumn passed. Impatient for spring, Colette and Maurice left for Monte Carlo a week into the new year. "My birthday," she told Moune early in 1952, "is assuming the proportions of a scandal."[4] The princes filled her suite with flowers, and Pierre was particularly assiduous with his attentions. The Polignacs paid their respects and swept her off to Grasse to meet their granddaughter, who was half Tahitian. Maurice, meanwhile, was occupied with the French stage adaptation of *Gigi*. Colette tried to help, "but the little work I venture to do here isn't any good." Perhaps, she mused, she was dining too well and seeing too many people. "The maharanee of Baroda let us go only after a lunch for seventeen which was luxury incarnate. But what do I need with luxury incarnate?"[5]

Cocteau arrived in Monaco late that February. Mauriac had attacked his latest play, *Bacchus,* and he raged to his diary about the "thirty-year manhunt of which I am the victim." His description of dinner with the Goudekets has often been quoted, but one should take into account the bleakness and petulance of the mood which color it:

> Fifteen days ago, a letter from Colette was quite legibly written, and she sounded content. Today I find her quite low and far away. I've already seen eyes like hers . . . they belonged to my green cricket when it was singing its death song. . . .
> Maurice rolls [her] chair into the bar. Then into the amazing velvet and gold dining room filled with draperies, caryatids, huge frescoes of naked women, peacocks and tigers . . . the gypsy violinist playing *Gigi* at Colette's shoulder seems out of another age, forming—with Colette, his violin, and that tune from *Gigi*—a kind of phantom group, invisible to the other tables.

Maurice penetrates the padded cell that encloses Colette as little as possible; only the essentials get through. Sometimes she hears me; sometimes she tries to hear me and can't. . . . Great sadness. Old age: this is how I will be. This is how the end begins.

Maurice seems to handle his wife's affairs admirably. . . . Colette is a peasant and a child. She goes on living, almost content inside that cloud that protects her against a cruel world no longer coincident with her flowers and her animals.

Colette does not disturb the world, and she is surrounded by respect. I do, and insolence surrounds me. Sometimes I envy her insulation, her wheelchair. I have all the afflictions of youth and none of its advantages.

Back to see Colette this morning. . . . She is transformed, and quite renewed. She hears us. She comes into the bar, wheeled by the bartender. I recognize her fine eyes swimming in the liquor of the best Marennes oysters, her olive-tree hair, her mouth like an arrowhead wound."[6]

The respect for Colette was not universal. Léautaud was still sniping at her in his journals. Her "books and her theater," he wrote, "are commercial literature. There is only one great writer today, and that is François Mauriac."[7] Mauriac received the Nobel Prize for Literature that November. "One of the first things he did," wrote Robert Phelps, "was to call on Colette, who should have had it, he felt, in his place."[8] It would be hard to think of two writers more spiritually dissimilar than Mauriac and Colette: he the devout Christian whose credo was "to believe is to love," she the pleasure-worshiping pessimist for whom love is the Fall. Yet her melancholy carnality seems to haunt his novels, and his nature poetry is ripe with what has often been called a "pagan" love for the landscapes of his native province. The crimes and passions of his characters—the secretive, wounded adolescents who love smoldering older women—are those of Colette's. He seeks redemption on their behalf as nobly and humanely, and as presumptuously perhaps, as he sought hers.

2

IN 1952, Glenway Westcott paid a visit to the Palais-Royal, armed with introductions from Cocteau and Anita Loos, the dramatizer of *Gigi,* and an armful of expensive bronze-colored roses. Colette couldn't receive him, said Maurice, who then proceeded to interview Westcott for nearly an hour. When he "became convinced that I truly, unselfishly loved Colette's work and would continually do my best to further a general love of it in vast and remunerative America," he ushered the guest into the red chamber.[9]

His audience, as he describes it, was somewhat farcical. It took place in

French, although the participants seemed to be speaking different tongues. Colette, thought Westcott, looked "immaculate and (so to speak) gleaming." She showed him her pretty feet and flexed her "strong and silken arches." When Maurice told Colette that their guest was a great fan of her writing, she asked him if he knew *The Pure and the Impure.* He didn't. "I believe it to be my best book," she told him.

Their subsequent discussion of her work was, he admits, "not very well focused on the cues that her husband and I gave her; she only half heard us. She devoted all possible cleverness to mitigating and disguising the vacuum between us." Maurice did his best to help them: "M. Ouess-cotte suggests that I ought to make a selection of your thoughts in aphoristic form . . . something like the *Pensées* of Pascal . . ." Colette was horrified. "I have no *pensées,*" she protested. "As a matter of fact, thanks be to God, perhaps the most praiseworthy thing about me is that I have known how to write like a woman, without anything moralistic or theoretical, without promulgating."

Westcott had been warned about Colette's hardness of hearing, but she had not been warned about his. He is in many ways an admirable critic, but he has a Yankee penchant for the uplifting, which he discerns in unlikely places. Now he delivered a "grandiose" lecture to Colette in which he insisted that she was a thinker and did philosophize. The central tenet of her philosophy was "belief in love; the particular passion in due course giving way to general loving-kindness, amor giving way to caritas, amour leading to amor fati. A part of it is just spectatorship and dramatic sense, with no admiration of evil, indeed not; only an appreciation of the part that evil may play in fate, as among other things it occasions virtue . . ."[10] Maurice looked "stupefied," and Colette listened politely, her face "turning masklike, as though she had suddenly grown much deafer."

As there was no reply to this oration, the visit ended. Colette and Maurice invited Westcott to return, and she promised, on that occasion, to dine with him at Le Grand Véfour. He took his leave of her with a lump in his throat and rushed out to buy a copy of *The Pure and the Impure.*

3

TWENTY YEARS EARLIER, Colette had told Gérard d'Houville (Marie de Régnier): "Perhaps we are the only two to understand something about death, you through serenity and me through indifference, because I have never been able to take an interest in what isn't life."[11] Colette sustained her interest in life to the end. "What is left to me is my avidity," she writes in *The Blue Lantern.* "Of all my forces it alone has not humbled itself to time."[12]

Her eightieth birthday was an occasion for an even greater outpouring of homage than she had received five years before. She accepted graciously, if a little distractedly, the high-minded praise of her wisdom and grandeur and the final honors that were bestowed upon her.[13] Yet she understood, as Cocteau did, that such awards are "given in extremis. How right she is to counter [the ceremonies] with the half-sleep of a mole, the deep and lucid irony that one perceives, as during a lightning flash, in her eye."[14]

That lucid irony is evident in her last letters. "I had a million things to tell you, and as many questions to ask," Colette tells Germaine Beaumont. "And naturally . . ." But she doesn't finish the sentence. "A writer who can't write anymore," she sighs to Moune, and she doesn't finish that sentence either. "Today, I'm worth nothing," she concludes her final letter. "But I love you."[15]

Colette's handwriting, like Sido's, grew spidery. She began to lose her short-term memory. Her pain, her deafness, and her torpor contributed to her isolation. There were moments when she rallied for a visit, and Cocteau records one of them: "This morning [December 5, 1953], Colette . . . sparkled. Everything that had gone soft in her face became sharpened. She told stories, she listened, she laughed."[16]

Claude Autant-Lara's film of *The Ripening Seed* had its première a month later. The screening was to benefit a student charity, and Colette recorded a message for the young audience: "Throughout my existence, I have studied flowering more than any other manifestation of life. It is there, for me, that the essential drama resides, and not in death, which is just a banal defeat."[17]

About this time, Bertrand de Jouvenel came to see her for the last time. "I brought some Algerian flowers," he recalled, "called *strelitzia*, which recalled to her the smell and light of an African garden; she remembered what she had once told me, that the Ouled-Nail dancers imitate with their fingers the shape of this flower, and she tried to do so but could not as her hands were cramped with arthritis." She gave him a book—*The Earthly Paradise*.[18]

4

THE GOUDEKETS MADE a last trip to Monte Carlo. "I'm writing to no one, not even my daughter," Colette told Moune from the Hôtel de Paris. "How to excuse this strange family?"[19] They were back in the Palais-Royal by the beginning of May. She wasn't ill, writes Maurice, but she was silent for increasingly long periods. As the trees were budding and the parks just coming into bloom, he arranged for two outings by car. Colette raised her hands shoulder high and turned her palms out in what he calls "a gesture of wonder." But it is also the classic gesture of surrender.

By the end of June, the little vitality that was left to her began to ebb. She no longer looked at the newspapers or opened her letters. She couldn't digest solid food, and she began sleeping most of the time. In her waking moments, she might ask Pauline to take her butterflies down from the wall, or to bring her an illustrated book of insects and flowers. Toward the end of July, she could no longer raise herself up in bed. A nurse was engaged to relieve Pauline, but it was the maid Colette "sought in the semi-darkness. To Pauline alone she could confess her lassitude, her weakness, her waning, and reveal her unvarnished face."[20] She gave Pauline precise instructions about her burial clothes, but she added: "People mustn't see me when I've died."[21]

Maurice and Bel-Gazou began their deathwatch. Occasionally Colette emerged from her torpor to give them "an angelic smile," and her husband could not resist observing to Cocteau, "What's so serious is that she's becoming sweet."[22] On the afternoon of August 2, she had an hour of "great lucidity." She and Maurice looked through an album of lithographs, and she read the captions aloud. The sky was as heavy as a pot cover—a thunderstorm was coming—and the swallows were swarming, with harsh cries, outside the window. With a sweep of her arm that embraced the rustle of live wings in the garden and the images on the page, Colette spoke her last coherent word: *"Regarde!"*

By the next afternoon, Tuesday, August 3, the heat was intense, and Colette was barely conscious. She drank a bowl of vegetable broth sent up by Raymond Oliver. To Maurice, she seemed radiantly happy. Her lips were moving, and she was lost, he says, in a silent conversation "addressed to no one among us." He summoned her doctor, Marthe Lamy, who told him that her heart was failing and that he should send for a priest. He declined to do so. That evening, Maurice briefly left the house for a walk. When he returned to Colette's bedside, there was no mistaking the harsh rattle of her breath. It stopped at seven-thirty.

5

"DEATH," WROTE COLETTE, "should never be something public."[23] The woman who hated funerals left no last wishes about her own. Maurice requested a religious ceremony at the Église Saint-Roch, but the archbishop of Paris refused him. Graham Greene's reproach to Cardinal Feltin was published on the front page of *Le Figaro littéraire,* with the prelate's reply, and the argument on both sides inspired a passionate public debate that had very little to do with Colette.

As a Catholic liberal, Greene argued for a display of charity and forgiveness from an institution built on those principles. Colette was a baptized Catholic. She had the right to the offices of a priest at her graveside. To deny them would certainly alienate non-Catholics and dismay enlightened believers. And was the cardinal really prepared, morally and spiritually, to deny her the hope of grace? The hope of grace, replied the conservative cardinal, was reserved for those who lived by the laws of the Church or had, in their last hour, showed signs of repentance. This did not mean, however, that Graham Greene and others could not offer their private prayers for God's pardon of Colette.

The readers of *Le Figaro* were, on the whole, in agreement with the cardinal, but the last words on this subject should be Colette's own impious ones. In the course of their interviews for the French radio, André Parinaud had asked her: "For you, Mme Colette, does life have any higher direction?" She replied dryly: "It only goes in one direction, as far as I know, which is toward the exit." But he pressed her:

> "I want to know if, for the writer and for the woman, there is an idea, a conception, an essential vision which she pursues, which is her goal, her cornerstone, and at the same time, her tuning fork?"
>
> "I see you're treating solemn subjects today, and I won't hesitate to say that they're beyond me. The meaning of life? Does one really have time to discover or create one? . . . Life got the habit rather early on of mistreating me a bit rudely, and . . . at the risk of being considered a passive animal, I didn't have much else to do than offer no resistance."[24]

6

SIDONIE-GABRIELLE COLETTE received the first state funeral that the Republic ever gave to a woman. At seven o'clock on the morning of August 7, 1954, her body was moved to the *cour d'honneur* of the Palais-Royal. The coffin was placed on a raised catafalque draped with the tricolor and flanked by a military guard in dress uniform. It was surrounded by a great embankment of flowers, most of them blue. There were wreaths from the French Parliament, the prefect of police, and the princes of Monaco. There was a garland of roses from the Queen Mother of Belgium, a sheaf of lilies from the association of music-hall artists, and a bouquet of country dahlias from "her compatriots in Saint-Sauveur-en-Puisaye."

The official ceremony for twenty-five hundred invited guests was to begin at ten-thirty, but by eight, a crowd of the uninvited had gathered in the rue Montpensier. It was so large that the police decided to open the gates early. For two hours, more than six thousand Parisians and tourists, most of them women, filed past Colette's bier. Some broke free from the strict ranks they were held in by the guards to deposit their own bouquets of wildflowers or violets, which, by the end of two hours, blanketed the pavingstones. All accounts of this procession remark on its silence. It was "strange," wrote the reporter for *Le Figaro*, "for the expressions bore witness to more than sympathy for an oeuvre; it was love for a woman."[25]

After the orations, her immediate family and a few close friends buried Colette in Père-Lachaise. As the dirt was shoveled into the grave, the rain began, the winds rose, and a storm broke—one of the most violent in a century. She would have enjoyed it.

Notes and Sources

IN THE NOTES and citations, I have used the following abbreviations. In quoting from Colette's published work, I have sometimes used the existing English translations, but in many cases I have translated from the French myself. All translations from Colette's correspondence, and from documents or text originally in French, are my own unless otherwise noted.

WORKS BY COLETTE

Collected Works

BQ1-3   *Colette.* Vol. 1: *Romans, récits, souvenirs (1900– 1919).* Vol. 2: *Romans, récits, souvenirs (1920–1940).* Vol. 3: *Romans, récits, souvenirs (1941–1949), Critique Dramatique (1934–1938).* Paris: [Collection] "Bouquins," Robert Laffont, 1989.

OCLF   *Oeuvres complètes.* 15 vols. Paris: Le Fleuron, 1948–50.

Pl. 1-3   *Oeuvres.* 3 vols. Bibliothèque de la Pléiade. Paris: Gallimard, 1984.

Individual Works

BL   *The Blue Lantern.* Translated by Roger Senhouse. New York: Farrar, Straus, and Giroux, 1977. Originally published as *Le Fanal bleu.* Paris: Ferenczi, 1949.

Blé   *Le Blé en herbe.* Original publication, Paris: Flammarion, 1923. GF (paperback) edition, Paris: Flammarion, 1969.

BOD   *Break of Day.* Translated by Enid McLeod. New York: Farrar, Straus, and Giroux, 1961.

BS   *Belles saisons* I and II. BQ3. Original publication, Paris: Galerie Charpentier, 1945.

BV   *Bella-Vista.* BQ2. Original publication, Paris: Ferenczi, 1937.

CAL   *Claudine à l'école.* BQ1. Originally published under the name Willy. Paris: Ollendorff, 1900.

CAL/LDP   *Claudine à l'école.* Livre de Poche edition, published under the names Willy and Colette. Paris: Albin Michel, 1956.

CAP   *Claudine à Paris.* BQ1 Originally published under the name Willy. Paris: Ollendorff, 1901.

CAP/LDP   *Claudine à Paris.* Livre de Poche edition, published under the names Willy and Colette. Paris: Albin Michel, 1956.

CEM   *Claudine en ménage.* BQ1. Originally published under the name Willy. Paris: Mercure de France, 1902.

CEM/Folio   *Claudine en ménage.* Folio paperback edition, published under the names Willy and Colette. Paris: Mercure de France, 1973.

Collected Stories   *The Collected Stories of Colette.* Edited by Robert Phelps. New York: Farrar, Straus, and Giroux, 1983.

CSEV   *Claudine s'en va.* BQ1. Originally published under the name Willy. Paris: Ollendorff, 1903.

CSEV/LDP   *Claudine s'en va.* Livre de Poche edition, published under the names Colette and Willy. Paris: Albin Michel, 1957.

Dialogues   *Dialogues de bêtes.* Originally published under the name Colette Willy. Paris: Mercure de France, 1904. Folio paperback edition, 1964.

Earthly Paradise   *Earthly Paradise.* Edited by Robert Phelps. New York: Farrar, Straus, and Giroux, 1966.

En tournée   *En tournée: Cartes postales à Sido.* With notes by Michel Remy-Bieth. Paris: Persona, 1984.

EPC   *En pays connu.* BQ3. Original publication, Paris: Ferenczi, 1950.

ES   *The Evening Star.* In *Recollections.* Translated by David Le Vay. New York: Colliers, 1986.

EV   *L'Étoile vesper.* BQ3. Original publication, Geneva, Paris, Montreal: Éditions du Milieu du Monde, 1946.

FB   *Le Fanal bleu.* BQ3. Original publication, Paris: Ferenczi, 1949.

HL   *Les Heures longues.* BQ1 or Pl. 2. Originally published under the name Colette Willy. Paris: Fayard, 1917.

JAR   *Journal à rebours.* BQ3. Original publication, Paris: Fayard, 1941.

JFM   *Journey for Myself.* In *Recollections.* Translated by David Le Vay. New York: Colliers, 1986. Originally published as *Le Voyage égoïste.* Paris: Ferenczi, 1928.

JN   *La Jumelle noire.* BQ3. Original publication, OCLF, vol. 10.

Képi   *Le Képi.* BQ3. Original publication, Paris: Fayard, 1943.

La Fin   *La Fin de Chéri.* Original publication, Paris: Flammarion, 1926. GF (paperback) edition, Paris: Flammarion, 1983.

L'Entrave	*L'Entrave.* Originally published under the name Colette Willy. Paris: Librairie des Lettres, 1913. Livre de Poche edition, Paris: Flammarion, 1919.
MA	*Mes apprentissages.* Paris: Ferenczi, 1936.
MDC	*La Maison de Claudine.* BQ2. Originally published under the name Colette Willy. Paris: Ferenczi, 1922.
MMH	*My Mother's House.* Translated by Una Vicenzo Troubridge and Enid McLeod. New York: Farrar, Straus, and Giroux, 1975, 1989.
NdJ	*La Naissance du jour.* BQ2. Original publication, Paris: Flammarion, 1928. GF (paperback) edition, Paris: Flammarion, 1984.
Parinaud	*Mes Vérités: Entretiens avec André Parinaud.* Paris: Écritures, 1996.
Paysages	*Paysages et portraits.* Paris: Flammarion, 1958.
P/I	*Le Pur et l'impur.* BQ2 or Pl. 3. Original publication, Paris: Aux Armes de France, 1941.
P/I FSG	*The Pure and the Impure.* Translated by Herma Briffault. New York: Farrar, Straus, and Giroux, 1966, 1967.
Places	*Places.* Translated by David Le Vay. Indianapolis/New York: The Bobbs-Merrill Co., 1971.
Prisons	*Prisons et paradis.* BQ2. Original publication, Paris: Ferenczi, 1932.
Retraite	*La Retraite sentimentale.* BQ1. Originally published under the name Colette Willy. Paris: Mercure de France, 1907.
RFL	*Retreat from Love.* Translated by Margaret Crosland. New York: Harcourt, Brace, Jovanovich, 1980.
Sido	*Sido.* Translated by Enid McLeod. New York: Farrar, Straus, and Giroux, 1975, 1989.
TOM	*The Thousand and One Mornings.* Translated by Margaret Crosland and David Le Vay. New York: Bobbs-Merrill, 1973.
TSN	*Trois . . . Six . . . Neuf.* BQ3. Original publication, Paris: Correa, 1944.
Vagabond	*La Vagabonde.* Originally published under the name Colette Willy. Paris: Ollendorff, 1910. Livre de Poche edition, Paris: Albin Michel, 1957.
VV	*Les Vrilles de la vigne.* Originally published under the name Colette Willy. Paris: Ferenczi, 1934.

Letters

AdP	*Lettres à Annie de Pène et Germaine Beaumont.* Edited by Francine Dugast. Paris: Flammarion, 1995.
GB	*Lettres à Annie de Pène et Germaine Beaumont.* Edited by Francine Dugast. Paris: Flammarion, 1995.
HP	*À Hélène Picard* in *Lettres,* omnibus ed. (of 3 titles). Edited and annotated by Claude Pichois. Paris: Flammarion, 1988.
LAMT	*Lettres à Moune et au Toutounet, 1929–1954.* Edited by Bernard Villaret. Paris: des femmes, 1985.
LAPC	*Au petit corsaire* in *Lettres,* omnibus ed. (of 3 titles). Edited and annotated by Claude Pichois. Paris: Flammarion, 1988.

LAPF   *Lettres aux petites fermières.* Edited and annotated by Marie-Thérèse Colleaux-Chaurang. Paris: Le Castor Astral, 1992.

LASP   *Lettres à ses pairs.* Edited and annotated by Claude Pichois and Roberte Forbin. Paris: Flammarion, 1973.

LDLV   *Lettres de la vagabonde.* Edited and annotated by Claude Pichois and Roberte Forbin. Paris: Flammarion, 1961.

MM   *À Marguerite Moreno* in *Lettres,* omnibus ed. (of 3 titles). Edited and annotated by Claude Pichois. Paris: Flammarion 1988.

SIDO, LETTERS

LASF   *Lettres à sa fille précédé de Lettres inédites de Colette.* Paris: des femmes, 1984.

UNPUBLISHED CORRESPONDENCE AND DOCUMENTS
(Please note that nearly all of this material is undated.)

ADC   Archives Départementales de la Corrèze, Brive.

BN   Archives of the Bibliothèque Nationale, Paris.

CASS   Archives of the Société des Amis de Colette, Saint-Sauveur-en-Puisaye.

Doucet   Archives of the Bibliothèque Littéraire Jacques Doucet, Paris.

GP   Letters of Colette to Germaine Patat from the archives of the Bibliothèque Nationale.

HRC   Harry Ransom Humanities Research Center, Austin, Texas.

MRB   Private collection of M. Michel Rémy-Bieth, Paris.

SMAF   Correspondence between Colette and Maurice Goudeket from the collection of the Société des Manuscrits des Assureurs Français, Paris.

OTHER SOURCES
(See Selected Bibliography for full bibliographic details.)

Arendt   Arendt, Hannah. *The Origins of Totalitarianism.*

Aury   Aury, Dominique. *Literary Landfalls.*

Barney   Barney, Natalie Clifford. *Souvenirs indiscrets.*

BdJ   Jouvenel, Bertrand de. *Un Voyageur dans le siècle.*

Binion   Binion, Rudolph. *Defeated Leaders: The Political Fate of Caillaux, Jouvenel, and Tardieu.*

Bonmariage   Bonmariage, Sylvain. *Willy, Colette, et moi.*

Caradec   Caradec, François. *Feu Willy.*

CC   *Cahiers Colette* nos. 1–20. Société des Amis de Colette.

CdJ   Jouvenel, Colette de. *Colette de Jouvenel.*

Chauvière   Chauvière, Claude. *Colette.*

Colette   Pichois, Claude, and Alain Brunet. *Colette.*

D'Hollander   D'Hollander, Paul. *Colette: Ses apprentissages.*
CSA

Discours	Cocteau, Jean. "Colette." In *Discours de réception à l'Académie Royale de Langue et de Littérature Française.*
Dormann	Dormann, Geneviève. *Colette: A Passion for Life.*
Douceur	Goudeket, Maurice. *La Douceur de viellir.*
Escholier	Escholier, Raymond. *Le Figaro littéraire.* Nov. 17 and 24, 1956.
F/G	Francis, Claude, and Fernande Gontier. *Colette.*
Hire	Hire, Jean de la. "Willy et Colette." In *Ménages d'artistes.*
Jullian	Jullian, Philippe. *Jean Lorrain: ou Le Satiricon 1900.*
Lanoux	Lanoux, Armand. *Amours 1900.*
Larnac	Larnac, Jean. *Colette: Sa vie, son oeuvre.*
Léautaud	Léautaud, Paul. *Journal.*
Lottmann	Lottmann, Herbert. *Colette: A Life.*
Maurois	Maurois, Michelle. *Les Cendres brûlantes.*
Mugnier	Mugnier, Arthur. *Journal de l'abbé Mugnier (1879–1939).*
Painter	Painter, George. *Marcel Proust.*
PdC	Goudeket, Maurice. *Près de Colette.*
Pougy	Pougy, Liane de. *My Blue Notebooks.*
Private Life	*A History of Private Life: From the Fires of Revolution to the Great War.*
Rdj	Jouvenel, Renaud de. "Mon Enfance à l'ombre de Colette: Lettres de Colette à Renaud de Jouvenel." *La Revue de Paris,* Dec. 1966.
Richardson	Richardson, Joanna. *Colette.*
Sarde	Sarde, Michèle. *Colette: Free and Fettered.*
Vérité	Jouvenel, Bertrand de. "La Vérité sur Chéri," Pl. 2.
Weber	Weber, Eugen. *France fin de siècle.*
Willy, *Indiscrétions*	Willy. *Indiscrétions et commentaires sur les Claudines.*
Willy, *Souvenirs*	Willy. *Souvenirs littéraires . . . et autres.*
Zeldin	Zeldin, Theodore. *A History of French Passions.*

ᴄ⟩ ᴄ⟩

INTRODUCTION

1. Willy, Preface to *Claudine à l'école,* Pl. 1, pp. 4–5.
2. *Gil Blas,* June 4, 1904; Caradec, p. 143.
3. Dossier Renée Hamon, MRB. The article, without any identifying name or date, is signed "Lucie Porquerol."
4. Aury, p. 57.
5. Pl. 2, p. 1547.
6. Colette to Willy, MRB. See also Pl. 1, p. xciv.
7. François Mauriac, "Le Roman d'aujourd'hui," *La Revue hebdomadaire,* Feb. 19, 1927, pp. 265–6.

8. *P/I*, BQ2, p. 887.

9. Colette, *JN*, Quatrième Année, "*Les Corbeaux*, d'Henry Becque, 25 avril, 1937," p. 1302.

10. *EPC*, "Trait pour trait" (Courteline), p. 875.

11. *Vagabond*, BQ1, p. 828.

12. *P/I*, BQ2, p. 903.

13. Maurice Dekobra, interview with Colette, cited by Claude Pichois, Pl. 2, Preface, pp. ix–x.

14. *Private Life*, Section 4, "Backstage," by Alain Corbin, p. 643.

15. The title of the original edition (Paris: Ferenczi, 1932) was *Ces Plaisirs . . .* (These Pleasures . . .). It's worth noting that Colette finds ellipses irresistible, and that they are ubiquitous in her writing—the thoughtprints of a fugitive creature forever escaping the trap of the definitive. The title was taken from a melancholy phrase that Colette left unfinished, but which has been quoted as a sort of caption for her legend: *ces plaisirs qu'on nomme, à la légère, physiques . . .* (these pleasures that are so lightly called physical . . .).

16. *MM*, p. 216.

17. *Vagabond*, BQ1, p. 930.

18. *MA*, p. 59.

19. Aury, p. 98.

20. Ibid. p. 80.

21. *P/I*, BQ 2, p. 947.

22. *JAR*, "La Chaufferette," pp. 60–61.

23. *Parinaud*, p. 151.

24. *P/I*, BQ 2, pp. 949–50.

25. *LASF*, p. 68.

26. *EV*, p. 67.

27. *MDC*, "La Petite," p. 217.

CHAPTER I

1. The château is now the Musée Colette, a charming destination for Colette pilgrims. There are imaginative installations of photography, film, books, furnishings, and documents.

2. *NdJ*, p. 579; *BOD*, p. 12.

3. The source for this and all subsequent quotes from Crançon is Escholier. His reportage was based on the notes of a retired schoolmaster from the Yonne, Émile Amblard, who did the archival research.

4. Assessed at half a million francs.

5. *MDC*, "Maternité," p. 246; *MMH*, p. 76.

6. Claude Francis and Fernande Gontier, authors of *Colette* (cited in Notes as F/G), who obtained the census records, give the nurse's name as Guille. The editors of the Pléiade refer to her as Mme Girard.

7. Colette, *MDC*, "Le Sauvage," p. 210; *MMH*, p. 11.

8. *LASF*, p. 100.

9. Letters of Olympe Terrain (OT) to Jean Larnac (JL), HRC.

10. Colette, *MDC*, "La Fille de mon père," p. 237; *MMH*, "My Father's Daughter," p. 60.

11. *Prisons*, "Voyages," p. 986.

12. *LASP*, p. 109.

13. F/G, p. 13.

14. *EV*, p. 631. Colette writes the word "colored" in English.

15. The retail tradesman wore an apron and served his customers with his own hands. "By giving orders and never touching his goods, [the wholesaler] could claim to be a bourgeois." Zeldin, vol. 1, p. 15.

16. *MMH*, "My Father's Daughter," p. 60.

17. Catalogue of the Exposition Colette, 1973, p. 113; BN C1136.

18. *F/G*, p. 22.

19. *MMH*, p. 12

20. *LASF*, pp. 258, 255, 36, 183.

21. *BL*, p. 47.

22. *MMH*, pp. 5–9.

23. *LASF*, p. 259.

24. *ES*, p. 197.

25. *MMH*, p. 14.

26. *LASF*, p. 380.

27. Ibid., p. 89.

28. Ibid., p. 56.

29. *MMH*, "My Sister with the Long Hair," p. 69.

30. Ibid., p. 70.

31. *ES*, p. 247.

32. *MMH*, "My Mother and the Books," p. 36.

33. *MDC*, "Ma Soeur aux longs cheveux," p. 246.

34. *EPC*, p. 911.

CHAPTER 2

1. HL, "Un Zouave," p. 1238.

2. Ibid., p. 1239.

3. Ibid., p. 1241.

4. *MMH*, p. 44.

5. Ibid., p. 178.

6. Pl. 1, p. xlix (footnote).

7. Letter of Adrienne Saint-Aubin to her son, 1880; Pl. 1, p. cxxvi.

8. Pl. 1, p. xlvii.

9. *LASF*, p. 441.

10. Ibid., p. 82.

11. Colette, "Mes Idées sur le roman," *Le Figaro,* Oct. 30, 1937; Pl. 3, p. 1831.

12. *LASF*, p. 266.

13. Pl. 1, p. xlix.

14. *ES*, p. 212.

15. *LASF*, p. 253.

16. *P/I*, BQ2, p. 950.

17. Ibid.

18. Zeldin, vol. 2, p. 48.

19. Pl. 1, p. l.

20. Escholier, Nov. 24, 1956, p. 3.

21. *LASF*, p. 405.

22. CC 8, p. 120.

23. Escholier, Nov. 24, 1956.

24. Pl. 1, p. li (footnote). The estate consisted of farms, woods, pastures, the house in Saint-Sauveur and the worldly goods it contained, including a well-stocked cellar, a sub-

stantial library, and a blue victoria in the carriage house. But he also left a hundred thousand francs' worth of debt, some of which, according to Crançon, had been incurred by Sido, and an earlier will promising the ten thousand francs to his former concubine, now Mme Cèbe, who had no doubt earned them and more.

25. Escholier, Nov. 24, 1956.

26. *ES,* p. 231.

27. According to Amblard, a religious ceremony was held in Brussels for Sido's brothers. Despite their atheism, they, like Sido—but unlike the consistently impious Captain—were concerned enough with public opinion to keep up certain appearances, such as proper weddings, funerals, and mourning rituals. If one is to believe Francis and Gontier, they were also not so freethinking as to accept their sister Irma's transgressions.

28. *LASF,* p. 315. The woman was Mme Steinheil. See chapter 12, footnote 1.

29. *MMH,* p. 35.

30. *EPC,* p. 956.

31. Ibid.

CHAPTER 3

1. Émile Zola, *Nana,* p. 11.

2. *MMH,* p. 38.

3. Ibid.

4. Ibid.

5. *BOD,* p. 27.

6. *BL,* p. 69.

7. *Prisons,* "Puericulture," pp. 1012–13.

8. Ibid.

9. *MDC,* p. 133.

10. *MM,* p. 334.

11. *BS* II, p. 565.

12. *Sido,* p. 186.

13. *LASF,* p. 433.

14. *MA,* p. 45.

15. Colette de Jouvenel (Colette's daughter), from an undated newspaper interview given in Colette's lifetime, in which she reminisces about her mother. BN dossier 18718. This rebuke made an unforgettable impression, and she repeats the story in a letter of 1973 to Bernard Gavoty, CdJ, p. 24.

16. *Sido,* p. 163.

17. Colette, "Autres bêtes" (Domino), BQ 3, p. 818. Originally published in OCLF. The dog, Domino, was a six-month-old puppy that had been crushed by a cart wheel. Achille insisted that it was hypocritically sentimental to eat adorable little rabbits and pet lambs but to balk at making a meal of kittens or puppies. Sido was horrified but did nothing to stop him. When the roast was served at the table and Achille began to carve it, his parents and brother declined their portions. Colette ran screaming from the room while Léo shouted, "She's going to vomit. . . . Get her out of here!"

18. *VV,* "Rêverie de nouvel an," p. 22. But for a contradictory description—the peasants go away "grateful and unpretentious"—see *JFM,* "Four Seasons" (Christmas Presents), p. 21.

19. *JFM,* "Four Seasons" (Offspring), p. 136.

20. When Colette was smitten by the sawyer's beautiful daughter who, at thirteen,

wore a chignon, a long dress, and heels, Sido remarked tartly that one couldn't have the chignon without the rest of the uniform: a greasy love letter in the apron pocket, a series of admirers smelling of wine and cheap cigars, and a bastard child hidden away somewhere. *MMH*, p. 86.

21. *JFM*, "Four Seasons" (Back to School), p. 147.

22. It's interesting to note that bridegrooms of the period sent their brides red and purple flowers, symbolically, on their wedding day—all previous floral offerings having been virginal white.

23. *Sido*, p. 164.

24. Ibid., p. 166.

25. *EPC*, "Des mères, des enfants. . . . ," p. 955.

26. *Sido*, p. 156.

27. *CAL*, p. 11.

28. OT to JL, HRC.

29. *MMH*, p. 22.

30. Ibid., pp. 23–4.

31. *CAL*, p. 11.

32. *VV*, "Jour gris," p. 45.

33. *JAR*, "Automne," p. 46.

34. *Sido*, p. 213.

35. Ibid., p. 203.

36. *LASF*, pp. 113–14.

37. *MMH*, p. 58.

38. *Sido*, p. 203.

39. The *peau de chagrin*, in Balzac's novel of the same title (1831), was a magic talisman—a goatskin—given to the hero, Raphael de Valentin, by a strange old man. Each time Valentin wishes upon it, his desire is gratified. But with each wish, the skin shrinks, and when there is nothing left of it, he dies. Letters of Sido to Colette, MRB.

40. Pichois, Pl. 1, p. l.

41. Ibid., p. li.

42. Pl. 1, p. cxxvi.

43. *Sido*, p. 176.

44. Ibid., p. 189.

45. *CAL*, p. 103.

46. *MA*, p. 102.

CHAPTER 4

1. GP.

2. *Paysages*, p. 220.

3. *MA*, p. 42.

4. Louise Kaplan's discussion of these practices in *Female Perversions: The Temptations of Emma Bovary* has been of particular interest and help to me in understanding this stage of Colette's life.

5. *CAP*, p. 272.

6. *MMH*, p. 78.

7. Ibid., p. 38.

8. Ibid., p. 134.

9. Ibid., p. 68.

10. In *La Maison de Claudine,* Colette spells her name Saint-Alban.

11. *Sido,* p. 172. But one has to wonder how she knew, at eleven, what the breast she had suckled at four months looked like.

12. *MMH,* p. 115.

13. *Sido,* p. 173.

14. They knew, for example, that the Captain had, the summer of the engagement, cut down a woods which was part of her dowry. OT to JL, HRC.

15. *PdC,* pp. 133–4.

16. *MDC,* "Maternité," p. 246.

17. Caroline Landoy to Juliette Roché, MRB.

18. The rich, lovely, and accomplished Caroline Landoy, née Cuvelier de Trye, was the daughter of a well-known contemporary playwright, and the best friend of Julie Considerant, the wife of Victor. She is the worldly and acerbic "Tante Caro" of Sido's letters.

19. Caro to Juliette, MRB.

20. *MMH,* p. 76.

21. Ibid., p. 173.

22. Élizabeth Charleux-Leroux, "Gabrielle Colette à l'école élémentaire," CC 12, pp. 143–54.

23. Francis and Gontier speculate that the girlfriend was in fact Sido's sister, Irma.

CHAPTER 5

1. His list of authors included Auguste Comte; Louis Pasteur; Pierre Curie; James Clerk Maxwell (of the namesake equations); Léon Foucault (of the namesake pendulum); the astronomer Flammarion; the chemist Saint-Claire Deville; the mathematicians Poincaré and Hermite; Édouard Branly, a father of the wireless; Henri Becquerel, who discovered radioactivity and shared a Nobel Prize with the Curies; as well as the inventors of color photography and the cathode ray. They were, as his son Willy might have said, *auteurs pas gai,* although Gauthier-Villars also published Charles Cros, a famous bohemian poet and humorist who took time from his lighter work—*Mucus* and *The Pickled Herring*—to conduct experiments in chemistry and invent a phonograph.

2. The Polytechnique, when Gauthier-Villars was a student there, was headed by Baudelaire's tyrannical stepfather, General Aupick, and Willy's father would later refuse to publish Baudelaire on the ground, he said, "that we are a Catholic house." Bonmariage, p. 52.

3. The issue of divorce was to their discourse what abortion is to ours, a lightning rod that channeled the conflict between the rights of the individual—and especially of women—and the sanctity of the patriarchal family.

4. Caradec relates that Willy sent his mother his books with the pages that he deemed unsuitable for her pinned together. The family kept the books, which they permitted me to examine, and the pins—never removed—have left rust stains on the pages.

5. Élisabeth Charleux-Leroux, "Réalité et fiction dans *Claudine à l'école,*" *Bulletin de la Société des sciences historiques et naturelles de l'Yonne,* vol. 113, 1981; and Paul D'Hollander, Pl. 1, pp. 1260–61.

6. *FB,* p. 766.

7. OT to JL, 1925, HRC. It is worth comparing this account to the novelist's description of the same encounter in *Claudine at School:* "Against the intruder, Mlle Sergent, I am sticking to a savage and rebellious attitude; she has already tried to tame me, but I've balked almost insolently. After several lively skirmishes, I have to acknowledge her as a thoroughly superior schoolmistress, sharp, often crisp, with a will that would be admirably lucid if it weren't sometimes blinded by anger. With more self-control, this woman would be

admirable: But if you resist her, the eyes blaze, the red hair becomes moist with sweat.... I saw her leave the room yesterday so as not to throw an inkstand at my head." *CAL*, p. 13.

8. See *Parinaud*, p. 102; also "Mélanges," OCLF, vol. 15; and *MMH*, "My Mother and the Books," p. 33.

9. In addition to his "Ode to Paul Bert," he delivered the funeral oration for the great General Mac-Mahon, with whom he had served.

10. "Mélanges," OCLF, vol. 15, p. 346; *Sido*, p. 176.

11. Mlle Terrain gives only one example. The inspectors asked Colette about the chemical composition of ink, to which she replied, "I buy mine at the grocer's." OT to JL, HRC.

12. There was a real and very recognizable model for each of the characters—Mlle Sergent, Aimée, Luce, Anaïs, Pomme, Dutertre, Rabastens—some of whom lost suitors, others promotions, and most of whom apparently suffered *"calomnies,"* or at least merciless gossip about their sexual proclivities, after the novel was published. Mme Charleux-Leroux and others have looked for evidence of the rampant omnisexual lewdness Colette describes but haven't found any, although Mlle Terrain did have an out-of-wedlock child.

13. Rachilde, *Portraits d'hommes*, "Willy: L'À peu près grand homme," pp. 15–59.

14. Colette, "L'Ouvreuse," *La Revue illustré*, 15.vii.07; also cited by Hire, p. 65.

15. *MA*, p. 93.

16. Hire, p. 13.

17. *MA*, p. 102.

18. Willy was christened Henri Gauthier-Villars but, ever the anglophile, he changed the spelling to Henry.

19. Caradec, p. 25.

20. Ibid., p. 28.

21. Ibid., p. 32.

22. Bonmariage, p. 54.

23. Hire, p. 65.

24. A pun on a pun. The title in French is "L'À peu près grand homme," the almost great man, but an *à peu près* is also a pun.

25. Willy, *Souvenirs*.

26. Willy, *Maugis amoureux*, p. 148.

27. Bonmariage, p. 152.

28. Pierre Varenne, Willy dossier, MRB.

29. Jacques Frugier's chronology for 1889, in Pl. 1, p. cxxviii.

30. Marthe Lamy, CC 12, p. 76.

31. "I've seen them," she writes of the pubescent sirens: "... already shapely of hip and ankle, basely abuse what one calls the privileges of childhood. Playing horsie on the knee of an older cousin or perched on a barstool, knees drawn up to her chin, an adorable little blond, with knowing eyes, shows all she can of herself and spies, with the cold look of a cat, the shameful discomfiture of the men." *CSEV*, p. 83.

32. *Képi*, "La Cire Verte," p. 335.

33. Ibid.

34. *LASP*, p. 244. Bert died suddenly in 1886, at the age of fifty-three, so the dates don't jibe. But as in all her recollections, there is an imprecision about dates that leaves room for error, and thirteen (which she would have been in 1886) was, according to Colette, "the most troubled age."

35. Colette, "Graphismes," CC 2, pp. 6–10.

36. Ibid.

37. *ES*, p. 266.
38. "Graphismes," op. cit.
39. *Képi*, "Le Tendron." Translated as "The Tender Shoot" by Antonia White in *Collected Stories*, pp. 421–80.
40. Caradec, p. 58.
41. Bonmariage, p. 75.
42. Willy, *Souvenirs*, p. 40.
43. *MA*, p. 32.
44. *GB*, p. 197.
45. Caradec, p. 58.

CHAPTER 6

1. *CAP*, p. 181.
2. *BV*, "Le Sieur Binard," pp. 1368–72. Translated as "The Patriarch" by Antonia White in *Collected Stories*, p. 324.
3. *BOD*, p. 25.
4. "The Patriarch," *Collected Stories*, p. 322.
5. Weber, p. 95. Seven female doctors as of 1882, 95 by 1903, and only 556 by 1928.
6. *BV*, "Le Sieur Binard," p. 1370.
7. Pl. 1, pp. lvi–lvii.
8. Varenne, Willy dossier, MRB.
9. Caradec, p. 78.
10. Pl. 1, p. lvi.
11. *BL*, pp. 134–5.
12. *CAP*, pp. 277–93.
13. Willy, *Indiscrétions*, pp. 22–3.
14. *MA*, p. 42.
15. Letters of Sido to Juliette, MRB.
16. Ibid.
17. "Noces," OCLF, vol. 7. Translated as "Wedding Day" by Herma Briffault in *Earthly Paradise*, p. 84.
18. Ibid.
19. Meg Villars, *Les Imprudences de Peggy*, "traduit par Willy." Paris: Société d'Éditions Parisiennes, 1911.
20. Sido to Juliette, Pl. 1, p. lx.
21. Dossier Renée Hamon, BN 18711.
22. Caradec, p. 64.
23. Ibid., p. 65.
24. Mme Sanda Goudeket to the author, June 1991.
25. Dossier Renée Hamon, BN.
26. Pl. 1, p. lx.
27. Caradec, p. 65.
28. Letters of Sido to Charles Roché, MRB.
29. Pl. 1, pp. lx–lxi.
30. *Earthly Paradise*, "Wedding Day," pp. 84–88.

CHAPTER 7

1. Élisabeth de Gramont, *Mémoires*, vol. 1, p. 13.
2. *MA*, p. 207.

3. Pl. 1, p. lxii.

4. *GB*, p. 150.

5. *MA*, pp. 12–30.

6. Caradec, p. 68.

7. Just so the allusion would be lost on no one, he specified, "Venusberg, as in the *mons veneris.*"

8. *MA*, p. 38.

9. Ibid., p. 41.

10. Pl. 1, p. lxii.

11. *MA*, p. 59.

12. *CEM*, p. 333.

13. *MA*, p. 32.

14. Bonmariage, p. 136.

15. Zeldin, vol. 2, p. 1128.

16. Arnold Hauser, *The Social History of Art*, vol. 4, pp. 200–1.

17. *MA*, p. 18.

18. Ibid., p. 31.

19. Willy to a friend, MRB.

20. *MA*, p. 35.

21. Ibid., pp. 42–4.

22. Albums of Madeleine de Swarte, Doucet, album 2.

23. Willy, *Souvenirs*, p. 132.

24. Ibid., p. 134.

25. *MA*, p. 55.

26. BN 18706.

27. Ibid.

28. Willy, *Souvenirs*, p. 136.

29. Ibid; and *MA*, p. 57.

30. According to a 1999 French biography of Colette by Claude Pichois and Alain Brunet, this was not the first infidelity Colette had to endure. They cite an extremely touching letter, dated 1893, from her to Willy about his relations with an actress named Louise Willy: "Oh, Willy! I have so much, so much pain! . . . You forget me with others and I adore you so much!" *Colette*, p. 60.

31. *Sido*, p. 759.

32. *MA*, p. 45.

CHAPTER 8

1. *MA*, p. 62.

2. Willy to Charles Roché, CASS.

3. Prof. Maurice Rapin, cited in Pl. 1, p. 1293.

4. BN 18706.

5. Sanda Goudeket to the author, 1991.

6. See below, chapter 10.

7. "The Kepi," translated by Antonia White, *Collected Stories*, p. 499.

8. *MA*, p. 65.

9. *LASP*, pp. 11–12.

10. Pierre Champion, *Marcel Schwob et son temps*, p. 96.

11. *MA*, p. 64.

12. Her name may owe something to one of Willy's more famous puns. He once called

Catulle Mendès, who was famously handsome in his youth, and as prolific a womanizer as a writer, M. Vain-du-rein—a pun on *vin du Rhin*, Rhenish wine, but which also translates "vain of his loins." It's a bit of a stretch, I admit, but Verdurin—*verre du Rhin*, a glass of Rhenish wine—is something rather heavy, heady, and a little vulgar, although perhaps one is supposed to read it as *ver du rein*—worm of the loins—the insidious worm of social decomposition. The reference would not have been lost on a small circle, at least, of Proust's—and Willy's, and Colette's—contemporaries.

13. Maurois, p. 142.
14. *LASP*, p. 15.
15. *Retraite*, p. 587.
16. *MA*, p. 69.
17. "The Kepi," *Collected Stories*, pp. 524, 498.
18. *MA*, p. 72.
19. *LASP*, p. 13.
20. Ibid., p. 14.
21. Ibid., p. 22.
22. Ibid., p. 18.
23. Ibid., p. 24.
24. Albums of Madeleine de Swarte, Doucet, album 1.
25. *LASP*, p. 24.

CHAPTER 9

1. Arendt, pp. 59–60.
2. Ibid., p. 68.
3. Jullian, p. 148.
4. Claude Dauphiné, *Rachilde: Femme de lettres 1900*, p. 32.
5. *P/I*, FSG, p. 18.
6. Dossier Renée Hamon, MRB. Colette can certainly only mean three serious, long-term lovers—a figure and a distinction which I accept.
7. *MA*, p. 179.
8. Dauphiné, *Rachilde*, p. 25.
9. Ibid., p. 26.
10. Edward Berenson, *The Trial of Madame Caillaux*, p. 117.
11. Arendt, p. 82.
12. Colette, "Marguerite Moreno," in *MM*, p. 10.
13. Chauvière, "28 rue Jacob, par Marguerite Moreno," p. 55.
14. *Retraite*, p. 555.
15. In the manuscript (conserved in the Bibliothèque Nationale), Colette had originally written *"un jeune youpin de lettres"*—a young jew-boy of letters—but Willy changed it to the more discreet *"un jeune et joli garçon de lettres."* BN MS 14609.
16. *CEM*, pp. 337–8.
17. Arendt, pp. 81–2.
18. *JN*, Troisième Année, "L'âne de Buridan," p. 1246.
19. Maurois, p. 100.
20. Ibid.
21. *MA*, p. 158.
22. *LASP*, p. 32.
23. *MA*, p. 170.
24. *VV*, "Jour gris," p. 45.

25. Weber, p. 159.
26. Caradec, p. 92.
27. Weber, p. 272.
28. Ibid., p. 159.
29. Cited by D'Hollander, *CSA*, p. 63.
30. *MA*, p. 173.
31. Caradec, p. 81.
32. There is a photograph in Showalter's *Sexual Anarchy* showing Wilde dressed as Salomé, which came from the private collection of Willy's friend Guillot de Saxe. Colette's costume in *Rêve d'Égypte* was almost exactly that of Wilde in the photograph.
33. Pl. 1, p. xxxvii.
34. Joris-Karl Huysmans, *Against the Grain*, p. 66.
35. Elaine Showalter, *Sexual Anarchy*, p. 13.
36. *LASP*, p. 34.
37. Pl. 1, p. lxiv.
38. Bonmariage, p. 58.
39. F/G, p. 122.

CHAPTER 10

1. OT to JL, HRC.
2. Ibid. Thirty years later she advanced the curious hypothesis that Willy and Colette were eager to attend the ceremony because they counted on meeting Dr. Merlou there— Jules Colette's old Nemesis—who was by then a member of Parliament, "and through whose offices Willy might have obtained a more lucrative position than that of a man of letters."
3. Colette to OT, MRB.
4. OT to JL, HRC.
5. Unpublished letter of Colette to Moreno, collection of Foulques de Jouvenel.
6. Caradec, p. 89.
7. Colette to OT, MRB.
8. Terrain Dossier, BN 18708.
9. *MA*, p. 89.
10. *LASP*, p. 27.
11. *MA*, p. 90.
12. *LASP*, p. 27.
13. *MA*, p. 95.
14. Ibid., p. 91.
15. *Retraite sentimentale*, Pl. 1, p. 873. *RFL*, p. 80. The translation that appears here is mostly my own.
16. OT to JL, HRC.
17. Larnac, p. 56.
18. Colette to OT, MRB.
19. *MA*, p. 36.
20. Larnac, p. 55.
21. Caradec, p. 90.
22. *LASP*, p. 444.
23. Jullian, p. 280.
24. Sarde, p. 140.
25. *MA*, p. 127.

26. Reported by G. Ravon, *Des yeux pour voir,* cited by D'Hollander, *CSA,* p. 77.
27. Ibid.
28. Caradec, p. 90.
29. *LASP,* p. 29.
30. BN 18706.
31. Maurois, p. 101.
32. Ibid.
33. Maurois, p. 102.
34. Ibid., p. 474.
35. Ibid.
36. Chauvière, p. 58.
37. *P/I* FSG, pp. 164–5.

CHAPTER II

1. Esterhazy's complicity in the affair had already been unearthed by Mathieu Dreyfus, Alfred's brother, and disclosed to the press. But it was Picquart who offered the first concrete proof, in the form of an express letter (the famous *"petit bleu"*) found in the intelligence files.
2. The socialist Jaurès had originally derided Dreyfus's judges for their "indulgence" and called for the death penalty. On the other hand, Scheurer-Kestner, vice-president of the Senate, was an early supporter of Dreyfus, and it was to him that Picquart addressed his exposé from Tunisia. He was, like Dreyfus, an Alsatian, and "regarded himself as the protector of all Alsatians in France." Jean-Marie Mayeur and Madeleine Rebérioux, *The Third Republic from Its Origins to the Great War,* p. 184—one of my principal sources, with Arendt, for the history of the Dreyfus Affair.
3. ". . . the vast majority of the comfortable Jewish bourgeoisie had only one aim—the peaceful enjoyment of its rights. It feared disorder and was pleased to present the French army as an admirable school of toleration." Mayeur/Rebérioux, *Third Republic,* p. 181.
4. Maurois, p. 146.
5. Séverine, the *pasionaria* of French letters, and Durand's collaborator, covered the trial for the paper and told her readers: "If we do not demand justice for a condemned man we have reason to believe is innocent, what right do we have to seek justice for ourselves!"
6. Weber, p. 122.
7. Maurois, p. 126.
8. Among the proposed solutions to the Jewish Question were stewing the Jews in oil and circumcising them "up to the neck." Arendt, p. 107.
9. Jules Renard, *Journal,* Feb. 17, 1898. Paris: Gallimard, 1959.
10. Dossier Renée Hamon, BN.
11. *LASP,* p. 46.
12. Caradec, p. 99.
13. *TSN,* p. 372.
14. "The Kepi," *Collected Stories,* p. 512.
15. *TSN,* p. 372.
16. *MA,* p. 36.
17. Ibid., p. 203.
18. Ibid., p. 86.
19. Jean de Tinan, *Aimienne ou Le Détournement d'une mineure,* 1899, quoted by Pichois, Pl. 1, p. lxvi.

20. *MA*, p. 98.

21. Ibid.

22. Even if Colette had signed her own first novels, Willy would, under the Napoleonic Code, which was still in effect—it wasn't modified until 1907—have received the royalties, owned the copyrights, and been entitled to dispose of them. Their country house, Les Monts-Bouccons, was sold in 1908, so for that he needed Colette's written consent. Which she gave him.

23. Colette, Préface to *Claudine à l'école*, OCLF, 1948, cited by D'Hollander, *CSA*, p. 89.

24. D'Hollander, *CSA*, p. 93.

25. Hire, p. 72.

26. Lanoux, p. 358.

27. Ibid., p. 359.

28. *CAL*-LDP, p. 93.

29. *CEM*-Folio, p. 18.

CHAPTER 12

1. In 1908, the husband and mother of Mme Steinheil were both found dead: they had been strangled. She was tried for the double murder, although the prosecutors believed it had actually been committed by her lover, a fiftyish country squire named Borderel, who declared: "To defend myself would be to accuse her." It was widely remarked how young and beautiful Meg Steinheil still looked at forty. She was acquitted—the verdict was wildly popular—left France, married an English nobleman, and died on July 20, 1954, two weeks before Colette.

2. Arendt, p. 119.

3. Lanoux, p. 375.

4. Sarde, p. 152.

5. The equivalence in modern money is difficult to establish, but the franc in 1900 was worth somewhere between $1.50 and $5.00 in current spending power—outside any major American or European city—although some of the more essential costs of living, such as rent and food, were much lower than they are today. The equivalence is easier to understand if one imagines life in fin de siècle Paris being roughly comparable, costwise, to what it is in a place like Guadalajara or Cairo. Also see my chapter 22, note 19.

6. See Lanoux, pp. 270–73.

7. Léo Taxil, *La Corruption fin-de-siècle*.

8. The popular press of the era—*Fantasio, Rire, Le Sourire, Fin-de-Siècle,* to name but a few of the reviews—serves up a *grande bouffe* of Woman-as-Confection. The monotonous and cloying menu barely varies from week to week: fat beauties in diaphanous veils; wood nymphs; bacchantes; ferocious gypsy girls; pert, busty ingenues in short skirts or knickers; exotic dancers—Africans, Hindus, Americans, Egyptians; pretty, languid addicts taking morphine or smoking opium, their images an early version of Heroin Chic. There are features on "the most beautiful busts of Paris"; memoirs of a satyr, a chauffeur, and an odalisque; half-nude models riding circus horses, splayed sumptuously on beds, jumping out of cakes or bathtubs; and in the same pages, advertisements for abortionists, pornography, condoms, and thyroid pills (for losing weight), cures for impotence, venereal disease, gout, anemia, and migraines, and contraptions to enlarge the breast. Colette would grace the pages, and sometimes the covers, of these reviews when she went on the stage.

9. Dumas, *L'Ami des femmes,* cited by Pichois, Pl. 1, p. xii.

10. Lanoux, p. 106.

11. Simone de Beauvoir, *The Second Sex*, p. 192.

12. Aucler's police dossier contained the opinion that she was suffering from "madness and hysteria, a disease that causes her to look upon men as her equals and to seek contact with them." *Private Life*, p. 165.

13. *La Vie heureuse*, 1904, BN Fol. ZN53.

14. Rachilde, Gyp, Marcelle Tinayre, Judith Gautier, Gérard d'Houville (Marie-Louise de Hérédia de Régnier), Colette Yver, Lucie Delarue-Mardrus, Renée Vivien, Anna de Noailles, Myriam Harry, Juliette Adam, Arvède Barine, Séverine—to name just the better known of Colette's contemporaries.

15. De Beauvoir, *The Second Sex*, p. 336.

16. *CAP*-LDP, p. 198.

17. *CAL*-LDP, p. 125.

18. Ibid., p. 136.

19. Ibid., p. 62.

20. Pichois, Pl. 1, p. lxvii.

21. Ibid., p. lxxii–lxxiii.

CHAPTER 13

1. *MA*, p. 137. The house was sold in January 1908.

2. Ibid., pp. 137–8.

3. Colette to MM, collection of Foulques de Jouvenel.

4. I have passed over these slight novels, *Minne* and *Les Égarements de Minne*, published in 1904 and 1905, respectively, and condensed in 1909 into one volume entitled *L'Ingénue libertine*, signed Colette Willy. In the first one, a well-brought-up young virgin runs away from home in search of rough sex with a hoodlum. In the second, the same character has grown up and married, but she's never had an orgasm. She takes a lover, hoping he'll provide one, but ultimately finds ecstasy in an unlikely quarter, the arms of her husband.

5. Or so said Willy's secretary Alfred Diard. Colette claims that she had no jewels, just a collection of glass beads. Caradec (p. 142) suggests that the truth is somewhere between "the beads and the pearls."

6. *MA*, p. 118.

7. *Parinaud*, p. 97.

8. *MA*, p. 168.

9. *Vagabond*, p. 32.

10. Ibid., p. 30.

11. Pauline Réage, *Story of O*.

12. For an enlightening and thorough discussion of this subject, see Jessica Benjamin, *The Bonds of Love*, and in particular the chapter "Master and Slave."

13. *CEM*-Folio, p. 242.

14. For an illuminating discussion of the function of jealousy and the cycles of "abandonment and reunion" in scenarios of bondage, see Louise Kaplan, *Female Perversions*.

15. Willy, *Indiscrétions*.

16. All quotes from *CAP*-LDP.

CHAPTER 14

1. Caradec, p. 148.

2. *Colette*, pp. 101–2.

3. *Discours*, p. 22. Georgie was married in 1891; Cocteau and Goudeket were both

born in 1889. So the young Raoul-Duval must have been two or three years, at least, behind them. According to Pichois, Georgie was the author of three books and a play, the latter produced in London by her sister, Mrs. Brown Potter, a well-known actress and friend of the Prince of Wales. *Colette,* pp. 103–5.

4. Willy, *Indiscrétions.*

5. *LASP,* p. 51.

6. Caradec, p. 149.

7. *LASP,* p. 49.

8. Ibid., p. 51.

9. *CEM*-Folio, p. 13.

10. Ibid., p. 16.

11. Ibid., p. 20.

12. Ibid., p. 56.

13. Ibid., p. 148.

14. *MA,* p. 177.

15. *CEM*-Folio, p. 241.

16. Writes Pichois: "One sees the formula: novel, play, play, novel, which permits the Willy factory to appear to multiply the products by diversifying the packaging." Pl. 1, p. lxix.

17. They combined their names to create the pseudonym Luvey.

18. It was she who immortalized "Ta-rah-rah-boom-dee-ay," a song I learned from my grandmother, Colette's contemporary.

19. She disliked Piaf herself, remarking in 1941 "that to be very ugly, infatuated, and without talent at the same time is too much." *LAPF,* p. 69.

20. Polaire, *Polaire par elle-même,* p. 118.

21. In her memoir, Polaire deplored the gossip that this exhibition aroused and denied that there had ever been anything improper in her friendship with Colette and Willy. Willy's statements over the years, public and private, support this assertion. So do Colette's; Polaire, she told a friend, had a horror of "unisexuality" and had never been her lover.

22. Caradec, p. 136.

23. *MA,* p. 163.

24. Ibid., pp. 165–66.

25. *La Vie heureuse,* no. V, 1904.

26. *TSN,* p. 372.

27. Caradec, pp. 141–42.

28. *Paysages,* p. 152.

29. Weber, pp. 213–17.

30. *Private Life,* p. 667.

31. *Paysages,* pp. 150–54.

32. *MA,* p. 195.

33. Caradec, p. 143.

34. Among the many distinguished witnesses who testified on Willy's behalf was Joris-Karl Huysmans, who asserted that Willy's novels provided "a true and valuable documentary on the customs of our epoque. In my opinion, they are works of an artist." Caradec, p. 155.

35. Ibid., p. 169.

36. *MA,* p. 199.

37. Caradec, p. 120.

38. *Dialogues,* p. 149.
39. *P/I* FSG, p. 171.
40. Willy, *Indiscrétions.*
41. Pl. 3, p. 1567.
42. *P/I,* Pl. 3, p. 634.
43. Ibid., p. 633.
44. Ibid., p. 637.
45. Ibid., p. 628.
46. Allan Massie, *Colette.*
47. Francis and Gontier resurrect old rumors about Colette and Moreno, Otéro, Augusta Holmes, and various actresses, but as Jean Chalon puts it, "*le tout Paris* had been attributing mistresses to Mme Willy for a long time because no one knew of her having any [male] lovers." Jean Chalon, *Colette, l'éternelle apprentie.* p. 91.
48. Barney, p. 191.
49. George Wickes, *The Amazon of Letters,* p. 263.
50. François Chapon, *Autour de Natalie Clifford Barney,* p. 6.
51. Barney, p. 189.
52. Jean Chalon, *Portrait d'une séductrice,* pp. 119–20.
53. Pl. 1, p. lxxxii.

CHAPTER 15

1. Colette to Louis de Robert, BN 18707.
2. *CSEV/* LDP, p. 139.
3. *MA,* p. 167.
4. Ibid.
5. Ibid., p. 141.
6. *Claudine au concert,* p. 53.
7. Willy (Maugis), Polaire, Natalie Barney (Miss Flossie), Jeanne de Caillavet (Rose-Chou), the composer Léon Payet (Louis de Serres) and his wife, Marthe (Liette), among others.
8. Willy later claimed that Colette wanted to use *Claudine s'en va* to "pillory all the women she had slept with, and a few others"—and that he had opposed her. "It would have taken six volumes of small print," he adds maliciously. Willy, *Indiscrétions.*
9. MS. of *Claudine s'en va,* BN 14620.
10. *CSEV/* LDP, p. 86.
11. Ibid., p. 131.
12. Ibid., p. 168.
13. *LASP,* p. 52.
14. Kiki is referred to as a Chartreux but described as an angora. Willy remembers him as an angora.
15. *LASP,* p. 56. Colette's "Translation for the Unitiated: I forget my mitts and Willy scolded me for coming home bare-armed. . . . Willy's leaving a day before me for les Clayes. . . . I dined alone with the cat. . . . I'm going to 'sleep' alone tonight, and I'm feeling a certain melancholy, because I'm in the habit of nesting in a conjugal right arm. The departure for les Clayes inspires me with a subdued enthusiasm, and I salute the Muhlfelds."
16. *Dialogues,* p. 30.
17. Ibid., p. 80.
18. Ibid., p. 150.

19. To respectful reviews, for the most part, notably from the faithful Rachilde. The major dissent came from a critic who was an avowed enemy of Willy's, Jean Ernest-Charles, writing an essay called "The Case of Willy" in the *Revue bleue*. He called Colette's book "unbearably pretentious," while noting that it contained certain merits found in the *Claudines*: namely a feeling for nature and a sensuous grasp of detail. Ernest-Charles, *La Revue bleue,* "Le Cas Willy," Oct. 7, 1905.

20. Pl. 2, p. 1284.

21. *Claudine à Paris,* Pl. 1, p. 279.

22. *Colette-Jammes, Une Amitié inattendue.* Doucet 10.592.

23. *Dialogues,* pp. 10–13.

CHAPTER 16

1. Albums de Swarte, Doucet, album 1. *"Pour mon Papa son poupon, Meg."*

2. Pichois quotes a letter from Meg to Colette, written in July of 1905 and signed "Ton Meg"—the familiar second person is significant—"who is not very precise about her sex." Pl. 1, p. lxxxvi.

3. Caradec, p. 181.

4. Pl. 1, p. xciv.

5. *P/I* FSG, p. 76.

6. The Paris of the Second Empire was famous for its tolerance of—indeed, its fascination with and encouragement of—sapphism. De Morny liked to claim that an experience of lesbian sensuality gave a young woman the best possible erotic schooling, and it is said that he liked to entrust his mistresses to an older woman with the command: "Perfect her for me." Frédéric Loliée, *Le Duc de Morny et la société du Second Empire.*

7. *ES,* p. 231.

8. *P/I* FSG, p. 78.

9. Michel Rémy-Bieth (MRB) to the author, 1991.

10. Dossier Louise Weiss, "Notes et documents pour *Les Mémoires d'une Européene,*" BN 17794.

11. *P/I* FSG, p. 79.

12. Jullian, p. 199.

13. The only time Missy ever reportedly wore a dress was for her sister-in-law's funeral—and her nieces and nephews were so upset to see their Uncle Max in "drag" that they begged her to go home and change. MRB to the author, 1991.

14. *P/I* FSG, p. 80.

15. Ibid., p. 76.

16. Simone de Laborderie, who was a friend of both Missy and Louise Weiss, confided to Weiss that Missy had given her her word of honor that she "didn't know what pleasure was—that pleasure she had renounced the possibility of experiencing, but which she wanted at all cost to give." BN 17794.

17. *P/I* FSG, p. 81.

18. Pl. 1, p. 528.

19. Caradec, p. 179.

20. Barney, p. 191.

21. *MA,* p. 211.

22. Caradec, p. 178.

23. *LASF,* p. 268.

24. Ibid., p. 76.

25. Ibid., p. 416.

26. Ibid., p. 409.

27. Ibid., p. 53.

28. *LASF,* p. 114. Neither Achille nor the Captain had ever forgiven Juliette for her part in ruining the family, and the Rochés were unwelcome in Châtillon. So Sido went alone on her infrequent visits to Charny, where the Rochés moved after leaving Saint-Sauveur, returning brokenhearted at the misery she found there. Yvonne, Juliette's daughter—whom Sido always refers to as "Roché's daughter"—was a morose, deceitful adolescent. Charles Roché suffered from heart and kidney trouble, for which he took narcotics, and probably from tuberculosis. Juliette kept checking under her husband's sickbed to make sure the housemaid wasn't hiding there. "Everything's an excuse for [Juliette's] jealousy," Sido told Colette. "She tortures Roché night and day."

29. Pl. 1, p. lxxxiv.

30. In a biography of Colette by Jeannie Malige, the close friend and associate of Bertrand de Jouvenel, Malige remarks that "Sido didn't know [the Willys'] lateness for the funeral was not the fault of mechanical problems, but of an unexpected flare-up of passion, which delayed the terrible spouses at Fontainebleau for the time it took them to extinguish it." She doesn't attribute the story, but other evidence suggests that it is quite plausible. (See below, chapter 26.) Jeannie Malige, *Colette, Qui êtes-vous?,* p. 40.

31. Catalogue of the Exposition Colette, 1973, BN C1136. Also Pl. 1, p. lxxxiv.

32. *Sido,* pp. 196–7.

33. *Sido,* BQ 2, p. 787.

34. *MA,* p. 128–30.

35. Thanks in part to Mélie, who had nourished her on folktales and superstitions, Colette was a lifelong believer in the occult—or pretended to be one. When Aunt Alicia tells Gigi that opals are bad luck, and Gigi asks if she really believes in such nonsense as cursed stones and evil eyes, her mentor replies that superstitions "also go by the name of weaknesses. A pretty little collection of weaknesses are our indispensable stock-in-trade with the men." Why? "Because nine men out of ten are superstitious . . . [and] they forgive us—oh!—for many things, but not for the absence in us of their own feelings." Colette, *Gigi and The Cat,* translated by Roger Senhouse. London: Penguin, 1958, p. 37.

36. *Sido,* p. 194.

37. *P/I,* BQ 2, p. 911.

38. *VV,* p. 40.

39. *P/I,* BQ 2, p. 906.

40. Claudine Brécourt-Villars, *Petit glossaire raisonné de l'érotisme saphique, 1880–1930.*

41. Willy, *Maugis amoureux,* p. 67.

42. Ibid., pp. 267–8.

CHAPTER 17

1. He was born Waag in Paris, Jan. 15, 1875.

2. Introduction to *L'Envers du music-hall,* BQ 1, p. 946.

3. In 1915, after nearly twenty years of friendship, romantic and professional, Mendelys and Wague finally got married.

4. Sarde, pp. 247–8.

5. Colette to Missy, April 1909, BN 18706.

6. Colette, *Fin de siècle,* April 5, 1906.

7. Caradec, p. 196.

8. Ibid., p. 181.

9. He did, and loyally reviewed Colette's performance in *Paris qui chante*, October 14, 1906.

> The débuts of Mme Colette Willy will, without a doubt, attract *le tout Paris* to the Olympia. The famous name, the talent and beauty of the debutante, make her one of the most important *vedettes* that a music hall director has discovered in a long time.
>
> Mme Colette Willy cannot do anything indifferently, and the passionate attention of her public is assured in advance. The decision that she has just taken will give rise to plenty of commentary. There are many people who will never pardon Mme Willy for wanting to command attention as a dancer and mime; she will need a great deal of energy and obstinate will to conquer the resistance of that segment of the Parisian public who resent the stars they love when they break free from their habitual mold.
>
> Furthermore, Mme Willy has committed the error of being one of the most delicious writers in France; one is scarcely unaware of her collaboration in that series of novels so universally famous. . . . The public is thus used to considering her as a great artist of the word . . . and here she is appearing in the charming but unexpected form of a capricious and wild little gypsy, barely covered by her rags, which reveal her white, nude flesh!
>
> Thus it wasn't without a certain fear that I waited for the apparition of Mme Colette Willy in one of those first-night concert halls, where the presence of her friends was enough to create a hostile atmosphere.
>
> She appeared . . . and while no one sought to deplore it, the spectators were astonished to perceive that she wasn't wearing a leotard. . . . Apart from the fact that the truth of the role demanded it, dispensing with a leotard has become one of the necessities of modern dance. . . . For that matter, Mme Willy isn't the first to have emancipated herself from the conventions and the constraints of the body suit: Miss Ruth Rhada, Suzy Deguez, Isadora Duncan . . . and all the dancers with pretty legs don't wear them anymore either . . . and the stability of Europe hasn't been affected by it. . . .
>
> Nevertheless, the hypocrisy of the audience did not go so far as to sulk at its own pleasure. . . .
>
> Then Mme Willy danced and mimed and knew perfectly how to enchant her skeptical and blasé audience. . . . She brought to her part all the nervous originality of her talent as a writer . . . and that sort of voluptuous brutality and winning savagery of those gypsy girls who pass, whom one adores, and who disappear.

10. Caradec, p. 188.
11. Bonmariage, p. 89.
12. *LASP*, p. 114.
13. Sido to Juliette, MRB. Sido may have been showing off. Renée Vivien was being kept, at the time, by an immensely rich baroness, born a Rothschild; she prided herself on her hospitality and the sumptuousness of her appointments. It seems odd, too, that an alcoholic wouldn't have owned any glassware.
14. "Printemps de la Riviera," Pl. 1, pp. 1060–63. A louis was twenty francs.
15. Ibid.
16. Ibid.
17. Caradec, p. 206.

18. Ibid., p. 207.

19. On which Willy and Georges Wague also collaborated.

20. Pl. 1, p. xci.

21. Ibid.

22. *LDLV,* p. 14 (Footnote).

23. *MA,* p. 216.

24. Ibid., pp. 216–17.

25. The "you" is plural: *vous.* Does it refer to Colette and Missy? Or have Colette and Willy concocted some peculiar story for Sido that has them still happily married but living separately?

26. *LASF,* p. 56.

27. *MA,* p. 184.

28. *LASF,* p. 57.

29. Fernand Hauser, *Le Journal,* Nov. 17, 1906.

30. Letter dated Nov. 25, 1906, which appeared in the *Cri de Paris* of Dec. 2 and was reprinted by *Fantasio* on April 15, 1907, as part of a story on the lawsuit for defamation of character that Missy filed in response to another gossip column in *Fantasio* of Dec. 15, 1906.

31. *Fantasio,* Dec. 15, 1906.

32. Missy sued for libel but won only a Pyrrhic victory. She had asked for damages of 15,000 francs. The court agreed that she had been libeled, but awarded her twenty-five francs—a slap in the face—on the ground that Colette had already "publicly flaunted" their relationship. *Fantasio* triumphantly printed the transcript of the judgment.

33. 100 francs for the boxes and 200 for front of the orchestra, according to Caradec, p. 194.

34. *Le Rire,* no. 204, Dec. 29, 1906, quoted by Pichois, Pl. 1, p. xcii.

35. Sido to Colette, March 1, 1909, MRB.

36. Ibid.

37. Caradec, p. 196.

38. In some commentaries, Missy is named as the author, but Pichois, generally authoritative, attributes the scenario to Willy and Wague.

39. "Une Cabale au Moulin-Rouge," *Semaine parisienne,* Jan. 6, 1907, p. 1.

40. D'Hollander, *CSA,* p. 359.

41. Colette, the petition specified, had left Willy's bed and board in November, making it clear in the most public fashion that she did not plan to return.

42. *LASF,* p. 67. Sido goes on to remind Colette that according to her marriage contract, she is due five thousand francs in case of divorce. There were also some complicated legal questions concerning the ownership of the Robineau house in Saint-Sauveur, toward which Colette had paid ten thousand francs, although Willy had signed the receipt. Sido wanted to know what provisions had been made by the separation agreement for reclaiming this property, and whether or not Les Monts-Bouccons was legally hers.

43. Fifteen thousand francs a year, according to Caradec.

44. D'Hollander, *CSA,* p. 363.

45. The Mercure de France, which published *Dialogues de bêtes.*

46. Pl. 1, p. xcv.

47. This correspondence exists only in fragments, mostly undated, which have been dispersed among various collections of Colettiana, but using the internal logic of the letters, I have put them in what I feel is a reasonably accurate chronological order.

48. Colette to Willy, Jan. 20, 1907, MRB.

49. Bernard Loliée mss. sale catalogue, no. 3, 1968, MRB.

50. *LASF,* p. 73.
51. BN 18706.
52. Pl. 1, p. xciv.
53. Colette to Willy, Feb. 17, 1907, MRB.
54. Caradec, p. 201.
55. *LASF,* p. 85.
56. Ibid., p. 87.
57. Caradec, p. 205.
58. Willy to Colette, BN 18708.
59. *LASF,* p. 101.
60. Ibid., p. 94.

CHAPTER 18

1. *MA,* p. 141.
2. The protagonist of *Claudine s'en va.*
3. *RFL,* p. 63.
4. Ibid., p. 220.
5. Pl. 1, p. 1536.
6. *LASF,* p. 80.
7. *ES,* p. 240.
8. Pichois, Pl. 1, Preface, pp. cxvii–cxix.
9. D'Hollander, Introduction to *Retraite sentimentale,* Pl. 1, p. 1498.
10. Ibid., p. 1499.
11. *VV,* p. 11.
12. *Comoedia,* Jan. 3, 1909.
13. Including a margin note that says: "Keep going, you charming little horror!" Pl. 1, p. 1531.
14. *LASF,* p. 123.
15. Ibid., p. 159.
16. When Colette took *La Chair* on tour, a number of local prefects forbade the nude scene. In April of 1908, when the play reopened at the Apollo in Paris, Sido read in the paper that the police planned to "interrogate those women who show themselves nude in the music halls, and it cites, among others, The Apollo. Will you be among those naked ladies? It would be extremely disagreeable." *LASF,* p. 173.
17. It was collected in *Les Vrilles de la vigne* under the title "Music-Halls."
18. *VV,* pp. 239–47.
19. *MA,* p. 132.
20. *LASF,* pp. 128, 152.
21. Caradec, p. 213.
22. Ibid., p. 209.
23. Ibid., p. 207.
24. *LASF,* p. 151.
25. Ibid., p. 196.
26. Caradec, p. 216.
27. *LDLV,* p. 21. Colette may not mention Meg, but Missy does. In a letter to Colette undated but of this period, she relates the gossip from their favorite haunts—the lesbian bistro Palmyre and The Farm, where Otéro gets drunk, slaps a friend of theirs, and is almost thrown out. "You must have learned a lot from that little madwoman Meg," she adds. The nature of Meg's example is not clear. Missy to Colette, MRB.

28. *LDLV*, p. 23.
29. Sido to Colette, May 6, 1908, MRB.
30. *Comoedia*, May 9, 1908.
31. *LDLV*, p. 25.
32. Colette to Missy, BN 18706.
33. Ibid.
34. Unpublished legal correspondence, MRB.
35. *En tournée*, p. 9.
36. *LASF*, p. 205.
37. Ibid., p. 209.
38. Ibid., p. 214.
39. *VV*, pp. 15–25.
40. Ibid., pp. 23–4.

CHAPTER 19

1. Another related Marthe—Marthe Payet—is the friend of Annie Samzun and the mistress of Maugis in *Claudine Takes Off*. Willy later confessed that she was modeled on his own mistress Liette de Serres—see below, chapter 20.

2. Colette, *En camarades*, OCLF, vol. 15, p. 256.

3. Two years earlier, Léon Blum, the distinguished socialist and man of letters, had published a controversial essay on marriage, arguing for what he considered a modest and reasonable reform of the institution: abolish illegitimacy; give children their mothers' names; instruct the young of both sexes in birth control; sanction, for women as well as for men, a period of sexual experimentation; fix the appropriate age for a first pregnancy around thirty. Marriage would then become a union of mature equals.

Toward the end of his essay, Blum raised the question he knew had been percolating in the minds even of his most sympathetic readers. "I keep insisting on this part of my subject," he wrote—the injustice of making a young girl sacrifice her instincts to her honor:

> The sufferings of young girls are so secret or so misunderstood—they themselves are so ashamed of them—that they should inspire our pity. I confess that I have been thinking about [those young girls] while writing a book that they won't read. And should I have wanted them to read it? . . . Would I dare to advise [a young girl] to break with the prejudices that enslave her? . . . Would I dare, if I had a daughter, to raise her with these views? No question has tormented me more, and I still can't settle it. The passage from the old moral order to the [new one] . . . is perilous and difficult; the first adventurers to risk themselves are always sacrificed. . . . But to live in conflict with convention and prejudice; to brave the isolation and the contempt to which such audacity exposes you; to profit from this brand-new liberty that you have conquered—it takes too much courage, and also too much clairvoyance.

Blum, who had given *Claudine at School* an enthusiastic review in his journal, *Les Droits de l'homme*, had followed Colette's career with interest and sympathy, and it is possible that Claudine had influenced his thinking on the subject of young girls and their sacrifices. His essay, in turn, may have influenced the character of *The Vagabond*'s Renée Néré—a woman who chooses "to break with the prejudices that enslave her." Léon Blum, "Du Mariage," *L'Oeuvre de Léon Blum*, p. 180.

4. *LASF*, p. 256.
5. Caradec, p. 218.
6. *En tournée*, p. 43.

7. Dec. 1908, MRB.
8. Willy to Missy, MRB.
9. Ibid.
10. Caradec, p. 222.
11. Colette to Willy, BN 18708.
12. *LDLV*, p. 30.
13. BN 18708.
14. Colette to Vallette, MRB.
15. Caradec, pp. 223–4.
16. *LASF*, p. 260.
17. Ibid., p. 286.
18. Caradec, p. 225.
19. *Vagabond*, p. 32.
20. Colette to Wague, BN 18708.
21. A family named Blum whom Colette refers to as a "devouring horde."
22. *LASF*, p. 241.
23. *LDLV*, p. 35.
24. *En tournée*, p. 30.
25. Ibid., p. 39.
26. Ibid., p. 7.
27. Ibid., p. 35.
28. Colette to Missy, MRB.
29. BN 18706.
30. Colette to Missy, MRB.
31. Colette to Missy, BN 18706.
32. *RFL*, p. 220.
33. *Vagabond*, p. 25.
34. Néré is an anagram of Renée, which means reborn.
35. *Vagabond*, p. 35.
36. Bonmariage, p. 315.
37. Ibid., p. 97.
38. Ibid., p. 100.
39. *LDLV*, p. 38.
40. Ibid., p. 39.
41. Lottmann, p. 83.
42. *LASF*, p. 113.

CHAPTER 20

1. Caradec, pp. 235–6.
2. Pichois, pl. 1, Preface, p. ciii.
3. Willy, *Lélie, fumeuse d'opium*.
4. Caradec, p. 247.
5. Or in professional reparations—it isn't clear. This detail comes in an unpublished (and unfortunately undated) letter to Wague written sometime after the publication of *The Vagabond*, because she addresses him as Brague. "Did you know that [Willy] is obliged to pay me a thousand francs a year? He played the bounced-check trick, but my stove doesn't burn that kind of wood. He finally paid the whole thing." Colette to Wague, BN 18708.
6. The cook was not the same servant—Francine—who had worked for Colette and Willy while they were married and whose services they had shared after their separation.

Francine remained loyal to Willy, and it came back to Sido through another servant that she had "extremely vile" things to say about Colette and Missy, but, as Sido tells her daughter, "mostly about you. She reveres Willy. Is that because she was his mistress?" *LASF,* p. 398.

7. One of them is in the de Serres dossier at the Bibliothèque Nationale. Most of it is illegible, but the gist goes: "marvelous, marvelous Willy. The toad is in Nice—[is this Colette or her husband?]; so the torments are starting up again. Au revoir, magic Willy, it's nearly a pathological case to be able to think in verse as you do. I'm still completely astounded." To which Willy notes: "It's sweet to see genius paying homage to merit." BN 18706. Francis and Goutier attribute this letter—mistakenly—to Colette. It is not in her very distinctive hand.

8. And gets the better of "Marthe" in *En camarades,* written as these events are taking place. See above, chapter 19.

9. BN 18708.

10. Caradec, p. 240.

11. *LASF,* p. 314.

12. Caradec, p. 241, and the Willy dossier, MRB.

13. Pichois, Pl. 1, Preface, p. ci.

14. Caradec, p. 241.

15. Ibid., p. 248.

16. On Nov. 18, 1910.

17. *LALV,* p. 44.

18. In one of the rare surviving letters from Missy to Colette, the marquise describes to Colette, who's on tour, a rowdy night at Palmyre, the Montmartre bistro, in the course of which Fersen gets drunk, insults everyone, is slapped by the proprietress, and throws a glass of wine at her; then "all the queens rose up as a single body (if I may put it that way) to throw him out." One of them pulled out a large hank of his hair, and in turn denounced the place to the police, calling it "a disgusting hangout of dykes and queers." Missy to Colette, MRB.

19. Colette to Missy, MRB.

20. *LALV,* p. 45.

21. Colette to Missy, MRB.

22. Valentine was also the name of her proper sister-in-law, Mme Albert Gauthier-Villars.

23. Le Palmyre.

24. *Paysages,* p. 38.

25. Among his unpublished papers at the Bibliothèque Nationale is a clipping from *Gil Blas* describing the scandal at the Moulin Rouge. It is marvelously witty, the formality of the language a fine foil for the vulgarity of the demonstration mounted by "the elite of Paris," and without approving of Colette and Missy, it is sympathetic to them. The tone, the detachment, and the scrupulous attention the author pays to the "qualities" of the participants—their rank—suggests that the count himself, who did contribute to the review, may have been its author.

26. Barbier to Montesquiou, BN 15301.

27. Montesquiou to Colette, CASS.

28. BN 15260.

29. BN 15293.

30. BN 15301.

31. In one of her letters, Renée tells Colette that she imported her servant from Hong

Kong, but because he had been a sailor on an American ship, he had the temerity to speak to her "face to face, without lowering his eyes." Should she send him back to China, she wonders, or sell him to Palmyre, for the use of her clients? Renée Vivien to Colette, MRB.

32. *P/I* FSG, p. 85.

33. *Vagabond,* p. 226.

34. *P/I* FSG, p. 93.

35. Renée Vivien/Colette correspondence, MRB.

36. *P/I* FSG, p. 88. But Renée actually announced the misfortune of her "fatness" to Missy, in a letter. Renée Vivien to Missy, MRB.

37. *P/I* FSG, p. 97.

38. Ibid., p. 98.

39. *Vagabond,* p. 221.

40. Ibid., p. 65.

41. Colette to Hamel, BN 18712.

42. Colette to Robert, MRB.

43. Painter, vol. 2, p. 185.

44. Louis de Robert, *De Loti à Proust.* pp. 156–60.

45. Ibid., p. 190.

46. Ibid., pp. 176–7.

47. Robert to Colette, CASS.

48. Ibid.

CHAPTER 21

1. Aury, p. 57.

2. *ES,* p. 185.

3. *LASF,* p. 392.

4. Ibid., p. 406.

5. *L'Entrave,* p. 13.

6. Ibid.

7. *LDLV,* p. 46.

8. *LASF,* p. 411.

9. Colette to Missy, MRB.

10. *Vagabond,* p. 212.

11. Colette to Missy, MRB.

12. *L'Âge dangereux,* the dangerous age, was the title of a novel by the Danish writer Karin Michelsen, first translated into French in 1911. It made an impression on Colette, for she refers to it in several letters, and Pichois credits the novel as an inspiration for *Chéri.* It's the story of a woman of forty who married young, for money, and a few years into her marriage, fell in love with a young man eight years her junior. He had no fortune, and she could only dream about him. When she inherits some money of her own, she leaves the husband and goes to live alone in the woods. She writes to the young man, who comes to see her, but their second meeting is a terrible disappointment. He can't love her. She then makes overtures to her husband, who has fallen in love with a younger woman. She has to accept her solitude and the wages of her decision. She loses her beauty, and grows old and bitter. See Pichois, "Notice à Chéri," Pl. 2. p. 1543.

13. Colette to Missy, MRB.

14. *En tournée,* p. 92.

15. Colette to Missy, MRB.

16. Ibid.
17. *LDLV*, p. 48.
18. Colette to Missy, MRB.
19. *LDLV*, p. 49.
20. Colette to Missy, MRB.
21. Colette to Robert, MRB.
22. Robert, *De Loti à Proust*, p. 179.
23. Robert to Colette, CASS.
24. *ES*, p. 265.
25. His birthday has always mistakenly been given as April 5. My information about the de Jouvenel family comes from the ADC.
26. Richardson, p. 50.
27. BdJ, p. 25.
28. Ibid., p. 34.
29. Binion, p. 123.
30. Founded by Ludovic Trarieux, a moderate republican. Colette would describe de Jouvenel as *"beau, impérieux, glorieux, et trarieux,"* a Willyish pun on *contrarieux*, which isn't a word, but suggests *contrariant*, contrary.
31. Pl. 2, p. xv.
32. Binion, p. 134.
33. The ubiquity of sobriquets among the characters in this biography—the Kid, the Pasha, the Panther (and there are more to come)—suggests the period taste, and Colette's in particular, for treating love affairs like theater pieces.
34. Pichois, Pl. 2, Preface, p. xv.
35. RdJ, p. 6.
36. *En tournée*, p. 97.
37. *LDLV*, p. 52.
38. *LASF*, p. 439.
39. *TSN*, p. 381.
40. *L'Entrave*, p. 112.
41. *LASF*, p. 441
42. *En tournée*, p. 96.

CHAPTER 22

1. *LDLV*, p. 57.
2. Ibid., p. 54.
3. Ibid., p. 57
4. Ibid.
5. *LASF*, p. 440.
6. BN 18706.
7. *LDLV*, p. 55.
8. Colette to Missy, MRB.
9. *LDLV*, p. 58.
10. Ibid., p. 60.
11. Ibid., p. 55.
12. *LASF*, pp. 445–7.
13. RdJ, pp. 17, 53.
14. *LASF*, p. 455.

15. *LDLV,* p. 59.
16. *LASP,* p. 157.
17. *LDLV,* p. 60.
18. Colette's expression, which means the code of shacking up.
19. Compared to Hériot, Jouvenel wasn't rich, but forty thousand pre-war francs was still a very comfortable income. Captain Colette's pension as a tax collector was three hundred francs a month. Colette's rent at the rue de Villejust (paid by Missy) was seventeen hundred francs a year. A room and bath at a first-class hotel in Paris was eighteen francs, a bottle of the best champagne at a fancy nightclub twenty francs, and the average dinner at a decent restaurant, ten francs. Housing costs were relatively low and servants plentiful; it cost three francs to cross Paris in a cab, and public transport was even cheaper. But the difference between a comfortable middle-class income like Jouvenel's and a great fortune was, then as now, immense. When Boni de Castellane married Anna Gould in 1894, she brought him a dowry of fifteen million francs—*in yearly income!*
20. *LDLV,* p. 57.
21. *LASF,* p. 480.
22. Ibid., p. 501.
23. Ibid., p. 455.
24. Ibid., p. 460.
25. I cite the other for comparison:

Monsieur,
You ask me to come and spend a week with you, which is to say with my daughter, whom I adore. As you live with her, you know how rarely I see her, how much her presence enchants me, and I am touched that you invite me to come and see her. However, I will not accept your kind invitation, at least for now. Here's why; my pink cactus is probably about to bloom. It is a very rare plant . . . and I have been told that it only flowers, in our climate, once every four years. As I am already a very old woman, I am certain—if I absent myself while my pink cactus is blooming—that I will never see it bloom again. . . . Have the kindness to receive, Monsieur, with my sincere thanks, the expression of my distinguished sentiments and regrets.

NdJ, pp. 169–70.
26. *Le Figaro littéraire,* Jan. 24, 1953.
27. *LASF,* p. 482.
28. Ibid., p. 455.
29. Ibid., p. 458.
30. Ibid., p. 467.
31. Ibid., p. 483.
32. Ibid., p. 485.
33. Ibid., p. 487.
34. Ibid., p. 500.
35. " 'Tell me, monsieur . . . why do you do this?' He smiles, a confidential and hateful smile, he looks around him as if he wished that we were alone: is he going to betray his appetite for domination, invoke the revenge of his past as a poor salesman, confess the disgusted misogyny of the man who manipulates so many females, the joy of making them ugly, humiliating them, subjecting them to his half-mad fantasies, of 'marking' them?" *La Chambre éclairée,* "Le Maître," Pl. 2, p. 929.

36. But ultimately, she would remember that she was always bored by air travel: "One is a terrestrial or one is not. . . . So I was bored, and descended again to the cry of birds, the sound of bells, and of human voices. I crossed . . . that low, invisible ceiling which presses all its scents to the earth. . . . The olfactory shock was more moving than I had imagined." See "Là-haut," Pl. 2, p. 1497.

37. "À Tours," BQ 1, p. 1303.

38. Notice to *L'Envers du Music-Hall* (Music Hall Sidelights).

39. *LDLV*, p. 75.

40. Ibid., pp. 68–9.

41. Ibid., p. 72.

42. "I'm stirring up trouble. . . . You'll find out why. It concerns nothing other than an escape attempt—a sensual escape. It will be useful." *LDLV*, p. 73.

43. Ibid., p. 75.

44. Ibid., p. 76.

45. Léautaud, vol. 3, p. 82 (Nov. 8, 1912).

46. *NdJ*, p. 70.

47. Pl. 3, p. 1422.

48. *LASF*, p. 507.

49. *MM*, p. 63.

50. *NdJ*, pp. 166–7.

51. *LDLV*, p. 77.

52. There is nothing in Sido's letters to support Colette's assertion that she didn't want her to wear mourning. Indeed, Sido reminds Colette, at the time of Juliette's death, not to forget her mourning clothes.

53. *LDLV*, p. 80.

54. Ibid.

55. *EV*, p. 680: *"le caractère accidentel de ma maternité."*

CHAPTER 23

1. *EPC*, "Trait pour Trait," p. 870.

2. Vincent Cronin, *Paris on the Eve*, p. 404.

3. Charles Maurras, *L'Avenir de l'intelligence*.

4. *LASP*, p. 169.

5. Ibid., p. 172.

6. In later years, Anna addresses Colette as "Dear Friend and Genius." They both speak of memorizing each other's lines, and of their "boundless" and "fervent" mutual admiration. But one feels Colette has her tongue firmly in her cheek when she tells the countess that she is going to "taste the pleasure of reading you with care, slowly, softly cry-ing 'oh' to myself, as one does before an excessively blooming tree." *LASP*, p. 67.

7. Colette, "Le Jardin d'Amphion," *LASP*, p. 101.

8. When *Les Vivants et les morts* was published in 1913, the *Times* of London called Anna de Noailles the greatest French poet of the century.

9. Cronin, *Paris*, p. 409.

10. "To die for the motherland." "Dans la Foule," Pl. 2, p. 598.

11. Who was virtually alone in continuing to believe that the international solidarity among workers would triumph over the warmongers in both countries.

12. "Dans la Foule," Pl. 2, p. 596.

13. *LDLV*, p. 81.

14. *Paysages*, p. 17.

15. *ES*, pp. 275–6.
16. Ibid., p. 276.
17. Ibid., pp. 277–8.
18. In very small doses, strychnine was used for indigestion.
19. BN 18708.
20. *LDLV*, p. 86.
21. BdJ, p. 54.
22. *LDLV*, p. 86.
23. Berenson, *The Trial* (ch. 9, n. 10), p. 45.
24. Pl. 2, p. 1396.
25. Tyrannical father, cowed mother, aristocratic pastimes and relations, house in the sixteenth arrondissement, intelligence, worldliness—and he is Renée's peer.
26. *L'Entrave*, p. 23.
27. Ibid., p. 55.
28. Ibid., p. 85.
29. *MA*, p. 94.
30. *L'Entrave*, p. 114.
31. Ibid., p. 120.
32. Ibid., p. 88.
33. *LDLV*, p. 70.
34. *L'Entrave*, pp. 156, 162.
35. *ES*, p. 279.
36. *LDLV*, p. 94. The "Rat" is a reference to the image of herself she uses throughout her pregnancy cited above: a rat dragging a stolen egg.
37. *Paysages*, p. 26.
38. Ibid., p. 30.
39. It is, of course, impossible to reckon the precise moment of a child's conception some eighty years after the event, but the baby is born at full term on July 3, 1913. Counting back 280 days, one arrives at September 25.
40. In a letter to Marguerite Moreno, Colette mentions that she has been taking a "purgative potion" to dry up her milk. *MM*, p. 35.
41. *ES*, p. 280.
42. Jane Austen, George Eliot, Emily Brontë, Charlotte Brontë, Emily Dickinson, Louisa May Alcott, Christina Rossetti, Lou Andreas-Salomé, Virginia Woolf, Olive Schreiner, Natalie Barney, Renée Vivien, Gertrude Stein, Christina Stead, Isak Dinesen, Katherine Mansfield, Edith Wharton, Anna de Noailles, Djuna Barnes, Simone de Beauvoir, Simone Weil, Willa Cather, Carson McCullers, Marianne Moore, Hilda Doolittle, Marguerite Yourcenar, Sigrid Undset, Else Lasker-Schüller, Eudora Welty, Lillian Hellman, Monique Wittig, to name a few.
43. *ES*, pp. 281–2.
44. Michel del Castillo, "De Jouvenel à Colette," CC 10, p. 9.
45. *LDLV*, p. 99.
46. CdJ, "Lettres," p. 26.
47. "At the Sea," *Earthly Paradise*, p. 207.

CHAPTER 24

1. *LDLV*, p. 94.
2. Colette to Charlotte Lysès, first wife of Sacha Guitry, Aug. 4, 1913, *LASF*, p. 13.
3. *ES*, p. 281.

4. Ibid.

5. *LDLV*, p. 97.

6. *Paysages*, p. 141.

7. Yvonne Mitchell, *Colette: A Taste for Life*, p. 170.

8. del Castillo, CC 10, p. 10.

9. *LASF*, p. 191.

10. *MM*, p. 36.

11. *Prou, Poucette et quelques autres*, published in 1913. *L'Envers du music-hall (Music Hall Sidelights)* was also published that year.

12. *TOM*, p. 48.

13. *P/I* FSG, p. 90.

14. Painter, vol. 2, p. 227.

15. Jacques Frugier, Chronology, Pl. 2, p. lxvii.

16. Berenson, *The Trial*, pp. 123–4.

17. *TOM*, p. 89.

18. Lanoux, p. 358.

19. *LDLV*, p. 106.

20. Patrick Cazals, *Musidora, la dixième muse*, cited by Pichois, Pl. 2, p. 1434.

21. BdJ, p. 41.

22. Marguerite Moreno, *Souvenirs de ma vie*.

23. According to his military records—although, according to Colette, he entered the army as a second lieutenant. He was probably promoted very quickly.

24. Pl. 2, p. xxiii.

25. Moreno, *Souvenirs*.

26. F/G, p. 263.

27. Louise Weiss, BN 17794.

28. Annie de Pène was the nom de plume of Désirée Poutrel, who was married very young in her native Normandy to a M. Battendier. She gave birth to their daughter, Germaine [Beaumont], in 1890, and left her husband shortly thereafter. Her autobiographical first novel, *L'Évadée*, an echo of Colette's *Je m'évade*, published a year after *The Vagabond*, tells the story of her life in an amusingly breathless style. Its heroine, Rosine, has been languishing in a depressing provincial milieu. Freshly divorced and reveling in her liberation, she arrives in Paris, penniless but determined to seek her fortune. She is befriended by her neighbor, a handsome young priest, who introduces her into a circle of bluestockings, and she is taken on as a private secretary by the rich Mme Morand. The priest also presents Rosine to his best friend, a "great man of letters" named Bernières. Bernières becomes her lover, and the priest, who has also fallen in love with her, goes off to a remote parish so that he won't betray his vows. Mme Morand, in the meantime, founds a journal and makes Rosine its editor. Love of Bernières has inflamed her own literary ambitions. "Ah! How I would like to be somebody . . . to have a little bit of notoriety, a little rank in that grand intellectual army of which [Bernières] is one of the great leaders." Annie de Pène, *L'Évadée*.

29. *AdP*, p. 31.

30. Téry was the publisher of a socialist political weekly, *L'Oeuvre*, of which Henry's brother, Robert de Jouvenel, was the editor. Henry admired Annie immensely. She sent him voluptuous food packages—truffles and stuffed chickens—and became what the French called his "war godmother," which is to say his pen pal. He wrote to her from Verdun, asking her to keep him informed about his "two Colettes." He also joked about his wife's extreme fondness for her. Colette, he said, couldn't "live without" Annie, so he might just have to cut his wife in two. Henry de Jouvenel to Annie de Pène, MRB.

31. Colette, "Marguerite Moreno," *MM*, p. 15.
32. *BL*, p. 119.
33. Moreno, *Souvenirs*, p. 236.
34. *LDLV*, p. 109.
35. "Blessés," *Les Heures longues*, Pl. 2, p. 481.
36. Pl. 2, 1440.
37. *AdP*, p. 38.
38. *LDLV*, p. 114.
39. *AdP*, p. 46.

CHAPTER 25

1. "To die for the motherland is the most beautiful fate, the most worthy to desire."
2. *HL*, Pl. 2, p. 498.
3. Painter, vol. 2, p. 227.
4. Michèle LePavec, *Les Manuscrits de Colette à la Bibliothèque nationale*, CC 10.
5. *HL*, Pl. 2, p. 521.
6. Ibid., p. 482.
7. Ibid., p. 497.
8. *AdP*, p. 48.
9. BdJ, p. 44.
10. Pl. 2, Preface, p. xxvii.
11. Anne-Marie Pizzorusso, "G. A. Borghese et Colette," CC 7, pp. 24–35. Aleramo argued that women writers had the right to more "diversity" than they had yet been able to claim, having "entered life and art as a miserable copy of man." There was no such thing as a specifically female language, but there had to be a specifically female rhythm and voice that would capture "the profound spiritual difference between men and women." Colette, she felt, had—exceptionally—been able to "forge her own unique style."
    Borghese, one of the most respected contemporary critics, agreed. "Colette Willy," he wrote very astutely, "belongs to neither of the two categories [of women writers], the Amazons and the spoiled little girls. She almost fulfills [Aleramo's] desire to see the birth of a feminine literature; to witness the appearance of a woman writer who is able to express her inner life with all the autonomy, all the independence, enjoyed by a man. Femininity, for Colette, is not an obstacle to surmount, any more than it is an ornament to polish." Borghese, "The Vagabond," CC 7, pp. 36–44.
12. "There are no human beings who so resemble us, even physically, more than [the Italians] do. When I regard the citizens of this country . . . I see my own people, our own people. . . . The proportion of the features, the rhythm of their bodies, are immediately familiar. . . . Everything here spares me from the inevitable anguish I used to experience in Germany, at any contact with the Prussian or Bavarian human animal, pink as a hog, often prognathous, with a short nose and a long lip, and strong paws . . ." "Impressions d'Italie," *HL*, Pl. 2, p. 525.
13. *LDLV*, p. 119.
14. BdJ, p. 32.
15. Dormann, p. 190.
16. Guy Tosi, "Colette et d'Annunzio," CC 8, p. 17.
17. Mugnier, p. 503.
18. Jean-Luc Barré, "Colette, Henry de Jouvenel, et Le Seigneur Chat," *Album-Masques*, p. 107.
19. Mugnier, p. 503.

20. "Impressions d'Italie" and the Appendix, "Notes d'Italie," Pl. 2, pp. 525–41, 581–90.

21. "Bel-Gazou et la Guerre," Pl. 2, p. 499. *Taube* is the German word for pigeon, and also for monoplane.

22. Colette to Annie, MRB.

23. Léautaud, Jan. 25, 1916, vol. 3, p. 220.

24. Barney, pp. 198–9.

25. Henry de Jouvenel to Annie de Pène, MRB.

26. *AdP*, p. 83.

27. *HL*, Pl. 2, p. 561.

28. Ibid., p. 557.

29. Colette to Annie, MRB.

30. *AdP*, p. 56.

31. *TSN*, p. 385.

32. Ibid., p. 383.

33. *HL*, Pl. 2, p. 570.

34. Ibid., p. 587.

35. Colette to Annie, MRB.

36. Ibid.

37. Pl. 2, p. xxxii.

38. Colette to Annie, MRB.

39. As one of the first serious writers to work for the movies, Colette was also an amusing critic of the crassness of the film business, and intrigues on the set were fodder for her letters to Annie: "After two or three days steeped in a murderous atmosphere, translation: talks with the producers . . . I'm swimming in another atmosphere: that of pure art. . . . Not only pure art, but also Truth, Life, and raw Reality: when you want to force open a drawer filled with letters, you always, don't you, use a meat cleaver? You never wait for your husband, your forehead pressed to the windowpane, without clawing at a lace curtain with your teeth and nails? I was sure of it. Thank you." *AdP*, p. 95.

40. Pl. 2, p. xxxiii.

41. *AdP*, p. 96.

42. MRB.

CHAPTER 26

1. *AdP*, p. 99.

2. *Earthly Paradise*, p. 211.

3. Colette never specifies the manuscript she lost. Most biographers have assumed that it was her novella *Mitsou*. But Bernard Bray, who annotated *Mitsou* for the Pléiade, argues convincingly that it was probably something much briefer and less important—she was, after all, able to rewrite it in a day.

4. *LDLV*, p. 126.

5. "Lumières bleues," BQ 3, p. 917.

6. *LDLV*, p. 127.

7. Preface, Pl. 2, p. xxxv.

8. Dormann, p. 197.

9. A melodrama that tells the story of a young woman (Annie Morin) who marries a rich fellow student instead of the poor boy she really loves. She then proceeds to ruin her husband, hoping to drive him to suicide, but dies herself in an explosion.

10. BN 18718.

11. Colette to Annie, MRB.

12. "Mausoleums," *JFM*, p. 128.

13. *LDLV*, p. 128.

14. "Mausoleums," *JFM*, p. 138.

15. Dormann, p. 177.

16. Ibid., p. 182.

17. Ibid.

18. Pougy, p. 97.

19. *ES*, p. 160.

20. France had the greatest casualties among the combatants, losing 10 percent of her able-bodied men.

21. Francis Carco, *Colette mon ami*, p. 11.

22. *LASP*, p. 207.

23. Carco, *Colette mon ami*.

24. *LASP*, p. 213.

25. *ES*, pp. 192–3.

26. Carco, *Colette mon ami*, p. 51.

27 Ibid., pp. 35–9.

28. *ES*, p. 179.

29. Zou, never with a last name, figures prominently in Colette's correspondence with Annie de Pène and others. She had a mother in Neuilly, and a daughter. Otherwise, almost nothing is known about her, except that the Jouvenel family kept trying to marry Robert off to someone else, and Colette and Annie kept trying to find a rich husband for her, which perhaps suggests she was not of the Jouvenels' class. The blue lieutenant's name is also Robert, and Mitsou's background and manners are an obstacle to their love.

30. Colette, *Mitsou: ou Comment l'esprit vient aux filles*. Paris: Fayard, 1919, p. 129.

31. Mitsou's epistolary seduction of Robert, and his disappointment at discovering a discrepancy between the marvelous letter writer and the uncultivated starlet, may owe something to Colette's experience with Louis de Robert who had, one will recall, complained that she had always enchanted him more through her letters than in person. "There's . . . something in your presence that disappoints me." See my chap. 20, p. 223.

32. *ES*, p. 242.

33. Jean-Luc Mercié, *Anacréon le Jeune*, p. 70.

34. *BL*, p. 143.

35. Ibid., pp. 143–5.

36. *LASP*, p. 215.

CHAPTER 27

1. Pl. 2, p. 878.

2. Interested readers should consult Claude Pichois and Madeleine Raaphorst-Rousseau's excellent annotations to *Chéri*, Pl. 2, p. 1536. Among the sources they cite are Racine's *Phèdre*, Rousseau's romance with Mme de Warens, Constant's *Adolphe*, Stendhal's *Charterhouse of Parma* and *The Red and the Black*, a long list of Balzac novels, Flaubert's *Sentimental Education* and *Madame Bovary*, *La Dame aux camélias* of Dumas *fils*, and Henry Bataille's *Maman Colibri*.

3. Pichois and Raaphorst-Rousseau, Pl. 2, p. 1541.

4. "The first time I applied myself to the study of Chéri, he was sitting on the edge of

a chaise longue upholstered in blue damask playing with the lady's lapdog. The long shadow of his eyelashes flickered on his golden, twenty-two-year-old cheek. . . . On the features of his friend, which shared the authority, the even temper, the healthy bloom of the one who ruled Chéri, I read the leonine love, a happy skepticism, the hostility, which all fanned the fires of a fine, womanly autumn." Pl. 2, p. 880.

5. *AdP*, pp. 87–8.
6. *LDLV*, p. 80.
7. *HP*, p. 36.
8. *HP*, p. 11.
9. Though for twenty-five years Colette used the familiar *tu* in addressing Hélène, and Hélène the formal *vous* with Colette.
10. *HP*, p. 15. There are other stories of Colette's braid-cutting. She also chopped off the hair of a friend named Irène Le Cornec, and would have done the same to Mireille, the singer. It seems to have been a minor fetish. Mireille to the author, 1991.
11. Ibid., p. 24.
12. GP; BN 18718.
13. Ibid.
14. *Parinaud*, p. 75.
15. Ibid., p. 120.
16. *NdJ*, p. 35.
17. Which is very New York 1980s: a black bathroom, purple carpets, a gym and swimming pool in the basement, a Chinese salon.
18. Most of the quotes from *Chéri* are cited from the translation by Roger Senhouse (New York: Farrar, Straus and Giroux, 1974; Penguin reprint); some are my own translations from the French edition (Paris: Fayard, 1920).
19. His distance of choice was the 400 meters.
20. Dormann, p. 227.
21. BdJ, p. 54.
22. Ibid., p. 55.
23. *MM*, p. 47.
24. *HP*, p. 31.
25. RdJ, p. 5.
26. Like Vinca, Pam would offer herself to the boy she loves in part to compete with the older woman who holds him in thrall, in part to discover the erotic mysteries that he has learned from her. But unlike Phil, Bertrand was either too gallant or too repressed to go through with the defloration. See my chapter 30, note 17.
27. *HP*, p. 33.
28. Ibid.
29. *ES*, p. 243.

CHAPTER 28

1. BdJ, p. 55.
2. GP.
3. The French slang word for depression is *cafard*—cockroach. Colette to Renaud de Jouvenel, HRC.
4. RdJ, p. 5.
5. *LASP*, p. 218.
6. "Vérité," p. lvi.
7. BdJ, p. 56.

8. "Vérité," p. lvi.
9. BdJ, p. 56.
10. "Vérité," p. lvii.
11. Dormann, p. 227.
12. Jeannie Malige to the author, 1991.
13. "Vérité," p. lvii.
14. Perhaps that was the reason Colette was willing to entertain and indulge Meg: she was one of the few people left with whom she could speak ill of Willy.
15. René Aujol to the author, Sept. 13, 1991.
16. Jeannie Malige to the author, 1991.
17. Ibid.
18. *LASP,* p. 218.
19. BdJ, p. 56.
20. Pl. 2, p. 1547.
21. Ibid., p. 1550.
22. Ibid., p. 1551.
23. *LASP,* p. 280.
24. Pl. 2, p. 1551.
25. Ibid., p. 1548.
26. Pichois, Pl. 2, Preface, p. xxxviii.
27. Ibid., p. xxxix.
28. *Parinaud,* p. 84.
29. René Aujol to the author, 1991.
30. *Blé,* p. 97.
31. Jouvenel was apparently the only person ever to call Colette Sido. Her full name, one will remember, was Sidonie-Gabrielle.
32. Colette to Henry de Jouvenel, Jouvenel archives, ADC.

CHAPTER 29

1. Maurice Martin du Gard, *Les Mémorables,* vol. 1, pp. 135–6.
2. When he later reread the novel, he would concede that it was "pretty much a masterpiece. But what a world! And to have us believe that fifty-year-old women are more desirable than young ones!" Ibid.
3. Ibid., p. 137.
4. Binion, p. 149.
5. Ibid., p. 148.
6. Mugnier, Jan. 5, 1921, p. 371.
7. *GB,* p. 142.
8. Ibid., p. 149.
9. *Celle qui en revient* contained one new and several previously published animal dialogues, which suffer from the preciousness inherent in the genre. *La Chambre éclairée* was composed of articles written for *Excelsior* and *Le Matin* before and during the war. It contains a number of lyrical landscapes, more beasts, and some doting sketches of Bel-Gazou, but the best of the essays have a tarter savor. Colette has her fun, and at times malicious fun, at the expense of bureaucrats, snobs, servile daughters, horny war widows, a couturier who hates women, the clichés of the cinema, and that great ancien régime workhorse Mme Vigée-Lebrun.
10. *GB,* p. 142.
11. *MM,* p. 58.

12. *GB,* p. 144.

13. He specifies them thus: "Colette taught me that bread has a taste, privet a scent, and poppies a color." BdJ, p. 56.

14. "Vérité," p. lvii.

15. *MM,* p. 53.

16. BdJ, p. 56.

17. *LASP,* p. 69.

18. Ibid., p. 38.

19. *La Maison de Claudine* in French—an exploitative and irrelevant title Colette agreed to only for commercial reasons.

20. Martin du Gard, op. cit. p. 135.

21. Jean Marais to the author, 1991. Marais also added: "She was always very motherly to me. She was the only woman who didn't get flustered when I embraced her. She had an enormous personality. I think it must have been a great burden for her own daughter."

22. *LDLV,* p. 144.

23. *LASF,* p. 17.

24. *LDLV,* p. 148. *Emmerdite* is untranslatable. It's a pun on the words mother *(mère)* and shit *(merde)* and enteritis *(enterite),* turned into a malady.

25. BdJ, p. 57.

26. She described it to Abbé Mugnier at a dinner party later that spring. It was, he said, about "a woman who's the reflection of another. She stops being it and ceases to exist." Mugnier, p. 394. The novel, transformed, became *La Seconde.*

27. *LDLV,* p. 149.

28. *Prisons,* "En Algérie," pp. 1028–1034.

29. GP.

30. "I have never been able to refuse him anything he asked," wrote Valéry of Jouvenel, "so pleasantly forceful and indefinably persuasive was his way of speaking." Binion, p. 124.

31. Mugnier, pp. 393–4.

32. Ibid.

33. Ibid., p. 394.

34. Ibid., p. 395.

CHAPTER 30

1. Sido, of course, had four children, but as Colette told André Parinaud, she always referred to "my three children," as if Juliette were not part of the family.

2. *MMH,* p. 25.

3. *Vagabond,* p. 238.

4. *La Chambre éclairée,* "Fantôme," Pl. 2, p. 888.

5. Ibid., p. 890.

6. *Parinaud,* p. 46.

7. *LDLV,* p. 151.

8. *HP,* p. 44.

9. GP.

10. *HP,* p. 41.

11. GB, p. 158.

12. *LDLV,* p. 152.

13. GP.

14. GP.

15. Colette, *The Ripening Seed,* translated by Roger Senhouse. New York: Farrar, Straus and Giroux, 1955, p. 157. See also *Blé,* p. 163.

16. *The Ripening Seed,* originally called *The Threshold,* was written and published in installments in *Le Matin.* Jean Sapène, solicitous both of his advertisers' and his readers' family values, censored certain, to his mind, overly voluptuous words and images. He was willing to permit Phil's seduction by Mme Dalleray, but when he discovered that Colette meant to have her two young heroes "commit the carnal act," as Claude Pichois so charmingly puts it, "he bestirred himself . . . and the order came down to Colette to cease publication." There were two chapters left, but, Pichois continues, "what did it matter if the work hadn't reached its climax or achieved its meaning? The morality of France was safe." Claude Pichois, Preface, *Blé,* p. 22.

Colette was then free to finish her manuscript without restrictions on its length and content, and did so that summer, at Castel-Novel. "The last page cost me my entire first day [here]," she tells Moreno, "and I defy you to doubt me when you read it. . . . Twenty lines without a jewel or an ornamentation. Alas, that's what it's like. It's the proportion that gives me such trouble. I have such a horror of the grandiloquent ending." *MM,* p. 66.

17. She gets her name from the Paris street, the rue d'Alleray, in the fifteenth arrondissement, where Hélène Picard had her blue aerie and where Colette had rented a garçonnière for her rendezvous with Bertrand. His *amourette* with Pamela hadn't stopped when his *amour* with Colette began, but it remained innocent. One day, however, Pam asked him to take her to his apartment. He agreed, but on the way his conscience balked. "I told myself that I shouldn't do this to a young girl whom I loved very much." Instead, he dropped her off at the Bienvenue Française, a center for foreign visitors which Claire Boas had founded during the peace conference. "Vérité," p. lviii.

18. *Blé,* p. 106.

19. Ibid., p. 92.

20. *Ripening Seed,* p. 115.

21. Colette to Louis de Robert, MRB.

22. *Parinaud,* p. 47.

23. RdJ, p. 10.

24. *LDLV,* p. 156.

25. The British wanted to stabilize the Continent and secure its future peace by reducing the size of its standing armies. This peacekeeping strategy had a hidden agenda—expanding British influence—and a hostile intent, aimed mostly at France, which was then by far the dominant military power, in both personnel and equipment. Jouvenel was disinterested enough to recognize the value of the disarmament proposal at a moment when France and all the other former Allies were still saddled with immense war debts. But before agreeing to reduce the French army, he insisted on a treaty with a better guarantee than the signatures of the League's members, particularly as Germany wasn't one of them. Working closely with Lord Robert Cecil, he drafted a "mutual assistance" clause to the original British document, obliging the signatories to come to the armed defense of any member whose sovereignty was jeopardized by an aggressor. This compromise was accepted by acclamation, and Jouvenel's wisdom and skill as an arbiter were widely praised.

26. BdJ, p. 65.

27. *LASP,* p. 283.

28. *JFM,* pp. 133–4.

29. Léautaud, vol. 5, pp. 55–6.

30. Though by whom it isn't clear.
31. *MM*, p. 59.
32. *LDLV*, p. 155.
33. Dormann, p. 231.
34. She had converted to Catholicism a few years before, and Abbé Mugnier was her spiritual adviser.
35. Ghislain de Diesbach, *La Princesse Bibesco.* pp. 312, 314.
36. Ibid., p. 315.
37. Ibid., pp. 323–7.
38. GP.
39. *HP*, p. 51.
40. *MM*, p. 71.
41. GP.
42. Ibid.
43. Ibid.
44. *MM*, p. 74. Marthe Bibesco had just published a long, pseudo-Tolstoyan opus on the Romanian peasantry.
45. GP.
46. Dormann, p. 232.
47. *MM*, p. 76.
48. BdJ, p. 57.
49. GP.

CHAPTER 31

1. Dormann, p. 233.
2. In a letter to Christiane Mendelys (Mme Georges Wague), who was having marital problems of her own, Colette advises that she leave home and find a refuge, immediately. "When he begins to miss you, even for a moment in a month's time, you will have gained a point. Besides that, everything is against you." *LDLV*, p. 171.
3. *MM*, p. 78.
4. *HP*, p. 64.
5. GP.
6. Ibid.
7. Lottmann, p. 174.
8. BdJ, p. 57.
9. A pun on *bonne à tout faire*, good at everything, which also means maid of all work. Racine's version of the Phaedra myth is considered the greatest tragedy in the French language. Phèdre falls in love with her stepson, Hippolyte, and on receiving false word of her husband's death, is urged by her old nurse to declare her love. Hippolyte is horrified, and leaves the court. The old nurse denounces him to his father for the sins his stepmother only dreamed of, and Thésée calls upon Neptune to destroy the boy, which he does. In her guilt and despair, Phèdre hangs herself.
10. Mugnier, p. 439.
11. *LASP*, p. 226.
12. *LDLV*, p. 171.
13. GP.
14. *MM*, p. 81.
15. GP.
16. Chauvière, p. 68.

17. Ibid., p. 64.

18. Mitchell, *Colette,* p. 170. Based on an interview with Colette de Jouvenel.

19. GP.

20. He had spent that spring with Beneš in Prague, where he was "received with a generosity that repaid all that my mother had done for Czechoslovakia during the war." Pl. 2, p. lviii.

21. "What triumphs, but what a frail carcass to bear them," she tells Hélène. And to Moreno: "In thirteen days [at Rozven] he gained two kilos."

22. *HP,* p. 67.

23. BdJ, p. 58.

24. Pl. 2, p. xlviii.

25. "Vérité," p. lviii.

26. "The Hidden Woman," translated by Matthew Ward, *Collected Stories,* p. 238.

27. *Aventures quotidiennes,* BQ 2, p. 446.

28. Ibid., p. 447.

CHAPTER 32

1. Pougy, p. 154.

2. *MM,* p. 68.

3. Ibid., p. 71.

4. That summer, having sent Colette the draft of her memoirs, she received this memorable writing lesson:

> You don't have the hang of it yet. You've retouched—and it shows—most of your guys (Proust, Jarry, Iturri) like a homework assignment—I know you, you old bugger—they bored you! . . . I say all this to you as I would say it to myself, pretty harshly. You are magic itself when you tell a story, but you lose most of your expressiveness when you write. You neglect or tone it down. Take Proust, for example. . . . If you were telling me the story, your stage direction would be stunning. You write it, and what do I find? "Mme A. manifested a critical mood, delivering her judgments without pity, etc. . . . A chorus of flatterers took to the defense—the conversation took a bitter turn . . . explosion of human nastiness, mocking exclamations, derisive phrases, etc." Do you understand that in all this there is not a word that *shows* or *reveals* something about the people you're discussing? If you were telling the same story, it would take you fifteen lines to paint old Ma Arman, old man France, the elder Caillavet, etc. etc. And if you transformed your "explosion of nastiness" into a bit of dialogue, it would come to life with the rest. No narration, good Lord! Strokes of color . . . no need for a conclusion. . . . "A charming and delicate dinner?" A "conversation which wanders from one subject to another?" What does that show me? Zippo. Stick in a description of the décor, the guests, even the food. . . . Free yourself [from the specter of the editor's wife reading over your shoulder]. And try, oh my darling, to conceal from us that it bores the shit out of you to write! . . . I love you, I embrace you, I want you to write "prestigious" stuff, you understand me? Ta Colette.

MM, p. 90.

5. He had been born in Paris on Aug. 2, 1889. His parents were attending one of the inaugural fêtes for the tower, and he believed the heat of the evening and the crush of the crowd precipitated his mother's labor.

6. *PdC,* p. 10.

7. *Douceur,* p. 32.

8. Pl. 2, p. 1556.

9. *JAR,* "Un Salon 1900," p. 54.

10. Gold and Fizdale, *Misia,* p. 101.

11. *JAR,* "Un Salon 1900," pp. 54–5.

12. Ibid., p. 55, and *LASP,* p. 266. Three notes of a few lines each, a brief letter about the 1925 production, and one slightly longer letter of 1919 in which Colette responds to a few of Ravel's questions: "Why of course, a ragtime. Why of course, some Wedgwood niggers. . . . And the squirrel will say everything you like."

13. Colette had originally called *L'Enfant* "Entertainment for My Daughter." She notes that she had "stupidly used" this working title until the day Ravel protested, "with an icy seriousness," that he didn't have a daughter. The childless bachelor did, though, keep up a whimsical correspondence with the children of his friends; in 1910, he dedicated his piano duet *Mother Goose* to Misia Natanson's young niece and nephew, both piano prodigies, hoping they might play the work at its première. See *LASP,* p. 266, and *EPC,* "Paradis Terrestre," p. 853.

14. *JAR,* "Un Salon 1900," p. 56.

15. Ibid.

16. Ibid., p. 55.

17. Colette's dreamlike libretto invites the kind of interpretation that the pioneer psychoanalyst Melanie Klein devotes to it in an essay on *L'Enfant et les sortilèges,* which she reads as a parable about the evolution of conscience. Her analysis is too clinical to be summarized simply, but she cites the conclusion of the opera to support her theory about the resolution of the child's "infantile anxiety-situation." He conquers his sadism when he makes a symbolic act of reparation by bandaging the squirrel's paw. His conscience has awakened, and he becomes capable of "object love," which is to say he acquires a capacity for pity and sympathy. His redeeming gesture transforms a hostile world into a benign one, and trust triumphs over infantile paranoia. "The child has learnt to love and to believe in love," she concludes. "The profound psychological insight of Colette . . . is shown in the way the conversion in the child's attitude takes place. As he cares for the wounded squirrel, he whispers: 'Mama.' " Melanie Klein, "Infantile Anxiety-Situations Reflected in a Work of Art and in the Creative Impulse" (1929), reproduced in *Love, Guilt, and Reparation,* pp. 210–18.

Many aspects of Klein's reading are helpful for a biographer, but others seem wishful and misinformed, in part because the analyst was working from a plot summary given by the reviewer of a 1929 Viennese revival of the opera, which in German is translated as *The Magic Word.* This title gives too much weight to the child's "conversion" and not enough to his actual torment. The French is both more sinister and ambiguous. The first definition of *sortilège* is "the evil spell of a sorcerer," and then, "figuratively: a means of doing harm." Colette prefers to emphasize the destructive impulses at work in the opera, not the redemptive ones that Klein discerns. There are, indeed, very few acts of redemption in the work of Colette, so the language of her last stage direction needs more scrutiny. Predisposed to a happy resolution of the child's crisis both by the German title and her own theories, Klein gets an essential detail wrong. The child does not whisper "Mama" at the end. It's the animals who cry "Mama." It is they who have the catharsis, the revelation, who learn to love and believe in love, but the child is silent. His charity to the squirrel redeems him in their eyes, but we don't know what it means to him, and we aren't privy to the scene of his reconciliation with Mama. There are many ways to read his final gesture, including Klein's optimistic one. But those outstretched arms may also signify surrender. The final scene recalls a similar scene in "The Little One," the central essay of *My Mother's House*. A child who has been dreaming of adventure and freedom stands alone and forlorn in a garden "grown suddenly hostile," which "menaces a now sobered little girl with the cold leaves of its laurels." She looks toward the lighted windows of a house, and toward "the essential light" and protection of her mama. There is great poignancy to both scenes, but the Little One's revelation is less of love—of object love, as Klein would call it—than of her own fragility and dependence. The child in *L'Enfant et les sortilèges* revolts against his dependence, too. *I'm free, free, bad and free.* At the end the animals counterchant, *He is good, so good, he is wise, he is good, so good.* In the French their words are *sage* and *bon,* and the meaning of *sage* when used of an animal is docile. Has the child really been redeemed or, like the little girl in the garden, merely sobered? Is he healed or just broken to obedience by his trauma? See discussion in chapter 30, pp. 321–2.

18. Colette, *L'Enfant et les sortilèges,* Pl. 3, pp. 151–69.
19. *Vagabond,* p. 226.
20. Emphasis mine. Ibid., p. 227.
21. *BOD,* p. 18.

CHAPTER 33

1. *PdC,* p. 12.
2. *LDLV,* p. 185.
3. *PdC,* p. 13.
4. Dormann, p. 250.
5. Ibid., p. 251.
6. "Vérité," p. lviii.
7. BdJ, p. 58.
8. *PdC,* p. 11.
9. *MM,* pp. 103–4.
10. Ibid., p. 106.
11. Ibid.
12. Ibid., pp. 108–9.
13. Ibid., p. 109.
14. *NdJ,* p. 35. Her books are signed Colette Willy until *The Ripening Seed,* in 1923, which is signed Colette. She uses Colette for most of her journalism from 1920 on, though some pieces written as early as 1913 are also signed "Colette."
15. OT to JL, HRC.
16. Ibid.
17. GP.
18. *LASP,* p. 226.
19. *HP,* p. 74.
20. *MM,* p. 112.
21. Ibid., p. 113.
22. *LASP,* p. 77.
23. *NdJ,* p. 26.
24. The abbé Mugnier, who encountered Colette and Goudeket at the Countess Murat's late that June, dismisses him as a "Dutchman" who's "with" Colette, and goes on to relate the conversations of everyone with a title, ending his entry for that evening with a veiled reference to Colette and "Hippolyte"—i.e. Bertrand.
25. *MM,* p. 108.
26. *HP,* p. 75.

27. GP.
28. *MM,* p. 117.
29. *La Fin,* p. 134.
30. *Parinaud,* p. 120.
31. *La Fin,* pp. 123–4.
32. *Chéri and The Last of Chéri,* translated by Roger Senhouse. Penguin Twentieth Century Classics edition, 1954, p. 247.
33. Ibid., p. 186.
34. Ibid., p. 193.
35. Yannick Resch, Introduction, *La Fin,* p. 23.

CHAPTER 34

1. "A word from her, a phrase, and I felt myself let go of one after another of my inhibitions. . . . She restored me to the world." *PdC,* p. 15.
2. "I love you until I'm sick with it. I have such an imperious need for you that your presence scarcely quells it. . . . Nourish me, even if it must exhaust you; enrich me, even if it must impoverish you; or else command . . . Nothing has any value for me except in the measure that you accept it as an offering. . . . The pain of love is a torture, doubt racks me, I'm on the edge of an abyss. Embrace me quick, before the dark boy . . . imprisons me again in his dank underworld from which, without you, I would never have emerged." MG to C, SMAF.
3. *NdJ,* p. 35.
4. C to MG, SMAF.
5. RdJ, p. 13.
6. *Prisons,* "Notes marocaines"; *Places,* "Morocco," p. 83.
7. *HP,* p. 81.
8. *Places,* p. 83.
9. *LDLV,* pp. 191, 192.
10. *MM,* p. 128.
11. Ibid., pp. 122, 126.
12. *MM,* p. 131.
13. *Places,* p. 40.
14. Ibid., pp. 40–42.
15. Larnac, p. 198.
16. The child, writes Winnicott, locates its inner world (as Léa does) in the belly, and the labor of producing some sort of pattern from the chaos "is not mental or intellectual, but . . . is closely related to the task of digestion." "Any love," Colette had long since observed, "no matter what sort, if one lets it have its way, tends to turn itself into a sort of alimentary canal." D. W. Winnicott, *Human Nature,* p. 77. *BOD,* p. 30.
17. François Mauriac, "Le Roman d'aujourd'hui," *La Revue hebdomadaire,* Feb. 19, 1927, pp. 265–6.
18. Mugnier, p. 481.
19. Ibid.
20. Pl. 3, p. xli.
21. C to MG, SMAF.
22. Bernard Loliée MSS. sale catalogue, no. 3, 1968, MRB.
23. Chauvière, p. 250.
24. GP.

25. Ibid.
26. C to MG, SMAF.
27. *BOD*, p. 79.
28. Francis Carco and his second wife, Éliane, had a house nearby. Through them, Colette met the painters Suzanne Villeboeuf, J. G. Daragnès, André Dignimont, Luc-Albert Moreau, and André Dunoyer de Segonzac, who would illustrate Colette's monograph *La Treille Muscate*. All of them became Colette's good friends and are mentioned in *Break of Day*. Other members of this coterie were the actress Thérèse Dorny, the violinist Hélène Jourdan-Morhange, and the sculptor Louis-Aimé Lejeune.
29. *BOD*, p. 115.
30. GP.
31. *MM*, p. 145.
32. Pl. 3, p. 1376.
33. MG to C, SMAF.
34. *BOD*, pp. 30–31.

CHAPTER 35

1. GP.
2. John Updike, *Hugging the Shore*. New York: Alfred A. Knopf, 1983, p. 152.
3. Chauvière, p. 199.
4. Sanda Goudeket to the author, 1991.
5. In Saint-Tropez, she lived almost exclusively on fruit, vegetables, grilled fish, and the occasional grilled chicken. In a letter to Goudeket, she speaks of sticking to her weight-loss regimen and of looking "practically thin" in a black dress.
6. Chauvière, p. 201.
7. GP.
8. Pichois, Pl. 2, Preface, pp. lii–liii.
9. *MMH*, p. 38.
10. *MM*, p. 63.
11. Colette reworks Sido's actual letters, polishing the prose and changing small though telling details to suit her purposes. See my chapter 22, page 239, for one example.
12. *BOD*, 34.
13. Beginning with Karen Horney and D. W. Winnicott, and continued by Dorothy Dinnerstein, Margaret Mahler, Janine Chasseguet-Smirgel, Daniel Stern, Nancy Chodorow, Edith Jacobson, Robert Stoller, Jessica Benjamin, and many others. Benjamin's surveys of the field, and her own theoretical work in *The Bonds of Love* and *Like Subjects, Love Objects,* have, in particular, been of great help to me in this chapter.
14. Benjamin, *Bonds of Love*.
15. Pl. 3, p. xlii.
16. He would also leave a keenly observed verbal portrait of her at her writing table: "Her fine and powerful arms served as buttresses on the lectern. She remained there, as if frozen, for hours.... Only the rustling page, as she threw it off with controlled rage, broke the silence from time to time." Lottmann, p. 195.
17. GP.
18. C to MG, SMAF.
19. *MM*, p 178.
20. Ibid., p. 161.
21. Mugnier, p. 502.

22. *MM*, p. 188.

23. Colette, *The Other One*, translated by Elizabeth Tait and Roger Senhouse. New York: Farrar, Straus and Giroux, 1960, p. 142. Originally published as *La Seconde*. Paris: Ferenczi, 1929.

24. *LASP*, p. 196.

25. Richardson, p. 133.

26. *Paradis terrestre*, published in 1932 by Gonin. The animals' lethargy in captivity depressed Colette, who much preferred to see them at the circus. There, at least, they were more "like actors" and not so bored. *PdC*, p. 153.

27. *MM*, p. 204.

28. *Regarde*, published by Deschamps with illustrations by Meheut, and *Paradis terrestre*, the zoo book.

29. Pl. 3, p. 1466.

30. Colette, Preface, *MMH/Sido*.

31. Pl. 3, pp. 1465–6.

32. *Sido*, p. 186.

33. Chauvière, p. 74.

34. *MM*, p. 208.

35. *LDLV*, p. 216.

36. André Billy, *Intimités littéraires*, pp. 149–54.

37. *MM*, p. 212.

CHAPTER 36

1. *Places*, p. 46.

2. *PdC*, p. 96.

3. *Places*, p. 48.

4. Léautaud, vol. 8, June 2, 1930.

5. Dauphiné, *Rachilde*, p. 129.

6. Claude Dauphiné, Rachilde's biographer, takes noble pains to explain the paradoxes of her violently expressed and sometimes incoherent beliefs, noting that, despite her chauvinism, she still loathed the High Church royalism of the extreme right, quarreled with Barrès over his "prejudices," and continued to despise bourgeois sexual conventions. He calls her "a free spirit whom no cult or cause could ever entirely claim." *Rachilde*, p. 105.

7. *Rachilde*, p. 125.

8. Ibid., p. 63.

9. Rachilde, *Portraits d'hommes*, p. 58.

10. Ibid., p. 60.

11. Colette to Rachilde, Doucet.

12. Author of *Les Caprices d'Odette*, *Mady écolière*, and *Fourberies de Papa*.

13. Bonmariage, p. 55.

14. Caradec, p. 305.

15. Ibid., p. 284.

16. Ibid., p. 306.

17. Richardson, p. 142.

18. Caradec, p. 304.

19. Ibid., p. 306.

20. Richardson, p. 142.

21. In 1927, Léautaud was visiting Vallette at the Mercure de France, and they received

a visit from Willy, who "looked like a ruin." He told them he was taking iodine. Joanna Richardson speculates that he was taking iodides, which were prescribed for venereal disease. Ibid., p. 143.

22. Caradec, p. 308.

23. Léautaud, vol. 8, p. 317.

24. *HP*, p. 122.

25. *The Pure and the Impure.* But she still didn't have a title, and asked Hélène if she thought *Remous* (Eddy) would do or, if not that, *Écume* (Foam). It would be published later that year as *Ces Plaisirs* . . . and revised considerably for its definitive edition in 1943. *HP*, pp. 129, 135.

26. *EPC*, "Le Cirque," pp. 959–60.

27. Colette to Missy, MRB.

28. In 1927, Natalie had organized a series of Friday performances to introduce the work of her French writer friends to the Anglo-Saxons and vice versa. Winnie de Polignac, née Singer, was the heiress to the American sewing-machine fortune and a great patron of music, whom Colette had known since the fin de siècle. Mme de Gramont—the duchess de Clermont-Tonnerre—wrote a four-volume memoir that remains an important social history of the early years of the century; both Gertrude Stein and Walter Benjamin, to name but two admirers, considered it practically on a level with Proust.

29. Cited by Michèle Causse in "Amazone, ange, androgyne," her preface to *Berthe: ou un demi siècle auprès de l'Amazone* (the memoirs of Berthe Cleyrergue, Natalie's housekeeper) p. 21. All other quotes from Natalie in this section are from this source.

30. Colette to Una Troubridge and Radclyffe (John) Hall, BN 18707.

31. Causse, "Amazone," p. 19.

32. *P/I* FSG, p. 116.

33. In a letter from Colette to Missy, Colette reassures her old friend that "Natalie has nothing against you, on the contrary." MRB.

34. Barney, p. 22.

35. Colette to Natalie Clifford Barney (NCB), Doucet.

36. Wickes, *Amazon*, p. 263.

37. Barney, p. 187.

38. It was they, apparently, who introduced her to the history of "The Ladies of Llangollen," the two aristocratic eighteenth-century lesbians she describes in her chapter on Lesbos, and whose correspondence was published in a definitive edition in England in 1930.

39. Barney, p. 193.

40. In 1930, Colette told Carco that "in the little book I am grinding away at without making much progress, I speak of certain beings who are 'alluring voids.' " *LASP*, p. 231.

41. During its composition, Colette asked Maurice to look up the word "Phebus" for her, hoping it would mean " 'obscurities,' 'complications,' hidden stuff, and other labyrinths," and noting that "it would make me a damn pretty title." C to MG, SMAF.

42. *P/I* FSG, p. 21.

43. Ibid., p. 34.

44. Ibid., pp. 54, 57, 58.

45. Ibid., p. 130.

46. Ibid., p. 50.

47. Ibid., p. 158.

48. C to MG, SMAF.

CHAPTER 37

1. *MM,* p. 220.

2. LAMT, p. 45.

3. He of the failed line. According to Colette, whose chronology is extremely vague, she and Maginot had talked about the beauty business one afternoon just after the war, when he had lunched with her at the boulevard Suchet. He told her that a new era was beginning, and that it would be propitious for entrepreneurs of every stripe. "I see perfectly how to launch the thing. On the door of the boutique I would write, 'My name is Colette, and I sell perfumes.' " *PdC,* p. 81.

4. Colette, "Avatars," Pl. 3, p. xxxiii.

5. *MM,* p. 225.

6. The duchess was, according to Colette, one of her role models. She had fixed up an elegant old apothecary shop and sold perfumes there, using the prestige of her title to attract a select clientele. As she had been a great friend of Annie de Pène's, Colette was counting on that connection to facilitate the deal, and just to be sure, she drafted the impeccably high-toned letter that she wanted Germaine to send and sign, asking her to be sure it wasn't on *Le Matin* stationery. "But if it bothers you, don't do it," she added. *GB,* p. 189.

7. *HP,* p. 145.

8. *LDLV,* p. 227.

9. *PdC,* p. 82.

10. Pougy, p. 245.

11. MG to C, SMAF.

12. "I knew that she could console herself if she failed, but not if she had failed to try. . . . It was not to be the only occasion on which I was forced to allow her to navigate dangerous waters, always ready to take over the wheel should shipwreck seem imminent, rather than fetter her." *PdC,* p. 83.

13. C to MG, SMAF.

14. "Avatars," Pl. 3, p. xxxiii.

15. Barney, p. 200.

16. *The Cat, Short Novels of Colette,* translated by Morris Bentinck. New York: The Dial Press, 1951, p. 482.

17. Ibid., p, 516.

18. Ibid., p. 498.

19. While Colette was writing *The Cat,* she heard from Vera van den Henst that Nouchette, for inexplicable reasons, had dropped a neighbor's cat into the stairwell of their apartment house, also a modern high-rise. The cat survived, and the act was an aberration for the otherwise gentle child. Colette urged Vera not to punish her. Hélène van den Henst Thomas [Nouchette] to the author, 1998.

20. C to MG, SMAF.

21. Binion, p. 166.

22. CC 16. Interview with Arlette Louis-Dreyfus, pp. 97–110.

23. They had met when Arlette was a little girl, at her parents' house. Colette, then still married to Henry, knew the Louis-Dreyfuses through Anatole de Monzie.

24. *MM,* pp. 215–6.

25. *HP,* p. 167.

26. C to MG, SMAF.

27. CC 16, op. cit.

28. *JFM*, pp. 128–9.

29. Her driving particularly worried Colette, who confided an interesting bad dream about it to Renaud. Mother and daughter had traveled by different routes to a strange hotel. Colette was given an immense room, where she found three enormous hedgehogs. Her daughter arrived in a small black and white car and told her it was the model that turned over most easily. While she was talking, Colette noticed that Bel-Gazou had grown pale, with dark circles around her eyes, and that she had gotten thinner. "Reassure me," she asked Renaud. This dream recalls a similar one she had once recounted to Missy, in which the marquise also appeared to her with a ghostly pallor and hollow eyes. The conscious Colette may have had no "interest" in death, but her dreams belie this bravado. C to RdJ, HRC.

30. Pl. 3, p. xix.

31. The evening, noted Colette to Maurice, was a mixture of scientific conversation, bohemian informality, and a propensity for sweet wine and Freudianism.

32. C to MG, SMAF.

33. *JFM*, p. 128.

34. De Max, Colette's friend from her Willy days, was one of the greatest actors of his time, and notorious for his flamboyant homosexuality. He figures both in *My Apprentice-ships* and *The Pure and the Impure*. Colette wanted to write a play about Don Juan for him but never did.

35. Yves Courrière, *Joseph Kessel: ou sur la piste du lion*, p. 215.

36. Ibid., p. 217.

37. Ibid., p. 219.

38. Ibid., p. 218.

39. Ibid., p. 220.

40. *Dictionnaire des littératures*. Paris: Larousse, 1985, vol. 1, p. 831.

41. Courrière, *Kessel*, p. 492.

42. C to MG, SMAF.

43. RdJ, p. 14.

44. Hélène van den Henst Thomas to the author, 1998.

45. C to MG, SMAF.

CHAPTER 38

1. Dormann, p. 239.

2. This column, entitled "My Diary," lasted only a month before Colette ran out of steam, for obvious reasons.

3. In addition to *Lac aux dames*, Colette wrote the French text for *Jeunes filles en uniformes*, adapted from *Mädchen in Uniform*, directed by Léontine Sagan (1932) and an American film called *Papa Cohen* (1933). In 1935, she wrote the screenplay and dialogue for Max Ophüls's *Divine* and worked on the French adaptation of the Kaufman-Ferber play *Royal Family*.

4. Richardson, p. 158.

5. Mercier, Notice, Pl. 3, p. 1674.

6. *Douceur*, p. 165.

7. *Discours*, p. 27.

8. Filling the chair that had been vacated by Anna de Noailles, who had died in 1933. Cocteau would fill Colette's chair when she died, giving the speech cited above. Paul Léautaud, notes Richardson (p. 160), "thought it 'comical and not very exalted . . . to become a Belgian Academician,' but it was an honor that touched Sido's daughter."

9. Ibid., p. 158.

10. Pl. 3, p. 1823.

11. Colette, miscellaneous unpublished correspondence, MRB.

12. Published originally in 1922, and again, with some additions, in 1928.

13. Dossier Renée Hamon, BN. Actually, the published text says "make love," but that wasn't the expression Colette used with Renée in their private conversations about sex. With certain friends, Colette used the profanities "shit" and "fuck" quite casually, as we do now, and Renée records the usage, although she also sometimes crosses it out. It seems needlessly prudish to censor Colette, so I have taken the liberty here of restoring the force with which that line was, undoubtedly, delivered.

14. Aury, pp. 50–57.

15. Barney, p. 207.

16. *Places*, p. 51.

17. *Douceur*, p. 121.

18. *ES*, p. 157.

19. Martha Gellhorn to friends of the author, Donna Tartt and Nicholas Shakespeare, London, 1993.

20. *JN*, p. 1318. Other sources for this section: Colette, "New York et la 'Normandie,' " *Mes Cahiers*, Paris: Aux Armes de France, 1941, pp. 146–53; *PdC*, pp. 99–105.

21. *LAPF*, p. 124. The letter was dated May 7, 1944.

22. GP; Richardson, p. 163.

23. Richardson, p. 163.

24. Colette to her daughter, MRB.

25. Ibid.

26. GP.

27. Richardson, p. 165.

28. *HP*, p. 175.

29. CdJ, "Lettres," pp. 27–8.

30. Michel del Castillo, CC 10.

31. C to RdJ, HRC.

32. GP.

33. The distinguished editorial committee included Tristan Bernard, Francis Carco, Jean Giraudoux, François Mauriac, and Paul Morand.

34. Pichois, Pl. 3, p. xxix.

35. Colette to Vuillermoz, HRC.

36. Unpublished legal documents, MRB.

37. Pl. 3, p. 1700.

38. Unpublished legal documents, MRB; Colette to Claude Chauvière, MRB.

39. In a letter to Pierre Chaulaine from the same period, Colette envisages a new edition of all four *Claudines* that would, "if not expurgate, at least eliminate" Willy's baleful influence. "But the *Claudines* don't belong to me," she concludes bluntly. ADC.

40. In an interview with *Nouvelles littéraires*, she declared, "I don't like to write. Not only don't I like to write, but I like above all not to write. . . . This forced labor!" What would she like to do if she didn't have to write? "Everything! Everything except write!" Pl. 3, p. 1822.

41. Dupont, Pl. 3, p. 1701.

42. Caradec, p. 312. Paulette Gauthier-Villars had remained close to Colette. Her schoolmate and companion Dr. Marthe Lamy was Colette's personal physician and trusted friend.

43. Weiss archives, BN 17794.

44. *JN*, p. 1283.

45. Bernard Bray (editor), "Colette, Nouvelles approches critiques, Actes de Colloque de Sarrebruck," p. 194. BN 103140.

46. Chauvière, p. 88.

47. *PdC*, p. 179.

48. Ibid., p. 29.

49. Colette, "Mes Idées" (full cit.: ch. 2, n. 11), pp. 1831–2.

50. *Collected Stories*, p. 497.

51. Writes Bellosta: "Colette accuses herself of a cowardice she doesn't commit. This lie would astonish more male readers than female ones: in the same fashion but in a more immediate political context, '343 women' whose names enjoyed a certain fame signed, on April 5, 1971, a 'Manifesto' which has become famous in the history of our customs, in which they declared that they had had abortions; of those '343' a good number were no doubt lying, thus honoring their feminine solidarity." Pl. 3, p. 1861.

52. "How can one understand such a thing?" she asks Carco. "He has written me an unacceptable letter. . . . I don't know what one does in such a case. It's a new emotion." Pl. 3, p. 1513.

53. *HP*, p. 183. Pichois tentatively dates this letter from the summer of 1936, so it probably predates the campaign to smear Salengro.

CHAPTER 39

1. *PdC*, p. 143.

2. *LAPC*, p. 35.

3. *PdC*, p. 175.

4. *LAPC*, p. 40.

5. Pichois, "Note biographique sur Renée Hamon," *LAPC*, p. 23.

6. *LAPC*, p. 33.

7. Colette, "Préface aux *Îles de Lumières* by Renée Hamon," Ibid., pp. 18–19.

8. Goudeket, Introduction to *LAPC*, p. 9.

9. The article, clipped from an unidentified newspaper, is undated, and I have not been able to trace it. The byline was "Lucie Porquerol," although it is possible this may have been a pseudonym for Renée herself.

10. Richardson, p. 165.

11. C to RdJ, HRC.

12. *LAMT*, p. 134.

13. *JAR*, p. 43.

14. *HP*, p. 199.

15. Colette to Alice Bénard-Fleury, BN 3318.

16. They were former schoolteachers who had given up their jobs to cultivate a little farm that belonged to Thérèse's aunt, moving to their own land during the Second World War and to a third property—their last—in 1946. Colette met them in the early 1930s. She admired their lives, their purity, their bond with the soil and with their animals, and she would correspond with them affectionately until the year before her death, taking comfort, in the darkest years of the war, from their piety and their devotion. They urged her to visit them, but she never did. After the war, they and the Goudekets also considered the possibility of buying a country place to share, but nothing came of the idea.

17. *LASP*, p. 133.

18. *HP*, p. 200.

CHAPTER 40

1. *LAMT,* p. 205. She wants to know what Luc thinks of the alliance between England and Russia, and one infers from certain notes in Renée Hamon's diary that she, like many conservatives, mistrusts "perfidious Albion."

2. *LAPC,* p. 103.

3. Colette, *De ma fenêtre,* BQ3, p. 255. Original publication, Paris: Aux Armes de France, 1942.

4. *LAMT,* pp. 198–9. She doesn't want anyone to know that she has refused—they might think her "disobliging"—but she also doesn't want anyone to know that she secretly sends Cain and his starving family packages of food.

5. Ibid., p. 209.

6. *JAR,* p. 7.

7. *LAPF,* July 16, 1941, p. 68.

8. Ibid., June 4, 1941, p. 63.

9. *LAPC,* p. 113.

10. Gilles et Jean-Robert Ragache, *Des écrivains et des artistes sous l'Occupation,* p. 245.

11. *JAR,* p. 37.

12. From her dedication of *Julie* to the little farmers: *"un roman dont le plus grand mérite est de ne pas parler—ou si peu!—de la guerre."* BN 1690.

13. *LAPC,* p. 102.

14. *JAR,* "Fin Juin 1940," p. 7.

15. Ibid., p. 9.

16. *PdC,* p. 177.

17. *Paysages,* p. 237.

18. The thief who stole Colette's purse made off with two thousand francs and all of her papers, but a few days after the crime was reported in the local paper, she received an envelope with a misspelled note that said, "I didn't know it was you." It contained the cash and then some—Colette had mistakenly given the police a figure of three thousand francs when she filed her complaint, and the thief had made up the rest from his own pocket. The saga was picked up by the papers in Paris, which accused Colette of inventing it to "publicize" herself.

19. *LAPF,* May 29, 1940, p. 34.

20. *PdC,* p. 186.

21. *JAR,* p. 19.

22. *PdC,* p. 191.

23. *LASP,* p. 402.

24. Confused by her Jewish-sounding nom de plume, the Nazis put Rachilde—an anti-Semite—on their list of Jewish writers. She wrote to protest, noting that there hadn't been a Jew in her family for three hundred years. When the president of the publishers' union told her he would intervene in her favor, she was furious, telling him: "Not to be a Jewess is my right. It's not a question of a favor!" Dossier Rachilde, Doucet.

25. *LAPF,* July 1941, p. 69. But the word doesn't seem to have any political significance for her. It wasn't only her work for *P.P.* that she considered *"moche"* but her articles on fashion for the *Officiel de la couture.*

26. Patrice Blank to the author, 1991.

27. Ragache, *Écrivains,* p. 203.

28. The list of writers published by Drieu's *Nouvelle Revue française*—Gide, Éluard,

Valéry, Aragon, and Sartre among them—reflects how blurry the lines were between collaboration or at least accommodation with the occupying powers, and the desire, as Mauriac would put it, to bear witness, before Europe, to the endurance of the French spirit (Ragaches, p. 62). For a while, Paulhan himself served on Drieu's editorial committee. Malraux refused to contribute to the review but maintained his friendship with Drieu throughout the war. So did Bertrand de Jouvenel.

29. *LAMT*, p. 187.

30. *De ma fenêtre*, BQ 3, p. 186.

31. Ragache, *Écrivains*, p. 202.

CHAPTER 41

1. *LAPC*, pp. 94, 96.

2. An untranslatable and indeed ambiguous phrase, which could mean "seeming" novel or "sham" novel. *LAPC*, p. 98.

3. *Parinaud*, p. 167.

4. *LAPF*, June 9, 1940, p. 34.

5. *GB*, p. 206.

6. Dossier Renée Hamon, BN 18711.

7. *LAPF*, April 19, 1941, p. 54; Nov. 25, 1942, p. 105.

8. *GB*, p. 203.

9. *LAMT*, p. 190.

10. Francis Steegmuller, *Jean Cocteau*, p. 441.

11. Ibid., 440.

12. *LASP*, p. 442.

13. *Discours*, p. 27.

14. *GB*, p. 208.

15. *De ma fenêtre*, BQ 3, p. 237.

16. The emphasis is Colette's. She sent the letter to Moune, for her amusement. *LAMT*, p. 219.

17. Pl. 3, p. 1515.

18. Colette, *Julie de Carneilhan*, translated by Patrick Leigh Fermor, in *Three Short Novels*. New York: Farrar, Straus and Giroux, 1952, p. 145. Original publication, Paris: Fayard, 1941.

19. Dossier Renée Hamon, BN, p. 210.

20. Here it is worth noting that Colette told Parinaud that she wrote *Julie* because she wanted "to tackle a great animal I didn't know very well—the horse." *Parinaud*, p. 169.

21. Among the other well-known writers who made literary, not political, contributions were Simenon, Paul Morand, Henri Bordeaux, and P. G. Wodehouse, who was living in France and had been arrested by the Germans in 1940 as an enemy alien. On his release, he did several "comic" broadcasts for the German radio, aimed at the United States. Their gist was that the Occupation wasn't so bad. After the war, he admitted that he had been "criminally foolish," but never that he had intended to commit treason, and he claimed that he never for a moment imagined he was being used by the Nazis for propaganda purposes.

22. *Gringoire*, summer 1941.

23. Colette reports Monzie's reaction in a letter to Germaine Patat (C to GP). Monzie, it should be noted, published his own "secret political diaries" in *Gringoire*, which ran concurrently with *Julie*. As minister of education in the early 1930s, he had offered a chair at the Collège de France to Albert Einstein, a refugee from the Nazis. But he later met with Pétain, Abetz, Brinon, Déat, and other key figures in the Occupation to explore the

possibilities of restoring the autonomy of a legally constituted French Republic. These associations tarnished his name. "All these former parliamentary representatives," writes Philippe Burrin, referring to Monzie and several other former deputies in his circle, "who had been ardently pro-Munich and who found Vichy too reactionary, were anxious to remain in the game, but without taking too many risks. Their behavior is yet another sign of the atmosphere of those first two years [of the war] that encouraged many French people to plan for the future bearing the Germans carefully in mind." Philippe Burrin, *France Under the Germans*, pp. 379–80.

It should be also be noted that while *Julie* was running, *Gringoire* used a quote from Henry de Jouvenel as the caption for a caricature of a grotesque and obese England. "Liberty," it said, "is the right of peoples to obey England's orders." But this was a gross and exploitative distortion of Jouvenel's complex positions on foreign policy and the balance of power in Europe. Given his lucidity and his commitment to peace and democracy, it is difficult to believe he would ever willingly have lent his name to support the agenda of *Gringoire*, Vichy—or Hitler.

24. From Colette's letter to Germaine Patat. GP.

25. *PdC*, p. 197.

26. Ibid., p. 198.

27. *HP*, p. 204.

28. Among those who have been given credit for brokering Maurice's liberation are Sacha Guitry, Coco Chanel, Drieu La Rochelle, Robert Brasillach, Hélène Morand (see n. 32, below), José-María Sert, and Jean Jardin, the head of Pierre Laval's cabinet.

29. *LAPF*, Dec. 15, 1941, p. 75.

30. Lottmann, p. 263.

31. *LAPF*, Feb. 3, 1942, p. 78.

32. Hélène Morand, the Romanian wife of the novelist Paul Morand, was a close friend of Frau Abetz's. Bertrand de Jouvenel was the confidant of her husband. For complex reasons beyond the scope of this biography, and which he plumbs at great length in his own memoir, Bertrand had served a compromising political apprenticeship in the Fascist party of Doriot, along with his intimate friends Drieu and Alfred Fabre-Luce. He had interviewed Hitler in 1936 and had been impressed with him as a leader committed to the renewal of his country and a man of peace.

His friendship with Abetz—a cultivated francophile his own age—was cemented in the course of several trips Bertrand made to Germany in the 1930s, both as a reporter and as a partisan of Franco-German rapprochement. After the Munich putsch, Bertrand repented in profound if belated horror at national socialism and his own embrace of its ideals. Knowing he was far too suspect to be accepted by the Resistance, he put his services and his credentials as a persona grata to the Nazis at the service of Allied military intelligence. On behalf of this mission, he kept up cordial relations with Abetz, Karl Epting—the head of the German Institute—and prominent Vichyites.

Bertrand had a flat in Auteil, though he sometimes stayed in town at the Hôtel Beaujolais, around the corner from Colette, who mentions his proximity in a letter to Germaine Patat. He was teaching a course in economics and writing a book, having refused to work as a journalist under the Occupation. Abetz, however, remained confident of his loyalty and often invited Jouvenel to lunch or dine at the embassy, where they discussed questions of policy or—when Suzanne Abetz was present—culture. Bertrand occasionally returned their hospitality, and he mentions having sent Frau Abetz a book—perhaps one of Colette's—though he doesn't give its title.

33. Lottmann, pp. 262–3.

34. *PdC*, p. 207.

35. *LAPF*, Feb. 7, 1942, p. 80.

36. *LAPC*, p. 115.

37. *GB*, p. 211; *LAPF*, June 10, 1942, p. 90.

38. *LAPF*, Aug. 17, 1942, p. 97.

39. *PdC*, p. 208; *LAPF*, June 25, 1942, p. 92.

40. Lottmann, p. 264.

41. *LAPC*, p. 96.

42. Ibid., p. 106.

43. *Gigi*, finished in September, was serialized in *Présent*, Oct. 28 to Nov. 24, 1943, then published in Lausanne by the Guilde du Livre in 1944 as the title piece of a volume containing two short texts—"Noces" and "Flore et Pomone"—and a longish story, "La Dame du photographe." In 1945, the collection was republished by Ferenczi, with "L'Enfant malade" replacing "Noces." The four other stories she finished that year, collected under the title *Le Képi*, were published by Fayard in March of 1943.

44. *LAPC*, p. 122.

45. *Parinaud*, p. 62.

46. Ibid., p. 63. Its subject was the long lines of theater "fanatics" lined up to buy tickets at the Comédie-Française. *Combats* should not be confused with *Combat*, a left-wing journal published after the war.

47. Lottmann, p. 268.

48. *Gigi*, translated by Roger Senhouse, in *Three Short Novels* (full cit.: ch. 41, n. 18), pp. 45–6.

CHAPTER 42

1. *LAPC*, p. 121.

2. *MM*, p. 248.

3. *LASP*, p. 416.

4. *Douceur*, p. 172.

5. *LASP*, p. 417.

6. *Douceur*, p. 175.

7. *LASP*, p. 418.

8. Ibid.

9. The proprietor of a famous nightclub, Liberty's Bar in the place Blanche, who was, throughout the war, one of her most faithful suppliers of black-market food.

10. *LAPC*, p. 148.

11. "Flore et Pomone," "Nudité," and "De la patte à l'aile."

12. "The Sick Child," translated by Antonia White, *Collected Stories*, p. 346.

13. *MM*, p. 279.

14. Guatemala had declared war on Germany and annexed the large holdings of resident German nationals, who were interned. Julio's Guatemalan relations managed to arrange a "prisoner exchange"—Vera, Nouchette, and Julio for some German captives. The family had a laissez-passer for Lisbon. Hélène van den Henst Thomas to the author, 1998.

15. An expanded edition of *De ma fenêtre*, entitled *Paris de ma fenêtre*, was published in 1944 by Milieu du Monde, and a third edition, by Ferenczi, in 1948.

16. *MM*, pp. 287–8.

17. André de Fouquières, *Cinquante Ans de panache*.

18. Anthony Beevor and Artemis Cooper, *Paris After the Liberation*, p. 40.

19. Ibid., p. 45.
20. *ES*, p. 171.

CHAPTER 43

EPIGRAPH: Nancy Caldwell Sorel, "Colette and Truman Capote," *The Atlantic Monthly.* Capote had come to Paris in 1948. He was a beguiling and provocative enfant terrible of twenty-three—not unlike Mme Willy had been—and had just made his literary début. Cocteau introduced him to Colette, and she asked him what he expected from life. He told her that he didn't know what to expect—that was partly why he had come to see her—but that he would like to be a grown-up.

1. Carco, *Colette mon ami*, BN L27 85732.
2. *PdC*, p. 244.
3. *Discours*, p. 28.
4. Ibid., p. 33.
5. Lottmann, p. 301.
6. *LAPF*, Dec. 5, 1949, p. 182.
7. *ES*, p. 159.
8. *PdC*, p. 252.
9. *LAPF*, April 26, 1944, p. 123.
10. Richardson, p. 197.
11. Chapon, *Autour de Natalie*, pp. 23–4.
12. *LAMT*, p. 277.
13. Dossier Renée Hamon, BN 18711.
14. *ES*, p. 159.
15. GP.
16. *FB*, p. 740.
17. Nearly all the Jews and members of other racial minorities had been killed. More than a quarter of the seven hundred thousand captured Resistance fighters, forced conscripts, and prisoners of war had also perished.
18. Beevor and Cooper, *Paris After the Liberation*, p. 151.
19. *LAPF*, April 2, 1945, pp. 140–41.
20. Simone was a diva who had played in *Divine* and sung *Pelléas et Mélisande* at the opera. She had been the mistress of the Glâwi and, with him, one of Colette's backers in the beauty business. In 1943, she had bought the Théâtre Antoine. (See my chapter 44, note 9.)
21. *Colette*, p. 475. The authors are citing from Sartre's inscription on the copy of *La Nausée* that he sent to Colette in 1938.
22. Ibid. The authors are quoting from Berriau's memoir, *Simone est comme ça.*
23. GP.
24. *LAPF*, June 3, 1945, p. 145.
25. The philosopher, linguist, Orientalist, and author of historical novels with exotic settings. While Judith's writings had considerable merit, her election, in the opinion of her biographer (and Colette's) Joanna Richardson, "owed much to the fact" that she was her father's [Théophile Gautier's] daughter and literary heir, and that he had "failed, repeatedly, for all his distinction, to enter the Académie-Française." Richardson, *Judith Gautier*, p. 224.
26. *FB*, p. 799, and *BL*, pp. 149–50.
27. Ragache, p. 302.
28. Mauriac, *Le Figaro*, Jan. 4, 1945.
29. *LASP*, p. 138.

30. Colette to Maître Jacques Isorni, Oct. 21, 1944, ADC.

31. Lottmann, p. 275.

32. *MM*, p. 304.

33. Ibid., p. 300. Her deformity was the result of her incurable bone disease.

34. *ES*, p. 228.

35. *HP*, p. 229.

36. *ES*, p. 228.

37. *MM*, 311.

38. *PdC*, p. 237.

39. Colette to Pata de Polignac, BN 18718.

40. *PdC*, p. 239.

41. Ibid., pp. 240–41.

42. *BL*, p. 13.

43. *LAMT*, pp. 286, 291.

44. *BL*, pp. 30–31.

45. Chalon, *Portrait d'une séductrice*, p. 248. One of Natalie's grandfathers was Jewish.

46. CC no. 18, p. 27.

47. Chalon, *Portrait*, pp. 301–2.

48. Pougy, p. 253.

49. *BL*, pp. 74–5.

50. Ibid., p. 78.

51. Ibid., p. 71–2.

52. Ibid., p. 69.

53. *Selected Writings of Jules Laforgue*, edited and translated by William Jay Smith. New York: Grove Press, 1956, p. 217.

54. Margaret Crosland, *Colette: The Difficulty of Loving*, p. 1.

55. CdJ, "Colette," p. 23.

CHAPTER 44

1. ADC.

2. Lottmann, pp. 277–8.

3. *PdC*, p. 244.

4. Jean Cocteau, *Le Passé défini*, p. 167.

5. Jacqueline Audry's 1949 film version of *Gigi*, starring Danièle Delorme, was an unexpected hit. In 1950, Audry directed *Minne, L'Ingénue libertine*. In 1950, Jacques Manuel directed *Julie de Carnheilan*, starring Edwige Feuillère. Colette's own stage version of *Chéri* was filmed in 1949–50 by Pierre Billon. In 1952, Rossellini based his "Envy" segment of *The Seven Deadly Sins* on *La Chatte*. In 1954, Claude Autant-Lara released his adaptation of *Le Blé en herbe*, which he had been working on for seven years, starring Feuillère as the Lady in White. Audry directed a remake of *Mitsou* in 1956. The American film version of *Gigi* was released in 1958. From *Colette at the Movies: Criticism and Screenplays*, edited by Alain and Odette Virmaux. New York: Frederick Ungar, 1980, pp. 211–13.

6. It's interesting, however, that in her memoir of Moreno, she disavows any such expertise. "My resolute ignorance about the screen and its diverse techniques makes me not only an elderly person but a person, as one says, of another age." *MM*, p. 20.

7. *Colette at the Movies*, p. 20.

8. Ibid., p. 7.

9. Simone de Beauvoir, *A Transatlantic Love Affair*, pp. 180–1. De Beauvoir wrote to Algren in English, a language she spoke very well but not perfectly, which accounts for the

schoolgirlish awkwardness of the prose. In the same letter, she gives an amusingly puritanical description of Simone Berriau, that suggests why Berriau was—as de Beauvoir probably could never be—a congenial friend to Colette: "the woman who owns the theatre, an ex-beautiful woman, [is] a dreadful whore having slept with thousands of men. . . . She is a curious Parisian figure, fifty years old, trying to look thirty, always speaking about obscene things in the coarsest way and showing legs, hips, thighs, all what she may show of her body and even what she might not show." Ibid, p. 180.

Her vehemence recalls Colette's youthful distaste for Mme Cholleton's flirting, and her observation that the "uncompromising" young deny their elders a right to an erotic life.

10. CC 20, pp. 122–3, quoted from Simone de Beauvoir, *La Force des choses.*
11. *MM,* p. 333.
12. Ibid., p. 341.
13. Ibid., p. 352.
14. Richardson, p. 207.
15. *BL,* p. 161.
16. *MM,* p. 351.
17. Ibid., p. 350.
18. *LAPF,* Dec. 5, 1949, p. 183; Oct. 29, 1948, p. 175.
19. GB, p. 226.
20. Michel del Castillo to the author, 1991.
21. *Vogue,* Nov. 1, 1945, pp. 207–9.
22. Lottmann, p. 277.
23. *Discours,* p. 29.
24. CdJ, "Notes et réflexions," pp. 5–6.
25. Michel del Castillo to the author, 1991.
26. CdJ, "Lettres," p. 27.
27. Michel del Castillo, CC 10.
28. CdJ, "Lettres," p. 24.
29. *LASP,* p. 442 (footnote).
30. Colette to Pata de Polignac, BN 18718.
31. Richardson, p. 208.
32. Colette to Pata, BN 18718.
33. Richardson, p. 221.
34. *PdC,* p. 268.
35. Ibid., p. 275.
36. *LAMT,* p. 380.
37. Ibid., p. 364.
38. *PdC,* p. 58.
39. *LAMT,* p. 344.
40. Lottmann, p. 300.

CHAPTER 45

1. *Belles Saisons, A Colette Scrapbook,* edited by Robert Phelps, p. 278.
2. *LASF,* p. 23.
3. GB, p. 238.
4. *LAMT,* p. 354.
5. Ibid., p. 359.
6. Cocteau, *Passé défini,* vol. 2, pp. 119–20.
7. Léautaud, vol. 18, p. 126.

8. Phelps, *Belles Saisons,* p. 269.

9. Glenway Westcott, *Images of Truth,* "A Call on Colette and Goudeket," pp. 142–8.

10. He had probably been reading too much Isak Dinesen. Westcott's essay on Dinesen immediately follows his two chapters on Colette in *Images of Truth.* "*Out of Africa* is her only truthful work," he says of Dinesen. "[The tales] are pure fiction, absolute fictitiousness." The reverse is rather more true.

11. *LASP,* p. 294.

12. *BL,* p. 104.

13. The Grande Medaille d'Or of the city of Paris in January of 1953; the cross of the Grand Officer in the Legion of Honor—its highest rank—that March; honorary membership in the [American] National Institute of Arts and Letters that May.

14. Cocteau, *Passé défini,* vol. 2, p. 45.

15. *LAMT,* p. 381.

16. Cocteau, *Passé défini,* vol. 2, p. 348.

17. Richardson, p. 225. But Pichois and Brunet relate that Colette's message was drafted by Maurice. *Colette,* p. 498.

18. Bertrand de Jouvenel, "Colette," *Time and Tide,* Aug. 14, 1954.

19. *LAMT,* p. 379.

20. *PdC,* p. 280.

21. Richardson, p. 228.

22. Cocteau, *Passé défini,* vol. 3, p. 158.

23. *LAPF,* March 7, 1940, p. 32. She was writing just after the death of her brother Léo and explaining why she wasn't telling anyone but her most intimate friends.

24. *Parinaud,* p. 150.

25. *Le Figaro,* Aug. 9, 1954.

Selected Bibliography

A COMPLETE BIBLIOGRAPHY of Colette's work, or even of her work in English translation, is beyond the scope of this biography. Interested readers may want to consult Donna M. Norell's excellent *Colette: An Annotated Primary and Secondary Bibliography* (New York and London: Garland Publishing, 1993).

The following is a selected bibliography of the works in book form (it excludes periodicals) that appear in the notes or have informed my research.

Album Colette. Iconography selected and annotated by Claude and Vincenette Pichois, with Alain Brunet. Paris: Gallimard, 1984.

Album Masques: Colette. Edited by Katy Barsac and Jean-Pierre Jœcker. Paris: Masques, 1984.

Arendt, Hannah. *The Origins of Totalitarianism.* New York: Harcourt Brace Jovanovich, 1979.

Aury, Dominique. *Literary Landfalls.* Translated by Denise Folliot. New York: Evergreen Grove Press, 1961. Originally published as *Lecture pour tous.* Paris: Gallimard, 1958.

Barney, Natalie Clifford. *Souvenirs indiscrets.* Paris: Flammarion, 1960.

———. *Traits et portraits.* Paris: Mercure de France, 1963.

Beauvoir, Simone de. *The Second Sex.* Translated by H. M. Parshley. New York: Alfred A. Knopf, 1953.

———. *A Transatlantic Love Affair: Letters to Nelson Algren.* Compiled and annotated by Sylvie Le Bon de Beauvoir. New York: The New Press, 1998.

Beaumont, Germaine, and André Parinaud. *Colette.* Paris: Seuil, 1951.

Beevor, Anthony, and Artemis Cooper. *Paris After the Liberation.* New York: Doubleday, 1994.

Belles Saisons: A Colette Scrapbook. Edited by Robert Phelps. New York: Farrar, Straus and Giroux, 1978.

Benjamin, Jessica. *The Bonds of Love: Psychoanalysis, Feminism, and the Problem of Domination.* New York: Pantheon, 1988.

———. *Like Subjects, Love Objects.* New Haven and London: Yale University Press, 1995.

Berenson, Edward. *The Trial of Madame Caillaux.* Berkeley: University of California Press, 1992.

Billy, André. *Intimités littéraires.* Paris: Flammarion, 1932.

Binion, Rudolph. *Defeated Leaders: The Political Fate of Caillaux, Jouvenel, and Tardieu.* New York: Columbia University Press, 1960.

Biolley-Godino, Marcelle. *L'Homme objet chez Colette.* Paris: Klincksieck, 1972.

Blum, Léon, *L'Oeuvre de Léon Blum (1904–1914).* Paris: Albin Michel, 1962.

Bonal, Gérard. *Colette par moi-même.* Paris: Ramsay, 1982.

Bonmariage, Sylvain. *Willy, Colette, et moi.* Paris: Charles Fremanger, 1954.

Bonnet, Marie-Jo. *Un choix sans équivoque.* Paris: Denoël, 1981.

Brécourt-Villars, Claudine, *Petit glossaire raisonné de l'eroticisme saphique, 1880–1930.* Paris: LaVue, 1980.

Broche, François. *Anna de Noailles: Un mystère en pleine lumière.* Paris: Robert Laffont, 1989.

Burrin, Philippe. *France Under the Germans: Collaboration and Compromise.* Translated by Janet Lloyd. New York: The New Press, 1996.

Caradec, François. *Feu Willy.* Paris: Carrère, 1984.

Carco, Francis. *Colette, mon ami.* Paris: Rive-Gauche, 1955.

Cazals, Patrick. *Musidora, la dixième muse.* Paris: Henri Veyrier, 1978.

Chalon, Jean. *Colette, l'éternelle apprentie.* Paris: Flammarion, 1998.

———. *Portrait d'une séductrice.* Paris: Stock, 1976.

Champion, Pierre. *Marcel Schwob et son temps.* Paris: Grasset, 1927.

Chapon, François. *Autour de Natalie Clifford Barney.* Paris: Bibliothèque Littéraire Jacques Doucet, 1976.

Chauvière, Claude. *Colette.* Paris: Firmin-Didot, 1931.

Claudine au concert. Edited by Alain Galliari. Paris: Le Castor Astral, 1992.

Cleyrergue, Berthe. *Berthe: ou un demi-siècle auprès de l'Amazone.* Preface by Michèle Causse. Paris: Éditions Tierce, 1980.

Cocteau, Jean. "Colette." In *Discours de réception à l'Académie Royale de Langue et de Littérature Française.* Paris: Grasset, 1955.

———. *Le Passé défini. Journal.* 3 vols. Edited and annotated by Pierre Chanel. Paris: Gallimard, 1953.

———. *Portraits souvenir.* Paris: Grasset, 1935.

Colette at the Movies: Criticism and Screenplays. Edited by Alain and Odette Virmaux. New York: Frederick Ungar, 1980.

Colette-Jammes: Une Amitié inattendue. Introduction and notes by Robert Mallet. Paris: Émile-Paul, 1945.

Colette: Nouvelles Approches critiques. Actes du Colloque de Sarrebruck. Edited by Bernard Bray. Paris: Nizet, 1986.

Catterall, R. D. *A Short Textbook of Venereology.* London: The English Universities Press, 1974.

Cronin, Vincent. *Paris on the Eve.* New York: St. Martin's Press, 1990.

Courrière, Yves. *Joseph Kessel: ou sur la piste du lion.* Paris: Plon, 1986.

Crosland, Margaret. *Colette: The Difficulty of Loving.* New York: Bobbs-Merrill, 1973.

Daudet, Léon. *Memoirs of Léon Daudet.* Edited and translated by Arthur Kingsland Griggs. New York: The Dial Press, 1925.

Dauphiné, Claude. *Rachilde: Femme de lettres 1900.* Paris: Pierre Fanlac, 1985.

D'Hollander, Paul. *Colette: Ses apprentissages*. Paris: Klincksick, 1989.

Diesbach, Ghislain de. *La Princesse Bibesco*. Paris: Perrin, 1986.

Dijkstra, Bram. *Idols of Perversity: Fantasies of Feminine Evil in Fin-de-Siècle Culture*. New York, Oxford: Oxford University Press, 1986.

Dormann, Geneviève. *Colette: A Passion for Life*. Translated by David Macey and Jane Brenton. New York: Abbeville Press, 1985. Originally published as *Amoureuse Colette*. Paris: Éditions Herscher, 1984.

Fouquières, André de. *Cinquante Ans de panache*. Paris: Horay-Flore, 1951.

Francis, Claude, and Fernande Gontier. *Colette*. Paris: Perrin, 1997.

Gold, Arthur, and Robert Fizdale. *Misia*. New York: Alfred A. Knopf, 1980.

Goncourt, Édmond, and Jules de Goncourt. *Paris and the Arts, 1851–1896. From the Goncourt Journal*. Edited and translated by George J. Becker and Edith Philips. Ithaca and London: Cornell University Press, 1971.

Goudeket, Maurice. *La Douceur de viellir*. Paris: Flammarion, 1965.

———. *Près de Colette*. Paris: Flammarion, 1956.

Gourmont, Rémy de. *The Natural Philosophy of Love*. Translated by Ezra Pound. New York: Willey Book Co., 1940.

Gramont, Élisabeth de. *Mémoires*. 4 vols. Paris: Grasset, 1928.

Halévy, Daniel. *Péguy and les cahiers de la quinzaine*. New York and Toronto: Longmans, Green & Co., 1947.

Hauser, Arnold. *The Social History of Art*. New York: Alfred A. Knopf, 1951.

Hayman, Ronald. *Proust*. New York: HarperCollins, 1990.

A History of Private Life: From the Fires of Revolution to the Great War. Edited by Michelle Perrot, translated by Arthur Goldhammer. Cambridge, Mass.: The Belknap Press of Harvard University Press, 1990. Originally published as *Histoire de la vie privée*. Paris: Éditions du Seuil, 1987.

Hire, Jean de la. "Willy et Colette." In *Ménages d'artistes*. Paris: A. D'Espie, 1905.

Huysmans, Joris-Karl. *Against the Grain*. Translated by Robert Baldrick. New York: Penguin, 1959.

Jouvenel, Bertrand de. *Un Voyageur dans le siècle*. Paris: Laffont, 1979.

Jouvenel, Colette de. *Colette de Jouvenel* [pamphlet], edited by Gérard Bonal. Paris: Société des Amis de Colette, 1982.

Jullian, Philippe. *Jean Lorrain: ou Le Satiricon 1900*. Paris: Fayard, 1974.

———. *Oscar Wilde*. Translated by Violet Wyndham. New York: The Viking Press, 1969.

Kaplan, Louise. *Female Perversions: The Temptations of Emma Bovary*. New York: Anchor Books, 1991.

Klein, Melanie. *Love, Guilt, and Reparation*. New York: Macmillan, 1984.

Lanoux, Armand. *Amours 1900*. Paris: Hachette, 1961.

Larnac, Jean. *Colette: Sa vie, son oeuvre*. Paris: Simon Kra, 1927.

Léautaud, Paul. *Journal*. Paris: Mercure de France, 1954.

Loliée, Frédéric. *Le Duc de Morny et la société du Second Empire*, Paris: Émile-Paul, 1909.

Lorenz, Paul. *Sapho 1900: Renée Vivien*, Paris: Juillard, 1977.

Lottmann, Herbert. *Colette: A Life*. Boston: Little, Brown, 1991.

Louys, Pierre. *Aphrodite: Moeurs antique*. Paris: Charpentier et Fasquelle, 1906.

———. *Chansons de Bilitis*. Traduit de la grècque. Paris: Georges Crès, 1894.

Malige, Jeannie. *Colette, Qui êtes-vous?* Paris: La Manufacture, 1987.

Marks, Elaine. *Colette*. New Brunswick, N.J.: Rutgers University Press, 1960.

Martin du Gard, Maurice. *Les Mémorables*. Paris: Flammarion, 1957.

Massie, Allan. *Colette*. New York: Penguin, 1986.

Maurois, Michelle. *Les Cendres brûlantes*. Paris: Flammarion, 1986.

Maurras, Charles. *L'Avenir de l'intelligence*. Paris: Fontemoing, 1905.

Mayeur, Jean-Marie, and Madeleine Rebérioux. *The Third Republic from Its Origins to the Great War, 1871–1914*. Translated by J. R. Foster. Cambridge: Cambridge University Press, 1987.

McDougall, Joyce. *Plea for a Measure of Abnormality*. New York: Brunner-Mazel, 1978.

Mercié, Jean-Luc. *Anacréon le Jeune*. Ottawa: Ottawa University Press, 1971.

Mitchell, Yvonne. *Colette: A Taste for Life*. New York: Harcourt, Brace, Jovanovich, 1975.

Moreno, Marguerite. *Souvenirs de ma vie*. Paris: Flore, 1948.

Mugnier, Arthur. *Journal de l'abbé Mugnier (1879–1939)*. Paris: Mercure de France, 1989.

Paglia, Camille. *Sexual Personae*. New York: Vintage Books, 1991.

Painter, George. *Marcel Proust*. 2 vols. New York: Vintage, 1978.

Pène, Annie de. *L'Évadée*. Paris: Messein, 1911.

Pichois, Claude, and Alain Brunet. *Colette*. Paris: Éditions de Fallois, 1999.

Polaire, *Polaire par elle-même*. Paris: Figuière, 1933.

Pougy, Liane de. *My Blue Notebooks*. Translated by Diana Athill. London: André Deutsch, 1979.

Raaphorst-Rousseau, Madeleine. *Colette, sa vie et son art*. Paris: Nizet, 1964.

Rachilde, *Portraits d'hommes*. Paris: Mercure de France, 1930.

Ragache, Gilles, and Jean-Robert Ragache. *Des écrivains et des artistes sous l'Occupation*. Paris: Hachette, 1988.

Réage, Pauline. *Story of O*. New York: Grove Press, 1965.

Renard, Jules. *Journal*. Paris: Gallimard, 1959.

Richardson, Joanna. *Colette*. New York: Franklin Watts, 1984.

———. *Judith Gautier: A Biography*. London, New York: Quartet Books, 1986.

Robert, Louis de. *De Loti à Proust*. Paris: Flammarion, 1928.

Romein, Jan. *The Watershed of Two Eras: Europe in 1900*. Translated by Arnold Pomerans. Middletown, Conn.: Wesleyan University Press, 1978.

Sarde, Michèle. *Colette: Free and Fettered*. Translated by Richard Miller. New York: William Morrow, 1980.

Shattuck, Roger. *The Banquet Years: The Origins of the Avant-Garde in France, 1885 to World War I*. Rev. ed. New York: Vintage Books, 1968.

Showalter, Elaine. *Sexual Anarchy*. New York: Penguin, 1990.

Silverman, Willa Z. *The Notorious Life of Gyp: Right-Wing Anarchist in Fin-de-Siècle France*. New York, Oxford: Oxford University Press, 1995.

Steegmuller, Francis. *Jean Cocteau*. Boston: Little, Brown, 1970.

Taxil, Léo. *La Corruption fin-de-siècle*. Paris: Nilsson, 1894.

Truc, Gonzague. *Madame Colette*. Paris: Corrêa, 1941.

Tual, Denise. *Au coeur du temps*. Paris: Carrère, 1987.

Uzanne, Octave. *Parisiennes de ce temps*. Paris: Mercure de France, 1910.

Weber, Eugen. *France fin de siècle*. Cambridge, Mass.: The Belknap Press of Harvard University, 1986.

———. *My France: Politics, Culture, Myth*. Cambridge: The Belknap Press of Harvard University, 1991.

———. *Peasants into Frenchmen*, Stanford: Stanford University Press, 1976.

Wescott, Glenway. *Images of Truth*. New York: Harper Colophon, 1960.

Wickes, George. *The Amazon of Letters*. New York: G. P. Putnam's, 1976.

Willy. *Indiscrétions et commentaires sur les Claudines*. Paris: Blaizot, "Pro Amicus," 1962.

———. *Lélie, fumeuse d'opium*. Paris: Albin Michel, 1911.

────. *Maugis amoureux*. Paris: Albin Michel, 1905.

────. *Souvenirs littéraires . . . et autres*. Paris: Éditions Montaigne, 1925.

Winnicott, D. W. *Human Nature*. New York: Schocken Books, 1988.

Zeldin, Theodore. *A History of French Passions*. 2 vols. Oxford: Clarendon Press, 1972.

Zola, Émile. *Nana*. Translated and with an introduction by George Holden. London: Penguin Books, 1972.

Acknowledgments

$\mathcal{T}$HIS BIOGRAPHY took nine years to research and write. I would never have survived them without the patient love of my family and friends, or without the help of the scholars, writers, archivists, collectors, and witnesses who contributed their insights to my work. I can never fully express the depth of my gratitude to M. Foulques de Jouvenel for his support and generosity from the beginning to the end of this project; to M. Michel Rémy-Bieth for opening his priceless collection of Colette's unpublished letters and related documents to me, and for his faith; and to the Succession Colette and its counsel, Maître André Schmidt, for permission to quote from these and all other *inédits*—an exceptional privilege which has enriched these pages inestimably.

My archival research would also not have been possible without the expertise and kindness of Mme Michèle Le Pavec, the curator of manuscripts at the Bibliothèque Nationale in Paris. I am also deeply grateful to Mme Samia Bordji of the Musée Colette for her generous permission to reprint photographs from the museum's archives; to Mr. Carlton Lake, Ms. Linda Ashton, and Ms. Kathy Henderson at the Harry Ransom Humanities Center in Austin, Texas; M. François Chapon at the Bibliothèque Littéraire Jacques Doucet in Paris; M. Guy Quincy and M. Étienne d'Alençon of the Archives Départementales de la Corrèze in Brive; and to the following for their permission to consult unpublished manuscripts: M. Pierre-Marie Moulins of the SMAF; Mme Renée O'Brien; M. Jean Chalon; and Mme Gina Franchina-Severini.

The interviews that I conducted with the following witnesses, and the documents and recollections they shared with me, were of inestimable value in giving depth to my portrait of Colette: Mme Anne de Jouvenel, Mme Jeannie Malige, Mme Sanda Goudeket, Maître René Aujol, Mme Michelle Maurois, M. Patrice Blank, M. Michel del Castillo, Mme Nicole Stéphane, Mme Marguerite Boivin, M. Gérard Bonal, Mme Berthe Cleyrergue, M. Gilles Gauthier-Villars, M. Jean Marais, M. Jean-Claude Saladin, Mireille, Mme Hélène van den Henst Thomas, and Mme Esa di Simone.

I would also like to express profound thanks to my publisher, Sonny Mehta; my scrupulous editor, George Andreou; my agent, Andrew Wylie; my research assistant, Sylvie Merlier-Rowen; my photo researcher, Bridgett Noizeux; and to the following for reading and criticizing my manuscript, for lending me books and refuges, and for providing references, introductions, and direction:

Gini Alhadeff, Angelika and Euan Baird, Dr. Jessica Benjamin, Mary Blume, M. et Mme Yves Bonnefoy, Mlle Soline de Boysson, Mlle Maria-Catherine Bouttrin, Holly Brubach, Suzanne Brøgger, Joan Juliet Buck, Milena Canonero, Beatrice Cazac, Camilla Cazac, Rosemary Davidson, Lynn Davis, Gloria Emerson, Robert Fizdale, Jonathan Galassi, Wendy Gimbel, M. Jacques Grange, M. Pierre Grobel, Alan Gurganus, Robert Hamburger, Richard Howard, James Thurman Kahn, Dr. Louise Kaplan, Drs. Rachel and Donald Klein, Jane Kramer, Julia Kristeva, Valerie Leacock, Nancy Lindemeyer, James Lord, Nieves Mathews de Madariaga, Laura Meisner, Anne Michel, M. Bernard Minoret, Honor Moore, Lilian Moore, Benjamin Moser, Matthew Naythons, Nancy Novogrod, Jacqueline Onassis, Mme Geneviève Picon, Mme Martine Picon, M. Pierre-André Picon, Mme Sylvie Rebbot, David Rieff, M. Jacques Robert, Susie Rogers, Paulette Rose, Kitty Ross, Philip Roth, Eleanor Rowe, Nina Salter, Nathalie Sarraute, Martha Saxton, Louise Schimmel, Robert Seidman, Betty Sih, Stanley Siegel, Philippe Sollers, Deborah Schneider, Nicholas Shakespeare, Susan Sontag, Jean Strouse, Donna Tartt, Roy Thurman, Agnès Varda, Marina Warner, Wendy Wasserstein, Edmund White, Michael Wollaeger, Rudy Wurlitzer. But this list is far from complete. It excludes many of my closest "civilian" friends, here and in Europe, as well as writers and biographers who have, in ways great and small, given me courage, fellowship, and support, sometimes—as Colette would say—"in the shape of a good meal," and sometimes "in the form of a solid, mystical engagement."

My deepest debt, however, is to the three people with whom I live: my aunt Charlotte (Arkie) Meisner, who moved to Paris at the age of eighty without a word of French to care for a household and a little boy; my son, William Thurman Naythons, who was born in 1989 and has never known his mother without Colette; and my husband and *meilleur ami,* Peter Miller. They have sustained me.

New York, N.Y.
July 4, 1999

Index

Permissions Acknowledgments

Grateful acknowledgment is made to Farrar, Straus and Giroux, LLC, for permission to reprint excerpts from *My Mother's House and Sido* by Colette, translated by Una Vicenzo Troubridge and Enid McLeod, translation copyright © 1953, translation copyright renewed 1981 by Farrar, Straus and Giroux, Inc.; excerpts from *The Pure and the Impure* by Colette, translated by Herma Briffault, translation copyright © 1967, translation copyright renewed 1995 by Farrar, Straus & Giroux, Inc.

A Note About the Author

Judith Thurman won the National Book Award for *Isak Dinesen: The Life of a Storyteller*. She lives in New York City.